SOUTH-WESTERN SERIES IN
HUMAN RESOURCES MANAGEMENT

RESEARCH METHODS IN HUMAN RESOURCES MANAGEMENT

Neal W. Schmitt, Ph.D.
Professor of Psychology and Management
Michigan State University

Richard J. Klimoski, Ph.D.
Professor of Psychology
Ohio State University

Consulting Editors:
Gerald R. Ferris
University of Illinois at Urbana-Champaign
Kendrith M. Rowland
University of Illinois at Urbana-Champaign

GJ61AA
PUBLISHED BY
SOUTH-WESTERN PUBLISHING CO.
CINCINNATI

Publisher: Roger L. Ross
Production Associate Editor: Thomas E. Shaffer
Production House: Bookmark Book Production Services
Cover and Interior Designer: Barbara Libby
Marketing Manager: David L. Shaut

1 2 3 4 5 6 7 M 6 5 4 3 2 1

Printed in the United States of America

Library of Congress Cataloging-in-Publication Data

Schmitt, Neal.
  Research methods in human resources management / Neal W. Schmitt,
Richard J. Klimoski : consulting editors, Gerald R. Ferris, Kendrith
M. Rowland.
        p.   cm. - - (South-Western series in human resources
management)
  ISBN 0-538-80246-4
  1. Personnel management - - Research - - Methodology.   I. Klimoski,
Richard J.   II. Ferris, Gerald J.   III. Rowland, Kendrith M.
IV. Title.   V. Series
HF5549.S2463   1991
658.3′0072- - dc20
                                                                    90-9671
                                                                       CIP

EDITORS' INTRODUCTION TO THE HUMAN RESOURCES MANAGEMENT SERIES

The effective management of human resources has been of interest to organizational scientists and administrators for quite some time. But, perhaps due to productivity concerns and the contemporary quality of work life focus, human resources management issues have never been more prominent. As a result of this renewed interest, there is a greater need and demand for educating people about human resources management in organizations, which has manifested itself as expanded curriculum in this area in business schools and labor institutes, as well as in management education and development programs.

The South-Western Series in Human Resources Management is designed to provide substantive knowledge and information on important topics in the field to researchers, students, and practicing professionals who wish to more fully understand the implications of theory and research for the management of human resources. The topics for books in this series are carefully selected with a concern for traditionally important issues, new topics in the field, and new, innovative treatments of traditional topics. Thus, the series is open-ended with regard to both content and size, with no constraints on the number of volumes that will be included. The volumes in the series are all written by notable scholars, recognized throughout the field of human resources management.

Gerald R. Ferris
Kendrith M. Rowland
Series Consulting Editors

PREFACE

This book is about research. It deals with such topics as the nature of research questions, research methods, research designs and the analysis and interpretation of research data. In short it covers most areas that one might find in any up-to-date and comprehensive social science research methods text. But it is also about human resources management. It reviews or considers the problems or functions that face those involved in designing, developing, implementing or managing the elements of human resources programs found in most modern work organizations. Thus models and theories of selection; individual, group and organizational performance; work attitudes and motivation; and employee development are described and woven into our discussion of various research methods. In doing so, we feel that it makes clear the relevance of the many design and methods issues covered. Moreover, it allows us to use numerous recent examples of applied research in order to stress the object lessons that must be a part of a course on research. Thus, we frequently highlight the choices made by various investigators as they conducted their studies, pointing out both positive and not so positive outcomes of these choices. In combining these themes throughout the text, we hope that we have produced a research methods text that will be more directly useful than other similar texts.

This book is also about theory and practice. In the content, tone, and examples used in the book, we have tried consciously to attend to the needs and point of view of those who are involved in research in order to develop, refine, or manage human resource programs or policies. However, we have also incorporated the perspective of investigators who are interested in creating and testing theories of behavior in work settings. In this regard, the reader will frequently have the opportunity to be able to compare and contrast the two orientations on various topics (e.g. research design). We feel that this broader treatment will promote a better understanding of the multiple functions that could be served by good research on human resource topics. To the extent that the message is absorbed by the diverse groups of readers, who we feel will be exposed to this book, cooperation between those working on the inside of organizations (human resource specialists) and those on the outside (academic researchers) should be enhanced when they join together in a research enterprise.

We would like to acknowledge the careful and detailed reviews of an earlier draft of this book provided by Richard Arvey, Michael Campion, Jack Feldman, and Eugene Stone. Their comments were very constructive. As a result, we feel that the book is not only stronger from a content point of view, it is easier to follow and digest. We also appreciate the support of Jerry Ferris and Ken Rowland. With their encouragement as consulting editors for South-Western, we were able to produce the kind of research methods text we feel is needed in the field. Finally, credit must go to Marcy Schafer for her diligence and skill in preparing the final manuscript for the book. She did an enormous job in bringing together chapters and figures produced by two authors hundreds of miles apart. Her work was thorough and professional in every respect.

Neal Schmitt
Richard Klimoski

ABOUT THE AUTHORS

Neal Schmitt is a 1972 Ph.D. graduate of the Industrial Psychology program at Purdue University. Since 1974, he has been at Michigan State University where he is now a Professor of Psychology and Management. He coauthored *Staffing Organizations* (1986) with Ben Schneider. His research on personnel selection and decision making has appeared in *Academy of Management Journal, Personnel Psychology, Journal of Applied Psychology, Applied Psychological Measurement,* and various other journals. He was President of the Society for Industrial and Organizational Psychology in 1989–90 and is current editor of the *Journal of Applied Psychology*. He has received several research grants and has consulted with a number of private and public organizations on various human resource problems.

Richard Klimoski is Professor of Psychology and Vice Chair of the Department of Psychology, Ohio State University, Columbus, Ohio. Richard joined the faculty at Ohio State University in 1970 after receiving his Ph.D. from Purdue University in Psychology and Management. His teaching and research interests revolve around the areas of organizational control systems in the form of performance appraisal and performance feedback programs. His research has appeared in *Journal of Applied Psychology, Personnel Psychology, Academy of Management Journal, Administrative Science Quarterly,* and *Journal of Conflict Resolution*. Richard is the past Chair of the Personnel/Human Resources Division of the Academy and holds positions on the Editorial Review Boards of the *Academy of Management Review* (consulting editor), *Journal of Applied Psychology, Human Resource Review* and *Personnel Psychology*. He served on the Editorial Review Board of the *Academy of Management Journal* (1985–1987) and *Administrative Science Quarterly* (1978–1988). He is a Fellow of the Society for Industrial Organizational Psychology (a division of the American Psychological Association) and of the American Psychological Society.

CONTENTS

CHAPTER 1

AN EMPIRICAL APPROACH TO HUMAN RESOURCE RESEARCH

In this chapter, we describe our objectives and the general outline of the text. A brief history of research on human resource issues in organizations is presented. Various approaches to the acquisition of knowledge are described as is the logic of research. Conceptualization and operationalization of the variables in research studies are of central concern in any research effort if the findings are to result in maximum gains in information. One primary purpose of research is to make causal inferences and we describe the features of research studies that are most critical when we seek to strengthen the inferences we make. Finally, we describe the issues that are important when one is interested in producing organizational change as a result of research efforts.

WHY RESEARCH

In this book, we describe a variety of ways in which to design research and use methods to gather data relevant to human resource issues. It is our belief that knowledge of the appropriate design of data collection efforts and the ability to draw correct inferences from the data collected are important for human resource practitioners and researchers alike. This belief is based on the premise that data-based human resource management is superior to intuition-based management.

Our objectives in this book are several, but the most important is to educate future practitioners and scholars about the methods used to investigate human resource issues. In so doing, we hope to convince the reader of the value of sound research in solving organizational problems and developing knowledge and theory in human resource management. We believe the value of research is apt to be most appreciated when it is clear that the research methods yield information relevant to a particular content area in which the reader has some interest. Hence, much of this book also contains discussion of theory (e.g., motivation as it relates to compensation plans) and practical concerns (how to do job evaluation) of relevance to human resource students, professionals, and academics. Finally, we recognize that many of our readers may not conduct research studies using the various methods described in this book, but we feel that anyone involved in human resource issues ought to be well-informed consumers of research studies. We feel that the student or professional who understands the various methods and logic of good research will be able to evaluate research proposals, reports, and studies that will be of importance to human resource personnel working in a wide variety of contexts.

Perhaps some examples will clarify the distinction we draw between data-based and intuition-based management. One of your authors was recently asked by a group hoping to start a small business to evaluate a test which supposedly yielded important insight into people's personality based on their preference for color. The business pitch was that the manager should take the test and perhaps give it to two other staff members, and score the test. With this "overwhelming" evidence of the test's accuracy, the cover letter read, the manager would surely want to use this procedure more widely. Use of this kind of salespitch clearly takes advantage of the consumer's lack of appreciation for appropriately validated and empirically supported selection procedures. It relies on the manager or the human resource staff person's tendency to respond intuitively. The example as presented here may sound ridiculous but many similar actual examples can be cited. Belief in the utility of handwriting analysis is widespread in various parts of the world. Polygraph testing and written honesty tests are often used even though empirical justification for these methods is weak, at best.

Consider the large manufacturing company whose vice president for labor relations called one of your authors in to ascertain what could be done to convince workers to accept contracts that paid less money to help the company to maintain a sizable profit margin. His thesis was that we should do something to change worker values and to increase their trust in management. While he was convinced that efforts in this regard would produce change in worker attitudes, he also acknowledged that the company had committed to building new facilities in regions of the country in which the work force would be kept "union free." The vice president was acting on his belief or intuition that workers' attitudes were faulty.

Perhaps the most common example of the use of intuition versus data is represented by the continued use of unstructured interviews to select people. Dozens of studies document the fact that unstructured interviews, in which the decision maker relies on her or his intuition to judge the interviewee, have relatively little predictive validity. On the other hand, structured interviews in which carefully and systematically developed job-related questions are presented to each job candidate and for which an attempt has been made through applied research to identify desirable and undesirable responses have been found to provide useful and valid data on which to make personnel decisions. The methods discussed in this text will contribute to (a) the development of better interviews, (b) increased ability to assess the claims of consultants who help to develop selection interviews, and (c) greater ability to evaluate the contribution of new selection programs.

Other examples include the use of casual customer surveys or unsolicited complaints or compliments regarding a training program as indices of the quality of a meal and restaurant service or the training program's effectiveness. These practices ignore the fact that many other factors determine who bothers to make these comments (e.g., how busy the customers are). Compliments or complaints about a training program may have a significant impact on the trainer but they may or may not be related to what the trainee learns or can translate into changes in work performance. Further, unless an appropriate sample of customers or trainees are interviewed or surveyed, we know nothing of the opinions of the group of persons who chose not to comment.

In each of these examples, the point is not that the decision made would always be wrong but rather that the manager is acting only on a hunch, belief, or intuition about human behavior. Such decisions could be much better informed and of better quality had an effort been made to collect data and specify how one's observations led to particular conclusions. In the case of the color preference personality test, the informed manager would know something about the validity of such procedures. Further, the manager also would recognize the need for more documentation of this test's utility either in other organizations or in the one in which she or he is employed. The vice president for labor relations would likely gain a broader perspective on workers' commitment to the company's long-term economic viability and their work values if some representative sample of the workforce were interviewed or surveyed with a well-constructed instrument. And certainly those who use unstructured interviews as the basis for employment decisions would realize their limitation if they took a moment to read the research literature on interviews or if they made an attempt to check interview validity in their own organization.

In data-based management, we *attempt* to be objective. All knowledge of the world, or of organizations, is affected and perhaps distorted to some extent by the predispositions of the observers. And the more complex our observations, the farther from physical reality and the greater the inferences that must be made, the greater is the probability of distortion. In recruiting and selecting design engineers in a high tech firm, there may be an attempt to ascertain how creative their ideas and research are, but people (including engineers) frequently have different notions about what represents creativity. Unless some agreed-upon method to make observations is adopted and followed, the actual reports of creative behavior are likely to be quite different. In this case *objectivity* is agreement among "expert" judges on what is observed or what is to be done or has been done in research. *Any* observers with minimal competence should agree in their observations. Further, when social scientists (e.g., human resource researchers) do experiments or collect data, they do so in a way (and describe what they do) that other researchers can replicate. In short, social scientists not only should tell you what they believe about human behavior, but also what was observed and how those observations led to a particular conclusion or belief. Moreover, these observations must be subject to verification. In this text we argue that interobserver agreement and replication are important indicators of objectivity.

A BRIEF HISTORY OF RESEARCH ON PEOPLE AT WORK

Research in human resource issues of the type discussed in this book probably originated with psychologists in the early part of this century. In the following sections we outline the nature of early psychologists' early participation in solving human resource problems. Clearly, individuals in other fields, such as industrial engineering, management, marketing, and sociology, contributed to the development of the methods and research described in this text. In fact, some of the individuals whose contributions are cited in this section were trained in these disciplines. Our material derives from the excellent works of Baritz (1960), Ferguson (1962), and Stagner (1981).

The Early Years: 1890–1914

Industrialists of this period initially were not particularly interested in what psychologists (or any other academic specialists) could do for them. They were confident that they could solve whatever problems that faced the companies because they had the requisite abilities and experience.

But several factors were operating to change this initial disinterest. First, it was a time of industrial growth and of labor unrest. Workers were demanding more. Baritz (1960) also notes that in the 1890's there appeared to be a greater acceptance by industry of the role of government in the affairs of business. Government commissions were often staffed with experts from universities. Perhaps it was felt that academics could, after all, bring some new and effective ideas to bear on their problems.

Psychology, too, was changing. Wilhelm Wundt's promotion of psychology as an experimental (empirical) science had a tremendous effect on the field. As an offshoot of philosophy, the emphasis to that point had been in the search for universal laws (or truths), especially those which could account for our mental processes. But these endeavors had been frustrated by a reliance on traditional methods of investigation, like introspection. Wundt and others promoted empiricism, measurement, and operational definitions as opposed to speculation. New researchers also began to study physical and psychological differences among people. For example, James McKeen Cattell (who took his doctorate at Leipzig where he worked for Wundt) became impressed with the work of Galton on the nature and measurement of individual differences. Moving to the University of Pennsylvania, he became the first American professor of psychology. It was not just the recording and listing of human variability (in physical and mental abilities) or investigating their implications that was of interest to Cattell. The issue for him and many others of the day quickly shifted to uncovering the *causes* of these measured differences.

Increasingly, the work of academic researchers seemed to have some relevence to many industrial managers. If individual differences (as in numerical or mathematical aptitude) could be shaped by experience, management might feel that it was appropriate to stress training their workers. But if this variability came about largely as a result of genetic (hereditary) factors, such an emphasis on training would be wasted. Instead, the key to good performance might lie in personnel selection.

The implications of research on human behavior also were noticed because of the work of another psychologist, William McDougall. A Harvard professor, McDougall published his book, *Introduction to Social Psychology*, in 1908. In it he described and promoted a theory of human behavior that stressed the role of instincts. Instincts were felt to be relatively enduring properties of individuals, perhaps genetically determined, which shaped perceptions and actions. For over 20 years, his book appealed to the public, and several editions sold out immediately. His theory of instincts became a popular way to think about what motivates people. Thus, it was especially valued by those who made a living trying to affect human motivation on a regular basis—the advertisers. The first application of psychological theory and research to the world of business and industry was probably in advertising (Baritz, 1960). Interest in applications of psychology to advertising was further promoted by the publication of the Psychology of Advertising by Walter Dill Scott. In this book he emphasized the possibility that ads might be used to appeal to people's instincts, such as hoarding and hunting.

By 1910, Scott established a successful relationship with industry that was to last for many years. In 1911, he wrote one of the original textbooks in the field of Industrial Psychology (Scott, 1911). And by 1915 he was working on selection programs for the American Tobacco Company, Western Electric, and National Lead Co.

As industrialists saw the value of behavioral science for the areas of marketing and staffing, and as more opportunities became available to them, the field itself began to take form. One individual who was to accelerate this process was Hugo Munsterberg. Munsterberg also was trained in Germany. He received an M.D. in 1885 and a Ph.D. under Wundt in 1887. While at the University of Berlin he developed a series of lectures that were first published in German and later translated into a classic book, the *Psychology of Industrial Efficiency* (1913). Munsterberg felt that this new science lay somewhere between basic psychology and economics. In his book he took care to detail its application and potential in areas as diverse as vocational guidance, training, personnel selection, and marketing. He also acknowledged an intellectual debt to scientific management theories of the time but felt that it was up to psychologists to represent and worry about the human element in organizations.

Munsterberg emphasized the importance of vocational guidance and personnel selection. The goal was to help organizations to select workers who would perform better and experience greater job satisfaction (Moskowitz, 1977). He also was explicit in his belief that industrial psychologists, as staff or as consultants, should stay out of policy decisions, even if they affected workers. He felt that psychologists should remain detached scientists who had no right to proclaim what effect (result) is good and what is bad. It was management who would decide when and where to apply the "psychological levers" that were uncovered from research. And, certainly, the profitability of the firm should always be kept foremost in mind.

It was not only Munsterberg's writings but also his work in industry that had a great impact. He developed tests for the selection of personnel in such diverse fields as sales (for the American Tobacco Company), bus driving (for the Boston Street Railway), and even ship captaincy. He was eclectic in his interests, doing work in advertising (especially in packing design and copyright infringement). Moreover, he was well read and built on the work of others such as Gilbreth, F.W. Taylor, and Woodworth (Moskowitz, 1977).

By the middle of the decade, the reputation of academic research in human behavior was growing, both within universities and in work organizations. Carnegie Institute (now Carnegie–Mellon University) in Pittsburgh under Walter Bingham (who received his Ph.D. from the University of Chicago in 1908) was the first to establish a program that offered a consulting service to industry. The modest program grew steadily. Bingham set up a Bureau of Salesmanship Research (focusing on the selection of sales personnel) and later created a Research Bureau for Retail Training. It is noteworthy that he persuaded several major retail companies in the area to contribute to the bureau as a consortium of sponsors. In return, he and his staff did work relevant to their concerns in the areas of employment tests, training manuals, and programs of work adjustment and better supervision. Also significant is the fact that Bingham was able to persuade Walter Dill Scott to come to Carnegie (from Northwestern) in 1916 as America's first professor of applied psychology (Baritz, 1960). These early efforts on the part of behavioral scientists were clearly interdisciplinary involving personnel interested in sales, marketing, management, training, etc.

The Great War

The period of the first World War was important to the development of both the work and the reputation of human resource specialists. In 1916, the National Research Council was organized in the United States. A year later the Committee for Psychology was formed and given the responsibility for finding ways of using this new group of specialists. The unit was led by Yerkes (on leave from Harvard) and involved Bingham and others with applied psychology interests. It was quickly decided that their expertise could best be utilized in the areas of training and selection.

In particular, it was this group that identified the work of Otis as relevant to personnel selection. Up until that point in time, most testing (for selection or other functions) was done on an individual basis. But Otis had developed the basic concept of the multiple-choice response format, thereby making it possible for truly large-scale testing, application, and efficient scoring. Otis's work became the basis for the Army Alpha intelligence test, which was ultimately given to over 1,700,000 men. And all of these people were to leave the military with some awareness (for better or for worse) of testing.

Theories and procedures of performance appraisal were also developed during those years. As early as 1912, the Larkin Company had used management ratings of its supervisors to make annual bonus awards. But they were not that popular. During this period, the Committee on Classification, directed by Walter Scott (with the assistance of Bingham and Watson, the founder of American behaviorist psychology), did a great deal of work on performance appraisal for purposes of promotion and future military assignments.

All this created a supportive climate for the use of the behavioral and social sciences immediately after the war. The growth of the civilian economy and the rapid demobilization caused managers to seek out and employ psychologists. In a survey of the period, many members of the

American Psychological Association would eagerly claim to be doing work in industry in such areas as selection testing, job analysis, and the measurement of worker attitudes and worker morale.

About this time, the *Journal of Applied Psychology* was founded (1917) and still exists today as a key professional journal. In 1919, Scott formed his own consulting company in Philadelphia and Cattell started the Psychological Corporation. The growth and acceptance of human resource specialists in industry was also occurring in other countries at this time, especially in Europe. For example, in Germany in 1922, 22 firms had personnel research laboratories.

The Post-War Years

While testing lost some of its appeal between the two world wars, an important series of research studies was carried out over a span of 15 years at the Western Electric Company. These are known collectively as the Hawthorne Studies because they were conducted at the Hawthorne works of the company in the Chicago area. Numerous descriptions of these studies exist (e.g., Baritz, 1960; Bramel & Friend, 1981; Parsons, 1974; Roethlisberger & Dickson, 1939; Whitehead, 1938), and their significance is still being debated. While we don't intend to resolve any of the points of controversy, we will briefly examine these studies for the insights that they give into the forces that shaped human resource research for years afterward.

In 1924, the National Research Council decided to support studies on worker productivity. In particular, it called for an examination of physical working conditions and the role of lighting in the workplace. After considering a number of offers from companies who wanted to cosponsor the project, Western Electric Company was selected. At the time Western Electric provided the telephones and switching equipment needed by AT&T. The company had over 20,000 employees and was considered a progressive (even a worker-oriented) company. Management was pleased to have been chosen as the site for such important and nationally visible research.

One of the Hawthorne Studies involved actual experiments on illumination. It was organized by engineers in cooperation with an industry-supported group called the Committee on Industrial Lighting (Bramel & Friend, 1981). Following reasonable experimental design and procedures, workers were assigned to a control or experimental condition. Levels of illumination were varied (manipulated) for the latter groups in a systematic manner, and records of worker productivity were kept.

These studies turned out to be somewhat frustrating to those conducting them. It was found that worker productivity actually did improve. But output was unrelated to the levels of illumination experienced. Moreover, during the same periods, those in the control group also raised their productivity. Clearly, something other than physical working conditions was operating to affect productivity. But they were unable to pinpoint what this was.

A second set of experiments was approached with a greater appreciation of the complexity of the problem. They were conducted from 1927-1930 on groups of workers in the relay assembly and mica splitting areas. The former were responsible for making electromechanical switching devices called relays; the latter prepared materials (mica) for use. Two things were noteworthy about this series of studies. One was that workers were selected for participation and relocated in special areas of the plant. This meant they could be isolated from other workers not in the studies and could be more closely observed which, it was thought, would lead to "cleaner" (less ambiguous) results. Another feature of this second series was that they marked the earliest participation of social scientists, primarily Elton Mayo, in the Hawthorne Studies.

It was the first study in this series which has been one of the most publicized. Five women workers were exposed to varying combinations of starting and stopping times and work breaks. But once again the results were complex and confusing. It did not seem to make a great deal of difference what combination of starting times, pauses, etc., was in effect. Worker productivity seemed to increase beyond levels typically found on the factory floor. After some deliberation, the conclusion drawn by Mayo (and others) was that productivity increased largely as a result of the unique social conditions surrounding the workers in the experiment. It was felt that the special attention paid to them by the researchers, and their friendly style, was reciprocated by the workers in the study in the form of greater effort and productivity. Over the years, this effect, in which the phenomenon under study is inadvertently influenced by the process of studying it, is frequently referred to as the Hawthorne Effect. In this case, the social scientists actually caused productivity to increase through their intrusive research methods. The subjects (workers) apparently were not affected so much by the formal manipulations (e.g., work break schedule) as they were by the questions being asked of them about their feelings toward the work breaks!

It should be noted that other interpretations of the reasons for the results of this well-publicized study have been offered. For example, Parsons (1974) argues that the more explicit measurement of worker performance used by the psychologists provided new and valuable feedback to the workers and that it was this that spurred effort and productivity. Others, like Bramel and Friend (1981) emphasize that the workers were responding to implied threats and pressures by management. In fact, they point out that there actually was resistance to the notion of higher productivity by some, who were ultimately dismissed during the course of the experiment.

In any event Mayo was convinced that something in the nature of the social relationship in the workplace (especially within work groups and between work groups and their supervisors) helped account for both worker attitudes (morale) and behavior (performance). He persuaded an anthropologist, W. Lloyd Warner, to come into the program to study these work relationships. Warner, in turn, chose to use a prevalent method of his discipline, the method of unobtrusive (non-participatory) observation.

In their studies of teams of men assembling complex electrical switching mechanisms, Warner and his colleagues discovered a complex network of social relationships that controlled a great deal of team behavior. Most startling was the way they regulated production. In fact, individuals were not working as hard as they could be, but performed at some level that they perceived as a "fair day's work." Group members, especially the informal leaders, used a variety of techniques (from teasing to social ostracism) to prevent deviation from this group norm. It also seemed clear that this arrangement protected the work group from management pressure for higher production. For if one team (or individual) demonstrated extraordinary output, management would be certain to expect and demand more work of everyone. Given our current understanding of work group dynamics, these "discoveries" seem less than impressive to us today. Nonetheless, they represented a radically different view of the workplace than was held by managers of the company. This view gave rise to what has been referred to as the Human Relations Movement.

During this period between the wars, more and more companies were using psychologists to design and conduct attitude or morale surveys for this purpose. In 1932, Rensis Likert developed a very valuable attitude measurement technique that was to become a standard in the field of survey work (Seashore & Katz, 1982). He also wrote an influential book (with Gardner Murphy) titled *Public Opinion and the Individual* (1938). Kornhauser and Sharp, at the University of Chicago, did survey work for Kimberly-Clark. Other companies active in the area of employee surveys included Armstrong, Sears, Roebuck & Co., and Proctor and Gamble.

The Wagner-Peyser Act of 1933 brought into existence the Occupational Research Program which produced the *Dictionary of Occupational Titles*, a reference tool that has been continually upgraded and is still in wide use today.

The 1930s also produced the widespread use of formal training programs in organizations. Casual (on-the-job) training had traditionally been used, but until then only a few companies (U.S. Steel, Eastman Kodak, Chrysler) had established classroom-like training programs. Much of this new formal training was aimed at managers and supervisors and, in the spirit of the Human Relations Movement, emphasized leadership skills.

The Second World War

The employment of psychologists and human resource specialists in government and the military during the Second World War increased rapidly. Over 1,700 were to be involved in the armed forces. They did research, development and implementation work in a wide variety of areas. Some worked in personnel selection, training (especially management training), and on problems of absenteeism, turnover, and morale. Others were involved in unusual assignments (e.g., selecting and training bomber pilots, espionage agents, submariners), in analyzing propaganda, in developing campaigns to sell war bonds, in training personnel to deal with foreign cultures, and in the design of military hardware and technology. With the advent of new, expensive and more complex and sophisticated weapons (especially aircraft), many psychologists got more interested in not only the selection of people to operate these weapon systems, but also in the optimal design of the hardware itself. They did research and development work on such things as gun sighting mechanisms, cockpit design, tank controls, etc. Thus human factors research received a great deal of prominence during this period.

The new technology of worker attitude measurement derived in the 1930's was also put to use in the war effort. For example, Likert worked for the Department of Agriculture to conduct surveys of farmers regarding crop planting habits and intentions. He also designed studies to determine civilian plans for war bonds redemption (Seashore & Katz, 1982). The federal government encouraged private industry to use attitude surveys to define potential employee problems. They were concerned with anything that might precipitate a strike which would cripple the critical industries. In a large-scale effort, Ford Motor Company sent surveys to over 124,700 production and salaried employees to assess their concerns (Baritz, 1960). Although "only" 22,000 replied, some major problem areas were uncovered in this way.

Performance appraisal programs also enjoyed a great deal of popularity at this time. The military had found them useful for making promotion decisions with regard to officer ranks. Industry took the lead of these successes.

Recent Decades

In this short historical review, we see the beginning of interest in various human resource content areas and research issues that comprise a major portion of this book. Interest in worker abilities and attitudes and the measurement of their abilities and attitudes, as well as the use of observational techniques, interviews, and experimental research (especially on human factors and safety issues) all had been introduced and applied to human resource problems by the end of World War II. Events since World War II also have had a significant impact on the research issues and methods used as well. The civil rights movement and civil rights legislation and litigation have had a major impact on selection research. Issues having to do with pay differentials between men and women have stimulated research on compensation and the methods large companies use to establish their pay policy. Interest in quality of work life programs in the 1970s stimulated renewed interest in worker attitudes and perceptions and how these perceptions might relate to productivity and perceived quality of life and job satisfaction. Finally the 1980s might be characterized by a great deal of interest in productivity and the evaluations of methods designed to enhance it. Moreover, increased litigation and union–management arbitration issues necessitate continued need for quality research data.

In many of the historical developments just described, the researchers have sought to collect data in an objective manner to better guide the way we manage people. But you probably realize any understanding of behavior in work settings requires more than a single study. Thus, we (the research community, in general) prefer to build on a body of research evidence or conduct a series of studies in which we gradually increase our knowledge of some aspect of human behavior. Confidence in our inferences and in our decisions is strengthened through replication.

In the next section, we briefly describe how scientific inquiry proceeds. This description represents an idealized scenario, but we believe that it is important to understand how best to conduct research so that we can appreciate the implications of various tradeoffs that almost inevitably must be made when conducting applied investigations.

THE ORIGINS OF RESEARCH

Research can be thought of as a way of knowing about aspects of behavior or phenomena in organizations. In many respects it also should be viewed as a means to an end, usually with that end being that we become more informed and make potentially more valid human resource management (HRM) decisions.

Research can be used for description, prediction, and/or understanding. But research work can originate for any number of specific reasons. Some of these will reflect the investigators motives, others will reflect institutional needs. Because these reasons will have a major impact on many of the choices made and the actual form that the research will take, it might be useful to list some of the more likely reasons involved.

For the academically based investigator, research might be conducted to:

1. Develop a new theory.
2. Test or refine an existing theory.
3. Compare or evaluate two or more theories or theoretical positions.
4. Resolve contradictory predictions derived from two or more theories in a particular area.
5. Reconcile discrepant findings reported in the published literature.
6. Bridge or build linkages among two or more streams of research.
7. Follow up on recommendations for future research offered by authors in their published work.

On the other hand, the practitioner, as a staff professional or as a consultant, may have still other reasons for conducting research. Such a person is likely to be interested in:

1. Assessing organizational needs for HRM programs or interventions (e.g., training needs).
2. Resolving conflicts or competing preferences by members of management with regard to practices or policies (e.g., whether a flexible or a traditional work schedule should be followed).
3. Creating components of HRM systems (e.g., establishing pay grades).
4. Evaluating current programs, policies, or practices (e.g., the impact of a benefits package).
5. Meeting government agency reporting requirements (e.g., compiling EEO data).

6. Providing data for arguments in litigation (e.g., product liability).
7. Diagnosing the causes for organizational problems (e.g., high rates of voluntary turn-over).

Thus, research can be self-motivated, generated by pragmatic concerns, or legally mandated.Throughout this book, however, we will argue that regardless of the impetus for the research or the particular form that it takes, the "rules" for quality research and for confidence regarding our findings will be the same. A person who masters these rules (and the skills associated with their implementation) will be more likely to produce higher quality decisions (conclusions) or recommendations. Thus, good research, like good thinking, is required in all domains of human resource management and organizational behavior.

WAYS OF KNOWING

Throughout this book we will emphasize that investigators have a wealth of options when it comes to learning about (knowing) organizationally relevant phenomena. Blackburn (1987) clusters these into anecdotal/observational approaches, survey approaches, and experimental approaches.

Anecdotal/Observational Approaches.

These approaches refer to the gathering and sorting of information through relatively informal methods. In its most typical form, managers or researchers may rely on personal experiences and the comments of colleagues. Or, issues of fact or the causes of events may be dealt with by asking a few people on an opportune basis what they think. In its most sophisticated versions, the manager or researcher might master and make use of the variety of techniques described in detail in Chapter 4.

Survey Approaches

As outlined in Chapter 10, survey methods and survey research data are very popular for a wide variety of applications. Moreover, the careful and appropriate use of survey data can provide a reasonable basis for organizational decision making. But the survey approach has limitations as well. For purposes of this discussion, it's important to emphasize the point that survey data can provide only the most indirect evidence for cause-and-effect relations. Because we often need cause-and-effect knowledge to make valid choices or decisions, this is an important limitation. We often use survey data and the relationships that they reveal to rule out certain factors as unlikely causes. Some might use survey information as a source of tentative support for a theory or policy assumption. However, all must remain tentative. Given the nature of survey study designs, survey methods and the resultant data, asserting knowledge of causality would be inappropriate. There are usually too many alternative explanations for the results.

Experimental Approaches

Experimental methods and designs have evolved over the years and provide the strongest evidence regarding cause-and-effect relationships. The many variations in experimentation outlined in Chapter 11 are, in a sense, testimony to the fact that it is very important to the organizational sciences for theory building and theory testing. We would argue that it also has an important role to play in the development and assessment of organizational policies and practices.

As you will learn, as powerful as the experimental approach can be, there are still major theoretical and practical limitations as to what it can do. More importantly, one should not be overly impressed with a study solely because it is portrayed as an experiment. Because there are so many options (or choice points) available to an investigator, it would be prudent to scrutinize carefully what was done to be certain that it is consistent with good practices as outlined in this book.

Even the best thought out and the most carefully executed experiments may have weaknesses. Given the realities of organizational life, this is especially likely to be the case when we try to investigate something in an actual organizational setting. The point here is that one must become skilled to recognize and distinguish between minor and major (or "fatal") flaws in any research design or method. In a sense, rather than reject the result of a study outright, we need to let our knowledge of good experimental research guide us with regard to just how much confidence we should have in a particular set of findings. Only under these circumstances will clear cut conclusions regarding the value of a study be possible or warranted (Runkel & McGrath, 1972).

Each of these ways of knowing has a place in providing insights into the nature of organizations and organizational life. However, it is the experimental approach that has the potential for producing research findings that will allow us to form conclusions with the least equivocality (Rosenthal & Rosnow, 1984). Thus it will be the focus of the section to follow.

THE LOGIC OF EXPERIMENTAL RESEARCH

In order to develop competence in experimental research it is important to understand the logic of this approach. Only then can the many issues associated with research design and research methods be fully appreciated.

The Conceptual Framework

Experimental research is usually built around some view or understanding of what is to be studied. Even in exploratory work using qualitative methods (Chapter 4) or in correlational/survey studies, the researcher must be reasonably articulate with regard to the factors involved in the phenomenon that is being investigated. In good experimental work, it is almost a necessity.

In its simple form, the characterization of an investigator's beliefs would be considered a framework. Thus, in some fashion (preferably in writing) the researcher would specify the number and nature of the variables involved (these are the factors of interest, each of which vary along some continuum) and the relationships thought to exist among these variables (e.g., variable *x* causes variable *y*, which in turn affects variable *z*). Usually the framework will include a number of such variables thought to be necessary and sufficient to understand or explain the organizational phenomenon of interest. In such a framework, it is common to think and speak in terms of the independent or causal variable and the dependent or resultant (criterion) variable. However, as pointed out later, most frameworks are more complicated than this.

Theories

In a more fully developed form the researcher's ideas might be offered as a *theory*. In general, a theory is more sophisticated than a framework in that it goes beyond just identifying the variables of interest and their approximate relationships; instead, it describes the functional or precise nature of how the factors interact. A theory would include a statement of the boundaries or conditions under which such relationships would be valid. It also would provide or imply propositions or conclusions which can be reasonably expected to follow from the model, based on logical deductions. Similarly, a theory is a creation of the researcher who attempts to model some aspect of the "real world" in order to simplify and understand it. A theory or theoretical model is scientific only if it is possible to subject the theory to an empirical test (Dubin, 1976a). A great deal of research on organizations involves testing or modifying some framework or theory.

There are many different types of theories. Bordens and Abbott (1988) classify theories along three dimensions: quantitative/qualitative, level of description, and the scope of the theory. Expressed mathematically, a *quantitative theory* specifies the variables of interest in numerical terms and relates the numerical states of these variables to one another. One quantitative theory of interest to human resource personnel is expectancy theory as described by Vroom (1964). According to this theory, effort at some task or job is the product of valence (an employee's feelings about work outcome), instrumentality (the perceived degree of relationship between performance and outcomes) and expectancy (the perceived relationship between effort and performance). Formally, where

$$W = E \left(\sum_{i=1}^{N} V_i I_i \right) \tag{1.1}$$

W = work, E = expectancy, V_i = valence of outcome i, I_i = instrumentality associated with outcome i, and $\sum_{i=1}^{N}$ indicates a sum of the $V_i I_i$ products for the relevant performance outcomes.

According to this theory, work effort will be a product of the degree to which you believe working hard will result in good performance and the sum of your beliefs that performance will lead to valued outcomes such as pay and a sense of accomplishment.

By contrast, Maslow's theory of motivation is *qualitative*. He theorized that individuals will be motivated first by the most basic needs in a hierarchy of needs ranging from the lowest needs to the highest human need as follows: physiological, security, social, self-esteem, and self-actualization. As lower needs are satisfied, they become less important and higher needs arise. If such higher need satisfaction is thwarted, then lower needs are resurrected. This theory does not specify the mathematical relationships between needs; in fact, some would say Maslow did not present testable hypotheses nor discuss how the needs he described ought to be measured.

Descriptive theories—the second dimension along which theories vary—provide only a description of some behavior as opposed to an explanation of the relationships among a set of variables that influence some behavior. Perhaps one example of a purely descriptive theory is *arousal theory*. Task performance is thought to increase with arousal up to some optimal point then decrease with increases in arousal. The proposed relationship between performance and arousal is an inverted U. Arousal and performance are general concepts which can be defined, or operationalized in a number of ways. Note the theory describes the relationship, but offers no explanation for it.

At the next level are *analogical theories*, which attempt to explain behavior by analogy to better-known models of phenomenon, usually from the physical sciences. An example of an analogical theory is Landy's *opponent process theory* (1978) of job satisfaction. Landy used the physiology of color vision as an analogue to explain emotional reactions to one's circumstances. If one is very happy, there is a physiological opponent response that serves to bring the person back to neutral. Over time, this opponent process becomes stronger, hence individuals become more neutral or bored about their jobs. Also the opponent process may over correct just as it does in color vision. This over correction means that persons who have had a very exciting experience will experience a "let down" later on during a period of time in which they may be less happy than if nothing pleasant had ever occurred.

Other theorists do not depend on analogy but propose a new structure that directly relates variables in a system. The structure, called *fundamental theory,* usually includes unobservable entities and processes that are invented to account for observable relationships. By assuming the presence of gravity and the strength of its force as it related to the mass and distance between planets, Newton was able to account for planetary orbits. Fundamental theories are rare in the behavioral sciences, though perhaps Festinger's dissonance theory (1957) represents one example. Festinger posited that whenever two attitudes or behaviors are inconsistent, a negative psychological state called cognitive dissonance is aroused. Individuals are motivated to reduce dissonance and do so by changing either their attitudes or their behavior. Festinger's theory described how dissonance leads to behavioral or attitudinal change.

Theories also can be distinguished by virtue of the domain of situations to which the theory can be usefully applied. Festinger's theory has been used to explain a wide variety of attitudinal and motivational processes. Most of the theories of human behavior are much more limited in scope. For an excellent treatment of issues involved in theory building in organizational research, the reader is directed to the special issue of the *Academy of the Management Review* (October, 1989).

As we shall see at various points in this text, theories serve as a source of hypotheses—they provide understanding of the phenomenon we study, they direct or stimulate research, and they can be used to organize and interpret research results. We turn next to a consideration of the more explicit purpose for which we conduct research—that is, to test hypotheses derived from our frameworks, models, or theories.

Hypotheses

The propositions or conclusions implied by a theory easily become *hypotheses.* The latter are really formalized statements specifying key variables and their supposed relationships. What is special about hypotheses is that they are worded to include appropriate empirical indicators needed for testing (Dubin, 1976a). Moreover, good hypotheses are stated in such a way as to be complete enough that the reader knows the conditions that would allow them to be tested (Runkel & McGrath, 1972). Thus, one of the hallmarks of a good hypothesis is that it is stated in such a way that it can be disconfirmed.

A hypothesis then can be thought of as a piece of a theory that tells us where to look if we want to "find" a particular experience. Runkel and McGrath (1972) also stress that in its better form it is specific with regard to the people involved (e.g., all first level supervisors), the behaviors of interest (giving rewards) and the contexts in which events might occur (in manufacturing organizations). A good hypothesis also implies a comparison or contrast of interest. In the example developed here, the contrast may be between people, behaviors, or contexts. Thus, the reward-giving behaviors of supervisors may be postulated to produce different effects than punishing behaviors. Or the reward-giving behaviors of supervisors may be thought to have different consequences than the same behaviors demonstrated by managers.

A hypothesis is a tentative statement and usually takes the form "If this . . . , then. . . . " But even so, Ellsworth (1977) argues that it is important to specify the context in which the hypothesis is felt to be true. In particular, she distinguishes between a *universal hypothesis* versus an *existential hypothesis.* The former type implies that were it to be true, the phenomenon must operate or be found to exist in all contexts (work groups, organizations, etc). In contrast, the latter suggests that something only has to occur somewhere or sometime to be true. This distinction is more than a semantic nicety for it sets up expectations with regard to the kind of evidence we should be willing to accept as proof of a hypothesis's correctness. One example that is contrary to a universal hypothesis would be enough to disconfirm it. The (implicit or explicit) claims in a hypothesis also place a logical burden on an investigator. To use Ellsworth's words: "Existential hypotheses can be confirmed but never disconfirmed, universal hypotheses can be disconfirmed but never confirmed" (p. 609). In the latter case, we might continue to obtain results as predicted, but we would never be certain that the very next study wouldn't turn up negative. In practice then, researchers get around some of these dilemmas by specifying the conditions under which the hypotheses should or should not be supported.

SOURCE OF HYPOTHESES

To say that hypotheses are outgrowths of the propositions of a theory still begs the question of where they come from. In fact their origins can be quite diverse. A number of writers stress the importance of having first hand contact with or knowledge of a phenomenon as a good basis for research hypotheses (e.g., Daft, 1983; Rosenthal & Rosnow, 1984). For a manager, it means being around when organizational events happen, or noticing what Lundberg refers to as *paradoxical accidents* (something that doesn't make sense), or having a problem to solve, or perhaps being intrigued by some practitioner or craftsman's rule of thumb (e.g., "If you treat a person fairly, he or she will work hard."). The scientist might be more systematic in identifying or developing hypotheses. Certainly it is quite common for scientists to refer to prior writings and research, many of which literally call for a test of certain notions. In some cases, conflicting research findings or the identification of alternative interpretations become the source of testable research ideas. But, just as in the case of the manager or consultant, for the scientists, there is no substitute for familiarity (direct or vicarious) with the object or area of study.

In research then, investigators would use a framework or theory to position or justify the statement of the problem they will address. The research hypotheses narrow this down to the specific relationships of interest. It also turns out that hypotheses usually imply (or shape) the measures to be used, the research design to be followed, and even the methods involved. Thus, hypotheses constitute an important bridge between concepts (theory) and the operations that will be used (practice).

LEVEL OF KNOWLEDGE DICTATES THE RESEARCH APPROACH

It may not be evident yet, but it seems worthwhile to point out that in order to do hypothesis testing research you must have a fair amount of insight into the nature of the objects or events you want to study. The deductive nature of hypotheses and the many choice points that you will encounter in the design and execution of research require a strong conceptual understanding of a phenomenon. Thus, experimental research is very demanding in this regard. Another way to say this is that the depth of our understanding of a problem often dictates the choice of research alternatives. Case studies, descriptive surveys or relational research efforts may be preferred over experimental studies in light of very limited scientific or practical knowledge about an area.

Strong Inferences

The phrase *strong inference* is credited to Platt (1964), who used it to characterize an ideal approach for the development of cumulative knowledge in science (MacKenzie & House, 1978). However in many ways, it has come to signify both the hallmarks of good systematic and programmatic research and the goal of high quality data.

According to MacKenzie and House (1978), the strong inference approach to research is as much an attitude or state of mind on the part of the investigator as it is a set of procedures. This means that the researcher has come to believe that all theories are in some ways incorrect and will undergo change over time. Upon close study, however, better theories will hold up for some conditions. The task of the investigator, then, is to conduct research that disproves or rejects theories or to discover those circumstances under which theories appear to be correct.

Platt (1964) uses the tree metaphor to describe this idealized approach to building up knowledge. In this, the trunk of the tree represents the basic propositions of a theory where the discovery of evidence for support for the theory contributes to the upward and outward growth of the trunk. Research efforts then may add a branch, twig, or leaf where the data fail to reject a major or minor feature of the theory. That is to say, where attempts to find contrary evidence have failed, we have some growth. To continue the metaphor, Platt observes cases where studies have been carried out where there really is no good basis for the effort. He likens this to "examining a twig on a dead branch" (p. 348).

It is recognized that even well-trained researchers may be uncomfortable with the notion that science advances through the disproving of the postulates of a theory and through the development and testing of hypotheses that are falsifiable. After all, it is quite easy to get emotionally involved with (even identified with) a particular theory. To counter this, Platt recommends the notion of using multiple, perhaps competing, hypotheses to guide research. Multiple working hypotheses "distribute effort and divide affections" (Platt, 1964 p.351). This allows for a more rigorous test of the ideas put forth as we are likely to be less personally attached to a point of view. In applied research, this often comes about somewhat spontaneously in that different managers may, in fact, hold differing expectations (hypotheses) with regard to the likely impact of a particular program, practice, or policy. It remains for the alert researcher to articulate or state these expectations in an appropriate manner and then go on to test them in well-designed research.

To recap, the strong inference approach involves many of the features of good experimental research described above. That is to say, it includes the following:

1. Creating or adopting a general theoretical framework.
2. Identifying general laws or principles to explain what is known.
3. Creating or identifying how the laws should manifest themselves in organizations if they were indeed true (so-called bridging principles).
4. Deducing specific hypotheses from the general laws.
5. Conducting careful empirical research to test the hypotheses.
6. Modifying the theory based on findings.

As noted, the wording of the hypotheses in the strong inference approach is important as it is related to the logic or rules of evidence that we are willing to follow for the tentative acceptance or rejection of a theory. This logic asserts that if our theory is indeed true, then our hypotheses derived from the theory are likely to be also. So if we can show from our research that the latter is not true, we would have to modify our belief in the theory. Thus, we have the tradition of phrasing our research hypotheses in the negative (e.g., variable X will not influence variable Y). To put it another way, "we can conditionally reach deductively valid rejections of a hypothesis but not achieve a deductively valid affirmation of it" (MacKenzie & House, 1978 p. 17).

The thinking associated with a strong inference approach tends to create certain efficiencies. Careful deduction from a theory limits the areas worthy of investigation and allows for the focusing and the coordination of research efforts. In many cases, this will give rise to what Platt (1964) calls *crucial experiments*. These are experiments derived from essential postulates of a theory, which, when carried out, will provide tremendous insight into the validity of the theory.

Our ability to design and carry out crucial experiments in the organizational sciences is often quite limited, however. The theory itself may be so poorly developed that the necessary derivations may not be possible. More often, limited resources or the poor execution of the study may be to blame. In any event, as noted earlier, it is uncommon to reject a theory based on any single study.

It is far more likely that we will evaluate theories or parts of theories based on what is referred to as the *test record* that exists at a given point in time (Rosenthal & Rosnow, 1984). The test record is the cumulative evidence that we have. Because this is so important a topic, Chapter 12 has been devoted to how this can be done. In actual practice, Popper (1959) points out that it is not so much that our old theories get rejected outright, but that they usually lose their intellectual value and become supplanted by new ideas.

Rival Hypotheses

The concept of competing or rival hypotheses is a major feature of the strong inference approach. However, it is also central to research in general.

The goal of much of research is to establish cause-and-effect relations among variables. Some variables in a research study are set to a particular value. These variables are called *independent variables* and are the hypothesized cause of some *dependent variable*. In the case of organizational interventions (e.g., a training program), this usually means that we are interested in knowing if the planned activity has had a desired and predicted effect on some aspect of organizational functioning (e.g., job performance). In this case, the independent variable (training) might have two levels (present or absent). We would observe various aspects of the dependent variable, organizational functioning, to see if training had any effect. The individuals or organizations who do not receive training would belong to what might be called *control groups*, while those who do receive training would be in the *experimental groups*. As will be obvious in various parts of this book, we sometimes designate some of our variables as independent and others dependent when in fact this is not true in any experimental sense. Diagrammatically, however, the relationship between these two types of variables might look like this:

$$X \longrightarrow Y$$
$$\text{Training} \quad \text{Job Performance}$$

Logically, for us to be able to assert that an actual or causal relationship does indeed exist, at least three conditions must be met (Cook & Campbell, 1976; Ellsworth, 1977; Rosenthal & Rosnow, 1984):

1. *Temporal antecedence.* Variable X has to precede variable Y in time. In this case, training would have occurred before there were noticeable changes in job performance.
2. *Reliable covariance.* This means that if X changes in order of magnitude, so does Y. In this instance, as more training is given to an individual (or as more individuals in a work

group are trained), we would expect to see higher levels of individual or group performance.

3. *Plausible alternative (rival) explanations (hypotheses) can be ruled out.* That is, even if the above two conditions were met, it could be that something other than a cause-and-effect relationship exists between two variables to produce the pattern of data that we obtain. The investigator must be sensitive to this very real possibility. To put it another way, the quality of a study will be closely tied to the extent to which it deals with or can rule out rival explanations.

When there is a reliable relationship between two variables of interest, the prudent investigator should consider a number of alternatives to the preferred explanation ($X{\rightarrow}Y$). Ellsworth has identified several common ones in social science research. These are diagrammed in Figure 1-1.

Our theory might lead us to predict that X causes Y (no.1 in Figure 1-1). However, given only knowledge of covariation or condition 2 above, it could be that the reverse is true (no. 2 in Figure 1-1). That is, Y could cause X. If in addition to covariation, we meet the requirement of temporal antecedence, this rival hypothesis would then become less viable. But several others would still remain.

In certain domains of study (e.g., leadership), it is reasonable to envision that a reciprocal causal relationship (no.3 in Figure 1-1) might exist. Thus, the behavior of the leader (X) will cause changes in the performance of a worker (Y), but the latter will also affect the former (Lowin & Craig, 1968). In a somewhat more complicated scenario, a fourth possibility exists. It could be that the apparent relationship between X and Y is a function of a third, and in this case the truly causal, variable Z (no. 4 in Figure 1-1).

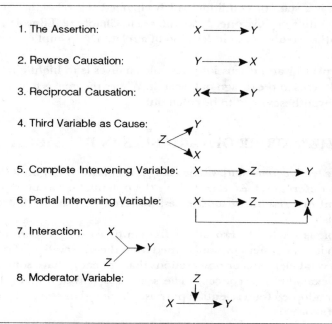

FIGURE 1-1   Alternatives to the Assertion that "X Causes Y"
Source: Reprinted with permission from Ellsworth, P. C. (1977). From abstract ideas to concrete instances: Some guidelines for choosing natural research settings. *American Psychologist, 33,* 604–615.

Ellsworth also identifies additional fairly common possible alternative relationships (and in a sense, rival hypotheses to the assertion that $X \rightarrow Y$). These are characterized in terms of the different roles that this third variable (Z) can play. Because these may be found in any area of research, they are worthy of some attention here.

It could be that a relationship exists between X and Y because Z serves as an *intervening variable*. As a complete *intervening variable* (no. 5 in Figure 1-1), X is viewed as causing Z which in turn, causes Y. To put it another way, if Z were not available, X and Y would no longer covary. Thus, it would be a mistake to conclude the simpler explanation. As a *partial intervening* variable (no. 6 in Figure 1-1), there would be some residual causal effect of X even if Z were to be taken away. Consequently, in the case of intervening variables, one gets into a discussion of proximal (most immediate) and ultimate causal relationships.

Two other possibilities regarding the true state of affairs regarding X and Y can be identified. As diagramed in no. 7 in Figure 1-1, it could be possible that variable X does indeed cause variable Y but only under certain circumstances. In this case such a causal impact will occur only when Z takes on certain values. If Z does not exist, the $X \rightarrow Y$ relationship may not be obtained.

The last scenario to be offered is where the variable Z acts as a moderator variable (no. 8 in Figure 1-1). In general, a moderator variable affects the nature of the relationship between two other variables (X and Y). It should be noted that in doing this it may not have any direct impact on these other variables. Thus, in general, we might note that highly directive or autocratic leaders (variable X) usually produce (cause) lower levels of worker satisfaction (variable Y). However, under conditions of time pressure or stress this directness is actually found to be associated with higher worker satisfaction. Apparently workers realize that, under time pressure, direct or unilateral action is appropriate and value or approve of a leader who is willing or able to behave accordingly. In this example, time pressure or stress, like variable Z, would be considered a moderator variable. It is a state or condition which changed the relationship between X and Y turning a negative one into a positive one. As we will see in Chapter 2, Ellsworth's last two cases do not differ from each other statistically. Moderation of a relationship implies that the two variables interact and vice versa.

The point of displaying and discussing these alternatives is to highlight the importance of considering rival hypotheses in the design of research. Where the goal is to establish strong causal inferences, such rival hypotheses need to be ruled out.

THE NATURE OF VARIABLES IN RESEARCH

We have used the term *variable* and will be using it regularly throughout this book to denote a symbol that takes on differing values. It must have the potential for assuming at least two states: It can be either absent or present. In most cases, however, we assume that variables will have multiple states or levels.

The term variable is related to two others frequently used by experimenters. The first is *concept*. A concept is an idea or generalization formed from the observation of particular instances. It is created to label several elements or observations that appear to have something in common. Job satisfaction is an example of a concept. The second is *construct,* a concept that has been deliberately created or adopted for a scientific purpose. As noted in several places, constructs are the basic elements of theories.

Concepts or constructs cannot be observed directly. They must be inferred. One of the functions of the observed or operationalized variable is to provide the empirical referents for concepts or constructs (Runkel & McGrath, 1972). In this case the empirical variable serves as an indicator of a hidden, presumed, or latent variable. We use one to infer the nature of the other. Unfortunately, a given term like "job satisfaction" may be used to refer to a concept, construct, or a variable. It should be kept in mind that not all variables need to imply a scientific construct.

We do, however, usually assume that operational variables reflect some underlying construct continuum. Thus, when we ask workers to complete a survey item regarding the number of different jobs that they have had prior to coming to work for a company, in all likelihood we will record and index this on a continuum from "none" to "many" and go on to relate this variable to others of interest. But notice that in doing this we are not invoking any notion of just what values on this continuum mean. It is only when we choose to label this variable "experience" that we are shifting from an empirical indicator, to one that is assumed to reflect some underlying construct.

In experimental research, we usually find ourselves concerned with the creation (or manipulation) of different levels of some factor of interest. As indicated above, this factor becomes the independent variable of the study. Thus, different groups of workers may be given different levels (amounts) of incentives in the expectation that those incentives will increase productivity. The impact of the manipulation is then assessed on actual levels of productivity (the dependent variable in the study). In this case it is reasonable to assume some underlying continuum (magnitude of incentive). However, in other instances, the manipulation (sometimes called the treatment) involves the creation of conditions which either reflect no underlying theme, or more likely, which amalgamate or confound (confuse or mix up) several factors at once.

The latter often occurs in experiments involving organizational policies or practices. In these circumstances, the manager may create or try out certain work arrangements (e.g., flexible working hours) because it is feasible to do so and because there is an assumption (hypothesis) that it will have a desired impact on worker commitment. But little attention is given to exactly what underlying variables are being manipulated. In the example of flexible working hours, a positive impact may occur primarily because being able to choose the times to start and stop work may cause the employee to feel a greater sense of self-control, thereby creating less frustration for the employee who no longer has to face peak traffic hours or because it allows for the better coordination of family (getting the children off to school) and work (starting work on time) roles (Hicks & Klimoski, 1987).

Notice in this example, that a desired impact (a more committed work force) may result from a flextime program. But because the manipulation (introduction of the program) affected several factors at once (intentionally or inadvertently), we cannot be certain what really is going on. We may have a reliable effect (prediction) but we do not know just why it occurs (explanation). To use the terms introduced earlier in this chapter, because specific causal factors were not conceptualized and actually manipulated, there are several plausible rival (competing) hypotheses for the obtained results. If the expected outcomes are obtained, it would be necessary to conduct further research to determine just which ones are responsible.

Operationalizing Variables

Runkel and McGrath (1972) argue that most social science research involves formulating and testing hypotheses that deal with some aspect of the *actor* (in our case, employee), *object* (that which the actor deals with), or *context* (the setting in which the actor is operating). It follows then that we are usually interested in studying one or more aspects of these three elements. To do so involves using any number of techniques for the operationalization (creation or indexing) of variables.

Because the investigator has several options, Runkel and McGrath (1972) suggest that an initial question that should be asked relates to the location of the property of interest. For example, in studying behavior in organizations, is it something that is an aspect of the actor (e.g., skill level), the object (e.g., task difficulty) or in the context (time pressure)? The answer will determine how the researcher will approach or create experimental conditions. Notice that all three factors could be relevant to job performance as a dependent variable.

We then would ask if the property is *inherent* in the actor, object, or context, or is it something to be *imposed*? For example, we may be interested in fact in an aspect of the employee, such as skill level, as it relates to job performance. We then would have to decide to what extent skill level should be considered something that is innate (inherent) or can be created (imposed) for purposes of our research.

In general, we can create or establish properties of interest in the "actor" through selection or intervention (Runkel & McGrath, 1972). To illustrate, if we wish to study the impact of skill level on job performance, we might choose to identify or select individuals who already have differing levels of skill by using observation, tests, or nominations from supervisors. People with high or low skill levels then would be observed or measured under controlled circumstances. That is, their job performance would be studied in a specific context. In this case we are using a selection strategy to establish or manipulate the independent variable (skill level) in the experiment.

Alternatively, an unselected but representative group of individuals might be brought into the research setting to be given certain experiences (treatments) designed to create different levels of skill. This could be done by giving some people a lot of instruction and practice on a relevant task while giving no such preparation to others. After this preliminary work was done, we would have contrasting groups to study. Our experiment comparing the impact of high versus low skill levels of performance could then be conducted. In this approach, the independent variable (skill level) has been created or induced according to the wishes of the investigator.

It may already be clear to you that each approach has certain strengths and disadvantages. In the case of selection, we may have problems with our measure. That is, it may not be perfectly reliable. As pointed out in Chapter 3, to the extent that the device that is used to identify high and low scoring individuals (groups, or systems) is not perfectly reliable, we would expect that a certain number of those chosen will, in fact, be incorrectly placed into extreme groups. Similarly, even if we were to validly locate high and low skilled individuals, it is possible that in selecting them for our experiment, we might end up with what is referred to as an *unknown sampling bias*. That is, there may be factors other than skill levels that distinguish one group from another. In this example, those labeled as high skill also may turn out to have greater aptitude to or be more motivated toward high achievement. Either or both of these attributes (high aptitude or motivation) are likely to have an effect on a variable such as performance, quite apart from skill level. Thus, any observed covariation between measured skill level (our ostensible independent variable) and performance may in fact be due to the operation of these alternative explanatory factors. In the event that either were operating, the data from our experiment would be misleading. Whether or not they came out as predicted, the findings could be subjected to a challenge. In this case, the method for operationalizing the key variable (skill level) gives rise to several rival hypotheses.

Establishing relevant properties by intervention is the classic approach used by researchers conducting experiments. In the example above, some participants are transformed into skilled workers. In dealing with aspects of individuals and groups, this can be done in any number of ways. Specifically, the investigator may use instructions, task experiences, feedback (often contrived), or confederates to create or modify attitudes, skills, or behaviors. The possibilities are quite varied. Yet, there are usually no established ways to create particular phenomena. This means that the researcher must review previous studies in the area and with the relevant constructs in mind, use professional judgment as to the best way to accomplish this. In any event, any time that manipulations are used to create levels of the independent variable of interest, there is a requirement that evidence be presented that the inductions were successful.

In many field settings the investigator does not have the time, power or the resources to create conditions of interest (e.g., consider what might be involved in actually manipulating work group success or failure). In some instances it may be considered unethical to do so. But in any event, if such an approach is used, the researcher must ensure that the techniques used will actually produce conditions that are consistent with the constructs of interest. Not only should the manipulation take, it should only involve the nature and range of phenomena being claimed. Much more will be said about the techniques for doing this in Chapter 11.

On the other hand, to select appropriate sets of individuals, groups, or organizations to represent experimental conditions in field settings is often reasonable. The researcher would identify them, sample from the pool of cases available, and solicit their participation in the experiment. Selecting and using subjects with existing attributes also contributes to what is referred to as face validity (e.g., to say "Ten master chess players and ten novices were contrasted in their responses to computerized opponents . . . " seems like a reasonable approach to use in the study of this topic to most people). Moreover, selection or classification is often the only way to experimentally study certain variables (e.g., gender, age, disabilities, work history). Under the best of conditions, it is possible that our construct is best represented by using subjects with existing attributes. The range and depth or complexity of certain phenomena of interest can only be assured this way (e.g., as in the study of creativity).

Even accepting the above arguments, however, it is clear that the planned and careful manipulation of conditions represents the most powerful approach to setting the stage for causal inference. By taking a representative sample (of individuals, groups, or organizations) and randomly assigning entities to participate in experiences designed to create the properties of interest, the researcher is able to make stronger arguments against the plausibility of rival hypotheses. In this and other chapters, we discuss the logic of these arguments under the concept of internal validity.

To this point, we have been talking about variables as they might be used in an experimental study. Much of the research on human resource issues is not experimental in nature; rather, we might examine only the degree to which one or more variables relate to others. However, even in this type of research we should be equally concerned about the adequacy of our operationalization of the variables. For example, studies of leadership behavior often refer to constructs such as consideration for subordinates and initiating work structure. The items in the consideration measure have to do with supervisors giving praise, explaining their reasons for action, asking opinions, etc., while items in the initiating structure measure include questions about goal setting and schedule maintenance. Operationalization of these two variables, like any others, needs to be preceded by a careful consideration of a conceptual or theoretical framework that specifies the meaning of the construct, distinguishes it from other constructs, and indicates how the measure of the construct should relate to other variables.

Measures of constructs attain further meaning after data are collected and analyzed. We find out how the measure actually does relate to measures of other constructs and how the measure is affected by such things as the format of the questions, the language level of the items, and the conditions in which the measure is given. Evidence about our interpretation of the measure also can come from data which indicate the degree to which the items in a measure are related to each other. If items are highly related, we have some confidence that they are measuring the same construct. Further, the measure should be related to measures of similar constructs (leader consideration should be related to leader supportiveness) and not very highly related to dissimilar constructs (satisfaction with the leader probably shouldn't be highly related to satisfaction with one's physical surroundings unless the leader was responsible for producing those surroundings). The meaning of questionnaire measures also can be increased by observation of the behavior in question or interviews with respondents. That is, we hope to increase our understanding of constructs by measuring or examining them in different ways. Issues of construct validity in relational research are more fully discussed in Chapter 3.

Relevant and Nuisance Variables

Thinking about relevant and nuisance variables must precede or accompany all research. *Relevant* variables are those thought to have an actual or potential impact on the phenomenon that you want to study. That is to say, based on theory, experience, or prior research, the investigator has some basis for believing that it would covary or affect the independent or dependent variables in the study. *Nuisance* variables are also thought to affect the phenomena of interest. But in this case, they are felt to have an undesired impact on what you want to study. Thus, sometimes the latter are called extraneous or confounding variables. (See Stone, 1978, for a similar discussion). While we will often select the specific variables to use in our research from among the set of relevant variables, we generally seek to reduce or minimize the action of nuisance variables. In any case in research, both types of variables can be thought of as the basis for potential rival hypotheses for explaining or predicting a phenomenon.

The distinction between a relevant and a nuisance variable is sometimes not an easy one to make. A given factor could be viewed as either one. Often the interests of the investigator determine the label given to a variable. It's somewhat like defining a weed as "any plant being in the wrong place." A variable will be considered a nuisance to the extent that its presence in the research situation is undesirable.

Design and the Treatment of Variables

As pointed out by Runkel and McGrath (1972), knowledge is the "knowledge of differences" (p. 51). Generally, in research we try to establish or create two or more types or levels of one variable (the independent variable) to observe its effects on another (the dependent variable). In doing this, however, we usually make choices as to how to deal with what are felt to be the relevant and nuisance variables. The outcome of thinking through these choices is an overall study design.

A research design is nothing more than a plan for conducting a study in such a way as to allow results to be interpreted with a minimum amount of ambiguity. In all research, we'd like to remove the most likely alternative explanations of hypothesized relationships. In experimental research, this means that when we are done we should be able to make statements as to the causal impact of the variables of interest. To put it another way, in a well designed study, you will be in a position to conclude that the variability of the scores for the study's dependent variable is a function of variability in the study's independent variable and not due to other factors.

In establishing a design, we must resolve or answer the following questions (Runkel & McGrath, 1972; Rosenthal & Rosnow, 1984):

1. Who or what will be the focus of the study?
2. What attributes of individuals, groups or organizations will be observed?
3. In what contexts will observations be made?
4. What methods will be used to analyze the data produced?
5. How are we going to deal with relevant and nuisance variables?

It should be kept in mind that there are numerous alternatives available to an investigator. Moreover, there is no one best design. The final choice for a study will depend on any number of factors. Certainly, the design will be a function of the specific hypotheses to be tested. But it also will depend on patterns established by previous research, the constraints and resources available, the needs or preferences of the sponsors or the ultimate consumers of the research, and the personal strengths or capacities of the researcher. These factors determine the research strategy, whether it be a survey or experimental, anecdotal or observational in nature.

For a design to be a good one it will have to meet at least four criteria. First, it must help test hypotheses or answer questions. Second, nuisance or extraneous factors must be dealt with or otherwise controlled. Third, while not strictly a design issue, the results must tell us how other people would react in different contexts; that is, the results must generalize to situations and people beyond our study. It turns out that a fourth key to good design is the manner in which we choose to treat variables.

Once we decide that a factor or a variable is relevant to the phenomenon of interest, we have a number of ways to treat the variable in a study. Thus, we may treat it as follows:

1. A design partition.
2. A measured variable.
3. A design constant (i.e., all subjects are equal on this variable).
4. Something to be dealt with through randomization (as we will see in Chapter 11, randomly assigning research participants to conditions has the effect of controlling for nuisance variables).
5. Something to be ignored because we believe it will have minimal effect on the other variables we study.

When a factor is turned into a design partition, we are giving it the importance or status of an independent variable in our research. It is a factor about which you want to make some conclusions. It has been judged to be a central or relevant variable.

In effect we are going to be dividing individuals, groups or organizations (or the observations we make on them) into mutually exclusive classes or parts and relate these to other variables. We already have described that this may be done through selecting and classifying cases or through manipulations. The partition may be coarse (yes/no; high/low; etc.) or it may be fine grained, involving many parts or levels. However, by definition it would have to have at least two levels in order to be a variable.

In relational research, we may have any number of independent variables or design partitions. However, in experimental research, for purposes of control and causal inference, the number will be limited (e.g., 1–4). In general, we only would invest effort in putting together two or more design partitions in a single study if we felt that there would be some unique information gained in doing so. More will be said about this in Chapter 11.

The dependent variable in research is usually a measured one. We are interested in understanding or predicting reasons for its variability, and we expect our independent variable to have an impact on the dependent measures. But we also may choose to measure a variable because we feel that it may be useful in helping us to better understand the forces operating in our study. If we are worried that a particular factor might confound or obscure our results, we might be able to put our fears to rest by measuring its magnitude, distribution across experimental conditions, or relationships with key variables. In the example presented above regarding the possibility of inadvertently getting more highly motivated research participants if we recruited, selected, and classified individuals into high or low skill groups, we could go on to measure levels of motivation to see if this is indeed the case. We could then attempt to rule out or statistically control for the effects of this variable.

In experimental research, we may measure or observe participants on a variable thought to be relevant because we may wish to consider it as a potential design partition later. In this case, after the experiment itself is over, we may choose to take scores on the measured variable and use them to create a new design partition. This is sometimes referred to as an internal (or post hoc) analysis in an experiment. It should be noted that, in doing this, we will be working with what is essentially correlational data so that conclusions about the causal impact of these post hoc variables are not possible.

A design constant is just what the phrase implies. It refers to using a variable to set a particular parameter and its level for all participants in the study. We might do this because we are only interested in studying a phenomenon at this level. Or we feel that it would be the best way to control a nuisance factor. As an example of the former, we may gather data only from managers or only under conditions of high (but not low) time pressure because these are what interest us. Alternatively, we might use only groups made up of hourly employees because we are concerned about but cannot predict the consequences of the impact of the independent variables in mixed hourly/managerial groups.

Occasionally, we also find it possible or desirable to randomly select subjects to participate in a study or we randomly assign them to conditions in an experiment. In relational research of the type we describe in Chapter 10, it is often impossible to collect data from all subjects about whom we hope to make some statements. However, if we sample randomly from some defined population, we can use the data from this sample to make statements about the whole population with specified levels of confidence. Various sampling strategies are discussed in Chapter 10.

Randomization has a special role in experimental research. This is because only a small number of factors can be manipulated or measured in an experiment. Yet, quite a variety of forces may affect the variability in criterion measures. In many instances, these factors are associated with or are reflected in the attributes of the objects (people, groups, organizations) being studied. To deal with this likelihood, the investigator might assign cases from a common pool to each of the experimental conditions in a study on a random basis. Thus, if particular attributes were to affect the dependent variable, they would not do so in any systematic way (i.e., spuriously inflate or deflate scores in any specific experimental condition). There still may be an effect of the factor; however, it would not produce a potentially undetectable bias in the results. At worst it would generate some "background noise" in the study. To say, then, that certain variables were dealt with through the technique of randomization is to imply a rational strategy and specific procedures. Randomization (of subjects to conditions, of specific treatment order to subjects, etc.) is a hallmark of true experiments and represents a way to deal with both relevant and nuisance variables.

A possible additional option to deal with these types of variables is to ignore them. In a sense those who do this are not really addressing their potential impact at all. Usually this does not really represent a choice at all but an outcome of poor pre-study analysis. That is, an investigator is likely to end up ignoring relevant or nuisance factors if he or she does not take the time to reflect on past experience, review previous research, or to approach the phenomenon at a conceptual or theoretical level. This is a very risky strategy to employ and will result in the likely discovery of several plausible, rival hypotheses or explanations for the results of a study, but only after the fact. To simply ignore key variables in a study (especially in an experiment) would be considered a fatal flaw and would result in the rejection of any inferences, conclusions, or assertions that may be based on the findings. This would be unfortunate insofar as many of the concerns may have been dealt with effectively by using any of the other modes of treatment outlined previously.

Information Gain and Research Design

The purpose of all research is to gain new information about a phenomenon of interest. In most studies in social science we are likely to obtain observations on at least one (usually a dependent) variable for a group of subjects. Thus, at a minimum, we will be able to get at descriptive data, such as average values, dispersion of scores, or the shape of a distribution for the sample at hand. In most work, however, our goals are usually much more ambitious. We are typically interested in *why* cases vary. To get at this we need to have a second variable that is usually measured, created, or manipulated. We then look at the relationship between the two as a way of learning more about the behavior and attitudes of the people involved.

The number and mode of treatment of the variables in a study (i.e., its design) will have a great impact on the potential information gained. As a general rule, potential gain will be a function of the number of relevant variables involved and the number of values that they can take on in the study (Runkel & McGrath, 1972). To illustrate, in some instances we may choose to hold a relevant variable at a single level while focusing on others. Thus, only males (not females) are used as subjects. Or only trained (but not untrained) subjects are involved. Alternatively, all participants in the experiment may be scheduled to encounter high (but not low) time pressure. Given the goals of the study these may be reasonable things to do. However, because knowledge is often the knowledge of differences, the treatment of a relevant variable as a design constant doesn't yield much information. At most we might be able to learn something about an observed relationship at the particular value chosen (i.e., for males, for trained individuals, etc.). (If we found no relationships or no effects of the other variables in the study, we might falsely conclude that this is the true state of affairs. In fact, a plausible alternative explanation is that we merely had chosen the wrong level of that variable for our study.)

On the other hand, if we were to allow the relevant factor to to be manipulated or measured—to occur at least at two values or levels—we would gain more definitive information. Thus, we could see if the relationship among variables holds for females as well as males, for untrained as well as trained participants, and for low as well as high stress conditions.

But the logic holds for going beyond two levels in many cases. It may be important in some instances that three or even more are used. It will depend on such things as the purpose of the study, the theory underlying the hypotheses, the nature of the variable, and the resources available. Given that a choice of multiple levels is made, the investigator will have much more information regarding the impact of that variable on and in combination with others in the study.

When we are in the beginning of an experimental research program, a useful strategy is to set a potentially important and relevant variable at two levels but at extreme values. Should the expected effects be found, the investigator might then go on to determine the appropriate or effective minimal range of that variable. Thus, subjects in a "trained" condition might be given extensive preparation and their behavior contrasted to those in an "untrained" condition. If effects are found, one could then reduce progressively the amounts of training given to see at what point the effects no longer hold. Of course, this would not be an appropriate strategy if the effects predicted for the variable were predicted to have negative or harmful effects. Here one might start with levels that might be very similar instead.

Whatever the goal of a research effort, it should be obvious that we will need to quantify the observations we make. This quantification of observations is measurement; in the next section we discuss how we assign numbers to observations and how those numbers attain meaning.

NATURE OF MEASUREMENT: HOW MEASURES ATTAIN MEANING AND LEVELS OF MEASUREMENT

Virtually all behavioral research demands the measurement of the objects in which one is interested and usually that measurement involves the assignment of numbers or symbols to objects or some property of the objects. The degree to which this assignment of numbers to people or characteristics of people results in data on which we can perform various arithmetic transformations is referred to as the scale or level of measurement. Various levels of measurement have been best described by Stevens (1946) who identified four types of measurement: nominal, ordinal, interval, and ratio. Understanding these different types of measurement is important because the level of measurement determines the types of statements we can make about the relationships among our observations and the types of statistics legitimately calculated with the numbers we collect.

Nominal Scales

A *nominal measurement scale* is one that has two or more mutually exclusive classes or categories of the variable in question. For example, if one is interested in gender, there are two mutually exclusive categories: female and male. Different past job experiences are likely measured on a nominal scale. The numbers, or categories, assigned to the people (in the case of gender) in these examples imply only that they are different in some way. The numbers do not signify any ordering of job experiences or members of different sex groups. We often use nominal values to index the existence or nonexistence of a treatment or intervention.

Ordinal Scales

An *ordinal measurement scale* is one that allows us to rank order people or objects on some variable. The color of hair of a group of individuals can be ordered from light to dark, so we would say that the lightness or darkness of one's hair color is an ordinal variable. If John's hair is darker than Judy's, whose hair in turn is darker than Joan's hair, then John's hair must also be darker than Joan's if our scale of measurement is really ordinal. In the human resource area, the kind of manipulations or treatments we usually create have clear ordinal relations (no training, some training, or a great deal of training). Usually, the variables we observe can be ordered in some way as well; for example, educational background levels can probably be ordered from high school diploma to doctoral degree though occasionally the ordering of technical degrees or community college education is problematic.

Interval Scales

A rank order, however, tells us nothing about how much difference there is among the ranked objects. To extend the example above, we might assign the number 10 to John's hair, 6 to Judy's hair, and 2 to Joan's hair. If we can establish that the color difference between John and Judy's hair, the color difference between Judy and Joan's hair, as well as any other difference of 4 on our scale is exactly the same, then we can say that we have *interval measurement*.

Note that variables measured in this fashion also allow us to make distinctions among objects (they are the same or different) as for nominal measurement and that we can rank order persons (ordinal measurement) on these interval scales. Interval scales do not have meaningful zero points (consider the meaning of zero intelligence) which, practically speaking, means we cannot meaningfully form ratios of objects measured on an interval scale. For example, it would not be useful to make the statement that John's hair (darkness = 10) is five times as dark as Joan's hair (darkness = 2) when darkness is measured on an interval scale. Finally, it should be noted that most of the measures (and resultant numbers) used in the measurement of human capabilities or attitudes are treated as though they meet interval assumptions without evidence that the scale units or differences are equivalent. For example, whether a difference between 65 and 75 on an intelligence scale is the same as the difference between 100 and 110 is debatable even though intelligence tests are probably one of the better developed measures of human capabilities.

Ratio Scales

As you have probably guessed, *ratio scales* of measurement are those in which the objects measured do have interval properties; in addition, zero is a meaningful measurement, hence we can form ratios of objects measured on a ratio scale. Zero is meaningful because it is possible to have zero length or weight; by contrast, it is difficult to conceptualize what it would mean to say someone has zero intelligence or zero empathy or motivation. Ratio scales are usually encountered only in the physical sciences; the usual examples include height and weight. It is meaningful to say that a person measuring six feet tall is twice as high as one measuring three feet tall. Some possible examples of *ratio measurement scales* in human resource areas include absenteeism and tardiness measures or the number of units produced in some jobs such as the number of letters typed by a secretary.

Practical Considerations Concerning Measurement Scales

The level of measurement with which we assign numbers to objects has practical consequences when we start summarizing our measurements or perform arithmetic operations on the numbers we use to represent the objects. For example, we can transform nominal data any way at all as long as we maintain the separate classification of objects in mutually exclusive categories. Numbers assigned to objects using an ordinal scale may be added, subtracted, multiplied, divided, squared, or transformed in any way that preserves their original rank order. Transformations of interval data must maintain both order and the relative size of scale intervals; that is, multiplying, dividing, adding, or subtracting from all values a constant number is fine, but taking the square root or squaring changes the size of the intervals between objects. Finally, the ratio properties of a scale are destroyed by the addition or subtraction of a constant number because the zero point changes.

Aside from considerations concerning appropriate transformations of numbers, the scale of measurement also has implications for the ways in which we summarize data and describe the relationships among variables. These summary statistics are described in Chapter 2.

Before we leave our discussion of the nature of measurement, it is important to note that most variables measured in the social or behavioral sciences are measured indirectly. Scientists frequently call this indirect measurement *measurement by fiat.* We have some commonsense notions about a concept or construct but we don't know how to measure it directly. So we measure some other variable that we presume is related to it. For example, psychologists have measured the galvanic skin response as an indirect measure of emotion, the number of trials it takes to learn a maze as an indication of learning ability, and the number of academic-like tasks a child can solve as intelligence. Now consider job motivation. We may judge employee or student motivation by the number of hours spent at a task, or success at the task, or by asking them questions about how hard they work. All three are indirect, imperfect measures: the person who spends hours at work may be daydreaming or avoiding another unpleasant situation, the successful performer may simply be more able, and the worker who describes how hard she or he is working may feel that this is the socially appropriate response. Part of the research process involves identifying or creating and then using these measures in a variety of situations while checking to see if the observations coincide with our initial commonsense or theoretical notion of what we are trying to measure. This, in effect, is the first requirement of strong inference noted above; namely, that we are really measuring what we intend. The basic problem is how to operationalize a construct discussed at length earlier in this chapter.

Whatever the level of measurement or the means by which our measures attain meaning, all measures we use must be reliable. Usually reliability means that we get the same values when we use an instrument (questionnaire, interview, observation) to measure some aspect of people in organizations. This basic notion of reliability is central to various ways of assessing the quality of our measurements, but as we shall see in Chapter 3 there are a variety of ways of assessing reliability in applied organizational contexts.

CAUSAL INFERENCE AND THE VALIDITY OF STUDIES

Throughout this chapter we have maintained that whether one is a manager attempting to make a policy or practical decision or a social scientist evaluating a theory, the goal of conducting a study is often one of causal inference. More specifically, the investigator usually wishes to be able to understand why, how, or when or where some form of intervention (manipulation, program, or practice) will have a predictable effect.

In general, when the goal is causal inference, we also have argued that the preferred approach is an experimental one. Whether conducted in a laboratory or a field setting under the right conditions, experiments will provide the kind of evidence on which to base strong inference. In this section, these conditions will be reviewed. While this discussion relates directly to experimental research, many of the conditions apply to other research designs as well.

Construct Validity of Studies

The notion of construct validity of measure was discussed above and will be further developed in Chapters 3 and 5. There we will be concerned with the extent to which a particular measure or test really does index the underlying or latent variable of interest. In the present context, we are concerned with the experiment as a whole.

Most basically, the *construct validity* of an experiment refers to the degree to which the investigator has been successful in creating or arranging for the conditions of conceptual or theoretical interest. For example, if the researcher wishes to study the effects of participation in decision making (PDM) on worker behavior, the notion of construct validity would be raised by questioning the degree to which he or she really did choose to define operationally or create both the essence of and the levels of participation correctly. As it turns out, at the time of this writing, the research literature is wrestling with just what the PDM construct really involved, so it is a good example (Cotton, Vollrath, Froggatt, Longnich-Hall, & Jennings, 1988; Dachler & Wilpert, 1978).

Cook and Campbell (1976) have highlighted several factors that affect the potential construct validity of experiments. These include the following:

1. *Method bias.* This refers to the possibility that the method used to create or produce variability (in the independent variable) is incorrect or flawed. The manipulation may

not capture the richness or complexity of the construct of interest. It could be contaminated (it creates forces that are not part of the construct). A special form of this is what is called a mono-method bias in studies, where a set of findings (even a theory) is incorrect because everything gets built upon a single method for operationalizing a construct. This is often of concern in survey research as we will see in Chapter 10. The point is, we would have far greater confidence in the construct validity of an investigation upon finding convergence of results of studies involving multiple approaches to manipulation and measurement.

2. *Hypothesis guessing on the part of subjects.* The results of a study may be an artifact of the ease with which research participants can guess correctly the purpose of the experiment and the observed tendency on their part to "give the researcher what he/she wants" (Rosenthal, 1967). In this case, the construct validity of the study would be in question because the observed behavior would not be a function of the purported independent variable.

3. *Confounding levels of constructs.* The investigator may create the wrong (e.g., weak) level of the construct. When no effects are found it may not reveal the true nature of the variable but reflect the fact that an inappropriate level had been created. This is a major problem for laboratory studies where the magnitude of the differences between the conditions created may be much less than the same phenomenon in the work setting.

The construct validity of an experiment can only be estimated. Much like establishing the construct validity of a test, it involves making inferences by the investigator about the appropriateness of the methods involved. At times the pattern of data obtained can also be used. And it can be difficult to do. Any time that the investigator makes claims for construct properties of the study, he or she has an obligation to do this. It then would be a necessary (although not a sufficient) basis for a quality study.

Statistical Conclusion Validity

Most research is conducted to uncover the magnitude of the effects (if any) of key variables of interest in a study or the magnitude of the relationship among variables. But the outcomes of a study may be influenced (unintentionally) by forces promoting instability or unreliability. To the extent that these forces are numerous or their impact great we would question the statistical conclusions made. (Cook & Campbell, 1976).

Statistical conclusion validity, then, is less concerned with bias (effects in a systematic direction) than with sources of error variance. Anything that may contribute to randomness in the data would be seen as a threat. Relevant factors include the following:

1. *Reliability of measurement.* This was mentioned above and will be treated extensively in Chapter 3.

2. *Reliability of a treatment or manipulation.* In large studies or those done over some time period, it is possible that the manner in which a variable gets "delivered" will change in ways unknown to the researcher. To the extent that its nature or its impact is not sytematic, such changes will add "noise" to the analysis and possibly promote incorrect conclusions.

3. *Sample size.* If a study involves a small number of subjects, there is an increased likelihood that the investigator will not detect real differences between experimental groups or real relationships between variables even when they, in fact, exist. This is another way of

characterizing the issue of statistical power. Occasionally, even the most sophisticated investigator succumbs to an erroneous belief in small numbers. Previous research on a topic, the level of confidence desired by the researcher and statistical power (calculations of the probability that you can conclude a real effect or relationship exists given the sample size) computations should guide sample size decisions (see Chapter 2 and 11 as well as Cohen, 1988, for a treatment of power in various experimental designs).

Other aspects of statistical conclusion validity are examined in Chapter 12 where the nature and logic of meta-analyses are covered.

Internal Validity

Internal validity refers to the extent to which the results of a study are unambiguous or cannot be explained by alternative factors related to the design and/or conduct of the study (Blackburn, 1987; Cook & Campbell, 1976). In the context of this chapter, the concept of internal validity can be thought of as focusing on a specific set of plausible rival (alternative) hypotheses for a particular pattern of results obtained from a study. A research effort with good internal validity increases our confidence that a particular manipulation, change, or intervention actually caused or accounts for observed outcomes.

We usually increase the level of internal validity by expending greater efforts at careful design and control of factors in the research setting. However, as will become clear, the specific factors we choose to be concerned with should depend on such things as the nature of the phenomonon itself and the setting in which the study is to take place.

Cook and Campbell (1976) have identified potential threats to internal validity. Several of these will be briefly described.

1. *Selection of participants.* Internal validity depends in part on how people (groups, organizations) became subjects or participants in the study or how they were assigned to various treatments or conditions in experimental research. To the extent that individuals are not randomly selected or assigned it is possible that the results may be due to preexisting differences in knowledge, skill, ability, attitudes, etc. In Chapter 10, we discuss various ways of sampling research participants in detail.

2. *Testing.* In research it is not uncommon to attempt to get measures or observations on subjects prior to the actual conduct of the study or the onset of an intervention. However, the process of doing this itself may sensitize or change people. Similarly, many studies involve taking repeated measures. This, too, may change respondents in some unintended manner. In the latter case, under certain circumstances this may produce fatigue or resentment which may cause poorer scores. Or it may induce participants to produce later answers that are consistent with previous ones. In any event the data would be suspect.

3. *Instrumentation.* The nature of the procedures or instruments used to take measures may have an effect on internal validity, especially if different techniques are involved during different parts of the study. Two different measures of job satisfaction may not be entirely equivalent. In a similar vein, self-reported or observer-generated data on stress may not show the same results. To conclude that true changes have occurred as a result of an intervention when, in fact, they are a consequence of using different instrumentation would be wrong.

4. *Statistical regression.* This is a special type of selection problem. In many contexts, an investigator may identify and select individuals (groups, organizations) for study or receipt of particular treatments because they scored extremely high (or low) on some measure as in the skill levels example provided earlier in this chapter. However, to the extent that the measure itself is unreliable, it is unlikely that such extreme scores reflect true score levels or differences. In fact, if the same individuals were to be assessed again, most likely the researchers would obtain different scores. In the case of an unreliable measure these would be less extreme and more like the typical or modal respondent. Thus, statistical regression reflects a tendency for scores, upon remeasurement, to change in the direction of the mean. We would be incorrect to conclude that such shifts in patterns of data were a result of some intervention. Regression effects could be a plausible alternative explanation.

5. *History.* For research that takes some time to carry out it is quite possible that events or factors other than those designed as part of the study have, in fact, produced the changes observed in the measured or dependent variable.

6. *Maturation.* Related to the notion of history, changes in scores on measured variables may be simply due to the normal evolution of things. Independent of our particular research intervention we would see such changes anyway.

7. *Mortality.* Some proportion of participants may drop out of the study before it is completed. To the extent that certain types of individuals (groups, organizations) choose not to come to sessions, complete surveys, or to provide data, our pattern of results over time may be more a function of mortality effects than any real change or impact of our intervention.

8. *Diffusion/imitation of treatments.* As noted, it is not uncommon for investigators to intervene or to provide treatments to some potential participants (experimental conditions) and to withhold or to postpone them for others (control conditions). They would then look for differences between these groups of individuals in terms of their scores on the dependent variable. However, if those in the control conditions were to inadvertently learn about or otherwise be affected by the intervention and change their own behavior as a result, such comparisons would be misleading. A finding of no differences between conditions could reflect the impact of this threat to internal validity rather than a lack of effect of the treatment.

9. *Compensatory effects.* Similar to the scenario just provided, individuals in the control conditions may learn about the fact that they will not be receiving the presumed benefits of the intervention. However, instead of adopting or self-administering the treatment involved, they might resolve instead to make up for having been left out with an increased effort or similar strategy aimed at making them look just as good on the dependent variable. Alternatively, such knowledge may produce a feeling of having been left out and of demoralization. Either dynamic can obscure the true effects of the variable in which the investigator is interested and lead to false conclusions.

10. *Interactions among the threats.* Cook and Campbell (1976) point out that more than one of the above factors may be operating at one time to affect a study's actual or potential results. In particular, selection procedures may either exaggerate or mitigate the consequences of maturation, history, or instrumentation. For example, the individuals chosen for the study may be more or less able to read, comprehend, and complete a complex survey than in the case of a different sample (selection x instrumentation effects).

Estimating the internal validity of a study is essentially a deductive process. Cook and Campbell (1976) characterize the investigator who does this as a critic, assessing the extent to which the study embodies one or more flaws. In point of fact, these and other "threats" to internal validity must be assessed as to how plausible and serious they are as early as possible in the design and development stages of research. That way certain changes or precautions can be taken beforehand. It might be added that in all of this, it is to the investigator's advantage to be well versed in the theoretical and empirical literature associated with the particular phenomenon. Finally it is also important to understand the setting in which the research is to be carried out. Ultimately these become the "lenses" with which to scrutinize the study and its design for any potentially serious weaknesses.

It can be argued that the main difference between true experiments and other study designs has to do with internal validity. True experiments allow for strong inference because the investigator can control most (but not all) threats to internal validity through the direct creation or manipulation of the independent variable(s) and the random assignment of participants to conditions. Much more about this will be said in the section on design of studies in Chapter 11.

External Validity

External validity is also referred to as generalizability. It reflects the extent to which the results of a study will hold up or generalize to other samples of participants, to other contexts (labs, departments or organizations), and to other levels of the variables under study but which were not actually created or manipulated.

In general, threats to external validity usually stem from interactions between the nature of the sample used, the intervention involved and the setting. More specifically these might include the following:

1. *The interaction of selection and treatment.* The impact of the intervention may be conditioned by (or even wholly the result of) the particular group of people who participated in our study. That is, they were more (or less) motivated, more (or less) capable, more (or less) prepared, etc., than a more typical or representative group. Thus, to conclude that our intervention does or does not work as a result of the study would be inappropriate as the data would be misleading.

2. *The interaction of setting and treatment.* It could be that the results of the study are largely a consequence of the particular location and/or the specific features of the intervention (or treatment) involved. If either or both are changed, the findings would be different in some important ways. We sometimes hear that experimental results cannot be replicated in a different lab. Or that a similar intervention in a different company did not produce the same impact.

3. *The interaction of treatments.* This threat refers to the possibility that the outcome of a treatment or intervention may be unique and depends on the particular combination of circumstances being created at the time. This becomes a serious threat when an investigator or consultant is using or trying out several things at once in an effort to improve organizational functioning. A given set of results may be hard to obtain under a different set of circumstances.

It should be stressed that the issue of external validity is not peculiar to attempts to generalize from laboratory findings to organizations. It is relevant to many field studies as well. In fact, any time participants in a field study are not randomly selected and assigned to conditions (treatments or interventions), one or more of the above threats are plausible. Or, in survey research the results of a study using subjects who are not randomly sampled may not generalize to other groups of subjects. Unfortunately, this is more often the case than not.

Deciding about the generalizability of a finding is largely an inductive process. We must look at multiple instances of when and where we obtain the same or similar findings as a result of some intervention (see Chapter 12 on the logic of meta-analysis). Thus, our confidence is bolstered with replications. But in the absence of a good track record, we must infer the potential for external validity from the sampling and design strategies used by an investigator (see Dipboye & Flanagan, 1979).

Relationships among the Four Types of Validity

It may already be obvious that the types of validity described above bear some relationship to one another. For example, in some ways internal and statistical conclusion validity are more like each other as are external and construct validity in terms of factors that promote them and the ways that we infer their existence (Cook & Campbell, 1976).

It also is true that there are tradeoffs involved as we might attempt to increase the potential level of one or the other. For example, we might introduce additional controls on a study to deal with one or more potential threats to internal validity. But this often has the consequence of limiting the naturalness of the setting to participants and limiting external validity. In fact, this is often what happens as we place a premium on internal validity in most experimental research.

The priority that we give to a particular type of validity will also depend on the purpose or the goal of our research. In theory building we might emphasize internal validity and construct concerns. In applied work we might pay greater attention to external (but by no means exclude internal) validity (Cook & Campbell, 1976).

RESEARCH IN THEORY AND PRACTICE

The entire research process as described above and as it is usually described in texts similar to this one is pictured in Figure 1-2.

When research is conducted in organizations with organizational objectives, we frequently find that the research process takes various twists and turns, and the sequence of events may look more like Figure 1-3. An examination of Figures 1-2 and 1-3 indicates that (a) there are a greater number of processes involved in organizational research, (b) there are a greater number of possibilities for interactions between stages in the research model, and (c) the purpose of the research shifts from a search for scientific fact to a search for the solution to some organizational problem. Boehm (1980), from whom these figures were "borrowed," advocates the use of both models to maximally advance knowledge in human resource management. She cites several instances in which involvement in rather messy organizational research has led to rapid advances in scientific knowledge about worker performance (e.g., development of theories about organizational careers, and the importance of individual ability as a determinant of work performance). In our next section, we consider some issues that are important when we do research with an aim toward translating the outcomes of that research into a successful intervention.

RESEARCH WITH IMPLEMENTATION IN MIND

Social scientists, in general, usually hope their research makes some contribution to knowledge regarding human behavior whether their work is descriptive, predictive, or of the theory-

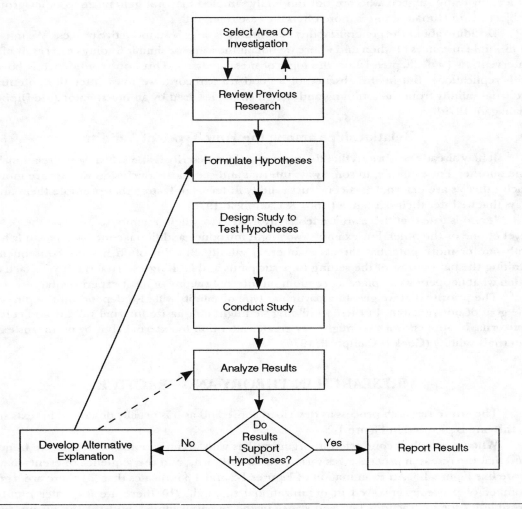

FIGURE 1-2   The Academic or Scientific Research Model
    Source: Reprinted with permission from Boehm, V.R. (1980). Research in the "real-world"—a conceptual
    model. *Personnel Psychology, 33*, 495–504.

testing type. Human resource researchers will have these goals but they also will usually want to see
the implications of their research used in some way by an organization.

How will an organization use the results of a study validating a selection procedure? What
score(s) will be considered satisfactory? What will be the impact on minority hiring if the procedure
is implemented? Who is apt to be included or excluded from hiring decisions and how does this
compare with the previous situation? How will the results of a survey on job stress be utilized?
Should the organization initiate training or medical programs to relieve stress? Are organizational
decision makers ready to change their policies or expend money to make changes in the physical
plant if necessary? Are researchers prepared to be receptive to unexpected information or are they
likely to discover it?

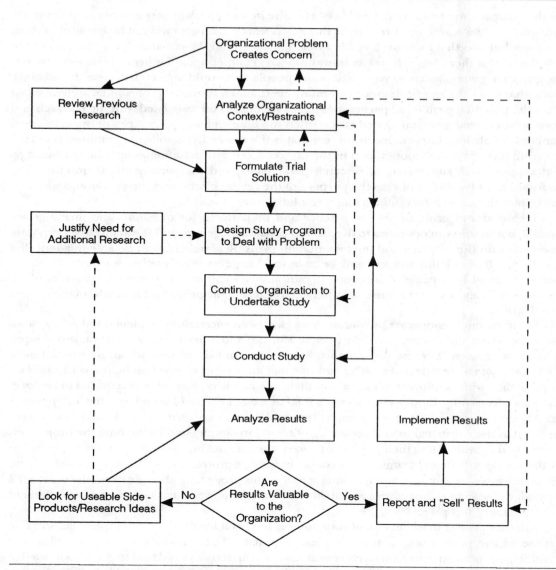

FIGURE 1-3 The Research Process within Organizations
Source: Reprinted with permission from Boehm, V.R. (1980) Research in the "real-world"—a conceptual model. *Personnel Psychology, 33,* 495–504.

Similar questions about applied research have been asked by Hakel, Sorcher, Beer, and Moses (1982) in a useful book titled *Making it Happen: Research with Implementation in Mind.* These authors presented a set of guidelines and suggestions that they claim will increase the likelihood that research results will actually be useful to organizations.

First on this list is the necessity that all parties realize what outcomes (costs and benefits) will result from the research. Organizational decision makers need to recognize that the study will provide information on some problem, that the outcome will provide a solution to a problem, or that the company will be more profitable or effective in serving customers as a result of the study. Participants in the search must recognize that any research outcomes will not be harmful to them in any way but also that their work or life situation may actually be enhanced as a function of the study. The researcher likely will receive some monetary compensation for her or his effort, but may also want to negotiate access to various data and people that would impact the research and make certain that he or she can (if desired) communicate research results to professional audiences. As well as the potential payoffs, all parties must be aware of the cost associated with the research and in our view, the major unanticipated cost is often the time and access required of organizational members. Of obvious importance in this context is the researcher's ability to communicate with the various groups whose cooperation in the project is crucial, including policy makers, management support staff, supervisors of research participants, and the participants themselves. The researcher must be able to discuss the purpose of the research, who sees the results and why, and what implications and interventions might result from the research.

Technical and professional competence and preparation for questions and meetings are essential, but so too is an openness to the ideas of constituent groups and the ability to incorporate these ideas into the research and implementation plans. Researchers must be able to admit that they do not have all the answers and be able to change as the situation warrants. In short, researchers must be capable of accepting organizational members as partners or participants in the research. They must feel a sense of ownership regarding the project if the results of the project are to be used.

Some research endeavors by your authors have been successfully implemented in organizations; others have not. In one particularly successful effort to introduce new selection procedures, we had management interest and support. Further, the individual with whom we worked most closely had done a great deal of reading and research on personnel selection before contacting us. We spent time with employees talking about their jobs and what they felt was required to perform their jobs successfully. Employees also were used as examiners and trained as raters of applicant performance in some of the job sample tests which were constructed and used. They were consulted in the construction and pretesting of these job samples and by the time the project was finished had identified it as their own. The procedures were not only adapted in their organization but the manager promoted similar procedures in outside professional organizations. Aside from the considerable researcher-employee interaction in this project, we also think that the manager's knowledge of selection procedures and ability to answer employee questions was a critical element in the success of this project.

Another project in which one of your authors has been involved was a complete failure. The purpose of the project was to test the possibility that efforts to increase the readability and attention-getting value of written safety communication materials would lead to greater knowledge of hazardous chemicals and safe behavior in the use of these chemicals. The safety director provided a letter of intent to cooperate in the research and was extremely enthusiastic regarding the contribution revised materials might make to the organization. Because of the initial enthusiastic reception, we did not pursue additional meetings with the supervisors of work groups and with other managerial personnel. When it came time to collect pre-intervention knowledge of the hazardous chemicals, supervisors and workers did not understand the purpose of the study, were suspicious of the intent of the organization and the researcher, and most workers refused to cooperate. Not only was there no adoption of revised safety communication materials, the study was never completed. Fortunately, we learned from our experience with this corporation and accomplished a similar project elsewhere, but only after a great loss of work and money.

Some of the determinants of successful and unsuccessful implementations such as those described previously were summarized by Hakel et al. (1982). Their summary is reproduced in Table 1-1.

LIMITATIONS OF RESEARCH

We will spend most of this book promoting the necessity for, and the advantages of, a research approach to human resource problems. However, research does have limitations, particularly when that research is conducted by persons who are not well-informed regarding the context in which the research is conducted and/or the conditions under which the results of the research are to be implemented.

An applied researcher must make the organizational sponsor (and very frequently the research participant) a partner in the research endeavor. They must participate in developing meaningful manipulations in an experimental study, responding to drafts of survey instruments and interview protocols, identifying appropriate research participants or groups of participants, anticipating organizational or environmental changes that might impact on the study, and interpreting the data that are collected.

While this type of involvement is costly in terms of the time commitment involved, it is essential to the success of this type of research. We can cite many examples like the one described above from our own research in which cooperative types of sponsor–researcher cooperation was missing or overlooked with the result being that either the research itself was meaningless or no one was interested in the final product. In the study cited previously regarding the evaluation of the effectiveness of changing written safety materials on the use of various hazardous chemicals, we were interested in measuring the number of worker requests for safety information over time. Our notion was that revision would increase requests. After several weeks, we asked a safety officer

TABLE 1-1
Summary of Determinants of Successful and Failed Implementation Efforts

Successful implementation most often occurs when one is able to

Identify interests of key persons and constituencies.
Define and negotiate the purposes of the project.
Identify and resolve policy issues up front.
Negotiate adequate resources and schedules.
Make contingency plans.
Model success behaviors.
Deliver results.

Failure is likely to occur when

Problem identification was incorrect.
Sponsor power is lacking.
There are changes in needs and/or key personnel.
The impetus for the project is not clearly specified or it changes.
There are unrealistic expectations for results or delivery schedules.
The researcher is insensitive to the social and political dynamics of the organization.

about the total lack of such requests. This officer responded that workers rarely, if ever, made such requests, that they normally depended only on their supervisors' verbal reports on the dangers involved in using various chemicals.

Perhaps the best solution to the problem of conducting meaningless research that will have only minimal impact is the involvement of the researcher in the organizational context in which the research is conducted and reliance on multiple methods of data collection. While we frequently will rely on the collection of quantitative data in controlled conditions as a major method of doing research, researchers also should conduct interviews with key people and research participants and observe data collection and the human behavior being studied directly. As noted this type of involvement is time consuming, but indispensable to the completion of successful research.

A second major problem is the cost of the research, particularly to small organizations. While the benefits of many human resource programs far exceed the investment, there can be considerable initial investment which smaller organizations could not justify or larger organizations may be unwilling to make. A competently conducted criterion-related validation of a selection procedure, for example, may easily cost $100,000 or more. The solution to this problem is to rely on cooperative efforts or consortia of similar organizations or to rely on meta-analysis of existing research (see Chapter 12) to make decisions about which human resource efforts are the best in a particular context.

OVERVIEW OF THE BOOK

In this book, we will introduce research methods using problems that human resource professionals and researchers frequently confront in organizations. It is our hope that this type of introduction to research methods will help human resource personnel make better data-based human resource decisions. We feel that this problem-oriented approach will be more likely effective in convincing some readers of the practicality of a research and data-based approach to organization problems. We also have emphasized the role of theory and knowledge regarding the content and context of problems as being very important in conducting informative research. Hence, major portions of some of our chapters will be devoted to summaries of theoretical positions and empirical research on human resource issues. In Table 1-2, we list, by chapter the various human resource issues we discuss. These issues include pay and compensation, safety training, selection, organizational development, turnover, absenteeism, job satisfaction, and others.

In this chapter we have introduced the reader to the rationale for research in human resource management, some of the assumptions one makes in conducting research, and some of the hallmarks of good research. In Chapter 2, we will discuss the descriptive and inferential statistics one uses in describing the results of a research study. Ways of assessing the reliability and validity of our measurement instruments are discussed in Chapter 3. And, in Chapter 4, we introduce the reader to observational and interview research which may, in some instances, be the only approach used to study a problem. In most instances, these qualitative approaches are used in conjunction with other research designs and data collection methods. Qualitative research provides unique insights about problems, but also contributes significantly to hypothesis generation and theory development.

TABLE 1-2
Chapter Titles and Human Resource Issues Addressed

Chapter Number and Title	Human Resource Issues—Illustrated or Implied
1. An Empirical Approach to Human Resource Research	History of research on resource issues Implementation of research
2. Data Analytic Strategies for Human Resource Research	Compensation
3. Determining the Quality of Our Measures	Individual differences (e.g., role ambiguity) Personnel selection Legal issues in test application Measurement theory
4. Understanding the Organization through Qualitative Research	Corporate culture Interviewing
5. Criterion Development at the Individual Level: Conceptual Issues	Criterion development for selection Training Job analysis
6. Defining and Measuring Effectiveness at the Individual Level	Performance appraisal Organization control system
7. Defining and Measuring Effectiveness at the Group and Organization Level	Group process Leadership Organizational theory Organizational change and development
8. Assessing the Potential for Effective Performance	Career path planning Performance appraisal Individual assessment
9. Decision Making on Human Resource Issues in Organizations	Utility theory Training Performance appraisal Selection
10. Assessing Employee Attitudes and Opinions	Motivation and compensation Leadership Attitude behavior Relationships Survey feedback
11. Evaluating Organizational Interventions	Training Safety Organizational change
12. Summarizing and Interpreting Human Resource Research Using Meta-Analysis	Selection Human Resource Interventions Goal Setting/Motivation

In Chapters 5, 6, and 7, we describe procedures that provide information about people and organizations that is necessary to guide selection research, survey research, or experimental research. In discussing measures of effectiveness, we begin with a discussion of a criterion on conceptual grounds, then talk about the nature of actual measures that can be used at the individual, group, and organizational levels. The central role of job, person, and organization analyses are emphasized.

Development and evaluation of selection procedures and the assessment of their usefulness in organizational decision making are addressed in Chapters 8 and 9. In the first of these two chapters, we discuss the relative merits of different selection procedures. In Chapter 9, we describe the use of these procedures to make organizational decisions and how we can evaluate the economic impact of those decisions. As will become obvious in Chapter 9, these assessments of the economic utility of selection procedures can be extended to other organizational interventions as well.

In Chapter 10, we outline how survey research can be used in organizations and how a survey is planned. Issues of sampling, questionnaire design, the analysis and feedback of responses are detailed. Finally, we discuss the importance of developing action plans as a function of the survey results.

The evaluation of organizational interventions using various research designs are treated in Chapter 11. In this chapter, numerous research designs are described. The nature of causality and the internal and external validity of research as discussed in this chapter are related to issues of design.

Finally, our last chapter deals with reviews of research literature and how best to summarize and draw conclusions from an existing body of research. Significant new approaches to meta-analyses have been developed in the last fifteen years and these can be useful and powerful tools. Before conducting an expensive new study on some issue, it is important that we know the existing data base and whether an additional study with potentially small sample size could significantly alter the conclusions drawn from that data base.

DATA ANALYSIS STRATEGIES FOR HUMAN RESOURCE RESEARCH

In this chapter, we present various methods of analyzing the data we collect about human resource problems. These data analyses techniques include basic descriptive indices as well as statistics that allow us to make statements about the likelihood that our observations are consistent or inconsistent with our hypotheses or theories regarding human behavior. While we do present computational formulas and numerical examples, our emphasis throughout is on understanding the logic and purpose of each procedure discussed. Correlation coefficients, regression analysis, factor analysis, as well as analyses of variance problems are discussed. Because we introduce a large number of terms in this chapter, we have included a table at the end of the chapter starting on page 86 that briefly defines each term. You may find it helpful to refer to this table as you read the chapter.

INDIVIDUAL DIFFERENCES AND THE NORMAL DISTRIBUTION

That people are different is a statement about which most people (human resources professionals included) would agree. *Why* people differ has been the major interest of various social science researchers. As an example consider your reaction to some human resource management class or training experience you have had in the past. Some of your classmates undoubtedly thought that the experience was one of the best they had at your company or university. Most likely others were just as adamant that much of their time and effort had been wasted. Why? One explanation might be the family background of the individuals in the class. Were their parents supervisors or managers or union employees? Another explanation might be their work experience. Have they had work experiences that they can relate to the problems discussed in this course that affect their reactions to the course? These are factors that a student or trainee brings to the classroom that may, in turn, produce reactions to the class that are different from those of their fellow trainees. There also are a large number of other factors that may influence trainees' or students' reactions to a course: the age and personality of the instructor, the format in which the course is offered, the time of day it is offered, the grading policy, to name but a few.

The presence of individual differences is assumed and the aim of behavioral researchers is to explain or account for individual differences. In research projects, it is important that the measures we use be sensitive to individual differences. If there are no differences in reactions to a training program or no differences in the level of pay satisfaction, then we have nothing to explain.

Sometimes a lack of differences between individuals is due to the way we measure some behavior or opinion or skill rather than the fact that there are no differences. For example, a human resource manager might evaluate a training program only on the basis of whether the participants would want to attend future sessions. Perhaps all would want to go again because the training content is useful to them or they enjoy being away from their usual work routine. However, a serious and much more useful training evaluation might allow for questions that yield more than simple yes no information about the desirability of future training. While all or most of the trainees might want to go again, some may not be very enthusiastic about the program as a whole. Using a scale that allowed responses from 1 (the worst program I ever attended) to 5 (the best program I ever attended) might reveal that there were differences in opinions about the program. These differences might relate to the background of the trainees or to their opinions about various aspects of the training (such as the trainer's presentations, audiovisuals, physical surroundings, perceived relevance of training to work).

While this example refers to the use of survey or questionnaire instruments (see Chapter 10 for further information on construction of scales) the importance of variability in persons also applies to experimental research (see Chapter 11). In Chapter 1, we made the point that we frequently select or create treatments in a way that ensures differences between different treatment groups. Sometimes in laboratory research those treatments are so extreme that similar treatments (and consequently similar results) cannot be created in a field situation.

In either experimental research or in research in which we are simply interested in measuring and relating two or more variables, it is assumed that individual differences exist and that it is the task of the researcher to adequately measure and capture the full extent of those differences. In this chapter, it is our objective to describe the ways in which researchers summarize the data they collect and how they analyze that data so as to make appropriate inferences or to reach justifiable conclusions about the behavior of people in organizations.

That individual differences in ability and attitudes exists is assumed by behavioral resarchers, but these researchers also assume that individual differences are *normally distributed*. This assumption implies that some relatively few number of individuals represent the extreme scores on tests or attitude measures and that most of the people's scores are in the middle of the distribution. The exact form of this normal distribution is illustrated in Figure 2-1. The basis for the assumption of normality lies in the distribution of physical characteristics, such as height and weight, that can be measured directly and that are distributed normally in the adult population. We assume by analogy to measures of physical characteristics that various psychological variables are normally distributed. We do not measure characteristics such as intelligence, personality, or attitude directly as we do height and weight. We assume a certain degree of intelligence when a person answers the verbal, perceptual, and quantitative items that appear in intelligence tests. To produce the desired assumed normal distribution of scores on psychological measures, we either choose test items whose summed responses produce a normal distribution or we transform people's scores in a way that produces a normal distribution. As we shall see below, this normality assumption is useful when we begin to summarize our data and draw conclusions from the data. Normally distributed data have interval properties that allow the computation of various useful descriptive and inferential statistics outlined below.

When we collect data or try to interpret the data someone else has collected, we compute or request access to summary measures that allow us to make interpretive statements about given cases. For example, if we know that a retail store clerk makes sales totaling $4000 in a given week, it helps to know the average clerk's sales for the same week. After you learn the average, usually the next question concerns the range of the weekly sales figures; or, if you've been exposed to

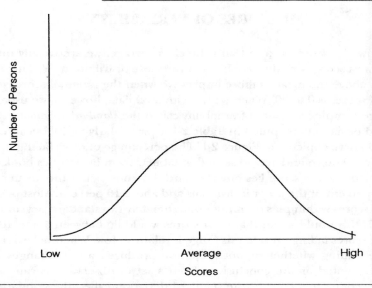

FIGURE 2-1   The Normal Distribution

statistical data frequently, you may realize the importance of the standard deviation. The sales figure of $4000 would be positive and impressive if the store average was $3500 and the range of sales figures was $2800–$4000. You would be much less pleased if the average was $4500 and the range of sales figures was $3800–$5200.

The average is one type of *central tendency* measure; the range is a measure of *variability*. Very often we also are interested in the degree to which the means or averages of one group of people differ from those of another group. In the next sections, we will (a) describe measures of central tendency and variability and (b) address how we conclude that groups of people are different on some variable.

CENTRAL TENDENCY MEASURES

The arithmetic *mean* or average of a set of data as described above is a measure of central tendency that is strictly appropriate only when the data we collect have interval or ratio properties. If we have only ordinal data, we correctly report the *median*, which is the middle score in a rank-ordered distribution of scores, as the measure of central tendency. The median of income statistics is commonly reported because a few millionaires in a group of people, most of whom have salaries around $20,000, would significantly distort the average. Even in large organizations, the computation of a mean annual salary might be a deceptive index of the earning power of organizational members as the chief executive officers' salaries sometimes approach or exceed a million dollars while the great bulk of the employees will make much less. The *mode* is the appropriate index of central tendency when one has only nominal data. If one is trying to decide at what height to construct tables and chairs at a preschool building and the mean height of the people were used to construct the chairs and tables, the teachers would find them too small and the children would find them too large. In this case, two sets of chairs and tables would be necessary. In Table 2-1, we present a distribution of scores obtained on a measure of pay satisfaction along with the computation of the mean, median, and mode.

MEASURES OF VARIABILITY

After we know our score on a test and the class average, we are usually interested in the highest and/or lowest scores—or the variability of the score distribution. We know intuitively that a score two points above the mean is more impressive when the range of scores is 16 to 20 than when the range of scores is 0 to 20. When we have interval data, however, we usually compute an arithmetically more complex measure of variability called the *standard deviation*.

The standard deviation computed in Table 2-1 is particularly useful because of its relationship to the normal curve depicted in Figure 2-1. The percentage of cases falling in any portion of the normal curve are known and are presented in tabular form in statistics books. For example, we know that a person whose score lies one standard deviation below the mean score lies below approximately 84 percent of the other individuals and above 16 percent. Most persons (about 96 percent) will have scores within plus or minus approximately two standard deviations of the mean score. In Table 2-1, this would mean that most scores would lie between 4 and 18 ($11 \pm 2[3.5]$). The probability of scores falling outside this range is relatively low. When behavioral scientists are interested in determining whether or not they have produced a real change or whether two variables are really related or the conclusions from a set of observations can be explained by chance alone, they compute a form of the standard deviation called the standard error to form confidence intervals beyond which it is unlikely to observe some value computed in a sample. We present the standard error later in this chapter in connection with tests of significance. Confidence intervals are computed to tell us how likely it is that the value of some statistic computed in a sample falls within a certain range. Usually, this range includes scores approximately two standard errors above and below the sample statistic in which we are interested.

STANDARD SCORES

Standard deviations are also useful in the computation of standard scores by which we can compare scores from different tests or performance ratings given by two different raters. An example of ratings coming from two different raters whose ratings differ both in terms of mean and standard deviation is presented in Table 2-2. Assuming there are no real differences between the two units of employees, and, if we want to compare Employee A with Employee I (or any other pair of employees across supervisory units), we must take into account the fact that Supervisor 1 gives ratings close to the center of the seven-point scale and that these ratings vary little. Supervisor 2 tends to give somewhat lower ratings but, in addition, she or he uses the entire 1–7 point scale. By expressing the scores in terms of *standard scores* (distance from the mean score divided by the standard deviation), we remove the differences among raters in the mean and standard deviation of their ratings and can make direct comparisons of individuals in different supervisory units.[1] Note that standard score distributions have a mean of zero and standard deviation of 1.00.

---

[1]Technically, standardizing scores will not produce exactly comparable scores unless the two supervisors' distributions of ratings are the same. Most of the time the slight differences in distribution make little difference. When they are important, however, then one way to make the scores comparable is to transform the scores to make both distributions normal.

TABLE 2-1
Measures of Central Tendency and Variability

Person	Level of Pay Satisfaction	Summary Statistics*
A	4	Mean = Total of Individual Scores/ Number of Persons = 220/20 = 11.0
B	5	
C	7	Median = Middle score in the ranked distribution = 10.5[†]
D	7	
E	8	
F	8	Mode = Most frequently occurring score = 10
G	9	
H	10	Range = 4 – 17
I	10	
J	10	Standard deviation = $\sqrt{\Sigma(X_i - M)^2/N}$
K	11	
L	12	$= \sqrt{282/20}$
M	13	$= 3.75$
N	13	
O	14	where X_i are the individual scores, M is the mean,
P	14	N is the number of scores, and Σ indicates the sum
Q	15	of the squared $X_i - M$ values.
R	16	
S	17	
T	17	
Total	220	

* The mean, median, and mode of a distribution of scores are equal only when the distribution of scores is normal, as in Figure 2-1.
† When there are an even number of scores, then the median is usually represented as the average of the two middle scores, in this case 10 and 11.

MEAN DIFFERENCES AND TESTS OF SIGNIFICANCE

Very frequently, there are reasons to compare the attitudes or performance of different groups of workers. We might be interested in differences in performance between trained and untrained groups, men and women, individuals who were recruited using different methods, workers being paid on a piece-rate basis versus those on a salary, etc. In this section, we use an example of an attempt to evaluate the economic worth of jobs to show how a researcher would reach the conclusion that groups differ on some variable.

In our example, the researcher used a point method to obtain evaluations of two jobs (forklift operator and secretary) by four different groups of men and women. One group of each sex evaluated both jobs. In the point method of job evaluation, jobs are graded as to their skill requirements (education, experience, initiative, and ingenuity), effort requirements (physical demand, mental or visual demand), responsibility requirements (equipment or precess, material or product, safety of others, and work of others), and job conditions (normal working conditions, hazards) most frequently on a five-point scale. Each of these factors can be given different degrees of importance or weight depending on the job. The weighted factor scores are added up to give each job an economic value rating. These values are then translated into dollar amounts depend-

TABLE 2-2
Ratings from Two Supervisors That Are Not Directly Comparable

| | Supervisor 1 | | | Supervisor 2 | |
| | | Standard | | | Standard |
Employee	Raw Score	Score	Employee	Raw Score	Score
A	3	-1.14	I	2	-.49
B	4	.38	J	7	1.67
C	4	.38	K	1	-.92
D	3	-1.14	L	6	1.27
E	5	1.89	M	5	.81
F	4	.38	N	1	-.92
G	4	.38	O	2	-.49
H	3	-1.14	P	1	-.92
Mean =	3.75		Mean =	3.13	
SD =	.66		SD =	2.32	

$$\text{Standard score} = \frac{\text{(Raw Score} - \text{Mean)}}{\text{Standard Deviation}}$$

ing on the total pool of money available. The data set which we are using in our example consists of the evaluations of two jobs by 32 people using this system.

The researcher was interested in whether men and women evaluating jobs that are typically held by one sex or the other (forklift operators by males, secretaries by females) would produce evaluations of jobs that differ from each other. Specifically, the data presented in Table 2-3 were used to address three questions: (a) Do men and women's job evaluations differ? (b) Do the evaluations of forklift operator and secretary differ? and (c) Is there some combination of job and gender of evaluator that results in different evaluations? The latter possibility would reflect what we referred to in Chapter 1 as *interaction*. For example, it may be that men evaluate jobs that are usually performed by men higher than do women and higher than they evaluate other jobs typically performed by women. We address the first two of these questions first using what researchers call a t-test of the significance of the differences explored.

In the middle of Table 2-3, we see that the mean of the men's job evaluations was 41.82 while the women averaged 37.82. Given the evaluative and subjective nature of these judgments, we would not expect these two averages to be exactly the same. But are these two judgments different enough that if we asked another sample of 16 men and 16 women to perform similar judgments that we would expect men's evaluations to be higher than those of women evaluators? In addressing this question, researchers typically express their confidence in experimental results in terms of a probability statement. That is, after evaluating the difference between men and women, we want to say that we would (or would not) expect to observe a difference this large between 16 men and 16 women more than five (or one or ten, etc.) percent of the time given there is *no real* difference between men's and women's judgments. In the jargon of scientific research, we seek to test the *null hypothesis* that there are no male-female differences in job evaluations. We reject the null hypothesis if the observed mean difference is so large that it is improbable (less than 5% or 1% are the two usual levels of probability used) that the null hypothesis is correct.

TABLE 2-3
Job Evaluations by Different Groups of Men and Women for Two Different Jobs

	Forklift Operator Job		Secretary Job	
	Men	*Women*	*Men*	*Women*
	A. 39	I. 36	Q. 44	Y. 35
	B. 41	J. 39	R. 43	Z. 40
	C. 49	K. 41	S. 41	AA. 39
	D. 39	L. 40	T. 38	BB. 44
	E. 41	M. 35	U. 37	CC. 36
	F. 44	N. 34	V. 45	DD. 40
	G. 46	O. 38	W. 39	EE. 37
	H. 47	P. 36	X. 36	FF. 35
Total	346	299	323	306
Mean ($\overline{X}$)	43.25	37.38	40.38	38.25

$\overline{x}_{women}$ = 37.82, $\overline{x}_{men}$ = 41.82, $\overline{x}_{FLO}$ = 40.32, $\overline{x}_{SEC}$ = 39.32

SD_{women} = 2.67, SD_{men} = 3.66, SD_{FLO} = 4.21, SD_{SEC} = 3.22

$$C = (346 + 299 + 323 + 306)^2 / 32 = 50721.125$$
$$SS_{sex} = (669^2 + 605^2)/16 - 50721.125 = 128.00$$
$$SS_j = (645^2 + 629^2)/16 - 50721.125 = 8.00$$
$$SS_{sex\ by\ j} = (346^2 + 299^2 + 323^2 + 306^2)/8 - 50721.125 - 128 - 8 = 28.125$$
$$SS_{p.w.\ group} = (39^2 + 41^2....37^2 + 35^2)-50721.125 - 128 - 8 - 28.125 = 292.75$$

To test the null hypothesis implicit in the first research question, we compute a t-value as follows:

$$t = (\overline{x}_{women}- \overline{x}_{men})/ \sqrt{(SD_{women}^2/N_{women}-1) + (SD_{men}^2/N_{men-1})} \qquad (2.1)$$

where $\overline{x}$, SD, and N refer to the mean, standard deviation, and sample size of the two groups.

$$\text{Numerically, } t = (37.82 - 41.82)/\sqrt{(2.67^2/15) + (3.66^2/15)}$$
$$t = -4/1.17$$
$$t = -3.42, df = 30, p < .05.$$

In this computation, the difference between the mean evaluations of men and women is divided by a value that is the standard error of the mean mentioned above. This is the standard deviation of the differences between means which we would expect if, in fact, there were no real differences between men and women. The observed mean difference must be significantly greater than the standard error for us to conclude there is a real difference.

The *t*-value is referred to a statistical table that gives the probabilities of achieving a given value of *t* when no difference is present. In this case, we refer to the tabled value for 30 (number of persons minus the number of groups) degrees of freedom (df), which indicated that any value greater than 2.04 had a probability value less than .05. This .05 is referred to as the *significance level*. Since this *t*-value was highly improbable, our conclusion is that men do, indeed, rate jobs higher than women.

Computation of the t-value necessary to test the significance of the null hypothesis that there are no differences in the evaluation of forklift operator and secretary jobs yields the following:

$$t = (40.32 - 39.32) / \sqrt{(4.21^2/15) + (3.22^2/15)}$$
$$t = 1.00/1.37$$
$$t = .73, \; df = 30, \; p > .05.$$

In this instance, the probability of achieving a t-value of .73 is quite high, higher than .05; hence, we do not conclude that evaluations of these two jobs are significantly different.

However, as you have probably guessed, these two tests do not give us the answer to our third question. In fact, the lack of consideration of the type of job and sex of the evaluator in the same analysis may hide the real explanation of some of the variability in these job evaluations. To assess the effect of these two variables in combination, researchers often use a technique called analysis of variance.

ANALYSIS OF VARIANCE

The analysis of variance provides a test of the significance of the effect of job, the effect of gender of the evaluator, and a test for the interaction effect. An interaction effect occurs when the effect of one independent variable (sex of evaluator or job in this case) on the dependent variable varies as a function of the effect of the other independent variable. To compute an analysis of variance we need to compute the sum of the squared values associated with various divisions of the data presented in Table 2-3. The following sums of squares (SS) are needed (the computations for these five falues are given at the bottom of Table 2-3

1. Add all the persons evaluations in each group (i.e., men and women evaluating each of the jobs). Square this sum and divide by the total number of observations ($N = 32$), in our example. To compute the portion of the sums of squares attributable to the two independent variables and their interaction, this value serves as a correction term (C).
2. To compute the sums of squares for sex (SS_{sex}) of evaluator, the values for men and women are totaled, squared, and then summed. This sum is divided by the number of observations on which the total is based. Finally, C is subtracted from this value.
3. The sums of squares for job (SS_j) are computed similarly. The values for forklift operator and secretary are totaled, squared, and then summed. This sum is divided by the number of observations on which the total is based. Then C is subtracted from this value.
4. The sums of squares for the interaction ($SS_{sex \; by \; j}$) is computed by squaring the totals of each of the four groups in Table 2-2 and dividing by the number of persons in each group. Then SS_{sex} and SS_j are subtracted from this total.
5. The sums of squares for persons within group ($SS_{p.w. \; group}$) is computed by first summing the squared values of all observations, then substracting C, SS_{sex}, SS_{job} and $SS_{sex \; by \; j}$.

These sums of squares are then divided by their degrees of freedom (df). For the effects of evaluator sex and job, df are equal to the number of groups minus 1. For the interaction, df are equal to the number of evaluator sex groups minus 1 multiplied by the number of job groups minus 1. The df for persons within group is the sample size minus the product of the number of sex and job groups. The sum of squares divided by df is called the mean square. The mean square for each source of variation in job ratings (sex, job, sex by job interaction) is divided by the mean square for persons within group to yield an *F*-test. The likelihood of various *F*-values, given no real difference between groups, is known and tables can be consulted for various *df* to determine whether the *F*-value is such that its probability is less than the .05 level of significance (or any other predetermined value). All of these calculations are summarized in Table 2-4. For *df* equal to 1 and 28, the *F* must be 4.20 or greater to be statistically significant at the .05 level. Hence, only the effect for sex of evaluation is significant indicating men evaluate jobs somewhat more highly than women.

The pattern of means for each of the four groups suggested that the difference between men and women might be due primarily to men's higher evaluation of the stereotypically male forklift operator job, but the test of significance for the interaction effect told us that this pattern of mean differences was not a statistically significant pattern.

Whether or not we conclude some effect is significantly different is dependent on a number of factors:

1. The size of the real difference between groups.
2. The level of significance we establish; that is, the probability associated with the possibility that we will falsely conclude that there is a difference. This possible error is called Type I error and in Table 2-4 we set the probability of this error at .05.
3. The sample size. The larger the sample size, the more likely it is that even small differences will be statistically significant.
4. The size of the differences within each group. Note that to calculate *F* for each of the effects, the mean square for that effect was divided by the mean square for persons within group. When there are large within-group differences, they may mask between-group differences.

The probability that we will be able to conclude that there is a significant difference when, in fact, there is a difference is referred to as the *power* of the test. The probability that we will fail to detect a real difference is referred to as a Type II error. Given we have a relatively small sample in the study summarized in Tables 2-3 and 2-4, there may have been low power to detect practically meaningful differences in job evaluations. We will address the issue of power again in this chapter when we discuss the statistical significance of correlations and in Chapter 9 when we present material on criterion-related validation of selection procedures.

It is useful to distinguish between practical and statistical significance in research. Practical significance in the context of our example of job evaluations would be the amount of pay difference implied by the difference in evaluations and whether workers or employers believe this

TABLE 2-4
Analysis of Variance Summary Table: Job Evaluation Results

Source of Variation	Sum of Squares	Degrees of Freedom	Mean Square	F
Sex of Evaluator	128	1	128	12.24*
Job	8	1	8	.76
Sex of Evaluator by Job	28.12	1	28.12	2.69
Persons within Group	292.75	28	10.45	

*$p < .05$.

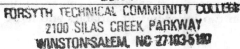

difference is important. After collecting these evaluations, they must be translated into pay amounts. This translation usually involves information gathered from a wage survey of other businesses that employ persons in similar jobs, decisions about merit increases and whether they are included in calculations of pay ranges, decisions about the number of pay grades and the dollar amounts assigned to different grades, etc. (see French, 1978, for more detail). Most such translations, though, would involve plotting current actual pay against the job evaluations and identifying jobs that appear to be underpaid or overpaid. To illustrate the practical significance issue, let's say that the one point mean difference between the evaluations of the two jobs resulted in a pay difference of $.10 an hour. Would workers be concerned with this difference ($208.00 for a year) or would they ignore it?

If we have evidence that employees are sensitive to this difference, then our experiment with job evaluators should have been designed to conclude that a difference this small was statistically significant. All research on human resource issues that addresses practical problems (as opposed to purely theoretical issues) should begin with a consideration of a practically significant difference and then select sample sizes and significance levels to assure adequate power to detect a difference if a practically significant difference does, indeed, exist.

When purely theoretical research is conducted, we may want to decide what a worthwhile mean difference is on other bases. Cohen (1988) defines a small mean difference in social science research as one equal to or less than .2 standard deviation units. Lacking other rationale, power calculations probably should be based on this difference. As you have probably gathered by now, researchers should design research with power in mind or else we run the risk of conducting expensive research projects with a high probability of falsely concluding that some intervention or factor is irrelevant or trivial. Cohen's book (1988) includes a detailed discussion of the issue of power in various research designs for various situations along with tables that allow the estimation of statistical power in research. We strongly recommend its use in planning research studies.

ANALYSIS OF COVARIANCE

Occasionally, we have an analysis of variance design but know that some important variable has not been controlled. In the job evaluation study discussed in this section, the experience of the evaluators in providing similar judgments might have played a role in determining their evaluations of the two jobs in this instance. If the researcher had the foresight to anticipate this or other similar possibilities, he or she could have collected data regarding the experience level of the judges. These experience differences then could have been used as statistical controls in a procedure called *analysis of covariance* (Winer, 1971). In an analysis of covariance, individuals are statistically equated on the covariate (experience in this case) prior to the analysis of the effect of the independent variables. Of course, another alternative is to experimentally control or equate the level of experience in each of the four groups. Experience, here, is an example of the nuisance variables discussed in Chapter 1.

MORE COMPLEX DESIGNS

In this section, we have provided an introduction to the analysis of variance and *t*-tests of group differences. It is possible, of course, to design more complex research in which there are more than two independent variables and more than two levels of each independent variable.

Occasionally the design also includes multiple measures from the same persons (a repeated-measures design). The logic used in analyzing the data from these more complicated designs is similar. We divide variance in such a way that it is attributable to various factors and interactions between factors and test to see if that variance is significantly larger than the variability within each cell (each combination of the various factors in the design). For detailed descriptions of these designs and the calculations involved in the analysis of data resulting from these designs, books on experimental design such as those by Winer (1971), Keppel (1982), or Kirk (1968) should be consulted (Also see Chapter11). Finally, some experiments include multiple-dependent variables in which case a text on multivariate analysis of variance would be helpful (See, for example, chapters in Bock, 1975, or Tatsuoka & Lohnes, 1988).

Analyses of variance more frequently are used in experimental research when the levels of a factor are deliberately manipulated or fixed and the objective is to determine how this manipulation affects some outcome. When the objective of the researcher is to observe how variables relate to each other in their natural, unmanipulated state, investigators more frequently have used measures of association or correlation. These measures are discussed in the next section, but it should be noted that the objective of analysis of variance and correlational analyses is similar; namely, to determine the degree to which values of one variable (or set of variables) are related to another variable(s). In fact, all analyses of variance problems can be translated to the correlation or regression problems (Cohen & Cohen, 1983) discussed in the next several sections.

MEASURES OF ASSOCIATION

As stated above, one frequently wants to know how two variables *vary* together as we observe them in a workplace. Or, we want to know what we can expect to observe concerning one variable when we know the value of a second. For example, if we know the scores of a set of employees on a number of tests, can we predict their job performance? Or, knowing the job performance of employees, can we predict their job satisfaction? Assessment of the degree to which variables *covary* involves the computation of a correlation coefficient. Similar measures of association are computed from analyses of variance, though correlations are probably the most frequently used measure of association. Observation of a sizeable and statistically significant correlation will allow us to predict one variable from another. In this section, we describe the calculation of some measures of association (correlation) and describe how this knowledge might be useful in making predictions.

Phi-Coefficient

With two nominal variables, the measure of association is a correlation called the *phi-coefficient*. We display an example of the calculation of this coefficient in Table 2-5. When collecting this data we might be interested in this question: Is high school graduation associated with job turnover? Simple examination of this table and the numbers in it would lead us to believe that high school graduation is related to turnover; that is, individuals with high school diplomas are most likely to leave their job within one year. The computation of the phi-coefficient gives us a summary measure of the relationship between these two measures— in this case, .60. The phi-coefficient is a special case of the Pearson product-moment correlation discussed in detail in a later section.

Several points about correlation can be made by examining the numbers in this table and considering other possibilities:

TABLE 2-5
An Example of the Computation of a Phi-Coefficient

		Turnover Within One Year		
		No	*Yes*	*Total*
High School	NO	40 (A)	10 (B)	50
Graduation	YES	10 (C)	40 (D)	50
		50	50	

$$\text{Phi-coefficient} = \frac{(A \times D) - (B \times C)}{\sqrt{(A+B)(C+D)(A+C)(B+D)}}$$

$$\text{Phi-coefficient} = \frac{(40 \times 40) - (10 \times 10)}{\sqrt{50 \times 50 \times 50 \times 50}}$$

$$= \frac{1500}{2500}$$

$$= .60$$

1. If all the high school graduates had quit, and all the persons who had failed to graduate are still on the job, the association between these two variables would be at its maximum. The reader can verify that the phi-coefficient would then be 1.00.
2. If the relationship were reversed; that is, all high school graduates had stayed and the remainder had quit, then the phi-coefficient would be −1.00.
3. If there were no relationships between high school graduation and turnover; that is, each of the entries in the table included 25 persons, then the phi-coefficient would be .00.

What is true in this simple example is true for correlational measures in general; that is, correlations range from -1.00 to 1.00.[2] Both negative and positive correlations are equally useful in prediction, but they describe a different type of relationship. A zero coefficient describes an absence of relationship between two variables or a relationship between two variables that is nonlinear. Nonlinear relationships, for example, may indicate that as values of one variable increase, the values of a second variable first increase, then decrease, or the reverse. The Pearson product-moment correlation described below is a summary of the relationship between linearly related variables (increasing values on one variable are directly related to increases or decreases on a second variable). Most of the relationships we observe in human resources research are linear and of the magnitude of .00 to .60. Cohen (1988) classifies correlations of 0.10 as small, correlations of .30 as modest, and correlations of 0.50 as large.

---

[2]Actually, phi-coefficients have this range only when the measurement of the nominal variable results in an equal percent of cases being placed in the categories of both nominal variables. The reader is referred to Magnusson (1966) or other texts on psychometrics for a full explanation of the reason why. One should expect a much lower phi-coefficient when the nominal variables do not classify individuals in equal-sized groups.

Kappa

Occasionally, researchers encounter instances in which we are interested in measuring the association between nominal variables that have more than two categories. For example, we might be interested in coding various nonverbal behaviors of interviewers to determine if such nonverbal behavior has any effect on applicant reaction to the interview situation. In this case, one important question is whether people who are asked to record the nonverbal behavior of the interviewer can agree as to the exhibited behavior. This agreement is a critical measure of the quality of our measure of nonverbal behavior. In Table 2-6, we present the agreement between two coders on the type of nonverbal behavior exhibited in 1000 time intervals each 10 seconds in duration.

As one index of agreement, we could calculate the percentage of times the coders indicated that the same behavior occurred; in this case, 78% ((450 + 138 + 192)/1000). However, the percent agreement is not a good index because it is dependent on the frequency of the use of the three categories. With large use of a single category (nods were recorded in just over half of the cases), percent agreement may be high by virtue of chance. An index, called *Kappa* (Cohen, 1960, 1968) is used to calculate agreement between raters above and beyond the agreement that occurs simply as a function of chance. As you can see, at the bottom of Table 2-6, we would expect the raters to agree almost 39% of the time, purely by chance. Corrected for the probability of chance agreement, Kappa indicates these two coders agreed 64% of the time. This is quite a reasonable level of Kappa, but we could also test to see if the agreement between these two raters exceeded chance by a statistically significant level using a standard error presented by Fleiss, Cohen, and Everitt (1969).

TABLE 2-6
Intercoder Agreement on the Categorization of Nonverbal Behavior

		RATER A				
		Nods	*Frowns*	*Leans Back*	*Totals*	*Percent*
	Nods	450	52	10	512	51.2
	Frowns	73	138	31	242	24.2
RATER B	Leans Back	18	36	192	246	24.6
	Totals	541	226	233	1000	
	Percent	54.1	22.6	23.3		

Kappa $= (P_O - P_C)/(1 - P_C)$

where P_O = proportion of times the two raters agreed on the behavior exhibited by the interviewer, which equals 78% here.

P_C = proportion of times that agreement would occur by chance, which is equal to the sum of the product of corresponding row and column proportions (i.e., percent/100).

P_C $= (.512 \times .541) + (.242 \times .226) + (.246 \times .233) = .277 + .055 + .057$

         $= .389$

Kappa $= (.78 - .389) / (1 - .389)$

         $= .64$

Pearson Product-Moment Correlation

The most frequently encountered correlation coefficient and the one we will be referring to throughout most of this textbook is the *Pearson product-moment correlation*. This correlation appropriately used with interval-level data is usually designated simply as *r* and its simplest computational form is as follows:

$$r_{xy} = \frac{\Sigma(Z_x Z_y)}{N} \tag{2.2}$$

where Z_x equals the standard score of an individual on variable X; Z_y equals the standard score of an individual on variable Y; Σ indicates that we sum all the $Z_x Z_y$ products for the group of cases on which the correlation is being computed; N is the number of persons available for the computation of the correlation; r_{xy} is the correlation between two variables designated as x and y.

A formula for the computation of r from raw scores and an example of its use is provided in Table 2-7 for a set of hypothetical data on job satisfaction and worker productivity. The formula above meets our primary objective of communicating the concept of correlation. Examination of

TABLE 2-7
Example of the Computation of a Correlation Coefficient Using Raw Scores and Standard Scores

| Job Satisfaction | Productivity | | | | | | |
	(X)	(Y)	X^2	Y^2	XY	Z_x	Z_y	$Z_x Z_y$
Kevin	6	4	36	16	24	.1	-.3	-.03
Abigail	8	5	64	25	40	.8	.1	.08
Dan	10	7	100	49	70	1.5	.8	1.20
Mary	9	10	81	100	90	1.1	2.0	2.20
Marcy	7	3	49	9	21	.4	-.7	-.28
Bob	4	2	16	4	8	-.6	-1.1	.66
Scott	3	6	9	36	18	-.9	.5	-.45
Sue	2	7	4	49	14	-1.3	.8	-1.04
Cheri	7	3	49	9	21	.4	-.7	-.28
Rick	1	1	1	1	1	-1.6	-1.5	2.40
	$\Sigma X = 57$	$\Sigma Y = 48$	$\Sigma X^2 = 409$	$\Sigma Y^2 = 298$	$\Sigma XY = 307$			$\Sigma Z_x Z_y = 4.46$

Standard Score Formula:

$r_{xy} = \Sigma Z_x Z_y / N = 4.46/10 = .44$

Raw Score Formula:

$$r_{xy} = \frac{N\Sigma XY - (\Sigma X)(\Sigma Y)}{\sqrt{[N\Sigma X^2 - (\Sigma X)^2][N\Sigma Y^2 - (\Sigma Y)^2]}}$$

$$r_{xy} = \frac{(10 \times 307) - (57 \times 48)}{\sqrt{[(10 \times 409) - (57)^2][10(298) - 48^2]}}$$

$$= .44$$

this formula will lead us to the same conclusions about correlation as we drew from Table 2-5 and the computation of the phi-coefficient. If all the values of $Z_x Z_y$ pairs tend to be similar; that is high positive Z_xs are associated with high positive Z_ys and high negative Z_xs are associated with high negative Z_ys, then the sum of products will be at its maximum and the correlation will be high. When positive Z_xs are consistently paired with negative Z_ys, the correlation coefficient will be negative.

Another method of presenting correlation coefficients is by means of a *scattergram*. A scattergram is a plot of the relationship between two variables. In Figure 2-2, we present scatterplots that represent a variety of possible relationships between two variables. A correlation coefficient is actually a summary measure of the degree of scatter one observes in a scatterplot. If all the dots in the scatterplot formed a straight line, the correlations computed by either of the formulas in Table 2-7 would equal to 1.00 or -1.00. Maximum dispersion of the dots in a scatterplot occurs when $r = .00$.

Correlations and Causality

When we find two variables are highly correlated, we often conclude that one of the two variables is the cause of the other. This is especially true because, in most cases, the reason for computing the correlation to begin with involved a guess or hypothesis that one variable caused another.

These attributions of causality are not necessarily correct, however. A good illustration of the problems encountered in the determination of causal relationships is provided by investigations of the job satisfaction-job performance relationship. Early investigations of this relationship were carried out with the assumption that happy workers were productive workers. The observation of a positive correlation between satisfaction and productivity could be representative of four different actual situations:

1. Satisfaction does indeed lead to performance as hypothesized.
2. Performance leads to greater satisfaction. This is certainly plausible as most individuals become more satisfied with jobs or classes when they find out that they can and do perform well.
3. Both satisfaction with a job and job performance are caused by a third factor, such as general satisfaction with one's marital/family situation or recent pay increases. It is certainly plausible that family problems would affect both job satisfaction and performance. Likewise, the level of pay raises a group receives could very plausibly affect both individual satisfaction and productivity. In fact, when we add consideration of a third variable, all of the cases outlined by Ellsworth (1977) and reviewed in Chapter 1 are possible.
4. Finally, the positive correlation could simply be a chance variation away from a true value or zero correlation. This would occur most frequently when we have a small sample of persons who are not representative of the complete population about whom we wish to make some statement. In fact, evidence exists that indicates job satisfaction and job performance are not highly related (Brayfield & Crockett, 1955; Iaffaldano & Muchinsky, 1985).

In our next section, we will discuss the way in which behavioral scientists evaluate the likelihood of the fourth possibility mentioned above. The degree to which we determine which of the first three

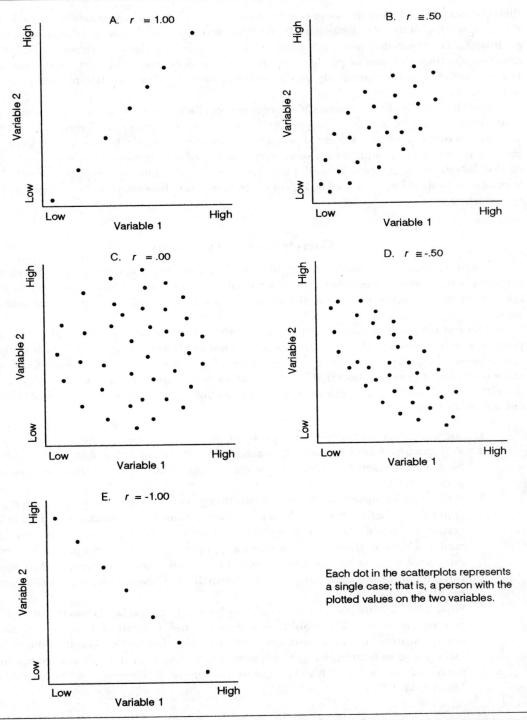

Each dot in the scatterplots represents a single case; that is, a person with the plotted values on the two variables.

FIGURE 2-2   Scatterplots Depicting a Variety of Correlation Coefficients between Two Variables Ranging from *r* = 1.00 to *r* = .00 to *r* = -1.00.

explanations is/is not likely is often dependent on how we design a research study and collect the data. Some issues regarding the causal relationships between study variables were addressed in Chapter 1. With more than two measured variables, we can ascertain under certain circumstances which of the various causal hypotheses (see Ellsworth, 1977 and Chapter 1) are most plausible. The latter method, called path analysis, is briefly described toward the end of this chapter.

STATISTICAL SIGNIFICANCE OF CORRELATIONS

Let us say that the correlation between job satisfaction and job performance for a group of 10 people (as depicted in Table 2-7) is .44. In collecting data on any project, we set out to discredit the notion that there is no relationship between two variables or that the true correlation is .00. As in the case of our hypothesis above that there were no mean differences in the evaluation of jobs, this is called a *null hypothesis*. In our example, a test of *statistical significance* tells us the confidence with which we can say, based on 10 observations, that the satisfaction-performance correlation is greater than zero. If we find that the probability of observing a correlation of .44 in a group of 10 is less than 5 times out of 100 (.05), we say that the correlation of .44 is statistically significant. (In our example, a correlation of .44 is not significant.)

The test of significance in this case again involves the computation of t and referral of this value to a table that tells us the value of t for a sample size of 10 at the .05 level of significance. In this case, t is given by this formula:

$$t = (r\sqrt{N-2}) / \sqrt{1-r^2} \qquad (2.3)$$
$$= (.44\sqrt{10-2}) / \sqrt{1-.44^2}$$
$$= 1.39, \ df = 8, \ p > .05.$$

The critical value of t needed for statistical significance with eight $(N-2)$ degrees of freedom is 2.31; hence, we conclude that the relationship between satisfaction and productivity is nonsignificantly different from zero.

If the correlation is significantly different from zero, the correlation can be negative or positive. If the researcher has reason to hypothesize that the correlation is positive (or negative), the probability value is doubled (i.e., .10) and the test is called a *one-tailed* test. The t-value needed for statistical significance at the .10 level is 1.86 in our example. Our obtained t is smaller than 1.86; nonsignificant, even in the event that we had formulated a one-tailed hypothesis.

Throughout this text and in other psychological literature, when authors speak of significance, they are usually talking of statistical significance, not social, economic, or political significance. The latter types of significance involve the value placed on changes/differences in measured variables. As mentioned above these considerations are often referred to as the practical significance of the results of a study.

The notion of statistical significance can be applied to nearly all statistics, such as percentages in polling studies or average differences between groups in a training experiment. A familiar example of the use of the statistical significance notion is the political survey. To say that the percentage favoring some candidate is 52% with a 3% margin of error means that the actual percentage favoring the candidate would not likely be greater than 55% nor less than 49% (recall the concept of a confidence interval described above), but that percentages among all voters who favor the candidate between these two figures would be likely.

As in tests of the significance of the difference of means, we also are concerned about power when we test the significance of some measure of association. The power situation for a correlation coefficient is depicted in Figure 2-3. In the figure we illustrate the expected distribution of correlation coefficients implied by both the null and alternative hypotheses. This situation involves a test of the null hypothesis that $r = .00$. The researcher felt that a practically and theoretically important correlation would be .20. Hence, this is identified as H_a or the alternative hypothesis. In the event that H_a is correct, the figure illustrates the probability of both Type I and II errors as well as the power of the statistical significance test. In this case, the standard error of the correlation coefficient was slightly larger than .10. To be significant with this standard error (N would be approximately 100), a correlation coefficient must exceed .20. About one-half of the time, we would expect the correlation to be less than .20. This is the probability of a Type II error which is indicated by the vertical-lined area under the curve. The slanted lines indicate the power of the

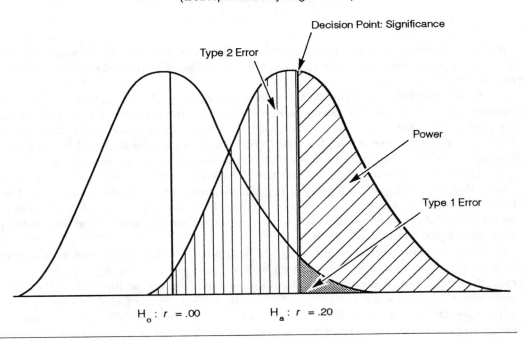

FIGURE 2-3   Illustration of Power

test. Both power and the probability of a Type II error are about 0.50 in this situation. We set a Type I error at .05.

From this diagram, one also can discern the effect of various procedures to increase power. If we increase the level of Type I error we allow, this would move the critical value we use to decide our correlation coefficient is significant to the left, thereby increasing power. Increasing sample size will have the effect of decreasing the spread of the two distributions of coefficients (i.e., they will become tall and skinny). This means they will overlap much less, thereby increasing power. If we are willing to entertain a different alternative hypothesis, that will also affect power. If our best guess of the true state of affairs or our estimate of the lowest practically or theoretically significant correlation is larger, say .30, the decision point will remain where it is but the whole distribution of coefficients implied by the alternative hypothesis will move to the right, thereby increasing power.

Incidentally, consultation of a power table in Cohen (1988) for the satisfaction-productivity example above indicated we had less than a .30 probability of concluding that there was a significant relationship even when the real relationship between these two variables is .50. Clearly, a researcher employing a sample size of 10 should prepare to discuss nonsignificant results since even with a relatively high estimate of the real correlation the probability of observing a significant relationship is very low.

REGRESSION ANALYSIS

Correlations are useful in describing the type of relationship existing between two variables, but applied psychologists frequently want to predict one of these two variables from the other. The procedure whereby prediction equations are developed is called *regression analysis* and the result is a prediction or *regression equation*. Let's say we are interested in the sensitivity of an organization to the external employability of its workers (see Fossum & Fitch, 1985, for a laboratory study of this issue). In this instance, the organization wants to know how likely it is that their employees can and perhaps will look for work elsewhere. This information would be helpful in planning interventions to decrease turnover among competent and desirable employees and to make plans to replace these individuals if they cannot be retained. We would then be interested in the correlation between some measure of the external attractiveness of employees and their salary raises across a number of years. Predictions of the size of one's salary raise could then be made on the basis of how likely an employee is to get external job offers. If both measures are changed to standard scores, then the prediction formula is simply:

$$z_{\hat{y}} = r_{xy} z_x \qquad (2.4)$$

where $z_{\hat{y}}$ is the standardized predicted salary raise; r_{xy} is the correlation between salary raise and external attractiveness; z_x is the standardized measure of external attractiveness. As you can see, predictions of salary raises are made by multiplying the external attractiveness score by the correlation between x and y.

If the predictions are made using raw scores on both measures, then the formula is more complex:

$$\hat{y} = r_{xy} \left(\frac{SD_y}{SD_x} \right)(x) + a \qquad (2.5)$$

where $\hat{y}$ is the predicted salary increase; SD_y and SD_x are the standard deviations of the salary raises and external attractiveness, respectively, a is a constant which corrects for differences in averages on the external attractiveness measure and the salary increase measure. Note SD_y/SD_x and a adjust for differences between x and y in standard deviations and means which do not exist when standard scores are used.

Suppose we had done a study of the relationship between the size of salary increases and the external attractiveness of a group of design engineers. The salary increase-external attractiveness correlation was .40. The standard deviation of the external attractiveness measure was 5; that of the salary increase measure was $2000. The mean of the attractiveness index was 10, and the mean salary increase was $12,000. The regression equation would then be:

$$\hat{y} = (.40) \ (2000/5)(x) + 10,400^3$$
$$\hat{y} = 160 \ (x) + 10,400.$$

The 160 value is called a *regression weight*. If we now encounter an individual whose external marketability index is 12, we can compute a prediction of the level of that individual's salary increases as follows:

$$\hat{y} = 160 \ (12) + 10,400 = 1920 + 10,400 \text{ or } \$12,320$$

This means that given an external attractiveness index of 12, we would predict that the person's salary increases over the period considered should equal $12,320 if we expect to retain the worker.

With less than perfect correlation (1.00) between x and y, we will make errors using this equation. The errors in our prediction over many cases are usually summarized by an index called the *standard error of estimate*. If we made a large number of predictions using the equation above, computed the errors associated with each of the predictions, and then computed the standard deviation of those errors, we would have the standard error of estimate. Fortunately, there is a simpler computational formula:

$$SE_{est} = SD_y \sqrt{1 - r_{xy}^2} \tag{2.6}$$

where SE_{est} equals the standard error of estimate; SD_y equals the standard deviation of salary increases; and r_{xy} equals the correlation between attractiveness and salary increase. If we have an observed correlation of 1.00, computation of the standard error using the formula above would yield .00, indicating no errors are made. When validity is zero, on the other hand, the standard error of estimate equals the standard deviation of y. Since this is the worst we can do by way of prediction, psychometricians frequently use the ratio of the standard error of estimate to the standard deviation of the criterion as an index of how much we reduce the error of prediction over random guesses. This approach to the consideration of a predictor's usefulness is called the *index of forecasting efficiency*.

Single versus Multiple Predictor Variables

In most situations involving human behavior, it is likely that several different factors or measured variables will be useful in making predictions. When we attempt to write regression

---

[3] To obtain 10,400 multiply the mean of the attractiveness measure by the regression weight ($r_{xy}/(\sigma_y/\sigma_x)$) and subtract the product from the mean salary increase.

equations involving two or more variables, those equations become increasingly complex. We present only the two-predictor case because of this complexity, but the principles underlying prediction with three or more predictors are identical to the two-predictor case.

How well two or more predictors combined improve the predictability of some behavior of interest depends on their relationship to each other as well as their relationship to the variable being predicted. If two predictors do not correlate with each other but both are correlated to some outcome variable or criterion, we could depict their relationship as in the set of circles in Figure 2-4a. In this figure, the central circle represents the variable we are predicting (sometimes called a criterion), the degree of overlap of the criterion with the two predictor circles is representative of their relationship with an outcome variable or validity. The combined relationship between two or more predictors and a criterion is called the *multiple correlation* (R). The multiple correlation coefficient, when the predictors are uncorrelated as in Figure 2-4a, is expressed quite simply as follows:

$$R = \sqrt{r_{y1}^2 + r_{y2}^2}. \tag{2.7}$$

In most cases, however, two valid predictors also are correlated with each other. The diagram relating the three appears in Figure 2-4b. Note in this figure that r_{12}, or the intercorrelation between the two predictors, is not .00. While each predictor is valid and predicts some unique portion of the criterion, all three variables overlap to some degree, which means, in essence, that the two predictors are predicting the same criterion variance. Under these conditions, the multiple correlation must be expanded to include consideration of the intercorrelation between the variables as follows:

$$R_{y.12} = \sqrt{(r_{y1}^2 + r_{y2}^2 - 2r_{y1}r_{y2}r_{12}) / (1 - r_{12}^2)} \tag{2.8}$$

Let's compute R for the two cases in Figure 2-4, assuming the same predictor validities in the two cases. First, the case represented by Figure 2-4a:

$$\begin{aligned} R &= \sqrt{.6^2 + .4^2} \\ &= \sqrt{.36 + .16} \\ &= .72 \end{aligned}$$

or the case in Figure 2-4b, assuming $r_{12} = .4$,

$$\begin{aligned} R &= \sqrt{(.6^2 + .4^2 - 2 \times .4 \times .6 \times .4)/(1 - .4^2)} \\ &= \sqrt{(.36 + .16 - .192)/.84} \\ &= .62. \end{aligned}$$

As is apparent from these calculations, it is best to have unrelated predictor variables. R decreased from .72 to .62 with the introduction of a .4 correlation between the two predictors. A common-sense interpretation and an example of this phenomenon might read as follows. Given a test of cognitive ability, we would likely learn more about a group of job applicants if we added a test of motivation than if we added another test of cognitive ability. This may be true even though the second test of cognitive ability is just as valid as the first cognitive ability test and more valid than the motivation measure.

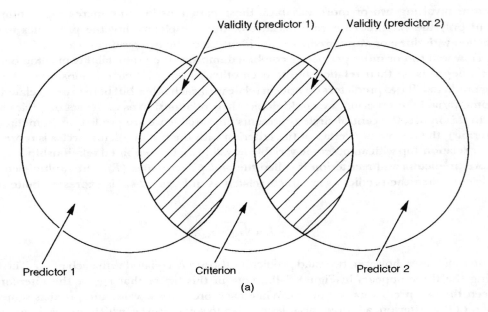

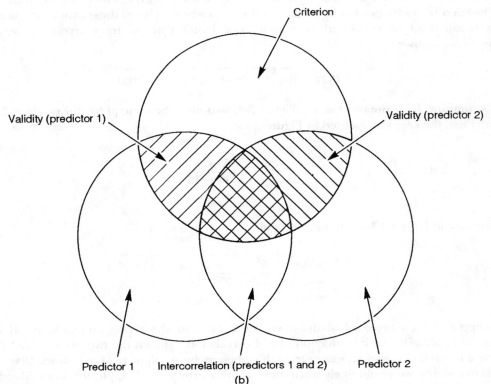

FIGURE 2-4   Diagrams Illustrating the Case of Uncorrelated and Correlated Predictor Variables

As you might anticipate, we also can compute regression weights for the predictors in a two-predictor case. Computation of these regression weights like the formula for R include provision for predictor intercorrelation. Calculation of the regression weights for the first of the two predictors in our example is as follows assuming $SD_y = SD_1 = 10$:

$$b_1 = \left(\frac{r_{y1} - r_{y2}r_{12}}{\sqrt{(1 - r_{y2}^2)(1 - r_{12}^2)}} \right) \left(\frac{SD_y\sqrt{1 - r_{y2}^2}}{SD_1\sqrt{1 - r_{12}^2}} \right) \tag{2.9}$$

$$b_1 = \left(\frac{.6 - .4 \times .4}{\sqrt{(1 - .4^2)(1 - .4^2)}} \right) \left(\frac{10\sqrt{1 - .4^2}}{10\sqrt{1 - .4^2}} \right)$$

$$b_1 = .52.$$

For b_2, values for predictor 2 and its correlations would be substituted in the above formula. In this case, b_2 is equal to .19. These regression weights are optimal weights in the sense that errors of prediction made when using them are minimal. However, the weights, themselves, are dependent on the particular sample on which they were calculated. Since this is true, these weights should be cross-validated (evaluated on a second sample of people). To cross-validate them, we collect predictor data on a second sample of persons from the same population and compute predicted criterion scores for these persons using the regression equation derived in the first sample. These predicted scores are then correlated with the actual outcome measures as an index of how well the regression equation will work in new samples. Usually, there is some *shrinkage* when one compares the R computed in the original sample with the R computed in a new sample. The shrinkage is greatest when the original sample size is small, when the number of predictors is large, and/or the R is relatively low. In fact, these three variables (sample size, number of predictors, and R) can be used to make predictions about the degree of shrinkage in the absence of an empirical cross-validation (Cattin, 1980) under certain circumstances. A shrunken R is reported frequently in research reports and is part of the standard output of most computer software packages that report regression results. While all rules of thumb are arbitrary, it is perhaps not wise to attempt any computation and application of regression weights to make predictions of some outcome when the sample size/number of predictor ratio is less than five. In these cases, it is best simply to add the predictor scores perhaps weighted by some judgment of the importance of the predictor variables involved.

As was true with correlation analysis involving just two variables, we can test the significance of the multiple correlation and the regression weights computed in multiple regression. For overall multiple correlation, we compute the following F-value:

$$F = (R^2(n - k - 1))/((1 - R^2)k), \quad df = k, n - k - 1 \tag{2.10}$$

where n equals the number of subjects and k equals the number of predictors. For the numerical example presented above, assuming $n = 100$,

$$F = (.62(100 - 2 - 1))/((1 - .62^2)2)$$
$$F = 48.89, \quad df = 2, 97, \quad p < .05.$$

We would again consult a table with a distribution of F values to determine if our F-value exceeded the established probability value ($p < .05$). In this case, it did, so we conclude there is a significant relationship between this combination of the two predictors and the criterion.

We would also be interested in the significance of the two regression weights. In this case, we divide the value of the regression weight by its standard error to compute a t-value which has degrees of freedom equal to n-k-1. The standard error formula for predictor i is as follows:

$$SE = \frac{SD_y}{SD_i} \left[\sqrt{(1 - R_y^2) / (n - k - 1)} \right] \quad \left[\sqrt{1 / (1 - R_i^2)} \right] \tag{2.11}$$

where R_i^2 is the squared multiple correlation of i with the other predictors. For predictor 1 in our example,

$$SE = \frac{10}{10} \sqrt{(1 - .62^2) / (100 - 2 - 1)} \quad \sqrt{1 / (1 - .4^2)}$$

$$SE = .0872.$$

Recall from above that b_1 equalled .52 so the t-value here is 5.96, which by consulting the values of a t-distribution for $df = 97$ $(n - k - 1)$, we find to be statistically significant.

Another issue that arises with multiple predictors is the order in which predictor variables are entered into the regression equation. Arithmetically, computer programs for regression analyses allow a variety of means by which to determine which predictors enter an equation. *Stepwise* procedures begin by choosing the predictor whose correlation with a criterion is highest, the contribution of this predictor is then removed using partial correlation analyses (see Ghiselli, Campbell, & Zedeck, 1981) and the remaining predictors are evaluated. The next best (in the sense of predicting the criterion) predictor is then entered. This process continues until additional predictors do not make a statistically significant or practical contribution to the prediction of the criterion. Entry of predictors in this fashion is determined by the correlations between the predictors and the criterion and their intercorrelations with each other. In terms of Figure 2-4, we are trying to maximize the prediction of a unique portion of the criterion variance at each step.

In a *hierarchical regression*, the researcher specifies the order in which predictors are to be entered into the equation. The researcher's desired order may be a result of practical considerations; for example, in selection, information from the least expensive selection procedures might be entered first, followed by more expensively collected information. Order of entry is more usually determined by theoretical considerations as will be discussed in a later section in this chapter.

Moderator Variables and Curvilinear Relationships

Use of a regression equation to predict job behavior assumes the performance of all individuals is predicted equally well. When individuals can be divided in two or more groups based on the predictability of their job performance, the variable used to group them is called a *moderator*. The concept of a moderator was introduced in Chapter 1 and is illustrated in Figure 2-5. In Figure 2-5a, we present the usual scattergram for a group of people who can be separated on the basis of some moderator variable; for example, method of payment (either piece rate or hourly). Hypothetically, let's assume the x's represent those persons receiving hourly pay; the 0's, those persons receiving piece-rate pay. If we take the scattergram apart and produce separate scattergrams for these two groups of people, we have Figures 2-5b and 2-5c. Figure 2-5a represents a scattergram in which the predictor-criterion relationship is likely to be about .40; in Figure 2-5b the relationship

● Employee Paid on Piece-Rate Basis
✕ Employee Paid on Hourly Basis

FIGURE 2-5   Illustration of Scattergram for Three Employee Groups for Whom Amount of Pay Earned-Job Performance Relationships Differ

depicted is likely near zero; while in the piece-rate situation, the pay-performance relationship appears substantially higher, perhaps near .60.

This hypothetical example is consistent with research and theory regarding pay-performance relationships (Lawler, 1971, 1981). Lawler maintains that theory and research support the contention that if pay policy is to motivate people, it must (a) create a belief among employees that good performance will lead to high pay, (b) contribute to the importance of pay, (c) minimize the perceived negative consequences of performing well, and (d) create conditions such that outcomes other than pay will soon be seen to be related to good performance. Our example is relevant only to the first of Lawler's conditions for an effective compensation system. And, of course, there are methods other than piece-rate pay in which compensation specialists can increase the perception that good performance leads to good pay.

The notion that a moderator variable could differentiate between subgroups of people on the basis of their predictability was introduced by Saunders (1956) and Ghiselli (1956a). Ghiselli (1956a) provided an example in which an interest measure moderated test-job performance relationships for different groups of taxi cab drivers. Seashore (1962) provided an example of a situation in which correlations between aptitude test scores and college grades were higher for women than men.

Statistically, the existence and importance of a moderator variable can be tested using regression analysis (Bartlett, Bobko, Mosier, & Hannan, 1978; Cohen & Cohen, 1983; Stone, 1988). Consider the situation pictured in Figure 2-5 in which method of payment is the moderator. The regression analysis used to predict job performance would include the following variables:

1. The amount of pay, which in this case is the predictor variable.
2. The method of payment variable (1 for hourly pay, 2 for piece-rate pay), which is the moderator variable. While reversing the coding of method of payment would not affect our data analyses, we usually code dichotomous variables consistent with some underlying continuum; in this instance, the coding is consistent with the idea that these two conditions represent points on a "degree of pay contingency" continuum. We will use the same practice in our discussion of *dummy coding* later in this chapter.
3. The product of the predictor variable and the moderator variable.

In this case, the researcher would require the entry of the predictor and moderator variable into the regression equation first, then the product of the two. If the regression weight for the product is statistically significant, then the researcher would conclude that method of payment *moderates* the relationship between the amount of pay and job performance.

As usual, we would be interested in the statistical significance of the addition of this product term. To evaluate the statistical significance, we calculate the following F-value.

$$F = \left(\frac{R_F^2 - R_S^2}{1 - R_F^2} \right) \left(\frac{n - k_F - k_S - 1}{k_F} \right) \tag{2.12}$$

where R_F^2 is the multiple correlation including all three terms and R_S^2 is the multiple correlation in the case in which only amount of pay and method of pay are included as predictors. The sample size equals n and k_F and k_S are the number of predictors in the two equations. Let's assume $R_F^2 = .30$, $R_S^2 = .27$, $n = 200$, then

$$F = \left(\frac{.30 - .27}{1 - .30} \right) \left(\frac{200 - 3 - 2 - 1}{3} \right)$$

The degrees of freedom for this F-value are 3 (k_F) and 194 ($n - k_F - k_S - 1$) and consulting a table of F-values we find that 2.78 is statistically significant ($p<.05$).

Having detected a statistically significant moderator effect in hierarchical moderated regression, it proves useful to describe its nature. With no moderating effect in the example above, the effect of amount of pay on job performance would be the same regardless of the method of pay. A statistically significant moderator effect could indicate a number of different possibilities with respect to the effect of the interaction of amount of pay and method of payment on job performance only one of which is consistent with the Lawler (1981) statements cited above on the motivating effects of pay. Various possibilities are presented pictorially in Figure 2-6. Figure 2-6a indicates a lack of a moderating effect, but all others would represent interactions, some of them more or less likely given the hypothesis that pay will be most effective in producing performance increments when it is contingent on performance. Figure 2-6b would represent results that are contradictory to the hypothesis because performance increases most directly as a function of pay in hourly pay situations. Figure 2-6c is consistent with the hypothesis. In Figure 2-6d, we depict an unlikely condition in which performance is high in piece-rate conditions regardless of the amount paid, although in hourly conditions we see an increase in performance with pay increases. This result would be consistent with the pay contingency notion. Finally, in Figure 2-6e we see another unlikely situation in which performance in hourly pay situations is uniformly high, while in piece-rate conditions performance varies as a function of pay. Note that in this sense (i.e., performance is contingent on pay) this latter configuration is consistent with the hypothesis. However, our point is that all four moderator effects would have very different implications for pay policy.

Cohen and Cohen (1983) showed that by rearranging the terms in a moderated regression equation one can produce new equations into which we can substitute different values, compute predicted outcome variables, and plot these values thereby producing a pictorial representation of the moderator effect. For example, the moderated regression equation described above can be written as follows:

$$\hat{Y} = b_0 + b_1 X_1 + b_2 X_2 + b_3 X_1 X_2 \tag{2.13}$$

where $\hat{Y}$ is the predicted outcome variable or performance in our example;

b_0 is the intercept value or the correction for differences in means as we described above;

b_1 is the regression weight for the predictor, in our example this is amount paid;

b_2 is the regression weight for the moderator or method of payment in this case;

b_3 is the regression weight for the product of amount of payment and method of payment;

X_1 and X_2 are the values of payment and method of payment respectively.

The rearrangement of terms necessary to allow plotting of the observed relationships are given by the following two equations:

$$\hat{Y} = (b_1 + b_3 X_2) X_1 + (b_2 X_2 + b_0) \tag{2.14}$$

$$\hat{Y} = (b_2 + b_3 X_1) X_2 + (b_1 X_1 + b_0). \tag{2.15}$$

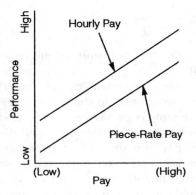

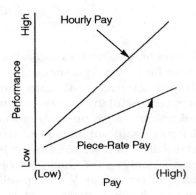

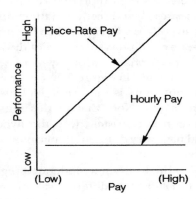

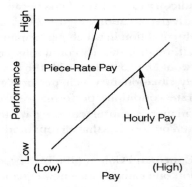

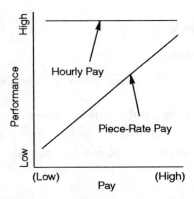

FIGURE 2-6 Various Possible Forms of the Moderating Effect of Method of Payment on the Relationship between Amount Paid and Job Performance

In the first of these two equations, one would substitute different values for X_1 (holding X_2 constant at its various values; for example, hourly versus piece-rate pay coded as 1 and 2). One could also use the second of the two equations by substituting different values of X_2 (holding X_1 constant), though in this particular example that would not make as much sense. These predicted $\hat{Y}$ values would then be plotted to illustrate the nature of the interaction as in Figure 2-6.

There are numerous examples of the use of moderated regression analyses dealing with various human resource issues. Phillips and Dipboye (1989) explained interviewers' appraisals of job applicant interview performances as a function of how the applicant actually did moderated by the perceived reasons or attributions the interviewer thought explained the applicants' good or poor performance. Locke, Mento, and Kutcher (1978) used hierarchical moderated regression to predict performance in a laboratory experiment using a job sample measure of ability as the predictor and motivation as a moderator. Champoux and Peters (1980) present a test of the degree to which jobs, which are perceived as being high on dimensions that are theoretically motivating, result in higher levels of worker job satisfaction. Consistent with the theoretical job characteristics model of work motivation, Champoux and Peters (1980) hypothesized that this relationship would be moderated by the workers' need for growth. While they found evidence for this interaction, they also found evidence for a curvilinear effect. This finding is worthy of special discussion.

Recall that earlier in this chapter we noted that a linear relationship is assumed when we correlate two variables and that a linear relationship implies that, as the values of one variable get higher, we see a corresponding decrease or increase in another variable. Champoux and Peters (1980) argued that the perceived motivating potential of a job might not be linearly related to job satisfaction throughout the entire range of motivating potential scores (MPS). To test this hypothesis, they computed the square of MPS and added it to the regression equation after the unsquared MPS, growth need strength, and the product of growth need strength and MPS had been entered in the equation. The squared term did add significantly to the prediction of job satisfaction above and beyond the other predictors. Through the calculation of satisfaction values using procedures like those detailed above for moderator effects, Champoux and Peters (1980) found an effect like that depicted in Figure 2-7.

The analysis and interpretation of moderator and curvilinear effects has been a controversial one in the human resource area. The rationale and defense of the use of product and power terms as outlined in this section is provided by Cohen (1978) and Stone (1988).

Suppressor Variables

A somewhat counter-intuitive result occurs in regression analyses when a researcher encounters *suppressor variables,* variables that add to the prediction of an outcome even though they are uncorrelated with that outcome. Usually, a predictor that is uncorrelated with the outcome of interest would be discarded, however, a suppressor is useful because it serves to remove predictor variance that is uncorrelated with the outcome. The usual suppressor variable case involving two predictors and a criterion is depicted in Figure 2-8.

Note the suppressor does not overlap with the criterion indicating its zero validity. It does, however, overlap with the valid predictor indicating the two are correlated. This represents the second way in which suppressors conflict with our intuition and the point we made above about multiple predictors; namely, that they should be as nonredundant or uncorrelated as possible. A suppressor's correlation with the nonvalid portion of the other predictor is actually the mechanism by which a suppressor increases R. Suppose we have the following correlations: predictor 1 correlates .50 with the criterion; predictor 2 correlates .00 with the criterion; and the two predictors themselves correlate .40. Then using Equation 2.8:

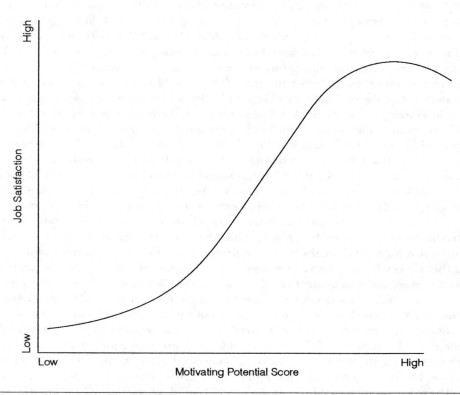

FIGURE 2-7 **Illustration of Curvilinear Relationship between Motivating Potential Scores and Job Satisfaction**

$$R = \sqrt{(.5^2 + .0^2 - 2 \text{ x } .5 \text{ x } .0 \text{ x } .4)/(1 - .4)^2}$$
$$= .54$$

Hence, the suppressor increased R from .5 (validity of predictor 1) to .54. In a regression equation, a suppressor variable usually receives a regression weight that is opposite in sign to its correlation with the criterion.

Suppressors are rarely reported in the literature. A possible example may be a case in which a paper and pencil mechanical ability test is used to select auto mechanics. This test is valid, but it requires a relatively high level of ability to read and this reading ability is not necessary to fix cars. A reading ability test would likely correlate with the mechanical ability test, but not with job performance measures of mechanics. In this case, the reading test may add to predictability through correlation with the valid predictor (mechanical ability test) not because it is correlated with job performance.

Even when identified, it may be difficult to use a suppressor for reasons unrelated to their usefulness in making predictions about a criterion. In a regression equation, suppressors would receive a negative weight, which means that individuals with high scores on the suppressor (the reading test in our example) would actually receive lower predicted performance. The concept of a suppressor is difficult to explain, hence will likely generate a questioning attitude regarding their

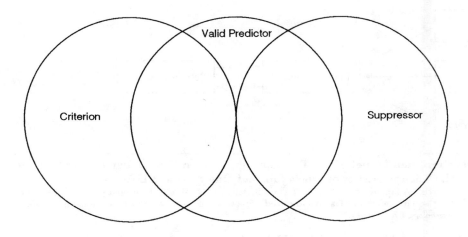

FIGURE 2-8   Illustration of a Suppressor Variable

use both from management and applicants who are informed that their scores on a test were too high! Use of a negative weight means that the higher one's score on the suppressor variable, the lower their composite score on the set of predictors used to make a decision.

While substantively interpretable suppressor effects are rare, they do occur frequently in regression analyses in which the predictor variables are highly correlated. In these instances, regression weights often take on negative values when the correlation for the same predictor with the dependent variable is positive. Unless one understands the effect of predictor intercorrelation on the computation (and resultant size and sign of the regression weights) of regression weights, serious misinterpretations of the nature of predictor-criterion relationships are likely.

Causal Analysis Using Correlations or Regression

In recent years, correlation and regression analysis have been used increasingly to provide tests of models that researchers develop concerning the interrelationships between sets of variables. Several different causal models were presented in Chapter 1 (see the discussion from Ellsworth, 1977 on page 16). One such model is depicted as Figure 2-9. While the complexities of the evaluation of some of these models is clearly beyond the scope of this book, an understanding of their purpose and the basic logic of the approach is useful. The arrows in these diagrams indicate hypotheses concerning causal relationships. In Figure 2-9, the researchers express the hypotheses (a) that marital status, self-esteem, and locus of control are the major determinants of life satisfaction; (b) that the characteristics of a job determine one's satisfaction with the job; and (c) that job and life satisfaction cause each other. The absence of other variables in this diagram indicates that there are no other major determinants of these variables. Further, the absence of arrows between some of the variables in the diagram indicates the researchers' hypothesis that these variables are not related, at least not directly so.

In evaluating this model, a researcher collects data on the variables in the model, computes correlations and regression weights as estimates of the paths in the diagram, and then evaluates the degree to which the few estimates made explain the entire set of correlations among variables. When the correlations among variables are relatively explained, the conclusion is that the

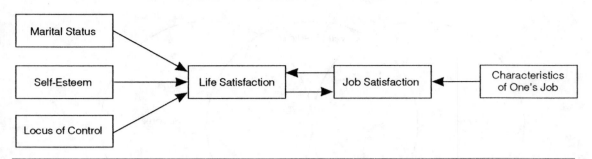

FIGURE 2-9 Simplified Model of the Relationship between Various Personality Characteristics, the Characteristics of One's Job, and One's Job and Life Satisfaction
Source: Adapted from Schmitt, N., and Bedeian, A. G. (1982). A comparison of LISREL and two-stage least squares analysis of a hypothesized life-job satisfaction reciprocal relationship. *Journal of Applied Psychology, 67,* 806–817.

hypothesized model represents one plausible explanation of the causal relationships among the variables. Other explanations, however, may also "fit" the data equally well.

Use of causal modeling of correlations requires some fairly restrictive assumptions that have been ignored by many users of the technique (James & Brett, 1984; James, Mulaik, & Brett, 1982). In addition to the usual assumptions underlying regression analysis, the most important of these assumptions is that our model includes all major causes of the endogenous or caused variables. The major advantage of the approach is the fact that it encourages researchers to formulate clearly and evaluate their hypotheses about the interrelationships among organizational phenomena.

Perhaps a simple example will reveal the logic of path analysis as well as some of its limitations as a means of supporting causal hypotheses. Consider three variables: level of pay, job performance, and job satisfaction. A researcher might hypothesize the following causal sequence:

$$+ \qquad\qquad\qquad +$$
$$\text{Level of pay} \longrightarrow \text{Job performance} \longrightarrow \text{Job satisfaction}$$

This model indicates that level of pay is positively and directly related to job performance and that job performance in turn is directly related to job satisfaction. The absence of an arrow from level of pay to job satisfaction indicates that the researcher hypothesizes that these two variables are related only indirectly through job performance. In this case, job performance represents an intervening or mediating variable.

Now, let's say the researcher collected data on these three variables and the correlation between level of pay and job performance was .60; job performance and job satisfaction were correlated .60. The correlation between level of pay and job satisfaction was .36. These correlations are completely consistent with the model presented above because the indirect effect (level of pay and job satisfaction) is equal to the product (.6 x .6 in the first figure below) of the direct effects that connect them. So the estimates of the paths relating the variables in the model would look like the following:

$$.6 \qquad\qquad\qquad .6$$
$$\text{Level of pay} \longrightarrow \text{Job performance} \longrightarrow \text{Job satisfaction}$$

Now this model is plausible given the data we have collected, but other models are equally plausible. Consider these:

$$\text{Job satisfaction} \xrightarrow{.6} \text{Job performance} \xrightarrow{.6} \text{Level of pay}$$

$$\text{Job satisfaction} \xleftarrow{.6} \text{Job performance} \xrightarrow{.6} \text{Level of pay}$$

Both of these models are consistent with the intercorrelations between the variables and represent plausible explanations. That is, the first model suggests that level of pay leads to job performance which in turn leads to job satisfaction. The second model indicates job performance causes both job satisfaction and level of pay. While the data do not allow us to differentiate among these three models, they are inconsistent with the hypothesis that level of pay and job satisfaction are directly related because the hypothesized indirect relationship totally accounts for the correlation between these two variables. Hence, the data are useful in rejecting one causal model of the relationship among these three variables, but not useful in confirming other causal models.

This relatively simple example is indicative of the logic underlying the evaluation of more complex models. We develop a theoretical model, we collect data, and then perform statistical tests of model fit and assess the degree to which the model fits the data. When data do not fit a model, we may proceed to modify the model. When data do fit a model, we have evidence of its plausibility, but should recognize that other explanations or models of the data also are feasible.

Hierarchical regression, for example, is often used to test intervening or mediating relationships (see, Brass, 1981 and Organ & Konovsky, 1989). For example, while we hypothesize above that job performance mediates the pay-job satisfaction relationship, it might be the case that level of pay mediates the job performance-job satisfaction relationship. Applying this technique to evaluate job performance as a mediator between level of pay and job satisfaction would have involved two hierarchical regressions; in both, job satisfaction would be the dependent variable. In the first regression, we would have entered job performance first then level of pay. In the second regression, level of pay would have been entered first followed by job performance. Given the correlations between level of pay, job performance, and job satisfaction presented above, entry of the first variable (job performance) into the first of these two regression equations would have yielded an R^2 equal .36 ($.6^2$). Using the formula for R^2 for the two predictor case (Equation 2.8), calculation of R^2 reveals an identical figure of .36. Hence, adding level of pay yielded no increment in R^2. In the second regression equation, entering level of pay first would yield an R^2 of .1296 ($.36^2$). Adding job performance to the equation increases R^2 to .36. The first combination of these two equations indicates that any observed correlation between level of pay and job satisfaction is completely mediated by job performance. The reverse (that level of pay mediates the job performance-job satisfaction relationship) is not plausible (because adding job performance to the second equation increased R^2 from .1296 to .36) which is the conclusion we reached by examining the intercorrelations of the three variables listed above.

Now, human resource problems are rarely this simple. We will discuss three potential complications introduced in Chapter 1: (a) partial mediation, ((b) reciprocal causation, and (c) moderated mediation. First, is the possibility that the mediation of the level of pay-job satisfaction relationship by job performance is not complete. This would have been revealed in our data analysis if the R^2 in our first regression equation had increased significantly when adding level of pay to the equation which already included job satisfaction. This result would have indicated a partial mediation and evidence that level of pay affects job satisfaction directly as well as indirectly through its influence on job performance. Diagrammatically the relationship would look like the following:

Level of pay —— >Job performance ——> Job satisfaction
|_____↑

To estimate the direct and indirect effects of these variables we must compute the standardized regression weights for two equations. In the first, job performance (JP) is the outcome variable; level of pay (LP) is the predictor and $r_{LP,JP}$ equals the standardized regression weight. In the second, job satisfaction (JS) is the outcome variable and job performance and level of pay are the predictors. Let's assume the correlation between level of pay and job satisfaction was .50 instead of .36. The standardized weight in the first equation is .60. In the second equation, the standardized weights are computed as follows:

$$b_{LP} = (r_{LP,JS} - (r_{JP,JS}\, r_{LP,JP}))/(1 - r_{LP,JP}^2) \qquad (2.16)$$
$$= (.5 - .36)/(1 - .36) = .22$$

$$b_{JP} = (r_{JP,JS} - (r_{LP,JS}\, r_{\,LP,JP}))/(1 - r_{LP,JP}^2) \qquad (2.17)$$
$$= (.6 - .30)/(1 - .36) = .47$$

In diagram form, the results of these analyses would look like the following:.

.60   .47
Level of pay ——> Job performance —— >Job satisfaction
|_____.22_____↑

In this example, job performance only partially mediates the relationship between level of pay and job satisfaction. This *indirect* effect is equal to the product of the weights connecting level of pay and job satisfaction in the diagram above (i.e., .60 x .47 or .28). The remainder of the effect (i.e., the correlation of .50 between level of pay and job satisfaction) comprises a direct effect (.22) between these two variables. When our hypotheses involve the relationships among three or more variables, partial mediation of the type described above is more common than complete mediation. Our model in the latter case will completely describe the observed correlations; normally, we test models such as the first completely mediated model that do not have the potential to fully describe the observed correlations. If these models fit reasonably well and others do not, then we have gained some information about the plausibility of causal hypotheses.

Reciprocal causation refers to models that posit a feedback loop. For example, it is certainly possible that job performance leads to increased level of pay which in turn leads to increases in job performance. A model like this also is presented in Figure 2-9 and introduces this section on causal analysis. The arrows in this diagram go from life satisfaction to job satisfaction as well as from job satisfaction to life satisfaction. Schmitt and Bedeian (1982) found that a model that included this reciprocal causation best fit the data they collected on these measures from a group of civil service employees.

Yet, another possibility is that one set of mediated relationships applies to one group of people and another set of mediated relationships occurs with a different group of people. For example, we might hypothesize that the relationship between level of pay, job performance, and job satisfaction varies as a function of whether people are paid on an hourly rate basis or on a piece-rate or incentive plan. Our hypotheses might be diagrammed as follows. For individuals paid on a piece-rate basis:

Job performance —— > Level of pay —— > Job satisfaction

For persons paid on an hourly basis:

Level of pay ——— > Job performance ——— > Job satisfaction

We developed a rationale for this series of relationships in the case of workers paid on a piece-rate basis above, but for workers paid on an hourly basis it might be reasonable to expect that job performance is affected by level of pay and that job performance leads to increases in job satisfaction. Method of payment in this instance serves as a moderator of the hypothesized mediating effects. This type of *moderated mediation* and the complexities of testing such hypotheses are described by James and Brett (1984).

While these techniques are useful in evaluating the plausibility of causal models, the user should be aware of the limitations and assumptions involved (see James & Brett, 1984; James, Mulaik, & Brett, 1982). These assumptions include the fact that the causal ordering of variables is justified theoretically. Also assumed is that all important causes of the outcome variables are included in the model. Failure to include all the variables has been labeled the unmeasured variables problem. All relationships are assumed to be linear and additive.

Finally, hypothesized causal models now are being evaluated using a procedure called linear structural equations analysis. This technique has become embodied in a program called LISREL developed by Jöreskog and Sorbom (1984). Researchers interested in causal modeling using LISREL will find Hayduk (1987) and Loehlin (1987) very helpful.

Nominal Variables and Regression Analysis

As we learned earlier in this chapter, very frequently our variables are not continuous (i.e., ordinal, interval, or ratio), but nominal in nature. Organization, region of the country, sex, and occupation all represent variables that most frequently cannot be ordered on any continuum. If we are interested in how groups formed by measurement on these variables differ, the usual method of analyzing data was to compute the means of these discrete groups (e.g., region of the country) on the variable of interest (maybe pay levels) and test whether the groups differed significantly. The traditional method used to test whether the groups differed significantly on a variable of interest was the analysis of variance. The objective in the analysis of variance was to show that differences in group means and the variance of individuals across all groups exceeded the variance of people within groups. In other words, the group variable helped to explain variability in the dependent variable of interest; in the case of our example, region of the country might explain some of the individual variability in pay levels.

Multiple regression analysis is virtually identical to analysis of variance when the independent variables are defined in terms of discrete groups, but the major advantage of using multiple regression analysis is that nominal variables and continuous variables as well as their interactions can be incorporated in a single analysis to answer questions not easily addressed by other methods of analysis. We will provide an example of the use of *dummy variable coding*, but the interested reader should consult Chapter 5 of Cohen and Cohen (1983) for a full and readable treatment of the use of nominal variables in multiple regression analysis.

The basic idea of dummy-variable coding is to render the information about the number of groups (g) in a series of g-1 dichotomies. So if we have four regions of the country, we can represent group membership in the form of three dichotomously scored variables. These groups could be naturally occurring groups as in our example or groups formed as a result of experimental manipulation as discussed in Chapter 1 and Chapter 11. The dummy-variable coding of our region variable is illustrated in Table 2-8. Note that individuals in G_1 would receive a score of 1 on X_1; all

TABLE 2-8
Dummy-Variable Coding of Supervisory Variable with Four Supervisory Units

Supervisory Unit	Independent Variables		
	X_1	X_2	X_3
G_1	1	0	0
G_2	0	1	0
G_3	0	0	1
G_4	0	0	0

other persons would receive scores of 0. Persons in G_2 would receive 1 on X_2 and 0 on the other variables and individuals in G_3 would receive 1 on X_3 and 0 on the other variables. Members of G_4 would receive 0's on all three independent variables. Note that with X_1, X_2 and X_3 we have uniquely defined membership in all four groups. These dichotomous variables are now correlated with the dependent variable (pay in this case) and with each other and regression analyses proceed as outlined above. Correlations of these dichotomous group variables with pay will be highest when the mean differences between members in the group are most different from mean pay levels in other groups. So the information carried in the correlation between group membership and pay is the same as the information we get when we compare mean differences in pay. You will note, however, that with several nominal variables each consisting of several discrete groups, we will quickly have a large number of independent variables. Our earlier cautionary statements about the sample size and number of predictors and the overestimation of R in a particular sample are relevant.

An example of a set of data involving the levels (expressed in hundreds of dollars per year) of individuals in four different regions of the country ($n_1 = 13$, $n_2 = 9$, $n_3 = 6$, $n_4 = 8$) is contained in Table 2-9. With group membership defined in this form, means, standard deviations, correlations, and multiple correlations can be computed as illustrated for our data in Table 2-10. The first column of numbers in Table 2-10 gives us the correlations between pay level and each of the first three regions of the country. Hence, living in region 1 is correlated positively ($r = .310$) with the amount of pay received, while living in region 2 is negatively correlated ($r = -.442$) with pay. The squared multiple correlation between the region of country and pay received is .355 while the shrunken R squared (see discussion above about shrinkage) is .294.

Notice that we dropped region 4. The reason is that we already have information on region 4 when we know the regional status of persons in the other three groups. Membership in the last group in any number of groups is always fully redundant with knowledge of membership in the other groups. This principle is most easily seen when we have only two groups; for example, males and females. If we scored females 1 and males 0 and correlated this variable with pay levels in Table 2-10 we might find a correlation of -.15 indicating women receive less pay. No second variable is needed for maleness. If we did produce another variable in which males are scored 1 and females 0, the correlation between this variable and pay would be identical although opposite in sign (.15). We will return to the computation of the correlation of pay and living in region 4 shortly.

The means and standard deviations of the X variables merit some comment. Since the X variables are coded 1 and 0, the mean of the X's is always the proportion of the people in a particular group. So, for example, if we count the number of persons in G_1 ($n_1 = 13$) and divide by

TABLE 2-9
Example of Data Regarding Pay Levels (Y) in Four Geographic Regions (G) Represented by Three Dichotomous Variables (X_1, X_2, and X_3)

Illustrative Data for Dummy-Variable Coding for $g = 4$ Groups

Case no.	Group	Y	X_1	X_2	X_3
1	G_2	61	0	1	0
2	G_4	78	0	0	0
3	G_1	47	1	0	0
4	G_2	65	0	1	0
5	G_2	45	0	1	0
6	G_4	106	0	0	0
7	G_1	120	1	0	0
8	G_2	49	0	1	0
9	G_4	45	0	0	0
10	G_4	62	0	0	0
11	G_2	79	0	1	0
12	G_4	54	0	0	0
13	G_1	140	1	0	0
14	G_2	52	0	1	0
15	G_1	88	1	0	0
16	G_2	70	0	1	0
17	G_2	56	0	1	0
18	G_3	124	0	0	1
19	G_4	98	0	0	0
20	G_2	69	0	1	0
21	G_1	56	1	0	0
22	G_3	135	0	0	1
23	G_1	64	1	0	0
24	G_1	130	1	0	0
25	G_3	74	0	0	1
26	G_4	58	0	0	0
27	G_1	116	1	0	0
28	G_4	60	0	0	0
29	G_3	84	0	0	1
30	G_1	68	1	0	0
31	G_1	90	1	0	0
32	G_1	112	1	0	0
33	G_3	94	0	0	1
34	G_1	80	1	0	0
35	G_3	110	0	0	1
36	G_1	102	1	0	0

Source: Adapted from Cohen, J., and Cohen, P. (1983), *Applied multiple-regression/correlation analysis for the behavioral sciences.* Hillsdale, N. J.: Erlbaum.

the total number of cases ($N = 36$), the result should be .361. The standard deviation also reduces to a simple form; that is, the square root of the mean times 1 minus the mean of the dichotomous variable. For X_1, this would be $\sqrt{.361 (1 - .361)}$ or .480. The standard deviation varies, then, with the proportion of members in a group, and since the correlation of the dichotomous variable with

TABLE 2-10
Regression Analysis of Motivation (Y) on Supervisory Unit Using Three Dummy Variables

		Intercorrelations				
		Y	X_1	X_2	X_3	r^2_{Yi}
	Y	1.000	.318	-.442	.355	--
G_1	X_1	.318	1.000	-.434	-.336	.1011
G_2	X_2	-.442	-.434	1.000	-.258	.1954
G_3	X_3	.355	.336	-.258	1.000	.1260
Mean		81.69	.361	.250	.167	
Standard Deviation		27.49	.480	.433	.373	$n = 36$

$$R^2_{Y.123} = .355 \qquad\qquad F = 5.869^* \ (df = 3,32)$$
$$\tilde{R}^2_{Y.123} = .294$$

*$p < .01$.
Source: Adapted from Cohen, J. and Cohen, P. (1983). *Applied multiple regression/correlation analysis for the behavioral sciences.* Hillsdale, N.J.: Erlbaum.

the dependent variable depends on the size of the standard deviation, the correlation will vary with the relative representation of members of a particular group in the sample (the maximum standard deviations and correlations occur when half of the total group belongs to a subgroup [i.e., G_1 . . . G_4]). This is important when the representation of different groups is very different. All other things being equal, the correlation of X_3 with pay level may be lower because of the relatively small number of persons in that group.

While Table 2-10 contains correlations for three of the geographic areas, there also may be an interest in computing the correlation between working in region 4 and pay level. While this could be computed directly from the data, it also can be computed as follows:

$$r_{YG_4} = - (\Sigma r_{Y_i} \sqrt{\overline{X}_i (1 - \overline{X}_i)}) / \sqrt{\overline{X}_4(1 - \overline{X}_4)} \tag{2.18}$$

where r_{YG_4} is the correlation between living in region 4 and 4 pay level, $\overline{X}_i$ is the mean of a given X variable, r_{y_i} is the correlation of a given X variable and pay, and $\overline{X}_4$ is the mean of X_4. For our data, this calculation would be as follows:

$$r_{YG_4} = -[(.318) (.480) + (-.422) (.433) + (.355) (.373)]/\sqrt{.222(1 - .222)}$$
$$= -.225$$

We usually would be interested in the correlation between region and pay, but as we noted earlier the sum of the individual squared correlations with motivation are not an adequate representation of the multiple correlation between area of the country and pay because the individual X_i are intercorrelated. In fact, they have to be correlated negatively since membership in one group means you can't belong to other groups. So the squared multiple correlation in Table 2-10 is .355 rather than .422 (i.e., the sum of .101, .195, and .126).

Tests of statistical significance for individual X_i as well as computations of partial and semipartial correlations, regression coefficients, and the means of each group on the motivation variable can be computed from dummy variable regression as in regression with continuous variables as we outlined above. Examples and detailed explanations of the calculations are available in Cohen and Cohen (1983).

In our next section, we discuss techniques that are used for a different type of research question. We have just concluded a discussion of the use of regression to maximize prediction of various outcomes and to test the plausibility of our theories about work behavior. We now turn to a discussion of how to summarize and integrate data on a great many variables and abstract from those analyses a relatively smaller number of psychologically meaningful dimensions or constructs. As you read the next section, it might be useful to read again the Chapter 1 discussions on page 19 on how variables attain meaning in behavioral research.

FACTOR ANALYSIS

Usually, human resource researchers will have available to them data on a large number of variables. This might be true when we measure the quality and quantity of job performance in different contexts, when we measure ability on several multi-item tests, or when we measure reactions to jobs and the job context. In this section, we will use an attempt to understand the basic dimensions that explain workers' satisfaction with compensation as our illustrative example (Scarpello, Huber, & Vandenberg, 1988). The need in this case was to reduce a large number of variables to a more manageable set of dimensions or underlying constructs which explain a large portion of the variability among the various measures. To achieve this goal, researchers examine the intercorrelations between all variables and may use statistical techniques called *factor analysis*.

First, consider the relatively easily explained correlation matrix in Table 2-11. The relationships depicted in this table are hypothetical but might represent the correlations between items from a job satisfaction measure called the Job Description Inventory (Smith, Kendall, & Hulin, 1969). Notice that a moderately high and positive correlation exists between all items. In examining the content of the items and in realizing that the descriptors refer to separate aspects of one's job, one might guess that the correlations in Table 2-11 could be summarized by statements about workers' satisfaction with work, supervision, and people. In looking at the correlations, we also observe that the highest correlations in the matrix are between items measuring the same facet of one's job, namely work, supervisors, and people. Further, the correlations across items from different facets are all relatively low. This matrix was deliberately constructed to fit the structure implied by the facet labels.

If all correlation matrices were this easy to interpret, there would be little need for more sophisticated statistical methods. However, there are at least three reasons why we rarely are able to interpret a correlation matrix as easily as we interpreted Table 2-11. First, factor analysis is usually used as an exploratory procedure. That is, we do not have a notion as to the major dimensions represented in the research participants' responses as we do in Table 2-11. So the content of the items does not always give us a clue as to what major factors to look for. Second, factor analyses are usually employed when there are a far greater number of items; obviously as we get 20 or 30 or more items, it will become difficult to see the factors in a correlation matrix as we did in Table 2-11. Finally, the correlations within a similar set of measures versus those between items belonging to different subsets of measures are rarely as distinct as those in Table 2-11.

TABLE 2-11
Hypothetical Correlation Matrix of Items from the Job Description Inventory

Work	(1)	(2)	(3)	(4)	(5)	(6)	(7)	(8)	(9)
Fascinating (1)	1.00								
Routine (2)	.40	1.00							
Satisfying (3)	.50	.35	1.00						
Supervision									
Impolite (4)	.20	.25	.15	1.00					
Hard to Please (5)	.15	.20	.10	.52	1.00				
Annoying (6)	.30	.18	.08	.41	.38	1.00			
People									
Boring (7)	.08	.12	.21	.10	.12	.21	1.00		
Ambitious (8)	.20	.25	.30	.11	.15	.18	.38	1.00	
Intelligent (9)	.15	.18	.20	.13	.14	.23	.42	.49	1.00

For all these reasons, researchers often employ factor analytic procedures to help them define the major dimensions or constructs underlying a correlation matrix and/or to reduce the number of variables with which they must deal. A factor is simply the linear composite of all variables that best explains the correlation among variables. Most correlation matrices can be relatively well explained by far fewer factors than variables. The part of the factor analysis that receives the most attention in interpretations of factor analysis and which is usually reported in research papers is the *factor loading* matrix. A factor loading matrix consists of the correlations between individual variables and the factors that explain or underlie these variables. A hypothetical factor loading matrix based on the data in Table 2-11 is presented in Table 2-12.

While we will not discuss the mathematics of factor analysis, it is important that the reader understand some of the characteristics of factor analysis. As expected from the correlation matrix, the factor analysis indicated a good summary of the workers' satisfaction could be made in terms of three underlying factors. The numbers in Table 2-12 represent correlations of each item with each of the underlying factors. In deciding which factor an item belongs to, we look at the factor loadings for that item. If its loading is high for a single factor, we say that the item best represents, or is best represented by, that factor. If the item's loadings are similar across factors or are all low, we usually conclude that the item is ambiguous with respect to the factors identified or that it represents some unique factor.

In interpreting a factor loading matrix, we go back to the content of the items and attempt to determine if those items loading highest on a given factor share some notion or measure some identifiable idea or construct. In the case of the factor loading matrix in Table 2-12, this is easy because the first three items all load highest on Factor 1 and they are all three "work" items. Similarly, the second three items load highest on factor 2 and are all "supervision" items. The last three items are factor 3, or "people," items.

Now let's consider the more complex satisfaction with compensation example mentioned above. Recently, Heneman (1985) has suggested that much of the research on pay satisfaction is confusing because researchers have assumed that people have only a general affect about their pay.

TABLE 2-12
Hypothetical Factor Matrix of the Job Description Inventory Items

Item	Factor 1	Factor 2	Factor 3
1.	.50*	.20	.05
2.	.61	.07	.13
3.	.70	.12	.08
4.	.10	.61	.08
5.	.09	.68	.09
6.	.12	.46	.12
7.	.08	.12	.41
8.	.15	.11	.42
9.	.09	.13	.50

*The underlined factor loadings represent the highest loading for that item.

Heneman (1985) argued that while employees may develop some general affect regarding pay, they also have specific attitudes about distinct aspects of financial compensation. After some preliminary work, Heneman and Schwab (1985) presented an 18-item pay satisfaction questionnaire (PSQ) that they believe reflects workers' perceptions of four underlying pay satisfaction constructs: pay level, raises, structure administration, and benefits. Scarpello et al. (1988) used the PSQ to test the Heneman and Schwab (1985) notions regarding the underlying structure of people's reactions to pay and pay policy and to test the notion that the existence (or nonexistence) of these constructs is influenced by employee job classification (salaried exempt, salaried nonexempt, and hourly).

In Table 2-13, we present the items in the PSQ and the factor loadings that resulted from a *principal components analysis* (a type of analysis similar to factor analysis) of the PSQ responses of a group of salaried exempt employees. While the principal components analysis did give evidence that there were four factors, the factor loadings were not entirely consistent with the Heneman and Schwab notions about the constructs underlying pay satisfaction. All the pay level items loaded on the first factor, but so did two of the raises items and the item asking employee's satisfaction with the company's pay satisfaction. The latter item also loaded highly on the third factor which seems to represent the structure-administration construct. Note that all six items that Heneman and Schwab thought represented issues of structure and administration load highly on factor three. The raises construct seems to be represented by factor 4 in Table 2-13, but again the results aren't completely consistent with the hypothesized definition of this construct. The second factor seems to be relatively unambiguously defined by the benefits items.

All items correlate with all factors in the usual factor analysis, but when items load highly on more than one factor, these factors are not perceived as discriminable by the respondents to our instruments. For example, items 9, 11, 13, 14, and 17 load highly on two different factors. This usually means the constructs are not clearly distinguishable and that the summed items representing these constructs will be correlated. In fact, Scarpello et al. (1988) did pursue additional analyses of the relationships between the factors they identified and concluded that the constructs underlying the PSQ were discriminable but correlated.

Scarpello et al. (1988) also did separate factor analyses of PSQ responses for hourly paid and salaried nonexempt employees and found evidence for only three factors. While the benefits and pay load items defined separate factors, the other two sets of items correlated with different factors.

TABLE 2-13
Factor Loadings of Pay Satisfaction Questionnaire Items
for a Group of Salaried Exempt Employees

Item*	F_1	F_2	F_3	F_4
1. My take-home pay	.78	.05	.30	.11
2. My current salary	.89	.10	.21	.22
3. My overall level of pay	.88	.14	.23	.19
4. Size of my current salary	.88	.09	.27	.20
5. My benefits package	.08	.83	.05	.07
6. Amount the company pays toward my benefits	-.00	.81	.11	.04
7. The value of my benefits	.22	.87	-.03	.02
8. The number of benefits I receive	.04	.89	-.02	.11
9. My most recent raise	.50	.05	.26	.42
10. Influence my supervisor has on my pay	.37	.03	.18	.69
11. Raises I have typically received in the past	.67	.18	-.00	.46
12. How my pay raises are determined	.27	.07	.18	.82
13. The company's pay structure	.52	.02	.58	.16
14. Information the company gives about pay issues	.09	.23	.47	.55
15. Pay of other jobs in the company	.23	.01	.76	-.05
16. Consistency of the company's pay policy	.34	.05	.65	.39
17. Differences in pay among jobs in the company	.41	-.01	.58	.24
18. How the company administers pay	.09	.07	.78	.27

*The first four items measure attitudes toward pay level, items 5–8 measure attitudes toward benefits, items 9–12 measure attitudes toward raises, and items 13–18 measure attitudes toward structure-administration. The underlined loadings represent those above .50, which was used by Scarpello et al. (1988) as the criterion to define factor composition.
Source: Scarpello, V., Huber, V., & Vandenberg, R.J. (1988). Compensation satisfaction: Its measurement and dimensionality. *Journal of Applied Psychology, 73,* 163–171. Adapted with permission.

Since pay raises and the structure and administration of pay systems often vary by job classification, this difference in perception seems reasonable. However, it does suggest that researchers may not be able to use the same instrument across classification groups or that they must use the existing PSQ items differently.

Recently, a form of factor analysis, called *confirmatory factor analysis*, has been used to test hypotheses about the nature of factors and may explain an observed correlation matrix. Confirmatory factor analysis has been used frequently to test hypotheses about constructs underlying various domains of interest to human resource researchers. Very often correlation matrices in which information on several traits (aggressiveness, originality, initiative) is collected by different methods (interviews, questionnaires, behavioral observations) are analyzed. In this approach, the investigator defines a set of hypotheses, or a model, regarding the nature of the trait and method factors and their interrelationships. Data are usually analyzed using the LISREL VI computer program (Jöreskog & Sorbom, 1984), which provides estimates of the loadings defined by the hypothesized model; the degree to which the estimates reproduce a set of correlations that are similar to the observed correlations; and tests of significance for the model fit as a whole, as well as tests of significance for each of the estimated parameters.

A relatively commonly estimated model is presented in Figure 2-10. This figure represents a model with six underlying factors (three traits [aggressiveness, initiative, and originality] and three methods [interviews, questionnaires and behavioral observations]); nine observed variables (Agg_I . . . $Init_{BO}$); and intercorrelations between method factors and trait factors. No trait-method relationships are depicted for both analytic and interpretive reasons (see Schmitt & Stults, 1986). Also estimated would be the uniqueness associated with each measured variable; that is, the degree to which the hypothesized factors do not account for variance in the individual measured variables. Lack of arrows from a hypothesized underlying factor to an observed variable indicates the hypothesis that the loading of that variable on the underlying factor is .00. The arrows in this figure indicate what we believe is causing variability in each of the nine observed variables (i.e., Agg_I . . . $Init_{BO}$). For example, Agg_I is caused directly by an underlying aggressiveness construct or trait and an underlying interview method factor as well as some uniqueness that is not depicted in the diagram. This model and variations of this model are presented in

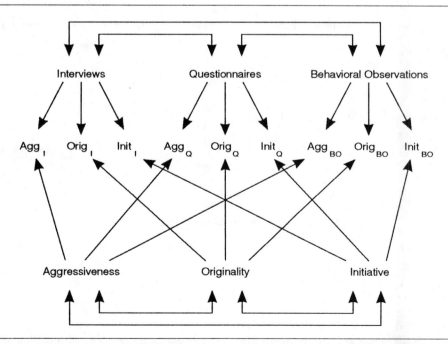

FIGURE 2-10 Model of a Correlation Matrix which Includes Trait and Method Factors

Widaman (1985), along with an outline of how comparisons between various models can be used to test hypotheses about the factors explaining correlation matrices.

　　An example of data that might result from a confirmatory analysis of the type depicted in Figure 2-10 is presented in Table 2-14. Analysis of similar models are available in Vance, MacCallum, Coovert, and Hedge (1988); Schmitt and Stults (1986); and Widaman (1985); A somewhat more complicated model is evaluated by Marsh and Hocevar (1988). In Table 2-14, the zeros all represent hypotheses that a variable does not load on a factor or that there is no relationship between method and trait factors. The loadings on the trait and method factors are modest and about equal; all observed variables have a large portion of unique variance associated with them. Since trait factors, method factors, and uniquenesses are uncorrelated and each observed variable is defined by one trait factor, one method factor, and its uniqueness, we can estimate the portion of trait and method variance in each variable. So, for example, trait variance accounts for 36% ($.6^2$) of the variance in *Aggi* while the method factor accounts for 9% ($.3^2$) and uniqueness for 49% (.72) of the *Aggi* variance (the total does not equal 100% because of rounding error).

　　The estimates in Table 2-14 also can be used to reproduce the correlations between the nine observed variables. Reproduced correlations can be computed by summing the products of the loadings of all paths connecting two observed variables in Figure 2-10. For example, the repro-

TABLE 2-14
Results of Hypothetical Confirmatory
Factor Analysis of a Model Like that Depicted in Figure 2-10

Factors

Observed Variables	Aggressive	Originality	Initiative	Interviews	Questionnaires	Observations	Uniqueness
Aggi	.6	.0	.0	.3	.0	.0	.7
Origi	.0	.4	.0	.4	.0	.0	.8
Initi	.0	.0	.3	.6	.0	.0	.7
Aggo	.4	.0	.0	.0	.4	.0	.8
Origo	.0	.5	.0	.0	.5	.0	.7
Inito	.0	.0	.4	.0	.6	.0	.7
AggBO	.5	.0	.0	.0	.0	.6	.6
OrigBO	.0	.3	.0	.0	.0	.7	.6
InitBO	.0	.0	.6	.0	.0	.4	.7

Factor Interrelationships

	1	2	3	4	5	6
Aggressive (1)	—					
Originality (2)	.3	—				
Initiative (3)	.4	.5	—			
Interviews (4)	.0	.0	.0	—		
Questionnaires (5)	.0	.0	.0	.5	—	
Observations (6)	.0	.0	.0	.3	.2	—

duced correlation between *Aggr* and *Init_Q* is (.6 x .4 x. 4) + (.3 x .6 x .5) or .186. The first product represents the loading of *Aggr* on the aggressive factor (.6), the loading of *Init_Q* on the initiative factor (.4), and the correlation between these two factors (.4). The second product is the loading of *Aggr* on the interview factor (.3), the loading of *Init_Q* on the questionnaire factor (.6), and the correlation between these two factors (.5). Similar rules for calculation of reproduced correlations are presented in Schmitt and Stults (1986, p. 16).

The reproduced correlations are then compared with the actual correlations and various indices of fit (see Bentler & Bonett, 1980) and tests of significance are calculated. The degree to which the reproduced and observed correlation matrices are identical is the degree to which the hypothesized model fits the data. This fit is indexed most frequently by the square root of the mean square of the residuals (differences between reproduced and observed correlations) and the rho index presented by Bentler and Bonett which represents a comparison of where the model being evaluated lies on the continuum between worst and best models of the data. An example of the application of these goodness of fit indices to several models and comparisons between these models is provided by Vance et al. (1988). Marsh, Balla, and MacDonald (1988) compared various fit indices and recommend an index developed by Tucker and Lewis (1973).

Clearly, confirmatory factor analysis can be used to test a variety of theoretically important hypotheses about the structure underlying a set of observed correlations and therefore represents a valuable analytic tool. However, modifications of the original model and subsequent evaluations of other models (see MacCallum, 1986) represent explorations of the data that are not unlike purely exploratory factor analysis. Such searches for the correct model should always be followed by tests of the refined model in a new set of data (Cudeck & Browne, 1983).

While we focus here only on a basic understanding of the purpose and interpretation of factor analyses, the user of these techniques will want to consult more thorough treatments of factor analytic techniques (e.g., Gorsuch, 1974; Long, 1983; Mulaik, 1972; Nunnally, 1978). This precaution is particularly appropriate given the easy accessibility (and consequent potential for abuse) of factor analysis techniques in various computer software packages. In consuming reports of factor analytic results, a reader should be wary of those reports which do not include (a) a full description of the technique used and the decisions made in using the technique (see Ford, MacCallum, & Tait, 1986); (b) a description and labeling of the variables included in the analysis; and (c) a full set of factor loadings and access to the correlation matrix among variables.

SUMMARY

We began this chapter with a discussion of basic assumptions— individual differences and the normality of the distribution of those differences. We then proceeded to describe ways in which we summarize the observations we make about a group of people and the degree to which we can use our observations on a sample of people to make inferences about some population. The summary measures we discussed included measures of central tendency, variability, and the degree of association between two variables. Tests of statistical significance were described as means by which we could make statements about the confidence with which we make inferences from the data collected from a sample to some broader population.

We then described regression analysis as a means by which our observations on one group of people can be used to predict behavior of some subsequent group of people and how we might use correlation and regression to test hypotheses about the interrelationships among variables. Factor analysis was described as a method that can be used to provide simpler descriptions of some phenomenon originally described along many dimensions.

If you have been able to understand our discussion in this chapter, we feel you will find the remainder of this book much more interesting and informative. We also believe you will be better able to read the research literature in human resource management. Perhaps most importantly, we think you will be better informed consumers of that research as it relates to the organizations and individuals you encounter in your everyday life. Finally, we include Table 2-15, which is a glossary of terms used in this chapter to help in summarizing the various issues and concepts introduced in this chapter.

TABLE 2-15
Glossary of Terms Used in Chapter 2

Alternative hypothesis—Hypothesis that is supported if we conclude that the null hypothesis of no relationship is not supported.

Analysis of covariance—Procedure for testing the statistical significance of differences between the means of different groups of observations while controlling for differences between cases in these groups that cannot be attributed to the manipulated variables.

Analysis of variance—Procedure for testing the statistical significance of differences between the means of different groups of observations.

Beta weight—Standardized regression weight; measure of unit change in criterion that results from unit change in the predictor.

Central tendency—The value that is typical of an observation from a particular sample.

Confirmatory factor analysis—A procedure that tests the degree to which a hypothesized grouping of variables into factors explains the observed covariances or correlations between these variables.

Covary—Degree to which values of one variable change along with values of a second variable.

Curvilinear relationship—Relationship in which the direction of relationship between two variables changes.

Dummy-variable coding—Designation of the members of a number of different groups as 0 or 1 (not a member or a member) to allow the analysis of nominal variables using regression.

Endogenous variables—In a path diagram representing hypothesized causal relationships, these are variables whose causes are specified in the diagram.

Exogenous variables—In a path diagram representing hypothesized causal relationships, these are variables whose causes are *not* specified in the diagram.

Factor analysis—Procedure used to identify major groups of variables from among a large set of intercorrelated variables; factors should be characterized by variables that are highly correlated with each other and not very highly correlated with other variables.

Factor loading—Correlation of a variable with a factor in factor analysis.

Hierarchical regression—Regression analysis in which the order of entry of variables into a regression equation is determined by the experimenter, not by the nature of the interrelationships among the variables.

Index of forecasting efficiency—Degree of reduction in the errors of prediction that results from use of a predictor expressed as a percentage of the standard deviation of the criterion.

Interaction effect—The effect of two variables on a third variable which represents an effect greater or less than the sum of the effect of either variable alone; the effects of the two variables are not additive.

Kappa—An expression of the degree of relationship between nominal variables corrected by the level of agreement that would obtain if they were related only by chance.

Linear relationship—A relationship in which a unit change in one of two variables results in constant change in a second variable.

Mean—Sum of the values of observations in a sample divided by the number of observations; the arithmetic average.

Measure of association—Measure of the degree to which values of one variable change as a function of values of a second variable.

Median—Value of the middle observation in a set of ranked observations in a sample.

Mediating variable—A variable that mediates the relationship between two other variables; the mediating variable is caused by one variable, but it, in turn, causes a third variable.

Mode—Value of the most frequently occurring observation in a sample.

Moderator variable—A variable whose different values determine the nature of the relationship between two other variables.

Normal distribution—A distribution of the values of observations that has a single mode, is symmetric and bell-shaped, and has limits of positive and negative infinity.

Null hypothesis—Statement of the *absence* of a relationship between variables or the absence of an effect for some experimental manipulation.

One-tailed test—Test in which only one alternative hypothesis is considered; for example, that the nature of relationship between two variables is positive.

Pearson product-moment correlation—A measure of the degree to which values of one value are associated with values of another; a number that describes the degree of dispersion of dots in a scattergram of the relationship between two variables.

Phi-coefficient—Product-moment correlation expressing the degree of relationship between two variables when both are dichotomies.

Power—Probability of rejecting the null hypothesis when it is correct.

Reciprocal causation—A case in which two variables both cause each other.

Regression equation—Developed on the basis of the means, standard deviations, and inter-correlations of predictors and criterion, the regression equation equals an intercept plus the regression weight(s) times the predictor or predictors.

Regression weight—Measure of how much a one-unit change in the predictor variable produces in some criterion variable.

Scattergram—Pictorial representation of the relationship between two variables.

Shrinkage—The degree to which the correlation between predicted and actual values of some criterion decreases when the regression weights from a regression analysis in one sample are used to make predictions about a second sample.

Significance level—Probability of rejecting the null hypothesis when it is true; probability of making a Type I error.

Standard deviation—Measure of variability of the values of our observations; square root of the average of the squared differences between the observation's value and the mean.

Standard error of estimate—Standard deviation of the errors of prediction made when using a regression equation to predict some criterion.

Standard error of the mean—Standard deviation divided by the square root of the sample size.

Standard score—The value of an observation minus the mean of the observations divided by the standard deviation of observations; also called a *z* score.

Suppressor variable—Variable in regression analysis for which the sign of the correlation with the criterion and the regression are different.

Test of significance—Test carried out to determine the probability of a given set of observations given the null hypothesis is correct.

Type I error—Rejection of the null hypothesis when it is correct.

Type II error—Nonrejection of the null hypothesis when it is false.

Variability—How much the values of our observations of a variable differ from each other.

DETERMINING THE QUALITY
OF OUR MEASURES

In this chapter, we describe various methods by which we evaluate the measurement of human resources. Our discussion of reliability theory begins with an assumption that any measurement is partly due to a true score on the underlying construct of interest and to errors of measurement. The proportion of the variability in obtained scores due to true score versus error was used as the basis for various definitions of reliability. The primary purpose of measurement is to draw inferences about the person being measured. The accuracy of the inferences (about job performance, absenteeism, buying behavior, safety behavior, etc.) is called validity. A discussion of the notion of validity and the various types of evidence researchers collect to support the inferences they wish to make from their measurements are described. While reliability and validity issues usually are discussed in connection with selection research, as they are in this chapter, it is important to remember that these issues are relevant to all areas of human resource research.

INTRODUCTION

In this chapter, we describe various ways of evaluating the quality of the measurement of human resources. These quality issues (i.e., reliability and validity) are equally relevant when one is considering the dependent variable in training program evaluation, the information obtained in a survey, the information regarding individual and organizational effectiveness measures discussed in Chapters 6 and 7, or data available in archival sources (see Chapter 4).

The reliability of our measurement procedures is basic; if we can't measure reliably in whatever sense is appropriate in a given research context, then we cannot conduct meaningful research regardless of the human resource problem with which we are engaged. However, evidence that a measure produces reliable data in applied organizational contexts must be accompanied by evidence that the measure has important theoretical or practical implications. That is, we must be able to demonstrate that the measure is a valid indicator of the construct in which we are interested. We speak to the role of systematically defining the content of our measures, correlating our measures with organizationally important outcomes, and collecting data and performing experiments that tell us whether our measure appears to measure the theoretical construct in which we are interested. All of these procedures, we maintain, are part of a construct validation process equally important to all domains of social science research. Certainly reliability is central in the discussion of procedures designed to assess human capability and motivation to do various types of work (see Chapter 8).

The standards for good measurement discussed in this chapter are important in assuring the best possible human resource decisions. Hence, the organization which uses reliable and valid measurement of its human resources to make decisions should realize substantial increases in productivity. However, it is also well to remember that the type of measurement and the manner in which measurement devices are employed communicates something about the way the organization views people. For example, it may be legitimate to use lie detectors in selection, but their use may also communicate to a prospective employee that the organization does not trust its workers. Asking employees to respond to a survey without giving feedback or indicating to the employee how survey results will be used will have long-term negative consequences for employee–management relationships. It is our position that the effort an organization places in the design and administration of human resource measurement systems communicates the organization's care and concern for its human resources.

In evaluating the quality of the measurements they use or construct, researchers usually discuss two properties: reliability and validity. *Reliability* most simply is defined as the degree to which our measures give us the same values when they are repeated. *Validity* usually is defined as the appropriateness of the inferences we draw from a test score. For example, in using test scores to make selection decisions, we are making an inference from a test score about a person's job performance. Both reliability and validity are more complex than these simple definitions would indicate. Likewise, there are several ways to estimate reliability and validity and these estimates are of varying importance in different research studies. In this chapter, we describe some of these methods and complexities.

RELIABILITY THEORY

Measurement in the physical sciences usually is more precise than measurement in the social or behavioral sciences. For example, when we use a measuring tape, we can count on achieving identical results regarding the length of an object. However, if this tape is made of material that expands or contracts as a function of the humidity in the air, then measurements will change slightly from time to time. Further, if the person using the tape does not obtain measurements when looking straight at the tape but rather from one side or the other (on a random basis), then there also may be a degree of inaccuracy or error in the measurements taken.

The values obtained with this expandable tape measure are affected not only by the distance of the object being measured, but also by changes in the weather and by the care with which the individual reads the tape. *Unreliability* is the result of an instrument's sensitivity to factors that do not affect the size of the measurement systematically or regularly, but change from one measurement situation to the next. Classical test theory, which is described in this section, deals only with this random error, not with constant error (error in the construction or calibration of a measuring instrument; that is, a yardstick, which is really 37.5 inches long). Constant error or bias will be discussed further in Chapter 5.

The extent of agreement between measurements on different occasions can be assessed by calculating the correlation coefficient between sets of repeated measurements. This correlation coefficient is called a *reliability coefficient.* If a measurement instrument is not affected by random factors (the weather or user carelessness in our example), then the reliability coefficient will be 1.00.

When measuring physical objects, we usually can take repeated measurements without concern that the object measured will change as a result of being measured. In measuring people, however, the very act of measuring may change these people because they remember the material presented or the questions asked stimulate them to search for answers or change their opinions about the concept being measured. This sensitivity to being measured means that their scores may be different upon readministration of the test or form. It is not necessary to make repeated measurements with the same test to estimate its reliability. Instead, *parallel* or *equivalent forms* are constructed so that the correlation coefficient between the parallel forms is the same as the coefficient between the scores resulting from two administrations of one of these forms. Of course, we assume that we can remove traces of the first testing on the occasion of administering the second test.

When constructing parallel forms, we try to make the items in the two identical with respect to content, instructions, and format. Parallel forms also should be arithmetically equivalent in their means, standard deviations, and the intercorrelations between their items. Classical reliability theory, and the various formulas presented in this chapter, are based on the definition of reliability as the correlation between parallel forms or scores on the same form given twice when administration of the first testing does not influence the second measurement.

Reliability theory is also based on the assumption that a person's score on a test is made of a true score and an error component. Since the errors considered are random, the true (t) and error (e) components in a test score (t_s) are independent, and a person's test score can be presented as follows:

$$t_s = t + e . \tag{3.1}$$

If we use equivalent measuring instruments or use the same instrument repeatedly to assess a person's ability (or attitude, perceptions, etc.) many times (each time erasing the effect of measurement), the scores obtained will be different if the measure has less than perfect reliability. These different scores will distribute themselves around the person's true level of ability on the construct being measured. The error component on any given administration of the test is the difference between the person's test score (t_s) and her or his true score (t). Errors have a mean of 0 (some will be positive, some negative), they will be uncorrelated with each other on repeated administrations of a test, and they will be uncorrelated with the true score component in the test as we stated above. Also, note again that defining errors as random excludes consideration of constant error of the type represented by the extra long yardstick mentioned above. Constant error is treated as part of the true score in this formulation.

Because of the fact that errors and true scores are uncorrelated, the total variance in a test (recall the discussion of variance in Chapter 2) will be a function of true score variance (σ_t^2) and error variance (σ_e^2):

$$\sigma_{ts}^2 = \sigma_t^2 + \sigma_e^2 . \tag{3.2}$$

Given the lack of correlation between errors on parallel tests and the lack of correlation between the true and error components of a test, we also can show (see Nunnally, 1978, for a formal proof) that the correlation between the true scores on parallel tests is equal to the ratio of the true variance in the test to the total variance in the test:

$$r_{tt} = \sigma_t^2 / \sigma_{ts}^2 . \tag{3.3}$$

Correlation between the true scores can be expressed, then, as the ratio of true score variance to total variance. The reliability coefficient (or correlation coefficient) between two parallel tests gives the numerical value of this ratio. As we shall see in the next section, there are various ways to think of error and true score variance and hence to operationalize reliability.

FORMULATIONS OF RELIABILITY

Our formulation of reliability depends on the purposes for which we collected data. In the following sections, we tie each of the definitions of reliability to issues of interest to human resource researchers.

Test-Retest Reliability

Most uses of tests[1] in human resource work involve selection of employees; hence, we are interested in their predictive value. In a predictive sense, a test must yield the same values when it is administered at two different points in time. In estimating test-retest reliability, we give a test or interview or other device twice to the same people and correlate their scores at these two different times. The two administrations of the test must be separated by a suitable time interval so that the examinees cannot remember their previous answers. We assume that the first administration of the test does not affect scores of individuals on the second administration of the test.

Using the notions of true and error variance developed in the previous section, it is clear that any nonsystematic changes in persons across time contribute to error variance. What is not perhaps obvious is that if all individuals change at the exact same rate, reliability will be perfect (recall that constant change or differences are treated as true score variance). Also, since the test includes the exact same items on both administrations, any idiosyncrasies (called item-specific variance) in the items are treated as true variance. Only changes in the relative position of the persons measured constitute error variance.

Parallel Forms Reliability

Occasionally it is not safe to assume that the responses of examinees to a second administration of a test will be unaffected by the previous administration of an examination, or perhaps it is impossible to get examinees together twice. In these cases, test constructors have estimated reliability by constructing two forms of the test and correlating the scores of examinees on both measures. The two parallel forms contain similar (in terms of content) but not identical items. Item difficulty (the proportion of people who get the item correct) as well as other item statistics (i.e., correlations of the item with other items) should be as similar as possible across forms. Note these parallel forms may be given at the same time or they may be separated by a suitable interval. Administered at the same time, the correlation between parallel forms really gives us an index of the degree to which the items in the two forms are similar in content or in terms of the ability the test is supposed to measure. When the two forms are separated in their administration by a time interval, the correlation between the two forms also may be lowered because of events that have occurred between the two test administrations. Consequently, parallel forms reliability with no time interval between test administrations yields what has been called a coefficient of equivalence (of the forms). When a time interval separates the administration of the two forms, the correlation

---

[1]We use the term test here and elsewhere, but the same considerations apply to any measure of human behavior, attitude, perception, intentions, etc.

between the two forms yields a coefficient of stability and equivalence. In the latter case, both time and the nonequivalence of the items in the two forms may serve to lower the reliability; these factors, then, constitute error variance. Frequently, this may be an appropriate measure of reliability since we would not be interested solely in a person's answers to specific items at a given point in time, but rather their general ability to answer all questions related to a particular knowledge or ability at any point in time. Differences across time and item content are, then, appropriately treated as evidence of a lack of reliability. If the parallel forms are administered at the same point in time (or close enough so that an intervening time interval should not have an effect on scores) then only changes in item content would make up error variance.

Internal Consistency

Frequently, researchers are faced with a situation in which two forms of an instrument are unavailable and there is no possibility for a second administration of a test (e.g., the examinees will be unavailable). One solution in this case is to take the items in the test and split them randomly in two halves and correlate the scores of the examinees on these two half tests. This correlation would be the reliability of a test one-half as long as the original. To obtain the reliability of the full length test, one needs to apply the *Spearman-Brown correction formula* which reads as follows:

$$r_{full} = 2r / (1 + r) \qquad\qquad (3.4)$$

where r_{full} is the reliability of the full length test and r is the correlation between the two half tests. As an example, let's assume that the correlation between two half tests is .60. Application of this formula would yield:

$$r_{full} = 2 \times .60 / (1 + .60) = .75.$$

The reliability of the full length test would be estimated at .75. Application of this formula is based on the assumption that the items in the two halves are statistically equivalent measures of the content one is interested in measuring. This means that one would expect the correlations of individual items with the sum of all possible item scores to be equal. This, of course, is most likely to happen when the content of the items in a measure is homogeneous. Internal consistency estimates are often used as an index of the unidimensionality or homogeneity of a set of items. Differences in items constitute error variance. A more formal exposition of the underlying assumptions for this formula and others in this chapter is contained in Nunnally (1978).

Another form of internal consistency is called *coefficient alpha*. If one were to split the items in a test in all possible ways, and average the split-half reliabilities (after correction with the Spearman-Brown) obtained in this manner, one would have coefficient alpha. Fortunately, there is a simpler way to calculate coefficient alpha. The formula for its calculation is as follows:

$$r_a = n^2 \overline{r_{ij}} / C \qquad\qquad (3.5)$$

where r_a is coefficient alpha, n is the number of items in the test, $\overline{r_{ij}}$ is the average intercorrelation between different items in the test, and C is the sum of all the items in the item intercorrelation matrix including items above and below the diagonal and the diagonal values (all 1.00 in the case of a correlation matrix). Actually the formula above is a standardized coefficient alpha, applicable when all items have the same standard deviation or when items are standardized before computing a test score.[2] An example of the computation of standardized coefficient alpha is given below (n is equal to 10, $\bar{r}_{ij}$ is equal to .50, and C is equal to 55:

$$r_a = (10 \times 10 \times .50) \, / \, 55 = .91.$$

It is not important to memorize these formulas, but the notions underlying their use is important. First, we assume that all the items in the test measure the same concept or construct when we apply measures of internal consistency; theoretically any one item could be an adequate measure of peoples' position on the construct being measured. However, none of our items is a perfect measure, hence we try to minimize the possibility of measurement errors by increasing the number of items. Both the formula for coefficient alpha and the Spearman-Brown formula include in their calculation the number of items. A long test is more reliable than a short test, provided the items measure the same construct. Intuitively, students would usually rather have their grades determined by an examination with many items as opposed to a single item exam even though the lengthier exam may be more threatening.

Finally, internal consistency estimates of reliability, like parallel forms administered at the same point, are affected only by changes in item characteristics. Hence specific item variance constitutes error variance.

Interrater Reliability

In applied organizational research, many of our constructs are measured by asking raters to make judgments of peoples' performance or behavior in various organizational situations as discussed in Chapter 6. The degree to which the judgments of various raters yield similar information about a group of people is termed *interrater reliability*. If we view the raters as items in a test, then all the forms of reliability we discussed above apply to raters' judgments. We can compute the consistency with which raters make judgments on two different occasions. If we compute the intercorrelations of the judgments of all raters, and compute coefficient alpha from this correlation matrix, we have a measure of the reliability of the sum of all raters' judgments. Sometimes we will want an estimate of the reliability of a composite of raters' judgments over time as, for example, when ratings are used as criteria in a test validation project.

If we return to our discussion of true and error variance in considering interrater reliability, we can see that these different alternatives will lead to different estimates of reliability. If we use a set of judges to evaluate the worth of jobs and are concerned that their evaluation of jobs might change as a function of time, then we would correlate their judgments of the same jobs (requiring the evaluation in a way that memory cannot influence the second evaluation) across time. In this case time differences would constitute error variance. If the number of jobs to be evaluated were so large that we would have to rely on different judges to evaluate different jobs, then interjudge reliability with an intervening time interval would be an appropriate estimate of reliability. Differences in judges and time would contribute to error variance. Additional issues with regard to interrater reliability and agreement are discussed in Chapter 4.

Whenever we measure some aspect of a person, we are really attempting to ascertain that person's "true" score on the construct we are measuring as opposed to a score that contains some

---

[2]Usually, we do not standardize item responses prior to computation of a total test score. So, in most instances, coefficient alpha is the appropriate index of internal consistency. In Equation 3.5, C would be replaced by the sum of all items in the variance-covariance matrix and $\bar{r}_{ij}$ would be represented by the average of the covariances.

element of error. In assessing reliability, we are estimating what proportion of variability in people's scores on a particular measure represents true variability on the underlying construct. But, if we have different methods of estimating reliability, then we likely will get different estimates of the degree to which our instrument is comprised of true and error variance. Which of these estimates is correct?

The answer to this question is that it depends on the purpose for which we are measuring individuals and what types of error ought to be considered and minimized when we use the measures to make decisions. Consider the case in which a supervisor observes an apprentice electrician trying to locate the source of a malfunctioning electrical circuit. The supervisor rates the performance of the apprentice on a nine-point scale ranging from "Completely inadequate, does not know how to proceed" to "Appropriately and efficiently searched for the problem." We want to determine to what extent such a rating reflects the "true score" of the apprentice and to what extent it reflects "error." In trying to provide estimates of the reliability of this rating, we might take any one or more of the following steps:

Steps Taken	Definition of Error
1. A second supervisor simultaneously observes and independently rates the same performance.	1. Rater differences in observing apprentice performance.
2. A second supervisor observes the apprentice solve a different problem immediately after the first one.	2. Rater differences and any differences in the problem the apprentice was given to solve.
3. A second supervisor observes the apprentice solving the same problem a week later.	3. Rater differences and any changes in the apprentice; for example, training, mood, or health changes.
4. A second supervisor observes the apprentice solving a different problem a week later.	4. Rater differences, differences in the electrical problem, and changes in the apprentice.

In this case, then, we have at least four different reliabilities. In the fourth example, reliability will be lowest because several potential sources of error (rater idiosyncrasies, time, and content of the test) serve to lower the reliability estimate. Which of these definitions we use depends on how we will use the data we collect to make decisions. If we always are going to use the same supervisor to make ratings of apprentices, then the supervisor should not be considered a source of error. Likewise, if we only are interested in apprentices' ability to solve a specific electric malfunction, then we would not want to evaluate the contribution to error which results from the use of different problem types.

A more complete list of the reasons why individuals differ in performance on a test or measure of job performance is presented in Table 3-1 taken from Guion (1965). In the various estimates of reliability presented above, we correlate two sets of measures of the same thing. True or systematic variance causes the individuals' scores to be the same on the sets of measures and increases the correlation. Changes in people on any of the factors in Table 3-1 lower the correlation between the two sets of measures and are defined as error.

TABLE 3-1
Sources of Individual Differences in Test Performance

I. **Reasons That Are More or Less Permanent and That Apply in a Variety of Testing Situations.**

    A. Some traits are general in that they influence performance on many different kinds of tests. General intelligence may influence performance on tests of verbal ability, numerical fluency, or knowledge of psychology.

    B. Some people are more "test-wise" than others; that is, because of more experience or special training in taking tests, they are able to come closer to their maximum potential scores in any kind of test situation.

    C. Some people grasp the meaning of instructions more quickly and more completely than others. Some may flounder through much of a test before catching on to what is required, regardless of the nature of the task; some never fully grasp any kind of test instructions.

II. **Reasons That are More or Less Permanent but That Apply Mainly to the Specific Test Being Taken.**

    A. Some of these reasons apply to the whole test or to any equivalent forms of it.
        1. *Some people have more of the ability or knowledge or skill or other trait being measured by the test.*
        2. Some people find certain kinds of items easy while others may be more confused by them. For example, some people are good at "outguessing" a true-false set of items.

    B. Some reasons apply only to particular items on a test. Of all the items that *could* be included, only a small number actually *are* in the test. There is an element of luck here; if the test happens to contain a few of the specific items to which the individual does not know the answer, his or her score will be lower than if he or she is luckier in the specific questions asked.

III. **Reasons That are Relatively Temporary but Would Apply to Almost Any Testing Situation.**

    A. The state of the individual's health may influence his or her score.

    B. A person may not do as well when he or she is particularly tired.

    C. The testing situation is, to some people, a challenge; they want to score high so that they can enjoy a feeling of achievement. The intensity of motivation to do well may fluctuate; the individual will score higher when highly motivated than when less motivated.

    D. Individuals react differently to emotional stress; a person tested under stress is likely to have a score different from that obtained when he or she is tested under emotionally secure conditions.

    E. There seem to be some relatively temporary fluctuations in "test-wiseness."

    F. A person varies from time to time in the extent of his or her readiness to be tested; such differences in set produce differences in attention to and comprehension of the test situation and, therefore, differences in scores. Those with favorable sets make higher scores.

    G. People respond differently to physical conditions (light, heat, etc.); individuals with the same abilities may score differently because of differences in their reactions to unusual or perhaps adverse physical conditions.

IV. **Reasons That are Relatively Temporary and Have Application Mainly to a Specific Test.**

    A. Some reasons apply to the test as a whole (or to equivalent forms).

(continued)

    1. People differ in their understanding of a specific set of instructions; those who under-
   stand the instructions do better than those who do not. However, a person who has
   only a dim comprehension of what he or she is to do at one time might understand
   better if tested at another time.

    2. Some tests require special techniques; some individuals may "stumble" into certain in-
   sights useful in tackling a particular test sooner than would others.

    3. The differences in the opportunities for practicing certain skills required in test perfor-
   mance produce differences in scores.

    4. An individual may be "up to" a test or "ripe" for it, at one time and not at another; indi-
   vidual differences in readiness cause differences in scores.

B. Some reasons apply only to particular test items.

    1. Momentary forgetfulness or lapses of memory while taking a test make a person miss
   an item he or she might otherwise get right.

    2. The same thing can be said of momentary changes in level of attention, carefulness,
   or precision in detail.

Source: Reprinted with permission from Guion, R.M. (1965), *Personnel testing*, New York: McGraw-Hill.

The factors in category I in Table 3-1 will probably stay the same across different testing situations and would therefore contribute to our estimate of "true" variability among persons. Some of those factors (B and C) may not be relevant to the trait we are measuring, however, and would detract from the validity of a test (see the discussion of construct validity later in this chapter). Category IIA are sources that likely would contribute to "true" score estimates when we are interested in specific aptitudes, but category IIB includes factors that would lower reliability when we use parallel forms or internal consistency estimates. All of the category III considerations would likely lower reliability when it is defined in a test-retest fashion and category IV factors might lower reliability estimated either in test-retest or parallel forms fashion. You will note differences in raters are not identified in Table 3-1, but everything that applies to written or oral test items also applies to raters. Raters are best conceptualized as test items when we are estimating their reliability.

Frequently, we also are interested in the exact agreement between raters on some dimension. Recall that constant differences across two raters are not considered error; that is, they are treated as true variance. The difference between reliability as we have been describing it and rater agreement is best illustrated by the data in Table 3-2 taken from Tinsley and Weiss (1975). In the first case, there would be complete agreement between raters as to scores of individuals A through G on the variable measured. In the second case, there is low agreement, but correlations between ratings provided by the three raters would be 1.00. Finally, in case 3, there is relatively high agreement, but correlations between raters (hence, reliability) would be low. Tinsley and Weiss have provided a measure of rater agreement. Computationally, this index is given as follows:

$$T = (N_1 - NP)/(N - NP) \qquad (3.6)$$

where N_1 = the number of agreements; N = the number of individuals rated, and P = the probability that raters would agree by chance. For case 3, the agreement between raters 1 and 2 would be computed as follows:

$$T = (5 - .12)/(10 - .12)$$
$$= 4.88/9.88$$
$$= .495$$

TABLE 3-2
Comparison of Interrater Agreement and Reliability

Subject	Case 1 High Agreement High Reliability Raters			Case 2 Low Agreement High Reliability Raters			Case 3 High Agreement Low Reliability Raters		
	1	2	3	1	2	3	1	2	3
A	1	1	1	1	3	5	5	4	4
B	2	2	2	1	3	5	5	4	3
C	3	3	3	2	4	6	5	4	5
D	3	3	3	2	4	6	4	4	5
E	4	4	4	3	5	7	5	4	3
F	5	5	5	3	5	7	5	5	4
G	6	6	6	4	6	8	4	4	5
H	7	7	7	4	6	8	5	5	4
I	8	8	8	5	7	9	4	5	3
J	9	9	9	5	7	9	5	5	5
Mean	4.8	4.8	4.8	3.0	5.0	7.0	4.7	4.4	4.1
SD	2.7	2.7	2.7	1.0	1.5	1.5	.5	.5	.9

Source: Adapted with permission from Tinsley, H.A., & Weiss, H.I. (1975). Interrater reliability and agreement of subjective judgments. *Journal of Counseling Psychology, 22,* 358–376.

The raters agreed five times (N_1), out of ten (N), and chance (P) was equal to the square of the probability that both would agree exactly on any given person by chance (given these were nine-point rating scales, this probability is the square of 1/9). Clearly, exact agreement on a nine-point scale would be difficult to attain in most instances, but in case 3 where there is no variability in the ratings provided to the ten individuals, the Tinsley formula would be an appropriate index of agreement. Chapter 4 provides additional approaches to estimating iterrater agreement.

Generalizability Theory

Cronbach, Gleser, Nanda, and Rajaratnam (1972) have developed an approach to reliability called *generalizability theory* that explicitly considers different sources of variance in measurements and describes ways of estimating the amount of variance contributed by these various sources. In generalizability theory, observations of people's performance are seen as samples from a universe of admissible observations. An examinee's universe score is defined as the expected value of her or his score over all admissible observations; this universe score is the *true* score. Generalizability theory emphasizes the notion that different universes exist and it must be up to the test user or constructor to define the universe. This definition must specify to what *facets* one is interested in making generalizations.

In the electrician apprentice example above, the facets might include supervisors, problems, and time. Clearly then we can have different reliabilities depending on the sources of error we want to evaluate or the facets to which we want to generalize. We can also desire generalization to any randomly selected level of a facet (e.g., any randomly selected supervisor in an organization) or to a fixed group of trained supervisor raters. Analyses of variance (see Chapter 2) are computed using the persons' ratings as the dependent variable and raters and dimensions are the independent variables or factors. In this instance, there are four levels of the rater factor and three levels of the dimension factor. The results of the analysis of variance are used to compute the variance attributable to people, raters, and dimensions and then the reliabilities. For computational details regarding various experimental situations, see Cronbach at al. (1972). All of these possibilities were computed and summarized in Table 3-3 for a set of data collected by one of your authors. In this example, four raters rated individuals on three dimensions. The ratees had taken part in an assessment program used to make promotions. This assessment program required the ratees' participation in various group and individual tasks in which their performance was observed and rated by four raters.

As you can see, reliability would vary considerably depending on the situations to which we desire generalization. If we want to generalize to other rating situations in which a randomly selected rater would provide a rating on a randomly selected dimension, reliability would be very low (.212). In this instance, any differences between raters and dimensions would be treated as error, only differences among ratees that are perceived by all raters using any rating dimension are treated as true variance. Fortunately, we usually want to generalize to other situations in which we use the same or a fixed set of trained raters to provide ratings on a fixed set of rating dimensions. In this case, that reliability would be .904. The raters and dimensions are constant, hence, treated as true variance.

The results in Table 3-3 also illustrate the effect of multiple observations (either by multiple raters or on multiple rating dimensions) on the reliability of the composite of these ratings. Going from three dimensions to a single dimension results in a significant drop in the generalizability coefficient. Dropping from four raters to one rater also results in a decrease in reliability, but the decrease is not as large. Also notice that we could afford to randomly select raters without a great drop in reliability, but a random selection of rating dimensions would result in a large drop in reliability. This makes sense; if the content of the rating dimensions is meaningfully different, we ought to see lower correlation coefficients between dimensions than between raters who are rating the same dimensions.

TABLE 3-3
Results of a Generalizability Analysis of Assessment Center Ratings

A. Generalizability to Randomly Selected Raters and Dimensions

Generalize To:	*Reliability*
Four raters, three dimensions	.611
One rater, three dimensions	.488
Four raters, one dimension	.296
One rater, one dimension	.212

B. Other Random and Fixed Situations

Dimensions fixed, raters random	.873
Dimensions random, raters fixed	.644
Dimensions fixed, raters fixed	.904

The strength of generalizability theory is that it forces the researcher to specify carefully what he or she considers true and error variance in the measurements that are collected.

Correction for Attenuation

When we develop a measurement instrument we are rarely, if ever, interested in the scores of individuals on that instrument only. We usually are interested in the way scores on the instrument we developed relate to other test scores, job performance, job motivation, absenteeism, or other behavior. The reliability of a test is important because it limits the size of any observed relationship with these external variables. In the extreme case, when reliability of a measure is .00, then a measure cannot relate to any other variable. When reliability is less than 1.00, and it almost always is, then we say that relationships with external variables are *attenuated.* Hence, reliability is a necessary condition for validity as evidenced by correlations with external variables.

Sometimes researchers are interested in the correlation between two variables when or if measurement error (lack of reliability) could be removed. They are interested in making an estimate of the degree of relationship between the underlying constructs or true scores being measured. The estimate of the true relationship (r_{xyc}) between two variables is made by dividing the observed relationship (r_{xy}) by the product of the square roots of the reliabilities (r_{xx} and r_{yy}) as follows:

$$r_{xyc} = \frac{r_{xy}}{\sqrt{r_{xx}} \sqrt{r_{yy}}}. \tag{3.7}$$

If one is interested in the true relationship between different measures of cognitive ability, for example, correlations for unreliability in both variables would be applied. A formal proof for this correction for attenuation can be found in Nunnally (1978, pp. 219–220).

If two different measures were correlated .60 and their reliabilities were .81 and .64 respectively, the corrected correlation between these measures would be:

$$.60/(\sqrt{.64}\sqrt{.81}) = .83$$

A frequent application of this correlation in personnel selection research involves the correction for attenuation for unreliability in the criterion (a job performance measure which we are trying to predict). Corrections to the observed correlation for lack of criterion reliability are made to estimate the true validity of a potential predictor. Similar corrections for predictor unreliability are not made because the use of the predictor in other situations will always involve a similar lack of reliability.

In making these corrections for unreliability, it is important that the right estimate of reliability be used. In the personnel selection instance, we usually are interested in prediction, hence assessments of criterion stability across time would be important. If we are using ratings of job performance as criteria, then rate-rerate estimates with an appropriate time interval and by different raters would be the appropriate estimate of reliability. If we are interested in construct validity issues (i.e., the degree to which test items measure the same construct), then internal consistency estimates would likely be the best choice.

Standard Error of Measurement

When a person's level of skill is being evaluated for a particular job or academic assignment, then a single score is obtained for each of the skill dimensions being measured. A relevant question, given the fact that all measures are subject to some error, concerns the accuracy of that single score as an index of the true ability of the individual being measured. Use of the standard error of measurement allows us to make statements about the confidence with which we have estimated the true ability level of an individual. Theoretically, the standard error of measurement would be the standard deviation of scores that a person would receive if we could obtain an infinite number of independent test scores from this individual. Because of lack of reliability, these scores would scatter around the individual's true ability level. Actually, the standard error of measurement (*SEM*) can be computed by using the following formula:

$$SEM = SD_{test} \sqrt{1 - r_{xx}} \tag{3.8}$$

where SD_{test} is the standard deviation of the test and r_{xx} is the test's reliability. So a test with a reliability of .84 and a standard deviation of 10 would have a standard error of measurement equal to 4.00.

Recall that approximately 95% of the cases in a normal distribution of scores fall within two standard deviations of the mean. This means, in this case, that the true score of persons with obtained scores of 20 could range between approximately 12 and 28 in 95% of the cases. So a person whose true score is 12 would be unlikely to have an obtained score as high as 20; likewise, a person whose true score is 28 would be unlikely to score as low as 20.

There are a number of uses for the standard error of measurement in personnel research and management. If one is trying to decide whether to hire two individuals whose scores are three points apart when the *SEM* is 4.00, we clearly know that the scores these two individuals received are not significantly different from each other and that on a subsequent test of these two people we shouldn't be surprised if the persons' relative position on the test changes. Note, however, that the probability that the higher-scoring individual will score higher on a second administration of the test is always greater than the reverse; that is, that she or he will score lower than the other person. Similarly, if we know this test is correlated with some important outcome measure, the probability is always greatest that the higher-scoring person will outperform the lower-scoring individual.

Similarly, if we are counseling an individual and we have available a variety of test scores on which to base statements about the person's skill or interest, the standard error of measurement can be useful in determining how confident we are that a person's measured mechanical ability is really superior to her or his musical ability.

Another use to which the standard error of measurement has been applied is to determine whether a person's obtained test score is significantly above or below a minimum cutting score. In this case, let's say that a personnel office is using the test described above to select only those persons who score above 18. The question then might be whether a person's obtained score falls significantly below 18. A person with a true score of 18 would receive a score of 14 or below only about 16% of the time (16% of the cases in a normal distribution fall beyond one standard deviation of the mean).

The latter use of the standard error of measurement has been commonly addressed in legal cases involving fair employment. Both the defensibility of a particular cutting score (dealt with in Chapter 9) and the significance of the difference between a cutoff and the obtained score of rejected applicants have been at issue. One alternative is to weigh other information more heavily when an applicant's score is relatively close to the cutoff—either above or below. In the absence of other information, however, it is well to remember that one would always be *more likely* to select an individual whose job or academic performance were superior if her or his tested ability were higher, assuming the test scores were valid indicators of the job or academic performance one wants to predict.

Finally, it is important to point out that a test's standard error of measurement may vary with the score range (Lord, 1984). While under most circumstances, the standard error of measurement in the middle range of scores is relatively constant, the standard error of measurement associated with extreme scores on a test may be very different. This is a technical point beyond the scope of this text, but one about which those who plan to use minimum cut scores should be informed (see Lord, 1984, for a brief statement and additional references).

To this point in Chapter 3, we have dealt with issues internal to a test. That is, we have presented ways of assessing whether the scores a test provides are sensitive to changes in time, whether the items in the test are internally consistent (i.e., measure the same ability or construct), and whether the test score is an accurate assessment of a person's true score on the tested construct. The purpose of giving a test, however, is usually to make predictions or inferences about people's behavior or performance in other contexts. Or, we want to know that our measure of a job's worth is a valid indicator of the real value of the job to the organization. We also might be concerned with the relationship between an attitude measure and employees' behavior. In the next section we present methods of assessing whether or not a test serves this purpose.

VALIDITY

As we stated above, validity refers to the degree to which a test measures what it is supposed to, or more formally, the degree to which inferences made from test scores or other instruments are correct or accurate. For example, knowing the content of various college admissions tests and the demands of a college curriculum, one might look at a college applicant's test scores and infer that he or she would do well in college. If such inferences are correct (relatively speaking) more often than expected by chance we would say that the college admissions test is valid in its predictions about college student performance. These statements suggest, and correctly so, that a test has validity for particular inferences or interpretations. While it may be valid for one set of inferences or interpretations, it may not be valid for other inferences or interpretations. For example, while a college admissions test may be valid in making inferences about the potential success of college applicants, it probably would not be valid in predicting the class attendance of these applicants.

Most textbooks on test construction and measurement indicate that there are three ways to establish the validity of a measure: content, criterion related, and construct. While we will follow the same format, we argue also that all validation work is really an aspect of construct validation. Content validity, as usually defined, is really an evaluation of the adequacy of test construction (Guion, 1977; Tenopyr, 1977). Researcher attention to issues of content validity in test construction is a necessary precondition for construct validity. Construct validation involves the systematic collection of data on a variety of potential interpretations of test scores. Criterion- related validity is one aspect of construct validation. The statements made in this paragraph will be more meaningful after our discussion of the various validation strategies and we suggest that you reread this paragraph after reading the validation strategies.

Content Valid Test Construction

Content validity refers to the degree to which the responses required by the test items are a representative sample of the tests, behaviors, or knowledge to be exhibited in the domain about which we want to make inferences. Consequently, in content validation, the researcher must:

1. Carefully specify the area of performance or behavior about which inferences are desired.
2. Clearly formulate the intended uses of the test.
3. Consider and then carefully specify the degree to which the test items sample the behavior or performance domain of interest.

The extent to which these objectives are met in any given test is assessed by asking a set of subject matter experts their opinions with respect to how well these various aspects of test construction were conducted and to evaluate the appropriateness of the end product of these operations (i.e., the test items). Frequently a group of judges is asked to give their appraisals of a test's content and these assessments are summarized in an index called a *content validity ratio* (Lawshe, 1975). This ratio is presented below.

Applications of content validation to industrial/ organizational psychology are very often difficult because the performance domains about which inferences are to be made are not as clearly specified as they are in educational applications where content validation procedures are commonly used. It is not always possible to assume that answering a paper-and-pencil test is representative of a job task, for example. Consequently, it is necessary to be more creative in constructing tests and test items to ensure content validity.

The important components of a content validation have been outlined in five steps by Mussio and Smith (1972) as follows:

1. Thorough and reliable job analysis that documents the nature of the tasks performed on the job and the necessary knowledge, skill, and ability requirements.
2. Construction of the test using data from the job analysis regarding the importance and relevance of particular knowledge, skill, and ability requirements in the performance of important job tasks.
3. Use of subject matter experts to make judgments of the content validity of the test items.
4. Establish job relevant ways in which to use the test; that is, the use of rank order or cutoff scores and the inferences made about persons above or below some decision point must be defensible. Decision making based on test data is dealt with in more detail in Chapter 9.
5. Analysis of the reliability and difficulty of the test and the test items as well as the readability of the test.

After the test is constructed in step 2 using the examination plan developed from job analysis data (see one such plan on p. 239 of Schneider and Schmitt, 1986), the items on the exam should be reviewed by a panel of subject matter or job experts. Mussio and Smith (1972) provided relevancy, accuracy (of the situation presented), and fairness scales by which judges could evaluate each of the test items. The job relevance question is most important. Lawshe (1975) has provided a way to quantify the independent relevancy ratings of the expert judges. Each judge is asked to indicate whether the knowledge, skill, or ability measured by the item is essential, useful but not essential, or not necessary to the performance of the job. A content validity ratio (CVR) for each item is calculated using the following formula:

$$CVR = (n_e - N/2)/(N/2) \tag{3.9}$$

where n_e is the number of judges indicating the knowledge, skill or abiliity (KSA) is essential and N is the total number of judges. By averaging the *CVR*s for all items in a test one can compute a content validity index for the test. The content validity index, then, is a summary of the degree to which the judges believe that the test domain and performance domain overlap. Judgment on the part of experts is obviously crucial in good test construction, but it is also central in other methods of validating the inferences we draw from test data.

Administering and scoring a content valid exam is no different than administering or scoring any other exam. Examinees should be informed of the test content, perhaps using sample items; efforts should be made to minimize extraneous variables, such as test anxiety, lighting and noise problems, etc.; and standardization of the testing situation for all examinees must be ensured. Item analyses and reliability analyses of the test should be made following test administration and these analyses should be followed by appropriate modifications of the test. While content validity is usually discussed in connection with employment tests, it is also relevant to measures developed and used in all areas of human resource research; for example, in determining training program content, performance appraisal, survey research, etc.

Criterion-Related Validation

In using a criterion-related validation strategy, a researcher collects data from a group of people concerning the appropriateness of the inferences made from test scores. Both test scores and the persons' standing on some performance or behavior are collected. The magnitude of correlation of these two sets of scores is taken as evidence of criterion-related validity. For example, if we have developed a measure of role ambiguity and we believe that ambiguity about one's role in some organization is stressful, then we should find sizable and statistically significant correlations between scores on our role ambiguity measure and the stress levels reported by the people from whom we collect data.

Criterion-related research in personnel selection involves several fairly well-defined steps:

1. *Job analysis is used to identify the major job duties and the knowledge, skills and abilities required to perform these duties.* Job analysis is also used to identify criteria, or relevant measures of job performance.
2. *Measures of job performance are developed.* These measures might include a variety of those discussed in Chapters 5 and 6. As with any other attempt to assess individual differences, these measures must be reliable and practical; but, most importantly, they must be relevant to the overall effectiveness of the organization.
3. *Measures of the knowledge, skills, and abilities required for successful job performance are developed or selected.* These measures are then given to job applicants whose performance is to be predicted. Various selection procedures are described in Chapter 8.
4. *Measures of job performance are collected and correlated with knowledge, skill, and ability measures.* These measures are taken after the applicants are hired and have worked for some period of time. Techniques described in Chapter 2 and in more detail in Chapter 9 are used to assess the degree of relationship between KSA measures and job performance measures. Ideally, measures of the knowledge, skills, and abilities are not used to make selection decisions until after the criterion-related validation study is complete.
5. *Decisions regarding the practical utility of the selection instruments are made and their use is introduced in the organization.* Ways of assessing the practical utility of selection instruments are described in the latter part of Chapter 9.

While the general outline of criterion-related research is well developed and widely employed, there are a variety of ways in which these steps are implemented. Usually these variations on the general model are a result of trying to do research in a functioning organization. In the next section, we describe some of the major design differences in criterion-related research and some of their potential implications.

Design of Criterion-Related Research in Personnel Selection. Criterion-related validity has probably been the most frequently employed validation strategy among human resource researchers interested in personnel selection. These researchers have used forms of two different validation strategies: concurrent and predictive. The difference between these two strategies is primarily one of the timing of the collection of the predictor data (selection instrument) and the criterion data (performance data). In a predictive criterion-related validation, the researcher collects test or predictor data from a group of job applicants, employs those applicants without reference to their test scores, and then on some later occasion collects data regarding their job performance. The correlation between the test data and the job performance data are taken as evidence of criterion-related validity.

In a concurrent criterion-related strategy, the researcher collects test data and performance measures at the same time from a group of job incumbents. As in the predictive strategy, the correlation between test and performance data is taken as evidence of the criterion-related validity of the test. Concurrent validation has been criticized because of potential differences in test taking motivation of job applicants and job incumbents; the possibility that experience on the job affects test scores; and perhaps most importantly, the possibility that the full range of applicant ability is not represented in a group of job incumbents. The latter problem is created by the fact that the least qualified applicants may not have been selected, the poorest performing individuals may have been fired, and/or the best performing individuals may have been promoted. This difficulty is referred to as the range restriction problem. While the preference among researchers has been the predictive criterion-related study, existing comparisons of concurrent and predictive studies yield small differences in validity coefficients (see Schmitt, Gooding, Noe, & Kirsch, 1984).

Perhaps one reason there are few differences between validities generated from concurrent as opposed to predictive studies is the fact that these types of studies rarely appear in the pure form in which they are described above. Sussman and Robertson (1986) identified 11 different approaches to the design of criterion-related research depending on: (a) when the selection instruments are administered, (b) how the selection decisions are made, and (c) when job performance or criteria data are collected. In the purely predictive study, tests of knowledge, skill, and ability are collected from job applicants prior to employment; selection decisions are made on a random basis; and job performance measures are collected later after employees have become relatively proficient at their jobs and performance levels have stabilized. Frequently, however, organizations do not wish to wait the considerable length of time a predictive validation effort often demands or they do not (or cannot) select employees randomly but use an existing battery or the very same instruments that are being validated to make selection decisions. Frequently, too, existing measures of employee performance are inadequate so special measures (often job samples or simulations) are developed to serve as criteria in the validation effort.

Restriction of Range. One problem associated with criterion related research in a functioning organization is the problem called *restriction of range*. As described above, organizations are understandably reluctant to hire people on a random basis; instead, they frequently use a selection instrument before it is validated or they might use alternate methods of selection that are related to those that are the subject of a validity study. If the organization rejects low-scoring individuals, no criterion data can be collected for these persons and they cannot be included in a criterion-related validation study. As mentioned previously, in the case of concurrent criterion-related validation, it is also likely that low performing individuals will have quit or been fired and high performing individuals promoted away from the group being studied. The problem of restriction of range is analogous to the conduct of an experimental study with a single level of the independent variable.

Fortunately, we can correct the observed validity coefficient (the correlation between a predictor and criterion) for range restriction *if* we have kept data on the scores of all hired and rejected job applicants and can compute the standard deviation of the applicants' scores on the selection instruments. The corrected validity coefficient is then computed using the following formula:

$$r_{xyc} = \frac{r_{xy}(SD_u/SD_r)}{\sqrt{1 - r_{xy}^2 + r_{xy}^2(SD_u^2/SD_r^2)}} \qquad (3.10)$$

where r_{xyc} and r_{xy} are respectively the corrected and uncorrected validities and SD_u and SD_r are the unrestricted and restricted standard deviations respectively. Consider a reasonably realistic situation in which the observed validity coefficient is .30 and half the applicants are accepted. With half of the applicants selected, the standard deviation of the selected group would be about 6.0 if the total applicant group's standard deviation was 10.0. Using these data and the formula above, the corrected validity coefficient would be as follows:

$$r_{xyc} = \frac{.30(10/6)}{\sqrt{1 - .09 + .09(100/36)}}$$
$$= .5/1.08$$
$$= .46$$

The corrected coefficient (.46) clearly indicates that the test has a higher functional validity than the empirically observed coefficient of .30. Such corrections may be routinely applied in making estimates of the criterion-related validity of selection instruments. Similar correction formulae are available for the situation in which predictors other than those we are interested in validating are used and for the situation in which the restriction has occurred on the criterion as in those cases in which people have been fired or promoted away from the work group (see Thorndike, 1949). These latter corrections, however, are unlikely to result in the rather substantial increases in estimated validity that occur when direct restriction on the predictor has occurred as in the example above.

Criterion Unreliability. If we are to come to an appropriate decision about the validity of a selection instrument based on a criterion-related study, the criterion must be a central concern. We mentioned earlier the degree to which lack of reliability in a criterion serves to attenuate observed validity coefficients and we presented a correction for this attenuation. Since we are interested in predicting the criterion, the estimate of criterion reliability should usually be of the test-retest type, but may also be of the alternate forms or internal consistency type. As indicated above, if ratings are the criterion, a reasonable estimate of criterion reliability might be the correlation between ratings by different raters across time. Lack of criterion reliability, range restriction, and the small sample sizes that are often available for validation work frequently make it unlikely that a researcher can conclude that there is a statistically significant relationship between scores on a selection instrument and measures of job performance. Schmidt, Hunter, and Urry (1976) have provided tables that indicate the sample sizes a researcher must have to do a validation study with a reasonable probability to conclude that the predictor and criterion are significantly correlated. This probability is called *power* by statisticians and researchers should always calculate the power of their studies (see Chapter 2) or consult the Schmidt et al. (1976) tables before spending the considerable amount of effort and money associated with criterion-related research.

One relatively realistic example based on the Schmidt et al. (1976) tables will serve to illustrate the importance of criterion unreliability and range restriction as they affect the power of criterion-related validation research. Let's assume we have used a valid predictor (true validity = .35) to select the top half of a set of applicants prior to estimating the correlation between the predictor and the criterion. Further, assume that the criterion is a rating for which we know the interrater reliability across time is .60. The expected validity in this case is .17, about half its true value. In order to have power of .90 (probability of concluding that the test is significantly related to the criterion), we would need 370 subjects. If no selection had occurred (i.e., there is no range restriction) we would have the same power with 213 subjects. If reliability were perfect and no range restriction had occurred, we would require 82 subjects to attain power equal to .90. Clearly, these two practical problems impact on the feasibility and outcomes of criterion-related validation research.

Of most importance in selecting or developing criteria is their relevance to the overall objectives of the organization. (A complete discussion of this issue will be presented in Chapter 5.) In an organization in which attendance is the primary determinant of successful job performance (which may be true in low-skilled, repetitive jobs the performance of which is regulated by assembly line speed), perhaps the most relevant criterion is absenteeism. In another case in which training or probationary period costs are very large, perhaps training success or turnover is the most relevant job performance criterion. Most frequently, some index of the quality and quantity of performance will be judged most relevant. The selection of a particular criterion or criteria is always a judgment—one which should be taken seriously. Judgments of criterion relevance can be made by several informed judges and their agreement as to relevance of various criteria should be high.

Dynamics of Criteria. In some previous discussions of criteria (e.g., McCormick & Ilgen, 1980) a concern for the fact that criteria change over time has been voiced. Recently, Barrett, Caldwell, and Alexander (1985) reviewed the evidence for three different kinds of criterion change: (a) change over time in the average level of group performance, (b) changes in validity coefficients over time, and (c) changes in the rank ordering of scores on the criterion over time. If measures of criteria exhibit real change (rather than change due to temporal unreliability) then the classic validation model we described above is inappropriate because our purpose in applying that model is to generalize from a one-time criterion measure to a long-term span of behavior.

Fortunately, the evidence examined by Barrett et al. (1985) does not indicate any real change in criteria in any of the three ways described above. Changes in group average performance do not seem to be substantial after some initial orientation or training period and, even if they were, these changes tell us nothing about the individuals' changes, which are the critical problem insofar as validation work is concerned. Changes in validity over time were reported at approximately chance levels (Barrett et al., 1985). Changes in the rank ordering of individual performance levels over time as reflected in test-retest reliabilities were more frequent than chance levels although a large number of the significant changes came from a single study. The issue of changes in criterion dimensionality will be discussed in more detail in Chapter 5.

Yet another definition of criterion dynamics holds that there are changes in the inter-correlations between different criterion dimensions, suggesting that the ability requirements of jobs change across time. This notion is reflected in the work of Fleishman and Hempel (1954), Fleishman and Fruchter (1960), and more recently in a paper by Henry and Hulin (1987). Data regarding these types of criterion change are relatively rare. In fact, in spite of the relatively large number of studies reviewed by Barrett et al. (1985), the issue of changes in criteria of any type often have not been the direct concern of researchers. They usually are incidental to the major purpose of a study. While Barrett et al. (1985) conclude by saying that researchers ought to focus on removing various sources of unreliability, we believe that in doing studies of reliability we might also be well-advised to examine the issue of criterion change directly.

Timing of Criterion Measurement. Another issue, at least in predictive criterion-related research and in some concurrent designs, is the length of time after employment one must wait to collect the criterion data. The usual guidance on this issue is that criterion measurement take place after job incumbents have learned the job; that is, after training and orientation are complete and the worker is a fully contributing member of the organization.

Schmitt and Schneider (1983) surveyed a group of 49 industrial psychologists all of whom reported that they had done selection research. These selection specialists were asked what amount of time after job entry should elapse before one would be able to collect stable performance and production data for people in various jobs. For professional occupations, the mean time was generally between one and two years; for most of the clerical and service occupations, the mean time was approximately six months; and for the remaining occupations, between six months and one year. Aside from providing some specific practical guidelines on this issue for various occupations, the Schmitt-Schneider data underscore the amount of time and effort that must be invested in predictive criterion-related research.

A very large number of criterion-related studies of the relationship between job performance measures and some kinds of tests, particularly cognitive paper-and-pencil tests, have been conducted during the past half century. Recently, these studies have been integrated using procedures outlined by Hunter, Schmidt, and Jackson (1982) and described in Chapter 12 of this text. This validity generalization work indicates that at least paper-and-pencil tests of cognitive ability have useful validities across a wide range of jobs (Hunter & Hunter, 1984; Schmidt & Hunter, 1981). Validity generalization work on various types of predictor variables will be summarized in Chapters 8 and 12.

Construct Validation

Construct validity of a measure is the degree to which certain explanatory psychological concepts or constructs account for performance on a measure. A psychological construct is an idea that is used to organize or integrate existing knowledge about some phenomenon. (Also see the definition of construct discussed in Chapter 1.) In addressing construct validity, we will use the example of a commonly studied construct, role ambiguity.

A researcher may notice that some employees seek more direction than others concerning the requirements of their work. Further, the researcher's observations are that this direction-seeking behavior occurs most frequently in those work units in which no clearly prescribed job duties exist, or in units in which the supervisors are inexperienced and not very knowledgeable about how best to use their employees. The researcher talks to employees in these units and discovers a great deal of concern about what they are supposed to do, how they stand with their supervisor, and how to get useful information about the organization and their role in it. The researcher calls this lack of direction and unease role ambiguity. Role ambiguity is not directly observable but we infer its existence through the behavior of people.

A Nomological Network. If we develop a measure of this role ambiguity and we want to establish its construct validity, we would collect a variety of pieces of information. We might conduct laboratory investigations in which we deliberately manipulate the degree to which various roles in the experimental situation are described. Responses by persons in various conditions to our measure of role ambiguity should reflect these differences in role specification. We might collect information from supervisors concerning how much direction they give their subordinates. Employees in those units in which the supervisors give a great deal of direction should experience less role ambiguity than employees in units where little direction is given. Or, the investigator could observe the supervisors in various units and rate their direction-giving behavior. These ratings should correlate with the role ambiguity responses in the units. Investigators may hypothesize that role ambiguity leads to stress; hence the role ambiguity measure should correlate with self-reports of job stress, as well as other behaviors and illnesses symptomatic of stress. All of these different studies or information should converge or lead us to the conclusion that role ambiguity is a meaningful explanation or construct and that it is central in explaining the behavior in these various studies.

Construct validation involves the testing of theoretical propositions or hypotheses concerning the construct in which we are interested. The constructs in our theory are operationalized by means of tests, observations, archival data, etc. The hypothesized or theoretical relationships then can be assessed through the observed relationships between our tests or other observations. A way of visualizing the relationships between theoretical and observable variables is by means of a *nomological network*. One such network for our role ambiguity construct is illustrated in Figure 3-1.

The upper portion of this figure represents our theory. We are hypothesizing that role ambiguity exists and that it is related to supervisory skill and worker stress, but none of these constructs is directly observable. In order to study these hypothesized constructs and relationships, we must operationalize the constructs or make them observable.

The bottom half of Figure 3-1 is an illustration of one set of possible operationalizations. Supervisory skill, thought to be directly related to role ambiguity, involves the supervisor's ability to give appropriate direction regarding the work that needs to be done. One way of operationalizing this construct might be to ask the supervisors to keep a diary record of their direction-giving behavior. Another possible way would be to observe their behavior in a simulated work task and count instances of direction-giving behavior as an index of this aspect of their supervisory skill. You probably could identify problems with both of these operationalizations and you could probably devise several others. In spite of their problems, however, information on these different measures should converge on a single interpretation: Role ambiguity as we conceive it is responsible for observed relationships among the measured variables. Role ambiguity, most frequently, has been operationalized using the level of workers' agreement to several attitude statements (Rizzo, House, & Lirtzman, 1970). Stress could be operationalized physiologically by measuring blood pressure or heart rate or we could ask the workers to report their level of perceived stress on some scale. Once the constructs are operationalized in a reliable manner, studies of the hypothesized relationships then can take place.

Thus, the process of construct validation involves three steps: (a) the construct of interest is carefully defined and hypotheses about the nature and extent of the construct's relationship to other variables are generated, (b) a measure is developed and its reliability is assessed, and (c) studies examining the relationship of the variable to other measures are assessed.

The Multitrait-Multimethod Matrix. The most frequently employed method used to assess the construct validity of a psychological measure has been the degree to which scores on the measure

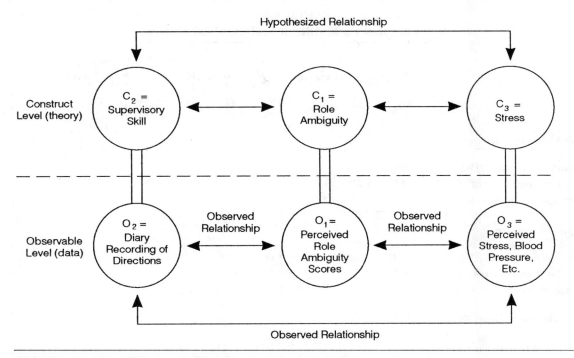

FIGURE 3-1 Illustrations of a Hypothetical Nomological Network
Source: Adapted with permission from Walsh, W.B., & Betz, N.E. (1985). *Tests and assessments.* Englewood Cliffs NJ: Prentice Hall.

correlate with scores on other measures of the construct as well as scores on measures of dissimilar constructs. These correlations usually are summarized in a *multitrait-multimethod (MTMM) matrix* and occasionally this matrix is subjected to confirmatory factor analyses (Schmitt & Stults, 1986; Widaman, 1985). Recall the introduction to this method of data analysis in Chapter 2.

An example of a MTMM matrix is presented in Table 3-4. In this table, we present the correlations between three different measures of personality constructs assessed in three different ways. If any of the three sets of scores being generated represent a meaningful construct, then they ought to correlate more highly with the other two measures of that construct than they do with measures of other constructs. So, for example, scores on organizational ability as measured in a situational interview should correlate highly with organizational ability as measured in the leaderless group exercise and on the questionnaire. Organizational ability scores should not correlate highly with scores on interpersonal skills measures and problem analysis measures if these are really measures of different constructs.

Campbell and Fiske (1959), who first presented the MTMM matrix and described its "logic," suggested four criteria by which to judge the matrix. These criteria, and examples of their application to the matrix presented in Table 3-4, are as follows:

1. The correlations between similar traits measured by different methods (called convergent validities) should be both statistically significant and high enough to warrant further consideration. The values in parentheses in Table 3-4 represent convergent validities. These values are relatively good when we consider the correlations between

TABLE 3-4
An Example of a Multitrait-Multimethod Matrix

	Situational Interview			Questionnaire			Leaderless Group Exercise		
	PA	OA	IS	PA	OA	IS	PA	OA	IS
Situational Interview									
Problem Analysis (PA)	1.00								
Organizational Ability (OA)	.41	1.00							
Interpersonal Skills (IS)	.35	.34	1.00						
Questionnaire									
Problem Analysis (PA)	(.68)	.40	.32	1.00					
Organizational Ability (OA)	.38	(.76)	.32	.36	1.00				
Interpersonal Skills (IS)	.31	.31	(.81)	.30	.29	1.00			
Leaderless Group Exercise									
Problem Analysis (PA)	(.42)	.41	.37	(.53)	.41	.28	1.00		
Organizational Ability (OA)	.37	(.45)	.36	.38	(.49)	.27	.50	1.00	
Interpersonal Skills (IS)	.29	.28	(.51)	.31	.29	(.38)	.45	.44	1.00

different traits as measured in the situational interview and the questionnaire, but convergent validities involving the leaderless group exercise are only moderate in size.

2. The convergent validities should be higher than the correlations between different traits measured by different methods. This criterion is definitely met for the questionnaire and situational interview measures but is generally not met for the leaderless group measures.

3. The convergent validities should be higher than the correlations between different traits measured by the same method. These values are located in the *monomethod-heterotrait triangles* enclosed by solid lines in Table 3-4. Again, this appears to be true for the situational interview and questionnaire measures, but it does not hold for the leaderless group exercise measures. In fact, the correlations between the three leaderless group measures are higher than the convergent validities involving these measures. When the monomethod-heterotrait correlations are high, we often conclude that there is *method bias*; that is, scores on these measures are more likely a function of the method of measurement (in this case, the leaderless group exercise) than they are attributable to individual differences in the traits being measured.

4. A similar pattern of trait intercorrelations should be apparent in the monomethod-heterotrait triangles as well as those triangles involving both different traits and different methods (called heterotrait-heteromethod triangles). This criterion is generally met throughout the matrix presented in Table 3-4. Correlations between problem analysis and organizational ability usually are higher than correlations between problem analy-

sis interpersonal skills and organizational ability and interpersonal skills. The latter two correlations are almost identical in all cases.

Measures that meet these four criteria are said to represent meaningful constructs in their own right—that is, one receives similar scores on a group of people no matter what method of measurement is used and the trait being measured appears to be different from other psychological dimensions. While the matrix in Table 3-4 is relatively easily interpretable, matrices that include more traits and/or a larger number of methods are not as easily interpretable. Problems also exist when the variables being measured are of different reliability. Further, the criteria presented above are not quantifiable. For all of these reasons a variety of methods to analyze MTMM matrices have been presented. These methods are summarized and illustrated in Schmitt and Stults (1986) and Widaman (1985).

The use of MTMM matrices has been an extremely popular and probably overused method of drawing conclusions about a measure's construct validity. Aside from the differential reliability problem noted above, whether or not traits converge across methods may actually be a function of the diversity of methods one uses. Further, in an applied context, one wants to know more about test scores (and the inferences drawn from them) than how the test scores correlate with other measures. While construct validation in applied research is still relatively rare, some good examples of other ways to assess construct validity are beginning to appear in the literature.

Arnold, Rauschenberger, Soubel, and Guion (1982) reported a construct validation of a set of physical ability measures for the selection of steelworkers. Their tests were relatively simple measures of the ability to lift or grip material. Evidence of the construct validity of these simple tests consisted of their correlation with performance on relatively elaborate job simulations. The job simulations were difficult and, in some cases, dangerous to administer in various locations to many applicants, but correlations of substantial magnitude between the simple tests and the complex simulations indicated that scores on the simpler tests represented the same underlying abilities or constructs required for successful completion of the tasks in the job simulations.

Borman, Rosse, and Abrahams (1980) present a study of the construct validity of personality tests used to select Navy recruiters. Their study involved the following steps:

1. A job analysis and factor analysis of job performance measures indicated the importance of selling skills, human relation skills, and organizing skills.
2. A trial inventory of 310 personality items and the Strong-Campbell Interest Inventory were administered to a group of Navy recruiters.
3. The responses to these items were correlated with the performance measures identified in number 1 above and the most highly correlated items were selected.
4. Responses to these "valid" items were factor analyzed.
5. The researchers then wrote new items, which they thought represented constructs similar to those identified in the factor analysis.

Correlations between the original set of items and the new items (number 5) represent the degree to which the researchers were able to understand the construct and write new items representing that construct. These correlations in the Borman et al. (1980) study were in the .50s and .60s.

A consultant, using psychological tests in industry draws on personal experience with the tests, knowledge of the relative predictive validities of various measures, and the interrelationships among the varieties of measures supposedly predictive of behavior, as well as knowledge of the situation in which the test will be used to formulate hypotheses about test scores and to further evaluate these hypotheses. This sort of informal construct validation has certainly received substantial empirical support from the validity generalization work described in Chapter 8 and the meta-analytic methods described in Chapter 12. It also has received support from a pair of studies by Schmidt and Hunter and their colleagues (Hirsh, Schmidt, & Hunter, 1986; Schmidt, Hunter, Croll, & McKenzie, 1983). In the first of these two studies, Schmidt et al. (1983) showed that expert judges could accurately estimate the validity of cognitive tests. In fact, their estimates were more accurate than actual criterion-related validities based on small samples. In the second study, inexperienced human resource people, who presumably did not have as complete a notion of the constructs being measured, were not as accurate as the "expert" judges who were trained and experienced personnel researchers.

Construct validation involves a series of data collection efforts in varying situations. The necessity of human judgment as to what evidence it makes theoretical sense to collect and how to interpret that evidence is obvious. The complexity of construct validation as well as its inherently time-consuming nature make it an infrequently used procedure in selection research. In a sense, construct validation is a continuing, never-finished process. For example, a great deal is known concerning the implications of scores on intelligence tests, but scientific work extending the understanding of these instruments continues. A criterion-related validity study investigating a particular predictor-job performance relationship in a given situation is only one part of the construct validation process.

While it may be difficult and time-consuming, basic construct validation work is absolutely essential in applied research. Unless we understand the measures we use to collect data, many of the results of our studies will appear confusing and inconsistent. Construct validation is also important because the labels we attach to our measures often convey different meanings to different people and a test with a given label may not operate the same in all situations. For example, a measure of role ambiguity might relate to issues of the type of tasks one is expected to do or the persons to whom one must be responsible. Further role ambiguity could be experienced both within a work organization and a family, but the same measure would not likely be useful in both contexts.

In concluding our discussion of validity, we would like to underscore the importance of human judgment in each of the validation strategies. In content validation, we rely on subject matter experts to review test materials and judge their job relevance. In criterion- related validity, we compute the statistical relationship between a predictor and some measure of job performance. However, some researcher or subject matter expert makes decisions regarding which job performance measures to collect. Indirectly, this judgment about appropriate job performance measures also represents a judgment about which predictor variables are valid. In construct validation, the researcher's judgment dictates what information to collect and how to interpret that information.

PRACTICAL ISSUES IN CONSIDERING
MEASURES IN PERSONNEL SELECTION

In assessing qualities of selection instruments there are three important practical issues to consider as well. First, concern for the impact of the procedure on minority groups and/or women dictates that we examine differences in performance for members of various groups. When the use of a selection instrument or a selection strategy results in a lower rate of hiring for a minority group than for majority individuals, we say the procedure exhibits *adverse impact*. The legal system has produced much external pressure on human resource professionals and organizations to justify use of instruments that produce adverse impact on legally protected groups. We outline some of the data reporting requirements in Chapter 9. The various tradeoffs one makes between affirmative action goals and organizational productivity goals in the use of different selection instruments and strategies are detailed in Schmitt and Noe (1986).

It also is important to note that various sets of professional guidelines on the use of tests and measures of human capabilities and attitudes have been written. Perhaps of broadest relevance are the *Standards for Educational and Psychological Testing* published jointly by the American Psychological Association, American Educational Research Association, and the National Council on Measurement in Education (1985). The *Standards* were intended as a basis for evaluating the quality of testing practices as they affect various parties. They include discussions of test validity and reliability similar to the discussion in this chapter but also include discussions of standards for the use of tests in particular contexts such as employment testing. Of more direct relevance to human resource professionals are the *Principles for the Validation and Use of Personnel Selection Procedures* published by the Society for Industrial and Organizational Psychology (1987). As the title suggests, *Principles* contains guidelines on good practice in the assessment and selection of human resources. Finally, four agencies of the federal government (the Equal Employment Opportunity Commission, the Department of Labor, the Department of Justice, and the Civil Service Commission) have jointly issued the *Uniform Guidelines on Employee Selection Procedures* (1978). These guidelines involve the reliable and valid use of selection procedures, particularly as these procedures might impact on the fair employment of minorities and women. As the *Uniform Guidelines* frequently have been cited and used in deciding fair employment issues in the federal courts, they are very important to the human resource professional engaged in selection research.

Yet another issue is the cost of using various selection instruments. Interviews and assessment programs are quite costly in terms of the time required for their administration and development. Paper-and-pencil tests may be costly to develop but relatively inexpensive to administer and quite cheap overall if many applicants are being evaluated. Work samples, or simulations, may be both costly to develop and administer.

Finally, a test or selection instrument usually represents one of the first contacts a job applicant has with an organization. Throughout this chapter we have been detailing the ways in which we can evaluate the contribution a selection instrument makes in hiring productive personnel. However, the process of selection certainly also communicates something to the job applicant regarding the way the organization treats people. Schmitt and Coyle (1976) documented the role campus interviewers played in determining college graduates' impressions and more recently Rynes and Miller (1983) have documented these effects in other contexts.

On the one hand, a rigorous process of applicant evaluation may communicate the fact that an organization takes its human resources seriously and is willing to invest a great deal of time and money toward their selection and development. If, however, the applicant gets no feedback regarding performance, the process seems arbitrary and difficult to understand, and the procedures do not seem job relevant, the applicant may feel anger at having been imposed upon, or feel that the organization has engaged in an unjustifiable invasion of privacy. This aspect of the quality of a selection procedure has received far more attention among European psychologists (e.g., Herriot, 1989; Schuler & Stehle, 1982) who have labeled it *social validity*.

Based on these postulated dynamics, it would seem best for organizations to inform their applicants fully regarding (a) the type and purpose of the selection instruments to which they are exposed, (b) the decisions being made in using those instruments, and (c) how they performed on each of the instruments. A fully informed applicant is more likely to feel that they have gained something as a result of the process even if they are not subsequently employed. Feelings of exploitation should be minimized.

SUMMARY

In this chapter, we have described various characteristics of a good measure of human resource capability, motivation, or attitude. These instruments should exhibit an appropriate level of reliability. In various contexts, changes across time, changes due to specific item content, or changes due to a particular rater may all contribute to a lack of reliable measurement. The decision to estimate reliability by test-retest, alternate forms, or internal consistency methods must be based on the way in which the measurement is used to make decisions.

The appropriateness of the inferences derived from test scores are likely to be most defensible when the test is constructed well following procedures usually labeled content validation and/or when we have evidence that the test scores are correlated with job performance measures (criterion-related validation). Guiding test construction, the choice of a criterion, and the types of data to collect to support the theoretical defensibility of an instrument should be a job analysis and/or a firm sense of the constructs one sets out to measure. As such, all information we collect regarding the meaning of test scores is construct validation.

Finally, in an applied situation, one cannot ignore the practical issues of cost, ease of administration, and impact on the people whose response we require to make our assessments.

UNDERSTANDING THE ORGANIZATION THROUGH QUALITATIVE RESEARCH

This chapter promotes the notion that an investigator can come to better understand the nature and functioning of organizations and the impact of Human Resource policy and practices through careful descriptive and analytic work. Toward this end, observation, interview, and archival techniques and methods are reviewed in detail. Such techniques are portrayed as having a special place in descriptive studies.

INTRODUCTION

Individuals who seek to understand the nature of organizations or to learn about the effects of Human Resource policies and practices may choose to do so through the use of any number of tools (techniques). They might also follow a wide variety of plans (or designs) for gathering the desired information. This chapter emphasizes the goal of careful and complete description of key organizational phenomena by following a relatively uncomplicated research plan (e.g., intensive case study) with the emphasis on three rather powerful and useful data gathering techniques—observation, the interview, and archival analysis. Taken together, these are offered as the essential tools of what has been called qualitative research.

It should be made quite clear that qualitative research is more an approach than a particular design or set of techniques, although these are admittedly difficult to separate in practice. It is an "umbrella" phrase "covering an array of interpretive techniques which seek to describe, decode, translate, and otherwise come to terms with the meaning of naturally occurring phenomena in the social world" (Van Maanen, 1979, p. 520). "Doing description" is therefore the fundamental act of qualitative research.

Qualitative research also implies a set of assumptions regarding the essential nature of scientific inquiry itself and its potential for discovering truths about organizational life. While the notion that research methods and assumptions are closely linked has been examined in previous chapters, it turns out to be particularly salient in the domain of qualitative research. And indeed, some of these assumptions are at the heart of disagreements as to how and where to make use of the approach. Thus it seems reasonable to start this chapter exploring the underlying philosophy of qualitative research before describing prevalent techniques and some contexts for applications.

ASSUMPTIONS UNDERLYING QUALITATIVE RESEARCH

Both proponents and critics tend to contrast qualitative and quantitative research to make their points. But as Morgan and Smircich (1980) point out, it is inappropriate to argue in the abstract for one or the other. Rather, the choice and appropriateness of method really depends upon what phenomena you are trying to understand and beliefs in how new knowledge can best be acquired. It turns out that choice of method is also related to assumptions about human nature as well.

Morgan and Smircich (1980) believe that social science researchers, regardless of preferred methodology, subscribe to the belief that behavior is "caused" and does not occur at random. Thus, there is some order and regulation to organizational life. Moreover, most researchers would agree that it is possible to discover something about these causes. This is probably why the natural science model of strong inference reviewed in Chapter 1 has so many proponents. Where investigators tend to diverge is in their assumptions regarding the complexity of these forces and the approaches suitable for inquiry.

Morgan and Smircich represent the issues involved on an objective/subjective continuum. At one extreme, the objectivist approach views the social world as a concrete structure to be discovered and characterized. It would emphasize the importance of studying patterns of relationships in order to uncover the causes of human behavior. It gives rise to a search for general, lawful, and often simple relationsips. On the other hand, one could view reality as completely subjective; that is, reality is what each person perceives, a projection of human imagination. A subjectivist approach also would stress an understanding of how people view their world and come to terms with it. In its extreme form, the latter would argue that there really is no "reality" to be captured in our theories and models, but that the goal is to understand how people shape the world in their minds and act accordingly. Figure 4-1 has been adapted from Morgan and Smircich (1980) to highlight the basic assumptions associated with these different research traditions in social science.

It also is true that varying assumptions about the world and about the best way to learn about the world have been associated with the use of particular research techniques. For example, those with an objectivist view tend to draw upon the techniques of the physical sciences (experimentation) as well as the latter's use of quantitative analysis. But it would be wrong to assume that various methods can be assigned easily to specific but different points along the continuum. This is too simple a characterization. In fact, a given technique stressed in this chapter (e.g., direct observation) often lends itself to a variety of uses, depending on the orientation of its user (Downey & Ireland, 1979). To put it another way, it's not the techniques that define an approach, it's the kind of intellectual effort it represents (Geertz, 1973).

This different attitude toward research by those who take a qualitative approach has been characterized in a slightly different manner by Evered and Louis (1981). They describe such individuals as conducting organizational research from the "inside." In contrast to the usual natural science paradigm, this involves taking an active or participative role in the behavior to be investigated. Usually, this means getting quite involved with the organization or the people that you want to study. Thus, we come to know our subject by being there or being involved experientially. We gain a personal knowledge this way. It also implies that we approach a situation or research question with an open mind and with few a priori assumptions. In practice, proponents of this view would argue that our hypotheses and the ways we categorize information should result from our experiences rather than be proposed in detail ahead of time.

As a qualitative researcher, our goal might be different as well. Traditional inquiry from the outside would stress the discovery of generalized statements that are universally applicable. In contrast, inquiry from the inside is directed toward creating a complete description of the specific case. The researcher is seeking a rich appreciation for the context and the conditions operating at that point in time. As Mintzberg puts it "we should ask ourselves whether we are better off to have each study 100 organizations, giving us superficial data on ten thousand, or each study one, giving

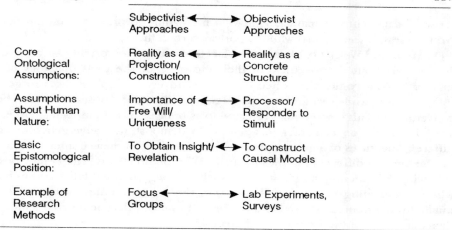

FIGURE 4-1   Assumptions in Research
Source: Adapted with permission from Morgan, G., & Smircich, L. 1980. The case for qualitative research. *Academy of Management Review, 5*, 491–500.

us in-depth data on one hundred" (1979, pp. 583–584). For the qualitative researcher, the answer is clear. Thus, as a rule, qualitative studies will typically involve small samples (of individuals, groups, or organizations).

The focus on small samples has several implications. As noted, the result may be greater insight into the particular case. On the other hand, small samples also imply a reduced capacity to detect valid but subtle phenomena. In the terms used in Chapter 2, the small sample qualitative investigation usually has low power. One other implication of using small numbers is limited generalizability. Even where the investigator has taken great pains to select individuals, groups, or organizations that are felt to be representative of the population of interest (e.g., managers or schools), there is a low probability that this really will be the case. This is another way of saying that the small sample study will have low external validity.

One other feature of inquiry from the inside is the willingness of the investigator to acknowledge the role of personal values in the research product. The way that data gathering methods are typically used in qualitative research is such that it is difficult to separate the person from the process. In a sense, like the clinician, the investigator becomes the research tool. Frequently, then, it is not unusual to see levels of skill, personal assumptions, expectations, and biases acknowledged openly at the outset by the qualitative researcher to allow the reader of the research to make an informed decision regarding the likely quality of the data.

To summarize, the person assuming a qualitative approach seeks an in-depth and rich description of specific cases based on the belief that this is the best way to know about some aspect of organizational life. He or she approaches the task with the realization that the data of interest must be generated from the participant's point of view inasmuch as it is the subjective interpretation of reality that accounts for much of the variation in the phenomenon of interest.

ATTRIBUTES OF QUALITATIVE RESEARCH

It already has been suggested that work in this area is diverse and that it is represented in both the attitude of the investigator as well as the particular methods for acquiring and making sense of data. Thus, it may be somewhat misleading to present common features or attributes. Nonetheless, it seems worthwhile to portray certain themes.

Webb and Weick (1979) stress the fact that qualitatively oriented investigators are particularly concerned about the weakness of their measures or the tools that they use to develop these measures. As a result, they often construct and use multiple indices to get at phenomena of interest. Thus, while recognizing the potential fallibility of any one measure, they seek evidence of convergence. This is sometimes referred to as *triangulation* (Campbell & Fiske, 1959).

Triangulation can refer to attempts to demonstrate convergence or agreement between different measures of a given construct or consistency of measurement using a given instrument on the same or different samples (Denzin, 1978; Smith, 1975). The latter cases represent types of reliability. It is not uncommon to adopt such a strategy in quantitative research as well, particularly when investigating new areas. However, in the present context, triangulation will refer to the qualitatively oriented researcher's tendency to make inferences or conclusions from consistent data derived from two or more methods.

To illustrate this, in a study of the impact of a company merger on employees, Jick (1979) reports on his use of multiple methods, direct and indirect, quantifiable and qualitative, used to describe behaviors in a sample of individuals over a 14-month period. The focus of the research was on the dynamics of anxiety and job security at the time of a company merger. Surveys were distributed to a representative sample of employees, a subsample of whom participated in a semistructured, probing interview. Also, direct observations of employees as well as surreptitious measures were taken.

To illustrate the latter, Jick discovered that one of the merging organizations had an archives/library that contained a variety of files, books and memorabilia from its 100-year history. It also contained a comprehensive collection of newpaper articles that cited the merger. Jick found that he could monitor library activity levels relative to these materials as a kind of anxiety thermometer. He reasoned that employees could refer to the public accounts of the merger to check out or verify past pronouncements against what they were now experiencing. In this study Jick referred to library records to get a sense of what types of employees were making use of the facility. He integrated this information into his conclusions regarding the impact the merger was having on workers in different functions and at different levels.

When triangulation is used in this way, the researcher becomes a builder or creator, piecing together parts of a complex puzzle. Convergence of conclusions creates confidence; lack of same promotes additional data gathering or the modification of an interpretation. Data that don't conform may, in fact, promote new theories. To put it another way, "Qualitative data and analysis function as the glue that cements the interpretation of multimethod results" (Jick, 1979, p. 609).

Webb and Weick (1979) also offer some other generalizations about those who carry out qualitative research. For example, the latter assume that information about a phenomena can come through the "noise" of organizational life—if one is prepared to look for it. Such investigators are willing to make use of existing data or systems of measurement if they can meet their needs (e.g., librarian's records). In other words, they don't believe they need to be the ones to construct the indices. They are particularly open to what might be called the *secondary analysis* of existing data. Qualitative researchers have been characterized as "finding foolishness functional" (Webb & Weick, 1979, p. 652). That is to say, they approach measurement with a certain lighthearted and playful stance. They are willing to entertain possibilities that haven't been tried before. As skillful observers, qualitative researchers are interested in the variance of measures as well as any central tendency. The deviant cases are looked to for new insights. Lack of variability is also informative.

Finally, Webb and Weick (1979) highlight the role of the expectations held by the qualitative investigation as a potential for control against making incorrect inferences. In research as in life, expectancies can be disconfirmed and can create surprise. They argue, however, that a sense of surprise is informative, as it reminds the researcher of his or her assumptions and values and the personal expectancies that are held. Just as important, discovering what people don't do, which individuals are left out of a meeting, etc., falls within this notion and also can be viewed as information. Thus, the sophisticated qualitative researcher tends to lay out in advance what he or she expects to find so that surprise can be documented (Webb & Weick, 1979, p. 653).

An articulate spokesperson for qualitative methods, Mintzberg (1979) describes an emerging strategy of what he calls *direct research*. This strategy was reflected in his doctoral dissertation in which he studied the work of five managers using structured observation (Mintzberg, 1973). It is characteristic of his work on corporate decision making (Mintzberg et al., 1976) as well.

According to Mintzberg, direct research can be characterized to varying degrees by seven themes:

1. *The research has been as purely descriptive as possible.* The goal has been to provide a basis for relevant theories, theories that are grounded in reality.
2. *The research has relied on direct methods, such as nonparticipant observation—sitting down in a manager's office and watching what he does, or tracing the distribution of memos to learn about the flow of decisions in organizations.* Sample sizes have been small, as well, in order to describe the phenomena in rich detail.
3. *The research has been as purely inductive as possible.* In general, the logic of scientific inquiry has emphasized deduction and has approached investigations with a theory or hypothesis in mind (Popper, 1968). As Mintzberg states, "It is discovery that attracts me to this business, not the checking out what we think we already know" (1979, p. 584).

   More specifically, he stresses detective work, and the tracking down of patterns and consistencies. This involves looking for order and following one lead to another. As he illustrates with historical examples, the search for order is itself not often orderly. There is a lot of recycling and one must remain open to serendipity (surprise results), making use of what might be termed as *peripheral vision* (Daft, 1983). The second step to induction he calls the *creative leap*, a willingness to go beyond what is actually known or expected, to form conclusions based on fragmentary or incomplete data. One should not be afraid to generate a new theory. Because they are abstractions, Mintzberg maintains all theories will be wrong to some extent anyway. The goal is "detective work well done, followed by creative leaps in relevant directions" (p. 584).
4. *The research is systematic in nature.* An important feature of his direct (albeit qualitative) research, is that he goes into an organization with a well-defined focus and collects specific kinds of data systematically.
5. *The research is conceptualized in real organizational terms.* The investigator attempts to understand and use employees' frames of reference, language, and insists on measuring things that really happen in organizations. This point is well illustrated in the frustration encountered by both investigators and managers as the former have attempted to impose such constructs as environmental complexity on the actual events that occur to the manager as he or she opens up a new territory (Downey & Ireland, 1979), or on the dollar value of improved performance in the battlefield on a military tank squadron commander (Eaton, Wing, & Mitchell, 1985).

6. *The research has ensured that data gathered according to the rules of the natural science model are supported by information derived from impressions and anecdotes.* This is another way of invoking the notion of triangulation. But for Mintzberg, while the former create the foundation for theories, the latter allow for actually building one. Rich description allows us to explain the relationships that we may uncover. Creative leaps require intuition, and this, in turn only can come from a sense of things or how they seem (Mintzberg, 1979, p. 587). At some personal level, we need to know the phenonema we are trying to understand.

7. *The research has tried to integrate diverse elements into some configuration of an ideal or pure type.* What Mintzberg means by this is that he attempts to go beyond investigating the relationship between two variables while holding everything else constant. He maintains that the latter is an untenable assumption because organizational life comes in complex configurations where everything else is, in fact, variable. In this regard, he has more faith in typologies than taxonomies. That is, he is less interested in a conceptual framework that clearly and completely articulates *all* of the potentially relevant variables associated with a phenomena, and more concerned with developing a prototype, an idealized configuration of many elements.

This is an admittedly personal view of qualitative research by Mintzberg. However, it does capture the spirit of the approach when applied to understanding behavior in organizations.

The qualitative research orientation also can be found in an approach to inquiry called *action research*. The latter was introduced by Kurt Lewin in the 1940s to characterize research of a social science nature that involved both theory testing and social change. At the time he and his associates were very concerned with social issues such as anti-Semitism, poverty, and intergroup conflict. In many ways, he pioneered the well- accepted scientist-practitioner model of training. Thus, his goal was to produce individuals who not only were committed to important social values and to solving social problems, but who had the skill to research critical issues and to promote change based on findings (Lewin, 1946).

Over the years, the action research philosophy has been applied with increased frequency to organizational problems where the goal is to produce data and insights that can help solve practical problems. Thus, Rapoport's (1970, p.499) definition seems to convey the message well:

> Action research aims to contribute both to the practical concerns of people in an immediate problematic situation and to the goals of social science by joint collaboration within a mutually acceptable ethical framework.

Sussman and Evered (1978) add that action research also is conducted with the aim of developing new competencies in the people or the system facing the problems to be researched. This is implied in the notion that action research is collaborative. However, Sussman and Evered are most explicit about the fact that those who believe in action research are genuinely committed to the development of what they call an infrastructure or new capacity in the client or host system. While most social scientists are concerned about inadvertently doing any harm to the organization in which they do research, this approach sets a higher standard. The action research-oriented investigator actually seeks to leave the organization better off as a result of the project. For example, Sussman and Evered describe elements of this infrastructure as both ad hoc and permanent groups that will remain intact to deal with future problems. In many respects, organizational practitioners who adopt a survey feedback model (Chapter 10) clearly personify the philosophy and activities of action research as they design and implement a survey process (research) that will produce information to help managers help themselves (infrastructure) to accomplish increased organizational functioning (action).

At the risk of simplifying a very evolutionary or organic process, Sussman and Evered (1978) offer the diagram reproduced in Figure 4-2. In it they portray five steps often found in action research: diagnosis, action planning, action taking, evaluating, and the specification of new learning. In the center of this activity, in a place of central importance and involvement, is the development of the capacities of the client system.

One additonal feature of action research that is also relevant but not evident in this figure is the belief that action research has a high likelihood of generating what has been called *grounded theories*. It helps to know that research is developed and tested in the context of organizational realities.

The skills and orientation of the qualitative researcher are very relevant to the conduct of action research. But the reverse is also true. Most qualitative researchers make use of most of the steps in Figure 4-2.

GENERAL PURPOSES OF QUALITATIVE RESEARCH

At several points in this chapter we already have alluded to why one might want to conduct qualitative research. However, it seems useful to be somewhat more explicit and systematic about this. We might wish to use a qualitative approach for any of the following:

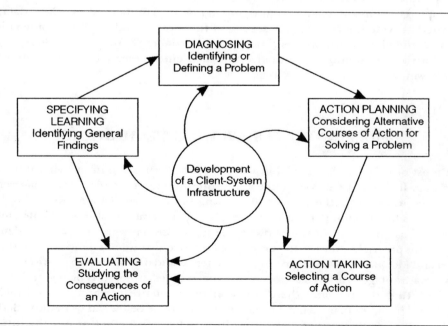

FIGURE 4-2   The Cyclical Process of Action Research
Source: Sussman, Gerald I. & Evered, Roger D. (1978). An assessment of the scientific merits of action research. *Administrative Science Quarterly*, p. 588.

1. *To gain familiarity or insights.* The researcher (or manager) may seek to gain a better understanding of a phenomenon. This may be in an entirely new area of interest. Or it could reflect a desire to increase the level of specificity or precision of existing knowledge. The latter conditions might exist for the individual who is attempting to formulate a research problem or specific hypotheses.

2. *Description.* Here the goal is to accurately portray the characteristics of a particular individual, situation, or group. In its purely exploratory form the investigator may initially have no idea, hypothesis, or theory about the nature of these characteristics. He or she enters into the activity with few preconceived notions about the phenomenon of interest. However, in practice, most of the time the investigator already is knowledgeable regarding the general issues involved and can specify certain domains or variables interesting at the outset.

3. *Frequency.* The investigator may be interested in the frequency with which something does or does not occur. This also may involve the detection of patterns of covariation among factors or variables. When these are done with no real preconceived notions, the work would be considered exploratory and or purely descriptive. With hypotheses in mind, the activity shifts into the domain of theory or hypothesis testing. For example, a current theory may assert that something does not or cannot occur (with or without the presence of other variables). This is what we have called an existential hypothesis. A qualitative study may uncover one or more nonconforming cases, thus weakening the credibility of the theory.

4. *Causal relationships.* The focus of this chapter is on the use of methods in preliminary or exploratory research work. However, a given technique (e.g., observation) may be adapted to or made suitable for the generation of quantitative data. These data, in turn, would provide the basis for the testing of theories or models of phenomena involving cause-and-effect relationships (Martinko & Gardner, 1985). Just how these steps might be carried out in more quantitative, causal-oriented research will be illustrated in the following text.

A FRAMEWORK FOR VIEWING TECHNIQUES

While most of us are rather casual in the use of the term data, in our view it has a rather precise meaning. It should be used to refer to our interpretations of recorded measurements or observations that we make in the context of carrying out an investigation (Runkel & McGrath, 1972). That is, it is the meaning or sense that we give to observations after we create and impose certain rules and assumptions. In this context, the term *observations* should also be defined in a specific way. More precisely, they are the empirical evidence that we obtain in research.

Runkel and McGrath (1972) make use of these terms and distinctions to provide a framework for viewing the advantages and weaknesses of the many specific methods or research techniques available. While they do not limit their attention to qualitative research, their insights seem particularly useful in this domain. That is to say, the points made below can be made with the intent of obtaining data using the various techniques irrespective of whether or not the investigation adopts a qualitative approach. But they will have special implications when the techniques are used for qualitative, descriptive research.

Multiple Sources of Data

In brief, Runkel and McGrath (1972) remind us that in social science research we usually are interested in understanding the behavior of an individual (or groups of individuals). They refer to this individual as the actor. Observations regarding the actor may be generated by the person himself or herself, by the investigator, by others in the work setting, or by someone in the past with no connection to the current study. For example, the latter could take the form of a performance appraisal currently stored in a file, or the minutes of a staff meeting. Both could give us insights regarding the actor. Thus, the researcher has several potential sources of empirical evidence from which to choose.

Each source has certain strengths, but each is vulnerable to weaknesses as well. It also turns out that the quality of data will be dependent on whether the actor knows or believes that he or she is being observed or measured. Unlike in the physical sciences, the act of observing a behavioral process can alter the phenomenon of interest. We have what is termed *reactivity of measurement*. And while this has long been understood, it often gets rediscovered by many new investigators.

Considering the source of data and whether the actor knows or believes he or she is being studied (awareness) simultaneously produces a matrix that can position (and help anticipate the usefulness of) commonly used techniques. This matrix is presented in Figure 4-3 along with examples of research techniques as entries.

The matrix in Figure 4-3 summarizes many of the points just made and highlights the fact that different, commonly used data generating techniques imply different assumptions and properties. It also can be thought of as a "menu" of sorts, wherein entries represent choices or options to be selected with care by the investigator. In this regard the matrix can be entered with the point of view of the source of information, the type of technique, or the level of concern over reactivity in mind, depending on what is most important to the research. In any event, it can serve to make explicit the interplay among these factors as it implies the probable validity of the data that we would be working with as a result of our choices.

Who Observes and Records Behavior	Is Actor Aware That Behavior is Being Recorded for Research?	
	Yes (may be reactive)	No (should not be reactive)
1. Actor	—Self-Reports	—Traces
2. Peers	—Public Peer Appraisals	—Private Peer Appraisals
3. Researchers	—Visible Observer	—Hidden Observer
4. Recorder in Past	—Records of Public Behavior	—Archival Records

FIGURE 4-3   A Context for Considering Techniques

Source: Adapted with permission from Runkel, P.J., & McGrath, J.E. (1972). *Research on human behavior: A systematic guide to method.* New York: Holt, Rinehart, & Winston (p. 177).

Potential Strengths and Weaknesses of Using Different Sources

As in any domain involving measurement, a researcher must be aware of weaknesses of potential techniques. Webb, Campbell, Schwartz, and Sechrest (1966) refer to these as sources of invalidity. Figure 4-4 displays an assessment of the various approaches used to obtain observations with regard to several of these sources. While these will be described briefly here, the interested reader is encouraged to read this excellent book on creative approaches to data collection for more complete information.

Sources of invalidity could include the following:

1. *"Guinea pig" effect.* This refers to the fact that, as already noted, people change their behavior when they realize they are being studied. This is usually in the direction of acting in a more normative or idealized way, although there are some cases where the tendency is to behave in a manner consistent with what the actor thinks is expected by the observer/researcher. This may not always be characterized as prosocial in nature (e.g., the researcher may want them to betray a confidence).
2. *Changes due to measurement.* The act of posing a question may actually change the actor. The actor is different as a consequence. Thus, if we start out by asking, "Have you ever thought about . . . ?" we are likely to cause people to think about the topic even if they had not heretofore. Once this has occurred, the actor is no longer the same as before the episode. Thus, a major weakness of obtaining self-reports through interviews or questionnaires is that the structure of the questions asked can unduly affect the way the respondent will think about a phenomenon. More to the point, if you were to go back to this same person, his or her second set of answers would be different, to some extent, as an artifact of past measurement.

| Sources of Invalidity | Method of Observing/Recording | | | | | |
| | Actor | | Researcher | | Third Party | |
	Self-Report	Trace	Visible	Hidden	Public	Archival
1. "Guinea Pig" Effect	H		H		M	
2. Change Due to Measurement	H		H		M	
3. Influence of Observer	M		H		M	
4. Instrument Change			H	H		
5. Population Restrictions		H	H	H	H	H
6. Content Restrictions		H	H	H	H	H
7. Stability of Content		H	H	H	H	H
8. Dross Rate		M	H	H	H	H
9. Closed to Serendipity	H					
10. Lack of Replicability	H		H	M		

Note: H = high susceptibility; M = moderate susceptibility; Blank = low susceptibility.

FIGURE 4-4 Potential Weaknesses of Techniques
Source: Adapted from Runkel, P.J., & McGrath, J.E. (1972) *Research on human behavior: A systematic guide to method.* New York: Holt, Rinehart, & Winston (p. 191).

3. *Influence of observer characteristics.* Personal and obvious features of the investigator such as race, gender, age, manner of dress, etc., will have effects on the actor. This is based on assumptions the actor might make about the investigator and what the latter would agree with or reinforce through approval. Thus, typical behavior of male athletes in a locker room is likely to be distorted if a female reporter is there conducting an interview. Racists are likely to modify their opinions in a more moderate direction if a black newscaster is asking questions.

4. *Instrument change.* The quality of data produced by many qualitative techniques are a function of the skill and conscientiousness of the observer or the investigator. The latter becomes the "instrument." But unlike a standardized questionnaire, the process of repeated use of human instruments can bring about change. Interviewers can get better at asking questions as a result of practice. Alternatively, nonparticipant observers can, over time, become bored with a resultant lack of attention to what is going on. Similarly, after many phone surveys, the staff person may start to anticipate answers to certain questions and stop really listening.

5. *Population restrictions.* This refers to a set of factors that can limit the validity of our assertions regarding the population to which we may want to generalize, and even those made about the sample itself. More specifically, who we choose to observe, measure, interview, etc., may be inappropriate. They could be of the wrong type or be nonrepresentative. Similarly, the times or the locations where we observe may cause us to include some people and not others. Studying work relationships at a single branch bank may lead to misleading impressions, especially if it were to be done on Saturday morning.

6. *Restriction of content.* This refers to the fact that different techniques may not be able to get at domains of interest. One of the reasons that self-reports (especially questionnaires) are so popular is that they are felt to be suitable for getting at inner feelings and intentions. These things are difficult at best to infer solely from other techniques like direct observation.

7. *Stability of content.* When we choose to take our measurements and where this occurs will have an impact on the information that we obtain. To study public sector managers at the end of a fiscal year will lead to different (potentially erroneous) conclusions than if it were to be done at different (perhaps randomly selected) times.

8. *Dross rate.* This is reflected in the proportion of observations that result in usable data. In a sense it's related to the efficiency of the technique for the purpose at hand. If one were to study industrial accidents through systematic observation, there would be a great deal of wasted effort in terms of the number of hours of observation needed to detect and describe a single accident. They are, in an absolute sense, rare events. On the other hand, reviewing accident reports in an archives would yield a great deal of information. It should be noted however, that the latter may have limited value for other reasons (e.g., they may reflect idiosyncratic reporting, their public/official nature may have induced a bias).

9. *Preclusion of serendipity.* It has been known for some time that a skilled researcher can make an important discovery by being open to and noticing aspects of a phenomenon that are not the initial focus of an investigation but which turn out to be important later (Daft, 1983). Certain methods are more likely to support this attitude than others and allow access to a wide range of properties of objects of study. One of the strengths of participant observation is that the researcher, once immersed in the context of interest,

can detect and process enormous quantities of information. In contrast, if relevant questions are not asked on a mail survey, potential data are lost to the investigator.

10. *Preclusion of replicability.* To what extent is it possible to go back and get new or independent observations on the same or comparable set of events? Field notes of a researcher may be limited in this regard because their content and quality are a function of the rapport he or she had with members of the organization, the unique skills brought to the task, and the transitory nature of the phenomenon itself (e.g., the strike episode studied is now over). It would have low replicability. On the other hand, conducting a second survey of a comparably sampled group of employees might be quite feasible for any number of research topics.

All of these sources of invalidity are potentially present in any set of observations. It is also true that some methods are better than others under certain circumstances. Webb et al. (1966) recommend that the sources should be treated as plausible alternative hypotheses for a given pattern of findings. Thus, they need to be evaluated in this light. The other message of this section is that there is indeed some advantage to using multiple methods of measurement to deal with the potential weakness of any one technique. This is another way of saying that triangulation is a relevant strategy in many contexts.

TECHNIQUES FOR QUALITATIVE RESEARCH

This chapter already has made reference to techniques used by qualitative researchers. However, in this section a set of those techniques that are used more widely will be discussed in some detail. Particular applications also will be described. Once again, remember that any of the methods described, with modification, can be used as well in research of more complex designs (e.g., experiments) with alternative goals in mind (e.g., theory testing). They are being introduced here because they have been found to be particularly useful for describing organizations and organizational life.

Systematic Observation

Nature of Systematic Direct Observation. While all of us have the occasion to observe and comment on human nature, scientific direct observation can be distinguished from this more casual version by several features. Bickman (1976) states that observation is scientific when it serves a formulated research purpose, is planned systematically, is recorded systematically, and is subjected to certain checks and controls for quality. To put it another way, Weick (1968, p. 360) describes scientific observation as "involving the selection, provocation, recording and encoding that set of behaviors and settings concerning organizations 'in situ' consistent with aims."

While many fields of social science have made use of observational methods (psychology, economics, organizational studies) it has been most refined in the hands of sociologists and anthropologists. When used by the latter it is sometimes referred to as part of (along with informant interviewing) the ethnographic method (Sanday, 1979).

When applied to cultural anthropology, the goal of systematic observation has been to obtain a complete understanding of a given group or society. Usually this includes one or more of the following objectives: (a) identifying the general themes of the culture, with reference to the way that functions get fulfilled (e.g., socialization of new members); (b) developing an appreciation of the native's point of view, including standards of thought and interpretation; and (c) gathering data in preselected categories of behavior (Sanday, 1979). The researcher usually is most interested in description but also seeks to gain some level of understanding as well.

To be effective in the ethnographic method, the field-worker must be trained in the method and—armed with notebooks, a tape recorder, and even a camera—must be prepared for a lengthy stay in the setting of interest. In practice the specifics of the effort will depend upon the personal tastes of the researcher and the goals involved, whether it be to focus on the whole, the meaning, or the particular behaviors of culture to be studied.

When done well systematic observation can provide insights regarding not only what occurred but the time and duration of phenomena. It can uncover the nature of the relationships of the various parts to the whole and characterize interpersonal and group processes over time. As pointed out earlier, it is sufficiently flexible to allow for the discovery of the unanticipated and the development of new insights. It also can be quantified. In short, systematic observation allows the researcher to get at the "deep structure" of person and systems properties along with the consequences of their interaction (Light, 1979).

One of the most often cited efforts in organizational research— the so called Hawthorne Studies—made heavy use of systematic observation. In particular, as noted in Chapter 1, the third series of studies conducted at the Hawthorne works of the Western Electric Company in Chicago during the period of 1931–1932 produced great insights into the nature of social relationships in the workplace (Baritz, 1960; Bramel & Friend, 1981; Roethlisberger & Dickson, 1939). In these studies, investigators from Harvard University spent many hours watching teams of men in the Bank Wiring Room assemble the telephone switching equipment in an effort to understand better what could account for levels of productivity.

At the time of this investigation, managers and researchers had a view of the worker and worker performance which emphasized financial incentives. In the case of the Bank Wiring Room, because the work involved five to seven men putting together a single large switching device, the company had instituted a group bonus plan to spur production. Under this payment plan, the greater the output (in terms of the number of switches completed) the more money would be placed into lump-sum payments to be equally divided among team members. This money for bonuses would be over and above the payment of any hourly wage.

Despite the potential for some fairly large bonuses, however, the output of the work groups was remarkably consistent. They typically made between one and two switching assemblies a day. Mayo, Warner, and their colleagues from Harvard chose to study these groups to see what could be learned about this (Roethlisberger & Dickson, 1939).

Using the method of observation, a great deal was uncovered. Over time, the researchers discovered that a complex network of social relationships actually controlled a large amount of work group behavior. Most startling was the way groups seem to regulate production. Individuals were found not to be working as hard as they could be, and they appeared to be performing at some level that was felt by the employees to be a "fair day's work." Group members, especially informal leaders, used a variety of techniques (from teasing to social ostracism) to prevent deviation from the group's expectations with regard to performance. It also seemed clear that this informal influence process protected the work group from management pressure for higher production as well. If one team (or individual) demonstrated extraordinary output during any one period of time, management would be certain to demand it of everyone.

Given our current understanding of work group dynamics (see Chapter 7), these discoveries seem less than impressive to us today. Nonetheless, they represent a radically different view of the workplace than was held by both researchers and managers of the company at that time.

The previous analysis of the various threats of observation and recording methods to the validity of research data identified the importance of the relationship of the investigator as observer to the individuals being observed. This theme is particularly relevant to direct observation as a technique.

Bickman (1976) distinguishes between situations where there is to be interaction by the subjects of study with the observer versus situations in which the latter is hidden or concealed. The researcher can act as a full participant, a participant observer, or a strict observer. Bickman also suggests that the researcher may adopt differing attitudes with regard to involvement. At an extreme, he or she may act as a provocateur and may attempt to affect the situation in order to be able to better study the phenomenon of interest.

The issue of concealment relates to concerns for potential reactivity or what Weick (1968) has termed observer interference. In many cases, the actual or presumed presence of the researcher will change a subject's behavior. Sometimes this effect is transitory. For example, in the Hawthorne Studies it took some time before the investigators came to be trusted and for the work groups to reveal their normal routines. More often, unconcealed direct observation continues to produce atypical behavior.

Johnson and Bolstad (1973) identified several factors which influence the effects of reactivity. Among them, the level of conspicuousness in the observation, the personal characteristics of the individuals being studied, and specific features of the observer (e.g., status). Most importantly, the purposes of the observation (real or imagined on the part of the subject) will affect the levels of anxiety or apprehension felt by those under scrutiny. To the extent that the latter perceive potential harm (e.g., loss of esteem) as a consequence of being studied by someone, one would expect efforts at self-protection in the form of behavior change. Unless the investigator is actually interested in studying the effects of being observed, the resultant changed behavior creates problems for valid inference.

As a participant observer, the researcher is involved in organization life in some regular way. Thus, he or she has a job to do or a role to enact while being an observer. Van Maanen (1975), for example, functioned as a police officer the entire time he was researching how that type of para-military organization went about socializing new recruits. In participant observation, occupying a particular role is felt to give the researcher special insights. Clearly, it places special demands on a person as well.

One of the central issues related to participative observation is the extent to which the people being studied are aware of the presence of the investigator. At one extreme, this fact can be completely hidden. A researcher, somewhat like an espionage agent under deep cover, gains entry into the organization without telling anyone about it. In fact, this may be more common in novels than in social science research (although there are some exceptions). A more common model is for the researcher to make arrangements with key people in an organization (e.g., a senior manager) to carry out a study, with a general announcement being made as to the project's existence and the methods to be involved. But this last arrangement does not ensure that particular employees under study are aware of their situation when they are actually in a conversation with the investigator. Such announcements easily can be forgotten. Thus, unless the researcher clarifies his or her role at the point of contact, the employees involved may remain ignorant of their role as subjects. Van Maanen (1979) describes how difficult it was building a trust relationship with coworkers in order to get around being misled by presentational data while still reminding subjects in subtle ways that they were the objects of his research. Moreover, he found it hard to keep his roles as a coworker and an investigator separate.

This last point raises aspects of another dimension of the observation technique that Bickman (1976) labels as intervention. By this he means both the intentional and unintentional ways in which the investigator can affect the processes under study (p. 285). As a hidden or passive observer, the hope is that there will be minimal effects from the act of observation. As a participative observer, this is most difficult to guarantee. Being an actor in the setting, the investigator is bound to have some effect. On the other hand, there are times when the researcher desires to stimulate or provoke the system in order to better understand certain dynamics. For example, the researcher may sit in certain proximity to others in a park to observe their reactions (e.g., Campbell, Kruskal, & Wallace, 1966). Or he or she may volunteer to help out the individuals to be studied. For example, Humphreys (1970) wished to study the behavior of homosexuals who used public bathrooms in parks for their activities. Rather than approach potential subjects as a sociologist, he joined the group to serve as a lookout for the police. Ethical risks associated with this plan have been debated at length, but it did allow him to observe the activities of interest without actually having to participate in them (Bickman, 1976).

In this regard, Salancik (1979) describes and advocates what he calls *field stimulations* in which the researcher "makes things happen" and then observes how the people and the system operate under these circumstances. The kinds of things he refers to would include sending memos to key people in organizations, simulating a need for help, or attempting to negotiate the price of a loaf of bread at a supermarket. He argues that this is a legitimate way to gain insight about organizations without having to get their permission to do so. He implies that this would tend to reduce a bias that has crept into organizational studies where findings have been based on data from only those companies who have been willing to be scrutinized. Moreover, it would reduce the amount of dross in a period of observation. The researcher would be on the spot of the event. In its most systematic form, the field stimulation would become a field experiment (see Chapter 11). He does acknowledge, however, legal and ethical parameters to this approach.

Methods of Observation. There are any number of specific activities associated with carrying out observations. However it is useful to distinguish between relatively unstructured versus structured approaches.

In general, the unstructured approach is a hallmark of the qualitative researcher. To reiterate, for many investigators the goal is to obtain a rich, in-depth description of an organization, its people, or one or more aspects of its functioning. In using *unstructured observation* a high degree of contact with the people or entities of interest is presumed. The investigator would start out with a set of tentative hypotheses and use these to guide, how, who, when, and where observations are conducted while being open to new directions.

Observations of this sort are usually recorded in field notes. Whenever possible, this would be done at the time of an event of interest. Where taking notes would be intrusive physically, skill in mental note taking becomes invaluable. In any event, ad hoc material must be reviewed daily and placed into a more systematic form. Thus, unstructured observation can still be systematic.

The content of field notes will be related to the research question involved. However, Bickman (1976), Bouchard (1976), and Weick (1968) would argue that they would include a description of the following: participants involved, the setting, the apparent purpose of the event/exchange, the activities or social behavior, and the frequency or duration of events.

The notes should be detailed and concrete. They should reflect what occurred with minimal inferences by the observer. They may however, make reference to the observer's feelings at the time, perhaps to indicate what was suprising or unexpected, or to reveal any potential bias created by his or her mood. Good field notes often will include quotations. To the extent that the notes "can communicate the rules for proper and predictible conduct as judged by the people studied" the observer has produced a successful product (Sanday, 1979, p. 529). More will be said about the issue of quality observations as applied to ratings in Chapter 6.

While the emphasis of this chapter is on description and on the theory generation goals of qualitative research, direct observation as a method is, more often than not, highly structured and systematic. It holds an important position in almost all areas of social science investigation. In fact, *structured observation* is usually conducted in such a manner so as to produce data suitable for quantitative analysis. Because it is so widespread, this approach to direct observation will be described in some detail.

Structured observation is based upon a clearly articulated definition of the important features of the people, behavior, or setting as envisioned by the investigator. These, in turn may derive from extensive prior experience, from a particular theory, or from past empirical research. To put it another way, the researcher has a good idea going into the study of who to talk to, and when to take observations, and what should be recorded. Just as importantly, the researcher also is relatively sure of what can be ignored (Smith, 1981).

The potential designated attributes of features to be attended to are enormous. Moreover there are no taxonomies or standardized lists of behaviors, actions, etc., to guide us. Ultimately these will relate to the goals for research. However, most of the time the recording activity will include rating or coding some aspect of the following (Smith, 1981):

1. *Form.* This is defined as the features of interest.
2. *Duration.* This is defined as the length of time the form lasts.
3. *Frequency.* This is defined as the number of times an event occurs (occasionally indexed in terms of rate of occurrence).
4. *Antecedent/consequent phenomena.* This is defined as what happens before or after the target event.

Weick (1968) distinguishes the following four classes of phenomena (forms) commonly of interest to social scientists:

1. *Linguistic.* This includes what gets said, to whom, with what apparent intent, and to what effect. This is a very prevalent focus, and several standardized formats for recording exist.
2. *Extralinguistic behaviors.* These are vocal dimensions of pitch, loudness, etc.; temporal features like rates of speaking; and stylistic aspects of speech (e.g., level of complexity).
3. *Body movement.* These include facial expressions.
4. *Spatial relations.* The focus here would be on how space is used and how people position themselves in relation to others.

In addition, investigators interested in studying some aspect of organizations might tend to focus on the following: (a) task relevant behaviors (including the sequence involved), (b) tools and technology used, (c) manifestations of affect/emotion, (d) levels of effectiveness, and (e) behaviors on which to base inferences regarding traits or qualities.

In the area of work measurement, structured observations are used to generate data for such practical purposes as work design, staffing levels, job classification, and compensation levels. Smith (1978) argues that here the focus should be on activities that have several key attributes. That is, they would be easily observable, mutually exclusive, collectively exhaustive, and reasonable in number. In light of the fact that the conduct of work measurement studies can be controversial and the outcome of such studies so relevant to so many people, Smith (1978) emphasizes that the nature and number of activities that are to be indexed be carefully determined and ultimately defensible.

The actual recording involved in structured observation rarely takes the form of prose as written in field notes. Instead, the investigator would be likely to develop worksheets to facilitate the structured observation. Frequently, these are formatted as checklists. The observer indexes whether something occurred or did not occur by placing a checkmark in the space provided. Here, the record of observation is the frequency with which something was seen. This is the essence of work measurement as practiced by human factors psychologists and industrial engineers (Smith, 1978). Figure 4-5 shows such a work sampling data form.

More likely, however, the observer will attempt to classify a behavior that is observed as belonging to one category or another. In other words, the bulk of structured observation in organizational research makes use of specially constructed rating scales. Here the investigator records, according to a pre-established format, impressions or inferences with regard to the frequency or the amount or the quality of something (e.g., work behavior). Figure 4-6 illustrates a behavior rating scale created for the purpose of indexing effectiveness in conducting performance appraisal interviews. Notice that the investigator must use judgments to use this scale (e.g., judgments as to what frequency of occurrence warrants a rating of "always" and judgments regarding lack of the behavior domains). More will be said about this in Chapter 6 when we apply such observation techniques to performance appraisal.

One area in which those interested in behavior in organizations have used observation is in the study of the nature of jobs. For a wide variety of practical reasons we often want to know just what duties, tasks, tools, activities, etc., are performed, used or exhibited by workers. In Chapter 5, for example, information based on job observations will be seen as relevant to establishing models of effective job performance. Similarly, any number of theories have been proposed where job attributes or characteristics are felt to be important to worker attitudes and behavior (e.g., Hackman & Oldham, 1976). These, too, require the measurement of jobs.

To illustrate, Jenkins, Nadler, Lawler, and Cammann (1975) investigated the use of observations to get at the characteristics of jobs. They trained 35 staff members in a two-day workshop in order to observe a total of 448 employees for two hours each. They also had the employees interviewed about their job. Thus, they could compare observation with interview-based impressions.

The observation instrument included 59 questions designed to get at a wide variety of job factors. An example of the items used appears in Figure 4-7. The majority of the items were responded to on six-point rating scales.

In the study, each worker was observed twice for one hour each time. The observations were carried out so that the two hours were separated by at least two days and were conducted at different times of a day. Two different staff people did the two observations. In order to cross-check their results, 48 employees were observed by the two staff people at the very same time. Finally, it is useful to note that the observation hour was structured so that the staff person spent 10 minutes becoming oriented to the worker and his or her job, 30 minutes observing specific job actions, and 20 minutes in the setting filling out the form. The staff then typically spent 15 minutes away from the job site completing the observation form.

In an unstructured observation the field-worker must make decisions as to what to record on a regular and continuous basis. In the structured approach a similar set of decisions are involved. In the latter case they are done a priori, well before data are gathered. Some of these

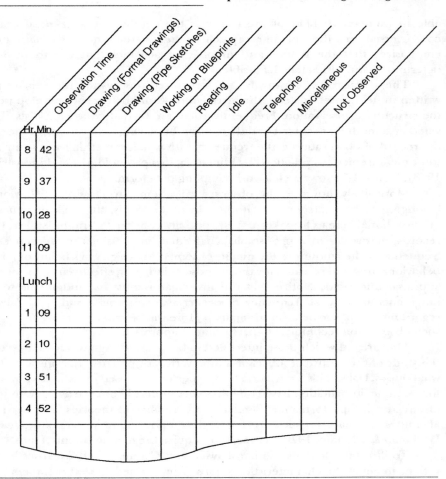

FIGURE 4-5 Work Sampling Data Form of the Sort Used to Record the Occasion of Occurrence of Work Activities
Source: Smith, G.L., Jr. (1978). *Work measurement: A systems approach.* Columbus, OH: Grid Publishing, Inc. Reprinted with permission.

decisions have already been alluded to, others have not (these derive from Bickman, 1976; Smith, 1981; Bouchard, 1976). Thus, prior to making direct observations, the researcher would need to resolve the following issues:

1. *Unit of observation.* What should the unit be? In particular, how molar or molecular should it be? For example, in behavior observation, one could record each activity exhibited (opening letters) or choose to cluster these into the tasks that are fulfilled by performing the activity in context (dealing with customer complaints).

   It's clear that while any number of actions or behaviors can be observed and recorded, investigators usually focus on instances or events that are theoretically or practically meaningful. For example, in a study of the behaviors of coaches, Curtis, Smith, and Smok (1979) chose to observe behaviors reflecting such things as reinforcement,

Use the following scale to index your observations of how the employee conducts performance appraisal interviews.

Always = 1
Often = 2
Occasionally = 3
Seldom = 4
Never = 5

_____ 1. Maintained control over the interview.
_____ 2. Probed deeply into sensitive areas in order to gain knowledge.
_____ 3. Asked appropriate questions.
_____ 4. Displayed insensitivity to the subordinate's problems.
_____ 5. Responded to the subordinate's outbursts in a rational manner.
_____ 6. Used appropriate complements regarding the subordinate's technical expertise.
_____ 7. Projected sincerity during the interivew.
_____ 8. Skillfully guided discussion through the problem areas.
_____ 9. Provided good advice about resolving conflict.
_____ 10. Appeared defensive in reaction to the subordinate's complaints.

FIGURE 4-6   Example of a Rating Scale Used to Characterize Job Behavior
Source: Adapted from Bernardin, H.J., & Beatty, R.W. (1984). *Performance appraisal: Assessing human behavior at work.* Boston, MA: Kent

encouragement after mistakes, or technical instruction. These were felt to be related to or to cause player behavior. Player behavior, in turn, would affect key outcome variables such as (in this study) player attitudes toward the team and ultimately the team's win/loss record. In fact, observations of the number of "punishment" behaviors observed correlated negatively with the team's win/loss record (-.35, and -.37) for the two years of their study. The coach's behaviors did make a difference, but in this case, in the negative direction!

2. *Intensitivity verses extensivity.* Just how much detail should be recorded? Or, are broad, general descriptions adequate?

3. *Observer knowledge.* How much information should the observer have with regard to the purposes of the study and/or the research hypotheses? On the one hand, more information might aid the observer by clarifying what to look for and allowing for serendipity. On the other hand, specific knowledge can induce a bias into the observations made. That is, knowing what the investigation is all about, the person might look for specific occurrences or might be prone to make inferences from observations that favor the research goals. Thus, as a rule, it is usually better to inform an individual generating observations for research only to the level needed for them to adequately do the job. In other words, it's appropriate for the observer to be blind as to the research hypothesis.

4. *Observer inference.* To what extent should the observer have to estimate, conclude, or infer what is to be recorded (e.g., some level of effectiveness). Or should he or she simply be describing what is actually seen or not seen? As noted, most structured systems do require some inference on the part of the investigator.

5. *Time unit for measurement.* The period of structured observation could last from a few seconds or hours. The stream of behavior or events can be arbitrarily broken into

Scale and Operation

Variety
1. How much *variety* is there in the job?
2. The job requires an individual to do the same things over and over again.
3. The job provides an individual the opportunity to do a number of different kinds of things at work.

Autonomy
4. How much *autonomy* is there in the job?
5. The job allows an individual to make a lot of decisions on his/her own.
6. The job *denies* the individual any chance to use his/her personal initiative or discretion at work.
7. He/she is given enough freedom to decide how to do his own work.

External Feedback
8. To what extent does the employee *find out* how well he/she is doing on the job from his/her *supervisor or co-workers*?
9. The co-workers of an individual working on the job never tell the person whether he/she is doing well or poorly.
10. Supervisors generally let a person working on the job know how well they think he/she is performing.

Task Feedback
11. To what extent does doing the *job itself* provide the employee with "*feedback*" about how well he/she is doing?
12. Just doing the work required by the job provides many opportunities for a person to figure out how well he/she is doing.
13. The individual can see the results of his/her work.

Rigidity
14. How *rigid* does the employee appear to be in his/her attitudes and manner of working?
15. The individual working on this job appears to be one who would have difficulty adapting to new and unusual situations.

Certainty
16. How much *uncertainty* is there in the job?
17. How *sure* does the employee seem in his/her job as to whether *certain things will work out as expected*?
18. The job requires the individual to be prepared to handle surprising or unpredictable situations.
19. The job is one that is highly predictable, and that rarely presents the individual with surprising or unexpected problems.

FIGURE 4-7 Scales Guiding the Observation of Work for Research on Task Properties
Source: Reprinted with permission from Jenkins, G.D., Nadler, D.A., Lawler, E., and Cammann, C. (1975). Standardized observation: An approach to measuring the nature of jobs. *Journal of Applied Psychology, 60,* 171–181.

shorter or longer episodes for classification or rating. Jenkins et al. (1975) chose to get two hours of observation in their study.

6. *Recording and coding of the behavior/event stream.* Should the behavior/event stream be recorded and coded in its entirety? Or, more likely, how should it be sampled? In this regard one can use time or event sampling. Bickman (1976) argues that to do event sampling (e.g., of accidents) requires a great deal of prior knowledge regarding the frequency, duration, and location of a particular phenomenon. The investigator must

be there exactly when the event occurs. On the other hand, time sampling implies not only precise definitions of what an event of interest is, but what time frame is most appropriate (five minutes or one hour). The issue of time sampling has been extensively investigated in the context of work measurement (Campion & Thayer, 1985; Fleishman, 1982).

In time sampling, observations are taken according to a plan. This may imply regular (every half hour) episodes or a random sampling. In the latter instance, electronic devices programmed for the purpose may be used to alert the investigator as to just when to record what is occurring. Observations taken on a random basis are frequently seen as part of a job analysis effort designed to obtain a complete description of what work is involved and the knowledges, skills and abilities required to perform it. Observational sampling is a complicated issue and, thus, the interested reader is referred to Bickman (1976) or Altmann (1973) for greater detail.

7. *The use of electronic recording devices.* Current technology is such that the researcher could record observations on film or video tape. These could then be viewed and coded later. However, unless disguised, this is likely to be quite intrusive and may interfere with the events to be studied. Alternatively, there exist very compact and portable event recorders that might be used instead of a checklist or rating scale. These are less obtrusive and can facilitate data reduction and coding. Indeed, with one it is possible to input data, maintain a cumulative record of the information of interest, and to have an immediate preliminary analysis of the results at the time that the last observation has been entered. Hidden recording, however, does raise ethical issues of informed consent. These are discussed in greater depth later.

Assessing the Quality of Observation Data. How do you ensure the quality of observational data? The answer is a complex one and depends to a great extent on whether the focus is on a structured or unstructured approach. As one might expect, the guidelines will be clearer in the case of the structured observations.

Several writers (Miles, 1979; Sieber, 1973) have commented on how little has been written with regard to how one makes sense of a large mass of qualitative data. In judging the quality of unstructured observations, they point out that traditional ways of checking on the quality of the information derived from unstructured observations prior to any data reduction, analysis, and interpretion may not be appropriate. For example, certain indices of reliability commonly applied to quantifiable data, don't make sense in the case of participant observation where, as a result of personal qualities, different researchers are likely to both affect and record a behavior episode in different ways. This is likely to occur even if the investigator has no preconceived notions about the phenomenon under study. Thus, estimating the quality of data from unstructured observations will in itself involve some subjectivity.

Sanday (1979) argues that good data in the form of field notes and summaries only can be obtained by individuals who are well trained and who are dispositionally suited for ethnography. Such individuals must have ample practice and experience in diverse and unfamiliar settings so that they come to understand what it means to see something as outsiders. Sanday suggests that the capacity for empathy and the ability to respond as a whole person are important personal characteristics. The field-worker must be willing to learn to use himself or herself "as the principal and most reliable instrument of observation, selection, coordination and interpretation" (p.528).

Assessing the quality of resulting descriptions is not easy. Because the goal is to "communicate the rules for proper and predictable conduct as judged by the people studied," the qualitative researcher, using unstructured techniques, will be considered successful if he or she "is like a linguist who has studied and recorded a foreign language so that others can learn the rules for producing intelligible speech in that language" (Sanday, 1979, p. 529). Somewhat more operationally, as a result of the summaries produced, can one anticipate the "scenes" of a society?

Van Maanen (1979) warns that the participant observer should be aware constantly of his or her own assumptions or misdirection caused by informants unable or unwilling to share key information. Ultimately, he suggests, when it comes to "analysis and verification . . . it is something one brings forth with them from the field" (p. 548). Jick (1979) relies on the triangulation model and looks for consistencies across data sets obtained with different methods. He especially relies on the extent to which qualitative and quantitative data help to explain each other. In his study of the effects of a merger between two organizations he found that archive and interview data were consistently related to high employee turnover. Thus, in general, many researchers come to have greater confidence in the validity of their data when they find consistency among observers and across methods.

Finally, a brief discussioin on how Miles (1979) approached the issue of assessing the quality of observation in data reduction and analysis for a study of innovation in public schools is offered to illustrate an actual case in assessing data quality. Miles acknowledges that it was a frustrating experience. Multiple techniques were involved. Each of six sites was visited weekly by a field-worker for a half or full day. Senior project staff would also go to sites from time to time. This took place over a period of almost three years! Direct observation and key informant interviewing were supplemented by document collection; a few retrospective interviews; a brief, individually administered questionnaire; and two waves of surveys directed toward teachers, administrators, students, and parents.

The qualitative data gathered in Mile's research were the most problematic. At first, the many pages of field notes were to be analyzed in terms of 202 categories of events reflecting combinations of actors and activities. Field-workers and coding specialists found this approach to be unworkable. Ultimately, 26 major themes were adopted and applied. By this time, it was the field-worker's own impressions that carried the most weight in any coding.

Originally, site summaries were produced. Some of these were direct summaries that could be fed back to organization members. Others were for staff use and contained more in the way of inference and interpretation. Miles learned through experience that a lot of the actual analysis was going on in the mind of the field-worker at the time of the recording. Site updates were added to site summaries to recap recent developments. All these, in turn, were reviewed in team meetings that occurred every few weeks. It was at these meetings that a great deal of discussion took place as to just what constitutes the innovation process in the school system. Once again the opinions of the field-worker were given great weight.

The project team developed a series of case studies built around the data and discussions. But the "actual process of analysis during case writing was essentially intuitive, primitive and unmanagable in any rational sense" (Miles, 1979, p.597).

The final cases looked good but some attempt at validation was tried through a feedback process to the sites. Once again, problems were encountered. It was discovered, for example, that there was no possibility of real anonymity in the cases. Even without being named, people at a site knew the actors involved. Some people felt vulnerable; information not previously shared was now widely available. There were attempts at self-aggrandizement and self-protection. Some threatened law suits. In the end, there were attempts at "rewriting history." Ironically, this tendency was most pronounced where the cases were most rich and detailed. While site members seemed to accept the pattern of survey results, they usually challenged quotes or direct descriptions of their behavior (p.97).

Finally, in the Miles study, evidence for quality was inferred through a process of comparing and contrasting data from the six sites. It is risky, although not uncommon, to look for and rely on expected or ostensibly reasonable patterns in the data as evidence of the adequacy of a methodology. This occurred in the present case. But Miles acknowledges that, if anything, the cross-site analysis was even less developed than the within-site analysis. Given the complexities and the problems encountered in this admittedly large-scale application of qualitative methods, it's no wonder that he has titled his paper "Qualitative Data as an Attractive Nuisance."

Structured observation techniques usually are favored because they can produce quantitative data. More to the point, this approach allows the investigator to assess the quality of data resulting from structured observation using well-developed, logical, and usually mathematical procedures. Thus, just about any approach found useful in establishing the reliability, the construct validity, or the content validity of a measure might be used for this purpose. Inasmuch as these notions are treated in Chapters 2 and 3, only a few points will be stressed here.

It goes without saying that the training of these observers who are to generate the structured observations is absolutely essential to attain quality. Individuals who are to be observers must have a clear and common understanding of the categories to be used and how to apply them. In general, it is easier to be accurate with smaller number of categories and with less inference required on the part of the observer to apply to these categories (Weick, 1968). However, the key to achieving quality through training will be the amount of practice (with feedback) involved.

Commonly, observers are trained with the use of videotaped stimuli, which allows for the presentation of standardized experiences for any number of potential observers, even when they might be at different locations. The use of videotapes provides a way to verify the accuracy (in terms of both what gets observed and what gets overlooked) of the trainee's recorded observations. Thus, the latter can be compared with what is actually presented on tape. Tape playback with discussion will also facilitate the correction of errors and provide a basis for constructive feedback. One word of caution might be noted, however. Despite the usefulness of this kind of training, it is not likely to be sufficient. Practice must be continued and include supervised experience in the field or in the setting in which the observational data of interest will actually be obtained.

The specific indexing of the quality of data from structured observations can be accomplished in a variety of ways. However, it is most common to demonstrate that the data show inter-observer (or interrater) reliability (Bickman, 1976). In its most simple form, this is accomplished by having two or more trained observers independently record their impressions of actual or programmed stimulus material using the same recording and coding system that has been developed. Computations are then carried out to determine the extent to which the observers agree in what and how they record what they see. Frequently, this is summarized in the form of a percent of agreement score:

$$\text{Score} = \frac{\text{Number of Agreements}}{\text{Number of agreements} + \text{Number of disagreements}} \tag{4.1}$$

Of course, a low score on this index may reflect the fact that one or more than one of the observers is in error. The investigator would have to determine who and what is in error. In Chapter 3, we described other approaches to the assessment of reliability as well.

In the Jenkins et al. (1975) study of the nature of jobs described earlier, the following three approaches were used to establish the quality of the observations obtained.

1. *Repeatability.* Recall that the observations were made in two ways. Staff studied jobs at two points in time for an hour each time and at one point in time. Indices of agreement between the two sets of observers could then be computed. While the authors considered the percent of agreement score just noted they chose to use a statistic known as Cohen's weighted Kappa (Cohen, 1960; 1968), which provides an estimate of agreement that corrects for chance and allows for partial agreement to be recognized in a set of scores. (See Chapter 3 for more on Kappa.)

2. *Homogeneity.* This refers to the extent a set of observations appear to be indexing the same thing (e.g., the actual amount of effort required by the job). Jenkins et al. (1975) wanted high homogeneity for those observations recorded on the same section of their rating form. They used a formula referred to as a homogeneity ratio (Scott, 1960), which produces evidence regarding the internal consistency of measurement across a set of items. The authors felt that it was superior to other options for indexing internal consistency, such as Cronbach's alpha (see Chapter 3).

3. *Convergence.* This aspect of data quality reflects the extent to which the data from the various scales of the observation form, when related to the data on the same scales obtained from the interviews, produced the same results. Thus, judgments of a worker's autonomy based on observations of the worker are expected to relate to autonomy judgments based on an interview with the worker. On the other hand, both sets of ratings should be different from those measuring other job dimensions (e.g., skill variety).

The authors used a form of a multitrait-multimethod matrix analysis (discussed in Chapter 3) to establish a degree of convergence for the five dimensions or constructs of interest. In this study, the observers did have trouble discriminating among the dimensions of variety, skill level, certainty, autonomy, and pace control; but, they could separate all of these from levels of cooperation with others displayed on the job.

It should be noted that the issue of observational quality is a complicated one and the indexes used will depend on both the assumptions that the investigator makes as well as the purpose of the research. For example, Jones, Johnson, Butler, and Main (1983) found that different indexes of interrater agreement (i.e., repeatability) did not produce the same scores for a given set of data. In their study, the weighted Kappa statistic produced the lowest (most conservative) values of the six approaches evaluated. But, the impact of using one over another was much more dramatic when dealing with items than dealing with clusters of items (like scales or dimensions).

Where observers are processing material that is presented in some standardized or programmed way (as when videotaped segments of work interactions are used), the investigator can go beyond simple agreement measures and compute accuracy scores. This is a prevalent approach in the determination of data quality produced as a result of training of those who are to observe and record aspects of job effectiveness (Bernardin & Beatty, 1984). Thus, with taped stimuli one can determine whose observations are in error and the nature of the errors made.

The analysis of data generated from structured observation usually parallels what would be done with quantitative data produced by other techniques (e.g., questionnaires). Thus, the computation of frequencies, means, and variances is typical. These in turn, can then be subjected to appropriate analytic designs (e.g., Analysis of Variance) and statistical tests.

Research Interview

Interviews are quite common in organizational studies. In organization practices, interviews are key assessment tools in personnel selection and promotion (Arvey, 1979; Schmitt, 1976). As a research technique they are most frequently seen in the context of survey work. Thus, Chapter 10 emphasizes the way the design and conduct of interviews carried out face to face or over the telephone can affect the outcome of systematic attitude and opinion surveys. In this chapter, special applications of the research interview will be reviewed. The point to be made is that it is an excellent vehicle for obtaining qualitative information as well.

Interviews have been characterized as conversations with a purpose. As a technique for qualitative research, they are used to gain insights regarding how individuals attend to, perceive, or otherwise deal with some phenomenon of interest. Another important feature to note is that interviews are dynamic. The nature of the exchanges that take place between the interviewer and the respondent will vary over time and be affected by such things as the needs and behaviors of both parties, their relationship, the skill of the researcher, the topics to be covered, and the context in which the interview is taking place.

This dynamism of the research interview is both a strength and a liability. On the one hand, it allows for flexibility and efficiency. Unlike the questionnaire that programs the respondent to answer a fixed set of questions in a prescribed order, the interview allows the researcher to pursue productive and appropriate lines of inquiry. In fact, unanticipated and entirely new directions of questioning can be conducted, if so desired. But this dynamism implies difficulty in imposing standardization on the process. Thus, it is hard to ensure that, across interviews, all respondents will face the same questions, in the same order, and posed in the same manner.

As a result of this dynamism, a special problem facing those who use the interview is the need to be responsive and to maintain rapport with the interviewee, while staying on track and following the research agenda. In a sense, the investigator is like a participant observer who must be a part of the process while remaining somewhat removed from it all. As will be pointed out below, this becomes even more complicated when a group interview is involved.

Issues to Be Addressed in the Research Interview. It seems rather straightforward to assert that the researcher should be attentive to the issue of who should be interviewed. In many situations the qualitative interview is conducted because very little is known about a phenomena or area. In fact, a study's objective very well may be to establish who should be targeted for a more systematic survey. It may even be appropriate, however, to use intact groups (e.g., club members) in the form of what are called *opportunity samples* if the kind of knowledge or experience of interest is thought to be widely shared. These points notwithstanding, normally those people (units, dependents, etc.) who are representative of the population of interest would be interviewed. If the population can be clearly defined, and the goal is to generalize with regard to findings, it is correct to select a scientifically drawn sample for the purposes of interviewing.

In organizational settings and in market research, there usually is some advantage to ensure that formal and informal (opinion) leaders are included in a sample. These people often have well-developed and articulated views and, thus, would constitute a rich source of data. Moreover, to involve such individuals early in an investigation conveys an importance and legitimacy to the effort (Bouchard, 1976). Key informants may be selected for their presumed specific knowledge. For example, more senior people may be interviewed because of their capacity to provide an historical perspective. Similarly, new hirees, the frustrated or disgruntled employee, or those who are outside of the mainstream of organizational life may be targeted because they are able to provide the desired insights (Dean, 1954). Of course, an alternative to focusing on these people is to be certain that they can be identified and indexed for later analysis. Thus, in the terms of Chapter 1, their status becomes a measured variable.

The various method of interviewing also present certain advantages and disadvantages. Personal interviews can be conducted in a face-to- face manner or over the telephone. The face-to-face interview method is emphasized in qualitative research because it establishes a personal relationship with the research subjects (see next section) and allows direct observation of the work context of the people involved. These factors, in turn, allow for the careful adjustment of lines of questioning and such subtle but important things as voice tone or quality and nonverbal body cues. In particular, when interviewing individuals of low verbal ability or those who are suspicious or mistrustful, it is useful to be able to work with several levels of communication (e.g., both verbal and nonverbal). Finally, in some investigations it is desirable to have the interviewee respond to physical or visual stimuli (e.g., proposed ideas for products or for ads), and face-to-face interview allows for this.

Yet, face-to-face interviews have some disadvantages. They are costly insofar as travel time is involved (either to get the interviewer to the respondent or the reverse). This also means that the collection of information will take longer as well, due to the number of research staff involved. Occasionally, there is the issue of safety—traveling to some locations may pose a potential threat to the researcher.

The telephone interview, on the other hand, can be administered by staff calling from various locations or from a single location. Most studies involve this method because those conducting the interview are in one place and can be better monitored or supervised. If problems occur they can be clarified quickly and consistently by a supervisor. Moreover, telephone surveys often can be administered quickly and can reach individuals anywhere in the country. In fact, one of your authors recently conducted a telephone survey of a sample of 650 managers in order to evaluate the impact of a development program. This was done in ten days' time (with a staff of 12), even though the respondents were scattered all over the world (including Malaysia).

All these considerations imply that telephone interviews can usually be conducted more quickly and at less cost than a face-to-face interview. And depending on the topic, interviews as long as 45 minutes to one hour are possible. This means that the method is desirable when quick results are needed (as in the case of research designed to evaluate the impact of the introduction of a new product or service).

When compared to the face-to-face interviews, the telephone interview has some weaknesses as well. In this day and age, many people are constantly being contacted by others over the phone for purposes of selling a product or service. This means that respondents may not be willing to participate in a real telephone study. That is, while telephone surveys have a good record in terms of what is called response rate (the number of individuals contacted who agree to participate), it is somewhat lower than the face-to-face interview. Moreover, the technique is subject to a "broken off" interview where respondents stop the process and refuse to answer more questions. This poses the problems of how to classify the case or to use the data.

Individuals have limited patience and capacities as well. The former implies that telephone interviews usually have to be shorter in length than face-to-face interviews (although, as mentioned, this will vary by respondent, characteristic, and topic). But realistically, it's often difficult to get support for a telephone interview that is much longer than 20 minutes. Limited capacity has implications for just what kinds of questions and what kind of answer formats are possible in a telephone interview. The investigator often has to plan on repeating questions for there is a heavy burden on aural and memory skills.

Telephone surveys may use either or both closed-ended or open- ended response modes. The former are choices presented to the respondent, who then picks an appropriate option (e.g., "strongly agree", "agree," etc.). In the open-ended format, the investigator or staff person needs to take down what is said as accurately as possible. Clearly, the nature of the material and the complexity of response options often precludes using a telephone interview. In these cases, it is better to collect data with face-to-face interviews.

It should be noted that both approaches require careful development and careful staff training, but, they are not always interchangeable. The nature of the research and of the resources available has a big impact on which is more appropriate.

A third major factor in interview research is the ability to create and that maintain motivation. There are a large number of factors that affect a respondent's willingness to be interviewed for research. To the extent possible the investigator should attempt to build on these as much as possible. The factors include the following:

1. *The perceived value of the research.* What the potential respondents believe to be the goals for the research will make a difference. If they believe it's for a "good cause" or if they will personally benefit from its outcome, respondents are more likely to get involved. In contrast, if they see negative consequences (in general or specifically for themselves), they will respond with at best superficial cooperation.

2. *The sponsor.* The decision to let respondents know who is sponsoring the research is a complex one. There are ethical reasons for favoring informed consent. Thus, all things considered, open disclosure regarding the sponsor is preferred. More practically, to the extent that the sponsor is reputable or well liked, it is more probable that questions posed will be answered. People will be more motivated to participate. On the other hand, knowledge of the sponsor under these conditions also is likely to create some bias. Individuals may distort answers. Instead of getting what is truly felt, the researcher may come away with a more socially desirable response.

3. *The rapport.* Rapport refers to the quality of the relationship that exists between the investigator and the study participants. It is especially important in the research interview. Rapport is affected by many of the factors already cited, but it is affected by the personal qualities and behaviors of the investigator as well. Greater rapport comes about when the interviewer is perceived as trustworthy, demonstrates empathy with and respect for the respondent without taking sides on issues, minimizes status differences in dress and in the use of language, and is a good listener. As noted, it is easier to establish rapport in the face-to-face interview but it needs to be established more quickly in the telephone interview (because of limited time usually available).

4. *The topic and format.* Some topics are more intrinsically interesting to respondents. However, the phrasing of questions, voice quality (tone and modulation), and sequencing can be designed to enhance interest levels.

5. *The setting.* Where interviews take place can affect the ability to establish or maintain motivation. In most cases this implies selecting a setting free from distraction or interruption. Executives might be questioned while away from their desk, operatives while away from their machines. Setting may impact on the level of privacy and confidentiality possible. The perception that the conversation will be overheard most likely will reduce candor. This especially is an issue in group interviews.

The fourth factor to be considered in planning the interview is the structure of the interview. Almost by definition, the qualitative research interview will be relatively unstructured. However, this does not mean that the investigator doesn't have a plan. In general, he or she will have goals for the session, a list of potentially useful questions, as well as some outline (mental or written) of the order in which they may be posed. In this regard the investigator is attempting to balance several factors in order to produce the desired result.

To the extent that the researcher knows little about the phenomenon, questions must be broad enough to stimulate respondent thinking. If the investigator has some strong ideas on the topic, he or she must be aware of the possibility of biasing the respondent with leading questions. Phrases like "Don't you think . . ." or "Wouldn't you agree . . ." should be avoided. They imply a preferred answer. Open-ended prompts like "Tell me about . . ." or "Describe how you feel . . ." are more in the spirit of eliciting unbiased information.

The sequence of questions asked and their level of specificity can have an effect on respondent motivation as noted. Sequence also will influence the way the respondent thinks about issues and opinions or conclusions. It is the task of the interviewer to elicit what thoughts and ideas the respondent already has—not to create them.

A number of authors recommend the *funnel technique* for eliciting valid and uncontaminated impressions from respondents in an interview (Bouchard, 1976). This technique involves first inquiring about a domain with general questions and unspecified response options. This loosely structured line of inquiry allows the investigator an opportunity to become familiar with the conceptual language and level of understanding of the respondent. With this insight, the researcher then can move to more specific questions, modifying them so as to be appropriate in language and direction. By going from general to specific, there is less of a likelihood that the respondent's answers will become contaminated or unduly influenced by the questions themselves. Over the course of a lengthy interview there might be several cycles of going from general to specific questions as one covers different topics or content domains.

There are other advantages of this format. The more or less free response format of the early questions are likely to be perceived as more natural by respondents. Thus, answers are likely to be more spontaneous and free flowing. Because the respondent feels less self-conscious, it should be somewhat easier to establish and maintain rapport.

A key feature of qualitative interviewing, regardless of specific question sequence, is the use of follow-up questions and probes. Short or incomplete answers to questions can be followed up with requests for elaboration. Apparent contradictions can be clarified. Additional facets of an issue can be covered beyond what was originally intended. When done with skill, such probes as "Please tell me more . . .," "What do you mean by that . . .," "I'm not sure that I am clear on that . . .," will produce additional relevant information.

In a great deal of research, the goal is to obtain information or data that can be readily analyzed by computer. Thus, the interview is designed to have a great deal of structure, both in the nature and order of questions used and in the way people answer. In its most extreme form, the highly structured interview is conducted by reading from a prepared questionnaire. As the respondent answers, the appropriate place on a form is marked or checked off by the investigator. In contrast to simply handing out a questionnaire (see Chapter 10) and hoping that it comes back filled out correctly, the interviewer can help respondents by clarifying items and motivating them to answer.

Usually, telephone interviews follow this very structured format. Figure 4-8 illustrates a page from a telephone survey conducted to assess the impact of a management development program. As a result of appropriate preliminary testing and advance promotion using company memos and media, the response rate was over 90% even though the questions were somewhat complex and the average time to complete the survey was 20 minutes.

A final issue peculiar to face-to-face interviews is whether or not to take notes in the interview. It is one thing to elicit information but quite another to record it with accuracy and in a way that

INTERVIEWER INTRODUCTION

All words in capitals and lowercase are to be read to respondents. Words in all capitals are not to be read to respondents.

Calling Procedure Note:

After three rings, a central answering service may answer. If that happens, ask for the person you are calling. If they are unavailable, identify yourself as a member of the Consumer Products Survey Team, and ask when would be a good time to reach the person you are calling. If asked if the call could be returned, give the number _____ . Our receptionist will bring the call to you.

Respondent's ID Number:
Interviewer's Name _____
Time of Interview _____ :00 to _____ :00
Phone # Called (___) _____

(Complete After Interview)

Respondent's Name _____   _____
                         (First Name)   Last Initial)
Gender of Respondent: Male (___)   Female (___)

Attitude of Respondent to Interview:
         Cooperative _____
         Neither cooperative or uncooperative _____
         Uncooperative _____
         Other _____

Questions Asked by Respondent:
_____
_____

         Begin Interview Here

         Hello. My name is _____ . Is this (respondent's name)?

If "no," ask for respondent. Leave your name and number and ask when would be a good time to call. Your number is _____ .

If "yes," go to "Introduction" below.
                         Introduction

I am calling as part of a study being conducted by an independent research firm for the Education Division of Consumer Products.

Are you aware of this study?   _____ yes   _____ no   _____ dk

Let me briefly (explain to you) or (remind you) of what's involved. The information we gather will be used to help the Education Division put together future programs. Your telephone number was drawn as part of a sample of Consumer Products management personnel.

Your answers are completely confidential. In fact, I don't even know your last name.

We'd like you to answer all the questions we'll be asking. However, if you feel there are questions you'd rather not answer, please let us know. Okay? (On Questions they decline to answer, write "88")

FIGURE 4-8 Example Format of a Telephone Interview Illustrating the Introduction Process

(continued on page 144)

The survey only takes about 15 to 20 minutes, and—again—all your responses are completely confidential.

Is this a good time to talk, or should we set a specific time to call you back?

Call back time: _____ a.m./p.m.
Call back number: _____
(Again, our telephone number is: _____)

I'll go through this as quickly as possible. However, if you're not clear about anything I say, please interrupt me and let me know.

Do you have any questions before we start?

If "no," continue.
If "yes," write in that question here:
_____
_____

Here's the way the interview works. I'm going to read a series of statements to you. After each statement, I need to know your level of agreement or disagreement with that particular statement.

It's really important that you know that there are no right answers. All that counts is your opinion.

Again, if you don't hear the statement clearly, let me know and I'll repeat it.

After the statement, let me know whether you Strongly Agree with that statement, Moderately Agree, Neither Disagree Nor Agree, Moderately Disagree, or Strongly Disagree with that statement.

SA	MA	Neither	MD	SD
(5)	(4)	(3)	(2)	(1)

Section I:

This first series consists of statements about the overall CP organization.

(Interviewers: Write in the number "88" for any statement the respondent declines to answer.)

_____   1. I have a good idea of the functions of the various units of the CO organization.

_____   2. If I were asked, I would be able to tell someone Consumer Product's ideal time frame for bringing out a new product.

_____   3. I can describe what constitutes the "wholesale" and the "retail" sides of our business.

_____   4. I can describe the needs and concerns of the various sales channels within the CP organization.

FIGURE 4-8 (continued)

is appropriate to the needs of the investigator. Clearly, some way of recording what gets said in the interview is imperative. But how and when to do it often presents a challenge.

The problem is that the straightforward solution of taking notes as the respondent is talking often interferes with the interview. It takes time and can interrupt the free flow of ideas. It distracts from the interviewer's thinking about and sequencing of questions. Moreover, continuous note taking produces something like a transcript. It will almost always have to be organized and copied. As noted earlier, this can be extremely time consuming. But most importantly, it makes what already is an intrusive technique, somewhat more so. Continuous and obvious note taking will cause most individuals to be more self-conscious and even uncomfortable. This, in turn, is most likely to reduce spontaneity and even promote self-censorship. The respondent will be careful in what he or she says in order to avoid disclosing any self-threatening information or in order to "look good" in the eyes of the interviewer or to those who will be reviewing the notes.

The particular setting may make a difference (e.g., a manager's office versus a shop floor) in note taking. Most experienced interviewers request permission to take notes first but, in fact, take only the briefest notes. This usually is done so as to reduce the intrusiveness of note taking and to maintain rapport. Thus, small note cards might be used instead of a pad of paper, and the noting of information would occur at convenient points of transition within the interview. It certainly would not be continuous. More to the point, it would not be done in a manner to convey to the subject that what was just said was noteworthy or unusual. It is most disconcerting to have the subject anticipating what is important by noticing what does or does not elicit note taking on the part of the interviewer.

It is tempting to make use of recording devices during the interview. This would free up the investigator from having to worry about real- time note taking. However, in most cases (unless they are disguised or hidden) these, too, are likely to produce undesirable consequences. The awareness of being recorded usually creates a mind set that everything said is "for the record." This will have inhibiting effects. On the other hand, it makes good sense to use recorders as dictation devices after the interview is completed as a way of quickly and easily capturing impressions and thoughts regarding the session. In any event, any recorded material still has to be reviewed and edited in order to be useful. This is inevitably time consuming. All these limiting facts, however, did not prevent one of your authors from using audiotape recordings in field interviews of railroad managers. The latter seemed to accept recording as an aid to good research. This did allow for the review and assessment of the quality of the interviews conducted by a research staff of four over a three-month period.

Typically, rough and cursory contemporaneous notes will be reviewed in privacy by the researcher immediately after the interview. This allows the former to become the basis or outline of a more complete documentation relying on (at most, short-term) memory. Ultimately, these too will have to be organized and summarized.

Analyzing and Reporting Interview Data. Once the interview has been concluded for qualitative research, the data must be summarized, analyzed, and reported. The treatment of this information is very similar to the treatment of information on observation presented earlier in this chapter. In general, notes are integrated around themes as they emerge from the responses to questions. Based on a thorough review of interview-produced materials, the investigator infers and interprets the essential meaning and "teases" out implications of what he or she has read and experienced. There is ample opportunity to emphasize or weight more heavily more informed or more credible respondents. It also is common to base interpretations on what the investigator may have deduced through means other than the interview. For example, personal exposure to relevant aspects of organizational life (i.e., several staff meetings) may color the interviewers descriptions and inferences.

The actual reporting of the qualitative interviews is a result of the larger research effort. At times, there is no real need for documentation. As a result of interviews, the investigator profits or grows from the experience and goes on to do his or her work in a different, hopefully more informed, manner. In other contexts, the interview data may be introduced into reports containing quantitative data in order to interpret or add substance. It becomes the "stuff" around which discussion sections of articles and dissertations are built. In some instances, however, the information stands alone. The investigator thus integrates the new knowledge or insights gained into an essay designed to characterize the phenomenon of interest. Examples from notes, anecdotes, even quotations may be used to support the points being made. In many respects, the final work product may look a lot like what is created by a good investigative reporter. The strength of the document lies in its organization, the persuasive tone of the arguments made, and the liberal and effective use of interview data (its appropriateness, consistency, specificity and detail).

When the structured interview format is used, the information obtained is a lot like what you would get from a questionnaire. This means that the response options chosen by research participants are translated into numbers. These numbers, in turn, are then subject to any of the analyses reviewed in Chapter 2. Thus, the analysis of the output of a very structured interview presents far fewer problems than the one arrived at via qualitative insights.

Special Applications of the Qualitative Research Interview. It seems likely that at one point or another any project involving information gathering will make use of the interview technique. This section is designed to highlight several particular interview applications that might be encountered with some frequency, and seeks to build on the work of Bouchard (1976) and others.

One special adaptation of the interview, *the tandem interview*, refers to an interview conducted by two individuals. Given the dynamics of the face-to-face interview described previously, it is easy to see how having two researchers involved might be quite functional. While one person is primarily responsible for asking questions, the other is taking notes or listening carefully to responses. The latter can be brought into a more active role from time to time to pose questions that seem to have been overlooked or are important and deserve elaboration.

Having a team of investigators work together in this manner allows for post-interview discussions in order to summarize what was learned. In this sense, points of agreement and disagreement can be part of the data base being built. In many cases this may be efficient as well. The researchers need not spend time orienting one another as they would have to if each were to interview informants individually and separately.

One other potential advantage of the tandem or team interview relates to the technical knowledge that researchers may have or share. At times, it may be that a fruitful session would only be possible if the researcher had certain subject matter expertise. To the extent that the appropriate knowledge base is not possessed by one individual, a second person brought into the team may allow for more complete coverage. For example, a research project calling for interviews of senior engineering managers regarding decision making associated with the introduction of innovative production technology might well use a team made up of a production technology subject matter expert and someone who understands decision making in complex organizations.

Of course, as with any technique, there are some disadvantages of the team approach as well. Most notably, by using it, a given interview ties up more than one investigator. This may limit the number of informants who might be contacted. Moreover, the team members must learn to work well together so as to create a climate that is free of tension.

Another form of the qualitative research interview is the *group interview*. There are times when it is advantageous to question more than one individual at a time. It can, for example, be very efficient. Such interviews can be conducted by one or more research team members as well.

The design and execution of successful group interviews involves several important considerations. Both the size and the composition of the group will make a difference for both process and outcomes. Larger groups are harder to manage and severely restrict the amount of time that a given individual can speak. It is harder to establish rapport as well. Groups made up of people who know each other may share the same enthusiasm (or reluctance) to participate. While they may be more spontaneous in their responses, it also is likely that their behavior and opinions will be affected by what each has been known to do and say in past interactions. Private (or inconsistent) thoughts may not surface. To the extent that there are status differences among participants, stylized response and deference to the senior member of the group may not be uncommon. In fact, a major task of the group interview leader is to manage to control the tendencies of some individuals to dominate "air time" while eliciting information and opinions from those who tend to be quiet or reserved. As Hoffman (1965) notes, there often is very little relationship between vociferousness and quality of contribution (see also Maier, 1950). Regardless of past acquaintance levels, individuals may vary in their experience and knowledge as it relates to the topic of interest. This, too, will affect group dynamics. Bouchard (1976) also points out that scheduling difficulties may be encountered when you try to get a group of busy people together.

One potentially important limitation of the group interview is that different or conflicting views and information may not be obtained. Questioning individuals separately will reveal particular points of view, perhaps in greater detail. Follow up and probing is more feasible. The same individuals in a group setting may be reluctant to go into such detail; or, just as common, they may be drawn into a particular way of thinking by what others say, in effect, overlooking or forgetting important points. Thus, descriptive richness, complexity, and accuracy may be sacrificed.

Group interviews may be especially useful where the investigator is interested in how attitudes, opinions, or ideas, might be stimulated by group interaction. Thus, there may be some real value in having individuals share the information or thoughts each has with one another in open discussion. Under these circumstances, group dynamics may work to some advantage.

The *focus group interview* is a term loosely applied to interviews conducted with small groups of individuals who are known to have had some personal experience with the phenomenon being researched. The interview thus focuses on respondents' impressions, interpretations, and opinions in this domain. Focus group interviews are used in market research by manufacturers and advertising agencies to determine consumer needs or preferences and their predilections to respond favorably to new products (Calder, 1977). As a type of group interview it is subject to the same dynamics outlined above.

Calder (1977) identifies three different applications of the focus group interview technique. First, it is used often in anticipation of quantitative research as an exploratory approach. The purpose of the technique, then, is to stimulate the thinking of the investigators. They may use focus groups to generate theoretical ideas or hypotheses that may be verified empirically at a later time. This approach concentrates on the creation of useful and important constructs that relate to those used in everyday life. For example, focus groups are very useful in planning both the content and wording of surveys. Alderfer and Brown (1972) report how qualitative interviews contributed to the appropriate wording of a questionnaire to be used to assess organizational attitudes. This is a prototype application of a qualitative technique for exploratory research.

Second, the focus group technique is used to provide generalizations from the information generated by the focus groups themselves. Calder refers to this as the *clinical approach*. The investigator thus uses the group as a way of probing deeply into a phenomenon to form certain conclusions. The validity of the inferences made will derive from the degree of rapport that exists with the group and the quality of the interactions that take place during the session. It is also highly dependent on the theories, knowledge and skill of the group leader as analyst. Calder is quite critical of this as a way of producing generalizable scientific findings. The results of such an effort are too dependent on the genius of the investigator; and, in practice, they are rarely subjected to verification with other means.

Third, the most prevalent application of the focus group technique is to use it as a way to experience the point of view of a sample of people from a population of interest. Calder refers to this as the *phenomenological approach*. Contact between the investigator and his or her subjects is viewed as necessary in order to better empathize with them and to anticipate their reactions to choices or decisions (e.g., about consumer products). This type of focus group emphasizes involvement with a group of people as they discuss and interpret things or events. The goal is to obtain a description of how they interpret reality in their own terms. Usually, one conducts focus groups of this nature until the investigator feels confident that he or she can "just about" anticipate what is going to be said.

Calder (1977) argues that the phenomenological focus group would be appropriate when managers or decision makers are out of touch with important constituencies. They also may be used when target segments (e.g., for marketing) are to be made up of minority or rapidly changing social groupings.

To illustrate the phenomenological approach, one of the authors was hired by a manufacturer of casual shoes to conduct focus groups made up of nurses. The company produced a type of sole that they believed was good for people who are usually on their feet a lot. The company had excess manufacturing capacity so it was looking for new markets. Nurses readily came to mind.

Focus groups were conducted over two sessions. In the first, nurses were asked to describe their work, their attitudes toward their uniforms (especially their "duty shoes") and their clothes, and their shopping philosophy and behavior. At the end of the discussion, they were given a pair of shoes of the type that would be manufactured and asked to wear them during the following week for at least three days. The second session then focused on the experiences that the nurses had with the shoes.

Through the use of this two-phase process it was discovered that nurses placed a great emphasis on quality work shoes purchased from special shops. Thus, if the company were to market their product they would have to work through an entirely different set of distribution channels. Further, it was found that the design of the shoe was not suitable for nursing work. The sole was too high and created instability problems when there was a need to lift patients. As a result of these insights, the company decided not to make and market shoes for nurses.

In the course of most experimental research the investigator often finds that he or she needs to better appreciate how the subject experiences and interprets instructions and manipulated conditions. In studies involving deception, there are the additional requirements of clarifying what did or did not occur and of ensuring that participants do not leave the session feeling less positive or more negative about themselves than when they came into the setting (Tesch, 1977). In each of these situations the research may use another special type of interview called the *debriefing interview*.

The debriefing interview is most often used in quantitative, usually experimental, research. However, it is discussed in this chapter because its conduct requires both the attitude and the skills of the qualitative researcher. For example, the investigator needs to gain a full understanding of the nuances of perceptions, reactions, and impressions of experimental participants and do it in a way that does not lead or bias answers. The investigator in the experimental study also wants to have such participants leave a session with a positive regard for the importance of the research. The debriefing interview may involve research subjects individually or in groups. As implied, it can be both an information-gathering and information-sharing event. The former will be emphasized here.

The design and implementation of experimental conditions requires a great deal of skill. The investigator may, on the basis of theory, want to examine the effects of a variable (e.g., work pressure) on some criterion of interest (e.g., performance). But he or she has many alternatives in the way the variable can be operationalized and created for experimental subjects. Theory, past research, personal experience, and observations of the phenomenon all will guide the method of choice. However, when first tried out, there is little guarantee of success. The debriefing interview is designed to obtain subject reactions and, under the right conditions, to obtain subject assistance in improving and strengthening an experimental manipulation.

Many experimental researchers attempt to refine their techniques in pilot work where differing versions of a procedure might be tried out. During and after the experience subjects may be asked to respond to questionnaires covering their state of information, their perceptions, their beliefs, and even their behavioral intentions. At the conclusion of the actual exeriment, the investigator scans this information and enters into dialogue with the subject.

In this debriefing interview, the researcher first attempts to understand how the written responses relate to the subject's state of mind. He or she then proceeds to relate both to the experimental condition experienced. If the subject wrote about moderate work pressure, the researcher would try to discern what this meant in his or her larger world view, and why it was described in this setting. Ideally, the investigator would like to discover that the experimental manipulation was perceived as intended. That is, subjects in the high pressure condition felt more pressure than those in the low pressure condition. But it would also be reassuring that, in an absolute sense, the former indeed feel a lot of pressure.

In many cases, however, the experimental conditions do not work appropriately. Under these conditions, the researcher needs to reorient the subject to think more like a coinvestigator (Fromkin & Streufert, 1976). Thus, in the debriefing interview the researcher must quickly establish rapport with the subject. The researcher says, in effect, "I have tried to create certain conditions (e.g., of work pressure). But apparently I have failed to do so. Why is this the case? What can I do differently that would be more effective?"

Even when the study has been designed and implemented, the debriefing interview is useful as an information-gathering tool. If the researcher is in a position to observe the subject in a session, he or she may wish to follow up on some behavior or action that was out of the ordinary. Thus, it becomes a means of remaining open to serendipity. When used on an occasional basis in the actual study it can provide an additional safeguard for quality (Aronson & Carlsmith, 1968; Tesch, 1977). The (hopefully) rare case of subjects who do not really understand the instructions or who are not convinced of the manipulation can therefore be detected. In many cases, one would not want to use the data generated by these subjects particularly if that data was very different from that generated by other research participants. Their data would be separately analyzed to understand why their responses were so different from other participants.

All of these special applications of the qualitative research interview require a great deal of competence and skill on the part of the investigator. He or she must be aware of and make use of interpersonal and group dynamics, have a wide-ranging behavior repertoire, and great sensitivity to the impact of nuances in choice of language. These are not capacities that are easy to acquire and refine. In most cases, they only can be developed under supervision with appropriate and timely feedback. As in the case of direct observation, the assurance of quality data is closely tied to the investigator as an intrinsic part of the technique itself. The value of the technique is related to who will be using it.

Archival and Trace Measures

Archival measures are based on documents and records that are generated in the course of day-to-day organizational life. These could include notes on desk calendars, schedule books, memos, speeches made by company representatives, and financial operating data (Bouchard, 1976; Webb & Weick, 1979). *Trace measures* are based on physical evidence and artifacts often presumed to reflect the attractiveness or popularity of activities or choice options. For example, the amount of floor wear in front of a museum exhibit might be used to infer the drawing power or level of interest created. Missing pages from the Yellow Pages section of telephone directories might be assumed to reflect frequency of need/use of services or products (Webb et al., 1966). For investigators interested in human resource management, a major source of archival and trace information is the personnel file (Owens, 1976).

There is no intrinsic reason that either type of measure must be used in a nonquantitative manner. That is, one could, for example, clearly create a coding system for analyzing executive speeches that would result in actual numbers (e.g., frequency counts) to serve as input to standard statistical analysis (Bouchard, 1976; Weick, 1968). However, for reasons covered below, it is more likely that an investigator will choose to make use of data from these measures in a subjective and qualitative manner. They often are gathered as incidental to other data and treated as supplementary and given a subordinate role to what gets generated by other methods (Miles, 1979; Pettigrew, 1979).

Both techniques are often classified as unobtrusive measures because they are presumed to be uncontaminated by reactivity dynamics (Bouchard, 1976). This is based on the belief that the actor would not be aware that he or she was being studied at the time the record or trace was being produced. However, there may be reasons to be concerned by reactivity bias (e.g., nos. 1 and 3, in figure 4-3) even here. For example, financial data in annual reports are often presented in a manner designed to make the company look good. Public speeches may tell us more about the speaker's assumptions with regard to what the audience wants to hear than what the speaker really believes. In a recent study of the analysis of the annual reports of publicly owned corporations and despite assertions to the contrary (Salancik & Meindl, 1984), it seems reasonable to assume that the text was carefully contrived for public consumption. Thus, a major limitation of these methods is that the investigator may never be certain regarding the level of self-consiousness felt by the actor responsible for the trace or artifact.

A second and somewhat related limitation of these measures is that their psychological meaning is problematic. More than with other techniques, the investigator must induce, and make a case for, the state of mind, intent, or motivation of the subject. To illustrate, the wear on floor tile may have little to do with the popularity of an exhibit but instead may be caused by such diverse factors as: a "right turn bias" known to occur as people enter public spaces, a bathroom located in that area, or the use of floor material in that area that simply wears faster (Bouchard, 1976). Similarly, memos written to the file may reflect a conscientious attitude and commitment to the organization or a deep distrust of the system by the actor. In other words, such measures may suffer from distortion. Variance in them may be caused by factors irrelevant to the phenomenon of interest. To put it another way, there are a large number of mediating factors operating between the measure and the phenomenon itself.

Nonetheless, a number of researchers have made skillful use of archival data. One who has done so (as sources of data for quantitative analysis) is Salancik (Pfeffer & Salancik, 1974; Salancik & Meindl, 1984).

Pfeffer and Salancik (1974) tested a theory of how departments or units in an organization gain power in a university setting. In their study most of the data came from university records. For example, subunit power was indexed by the number of department faculty who served on important university committees and the amount of money they had in their budget (controlling for number of faculty). The authors found that contrary to popular belief, the number of courses or students taught (also obtained from archival records) did not relate to the amount of power held as well as other, more political factors. Similarly, Salancik and Meindl (1984) used company archives to get copies of annual financial reports. By looking over such reports for a period of 18 years, the authors found that the words used by CEOs in the reports were related to the nature of the context in which the organization had to operate (its environment). Where the environment was changing or unstable, top managers used carefully chosen words to create "strategic illusions" for the causes of their firm's performance over the preceding year. This was less likely in companies where the environment was much more understood and predictable. That is, in this latter case few attempts at such structuring of opinions took place. Through the use of archival data, this study was able to contribute to the refinement of theories of organization and environment interactions (see Chapter 7 regarding models of organizational effectiveness).

In the end, the usefulness of archive and trace measures, like other measures, may be most evident in a research effort following a triangulation philosophy. In recognizing the limitations of any single technique and the benefits of multiple operationalism, the investigator would not place undue weight on these data. To the extent that the results converge, we have greater confidence in the generality and utility of the findings. While lack of convergence should justifiably instill caution, it too can promote new insights into the investigator's assumptions, the nature of the phenomenon, or the strengths and weaknesses of a given method (Bouchard, 1976; Jick, 1979; Webb et al., 1966).

ADVANTAGES AND DISADVANTAGES OF QUALITATIVE DATA

The data created in qualitative research would seem to have many attractive features. According to Miles (1979), they are rich, full, holistic, and usually match the complexity of that which is being studied. They appear to have face value due to this detail and specificity. They can add credibility to research reports when presented as vignettes or illustrations.

From both a scientific and practical point of view, many methods outlined in this chapter lend themselves to the uncovering of serendipitous findings and new insights as well. Webb and Weick (1979) stress the fact that certain classes of data (e.g., those based on unobtrusive measures) are particularly well suited for research on less-articulate populations, because the latter have neither the time, the interest, nor the talent to work with traditional self-report measures. Finally, many believe that qualitative data, when combined with quantitative results, can produce more valid inferences than either one separately.

On the other hand, there are some obvious limitations and liabilities associated with the use of the methods reviewed for obtaining qualitative information. Again, as reviewed by Miles (1979), collecting and analyzing qualitative data is laborious and time consuming. Mintzberg (1979) asserts that in his study of strategic decision making in organizations that he and his team spent a number of months on site to gain an appreciation for the context. To learn about socialization dynamics, Van Maanen (1975) actually joined and worked as a police officer for the better part of a year. It was only after and being accepted as a participant observer that he came to understand what were indeed the "facts" and what were indeed the "theories of facts" that he held as an outsider. It also took time (and trust) to discover what he calls *presentational data*. This is an idealized or manufactured image presented to outsiders and designed to protect the system and the esteem of its members. As pointed out by Van Maanen (1979 p. 544), "a central postulate of the ethnographic [participant observation] method is that people lie about those things that matter most to them." "Penetrating fronts" then becomes one of the important goals of the field-worker. This takes time and effort.

Miles (1979) describes the physical, emotional, and intellectual demands placed on those working with qualitative information. The researcher is almost totally responsible for the quality (validity or accuracy) of the data. The range of phenomena to be observed and documented; the volume of notes; the time required for write up, coding, and analysis can become a source of major stress. To illustrate, Miles points out that in his study of innovation in public schools, an-all day contact usually resulted in 60 to 90 minutes of taped notes which took a field-worker 2 to 2 1/2 hours to produce, and a secretary 6–8 hours to transcribe, and the field-worker another hour to review and correct. In this project he felt that this level of effort could not be reduced appreciably without losing many of the direct quotes and details that make such data so attractive. Moreover, on any major project this process must be multiplied by the number of sites, field-workers, and periods of observation!

But a major limitation of qualitative data, and perhaps the one most serious, is that the methods of analysis are not that well formulated. That is to say, for quantitative data there are clear conventions for analysis. But for the qualitative researcher, there are "very few guidelines for protection against self-delusion, let alone presentation of 'unreliable' or 'invalid' conclusions to scientific or policy making audiences" (Miles, 1979, p. 590).

CONTEXT FOR QUALITATIVE RESEARCH

At the outset of this chapter we characterized qualitative research in terms of an orientation or an approach rather than in terms of particular methods or techniques or special research designs. Indeed, throughout our treatment of the methods of observation, interview, and archival analysis, we have tried to illustrate applications of these methods in both qualitative and quantitative studies. However, one impression that comes from reading research of a qualitative nature is that, as a general theme, there is a great deal of interest in characterizing and understanding organizational culture.

Ashforth (1985) describes a corporation's culture as essentially the shared (and usually taken-for-granted) assumptions and values that guide decisions and behavior in that setting. He relates it to a more familiar term, *organizational climate*. While culture reflects shared values and assumptions, climate deals with shared perceptions regarding the manifestations of values and assumptions (e.g., company policies, practices, manager behavior). And while arguing that these constructs are distinct, Ashforth (p. 841) agrees that they "do slide greyly (sic) into one another."

Issues of definition notwithstanding, qualitatively oriented researchers often attempt to come to grips with the essence of culture. They want to measure it and study its causes or consequences. For example, Schall (1983) used a combination of group interviews, observations, archival records (e.g., memos), questionnaires, and face-to-face interviews with senior managers to uncover the cultural values and assumptions associated with communication rules and patterns in an organization. She found that observations and company records (of who wrote memos to whom) were better descriptions of this aspect of culture than the information gleaned from top management interviews. Similarly, other investigators have been interested in aspects of culture as diverse as the meaning, nature, and impact on behavior of organizational time dimensions of work (Schriber & Gutek, 1987), management ethics (Brady, 1986), and differentiation in the context of corporate acquisitions and mergers (Nahavandi & Malekzadeh, 1988).

In all these instances, the researchers need a comprehensive and clear description of some aspect of organizational functioning. While questionnaires and surveys could be used to some extent, there is the belief that actual contact between the investigator and the organization is critical. The former wants to come to "know" the phenomena intimately. Thus, the methods of observation and interviewing, in particular, prove to be invaluable.

ETHICAL IMPLICATIONS

A major implication of the use of most approaches reviewed in this chapter is that the investigator must deal with the issue of informed consent. The position taken by most social scientists is that subjects in research should have the option of not participating—subjects should give their consent before they become the object of study.

Informed consent in participant observation implies that subjects are aware that the investigator is going to be among them fulfilling multiple roles. When dealing with organizations or large groups this may be difficult to accomplish. It is especially true when the study takes place over a long period of time. People tend to forget about the arrangement. New people come into the system. Moreover, while the investigator contributes to the texture of daily life as a participant, it is difficult to maintain the balance between being unobtrusive and reminding coworkers that they are the object of a study.

As part of the organization, the investigator must deal with the possibility of changing the phenomenon intentionally or inadvertently. To illustrate, a colleague who is a university professor is also on the board of directors of a company that she wishes to study. Her actions as a board member will definitely affect the system. This becomes even more problematic if we adopt Salancik's attitude toward the benefits of field stimulation. As mentioned earlier, this involves deliberately "tweaking" the system to see how it responds so as to learn something about it (Salancik, 1979). The question is: What right do we have to do this?

Informed consent is especially relevant if the study makes use of hidden observation. Almost by definition, the subject is not to know that he or she is the object of study. Many investigators deal with this dilemma by publicly inviting participation and securing cooperation. Then he or she trusts that over time, memory lapses and the use of unobtrusive measurement will desensitize subjects so that they will behave naturally.

Other researchers argue that any behavior exhibited in public is open to study without formal consent. Such behavior, they maintain, is available to any and all to observe. Under this assumption, why should social scientists be required to go to any length to advise people that they are under scientific scrutiny? There is no simple or easy response to this. We would suggest that the need of informed consent in this public context will depend on the type of phenomenon of interest (e.g., pro-social versus illegal), the significance of the problem, the absolute need to use the method, the probable quality of the discoveries that might come out (based on theory and strength of the design), as well as the potential for harm to subjects as a result of the investigator's actions or work products. As we have said in other chapters, there is no substitute for good peer review when it comes to assessing these features before any work gets started.

Informed consent also is relevant to the use of archival or trace measures. It will be recalled that the latter's benefits derive, in part, from the fact that subjects are presumed to be unaware of the probable use of such artifacts for research. Most often, investigators assume that if they get permission from the current custodian of materials of interest they are behaving in an ethical manner. However, this does not relieve the researcher from considering ways to contact and obtain permission from the original source. Archival records of a public sort will not require such diligence.

A second area of concern is confidentiality. Interviews, in particular, usually are conducted with the assumption that what is shared with the investigator will only be known in detail to members of the research team. Great care must be exercised so as to not violate this trust in talking to other respondents (especially when attempting to verify the accuracy of accounts of events) or when writing up or documenting findings. Miles (1979) reports how difficult it is to "sanitize" reports in a way that keeps the desired richness of detail while still protecting sources. Confidentiality is especially difficult to maintain when the investigator, as participant observer, uncovers information shared in confidence that, for the good of the system, really should be revealed.

One last ethical dilemma to be mentioned in this section relates to certain features inherent in the use of the methods described in this chapter for strictly qualitative research. As stated many times, in most qualitative research, the knowledge, skills, attitudes, and abilities of the investigator are inextricably tied up with the nature and quality of the data produced. What this means is that the data, summaries, and inferences are not often subject to verification. Consequently, errors, biases, and distortion may not be detected.

There is the remote possibility that an investigator will consciously manipulate or distort findings. One can find examples of this where pressure for publication or the need to maintain or enhance a reputation has caused outright falsification to occur. Unfortunately, there is little that a text like this can do to prevent intentional deception. Much more insidious, however, is the well-known tendency for a person's beliefs and expectations to guide attention, to color perceptions, and to shape inferences and conclusions. Because what gets observed, recorded, and emphasized in qualitative research is largely a function of the investigator, it is quite possible that the final product reflects the latter's biases as much as the reality of the phenomenon. And more to the point, it would be difficult if not impossible to detect this distortion.

The ethical researcher must become aware of his or her biases and assumptions regarding that which is to be studied. Ethnographic training places great stress on this (Sanday, 1979). With such an awareness several actions might then be taken. At a minimum, the investigator might discipline himself or herself to follow a "devil's advocate" strategy during critical phases of the research. This would involve regularly challenging personally held assumptions by trying out reasonable, alternative perspectives on the evolving data base. Alternatively, it may be possible to create and configure teams of researchers with divergent personal views. Thus, any individual biases might be detected and minimized as a result of vigorous discussions during staff meetings. An interesting version of this was recently reported in a lengthy published study wherein two teams with different beliefs on the nature of a motivational technique, called *goal setting*, came together to design, develop, and implement some "crucial" studies (see Chapter 1). They did this under the watchful eye of a third neutral researcher who also was quite knowledgeable about the goal-setting area. As it turned out, the dialectic exchange in the design of the studies resulted in new ways of examining the theoretical issues involved. In the end, important limiting or boundary conditions were identified which could account for some of the conflicting findings of previous research (Latham, Erez, & Locke, 1988). Both sides were found to be partially right and partially wrong!

It is necessary that the investigator's biases and assumptions are clearly stated. As the author of a technical report, journal article, or book, the researcher should clearly preface his or her preconceived notions held at the time of the study. While we don't believe that research can (nor should) be value free, we do recognize the need for mechanisms to at least make it clear how and where values might have an impact on the quality (and accuracy) of the data and the conclusions derived from them (Morgan & Smircich, 1980). This is especially important in studies using the methods described in this chapter on qualitative research.

SUMMARY

In this chapter, we have taken the position that qualitative research involves a set of assumptions and a particular attitude as much as a set of techniques. In fact, any of the methods reviewed can be used to generate quantitative data as well. Some attempt has been made to show how this might occur.

Another important aspect of qualitative research is the key role of the investigator in the methods used. This individual not only chooses a particular technique, but also functions as the guardian of its ethical use and the ensurer of the quality of the data generated. This is not a small responsibility, or small task.

CRITERION DEVELOPMENT AT THE INDIVIDUAL LEVEL: CONCEPTUAL ISSUES

This chapter describes a way of thinking about the construct of individual effectiveness. Investigators and managers often are not only interested in measuring effectiveness, but also desire to predict it or bring about increased levels of functioning. The chapter provides a framework with which to develop or identify potential measures that might be used in research or practice. It also emphasizes the complex nature of criteria and the level of attention criterion development efforts deserve.

INTRODUCTION

Social scientists and managers alike have frequent and enduring needs for defining and measuring effectiveness. It is a fact that has promoted many programs and corporate practices and has generated extensive research. Moreover, designing and implementing systems for measuring effectiveness (usually at the individual level) constitutes one of the fundamental domains of practice for human resource specialists. Beyond this rich tradition, the topic recently has enjoyed the infusion of a great many new ideas. There are major shifts in thinking and conceptualizing about effectiveness. This has been evident in new models describing the dynamics of performance appraisal in organizations (Landy & Farr, 1980; Ilgen & Feldman; 1983; Wexley & Klimoski, 1984). As more has been learned about human information processing, it has become increasingly clear that we must reexamine our assumptions and approaches with regard to construct definition and measurement.

Clearly, designing or selecting effectiveness measurement systems requires informed choice. More specifically, we feel that it is unlikely that high quality decisions will be made if the researcher cannot link operational indicators with clearly articulated concepts of effectiveness. Therefore, in this chapter some effort will be expended to describe alternative views regarding the nature of effectiveness. To reiterate a point made in Chapter 3, an instrument that is reliable but of uncertain construct validity will be of doubtful value to either the scientist or the practitioner.

We already have stated that effectiveness measurement in the context of organization research and practice may involve a consideration of more than one level of analysis. Of primary interest to many, however, is the nature of individual functioning. We are interested in how well a person performs and, perhaps, the reasons for this. In this regard, this chapter on conceptual issues will emphasize theoretical and measurement issues at the individual level. A great deal of conceptual insight exists in this domain. It also is the opinion of the authors that applied experience available at the individual level of analysis is particularly useful. Experience and theory at the individual level do a good job of informing us as to how to approach measurement and research at other levels of interest.

CONTEXT FOR MEASURING EFFECTIVENESS

There are any number of reasons why a person might be interested in defining and measuring the effectiveness of individuals in organizations. These include the following:

1. *Measures of effectiveness frequently serve as dependent variables in research.* Most researchers who are concerned with developing or testing theories of behavior in organizations (as well as theories of organizations) quickly find themselves speaking in terms of effectiveness. Thus, models of leadership, for example, not only are focused on variables thought to define the relevant processes (Yukl, 1981), but on relating such processes to a criterion, very often individual performance. Similarly, investigations into the nature and significance of individual differences in ability (Reilly, Zedeck, & Tenopyr, 1979) usually involve linking such variables to productive behaviors. In this manner, effectiveness information contributes to our understanding of the empirical relationships among theoretically linked variables (the network of relationships expected based on theory) associated with a content domain or a construct (Betz & Weiss, 1987). Our emerging theories become more complete when we are informed of these data.

2. *Good measures are absolutely essential to applied research as well.* We need to be able to define and index levels of effectiveness in each of the following instances: (a) selection system validation, (b) compensation program design, (c) training program design and evaluation.

3. *Administrative demands require good measures of effectiveness.* In organizations, decisions must be made that affect the attitudes and behavior of personnel as well as the function of the organization itself. These include the allocation of organizational rewards, such as raises and promotions, the determination of who to lay off in times of financial difficulties, and who to try to retain when individuals working for the company get competing offers for employment. The availability of accurate and valid information on individual effectiveness levels not only results in better decisions, but its use promotes the idea that organization personnel decisions are fair. That is, such decisions reflect procedural justice (Greenberg, 1982). This, in turn, has desirable consequences in terms of worker satisfaction and loyalty (Aram & Salipante, 1981; Dalton & Todor, 1985) and even productivity (Greenberg, 1988).

4. *Employee development efforts are based on measures of effectiveness.* In many organizations, the purpose of assessing individual effectiveness is to provide a basis for personal development. That is, workers are appraised of their effectiveness levels in order to motivate and guide improvement. Under these circumstances, it is important to develop a measurement system that accurately portrays a person's strengths and weaknesses because developmental actions will be assigned or initiated based on what is found. Moreover, effectiveness measurements have implications for the way others tend to view the worker (in terms of personal traits or qualities) as well as how the worker comes to view himself or herself. Over time, assessments (and inferences regarding the causes of levels of effectiveness) can affect self-definition and self-esteem (Brockner & Guare, 1983; Tharenow & Harker, 1982).

5. *Effectiveness measures are central to management control efforts.* Information and control systems are two related organizational tools that are aimed at producing both reliable behavior on the part of employees and quality in personnel relevant decisions (Lawler & Rhode, 1976). Both are based on the fact that organization decision makers need to have accurate and detailed information about employees. In particular, they need information on current levels of performance of both individuals and groups of workers as well as their capacity or potential for meeting future job demands. Through such systems management is able to obtain a clear picture of the talent (human resources) available to run the organization. Moreover, it can determine if individuals are behaving in a manner consistent with their job description and with management expectations. At the heart of such information and control systems are carefully developed measures of effectiveness.

6. *Strategic planning efforts require accurate appraisal of effectiveness.* Managers and investors frequently find themselves in the position of having to assess the value of individuals and systems for purposes of acquisition/merger and selling parts of the organization. What is an organization or division worth? How much should it be sold for? Ultimately, the answers to questions of this nature rely on an appraisal of the actual or potential effectiveness of the units involved. Once again, good measurement is essential for high-quality decisions.

In all these contexts the applied researcher, consultant, or manager usually is interested in being able to evaluate, recommend, or promote certain individuals. We maintain that such assessments and advocacy should be based on defensible measures of effectiveness and that this begins with a thorough understanding of the effectiveness construct itself.

WHAT IS A CRITERION FOR EFFECTIVENESS

In research, the term criterion usually refers to the dependent variable. It is that which the investigator wishes to predict or to understand. In terms of research design, it is sometimes referred to as an observed or measured (as opposed to a manipulated) variable (Runkel & McGrath, 1972). It is a variable that is created, made operational through measurement, and then allowed to vary as a function of the effects of other (independent) variables. Thus, in research on stress it is a variable that is used to index the level of stress felt by subjects, perhaps as a result of specially created working conditions. Or it could refer to the output of work groups in studies directed at understanding this domain. In short, as emphasized in Chapter 1, the criterion (variable) usually reflects the focus of interest for the investigator.

In applied research and in the practice of management, a criterion is an evaluative standard, something we can use to index the level of person, group, or organization effectiveness. At the level of the individual, it usually represents a variable that reflects the degree to which an employee can be considered successful on the job (Blum & Naylor, 1968; P. C. Smith, 1976). We are all familiar with such criteria as "the number of houses sold" (for real estate people), the "number of patents awarded" (for scientists), "student evaluations of teaching" (for college professors), or "speed of response" (for fire fighters). All of these are regularly used examples of standards of excellence. Similarly, work group output or a company's product market share are frequently given the status of criterion variables. Where do these variables come from? How do we know that they are the right "things" to measure? The answer lies in the logic and care with which they were identified and developed in the first place.

THE CRITERION AS A CONSTRUCT

In most basic and applied research, variation on a criterion variable is meant to reflect more than simply a score on an operational index. Instead, it usually is viewed as representing the observed effects of some underlying or latent construct. To put it another way, most criteria are treated as if they have construct validity.

As noted earlier, a construct is a concept that has been specifically created or invented (constructed) by the researcher for scientific purposes (Kerlinger, 1973). It is a basic element of a theory and usually used to characterize certain postulated attributes or features of the theory. A construct is an abstraction that develops out of our experiences with some phenomenon and comes into being as we find the need to communicate our observations with others. In a sense it is a generalization formed from the observation of particular instances or events (Runkel & McGrath, 1972).

It is important to recall that because they are abstractions, you cannot see constructs directly; rather their existence, their nature, and their effects must be inferred. More specifically, they need to be made observable through our operational definitions.

Operational definitions are the actual procedures used to create or measure a variable in a concrete manner. An important quality of an operational definition (sometimes called an indicator) is that it is conceptually linked to the construct of interest. That is to say, a measure must reflect the theoretical nature of the construct, including its complexity. It should also have the attribute of being defined with some precision so that its essence can be communicated to others. This is critical to progress in research—with clearly specified operational definitions others will be better able to replicate a study and, hopefully, its findings.

Because a construct is an abstraction and can't really be seen or measured directly, we usually rely on the operating characteristics of the measures that we have chosen to provide clues as to its nature. This clearly presents a challenge. When we attempt to learn about a construct (e.g., numerical ability) using an operational indicator, how do we know we have done this appropriately? The answer is that we cannot know for certain. The scores that we get on a particular measure may reflect the nature of the construct, or it might reveal only something about the measure we have chosen, or about the sample we have studied. Ultimately, insight into a construct must depend on the process of inductive reasoning used by the user and his or her willingness to make inferences about the measure and its underlying construct from a variety of instances. Recall the discussion of construct validity in Chapter 3.

There is one additional strategy that we might employ to strengthen our confidence in asserting that we have measured a construct of interest. This approach has been referred to as *multiple operationalism* (Cook & Campbell, 1976). Simply stated, this involves using more that one indicator in an attempt to ensure that an underlying variable is, indeed, being reflected in obtained scores. This originated in the belief that it is inappropriate to rely on one potentially imperfect measure and that is reassuring to see convergence across more than one such indicator.

EFFECTIVENESS AS A CRITERION

The construct to be emphasized in this section is individual *effectiveness*, an all-encompassing concept to capture the notion of an ideally functioning individual. This term subsumes the terms performance, productivity, and efficiency. While these related concepts will be dealt with and used from time to time, the word "effectiveness" is preferred.

The remainder of this chapter is devoted to a discussion of criterion concepts as they relate to the definition and measurement of effectiveness at the individual level. In part, the latter is used as a focus because so much has been written in the area; but the logic of the analysis will be equally applicable to groups and systems (see Chapter 7).

CRITERION CONCEPTS

In the process of selecting potential criteria, we must go from the ideal to the practical, from the abstract to the specific (Guion, 1965). We will illustrate this process for the case of an account representative. To measure the effectiveness at the individual/job level of an account representative, we would start with or envision the essential features of effectiveness. This is referred to as the *ideal criterion*, or sometimes as the *ultimate criterion* (Blum & Naylor, 1968). In the case of the account representative we might conceive of a model of effectiveness that would include excellence in several areas or domains, including those of selling, follow-up policies and client service. This image of effectiveness is depicted in part A of Figure 5-1, which is intended to convey our image of the total range of effectiveness. This section has been subdivided into smaller spaces labeled with the components of effectiveness just mentioned. These are usually called criterion dimensions, criterion elements, or subcriteria. Thus, our image of effectiveness for the account representative has several aspects.

An ideal criterion, however, is an abstraction. It can be thought of as a construct. To be useful it still must be operationalized. In criterion development terminology the measures that we choose to use for this purpose are referred to as the *actual criterion measures*. Part B of Figure 5-1 represents the measures a company actually might use to index an account representatives' effectiveness. These include the number and dollar value of sales (selling efectiveness), the accurate completion of forms (following policies), and the calling of clients and the answering of their inquiries (client service).

The actual and ideal criteria are compared in Figure 5-1 by means of solid lines. This comparison is drawn to illustrate the typical case where our actual measures and our ideal measures have a fair degree of similarity. But, there is some slippage as we go from the abstract to the specific. Under these circumstances, part C illustrates three areas that have been given names in criterion development theory.

Criterion relevance is the term used to describe the extent to which the actual criterion measures do, in fact, get at or index our concept of effectiveness. To put it another way, we would say that we have relevance if variation in scores of our actual measures reflect true variation in effectiveness. Relevance corresponds to the validity of our criterion measures. Another area in part C is given the term *criterion deficiency*, which represents features of the ideal model of effectiveness that are not included or covered by the measures we are using. Certain components are missing either entirely or in part. Under these circumstances we say that our actual criterion measures are deficient. This is undesirable.

Criterion contamination is the term used to describe the third area of the diagram. We say we have contamination when variation in our actual measures is not a function of true effectiveness. This also is to be avoided. Criterion contamination can result for a number of reasons. Refer back to the account representative's example in Figure 5-1. A part of the space representing the actual criterion has been labeled "enthusiasm at sales meetings." A manager might try to measure this and make it part of an index of effectiveness. For the sake of the illustration, we might assert that this potential indicator is largely irrelevant to being a good account representative. In other words,

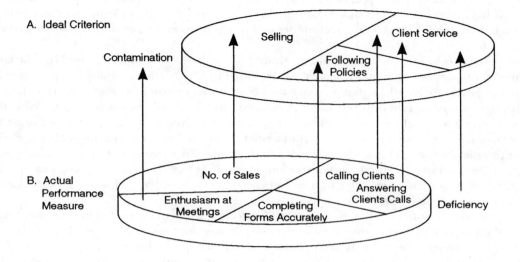

A. Ideal Criterion

B. Actual Performance Measure

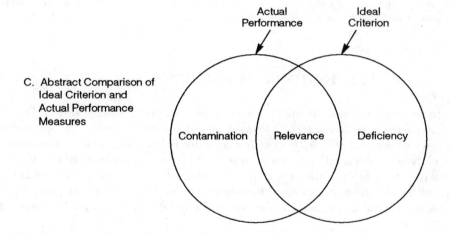

C. Abstract Comparison of Ideal Criterion and Actual Performance Measures

FIGURE 5-1   Criterion Concepts Applied to the Account Representative's Job

enthusiasm at meetings is just not part of our model. To the extent that assessments of the representatives do include enthusiasm "scores," we would say there is criterion contamination.

Contamination can occur for other reasons. An employee's scores on an actual measure (that are in some ways appropriate) still may be systematically affected by factors that are outside the control of a person. A good example of a biasing factor is the nature of a sales territory assigned to an account representative. Features of that sales area, such as size, population, affluence, etc., are bound to affect sales volume. The key here is that they act to affect it in a systematic way. That is, given a sales territory with certain attributes, *any* sales person would do better (or worse) there. The key to this effectiveness measure is the territory, not the person. Such systematic contamination is called *bias*. In this example, the actual measures of "number of sales" and "dollar value of sales" may have a built-in bias. It should be noted that it is often difficult to know if, in fact, actual criterion measures are biased. Some techniques that might be used for this purpose are described in Chapter 6.

Another reason for contamination also should be mentioned. It can be caused by a lack of reliability in our actual criterion measures. As described in Chapter 3, reliability refers to consistency of measurement and the extent to which a set of scores is free from random or error variance. Many things can affect criterion reliability. A result of low reliability means that an individual's score on a measure might be erroneously low or high at a given point in time. In contrast to contamination that takes the form of bias, contamination that is due to low reliability affects scores in an unpredictable way. This makes it harder to deal with. Specifically, criterion reliability sets important limits on the potential validities we can obtain in selection research. In the example of the account representative, an index of time to process orders may have a low reliability because of all the random factors that influence it.

In contrast to contamination, the concept of criterion deficiency is rooted in the notion that the actual measures used by an investigator or manager may not adequately cover the conceptual or theoretical domain of interest. What we are measuring may not be bad or incorrect per se (i.e., not contaminated), but it may be lacking some important components. In the example of the account representative, we have drawn an aspect of an ideal criterion that is left uncovered deliberately. For example, a client's perception of service may be strongly determined by feelings of rapport with the representative. If rapport skills were not a factor in the actual measurement of effectiveness, one would say that these measures were deficient.

CRITERION COMPLEXITY

It is possible to encounter situations where effectiveness is viewed as simple and unified, and thus a single actual measure (often referred to as a global measure) would be appropriate. However, in most cases where we see a single criterion measure being used, such as "commissions earned" (in sales) or "win/loss record" (in sports), it is used because of convenience or tradition rather than because it is thought to be the only index. The fact is that, for most jobs, even at lower levels in the organization, criterion complexity is the norm (Dunnette, 1963). By *criterion complexity* we mean that there are several facets or components to the ideal concept of effectiveness. It is multidimensional.

Under some circumstances, when it comes to making use of criterion data, this multidimensionality can be dealt with by keeping information separate regarding a person's effectiveness in each area. Much like the physician who makes use of the patient's medical chart, data on each area of an employee's strengths and weaknesses can be read and processed as distinct and useful. To illustrate, a manager might review an account representative for purposes of determining a merit raise by examining information arrayed as these multiple criteria. This could take the form of a list of factors to consider or even a profile, as in Figure 5-2. Presumably, a salary decision would come out of the impression generated by the available data.

Many organizations, however, do not like to make such important personnel decisions in such an impressionistic manner. Thus, methods have been developed to systematically gather and combine complex criterion information.

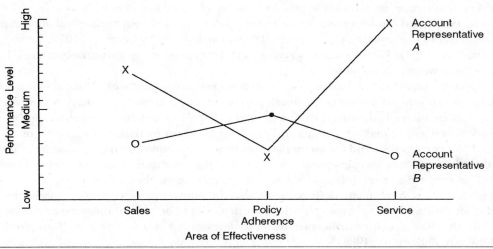

FIGURE 5-2   Multiple Criteria Arranged as a Profile of Scores

Building Criterion Composites

The combination of data on several performance dimensions results in a *criterion composite*. The goal of creating a criterion composite is to integrate effectiveness information in a variety of areas into one number or score. This could then be used to compare individuals or to make personnel-related decisions.

In order to create a composite, three types of decisions must be made by the personnel specialist. First, the relevant criterion dimensions must be identified. Second, the relevant importance of the criterion elements must to be established. And third, the rule for combining subcriterion data must be agreed upon.

Criterion Dimensions. To this point we have been rather general with regard to just where the conceptual or ideal criterion comes from. When reading the example of criterion issues relating to the account representative you might have noticed that the criterion elements appear to have been derived from a direct consideration of the representative's job itself. This is, indeed, the preferred starting place. Thus, in general, criterion definition and dimensionality will be established through a job analysis.

Job Analysis and Criterion Development. The term *job analysis* refers to the activities associated with the determination of the tasks, duties, and responsibilities carried out by job incumbents. That is, the person conducting the analysis wants to know just what the job is all about (job description). In most cases, a job analysis also defines worker requirements. These include the knowledge, skills, abilities, and other related qualities that a worker needs to have in order to perform the job adequately.

There are a large number of approaches to job analysis. However, most will make use of several techniques (e.g., interviews, observations, questionnaires) and involve gathering information from multiple sources (e.g., the job market, supervisors, staff specialists) in order to come up with the most comprehensive and accurate picture possible. In this regard, many of the issues discussed on qualitative research in chapter 4 would be relevant here as well. Moreover, while a job analysis can be carried out by a manager or nonspecialist, there is both theoretical and empirical literature to guide the practice (e.g., Cascio, 1987a; Gael, 1988; McCormick, 1979; Levine, Ash, Hall, & Sistrunk, 1983). Therefore, it is recommended that people trained and experienced in job analysis be used whenever possible.

Job analysis provides the basis for many human resources practices. While it is introduced here as the starting point for criterion development efforts, it serves a similar purpose for such things as identification of potential selection devices (Chapter 8), recruiting and training (Chapter 11), promotion decision-making systems and job design and compensation programs. In all these areas valid job descriptions and/or a complete set of worker requirements are needed. Similarly, job analysis is important for personnel research including test validation research. Finally, the nature of jobs as defined by job analyses is often the focus of theoretical work. Task and job characteristics often have been defined as central in many theories of work motivation and leadership, for example. The investigator frequently needs to be able to measure and classify (or create) jobs that have specific attributes in order to develop or test these theories (Campion, 1988; Kulik, Oldham, & Langner, 1988).

As noted, there are a variety of job analyses methods available to investigators. However, to illustrate what steps could be involved we briefly will describe a job analysis conducted by one of your authors for purposes of understanding the nature of effectiveness of the job of emergency telephone operators.

The effort began with a review of existing materials: job descriptions, training manuals, position announcements, etc. Interviews with supervisors and/or expert job incumbents were then conducted by the investigator in order to gain an overall picture of what those in the position do and how they fit into the organization. A meeting was then held with a group of five subject matter experts to generate a list of task statements. Any special environmental conditions affecting performance would be noted at this time.

In this meeting the investigator provided a definition of what a task statement consisted of and gave examples of possible tasks generated from his own preliminary review of the job. While the people in this panel could have been asked to write down task statements, it was done orally with the investigator. It was felt that interaction among the people was desirable and would produce additional task information and clearer definitions than would have been obtained otherwise.

The investigator then edited the task statements and removed duplicates and prepared a preliminary grouping into major dimensions. This served as input to another group of experts who were asked to react to the lists and groupings and to make deletions, changes, or additions. This process of using additional groups continued until very few new tasks were generated. (Usually this involves no more than three or four such meetings.)

At this point the investigator had a slightly larger (ten) group of incumbents rate the task statements using a questionnaire developed for that purpose. Individuals were instructed to rate each item on three scales as recommended by Levine (1983): time spent, task difficulty, and criticality. The nature of the rating continua involved can be seen from a review of Figure 5-3. Raters were asked to focus on the job as a whole, rather than on any one particular individual performing that job. Overall task importance values could then be computed by multiplying difficulty and criticality ratings and adding the value for the time spent. Tasks then can be organized by category and ranked in terms of importance. In Figure 5-4 we present some tasks and examples of the ratings made.

At this point the investigator had to decide whether to use task information directly to construct instruments designed to assess effectiveness (as in a behavior checklist), to use the task

A. Time spent—a measure of time spent per week doing a task relative to all other tasks within a given job.
_____ 1. Rarely do
_____ 2. Very much below average
_____ 3. Below average
_____ 4. Average (approximately 1/2 tasks take more time, 1/2 take less)
_____ 5. Somewhat more than average
_____ 6. Considerably more than average
_____ 7. A great deal more than average

B. Task difficulty—difficulty in doing a task correctly relative to all other tasks within a single job.
_____ 1. One of the easiest of all tasks
_____ 2. Considerably easier than most tasks
_____ 3. Easier than most tasks performed
_____ 4. Approximately 1/2 tasks are more difficult, 1/2 less
_____ 5. Harder than most tasks performed
_____ 6. Considerably harder than most tasks performed
_____ 7. One of the most difficult of all tasks

C. Criticality/Consequences of Error—the degree to which an incorrect performance would result in negative consequences.
_____ 1. Consequences of error are not at all important
_____ 2. Consequences of error are of little importance
_____ 3. Consequences are of some importance
_____ 4. Consequences are moderately important
_____ 5. Consequences are important
_____ 6. Consequences are very important
_____ 7. Consequences are extremely important

FIGURE 5-3 Task Rating Scales

clusters or dimensions to create a rating scale, or to continue the analysis to get at the knowlege, skills, and abilities that are needed to perform the tasks.

In the latter case, such information also was gathered in small group meetings. With a well-defined list of tasks at hand, job experts were asked to generate the worker requirements involved. Once again, an iterative process was used in which the investigator edited the output of one group to serve as the input of another until a consensus was reached. Finally, ratings of the importance of the particular knowledge, skills, or abilities uncovered were obtained. These were specific to the needs of the investigator and related to the purpose of the analysis in the first place (e.g., whether to develop criteria for test validation, promotions or the evaluation of training interventions). Table 5-1 provides a summary of the job analysis steps used to understand the work of emergency telephone operators.

Just about any method of job analysis can be used for criterion development. In their excellent review of this area, Bernardin and Beatty (1984) describe specific applications of different job analysis methods in developing criterion measures: the critical incident technique (Latham, Fay, & Saari, 1979), the task analysis approach (Schoenfeldt & Brush, 1980), the job element method (Clark & Primoff, 1979), the Functional Job Analysis (Olson, Fine, Myers, & Jennings, 1981), and the Position Analysis Questionnaire (PAQ) (Cornelius, Hakel, & Sackett, 1979). Several elements of these job analysis approaches can be found in the emergency telephone operator case illustrated above.

Bernardin and Beatty (1984) point out that there is no one best method of job analysis for establishing measures of effectiveness. Each has advantages and disadvantages. Some are very

Task	Time	Difficulty	Criticality	Importance
Types reports from information given by officers or phone callers into LEMS computer using appropriate standard formats to maintain a record of the call and to get a complaint number for later access.	3	3	5	18
Fills out stolen car reports on UDAA card according to standard format after verification from officer so dispatcher can publicize this information to field units and LEIN operator can maintain a file of reports.	2	2	4	10
Monitors status of all field units knowing their activities and location at all times for safety of officers and to provide prompt dispatching and responses across jurisdictions.	7	5	6	37
Asks for and records pertinent facts from caller obtaining location, nature of incident, injuries and/or weapons present to relay information to dispatcher.	7	6	6	43

FIGURE 5-4   Examples of Tasks and Task Ratings from the Job Analysis for Emergency Telephone Operators

structured and amenable to quantitative analysis (e.g., the PAQ); others can be used to generate qualitative information (e.g., interviews with job incumbents or supervisors). The most appropriate method will depend on the purposes to which the final effectiveness data will be put. This is because purpose will dictate the level of specificity required, and the techniques vary in this regard (Bernardin & Beatty, 1984). For example, the task approach to job analysis might be particularly useful in producing measures that are to be used establish employee training needs since inferior performance in specific task areas implies specific remediations (i.e., training and practice in those tasks).

The Cornelius, Hakel, and Sackett (1979) study using the PAQ is noteworthy because it highlights some of the difficulties of establishing criterion dimensions for jobs in large organizations. In this study the researchers had to develop criterion dimensions for over 100 positions in the U.S. Coast Guard. By administering the PAQ to a sample of Coast Guard personnel and analyzing the resultant data, they were able to establish the existence of job "families." The employees in relatively homogeneous jobs then could be evaluated on a common set of criterion dimensions. This reduced the number of different appraisal forms needed considerably.

The use of job analysis information in this manner is likely to occur with increased frequency as organizations attempt to achieve a balance between the use of a common set of criterion dimensions to be applied company wide (and hence to be so general as to be almost useless) or

TABLE 5-1
Steps in Job Analysis

I.   Review of Existing Documentation on Job, Unstructured Interviews/Conversations with Supervisors and Expert Job Incumbents

II. Task Analysis

    A.   Generation of tasks in group meetings with subject matter experts (SMEs)
       1. Special conditions
       2. Task statement defined
       3. Writing task statements
       4. Editing and grouping task statements by job analyst
       5. Review of task statements by SMEs
    B.   Task rating (difficulty, criticality, and time spent)

III. Analysis of Knowledge, Skill, Ability and Other Characteristic (KSA) Requirements

    A.   Generation of KSA
       1. Distribution and review of task statements
       2. Define and give examples of KSAs
       3. Generate and record KSAOs for each major task dimension
       4. Edit of KSA
    B.   Ratings of KSA

the use of a different set of dimensions for each job title (which is perhaps unrealistic and, in any event, burdensome).

Criterion Weights. Once criterion dimensions have been identified, a second step is to determine their relative importance. Are all factors to be considered equally critical to overall effectiveness? Or is it the case that some are more central to our definition of success? In more technical terms, we need to establish the weights to be given to criterion components.

It should be noted that the weights given to criterion elements in a composite criterion may be only weakly linked to the weighting judgments obtained in job analysis. This is because criterion dimensions represent constructs that are often at a higher level of abstraction than, say, the task domains of a job analysis. Thus, it is usually appropriate to establish such weights independently of establishing the importance of individual tasks, once the nature of preferred wording for the dimensions is determined.

The phrase *criterion distortion* has been used to describe the situation in which the relative importance given to components in a criterion composite are at variance with what is envisioned in the model of the ideal or ultimate criterion (Brogden & Taylor, 1950). To the extent that this occurs, an organization may make personnel decisions and take actions that are contrary to its best interests (e.g., it may promote the wrong people). In the example of the account representative, if we promoted people only on the basis of how well they comply with company policy and largely ignored their client service activity, criterion distortion would result. Over time the entire company likely would become less effective. Because of the possibility of criterion distortion, a number of techniques have been developed to systematically and correctly establish these weights (Blum & Naylor, 1968; Bernardin & Beatty, 1984; Guion, 1965).

Carroll and Schneier (1982) identify seven different ways that human resource specialists can deal with the issue of criterion weights in creating composite measures of effectiveness. Four of these briefly are reviewed here.

1. *Judgment.* Perhaps the most direct way to determine the relevance of criterion dimensions is to ask experts, such as the job incumbent, the supervisor, or the personnel specialist, to provide the weights to be used. If more than one expert is involved, their judgments could be averaged. This method frequently is referred to as the Kelly Bids System (Schmidt, 1977). Schmidt argues that this is a straightforward and practical approach. For example, experts might be given a total of 100 points to allocate to criterion dimensions on the basis of relative importance. This is something all can understand and accept. On the other hand, Bernardin and Beatty (1984) feel that the Bids method doesn't take into consideration the ease or difficulty with which the different dimensions can be measured. For instance, large weights might be given to important factors that cannot be operationalized reliably. But obviously we would want both relevance and reliability. In any event however, difficulty in measurement should not be an excuse to ignore (or give zero weight to)important factors.

2. *Reliability.* The various criterion factors may be emphasized in proportion to the ease (accuracy) with which they can be measured. Kane (as cited in Bernardin & Beatty, 1984) stresses the importance of observability and uncertainty. Presumably, criteria that are readily observed and can be established with minimal uncertainty should be given greater weight. However, our view again is that the most important consideration should be the relevance of the criterion dimension.

3. *Dollar value.* Brogden and Taylor (1950) were the first to suggest that a common and relevant metric, the dollar value, could be used as a basis for weights. Criterion elements would be stressed in proportion to their contribution to the value of effective job performance in an organization. Recently, a variety of ways to do this has been proposed (Cascio, 1987b; Landy, Farr, & Jacobs, 1982). But it should be noted that these all require some judgment on the part of experts. In a sense we are getting importance ratings as in the Kelly Bids method. However, in this case it is with regard to a common denominator—money earned for the organization.

4. *Unit (equal) weights.* Upon reflection, personnel specialists may come to the conclusion that it would be most accurate to consider each criterion component equally important. Thus, they should get equal weights. If this were to be the case it is important to note that some action regarding weights is still necessary. For example, Tiffin and McCormick (1965) state that unless scores on sub-criteria are put into a standard score format and then combined according to an equal weighting scheme, the effective weights might be quite different. Combining data without first converting to standard scores leads to giving (inadvertently) greater weight to those factors that manifest the greatest variation in the data set. This, of course, is true of any composite scheme, but it can show up most dramatically in the case of presumed unit weights.

Combining Criterion Components. The final issue to be resolved when creating composites is how one combines the elements once they have been weighted. A variety of combination rules could be used; however, one has evolved as the most useful. In building criterion composites it is common to *add* the weighted subscores together. Let's go back to the example of the account representative to demonstrate how this might be done.

First, to simplify things a bit, let's assume that overall effectiveness of an account representative is a function of just three factors: selling, follow-up policies, and service. Diagrammatically, we might start to build our composite as follows:

$$\text{Overall effectiveness} = \text{Selling, Follow-up policies, Service} \tag{5.1}$$

Second, suppose the account representative is located in a relatively new company where the policymakers feel that superior service will make one distinctive in the marketplace. Follow-up policies are expected, of course. But it is recognized that some selling is also expected. More operationally, an investigator using the Bids system determines that service is five times as important as follow-up policies, while selling is two times as important. Our evolving composite would reflect these weights as follows:

$$\text{Overall effectiveness} = 2 \text{ (Selling), } 1 \text{ (Follow-up policies), } 5 \text{ (Service)} \tag{5.2}$$

Third, a combination rule is imposed. Because the additive function is widely used we will follow suit. Doing this results in the following equation:

$$\text{Overall effectiveness} = 2 \text{ (Selling)} + 1 \text{ (Follow-up policies)} + 5 \text{ (Service)} \tag{5.3}$$

With this criterion composite formula, a manager then determines the overall effectiveness of the account representative. In this case, the manager carries out the following steps:

1. Operational measures for each of the criterion areas first are selected or developed. Examples of several of these are offered in Figure 5.2. Notice that any number of operational indicators could be created or adopted. This step does depend greatly on informed judgment based on job analysis data.
2. The employee is then measured on each of the sub-criteria.
3. The scores then are converted to standard scores. (subtract the score mean from a score and divide the result by the standard deviation of the scores)
4. The standard scores then are multiplied by the weights that had been established.
5. These weighted standard scores then are added.

The resulting composite score then represents the level of effectiveness of an individual account representative. The score still has to be interpreted. Is it high or low? Compared to what? Compared to other representatives, to past scores earned by this person, to levels aspired to by this individual? Regardless of what standards the manager uses, he or she is able to make use of a great deal of information in a systematic way. This is the strength of a systematic approach to the development of criterion composites.

Some other points about the development of composites are worth emphasizing. One has to do with the pattern of weights used. In the illustration just described, the account representative's work setting is a very new company that is trying to become known for quality service. The weights were chosen to reflect the values usually stressed in this context. Notice that the same sub-criteria, given different weights, might be quite appropriate for a different organization. For example, Equation 5.4 might be used in a setting where the need for revenues (through sales) is great.

$$\text{Overall effectiveness} = 5 \text{ (Selling)} + 1 \text{ (Follow-up policies)} + 1 \text{ (Service)} \tag{5.4}$$

Recently, a number of writers have emphasized the need to manage human resource practices (including criterion development) in a way that is consistent with organizational strategy and what might be called the *organizational life cycle*. For example, Schuler (1988) suggests that when an organization is new and agressively growing (the "entrepreneurial" stage), it seeks to hire employees who demonstrate innovation, initiative, and the ability to take risks. Thus, these factors should be part of the definition of the ideal criterion for employees in this type of organization. In contrast, in the case of what Schuler calls the *extract profit* strategy of a mature organization, managers want individuals who function well in a low-risk, repetitive behavior environment. Thus, both the dimensions and the weights given in a composite of individual effectiveness are different as a result of company strategy.

Another issue relates to the type of combination rule that is used in the composite. Under some circumstances subtraction is more logical, if high scores on some indicators reflect an undesirable state of affairs. To illustrate, effectiveness in the job of data entry clerk may be captured in the following composite involving a subtraction:

Overall effectiveness = 3 (Number of keystrokes/hour) - 2 (Number of errors)   (5.5)

A third combination rule—that of multiplication— also is possible. By using multiplication, we follow what is, in effect, a noncompensatory decision rule. In contrast to the case where we use an additive rule, in this model a high level of functioning in one area (e.g., Service) cannot offset or compensate for extremely low levels of effectiveness in another area (e.g., sales). This is clear if we modify the composite formula as in Equation 5.6.

Overall effectiveness = 2 (Sales) x 1 (Follow-up policies) x 5 (Service)   (5.6)

Notice that a very low score in one area (e.g., a zero), causes the whole expression to go to zero. Whether this noncompensatory combination is appropriate or not, of course, depends upon priorities established by policymakers.

Weakness of Criterion Composites

The steps outlined also reveal a major weakness of the composite approach. A good deal of time and effort is required. Thus, it might make sense only if an organization must make many personnel decisions based on carefully estimated levels of success. Schmidt and Kaplan (1971) point out that composites also can obscure essential information if the goal is to develop an understanding of certain relationships. For example, in both research and practice, scores that are obtained on other measures are frequently related to criteria of job effectiveness. This often occurs when we develop selection programs (see Chapter 8). By using a composite score as a criterion we might find an empirical relationship but not be able to tell exactly why it exists.

The use of criterion composites has been criticized for other reasons. Ghiselli (1956b) outlines a set of concerns that focus on what he calls *criterion dimensionality*. He argues that composites, despite their seeming complexity, still do not adequately reflect the dynamics of effectiveness as a construct. More specifically, Ghiselli identifies three types of dimensionality that must be dealt with. The first is *static dimensionality*. This is already explicit in the composite approach. That is, effectiveness should be thought of as multidimensional. The second one he terms *individual dimensionality*. This means that two individuals might be considered equally effective, but for different reasons. Thus, a set of weights might be appropriate for one person but not for another. The third aspect of criterion dimensionality involves the notion of *change*. The pattern of subcriteria considered desirable for a given individual may, in fact, change over time. For example, an individual may be expected to do different things as a new account representative than as a more senior employee. These observations imply that to make use of a common set of criterion elements and to rely on a single set of criterion weights would be both inappropriate and misleading. While Ghiselli doesn't claim to have the answer to the problem, he does suggest that perhaps the multiple criterion approach described earlier might be appropriate in many cases. Criterion dynamics present the investigator with other issues that have to be resolved as well. Chapter 7 will highlight some of these.

ASPECTS OF A GOOD CRITERION

We already have alluded to several important features of actual criterion measures. To recapitulate, our measures should be relevant, not deficient, and free from contamination. Composites should reflect minimal distortion; that is, the weights applied to various criterion dimensions should be appropriate. Actual criterion measures should be reliable.

Some additional "criteria" for criteria also have been identified (Bernardin & Beatty, 1984). One is *practicality*. In some cases we might be able to get actual criterion measures that possess many of the above qualities, but at too great a price. It's just not cost effective. A second issue is that of *acceptability*. Measures of effectiveness must be viewed as correct or appropriate by the people affected—management and workers alike. It is interesting to note that one of the ways to accomplish this is to ensure that the measures really do get at the important aspects of a job (that they have relevance). Third, good criterion measures must *discriminate*—they must differentiate truly effective from ineffective individuals, groups, or systems. In most organizational settings, this means that there will be variability in the scores of individuals. These and related issues will be addressed in a slightly different fashion in Chapter 6 when we will discuss actual techniques used in organizations to measure effectiveness.

Guion (1987) recently has added that a good criterion measure also has *requisite complexity*. By this he means that it captures most, if not all, of the components of the idealized or conceptual image of that which we are interested in studying. This is particularly important in research associated with theory building or testing. Otherwise, the results of studies of this sort might be misleading. That is, certain findings may incline us to reject or modify a theory when, in fact, the problem lies with the particular measures used. To avoid this problem, he recommends matching the specificity and complexity of the independent and dependent variables involved. For example, if the nature of the theorized antecedent or predictor variable is simple, it would be inappropriate to use a criterion measure that is multidimensional. Instead, a similarly simple measured (dependent) variable would be called for.

The criterion concepts and the notions of complexity and composites have been introduced and illustrated using the individual as the unit of analysis. However, they are equally applicable to groups and systems (Campbell, 1976). In particular, it is common to see both basic and applied researchers wrestle with the need to capture what is intrinsically a complex phenomenon using a limited set of measures. Frequently, what results is a compromise wherein certain levels of criterion deficiency are tolerated. Rather than apply the concepts to groups and systems at this point, in the interest of continuity, they will be reintroduced as needed in Chapter 7.

SUMMARY

In research or in managing organizations, there is a fundamental need to define and measure effectiveness. While this is often done on an intuitive and ad hoc way, there are well-developed conceptual and empirical approaches to accomplish these goals. This chapter has described a conceptual framework. It does not prescribe the solution, however. It should be quite clear that the content, nature, and complexity of criterion measures must be related to the nature of the phenomenon under study. They also should depend on the purposes and needs of the user (Guion, 1987). Whether to use global or specific measures is ultimately a judgment call. Hopefully, this chapter provides some guidance in the factors to be taken into consideration while making such decisions. More specific advice will be offered in Chapter 6 as we address the special considerations relevant to directly measuring the effectiveness of individuals.

DEFINING AND MEASURING EFFECTIVENESS AT THE INDIVIDUAL LEVEL

This chapter deals with concepts associated with defining and measuring effectiveness in work organizations at the individual level. We first attempt to place the measurement of effectiveness in a context of specifying the criterion domain. Major sections are then devoted to an examination of forces affecting and controlling the quality of such measures. Finally, the chapter presents a fairly extensive description of the numerous options available to those who need (for reasons of research or practice) to select, modify, or develop measures of effectiveness at the individual level.

SPECIFYING THE CRITERION DOMAIN

In the previous chapter, we reviewed the thinking that goes on in the development of criterion or effectiveness measures. However, at this point we want to be explicit with regard to just where our actual criteria come from. That is to say, we will review how we decide just what should be included in a good operational measure.

Systems Perspective

In general, when selecting or developing criterion measures for individuals, the researcher or practitioner should attempt to establish the abilities, behaviors, or work products that are important for the job, tasks, or persons of interest. To do this well we recommend a systems approach.

In this context, a *systems approach* implies gathering information regarding the necessary abilities, behaviors, or work products from more than one perspective. More importantly, this means taking into consideration the setting or context in which effectiveness is to be demonstrated. To do this involves conducting two or more of the following: job analysis, worker analysis, and/or organization and environment analysis.

Job Analysis. When reading the example of the account representative used to illustrate criterion issues in the previous chapter, you might already have noticed that the criterion elements identified could have been derived from a direct consideration of the job itself. This is, indeed, the preferred starting place. Thus, in general, criterion definition and dimensionality will be established through the conduct of the job analysis, which is why we stressed job analysis in Chapter 5.

Worker Analysis. The purpose of worker analysis is to come to a better appreciation of the nature of effectiveness by focusing less on the job and more on the individual (or groups of individuals) who are performing the job. This can be done in a number of ways.

When the goal of the researcher is to establish the content of effectiveness measures it is not unusual to enlist the help of people who are knowledgeable with regard to the job or job type of interest (usually these are supervisors) and use what is commonly referred to as the *critical incident technique*. In brief, this technique involves having individuals think about incidents (on-the-job events), actually seen or experienced that reflect examples of especially effective or ineffective behavior or performance on the part of known workers. Through a process of collecting and distilling many such incidents, the investigator comes to better understand the nature of effectiveness and its complexity for the job or job family (e.g., all types of account representatives). As applied to the development of behaviorally anchored rating scales (described later in this chapter) systematic analysis of the critical incidents also can provide the words to be used in the phrasing of the dimensions and of the scale response points as well.

The practicing manager may perform such a worker analysis in a different manner. In this regard, he or she might review the observed performance of several employees. This could involve summarizing existing assessments of employees recorded on a standardized instrument as part of the organization's formal appraisal program. Through such an effort, the manager would constantly reflect on what factors have caused or created impressions of effectiveness or lack thereof. By focusing on specific individuals, the manager as investigator can thus clarify what it is that is important and promotes effectiveness. Moreover, by comparing stongly held beliefs regarding the overall effectiveness of a given person with assessments of the various factors found on a standard form, he or she will become sensitive to instances of deficiency. Thus, aspects of functioning, important to the notion of an effective worker that are not captured on the form, should be detected. This in turn should produce a necessary and sufficient set of factors that can serve to define effectiveness.

Finally, a worker analysis may be carried out by examining the qualities of individuals who represent extremes. In this approach, supervisors might be asked to identify or nominate workers who are (all things considered) very effective or very ineffective. By probing the basis of these nominations, the investigator may be able to discern the factors that go into a conceptual model of effectiveness implicitly held by these key members of the organization.

Organization and Environment Analysis. A third way to uncover the true nature of what must be included in measures of individual effectiveness is to examine the context of the job and the worker. Most contemporary views of the nature of organizational life emphasize the fact that individual employees are, to a large extent, interdependent with others when it comes to doing their job (Katz & Kahn, 1978). The performance of a sales person is affected by the performance of the market researcher (who might advise on selling strategies) or by the department secretary (who relays messages and leads about possible customers). A manager's decisions are strongly affected by the data and summaries created by an analyst. Any number of examples can be given. While these interdependencies may be detected in a good job analysis, an organization analysis ensures a good look at them.

Similarly, organizational analysis uncovers practices and policies that serve to affect (enhance or limit) individual effectiveness. For example, Cravens and Woodruff (1973) sought to devise performance indicators for sales personnel employed by a manufacturer of consumer goods. Their approach involved going beyond a job and worker analysis as they reasoned that sales performance could be influenced by a number of factors outside of the employee's control. Thus, in their study, they indexed (and controlled) for the company's experience and its reputation in each sales territory and the amount of effort it was spending there promoting its products. Clearly, a sales person's performance would be affected by such factors and they needed to be factored in any evaluation of sales personnel from different sales territories.

Another advantage of considering the context in which job performance is to take place is that it can provide a description of individuals or groups who may be considered as *stakeholders*. By stakeholders we mean those who have a vested interest in and valid point of view regarding the behavior and performance of the individual (or job) of focus. Stakeholders may be outside (e.g., customers or suppliers) as well as inside the boundaries of the organization. For example, Yukl and Kanuk (1979) in their investigation of the effectiveness of beauty salon managers obtained information on a sample of such managers from a representative of a major cosmetic company who called on all of the salons and who also knew the managers well. As the United States moves to a service-based economy, customer perceptions and satisfaction in particular will become increasingly relevant.

The importance of a stakeholder inventory to the defining of effectiveness is quite direct. It promotes a consideration of effectiveness from multiple points of view. Thus, the question of what constitutes a good performance, in effect, is followed by another related one: From whose point of view? What is effective from your secretary's perspective may have little to do with what your manager wants. Through a stakeholder analysis the investigator attempting to define and measure effectiveness may find the need to create multiple relevant indices in order to cover the criterion domain. This also implies that effectiveness might best be assessed using more than one set of informants or sources (see Klimoski & London, 1974). More about stakeholders will be covered in Chapter 7.

These three approaches to identifying the criterion domain for purposes of measurement should not be seen as interchangeable. Under most circumstances, one cannot substitute for another. They just don't provide the same information. In particular, we find it highly unlikely that good effectiveness measures can ever be constructed without a job analysis. In this regard, these other ways of obtaining information regarding criterion dimensionality might be viewed as supplemental and providing an expanded, and in our judgment a better, view as to the nature of effectiveness at the individual level.

Three Alternatives

Some years ago Campbell and his associates (Campbell, Dunnette, Lawler, & Weick, 1970) described the numerous options open to personnel specialists regarding the content or substance of the assessments of effectiveness at the individual level. They suggested that measurement programs can emphasize person, process, or products. By *person* they mean an appraisal can focus on evaluating the personal traits or qualities that are felt to be important in employees. Thus, an effective employee is one who has or exhibits key attributes such as initiative, loyalty, dependability, etc. This is a very common approach and has been a part of many programs for years (Tiffin & McCormick, 1965). Despite its popularity and the documented preference of people to use trait categories in the way they relate to one another, Campbell et al. (1970), and others (Bernardin & Beatty, 1984), strongly argue against this type of orientation. Making trait assessments is quite difficult, even for individuals trained as specialists (psychologists). Traits are not tangible or clearly defined entities. They must be inferred from what people do or say. Yet arguments can (and will) be made for the use of trait-based assessment programs under certain circumstances.

Alternatively, measurement efforts can stress what have been called *products*. Guion (1965) labels the product of effort or work a secondary outcome. These are the things accomplished or produced as part of one's job. Sometimes they are referred to as outcomes. The attraction of indexing effectiveness in terms of "number of units produced," "commissions earned," "scrap levels," etc., stems in large part from the apparent objectivity involved. Such things can be counted or measured directly. But, as pointed out in our discussion of criterion contamination, these indicators, too, have their problems. Sometimes things become criterion measures just because they appear to be easily measured. Such measures often are deficient and contaminated. Finally, the objective nature of these types of criteria is frequently overstated. Subjectivity and human judgment enter into the measurement process at many points (Smith, 1976).

Process data refer to job-relevant behaviors. Instead of emphasizing personal qualities or job results, this approach focuses on what a person does or does not do on the job. The attention to job-relevant behavior appears to have at least three advantages. First, behavior is observable. We can see and record it with some reliability. Second, it is likely to be under the control of the individual. It is something to which he or she can be fairly held accountable. Finally, it usually can be changed or modified. This is related to the second point. Dysfunctional or inappropriate behavior patterns, if isolated, often can be useful input to programs designed to bring about improvement in effectiveness.

Getting at relevant processes can present quite a challenge if what is truly important for effectiveness is how a person thinks or makes decisions in contrast to any particular job behaviors. In this case the phenomenon of interest is mental and cannot be observed or noticed under normal conditions. Thus, we may have to rely on self-reports of how a problem is approached intellectually (through interviews or diaries) or develop observable indicators of the underlying mental processes. For example, Martin and Klimoski (1989) had managers speak aloud under controlled circumstances while they conducted an evaluation of their employees. This provided information regarding their mental processes on this task. These data, in turn, could be evaluated for correctness or effectiveness. Similarly, cognitive psychologists have devised procedures to allow for the measurement of mental processes through such observable behaviors as decision time, the way people search for information as they solve problems, or the choices that they make (Ford, Schmitt, Schechtman, Hults, & Doherty, 1989). Finally, some worker-oriented job analysis techniques (e.g., McCormick, 1976) do attempt to get at the relevance and importance of on-the-job thinking and decision making as it relates to job effectiveness.

To appreciate the distinction between persons, process, and product, consider the following example where we might want to evaluate a manager on the criterion dimension of dependability:

Person	Process	Product
Judged on dependability	Observed tendency to review own work and the work of subordinates daily	Number of deadlines missed

As you can see, while the concept of dependability is retained in each case, the operational indicators are different.

Current thinking among personnel specialists is that there are advantages to using job-related behaviors (process data) as the substance of effectiveness measures. However, each approach appears to have features that might make it attractive under certain circumstances. For example, trait measurement would be appropriate and even necessary if the purpose of assessing effectiveness is to select individuals for new or different assignments (Bernardin & Beatty, 1984). Evaluating individuals on the basis of behavior would seem useful for the planning of training or development activities for an employee or a group of employees or for evaluating training programs (Wexley & Latham, 1981). And, outcome measures may be appropriate as a basis for administrative decisions like compensation (Carroll & Schneier, 1982). Regardless of the choice of person, process, or product, it should be kept in mind that the problems of contamination, deficiency, reliability, etc., still must be dealt with. To put it another way, the purpose of the measurement of individual effectiveness should determine which approach(es) you would use.

RELIANCE ON HUMAN JUDGMENTS IN OBTAINING INDIVIDUAL EFFECTIVENESS DATA

In later sections of this chapter it will become increasingly clear that the measurement of individual effectiveness usually involves human judgment. Even nominally objective data (e.g., number of products produced) will require decisions by managers about such things as the quality or timeliness of production (i.e., does it meet standards for a completed product).

Social Cognition Theories

In recent years, researchers have come to believe that the key to improving the quality of individual effectiveness measures lies in a better understanding of the way individuals gather, process, and use information (Bernardin & Beatty, 1984). While this notion had been put forth years ago by Thorndike (1920) and Wherry (1952), the work of Landy and Farr (1980) and of Ilgen and Feldman (1983), in particular, have set the tone of current thinking.

Accurate data regarding individual effectiveness are difficult to obtain, it is argued, because of the cognitive (and some might say emotional) demands that are placed on individuals charged with this task. Thus, basic research in the areas of person perception, impression formation, human memory and cognition, decision making, and group dynamics is referred to for guidance in the design and implementation of measurent programs.

One of the more useful frameworks in this regard comes from research on social cognition. This area of study attempts to understand how people come to perceive, understand, and make use of their social (i.e., interpersonal) environment.

Of particular relevance are the theories and the research data that help to explain how we form impressions of other people. In this view, the process that a manager or supervisor experiences in providing estimates of effectiveness is assumed to represent only a special case of impression formation. Carroll and Schneier (1982) portray the dynamics operating in a diagram (Figure 6-1).

Like anyone who must relate to someone else, the supervisor is thought to be trying to "make sense" of his or her subordinate in order to respond to the demands of a performance measurement effort whether for administrative reasons or for research. More specifically, he or she must reach some conclusion regarding the employee's recent level of performance and/or effectiveness, and (especially in the case of the poor performer) the reasons for this level of functioning. According to theories of social cognition, this is a complex process, one which often results in poor quality (inaccurate) evaluations.

Implicit Personality Theory. A useful construct derived from this literature is the evaluator's *implicit personality theory*. This refers to the beliefs or assumptions held by a person regarding the way in which various aspects of behavior are related. It also involves mechanisms that promote the tendency for individuals to make inferences or to form conclusions about others based on limited information (Schneider, Hastorf, & Ellsworth, 1979; Hakel, 1971; Rassenfoss & Klimoski, 1985).

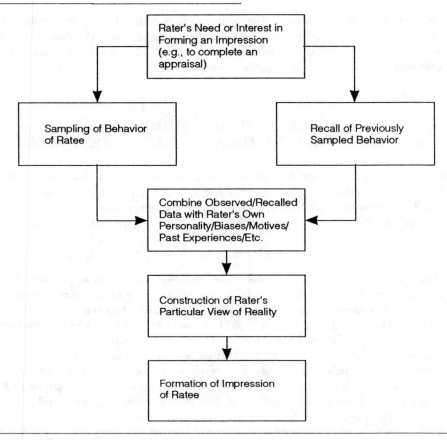

FIGURE 6-1   A Model of Impression Formation

Source: Reprinted with permission from Carroll, S. J., & Schneier, C. E. (1982). *Performance appraisal and review systems.* Glenview, IL: Scott Foresman.

For example, when a person states that a muscular worker also can be expected to be aggressive we are getting some insights into his or her implicit theory.

Implicit personality theories are mental frameworks within which we deal with information about other people. They also reflect the fact that, as social perceivers, we are not passive and do not process things as they actually are. Instead, we frequently create meanings in the behavior of people and in the events around us (McCauley, Stilt, & Segal, 1980; Cooper, 1981). More specifically, these implicit theories (like stereotypes) affect what information we attend to, demand, or generate; how we store and organize this information; how we retrieve and integrate this with new knowledge; and, ultimately, how we behave towards others (Feldman, 1981).

As noted, central to the notion of implicit personality theories is the presumed covariation among elements or aspects of personality or behavior on the part of a perceiver (manager, worker). Cooper (1981) calls these *illusory correlations* because while they may have a basis in reality, it is more likely that they come about because of several rather natural yet erroneous tendencies on the part of individuals. Moreover, when the person that we are talking about is the manager making assessments in the form of ratings, the result of these illusory correlations is usually a biased estimate of effectiveness. More specifically, we tend to get evaluations that exhibit a symptom of poor quality called *halo*.

By way of illustration, Rassenfoss and Klimoski (1985) investigated the effects of implicit theories on ratings and recommendations made by student subjects in a simulation study. Students' implicit theories of a dormitory counselor were measured and integrated into the study. The task they had to perform required that they evaluate the behavior and effectiveness of applicants for the job of counselor. When subjects were given some preliminary information regarding the applicant that was relevant to their implicit theory regarding dormitory counselors, it was found that they perceived or "read into" the behavior of the applicant certain features which were consistent with their theory. For example, applicants who were discovered to be *trustworthy* (a theory-relevant trait) through the presentation of preliminary information, were characterized as *careful* (also theory relevant) in their work performed as part of the application process, even when they were not. In contrast, they were not viewed as more or less *honest*, a quality equally attractive but which was not part of this implicit theory. In both instances, no information was actually presented regarding how honest the candidate might be.

Implicit theories also have been investigated and found to be important in the assessment or description of managerial effectiveness or leadership. In the study of leadership, it is quite common to use ratings or descriptions of effectiveness supplied by group members or followers. This has been especially true for research testing theories that emphasize the importance of leader behaviors. In such theories, leader behavior is thought to be the key to effectiveness. That is to say, effective leaders are thought to be this way because they demonstrate different behaviors or more of certain behaviors than less-effective leaders (Stogdill, 1969; Yukl, 1989). Thus, there has been a tradition of using subordinate (or follower) ratings of leader behavior as measures.

Recently, Lord and his colleagues (Lord, Binning, Rush, & Thomas, 1978; Rush, Thomas, & Lord, 1977; Lord, 1977) have investigated the nature of and basis of the judgments that go into ratings of leader behavior. In carefully designed laboratory experiments he has been able to demonstrate that, at times, actual leader behaviors bear only a weak relationship to what followers report. For example, the apparent success or failure of the group has been found to influence subjects' ratings of certain categories of leader behaviors. He postulates that subjects' "implicit leadership theories" may be operating to influence attention, encoding, memory, and recording dynamics. Another finding is that raters (followers) tended to ascribe more behavior to the leader that was consistent with their images of a leader than behavior that was not consistent or irrelevant to the image. This was especially true when there was any delay between the observation period and rating period (Phillips, 1984). While we would not argue that all follower reports of leader behaviors are suspect, it would be important to rule out implicit theory processes as an alternative explanation for a particular pattern of results.

Finally, Krzystofiak, Cardy, and Newman (1989) have demonstrated the impact of implicit personality theory dynamics in a field setting where management students were required to judge the performance of professors. While actual performance differences among professors were detected in student judgments, inference about traits had significant and independent effects. However, Krzystofiak et al. suggest that trait categorization may be a natural and automatic process in human judgment and memory. Contrary to some other authors, they recommend that, rather than try to eliminate the tendency, we might do better to use multiple rating formats that allow us to capture more of the information that raters are (appear to be) using.

Two related concepts, prototypes and schemas, also have been found to be useful to understanding the cognitive processes operating in performance appraisals. In order to deal with the tremendous amount of information available to managers as they evaluate employees, psychologists feel that people construct cognitive blueprints called schema or prototypes. *Prototypes* are abstract images that capture the essential features of categories. *Schemas* are somewhat more complex and include elements like causal relationships. Both are thought to be important because they, like implicit theories, affect the way that we perceive and organize information (Feldman, 1981). In particular, they seem to guide our attention and search for information. Like a mental set, they predispose us to notice or detect information that is consistent and to ignore what is discrepant.

Prototypes can exist for a variety of phenomena, but we are most interested in those that might be held for various categories of workers like "high performer" or for types of jobs—secretary, vice president, etc. To the extent that a subordinate is considered to belong to a category (e.g., a good worker), his or her behavior or performance comes to be viewed from this perspective. The process of labeling someone has profound implications for attention, retention, and retrieval or recollection of information. Furthermore, while there is some evidence that valid prototypes can enhance personnel decisions (Schmitt, 1976), it is far too common for them to be incorrect or incomplete in some important ways.

Attribution Processes. A final concept, *attribution process*, which derives from the social cognition literature, is useful in understanding how we come to *interpret* performance and performance-related behavior. It is assumed that our evaluations of other people are not merely the result of only automatic processes. Instead, we appear to spend effort trying to figure out just *why* someone behaves (or performs) the way he or she does (Kelley, 1973; Jones & Davis, 1965; Mitchell & Kalb, 1981; Feldman, 1981).

Contrary to the old adage, *attribution theory* states that a person's actions do not speak for themselves. We must interpret or make sense out of them. Especially under circumstances that are important or where a decision has to be made (e.g., as in a performance appraisal), we usually go through a process of trying to infer what personal qualities (traits or dispositions) are relevant to the behavior that we see. These, in turn, serve to guide our actions toward the person.

According to Heider (1958) and others, we act like a naive psychologist or detective. Upon observing behavior (like an instance of poor performance), we first attempt to determine if it was caused by internal or external forces. That is, was it caused by the individual or by something in the setting or the environment? If you, the observer, conclude that it was caused by the individual, you then might try to establish just what it is about the person (ability, effort) that is causing what you see.

Kelley (1973) suggests that we use certain clues or decision rules as we go about making attributions. One is behavior consistency. Consider the case of the poorly performing worker. Attention to consistency cues would involve asking questions of the following type: Does he or she do poorly on a variety of tasks and in different situations? What about past performance? Was it ever at higher levels? To the extent that behavior is consistent, we are more likely to conclude that something about the individual is responsible.

Related to this is the notion of distinctiveness. Does the worker perform in other situations at the same low levels? Or is there something unique about the particular task, work group, or supervision experienced? A third rule we might use is called consensus. How are other workers performing under the same circumstances? If all of our salespeople did poorly last month, it would be reasonable to conclude that something in the environment most likely is having an effect to dampen performance (e.g., a poor economy).

The most common causal attributions that we might make for (especially poor) performance include worker ability, levels of effort, task difficulty, chance factors (luck), or the quality of supervision. Notice that some of these can be thought as stable or hard to change (ability). Others are transitory (luck) or can be more easily modified (effort). Moreover, some attributions are more self-serving than others. To infer that poor performance is primarily due to the employee's personal and stable qualities, rather than to inadequate supervision, frees the manager of a lot of responsibility (and work!).

Most of the research evidence relating attributional dynamics to performance appraisal comes from specially designed simulations of work and not from actual organizational settings. Thus, the results must be interpreted with some caution. However, what has been discovered seems very relevant to our goal of understanding performance measurement processes.

In many cases, however, it has been deviations from theory that have been the most provocative. For example, several studies have documented the tendency of people to *underestimate* the importance of the situation in causing or explaining behavior. When performance is observed, it is usually presumed to be due to personal factors like ability or effort rather than to the situation. This, in turn, affects how we react. In a simulation study, Heilman and Guzzo (1978) found that rewards and punishments were given out as a result of attributions for performance. Employees perceived as successful because of such factors as luck or an easy task were less likely to be considered for promotion than those whose performances were thought to be a result of high ability. On the other hand, Mitchell and Kalb (1981) report that this tendency can be modified. In their study, subjects (acting as supervisors), who were given experience on the same task that their future subordinates would be working on, demonstrated greater sensitivity to the situation as a cause in their later evaluations of poorly performing subordinates on the same task.

Implications of Social Cognition Dynamics

The theories and findings of the research on social cognition are only beginning to be recognized for how they might contribute to personnel measurement. Still, it might be useful to point out implications as seen by your authors.

The pervasive impact of implicit theories of personality on performance judgments implies that the person responsible for measurement system design needs to be sensitive to their nature and the extent to which they exist in the work setting. To the degree that this is done, he or she might use the insights gained in both scale design and in training raters. In the former instance, where the prototypes are valid (i.e., they reflect what would be uncovered by a job analysis), they could become the bases for the selection of scale dimensions to be used. Alternatively, erroneous implicit theories might be acknowledged and treated in the training activities carried out to implement the appraisal program. By making explicit these implicit ideas and by confronting them in training, the individuals responsible for producing effectiveness data will be less likely to be susceptible to their influence. Something like this is being done in frame of reference training as described later in this chapter.

Work on attribution theory implies that the evaluation of the effectiveness of someone is a rather personal process. That is to say, the rater's needs, feelings, and expectations play a part in what gets perceived, encoded, stored, and retrieved from memory. Once again, discussing these tendencies in a training program for those responsible for appraisals may serve to mitigate some of their unintentional, but powerful, effects. However, beyond this, there is evidence that increasing accountability also may be an appropriate way to deal with them (Mitchell & Klimoski, 1985; McAllister, Mitchell, & Beach, 1979). In general, *accountability* refers to the requirement that one's evaluation (e.g., an appraisal) or decisions (e.g., regarding pay) will have to be reviewed by someone else. This usually raises what might be thought of as evaluation apprehension, a concern on the part of the rater that he or she might not come across as an effective person, rater, or manager. Thus, ironically, the rater's concern over an evaluation (his or hers) may lead to a higher quality (more accurate) evaluation of someone else. Accountability appears to increase the care and rigorousness with which an evaluation is made. This, in turn, reduces the tendency to rely on strictly habitual or more or less casual attribution formation. The end result is fewer attribution errors.

Many companies appear to recognize the value of accountability in increasing the quality of the data obtained in their performance appraisal program. For example, it is quite common to require a manager to review an appraisal with the worker before it becomes part of the latter's personnel file. Presumably, having to face the worker (who is likely to challenge an erroneous appraisal) causes the manager to exert more care in the evaluation. More recently, some organizations have instituted an additional review of appraisals by requiring that they be further checked by the manager's boss. If an anticipated review by the subordinate encourages any distortion of appraisals in an overly positive direction, then having an upper manager get involved might mitigate this tendency. Thus, the cure for faulty attributions by increasing accountability will not create additional problems.

One final implication of the emerging evidence from research on social cognition is worth highlighting. There is a need to recognize that when it comes to subjective estimates of effectiveness the observer/rater is an intrinsic part of the measurement process. No matter what appraisal format described in this chapter may be used, human judgment is involved. Thus, we might wish to consider individual differences in the capacity to form valid inferences and judgments. In this manner individuals might be classified with regard to their skills in social judgment. Some will be much better than others. As outlined by Banks and Roberson (1985) this would mean considering each appraiser as a test. In particular, Banks and Roberson emphasize the importance of domain sampling for appraisers-as-tests. We thus would need to determine the capacity of observers/raters to correctly attend to the right aspects of work behavior as a basis for their judgments. Observers who cannot do this well should be identified and dealt with. Instead of rejecting such individuals as unsuitable, Banks and Roberson (1985) recommend that evaluation skills be increased by teaching them how to differentiate between levels of performance, to avoid judgmental errors, and to appropriately sample behavior on the job. For example, they recommend that we might attempt to change appraisers' prototype categories or schemas in a direction more in line with actual job requirements.

Irrespective of the way one might bring about the situation where appraisers are less susceptible to incorrect social judgment processing, we need to be aware of the wide range of individual differences in this area. These will certainly show up in the quality of the effectiveness data that we will obtain.

Status of Theories of Social Cognition

A recent review of this area by DeNisi, Cafferty, and Meglino (1984) was very supportive of the potential usefulness of these theories for understanding individual performance measurement in work organizations. However, they stress the need for more research before we can form any definite conclusions regarding the way different conditions in the workplace affect cognitive processes. In particular, they argue for more studies on the way people search for information. DeNisi et al. (1984) feel that it is very important to learn of the impact of such things as the purpose of an appraisal (e.g., developmental, salary decision), the time pressures faced by a manager, and the type of rating instrument used. These are all thought to affect the nature of the information gathered, the processing of information, and the attributions made. And these, in turn, will influence the quality of the resulting data.

ESTIMATING THE QUALITY OF MEASURES
OF INDIVIDUAL EFFECTIVENESS

Based on criterion development theory, we would say that the quality of an operational measure is the extent that it reflects the effectiveness of an individual in the areas defined by our conceptual or ideal criterion. The fact of the matter is that we almost never have a way determining this directly. Instead, we have to rely upon inferences from accumulated evidence that our measures are any good. Over the years, researchers have come to use what Bernardin and Beatty (1984) call *surrogate measures,* or indicators, of the quality (or validity) of performance data, most of which are psychometric in nature. Among these are: (a) evidence of central tendency, range restriction, leniency and severity, halo; (b) levels of reliability, contrast, or order effects; (c) freedom from unfair bias; (d) degree of documentation; and, more recently, (e) accuracy. Each of these will be described briefly.

Central Tendency

Central tendency reflects a pattern where scores on an effectiveness measure cluster at or near the middle of the distribution of potential scores. In the case of ratings, managers would not be using the extremes of the scales and all workers would be described as average. Central tendency is viewed as an error or as a manifestation of poor data because it is believed that this is not really the true state of affairs in most work situations. Some employees are bound to be better or more effective than others. Where there are large numbers of people being evaluated we might expect that the distribution of their evaluations ought to resemble a normal distribution (see Chapter 2).

We frequently find central tendency error under circumstances where managers don't really know the people to be evaluated or where the appraisals are not believed by managers to be very important. In the latter case, rather than work at making valid assessments or taking the chance of alienating some workers by giving them a (perhaps warranted) low evaluation, everyone receives the same middle score. The end result is low discriminability as the measurement program fails to differentiate among employees. Such data are not particularly useful for most purposes.

Notice that we are making assumptions when we say that obtained scores with limited variability clustered about the middle of the distribution are in error and that we have low quality data. None of the measures of range restriction or central tendency can tell us if, in fact, this might not be the correct distribution. In some contexts (e.g., where we have a preselected group) it might well be. Thus, it would not be an error; it reflects the true state of affairs! This is a problem of many of these surrogate indicators of quality. Whether or not measurements are appropriate or are in error must be determined through additional analyses.

Leniency and Severity

Leniency and *severity* also refer to the tendency of people to use only a limited part of the effectiveness continuum of a measurement system. However, this time evaluations are represented as universally high (lenient) or low (severe). This is an error or reflection of questionable data because, once again, it is presumed to be an inaccurate picture of the true situation. It is thought to be unlikely that all individuals are truly great or really poor.

The causes of leniency and severity effects are numerous and complex. In some cases they can be a function of the personal style of the manager doing the evaluations. Some are just tougher in their standards than others. Far more likely causes though, are forces in the measurement situation that promote this type of distortion. For example, leniency is frequently observed when the evaluations are not to be used as input to any important decisions, where the supervisor is not very self-confident and desires the positive regard of the people being measured (who are likely to see their scores), or where the supervisor believes that low appraisals reflect badly on his or her own ability to manage. Under all these circumstances, the motivation of the manager to be accurate would be low and the desire to be discriminating weak. The result is poor quality data.

Reliability

As mentioned in the section on criterion contamination, high reliability is a desired feature of actual criterion measures. As advanced in Chapter 3, *reliability* is the extent to which a set of scores are free from error variance. To the extent that we have low reliability in evaluations we would infer that they are of poor quality. From an operational viewpoint, we might desire three types of reliability evidence. The first relates to consistency in evaluations over (a somewhat short) time. Apart from the effects of memory, would the manager produce a similar evaluation if asked to perform one on the same worker a second time? The second involves the degree of consensus obtained in assessments. Do two or more managers (who are in a position to do so) give similar evaluations for a set of workers? And finally, would we get the the same level of appraised effectiveness if we used a different appraisal instrument? Or are the results a function of the particular form or evaluation format that is used? Evidence of more types of reliability gives us greater confidence that our appraisals are of high quality (Bernardin & Beatty, 1984). These concepts of reliability have been discussed with regard to measures in general in Chapter 3.

Guion (1965) notes that, by gathering effectiveness data from more than one person, an investigator can check on the extent to which one or more appraisers don't go along with the others, thus providing a check, of sorts, on the quality of data. He describes a formula by Shen (1925) whereby a set of ratings made by one rater can be correlated with the composite of all the others (η_c in the equation below). This is reproduced as follows for Rater 1:

$$\eta_c = \frac{(k-2)(\eta_i^2)}{kr_{ij} - 2\eta_i} \qquad (6.1)$$

where k is the number of raters, r_{1i} is the average of the correlations of rater 1 and other raters, and r_{ij} is the average of the intercorrelations between ratings. Guion points out that this value can be computed for each rater contributing to the pool of ratings, differences can be tested for significance, and the ratings of those whose correlation with the pool are significantly lower than others may be considered as suspect (Guion, 1965, p. 112).

Halo Error

As outlined in Chapter 5, effectiveness in most jobs is considered to be multifaceted or multidimensional. This means that it is quite possible for an individual to be strong in one area (e.g., selling) and not to be as effective in another (e.g., follow through or service). Halo is the tendency to evaluate a person in an undifferentiated manner so that he or she is regarded as equally effective or ineffective in all domains.

While the general notion is clear, how or why halo comes about is not. For instance, we might manifest halo because we get a global or overall impression and we let this affect our judgments in the specific areas to be evaluated. Cooper (1981) calls this *engulfing*. Or we might not have enough opportunity to observe the person being evaluated. Or it might occur because we let our (possibly accurate) assessment in one area of effectiveness determine our evaluations in the others. Cooper (1981) elaborates on these and other processes that might be involved.

The fundamental assumption that underlies the notion of halo as an *error* always must be questioned. That is, in a given circumstance can we assume that a person could be all good or all bad? We always must be sensitive to the possibility that the extremely high covariation among dimension scores just might reflect reality. We may have a group of truly effective (or ineffective) individuals.

The measurement or assessment of halo in a set of evaluations on individuals is complex. As pointed out by Becker and Cardy (1986), Fisicaro (1988), and others, the two most frequently used measures of halo are the *average ratee standard deviation scores across performance effectiveness dimensions* and the *average intercorrelation across preformance dimensions* rated (often transformed to Fisher z values). Cooper (1981) points out that these two indices are both conceptually and empirically distinct. While Murphy and Balzer (1981) found the two measures to be relatively independent in their study, Pulakos, Schmitt, and Ostroff (1986) warn against the current practice of using the standard deviation across dimensions within ratees to measure halo. Pulakos et al. (1986) recommend that each rater's average observed and standardized intercorrelation among the dimensions be used as an index of halo.

Order Effects and Contrast Effects

It has been argued that the evaluation of performance involves processes that are quite similar to those occurring in impression formation. Moreover, both imply the obtaining, storing, retrieval, and use of information. This, in turn, is greatly influenced by cognitive processing dynamics. Order effects refer to the fact that the sequence in which we receive information can alter or distort our perceptions and evaluations.

The first performance data or cues about a person that we become aware of frequently get too much weight in our thinking. This is referred to as a *primacy effect* (Latham, Wexley, & Purcell, 1975). On the other hand, under certain circumstances evaluations can be biased by something that has just happened. This is referred to as a *recency effect.* The term recency effect is also used to refer to the fact that events which have happened some time before a manager is expected to do a performance review often are forgotten or, at least, given very little weight in the evaluation. In theory, our impressions will reflect a balance of both tendencies. It seems clear that first impressions do a great deal to set up certain expectations or cognitive structures which will have direct effects on what we attend to later (Feldman, 1981; DeNisi et al. 1984; Rassenfoss & Klimoski, 1985).

It is also true that our judgments of a person's effectiveness are going to be affected by the performances of others doing the same kind of work. This is referred to as the *contrast* effect (Landy & Farr, 1980). In a very clever study, Grey and Kipnis (1976) discovered that a manager gave unusually high recommendations to an employee if he or she was a good performer in a work group made up largely of low performers. Presumably the former stood out in contrast to peers. This phenomenon also has been found in selection interviews where a manager must meet with and evaluate a large number of applicants in quick succession. The quality of preceeding candidates can cause a bias in impressions, especially at the end of the day (Schmitt, 1976).

Finally, Smither, Reilly, and Buda (1988) describe contrast effects of a different sort. In their experiment they found that knowledge of prior performance influenced evaluations of effectiveness. Awareness of prior poor behavior depressed later ratings of the same individuals. But this effect was only pronounced when the two sessions of evaluation were close together (one hour). No such effects occurred when a more realistic interval of three weeks was used.

Freedom from Unfair Bias

Personal prejudice should not enter into estimates of job effectiveness. It is a bad business practice because the real levels of effectiveness are unknown when this occurs and inferior personnel decisions are likely to result. Most importantly, it also is against the law to discriminate on the basis of race, sex, religion, age, handicap, or national origin. For example, data that reflect systematically lower scores for employees belonging to groups identifiable by one or more of these factors (e.g., blacks, women, Jews, Mexican-Americans, etc.) could be the result of bias or prejudice. In particular, however, care should be taken to minimize the possibility that one or a few supervisors could be destroying the future opportunities of workers by unwarranted low evaluations.

The actual detection of unfair bias in effectiveness indicators is difficult. Often, researchers and managers compare the psychometric properties of effectiveness scores (e.g., means and standard deviations) for known groups. Thus, ratings given to blacks and whites might be contrasted to see if the former are systematically lower than the latter. More sophisticated analyses will involve the careful examination of patterns of relationships among indicators of effectiveness or the presumed correlates of effectiveness. In this regard, Huber, Neale, and Northcraft (1987) used hierarchical regression to determine the effects of ratee characteristics (gender, age, etc.) over and above performance factors on subjective assessments of effectiveness. While actual performance accounted for the largest amount of variance in the judgments of the managers in this study, ratee characteristics also had direct effects (see also Madden, 1981).

In many investigations, the assessment of bias is done using analysis of variance designs. This is because variables such as gender and race usually are treated as having discrete values (male/female, black/white, etc). Thus, the inference that unfair bias may be operating is made where, for example, there is an effect of the sex of the rater or the sex of the worker, or where the various interactions reported in complex factorial designs (sex of rater by sex of worker) are found to be significant (c.f., Mobley, 1982; Shore & Thornton, 1986).

Finally, it should be mentioned that bias also has been inferred from analyses of subjective effectiveness data gathered from known groups, wherein the apparent dimensionality of these data are found to be different. For example, Klimoski and London (1974) obtained ratings from three groups: job incumbents, coworkers, and supervisors. These ratings were subjected to hierarchical factor analysis. It was found that the apparent dimensions of judgment used by these three groups were different. The groups appeared to approach the rating task with different concepts of just what was meant about effectiveness (much like implicit personality theories). It is interesting that Klimoski & London (1974) preferred not to label these differences as bias as it might imply one or more of the groups was systematically wrong. Instead, they argue that, when it comes to the three groups studied, each party could have a valid point of view. This point will be discussed later in this chapter when the focus is on what choice of agent should be used by an investigator.

For those who are particularly interested in theory and a model of discrimination dynamics in effectiveness ratings, consult the works of Dipboye (1985) and Jacobson and Effertz (1974).

Accuracy Scores

Indications of the quality of effectiveness measures discussed so far all have relied on inferences based on statistical or psychometric evidence. However, as noted, many researchers have raised methodological and theoretical issues about the usefulness of such indicators. Thus, a number of investigators have turned to measures of accuracy.

Accuracy is inferred from both the strength and kind of relationship between one set of measures and another true or target set felt to be an accepted standard for comparison (Sulsky & Balzer, 1988). Unlike reliability or validity measures, accuracy indices focus as much on the kind of relationship as on the strength of relationship between two score distributions.

In general, *accuracy* is determined by comparing rater judgments of effectiveness for several individuals on several dimensions with corresponding evaluations provided by experts. Or, in the case of investigations where simulations are used, one can compare obtained ratings with what had been designed or scripted. For example, Borman (1978) used videotaped examples of people performing the task of a recruiter/interviewer as stimuli, while Becker and Cardy (1986) used written stories or vignettes. In both cases, the researcher knew in advance and could refer to scripted performances as the true or target values in a computation of an accuracy score.

Most researchers studying accuracy draw heavily on Cronbach's (1955) work in which he argues that overall rater accuracy can be divided into four components:

1. *Elevation.* Level of ratings given across several dimensions.
2. *Differential elevation.* Variability in ratings across dimensions.
3. *Stereotype accuracy.* The match between the profile of ratings given and a target or true score profile.
4. *Differential accuracy.* Accuracy for specific dimensions.

Thus, when it comes to describing accuracy each of these indices has potential value. Cronbach also provides for an overall index of accuracy (D^2) making use of the information in all of these indices.

Sulsky and Balzer (1988) point out that, while the large number of potential accuracy scores all tend to involve a companion with a standard, the various measures are not highly related to one another. In their review of this topic they conclude that the different measures may uncover different facets of rating performance or even ability. Thus, the investigator needs to be clear about just what type of accuracy is of interest. In general, these authors urge extreme caution in the use of accuracy measures, insofar as there are so many options to choose from and no consensus exists in the literature.

Cronbach (1955) developed his ideas from research on person perception. They were adapted to the area of personnel ratings and evaluations by Borman (1977). Thus, the various indices that have been derived and the research plans followed in this area are sometimes called *person perception designs* (Dickinson, 1987). However, there is no reason why effectiveness data of any sort can't be compared to some standard or ideal in order to assess accuracy. A case in point can be found in the work of Vance, MacCallum, Coovert, and Hedge (1988). In their study, ratings obtained from job incumbents, supervisors, and coworkers (peers) were assessed relative to an objective proficiency test. The subjects in this research were U.S. Air Force personnel who rated the effectiveness of jet engine mechanics. The target for comparison, then, was the score the mechanics got when they actually did repairs under controlled conditions. Vance et al. (1988) then used multitrait-multimethod-type data in a confirmatory factor analysis (see Chapter 2) to compare and contrast the various ratings with this true score index.

In a very useful paper, Dickinson (1987) describes and develops various research designs for evaluating the validity and accuracy of effectiveness ratings. He goes through the logic of the multitrait-multimethod analyses as interpreted in analysis of variance terms. He then does this for the person-perception designs just described. Finally, he offers a plan for what he calls a combination design, which is presented in Figure 6-2. Dickinson (1987) argues that if investigators gathered data according to this design, a great deal of information regarding the validity and accuracy of sets of effectiveness ratings would be known.

Documentation Deficiencies

The goodness of effectiveness data can sometimes be inferred from the care and effort that a manager gives to the measurement task. Like many of the other indices of quality described above, the evidence here is usually circumstantial. How much time does the manager spend preparing for and gathering effectiveness data? Are evaluations carried out in a timely manner? In operational and routine programs, are forms carefully completed? And in the cases where it is appropriate, how much documentation is provided? By this documentation we mean annotations and examples of behavior or accomplishments that can serve to illustrate and anchor the evaluations made. Such documentation serves as a clue to quality.

GENERAL FACTORS AFFECTING THE QUALITY OF APPRAISAL DATA

The various indicators described in the previous section all imply ways of determining if an effectiveness measurement program is generating high quality data. There are, however, some general rules or principles to follow in this area. That is, to the extent that the following conditions are problematic, we are not likely to get the quality that we desire (DeCotiis & Petit, 1978).

Opportunity to Observe

This rule appears straightforward. Only those who have an adequate opportunity to see the employee in job-related settings and over a suitable period of time should be used to supply

---

SUMMARY TABLE OF PSYCHOMETRIC INTERPRETATIONS OF THE COMBINATION DESIGN

Source	Psychometric Interpretation
Rating sources (S)	Elevation accuracy
Ratees (R)	Convergent validity
Traits (T)	Trait bias
Methods (M)	Scale bias
S x R	Differential elevation accuracy (Differential convergent validity x rating sources)
S x T	Stereotype accuracy
S x M	Differential scale bias x rating sources
R x T	Discriminant validity
R x M	Method bias
T x M	Trait x scale bias
S x R x T	Differential accuracy (differential discriminant validity x rating sources)
S x R x M	Differential elevation accuracy (differential method bias x rating sources)
S x T x M	Differential stereotype accuracy x methods
R x T x M	Differential discriminant validity x methods
Error	Measurement and sampling errors

FIGURE 6-2 Interpretations of Psychometric Output of Combination Designs
Source: Reprinted with permission from Dickinson, T. L. (1987). Designs for evaluating the validity and accuracy of performance ratings. *Organizational Behavior and Human Performance, 40,* 1–21.

effectiveness information. Sometimes formal reporting relationships can be deceiving in this regard. One normally would expect that the immediate supervisor would be in an excellent position to supply evaluations. However, in highly decentralized systems this may not be the case. Opportunity to observe needs to be verified. Conversely, a second opinion regarding an employee should not be given weight if it comes from someone who is quite removed from the day-to-day functioning of the employee.

Capability to Evaluate

Not all individuals are able to do a quality job in estimating effectiveness or in supplying data. There is some evidence that reliable individual differences exist in this regard (Borman, 1977; Taft, 1955). The key here would be to find a way to identify just who these individuals are in a given context. Alternatively, individuals' capabilities might be enhanced by their involvement in the careful development and application of evaluation tools or instruments. Finally, managers responsible for producing effectiveness information might have their capability increased by training programs designed for this purpose.

Motivation to Be Accurate

Several of the biases or errors that we detect in effectiveness data stem from the fact that managers frequently lack the motivation to be accurate in their data gathering and reporting. There is some evidence that this factor may account for the greatest amount of variance in the quality of data. This, too, implies careful attention to the process of program implementation.

TECHNIQUES FOR MEASURING INDIVIDUAL EFFECTIVENESS

As a reflection of the many forces operating to reduce the quality of assessments, a large number of techniques have been created to measure individual effectiveness. Over the years the goal has been to uncover the best technique or scale for the job. However, it is important to note at the outset that no one technique has been found best, even for a given purpose (Bernardin & Beatty, 1984). In fact, some have argued that looking for the perfect scale or instrument is not a fruitful way of dealing with the issue of improving quality (Landy & Farr, 1980).

Ratings

Ratings are perhaps the most prevalent technique for obtaining effectiveness information. In fact, the term "rating" is almost synonymous with the measurement of effectiveness. In this technique, managers are asked to form an impression of an employee's performance or effectiveness relative to some standard of excellence. Usually the standard is with regard to certain expectations held for anyone in that job. Thus, ratings are assumed to involve what are called *absolute judgments*. Ratings reflect how much effectiveness there is. Inasmuch as it is felt that the particular scale used for recording these judgments also plays a role in their formulation (DeNisi et al., 1984), a great deal of attention has been given to scale format.

Graphic Scales. The *graphic scale* is the oldest and perhaps the most popular type of rating scale; it is also one of the most simple. In its most basic form, the scale takes the shape of a line upon which the rater places a mark at the point that best reflects his or her judgment. However, the continuum is usually broken into a number of parts or segments (called *scale points*) each representing a discrete level or degree of effectiveness. A wide variety of graphic scales can be seen in Figure 6-3.

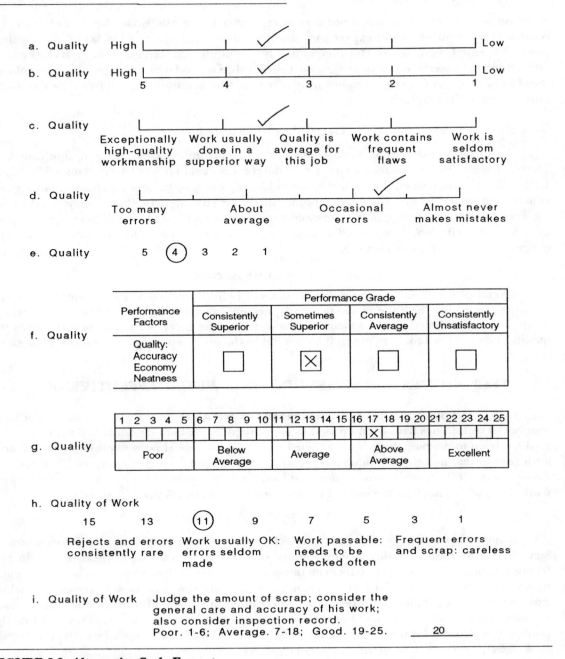

FIGURE 6-3 Alternative Scale Formats
Source: Reprinted with permission from Guion, R. M. (1965). *Personnel testing*. New York: McGraw-Hill.

It is clear from Figure 6-3 that graphic scales can differ in the number of scale points used to reflect effectiveness. At a minimum, a scale might have just two points or levels. A person can be judged "good" or "bad" at some behavior, judged to have or to not have a trait or quality, etc. Most of the time, however, more than two levels of effectiveness can be perceived. It also has been discovered that managers don't like to be forced into making such simple assessments; so, more scale points are typically used. On the other hand, too many points on a continuum cause problems with reliability. Simply put, you are asking the rater to make discriminations that are too fine grained and unrealistic, given the limits of human nature. While we may conceive of 100 levels or degrees of effectiveness, we simply cannot make this level of differentiation with any level of reliability. Over the years, several studies have been conducted to establish the appropriate number of scale points (e.g., Bass, Cascio, & O'Connor, 1974; Lissitz & Green, 1975) and, for most purposes, five to nine levels would be recommended (see Figure 6-4).

Graphic scales differ in the way that the scales and scale points are labeled or anchored. The attribute or factor to be rated simply may be listed or attached to each scale, or short paragraphs may be provided. Similarly, the scale points may be defined by numbers, by adjectives, by adverbs, or by more elaborate descriptive phrases. As you will see shortly, the trend in the construction of scales is to make use of more complete descriptions employing behaviors as anchors. Ultimately, even these latter variations will have implicit or explicit numerical values. Thus, a person's score on the graphic scale becomes the sum or total number of points produced by the choice of scale location.

Summated Scales/Behavior Observation Scales. This format also is simple to use and builds on features of graphic scales. Based on a job analysis, a large number of statements related to work behavior are generated. Using various forms of item analyses, a subset is retained for scale use. If the instrument is to get at several dimensions of effectiveness (e.g., customer relations, technical knowledge), multiple items can be used to define each dimension. In any event, each statement becomes a stimulus to which a rater must respond.

In the summated scale format, possible response continua include frequency, degree of goodness, and amount or intensity. Thus, the scale points (regardless of their number) would be

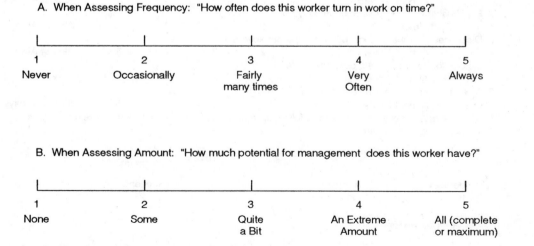

FIGURE 6-4 The Best Scale Anchors for A Five-Point Summated Scale
Source: Adapted with permission from Bass, B. M., Cascio, W. F., and O'Connor, E. J. (1974). Magnitude estimations of expressions of frequency and amount. *Journal of Applied Psychology, 59,* 313–320.

anchored according to the type of judgment desired. Figure 6-4 shows the results of one study (Bass et al., 1974) that identified the best words to use if you wanted to anchor a continuum of frequency or amount for a scale involving five points. The Bass et al. (1974) study could be consulted if you wanted the optimal anchors for various numbers of scale points.

To use the resulting summated scale, raters place a mark at an appropriate place on the continuum associated with each item. An employee's overall score is the sum of the values represented by the scale points given.

More recently, Latham and Wexley (1981) have presented a type of summated scale called the *behavior observation scale* (BOS). A key feature of BOS development is a careful job analysis. The items are specific job-relevant descriptions of behavior. The manager is required to indicate the frequency with which each occurs on the job. In practice, several items are used to measure effectiveness in a particular area. Further, numerous dimensions are required for most jobs. An example of a BOS scale used by managers to measure effectiveness in the area of dealing with organizational change is presented in Figure 6-5 (see Latham & Wexley, 1981).

Part of the appeal of the BOS approach is that it is likely to produce higher quality ratings by making appraisals less difficult to perform. Only basic judgments of frequency are called for; few inferences are required. Moreover, the fact that the statements are so job related promotes the impression that the scale is appropriate and valid (which it should be, if developed properly). And this, in turn, encourages conscientious effort in the conduct of the appraisal.

Weighted Checklists. The scales described to this point have a common feature in that the person completing them has a pretty clear idea of the score he or she is awarding to someone being rated. The values of the various scale points usually are obvious. Thus, should the manager want to, it

---

Example of One BOS Criterion or Performance Dimension for Evaluating Managers
1. Overcoming Resistance to Change*
   1. Describes the details of the change to subordinates.

Almost Never	1	2	3	4	5	Almost Always

   2. Explains why the change is necessary.

Almost Never	1	2	3	4	5	Almost Always

   3. Discusses how the change will affect the employee.

Almost Never	1	2	3	4	5	Almost Always

   4. Listens to the employee's concerns.

Almost Never	1	2	3	4	5	Almost Always

   5. Asks the employee for help in making the change work.

Almost Never	1	2	3	4	5	Almost Always

   6. If necessary, specifies the date for a follow-up meeting to respond to the employee's concerns.

Almost Never	1	2	3	4	5	Almost Always

Total = _____ .

Below Adequate	Adequate	Full	Excellent	Superior*
6–10	11–15	16–20	21–25	26–30

*Scores are set by management.

FIGURE 6-5   An Example of a Behavior Observation Scale
    Source: Reprinted with permission from Latham, G. P., & Wexley, K. N. (1981). *Increasing productivity through performance appraisal.* Reading, MS: Addison-Wesley.

would be very easy to give someone a score that is unwarranted (too high or too low). In many organizations this generally means inflated ratings (evidenced as leniency). Weighted checklists are thought to reduce this possibility by not giving the rater scale value information.

When originally introduced in the 1940s (Knauft, 1948), the items in a checklist would have been adjectives, statements, or phrases. Today, they more often are short descriptions of behavior, not unlike BOS items (Bernardin & Beatty, 1984). To construct this type of scale, a large number of items are generated by people familiar with the job in question, often using the critical incident method. Participants are asked to recall specific examples of on-the-job behaviors which reflect something that is noteworthy, either because it was something very good or very poor. These descriptions of incidents are edited down to short phrases. Job experts are then asked to scale the items in this large pool according to the level of effectiveness they reflect. One way to do this is to use the method of equal appearing intervals developed in attitude measurement research. In using this method, the items are sorted into 11 piles or categories, each representing distinguishable levels of effectiveness. Items for which there is a consensus are then selected for use on the rating instrument. Their value becomes the mean of the scores obtained from the scaling that was conducted.

The final appraisal instrument that is presented to raters consists of a series of short behavior descriptions. Usually, the items are mixed up with regard to the level of effectiveness that they convey and, in the case of a multidimensional instrument, the areas of effectiveness as well. In all cases, the scale values of the items are not given. To use the instrument, the rater is required to check off those items that are felt to be descriptive of the employee being assessed. The score received by that employee would be a function of the sum of the scale values of the items selected or the median of these items. In actual practice, the rater presumably would not have access to the weights so that the scores might be computed by someone in the personnel area.

Forced Choice Scales. In some respects, *forced choice scales*, in which the rater is forced to make a choice of statements about an employee from a group of potential statements represent an extension of the weighted checklist approach. They were developed mainly because of a growing dissatisfaction with the way evaluations were being made and recorded on more conventional scales. Wherry (1952) is credited with creating them with the goal of reducing error of leniency and, hopefully, of increasing accuracy. Initial evidence has confirmed that, compared to graphic scales, ratings on these scales are more normally distributed. Not all individuals have been given high evaluations. The key seems to lie in the fact that, as in the case of the checklist, the rater does not know the scale values of the items and that they are hard to discern intuitively.

In the forced choice format, items are grouped so that they have equal desirability in the eyes of the rater. He or she is required, or forced, to choose one or more items from each cluster that best describe the employee. The scale value of the items selected (unknown to the rater) then becomes the employee's score.

To understand this approach, it is important to understand the procedure used to create, scale, select, and cluster the items. Items usually are generated by job experts and edited into short phrases. They then are scaled for and arranged by two properties. The first is referred to variously as *importance*, or *favorability*. This is the extent to which the attribute or behavior reflected in the item is attractive or makes a person manifesting it look good. The second property is referred to as *discriminability*. This is the appropriateness of the item for describing a truly superior employee. In a sense, it's the item's validity. Statements are arranged so that in a cluster of two or four all would have about the same importance or favorability; however, only one might truly reflect effectiveness.

Constructed this way, the scale is resistant to carelessness or deliberate distortion. Checking a statement at random should not introduce a particular bias into a score. More importantly, a person who wanted to give an employee a very high (or low) evaluation where one was not warranted would have a difficult time. He or she would not be able to use the apparent favorability as a clue to just which ones to select.

There are several ways to scale statements for favorability and discriminability, but there is no conclusive evidence that one might be better than another (Bernardin & Beatty, 1984). On the other hand, there seems to be a professional consensus that the use of clusters of four favorable or positive items, two of which have some relation to effectiveness and two of which do not, is the format that is preferred (Berkshire & Highland, 1953). In this situation the rater is required to select two of the four that he or she feels is appropriate. The ratee's score then becomes the number of valid statements chosen.

Research on this type of scale appears to have been carried out in two "waves" of activity—when it first was invented (e.g., Sisson, 1948) and more recently (King, Hunter, & Schmidt, 1980). While there seems to be a fair amount of data to support the view that its use does result in ratings that have higher psychometric quality, the extent to which it is a format that is liked or accepted by users is not so clear. Some managers resent not being able to talk about the kind of evaluation that they have just given their subordinate. In fact, some supervisors have attempted to outwit the system by keeping good records of their ratings and relating these to what evaluations come out of personnel for their employees. Others have tried to do this by not actually rating the person they are supposed to rate. Instead, if they wished to give an overly favorable evaluation they might imagine the most effective worker they have known on the job and complete the form with him or her in mind. In theory, at least, this should increase the likelihood that they would select the valid items.

Behaviorally Anchored Rating Scales. Introduced relatively recently by Smith and Kendall (1963) amid a great deal of optimism that they would deal with many of the forces that reduced the quality of ratings (Campbell et al., 1970), *behaviorally achored rating scales* (referred to as BARS or BES, for behavioral expectations scales have been heavily researched in the last 15 years. While the evidence is not as clear as it should be to make firm conclusions at this time, it seems safe to say that BARS represents, at most, only a small advance in scale technology (Bernardin & Beatty, 1984).

There have been several versions of BARS. With one important exception (the way they are actually used), they have a lot in common. In contrast to other approaches (e.g., the forced choice method) that have tended to look for ways to outsmart or trick the rater into giving good quality evaluations, the philosophy behind the development and use of BARS has been to do things to *help* the rater to be accurate. In particular, every effort is made to be certain that potential scale users provide a lot of input into the critical features of its design.

Behaviorally anchored rating scales usually are constructed for a particular job or cluster of jobs that have a great deal in common (e.g., college teaching). They employ a multistep procedure that involves participation of several groups of supervisors or employees at critical points. While in practice these could vary, the steps outlined below follow those presented in the original version (Bernardin & Beatty, 1984):

1. *Because effectiveness in most jobs is multifaceted, the performance dimensions must be identified and defined.* This usually is done by having a group of future scale users meet to discuss the job in question and to reach a consensus. This same group is asked to write statements clarifying what is meant by being high or low on each dimension.

2. *A second group of future users then is given the dimensions with these general anchors.* Their task is to come up with a large number of behavioral examples for each dimension. They may be instructed in the use of the critical incident framework for structuring this activity in order to keep focused on job effectiveness and to come up with the necessary number of examples.

3. *The examples are usually edited by the personnel specialist conducting the project into short behavioral phrases.* These are then given to another group. They receive the list of dimensions and the behavioral examples produced so far, but the latter are deliberately mixed up with regard to dimensions. This groups' task is to match each example with its appropriate dimension to double check the work of their predecessors. Usually, an agreement of 80% is required for a given statement to be assigned to a dimension.

4. *Still another group is then asked to rate or scale the examples that have survived to this point.* This group is to indicate the extent to which each example reflects effectiveness on the dimension to which it has been assigned (usually on a 1–7 scale). This is done independently by each person. A standard deviation is then computed on the scores given to each example. Those examples with a large standard deviation are rejected. This reflects a lack of agreement among raters due to the level of effectiveness described by that example.

5. *Examples are placed as anchors at appropriate points on the scale of effectiveness for each dimension.* Usually, this is done for only some of the points along the continuum but in a manner that still covers the full range of effectiveness. A resulting scale might look like Figure 6-6.

The "retranslation" step in number 3 is important and is a unique aspect of BARS methodology. It sometimes uncovers dimensions that were overlooked in the earlier steps because it is discovered that there are some examples "left over" that also seem to go together. On the other hand, the importance or relevance of dimensions that arise from this process with none or very few examples is questionable. The requirement for a high degree of consensus also eliminates examples that might be appropriate for more than one dimension, thus reducing the potential for halo error when they are used as anchors in the final scale. In a sense, these steps in the BARS development process tend to ensure that the concepts and language of the scale will be accepted and understood by everyone.

The actual way BARS are used or applied appears to have evolved somewhat since it was invented (Bernardin & Smith, 1981). Originally, the scales were to serve as a structure for systematic observation and record keeping by managers prior to making ratings. That is, over some period of time managers were to notice the job behavior of a person due for a review and to record examples of good or poor performance on the relevant scale dimension. This was to be done at an appropriate point on the continuum. They were expected to use the scaled anchors to make this judgment. Later, they would review these entries and make a summary rating on each dimension. These then would become an employee's scores.

More recently, however, BARS have not been used in this future-oriented or prospective manner. Instead, much like any rating scale, it is completed at the time an appraisal is called for. The manager is expected to reflect on the employee's behavior in a particular performance domain during the period of time in question, integrate this information in the form of a judgment, then record this impression on the scale at a point he or she feels is correct. The scale definition and description and the behavioral anchors presumably help to do this accurately.

Organizational skills: A good constructional order of material slides smoothly from one topic to another; design of course optimizes interest; students can eaily follow organizational strategy; course outline followed.

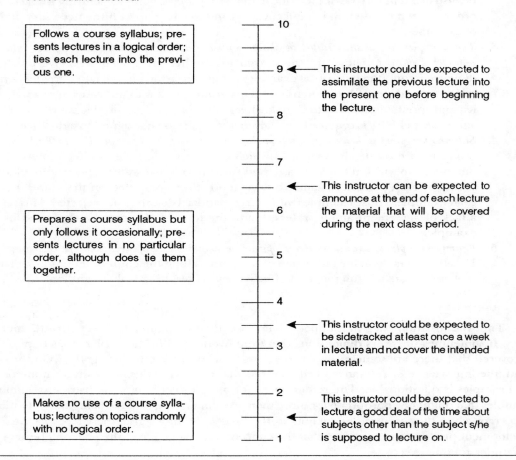

FIGURE 6-6   A Behaviorally Anchored Rating Scale for College Professors
Source: Reprinted with permission from Bernardin, H. J. (1977). Behavioral expectation scales versus summated scales: A fairer comparison. *Journal of Applied Psychology, 62,* 422–427.

Personnel Comparison Systems

Despite the diversity apparent in the various scales just described, they all represent formats in which the person doing the assessment makes judgments with regard to job relevant or absolute standards. A poor worker, for example, is thought to be poor because he or she cannot or will not do the job. In general, this is a property of ratings. In contrast, personnel comparison systems are based on a different set of assumptions. As a group, their advantage is that the distribution of scores is "spread out." A discussion of various personnel comparison systems follows.

Personnel Rankings. All of us are familiar with the concept of ranking. We see it every day in the popular press or hear it used in conversation. When applied to personnel evaluations, *personnel rankings* involve the ordering of employees on a continuum of (usually overall) effectiveness so that individuals who are placed higher are felt to be better than those who come later. Because it is an easily understood and straightforward way of evaluating and recording evaluations, it is very popular.

When there are a fairly large number of workers to consider (say, over ten), it is sometimes difficult to differentiate among them, especially in the middle ranges of effectiveness. Thus, Guion (1965) recommends that a variation of this method, known as *alternation ranking* might be used. In this approach the manager works from a list of employees. He or she first selects the most effective and the least effective persons on the list. These are then given the first and last place (rank) respectively. Their names are taken off the initial roster and the choice of first and last place is again made with regard to the people who are left. These are assigned the second best and the second worst ranks. Then their names are dropped from the list. This process is continued until the list is exhausted. Alternation ranking is based on the premise that it is easier to make extreme judgments. It is sometimes called the peel off method because the process is as if one is peeling away layers.

If more than one manager is in a position to provide ranking information on a group of workers, it is quite feasible to average the data that they provide. However, if this is done it is unlikely that the resulting numbers will be whole integers (e.g., the top person might get an average rank of 1.7). Moreover, with more than one set of rankings it also is possible for two or more individuals to be tied with the same average rank score. In any event, the appropriateness of averaging ranks should be carefully considered insofar as the different judges may not be equivalent in opportunity or capacity to evaluate personnel.

Forced Distribution Method. Ranking requires that each individual is given a unique position in the ordering. There are times, however, when all that is desired is some notion of how groups of workers compare in a relative sense. In the *forced distribution method* the manager is only expected to place workers into five or seven groups or categories of effectiveness, usually in specified proportions. Thus, in a five category system, 10% of the workers are to be assigned to the extreme high and low clusters, 20% are to be placed into the next highest and lowest categories, and the remaining 40% are to be clustered in the middle.

It is no coincidence that the distribution described above approximates a normal distribution. The use of the forced distribution method is most appropriate when one is willing to assume that the true levels of effectiveness of the workers are, in fact, distributed in this way. This should be the case when fairly large numbers of employees are being evaluated. Even when it is not the case, the final arrangement of people must conform to this pattern. Hence the technique also is called a *forced distribution*. It would be possible, however, to force placements into something other than a normal distribution, if that is what is believed to be fair given what is known about the people being evaluated (e.g., they all may be competent and experienced personnel so one may not want to use the whole effectiveness continuum). In general, however, forced distribution systems do not appear suitable when only a small number of employees are to be evaluated.

This approach is sometimes used to narrow the field of workers for future consideration. For example, under such circumstances, the 10% in the topmost category might then be ranked individually in order to determine the person most deserving of some honor (e.g., a teaching award).

It's clear that both simple ranking and the forced distribution method require that individuals get placed in some kind of order of effectiveness, even when it may not be warranted. They may not allow for the possibility that two or more individuals are equally effective. Moreover, they only provide what is essentially ordinal data. We know that a person ranked fourth is better than one ranked fifth, but we don't know how much better. Similarly, we cannot rely on differences between ranks at different parts of the distribution to reflect equivalent differences in effectiveness. For example, Figure 6-7 shows a situation where a decision to promote the top two candidates based only on rank information would unfairly disenfranchise the next runner up who is, in fact, barely distinguishable from one who would be chosen. While the next method to be described, the paired comparison method, does not deal with the issue of forcing differences, it does provide a mechanism for deriving some insight into the magnitude of the differences in effectiveness of individuals who are to be compared.

Paired Comparison Method. The *paired comparison method* systematically compares all workers with regard to their effectiveness. A formula for determining how many judgments are required of a manager is as follows:

$$[N(N-1)]/2. \tag{6.2}$$

Thus, if you had five subordinates you would make 5 x 4/2 or 10 paired comparison judgments. More specifically, a list of all workers, taken two at a time, and in all possible combinations would be prepared. The supervisor then would indicate which person of each pair was the more effective. In determining someone's score the supervisor analyzes the proportion of judgments in which the employee is chosen over all the others. Those proportions are frequently standardized/normalized, yielding interval data. Thus, one also can tell by what degree each worker differs in judged effectiveness (Blum & Naylor, 1968), although these scores, too, are based on the assumption that individual performance is distributed normally.

   Despite the apparent simplicity of this approach, as in the case of rankings and forced distributions, it is believed that when work groups are large it is quite tedious to use. And, in fact, research has been conducted to discover modifications that can be made so that the number of pairs to be evaluated can be reduced and can result in a valid coverage of employees (McCormick & Bachus, 1952). However, a principle concern with regard to this method remains in that it asks for a global or overall judgment of effectiveness, one that is not well defined or anchored. This makes it difficult to know on what basis the judgments have been made (Bernardin & Beatty, 1984).

   An additional feature of the paired comparison method is also true for personnel comparison appraisal systems in general. It is very difficult, except under unusual circumstances, to compare evaluations across departments or organizational divisions. The best person in one area may not be

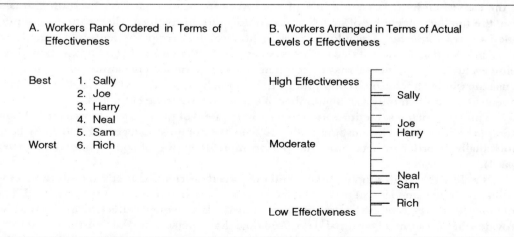

A. Workers Rank Ordered in Terms of Effectiveness

Best	1.	Sally
	2.	Joe
	3.	Harry
	4.	Neal
	5.	Sam
Worst	6.	Rich

B. Workers Arranged in Terms of Actual Levels of Effectiveness

High Effectiveness
— Sally

— Joe
— Harry

Moderate

— Neal
— Sam

— Rich

Low Effectiveness

FIGURE 6-7   When Rank Order Information is Misleading

as effective as a person ranked at the middle of the distribution in another work group. Thus, it would be rare to see these techniques used where there is a need for system-wide personnel data.

Techniques of Scaling. As seen from this review, items, people, or potential anchors on evaluation instruments can be scaled using any of a number of procedures. The various techniques described represent a mixture of approaches, adapted for use to the measurement of individual effectiveness. By way of recapitulation, it might be useful to highlight these by using traditional names for the scaling technique involved.

Thurstone Scaling (Method of Equal Appearing Intervals). A pool of items is sorted by a panel of judges into piles (or given category values) representing steps along a 7-, 9-, or 11-point effectiveness continuum. After all judgments have been made, mean and standard deviations are computed for each statement. The scale value for these statements then is based on the mean of the judgments. Unambiguous (consistently rated) statements or items representing the full range of the scale then are assembled for use.

Likert Scaling. Items or behavior statements are rated on an a priori scale (e.g., 5 points) by judges with regard to how appropriate or descriptive they are of a target or criterion group (e.g., the excellent performers). Items or statements then are selected for use in an instrument based on the means and standard deviation of the ratings they receive.

Ratio Scaling. An item or phrase dealing with *frequency* or *amount* is assigned a number (0–100) by judges relative to a zero (0) level or amount. Other items or phrases are judged in relation to this benchmark or referent. Means and standard deviations of the numbers (points) given to an item or phrase become its scale value. Depending on how many points the investigator seeks for an effectiveness continuum (3, 4, 5, etc.) he or she would choose an appropriate set from those that have been scaled.

Ranking. Judges are asked to place items (or people) on a continuum (e.g., of effectiveness) in serial order so that each successive one is greater (or less) than the preceding one. When several judges are used, means or medians can be computed and used as a best estimate of the apparent width or value of each item.

Pair Comparison. Items (or individuals) to be scaled (or evaluated) are taken two at a time and compared relative to the dimension of interest. The investigator then tallies the frequency with which each item (or person) is chosen as better or greater on the continuum across all of the pairs. The item score is related directly to this proportion or can be transformed to a standard score.

Proficiency Testing

A *proficiency test* involves the selection of a task or set of tasks that are representative of the work typically carried out by the employee and that subsequently are used as the basis for the appraisal. Persons being evaluated are asked to perform under standardized circumstances in the presence of the individual(s) conducting the appraisal. The audition that a performing artist goes through, although it most often is used in the service of making a selection decision, is a good example. A proficiency test can be thought of as a work sample. In its most carefully developed format, each set of behaviors or products of these behaviors is noted and scored according to specified rules. A person's evaluation then is a function of the number of points earned (Campion, 1972).

Ordinarily, proficiency based appraisals are conducted under circumstances where it is critical that workers have high levels of skills in certain areas of work not frequently used or observed on the job. For example, police officers are regularly evaluated on their use of firearms observed on the job. For example, police officers are regularly evaluated on their use of firearms in simulations involving their use. Pilots are expected to demonstrate their knowledge and skill in dealing with an emergency on a regular basis, once again usually under contrived circumstances. As mentioned earlier in this chapter, proficiency tests have been used as criteria for research on other types of effectiveness measures (Vance et al., 1988).

Assessment Centers

One type of program that has elements of proficiency testing is the assessment center. Although it will be described in Chapter 8 as a technique for selecting future managers, its use for measuring effectiveness deserves some elaboration.

Assessment centers involve the systematic observation and evaluation of personnel as they behave and perform in standardized settings. Specially trained staff use techniques like interviews, psychological tests, work samples, and group-based simulations to make inferences about the strengths and weaknesses of candidates for promotion. As originally conceived, the assessment center method was built on the following assumptions:

1. Promotion decisions should be made in the most systematic manner possible.
2. Effectiveness at higher level jobs (i.e., management) require certain knowledge, skills, abilities, and dispositions.
3. These cannot be detected in the behavior and performance of people in lower levels. That is, they may not be required, or the job doesn't even allow for their manifestation.
4. Standardized settings can be designed to produce activities and behavior that allow trained observers to make inferences with regard to whether or not a person has these necessary attributes.
5. Based on these observations and inferences, staff members can estimate or predict an individual's likely success if promoted to a higher level.
6. These estimates increase the validity of promotion decisions.

Currently, assessment centers are being used by hundreds of companies, both public and private, to make evaluations of management potential. Yet, as popular as they are, we still do not know under what conditions they will be useful or, when they are predictive of future success, just why they work (Klimoski & Strickland, 1978; Klimoski & Brickner, 1987).

Output Measures

In our examination of criterion development theory, we described the tendency of many organizations to establish and rely upon work products or outputs to index effectiveness. This is done in the belief that such indicators are less subjective (and hence less prone to the errors and biases described earlier). Moreover, they are attractive to many managers because they can be more easily translated into a dollar value, which is a metric that most people can understand and use. The "amount of goods produced" or "customers serviced" is the stuff that industry is built on.

The use of any output measures for indexing the effectiveness of personnel however, requires some basis for comparison. Several options exist. A person's performance can be assessed relative to his or her past performance, the performance of others, some established standard, or a set or an implied goal (Carroll & Schneier, 1982). Of these possibilities, the one that is most widely used involves the determination and use of engineered standards.

The application of performance standards has a rich tradition in industry, deriving from the Scientfic Management movement. Thus, it is not suprising that a variety of techniques for their derivation have been invented. For example, historical (typical) performance levels are used as standards in this way. The most common techniques to establish standards are *time study* and *work sampling*. Both involve the systematic observation of workers as they perform the job or elements of the job. Job behaviors and activities are then classified and timed. As a result of this developmental work, the specialist can estimate fairly accurately the amount of time it takes the typical worker to do the tasks that make up a job and, consequently, how much work can be performed in a period of time (e.g., an hour or a day). Some aspects of the methods involved have been outlined in Chapter 4. For a complete treatment of this topic, the interested reader is referred to Smith (1978).

Output data can be gathered in any number of ways. A supervisor can count the products produced, the worker can do this, or, it might be done rather automatically. The U.S. Navy, for example, employs many civilians whose job it is to enter information into military computers at seven centers throughout the country. Recently they have come to emphasize the "number of keystrokes per hour" as an output measure of the effectiveness of personnel. One advantage of this measure is that these data can be recorded directly by the computer being fed the information. A standard of 9000 strokes per hour has been established as reasonable for entering data, and a somewhat higher rate is expected for the verification of data.

To index a worker's effectiveness one can look at their performance relative to a standard. Usually this is done by computing an efficiency index (*EI*) and comparing employees on this basis. An efficiency index is created by dividing the person's output, in units, by the standard, in units, for some unit of time (e.g., an hour), and then multiplying by 100 as follows:

$$\text{Efficiency index} = \frac{\text{Output in units}}{\text{Standard in units}} \times 100. \tag{6.3}$$

Productive efficiency or productivity then is a function of the employee's efficiency index and the number of hours worked relative to the number authorized or expected.

It may not be obvious from this brief description that a great number of choices or decisions have to be made in order to come up with such objective indices of effectiveness. For example, the analyst has to choose the method for studying the job, a "typical" group of workers has to be selected and observed, levels of effort exerted by these people must be estimated, etc. As Smith (1976) points out, human judgment enters into every performance measure.

Output measures frequently reflect factors outside the worker's control (they are contaminated criteria). The rate of work may be determined by product demand more than worker ability or motivation. Even for jobs that lend themselves to such measurement, it is inappropriate to think of them as capturing the worker's true value to the organization (they are deficient criteria). The worker's output may vary in quality, there may be requirements to help coworkers, etc., that are not part of the productivity measure. To the extent that such measures are available, we recommend that their nature be scrutinized carefully before being used for purposes for which they were not originally designed.

Management by Objectives

One approach to the use of output measures to index individual (usually, managerial) effectiveness that has received a good deal of support is *management by objectives* (MBO). At the outset, it should be noted that MBO usually is viewed as more than just an effectiveness measurement technique. When it first was introduced 30 years ago, it was thought by some to be a way of improving the practice of management by making goal setting and work goals explicit and perhaps even increasing the compatability of the goals of the workers and the goals of the company (Greenwood, 1981). Other writers felt that MBO would provide a mechanism for making organizations more participative and humane (McGregor, 1957). Even today it is viewed variously as a way of encouraging systematic planning, increasing individual accountability (control), administering compensation, and motivating workers (McConkie, 1979). The multiple functions of MBO programs make them a difficult thing to describe and to evaluate. The emphasis here is on the use of MBO programs as a technique for establishing the effectiveness of individuals (usually managers).

There is a great deal of variation in the specific form that MBO programs take. This is due to the fact that many of the components involved can be used alone or in different combinations. Thus, when a company says it uses MBO it may mean several different things. However, most MBO programs have a common set of features (Carroll & Tosi, 1973). Figure 6-8 outlines these in the form of steps that are usually followed in programs that would be considered relatively complete (Carroll & Schneier, 1982, p.140).

An essential feature of MBO is to establish for the manager a set of goals or objectives that are consistent with the goals and mission of the company. On face value, this does not seem to be a difficult starting point. However, numerous writers have pointed out that top managers frequently do disagree as to why their company exists. It's not that they haven't any ideas in this regard, but that there often is no consensus among them. Moreover, Porter, Lawler, and Hackman (1975) make a distinction between several types of goals that may be considered. There is usually a goal or set of goals that get written into charters, official pronouncements, or statements at public ceremonies. These are called *official goals*. Most of the time these sound like advertising slogans. Thus, a company might say that it seeks to be the best business machines company in the world. More down to earth are what are called *operative goals*. These represent the actual things that the company appears to be working toward. They may or may not be consistent with their official goal statement. For example, the business machine company really may be trying to become the most service oriented of its type. The third class of goals are called *operational goals*. These come closest to the things that drive the day-to-day activities of departments or divisions. Considering the operative goal just cited, managers may refer to aspects of customer service, like delivery delays, or speed of service, or proportion of repeat business, when they consider that their operational goal.

To initiate a good MBO program the company must define or clarify what it is they are working toward. The goals or objectives for a given manager are then placed within this framework. To get from the perspective of the system to the level of a manager still requires further development. Usually, this involves a process of building what are, in effect, cause-and-effect linkages. That is, certain activities and accomplishments (causes) must be achieved to allow for other overarching objectives (effects) to be met. This process is sometimes referred to as the *cascading of objectives*. Basically, this means an analysis is carried out where the resources (talent and capacity) and activities of subordinate individuals and groups are considered in light of how they can be used in the service of increasingly higher level goals. For instance, the warehouse facility of the business machine company would be expected to develop goals which, if carried out, would move the company toward a major objective. More specifically, the warehouse manager might strive to establish forecasting techniques that allow it to anticipate customer demands for parts. Thus, customer service needs can be met in a timely manner, without maintaining an enormous and expensive inventory. The latter consideration, incidently, might be consistent with another company goal, that of reducing overhead costs. In Figure 6-9, we illustrate this process. The issues involved in establishing and operationalizing organization and subunit goals also will be relevant

STEPS
1. Analyze environment.

⬇

2. Set organizational goals.

⬇

3. Set goals for individuals and groups derived from organizational goals.

⬇

4. Develop action plans for each goal.

⬇

5. Determine performance indicators to use in evaluating goal progress and accomplishment.

⬇

6. Periodically review goal progress.

⬇

7. Conduct final review of goal accomplishment at end of time period.

⬇

8. Establish self-improvement objectives for next period based on any deficiencies identified in goal accomplishment in previous period.

⬇

9. Establish performance objectives for next period.

FIGURE 6-8   The Management by Objective Process
Source: Reprinted with permission from Carroll, S. J. and Schneier, C. E. (1982). *Performance appraisal and review systems.* Glenview, IL: Scott Foresman

to the process of defining and measuring group and organization effectiveness. More will be said about this in Chapter 7.

In actual practice, it usually is assumed that a manager and his or her boss understand how the daily work activities and special projects of the department fit into the big picture. Thus, the focus of many MBO efforts is on (a) goal setting, (b) the development of the action plan, and (c) the performance review.

The action plans specify the means by which the objectives will be accomplished. Usually, they include the resources needed, the kind of cooperation expected from various individuals, the amount of time required, and the standards which are to be used in judging the work accomplished.

To use MBO as a format for measuring individual effectiveness it is critical that the goals or objectives-setting phase be done well. These must be inclusive enough to cover the work domain (not be deficient) yet not involve factors that are irrelevant (be free from contamination). Furthermore, results relative to objectives in various work responsibility areas must be specified in terms of operational measures. If this is the case, it is easy to determine if a person is performing appropriately in his or her job. Performance relative to standards would be a matter of record for all, including the subordinate, to see. A person's evaluation could then be characterized in terms of either an index reflecting a percentage of goal attainment or a profile. In the latter case

FIGURE 6-9 Establishing Organizational Goals
Source: Reprinted with permission from Carroll, S. J., & Schneier, C. E. (1982). *Performance appraisal and review systems.* Glenview, IL: Scott-Foresman.

accomplishments could be arrayed in a manner clearly portraying success relative to each of the objectives. Figure 6-10 illustrates this latter format. To use the jargon introduced earlier, these would be the products data with which to measure effectiveness.

Alternatively, the action plan could provide the basis for assessment. In this approach what gets emphasized is not so much what got accomplished during a specific period, but how it was done. Thus, the manager would be evaluated in terms of the nature, timing, and sequence of work behaviors or activities performed. In this regard, effectiveness becomes defined in terms of process data.

The performance review is an important feature of most MBO programs. Because such reviews are not really a part of the measurement process, only a few points will be mentioned here. In MBO programs the cycles of review should be related to the work to be done. That is, instead of taking place at regular intervals like once a year, meetings would be held after some unit of work has been completed. These sessions would review what was or was not accomplished, and anticipate what is likely to be done in the next period. In some cases, objectives might be modified, or the action plan adjusted. This process of multiple reviews implies that, at times, we are performing what could be called a *formative evaluation*. We are considering work in progress so to speak. At others, we are doing a *summative evaluation*. In this latter case, we are less interested in using data to make some adjustments in instructions or assumptions to or about an employee and seek instead to reach a conclusion or a decision (e.g., what level of compensation to offer him or her).

The research literature describing and evaluating MBO programs is quite large. For example, Kondrasuk (1981) reviewed over 180 studies in the area. However, most of these studies deal with the potential effects of MBO on individual and organizational performance and less on measurement issues. What is important to note at this time is that MBO doesn't really provide a system of measurement that permits easy direct comparisons across employees (Bernardin & Beatty, 1984). It allows for what is essentially idiographic measurement. This means that the performance of an individual is to be evaluated relative to a unique set of goals that were accomplished under a negotiated set of contingencies and constraints. Thus, it is very difficult to compare two or more individuals, especially if they are working for managers who might hold different standards or are performing in different functional areas. Of course, if an organization were to use some other

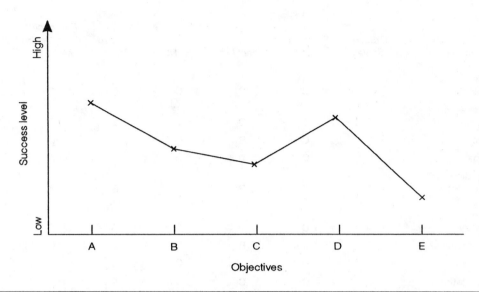

FIGURE 6-10 An MBO Accomplishment Profile

system for making evaluations of effectiveness in addition to MBO (e.g., overall ratings), this problem would be alleviated somewhat. When comparisons are warranted, the manager or researcher could make use of this other method.

CHOOSING AMONG APPROACHES IN THE MEASUREMENT OF INDIVIDUAL EFFECTIVENESS

This chapter has described various approaches to measuring effectiveness that are valuable to human resource specialists. They all reflect attempts to obtain valid measurements of individual effectiveness. The fact that there are so many versions is a testimony to both the creativity of people working in the area and the difficulties involved. As stated at the outset of this chapter, it is clear that the perfect measurement approach has yet to be developed. Each has its strengths and weaknesses. Recently, Bernardin and Beatty (1984) have evaluated some different formats with regard to several standards. Figure 6-11 has been adapted to reflect their findings.

It can be seen from this figure that no one method is clearly best. As Bernardin and Beatty stated: (1984, pp. 232–233)

> The good news is that it appears that some methods work better than others. The bad news is that those methods with the best empirical track record are also the most impractical, time consuming, and expensive.

We also have implied three other criteria for effectiveness measures that should be considered by researchers and practitioners as they select one or more of the options described in this chapter. A listing of these criteria follow:

Criteria	Graphic Scales	Summated Scales	Checklists	BARS	Forced Choice	Personnel* Comparison Methods	MBO
Utilization:							
Feedback	C	C	C	C	F	C	C
Administrative Decisions	C	C	C	C	B	C	C
Research	C	C	B	C	B	C	C
Training	C	C	B	B	B	A	A
Organization Development	C	C	B	B	B	A	A
Subjective:							
Practicality	A	B	B	C	D	C	C
User Acceptance	B	C	B	B	D	C	B
Ease of use	A	B	A	C	D	C	D
Documentation	F	C	C	C	F	F	B
EEO Requirements	F	B	B	D	D	F	A
Interpretability	F	B	B	C	D	F	A
Score Comparability	F	A	A	C	D	F	F
Psychometric:							
Leniency, Discriminability, Etc.	D	C	C	C	B	A	B
Reliability	C	B	C	C	B	A	A
Halo	F	D	D	D	F	F	–
Validity	D	B	B	B	B	B	B

FIGURE 6-11 Evaluating Various Techniques (A = Best, F = Worst)
> Source: Adapted with permission from Bernardin, H. J., & Beatty, R. W., (1984). *Performance appraisal:*
> *Assessing human behavior at work.* Boston, MA: Kent.

1. *The way effectiveness is defined.* The investigator has to be clear as to what is meant by individual effectiveness as a construct. This will influence the choice of operational measures to use. For example, recently Sackett, Zedeck, and Fogli (1988) reported research examining the relationship of effectiveness measures aimed at getting at either typical or maximum job performance. The former would be designed to get at how an employee performs on a day-to-day basis; the latter would index performance where the employee is exerting the greatest effort that he or she can bring to bear. Logic would suggest that these would not be the same for most of us. This is what Sackett et al. (1988) found. But more to the point at hand, it would appear that you might use different types of measures (or at least different instructions) depending on what you are interested in. Sackett et al. (1988) found very low correlations between supervisor ratings and several typical performance indicators obtained from machine records for check out clerks.

Instead, they found evidence that such ratings were more associated with episodes of maximum performance levels.

In a similar manner, the construct of effectiveness may be defined using different standards. We can think of effectiveness in terms of performance contrasted to job requirements, relative to others who might be doing the same job, or in comparison to some absolute level. Arguments for the appropriateness of all three standards can be found in the literature. But once again, which one you choose will imply the use of a different type of measure. As pointed out, ranking methods are well suited to obtaining a relative index of effectiveness but may not tell you much about absolute or job-relevant standings.

2. *The purpose of using the measure.* This is related to the points just made but is worth reiterating. There are times when the practitioner needs effectiveness data for very different purposes. As noted in the chapter, a format that would be very good for gathering effectiveness data for the assessment of promotion potential may be inappropriate for obtaining data in order to make compensation decisions. Unfortunately, many organizations use and expect one method to accomplish multiple objectives. The result usually is dissatisfaction and disillusionment and the continued search for the perfect all purpose measure.

3. *Cost effectiveness.* The notions of the costs and benefits associated with human resource practices is highlighted in a later chapter. However, it's worth mentioning that there is a great deal of variation in the costs associated with designing, developing, and implementing the different techniques described in this chapter. For example, assessment centers and job simulations (job samples) are quite expensive to develop and use. Thus, the investigator must determine if the potential benefits (e.g., improvements in accuracy or validity, greater acceptability) are worth these extra costs.

Unfortunately, there are no easy rules, as this kind of analysis will be influenced by personal, professional, or corporate values and the intended use of the effectiveness measures. For instance, how important is it to pick the very best person for a promotion? Alternatively, in theory testing research, how consequential would it be if a set of predicted relationships were not uncovered because an inferior or inappropriate measure of effectiveness was used? One strategy that has been used to deal with the issue of expense associated with some measures of effectiveness is to conduct preliminary, *calibration research.* In this approach, data are gathered using a very expensive but highly valid technique for purposes of research. Less expensive techniques and the data they produce can then be related to what is known about a sample of employees. To the extent that there is a reasonable correspondence between the inferences of effectiveness from the more and less expensive measures, the latter might be used as a substitute for the former in future theoretical or applied work. The reader might recall that this strategy was used by Vance et al. (1988) as they compared ratings (inexpensive to get) with job sample performance data for aircraft engine mechanics.

IMPROVING THE QUALITY OF INDIVIDUAL EFFECTIVENESS MEASURES

When it comes to the use of subjective measures, there are ways other than changing techniques that will improve the quality of individual effectiveness data. These include ensuring the motivation to rate accurately, training, and using multiple points of view in the evaluation process. In fact, some would argue that these alternatives are more likely to make an impact on quality than the choice of scale that is made.

Motivation to Be Accurate

It is well known that people are frequently uncomfortable with the responsibility of completing performance evaluations (McGregor, 1957). Most managers realize that it is a part of their job, but they also know that it can affect the nature of their relations with subordinates. It emphasizes the power differences and frequently places two people who should normally be working closely together as a team in an adversarial relationship.

In general, people try to avoid giving negative or unpleasant information to others (Blumberg, 1972; Tesser & Rosen, 1975). Thus, Stone (1973) reports that a majority of managers surveyed dislike giving negative evaluations. And several laboratory studies have documented the tendency of evaluators to raise the evaluations of poor performers and to give more positive feedback to subordinates than is warranted (Ilgen & Knowlton, 1980; Fisher, 1979). In some cases this tendency has been viewed as subconscious or perceptual (Mitchell & Klimoski, 1985; Weary, 1979). However, many writers conclude that people do recognize poor performance when it occurs but that they just don't record it as such (Ilgen & Knowlton, 1980; Larson, 1984). They are just not motivated to rate accurately.

In terms of organizational practices, there are several things that can be done to change this. Most fundamentally, senior management can create the climate for high quality assessments. This means attending to the perspective and needs of the managers who will use the system, understanding the views of employees, and being certain that the performance measurement program is consistent with other policies and practices. But there are more specific things to do as well.

Supervisor Support

In order to increase supervisor support for the system (and hence motivation to do a good job as a rater), Carroll and Schneier (1982) cite the following as important:

1. *Understand the system.* People resist things because they do not know what they are, what their role is, or why the program has come about (for example Beer, Ruh, Dawson, McCaa, & Kavanagh, 1978). Quality appraisals take time and effort, and will not be forthcoming if these issues are not understood.
2. *Perceive how to use the system.* Even if managers know and understand the system they may still not have the needed skills to do what is expected of them. This, in turn, produces resistance and a half-hearted effort. When the manager must report or justify the appraisal in particular, these result in a tendency toward a leniency bias. To put it another way, to increase acceptance managers need to have a sense of self efficacy in the conduct of performance appraisals (Bernardin & Beatty, 1984). Usually this can be created through extensive training.
3. *Perform quality appraisals.* Simply stated, low motivation to do a good job in the conduct of appraisals may stem from the fact that there are few positive and many negative consequences (outcomes) for being accurate. Senior management may not really care. They themselves may not carry out the appraisal of their own direct reports conscientiously. In fact there is a lot of evidence that there may be more incentives operating in most organizations to promote distortion than accuracy in appraisals (Barrett, 1966).

4. *Perceive the relevance and legitimacy of the measurement system.* A program must do what it is intended to do. It must be well designed to produce appropriate and useful information or it will not receive support (Decotiis & Petit, 1978). Usually, this implies that it should be developed with the help of individuals professionally trained in the individual effectiveness measurement area. However, there also is some evidence that managers who have had a role in the shaping of choices made by program designers are more likely to perceive its relevance and legitimacy (Friedman & Cornelius, 1976). Indeed, this is one of the presumed benefits of the construction of BARS, inasmuch as several groups of potential users are involved at various stages of the process.

Individual Support

Working relationships being what they are, it is not surprising to find that the enthusiasm and support that managers give to a measurement program is, in part, a function of how their employees feel about it. Given the intrinsic difficulty of the appraisal task, criticisms or challenges from those being evaluated are likely to undermine efforts at producing quality data and, instead, to promote sloppiness or bias (usually reflected in leniency and range restriction where judgments are involved). Carroll and Schneier (1982) suggest that subordinate acceptance of measurement programs also is likely to be affected by several factors:

1. *Perceived relevance and accuracy of the measures used.* Most employees want to be evaluated in those areas that are legitimately part of their job. But they only should be held accountable for those things over which they have some control. They also want to know that the techniques used are appropriate. Many of these expectations are violated in practice, however. For example, it is common for organizations to use the same scales or criterion dimensions for all employees. While this makes for ease of comparison of scores coming from different departments, it also implies that a lot of employees are being assessed on factors which may be irrelevant to the work performed. To deal with the problem (and at the same time keep the number of different scales to a minimum), some organizations are clustering jobs into families that share common tasks and responsibilities. Those jobs within the cluster would then get the same appraisal form. Of course, an approach like MBO deals with the issue of relevance directly by having the subordinate actually influence the areas in which an evaluation will be made.

2. *Fairness of measurement system administration.* Even a system that is carefully developed can be implemented and administered in a haphazard fashion or in a manner that encourages cynicism. In particular, employees are concerned with apparent favoritism, or even worse, with being blackballed by a boss. In an era of automated personnel information systems, there also is a concern for the confidentiality of data and of threats to privacy. This too can create concerns regarding administration. There is no easy resolution to these issues. Perhaps they can be dealt with best by having a professionally trained human resource staff, one that can develop a relationship of trust with employees. But other things like top management support for the independence of the personnel function in the organization, well-developed and documented measurement procedures, and an effective appeals process to which dissatisfied employees might turn (if the data were to be used for administrative purposes) would help promote the feeling that the system is fair.

3. *Values congruence.* The various approaches to effectiveness measurement have different underlying assumptions or philosophies. For instance, personnel comparison systems

(like rankings) require evaluations on a relative basis and tend to promote competitiveness. On the other hand, MBO usually involves participation, reflecting confidence in an employee's maturity. Similarly, evaluations may be put to a variety of uses. The major distinction in terms of use is between data gathered for administrative as opposed to developmental or research purposes. These purposes imply a different flavor to a program. The point is that employees have needs, values, and expectations that may be incompatible with implicit or explicit program philosophies. This too would reduce levels of employee acceptance.

Compatability with Policies and Practices

The motivation of both managers and employees to carry out their roles in a performance measurement program is also going to be affected by other personnel policies and practices. To the extent that requirements of the program are not consistent with those in these other areas, reduced support is likely to result. An area that is most problematic is how data are used in compensation decisions. Organizations vary greatly in the extent to which they emphasize assessed merit. Obviously, to the extent that they do, their program must be particularly well conceived and administered, for few things are more upsetting to employees than to feel that their compensation is subject to arbitrary forces. Policies in areas of reduction in force, promotions, dismissals, and rehiring, also are likely to affect and to be affected by policies and practices associated with performance measurement programs (Lawler, 1971).

With supervisor and subordinate support for the measurement program and compatible policies, there is a high likelihood that, given a reasonably designed scale, high quality data will be obtained.

Motivation in Research

Investigators who are gathering effectiveness data for research also have to be concerned about the motivation of those who are supplying the data. If the research is being conducted in field settings, the motivation of those involved will be strongly affected by the way that the study is introduced to participants, the degree to which the integrity of the data will be maintained, and the credibility of the research team.

Thus, the forces and factors described in great detail in Chapter 4 related to conducting observations and interviews in organizations will be of relevance here as well. To the extent that the study is presented and accepted as important, the data are only to be used for research, the sources of the data are confidential (or anonymous), and the existence of the data cannot come to hurt the participants (raters and employees), the investigator is more likely to get cooperation and expect acceptable levels of motivation to complete or carry out the assessment task. As in the case of observations and interviews, the establishment and maintenance of trust between the investigator and respondents is very important.

When effectiveness data are gathered in artificial or laboratory settings, the investigator usually has the capacity to seek out (even pay) individuals to conduct ratings for research purposes. However, even here issues of motivation should not be overlooked. In particular, it is quite common to conduct research in a laboratory where undergraduate students are used as raters and their behaviors (ratings) are the focus of attention. Under these circumstances, the motivation of the rater (subject) actually may be a variable of interest and subjected to experimental manipulation (e.g., Klimoski & Inks, 1990). But more often, motivation is assumed to be consistent and relatively high for all subjects, across all conditions and over the period of the session. We should never assume this much. Procedures need to be implemented as part of the investigation so that high motivation does indeed occur. For example, being paid for participation might help. Alternatively, creating accountability forces might be warranted (e.g., Klimoski & Inks, 1990). In any event, it would also be prudent to check on the level of motivation of research participants who are providing effectiveness data as a matter of practice.

TRAINING FOR QUALITY MEASUREMENTS

Once again, with regard to organizational practices it seems reasonable to assume that one will get higher quality effectiveness data if the people responsible for them are well trained. As straightforward as this is, there continue to be numerous instances where managers, often newly assigned to their roles because of a promotion, are asked to do evaluations with minimal guidance. Moreover, while there may be no doubt that training is indeed warranted, only recently has a consensus developed in the technical literature regarding what kind of training is appropriate.

The traditional approach to training has been to offer a workshop to potential users in which the philosophy of the effectiveness measurement program is reviewed and the forms and expected "paper flow" are outlined. But the core of traditional training has been to emphasize the nature of potential bias and errors (leniency, central tendency, halo, etc.). These usually are defined and examples are given. The future raters are told to avoid them if at all possible (Levine & Butler, 1952; Wexley, Sanders, & Yukl, 1973). Instruction is usually in a lecture/ discussion format. The training itself might last anywhere from an hour to a day.

When these training programs have been rigorously evaluated, however, there has been little evidence that they had the desired effects (Bernardin, 1978; Spool, 1978). Although managers might come away with an understanding of what the appropriate forms are and might be able to define errors, their actual evaluations would continue to manifest poor quality. It seems clear that merely imparting knowledge is not a sufficient basis for rater training (Wexley & Latham, 1981).

In the last ten years, however, there has been something of a revolution in the area. In fact, it represents a good example where advances in theory have contributed greatly to changes in professional practice. Much of the credit is due to the scientists whose research has led to a more complete understanding of the social judgment process. As outlined earlier in this chapter, we now know much more about the causes of rating bias and distortion. Developments in training theory and technology also have occurred. Thus, both training content and training process have been affected.

The best evidence is that rater training should focus on improving observation and categorization skills (Bernardin & Beatty, 1984), while stressing accuracy (Bernardin & Pence, 1980), and using a training format that requires active participation and practice on the part of trainees (Latham et al., 1975).

Frame of reference training has been suggested as one approach that is useful in increasing the accuracy of observations (Bernardin & Beatty, 1984; Borman, 1979). In this approach, individuals are taught what job behaviors to look for when assessing employees and how to evaluate (how much weight) differing behavior patterns. In particular, trainees are allowed opportunities to make and record their own observations and to learn how their processing and use of information differ from others. In a sense, the training attempts to make explicit the performance schemas and prototypes actually held by the trainees and highlight those felt to be more appropriate. The desired schema thus becomes a common frame of reference to be used by everyone. In a related vein, Bernardin, Cardy, and Abbott (1982) found that managers who held performance schemata were compatible with the rating dimensions of a BARS instrument appeared to make better ratings on that scale. This should occur in the case of BARS insofar as they are constructed with a great deal of input from future users of the scale.

There also is some evidence that the quality of data (if ratings are to be used) can be enhanced if rater training includes an emphasis on a more systematic approach to documenting and recording observations of relevant job behaviors. Bernardin (1978) recommends the use of a diary to do this. In a study involving the measurement of teaching effectiveness, some student raters were trained to keep a diary of critical incidents in instructor behavior throughout the school term. It was found that ratings of this group had less leniency and halo than another group of student raters who did not receive this training. The trained group found the diary very helpful in making their ratings (Bernardin & Walter, 1977; Buckley & Bernardin, 1980). It also might be recalled that one of the strengths of the BARS method as originally developed was that it helped structure on-the-job observations of workers. Raters were to record these on the actual instrument to be used later when appraisal judgments were required.

A final point might be made with regard to advances in the technology of rater training. As mentioned, more successful programs require a great deal of active participation on the part of trainees. In particular, they get a lot of practice making ratings of people in a very standardized context. Usually, they will make ratings of workers (actors) who are portrayed on videotape. Not only does this provide a constant stimuli for all trainees, but because it has been scripted in a particular manner (e.g., to represent a poor performer) it also is possible to assess and feed back the accuracy of ratings. Unlike most performance evaluation situations, there is a true score to serve as the basis for examining the quality of the ratings supplied by trainees and for providing feedback to them (Ivancevich, 1979; Warmke & Billings, 1979). It appears that information regarding observational errors at this level of specificity and detail is what is needed by trainees to improve the quality of their performance appraisals (Nemeroff & Cosentino, 1979; Thornton & Zorich, 1980).

Almost all the points just made about the training of organizational members who will be supplying effectiveness data are also relevant to the preparation of assistants or subjects in laboratory research. Thus, those who will be giving ratings or who otherwise will be assessing effectiveness, also need to be capable of doing the job. Any number of programs or techniques found useful in actual organizations (e.g., use of videotaped stimuli, frame of reference training) can be adopted for the purpose of ensuring this capability.

CHOICE OF APPRAISAL AGENT

Throughout this chapter we have regularly referred to the manager or supervisor as the agent responsible for carrying out evaluations and for producing effectiveness data. This was done to reflect the reality of the way these programs are carried out in most organizations. However, it is possible to obtain evaluations from a number of sources, including the employee (self-ratings), coworkers (peer ratings), superiors, subordinates, and personnel specialists. Moreover, there is evidence that the quality of ratings can be related to their source under different circumstances. And there will be times when we will want information from multiple sources for maximum appraisal validity.

Wexley and Klimoski (1984) stress that, when it comes to the selection of who is to be conducting evaluations, four factors should be considered. The person must: (a) be in a position to observe the performance and behavior of the worker, (b) be knowledgeable about what constitutes effectiveness, (c) have an understanding of the measures to be used, and (d) be motivated to be accurate. Some of these factors already have been reviewed, but they take on different implications when the issue is the appropriate source of data.

A great amount of accumulated evidence has established that evaluations made from these various perspectives are different and should not be considered interchangeable (Borman, 1974; Klimoski & London, 1974; Holzbach, 1978). But the interesting thing is that while they may be different, it's possible that each might be valid, at least under various circumstances. In particular, the five potential sources of appraisal data listed above are in positions that encourage somewhat different definitions of effectiveness, allow for different opportunities for observation, and imply different levels of motivation to be accurate (Carroll & Schneier, 1982).

Superiors, of course, should have a good understanding of what constitutes effective job performance; but they may not be in a position to see a subordinate's behavior in key areas. Coworkers can observe a person's day-to-day activities, yet when it comes to what is desirable behavior, they may have a limited perspective. One must assume that self-ratings are made with the benefit of insight as to what the worker actually does on the job but they are characteristically inflated and reflect a great deal of halo. One could go on. The fact is, each perspective has certain strengths and weaknesses. Figure 6-12 highlights this point.

One of the most critical factors to influence the appropriate choice of rater is the purpose for which the evaluations is being made (Wexley & Klimoski, 1984). This is because of the impact that purpose appears to have on the motivation of the different agents to be accurate. In general, assessments being made exclusively for research tend to generate the least anxiety and resistance (and hence distortion) from all of the sources. However, if they are to be used for administrative

	Strengths	Weaknesses
Supervisors	Legitimate authority; Controls rewards, punishments; Knowledge of subordinates' job responsibilities	Subject to self-interest; Poorly motivated to be accurate
Peers	Knowledge of coworkers' duties; Opportunity to observe coworkers closely	Frequently in competition; Subject to collusion; Subject to friendship bias; May not see full range of colleagues' responsibilities
Subordinates	Opportunity to observe supervisor closely; Can evaluate personnel management component of supervisor's job	Subject to intimidation; Subject to loyalty forces
Self	Intimate knowledge of intentions, effort; Knowledge of job performance; Encourages self-development	Subject to self-serving bias
Personnel Specialist	No vested interest in rating outcome; Well trained and practiced; Able to get information from multiple sources	May not have adequate opportunity to observe performance; May take away legitimate responsibility from supervisor

FIGURE 6-12 Strengths and Weaknesses of Appraisal Agents
   Source: Adapted with permission from Carroll, S. J., & Schneier, C. E. (1982). *Performance appraisal and review systems.* Glenview, IL: Scott Foresman.

action (e.g., for salary recommendations), there is reason to avoid having peers (DeNisi & Mitchell, 1978) or the employee (Thornton, 1980) supply the information.

Subordinate ratings of an employee are best used when the goal is to improve the latter's effectiveness. However, there is some evidence that peers are good at describing a colleague's strengths and weaknesses as well (Greller, 1980; Kane & Lawler, 1978). And, if gathered for developmental purposes, even self-appraisals appear to have potential (Mabe & West, 1982). In fact, Klimoski (1983) reports a project with a municipal agency where a combination of self-, peer, and subordinate ratings were used successfully to provide data on the developmental needs of managers. These then served as the basis of an individualized training program designed to increase the manager's effectiveness as a supervisor of workers.

When it comes to research conducted in artificial settings or laboratories, the investigator has the full range of options as to the choice of agent. Subjects in laboratory studies who are being observed can be evaluated by other subjects, by assistants to the researcher, or they themselves may provide data. In several areas, it is even common to create hierarchical relationships in the lab. Thus, it is possible to have subjects (as supervisors) rate subjects (as employees). That is to say, one might produce different roles as part of a study (e.g., Fisher, 1979).

The main difference between lab and field settings, however, is with regard to how well the investigator can ensure that the rater has the opportunity to observe and how well the essential dynamics of the roles are, in fact, operating. In these areas, research in simulations provide a mixed case. Thus, the investigator *should* be able to guarantee (or control) exposure to the individuals being evaluated. After all, this is a strength of using a simulation—unless, of course, opportunity to observe is a design variable (c.f., Heneman & Wexley, 1983). On the other hand, it is much more difficult to ensure that the role dynamics of organization life are being captured. In this regard, there has been a great deal of criticism of simulations for research on performance appraisal (Ilgen & Favero, 1985). Under normal circumstances, they may not ensure that the points of view of the self, peer, or supervisors as found in organizations are being captured. This leads to the question of generalizability of the results obtained in the simulation.

How might an investigator ensure the quality of subjectively produced effectiveness data? The answer appears to be that he or she should operate on one or more of the factors just described: scale format, motivation, training, and the appropriate choice of agent. The greatest success is likely to occur when all of the factors are considered in the implementation and administration of a measurement program (Beer et al., 1978).

As stressed earlier in this chapter, the quality of objective data on individual effectiveness should not be assumed. Such data should be scrutinized carefully. But here, the issues associated with quality and its improvement are somewhat different than in the case of subjective assessments.

Objective (usually performance) data should be reviewed to determine if they are either contaminated or deficient. This would be particularly true of researchers using effectiveness data from organizational records. There are any number of factors which might affect operational indicators used by organizations that cause them to be relatively insensitive to individual worker effort or ability. For example, the performance of a welder in terms of "number of units produced" or of a programmer in terms of "amount of time on a mainframe computer" (central processing time) may be strongly influenced by outside (even seasonal) factors. Thus, the careful investigator might look for evidence of temporal stability of such measures before accepting them as valid. Similarly, the distinction of typical versus maximum performance has relevance here. Objective indicators must be examined to see if they are indeed appropriate for a study where the investigator is interested in one or the other of these aspects of effectiveness.

Finally, one should be sensitive to the possibility of random errors creeping into the data set. Errors of worksheet recording or errors of key entry of the data into the computer can compromise data quality and reduce the possibility of detecting real relationships. To this point, Smith, Budzeika, Edwards, Johnson, and Bearse (1986) offer 13 rules to detect common mistakes (e.g., one should print out the raw data once it has been coded and entered into a computer) . In fact, many of the issues dealing with quality of measurement in paper and pencil tests (Chapters 2 and 3) can be raised with regard to objective measures of effectiveness. It would be prudent to review these when considering creating, adapting, or directly using objective measures of individual effectiveness.

SUMMARY

This chapter has explored, in some detail, the ways individual effectiveness is defined and measured in organizations. Implications for research and practice also have been described. The emphasis has been on the forces that affect the quality of the information obtained because the issue of poor quality is one that must be resolved at the outset by anyone seeking to use individual effectiveness data. In the end, it is quite likely that the conditions of opportunity, motivation, and capability will be as important as the particular scale format when it comes to ensuring high quality individual effectiveness information.

DEFINING AND MEASURING EFFECTIVENESS AT THE GROUP AND ORGANIZATIONAL LEVEL

This chapter includes a discussion of group and organization effectiveness. We review what objectives or goals are associated with groups and organizations and what special indices must be developed to do research on groups and organizations. These indices often present special problems of measurement. Sample sizes are almost always smaller, multiple interested constituencies may define effectiveness differently, and the large number of variables typically involved make it difficult to isolate cause-and-effect relationships. In this area, perhaps more than in any area of human resources research, the theoretical assumptions and values of the researcher are important and must be articulated clearly.

This chapter is designed to address issues associated with defining and measuring effectiveness of groups and organizations. In many ways it serves to complement our treatment of individual effectiveness (see Chapters 5 and 6).

INTERDEPENDENCY IN WORK

Why should we be interested in group and organization levels of analysis? Actually for both practical and theoretical reasons the manager or researcher frequently will find that the focus on the individual is inappropriate. In particular, there are many instances where the nature of the work to be done is such that there are many complex elements of information sharing or effort coordination involved in order to do what is required. To put it more technically, there are *task interdependencies*. In particular, as Steiner (1972) points out there are two classes of task situations where such interdependencies are pronounced. He terms these disjunctive and conjunctive conditions.

In *disjunctive task* situations the nature of the work is such that successful performance can occur if any one individual in the work group provides a particular contribution. This condition often exists in problem-solving or decision-making contexts. Thus, the group is moved closer to its goal if any one of its members comes up with an answer or provides a solution to the problem. Committees, task forces, project teams, or creative departments of organizations frequently face this situation.

In contrast, success on *conjunctive tasks* comes about as a function of the contributions of the least effective member. In the context of intellective tasks, this occurs when the group feels that it cannot move on to new issues until all participants (including the person who is slowest to assimilate the facts) understand what is going on. More often this notion is relevant when physical skill or effort is involved. Thus, a team scaling a mountain (and literally tied together by safety ropes) can move only as fast or as aggressively as the least capable or prepared member.

There also are times when managers, coaches or policymakers believe that task accomplishment can best occur under what is termed *fate interdependence*. This means that the nature of the task or the rules for working are such that the fortunes of the people involved are intertwined or linked together. In other words, to the extent that all group members do their individual subtasks well and/or work in a cooperative and mutually helpful way, everyone profits from the experience. Steiner (1972) labels these as *discretionary work* or task situations wherein individual contributions are encouraged (or played down), weighted, and combined by the group according to what its members feel is appropriate under the circumstances. Thus, a crew on a sailboat can be successful to the extent that there is a continuous and real-time orchestration of individual efforts and talents. Notice here that the nature of the job at hand is such that the contributions of one group member can offset the failings of another if they are introduced in a timely manner.

Individuals can be made to be fate interdependent by the reward system of organizations. That is to say, individuals can be paid in proportion to group not personal, accomplishments. This, in turn, is likely to occur where managers feel that there is the need for collective effort. Team rewards also will be likely in those situations in which there is also a fair amount of task uncertainty. By this we mean that not a lot is known about just how to go about the job of producing a product or of providing a service. In fact, in many circumstances there may be a lot of uncertainty surrounding the nature of the demands that will be placed on the group. Thus, a sales team may never really know what their largest customers will demand or what the competition will throw at them. Team members will need to improvise and to coordinate their efforts and talents to make the sale. Moreover, in many work settings, the actual level of task interdependencies will vary and often depend on what is required at the time. Under all these circumstances, mutual assistance and adjustment would be expected and necessary. Thus, it seems reasonable for organizations to put in place information and reward systems that encourage timely coordination and cooperation— that is, create fate interdependence (Lawler, 1986).

In situations of fate or task interdependencies, effectiveness measures need to be taken at the group level. To look at and to assess the contributions of individuals would be misleading. Similarly, to recognize or reward the performance of individuals would be inappropriate. While personal effort is not irrelevant, the ultimate success of all the individuals involved depends on how well the group functions. Under conditions of high interdependency, criterion measures taken at the level of the individual would be both deficient and contaminated.

There also are circumstances when the decision to use the group (or organization) as the unit of analysis is based on empirical evidence. In many cases investigators examining the variability in criterion measures are able to detect a reliable difference in scores as a function of group membership. At times, this may be an added effect to the impact of other variables of interest (either manipulated or measured). For example, in addition to determining from a survey (see Chapter 10) that employee attitudes are related to individual differences in age or experience, it also may be observed that the work group the respondent is in makes a difference. On average, different work groups can be shown to produce different levels on the attitude measure as well. We have what we would call a group effect.

On other occasions group effects (if not measured) may actually mask certain phenomena. Markham (1988) determined this in a study of the relationship of pay and job performance using a sample of 71 managers and professionals in a manufacturing organization. Markham (1988) concluded from a review of past research that even though an organization's policy might emphasize contingent pay (pay for performance), records may show no apparent relationship.

In his study, Markham was able to show that this was indeed the case when measures were taken using the individual as the unit of analysis. That is to say, Markham found no correlation between measured individual performance and size of merit raise received by these individuals. However, when the work teams (or groups) were compared, a clear pattern emerged. Consistent with the merit policy of this organization, work units with higher levels of performance had group members (on average) who got bigger merit raises. Markham reasoned that a pay and performance relationship at the group level came about because the supervisor's overall raise budget was increased as a function of the average performance of team members. Thus, he or she had more money for merit raises. However, for practical reasons the supervisors in the organization tended to reward all team members about the same. Thus, while there still might be some differences in performance levels across people in the team, the raises given were all similar. This latter dynamic tended to eliminate the possibility of finding any correlation at the level of the individual. This phenomena can be seen in the two diagrams used by Markham (1988) to characterize what he calls the individualized dyadic model (the traditional way of thinking about pay and performance) with the cohesive team model (Figure 7-1).

Markham described, in this study, two sets of analyses that can be used to determine if there is, indeed, a group level effect. The first he refers to as a *within and between analysis* (WABA). This involves computing a series of correlation coefficients between performance and merit raise size at both the individual and group levels and contrasting their relative sizes. The second technique is called *contextual analysis*. This is a type of regression analysis where several individual and group level variables, singly and in combination, are considered as potential predictors of the size of the merit raise received by individuals. The statistical significance of the effects of the group variable would imply that the group should be considered a relevant unit of analysis. As noted, both types of analysis revealed a pay and performance relationship at the group, but not at the individual, level.

There is one other context in which the empirical effects of some phenomena at the group level deserve to be mentioned. As you can see in the examples of experimental research reviewed throughout this text, for a variety of reasons it's not uncommon to conduct studies aimed at individual phenomena with groups of individuals. For example, while a survey could be administered individually, it is usually more efficient if potential respondents are brought to a conference room, a cafeteria, or an auditorium to complete the instrument. But because it may be impossible to take all people off the job at once, several groups of workers might be brought in over a period of time (e.g., days). Similarly, in order to get an adequate number of data points, laboratory studies often are conducted over many sessions. In effect, groups of subjects are brought in to be exposed to some manipulation or treatment (see Chapter 11). Many more instances could be given. In any event, under such circumstances the prudent investigator would assess whether or not there is a session (i.e., group) effect on the measured variables of interest. It could be that the typical or average scores for various groups differ significantly by chance. Such a discovery would imply that a group or session factor would have to be incorporated into any planned analysis (usually as a measured variable). To put it another way, the group or session would have to be recognized as a potential causal (or nuisance) variable for the phenomena at hand.

Arguments for paying attention to the interdependencies of individuals in group contexts also are valid when applied to larger aggregations like departments or whole organizations. The nature of manufacturing and distributing a product, or producing and delivering a service, requires collective effort and talents. These result in interdependencies. Even while recognizing the potential value of focusing on the individual and the group, at times there are important benefits from using measures of effectiveness at this higher (organization) level of aggregation.

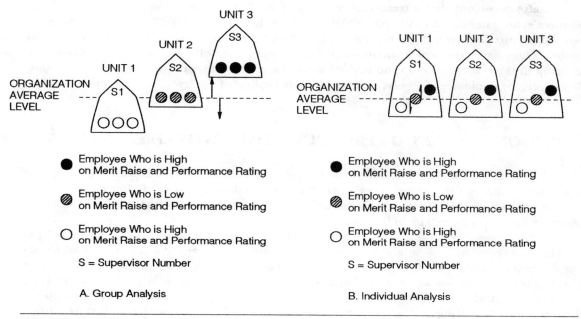

FIGURE 7-1 **Discovery of Relationships at the Group Level that May be Obscured at the Individual Level**
Source: Markham, S. E. (1988). Pay-for-performance dilemma revisited: Empirical example of the importance of group effects. *Journal of Applied Psychology, 73,* 172–180. Reprinted with permission.

GROUPS AND ORGANIZATIONS AS THEORETICALLY INTERESTING

The nature of work and of working is not the only reason to consider measurement at the group and organization level. In many cases, attention is given to these entities because they are interesting in and of their own right. Many researchers seek to define and measure effectiveness here because they are trying to develop, refine, or even test theories of groups or of organizations (e.g., Gladstein, 1984; Woodman & Sherwood, 1980). For these people, the effort at good measurement is not driven by practical concerns as much as the fact that it is needed to move theoretical developments forward.

MULTIPLE APPROACHES

As in the case of defining and measuring effectiveness at the individual level, there is no one approach to measurement that is currently regarded as definitive. Whether you are involved in measurement at the group or the organization level, quite a few options are available. This means that the investigator will be called upon to make many judgments regarding the nature and use of measures. For these judgments and choices to be informed, there is a need for a certain amount of subject matter knowledge and expertise. The investigator, whether manager or scientist, must be aware of existent theory, research, and practice.

It also turns out that a treatment of measurement at the group and organization levels requires some attention to the conceptual issues involved. Thus, this chapter is structured to provide an introduction to some theoretical models or frameworks relating to groups and organizations. Once again it is worth mentioning that we merely are offering an overview of current thinking in these areas. There is no real substitute for scholarship prior to attempts at selecting, developing, or implementing good measurement, regardless of the level of measurement.

PERSON, PROCESS, OR PRODUCT MEASURES OF EFFECTIVENESS

In an examination of the nature of individual effectiveness in Chapter 5 we found it important to distinguish between person, process, and product measures of effectiveness. These notions will be useful to us in this chapter as well. We will apply these terms to the locus of attention and measurement involved in an investigation.

In the discussion of individual effectiveness, *person* referred to traits or qualities thought to be relevant to effectiveness. Similarly, at the level of groups and organizations, certain distinguishing attributes or features will be linked to or viewed as hallmarks of effectiveness. In the earlier chapter, the term *process* was used to capture the notion of effectiveness that is rooted in an individual's behaviors. There will be parallels in groups and organizations as well. That is to say, the behaviors or activities of groups or organizations can be scrutinized for clues regarding effectiveness. Finally, just as *products* implied output-type effectiveness indicators for individuals, we will see that a number of writers favor such measures of groups and individuals. Certain group and organizational achievements have come to be considered good indicators of effectiveness.

As in the case of dealing with individuals, there will be times that any or all of these types of measures will be appropriate or preferred. Thus, the goal for those who are starting to work in the areas of groups or organizations should be to learn the alternative measurement concepts and techniques involved as well as to be able to apply them under the right circumstances.

DEFINING AND MEASURING GROUP EFFECTIVENESS

The following sections review theoretical and practical notions about defining and measuring effectiveness at the group level.

The Nature of Group Functioning

At the time of this writing there is no consensus regarding the correct framework or model of task group functioning (Guzzo, 1986). It's not for lack of effort. The fact is that any number of writers have attempted to come to grips with a solution to this dilemma (Gladstein, 1984; McGrath, 1984; Steiner, 1972). But the complexity of groups and of group dynamics has made it difficult to reach firm conclusions. For purposes of this chapter, however, a framework that would seem to have great heuristic value for a treatment of measurement issues associated with group effectiveness has been offered by Hackman and Morris (1975) and recently modified by Hackman (1986). Figure 7-2 has been adapted from these works.

According to the framework portrayed in Figure 7-2, to understand group functioning, you need to be able to characterize certain aspects of the group itself, the group dynamics that take

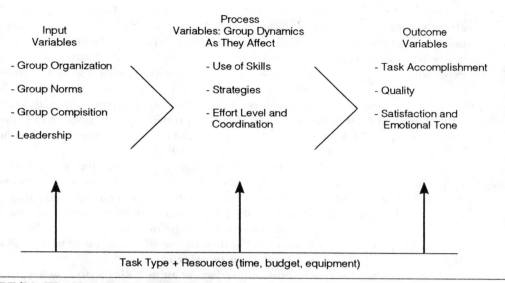

FIGURE 7-2 The Nature of Group Effectiveness
Source: Adapted with permission from Hackman, J. R. (1986). The design of work teams. In J. Lorsch (Ed.), *Handbook of organizational behavior.* Englewood Cliffs, NJ: Prentice Hall.

place (and critical intermediate factors), as well as group outcomes. Put another way, we must attend to analogs of person and process variables if we are to understand group products.

Defining Group Input Factors

According to the framework offered in Figure 7-2, group functioning (and hence potential effectiveness), much like individual functioning, will be strongly influenced by certain input variables. Four of these are identified as follows:

1. *Task organization (or group structure). Task organization* refers to just how the work to be done is divided up among group members. It implies a division of labor with regard to duties and activities. It also includes the notion of responsibility and authority. That is to say, task organization will subsume issues as to who has the power and final authority to make decisions. Finally, the concept of task organization reflects group size. Discussions regarding the division of labor inevitably include an examination of how many people are needed to get the job done. Do we need five or twenty-five individuals in the group? We already have touched on the idea behind organization or structure in discussing interdependencies in groups. However, it is important to point out that while task group structure sometimes derives from or is dictated by the essential properties of the task itself, in most contexts decision makers have a lot of discretion in this area. They can decide just what work will be performed by which group members.

2. *Group norms. Group norms* are the informal rules that groups develop or adopt to regulate members' behavior (Feldman, 1984). Norms exist and are enforced by group members in order to facilitate working together and to make the behavior of group members more predictable. To the extent that norms clarify what is expected of individuals, they

also are felt to be important to group survival (Feldman, 1984). Finally, the existence of group norms increases the likelihood that groups can effectively regulate members' behavior by rewarding conformity and punishing deviance (Hackman, 1976). Norms derive from a number of sources. Critical events in a group's history may determine expectations for key behaviors well into the future (e.g., with regard to vigilance or reliability). Indeed, there often is a carryover into the current situation of "lessons learned" from the past experiences of individual group members. But it also turns out that norms can be shaped by the behaviors and statements of important or respected group members. Thus, managers, supervisors, and leaders will have an impact on what will become normative for the group (Feldman, 1984).

3. *Group composition.* The nature of the individuals making up the group imply *group composition.* It is the mix of types of people in the group. In the theory and research on groups, quite a large number of composition variables have been explored (Shaw, 1981). Thus group composition can refer to the proportion of males and females in the group, the age distribution of the people involved, and the mix of members' abilities or their personalities. In some contexts, even the distribution of height (as in basketball teams) or weight (for hot air balloon crews) may be relevant.

4. *Leadership.* In this discussion, group *leadership* includes both the formal assignment of leadership duties and the actual, informal, and ad hoc attempts at influence that take place in the group. While there is no agreed-upon system for classifying leaders and leader behaviors, there are a lot of approaches available (Yukl, 1989). For example, it is common to describe leadership in groups in terms of the extent to which it is centralized or shared, or whether leadership efforts are aimed at task accomplishments (e.g., efforts at structuring, clarifying, summarizing), group maintenance (supporting and harmonizing), or both (Cartwright & Zander, 1968; Shaw, 1981; Yukl, 1989). The importance of group input variables stems from the fact that they set the stage for process and outcomes. A particular combination of group organization, norms, composition, and leadership will have predictable consequences. The wrong combination will retard group accomplishments. It may even produce a disaster!

Measuring Group Input Factors

The definition and measurement of input factors is not well developed. This means that the manager/researcher will frequently be challanged to innovate and improvise.

In instances where task organization or structure is of interest, it would be useful to start with a consideration of the way the manager/researcher has set up the division of labor within the group. This may be reflected in the description of the group's task or in the job titles given to specific individuals. Of course when studying ad hoc laboratory groups, the most direct way to index the task structure is to uncover what had been created by way of task properties. For example, Shaw (1981) describes work group organization in terms of within-group communication channels. Figure 7-3 provides an example of such structures.

In most cases however, the structure of within-group activities relative to the division of labor must be assessed by something other than a review of position descriptions. Investigators frequently will use interviews or questionnaires to assess group member perceptions of group structure. Finally, group organization can be indexed by careful observation of the group members as they work. Thus, the techniques for process measurement described shortly will be found useful.

The measurement of group norms is also problematic. While the concept of norms has been around for many years, it is only recently that the elements of norms have been articulated

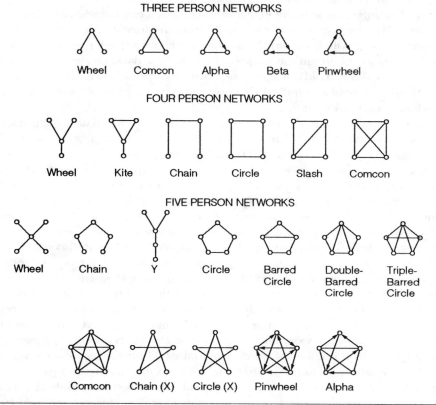

FIGURE 7-3   Possible Communication Structures in Groups

Source: Reprinted with permission from Shaw, M. E. (1981). *Group dynamics: The psychology of small group behavior* (3rd ed.). New York: McGraw-Hill.

(Hackman, 1976). Thus, Jackson (1965) identifies the importance of indexing norms in terms of both the pattern and intensity of approval and disapproval associated with various possible behaviors. Jackson's theory predicts that group member behavior will be regulated to the extent that expectations have been crystalized, that is, where there is a high degree of consensus among group members regarding what should or should not be done. This will be moderated by the intensity of feelings held by group members with regard to deviance from expectations. Where there are both crystallized expectations and strong feelings, group members will be very likely to expect conformity from one another.

Group norms may be measured by obtaining reports from group members using questionnaires and/or individual or group interviews. However, because of the emotions or affect usually associated with norms, these approaches might prove to be too obtrusive (see Chapter 4). Direct questions might prompt distortion or concealment. Thus, once again, norms may be best measured by careful observations of actual behavior, with the goal of capturing norm-relevant influence attempts. As in the case of indexing group organization, we must rely on inferences from careful observation and attention to group process.

In a study of work norms as they relate to communications, Schall (1983) used several techniques. She examined company documents and manuals, constructed a questionnaire designed to get at communication norms (especially the informal, operational rules), and administered it to workers. She interviewed top managers and had them rate the salience of the norms she had uncovered, and did some scaling of norms. In the latter instance she had a group of employees from all levels sort cards on which was written a single work norm. Each pile of cards was used to define some level of norm potency in the workplace. From these data she was able to identify what organizational members did and did not agree on (consensus) and what rules of behavior (norms) were, in fact, operating. She also required that, when done, the piles of sorted cards represent distinct points along an intensity continuum.

In contrast, the measurement of composition factors lends itself to a direct approach. In fact, composition is often a variable of interest in group research so it becomes a measured or manipulated variable. To illustrate, Tziner and Eden (1985) experimentally varied the composition of three-man military tank crews to assess its effects on performance. Specifically, both crew members' ability and motivation were assessed and crews were made up on the basis of the scores obtained. The ability index was a composite of performance on an intelligence test, level of formal education achieved, Hebrew language proficiency (the study was conducted in the Israeli Army), and ratings derived from a semi-structured interview. Motivation levels were estimated from answers to items embedded in a questionnaire. A given soldier was designated as either high or low (relative to the median) on the two composition factors. Then the tank crews were configured to allow for all possible combinations of crew types. In this study it was found that ability and motivation levels had additive effects on crew performance. But ability levels were more important. Not surprisingly, crews composed of uniformly high ability outperformed the typical crew.

In a management development program that one of your authors has been involved in, group composition also was felt to be relevant. The program took place over a week-long period wherein managers were exposed to a number of developmental experiences, including a very complex business game. Participants were to go through the program in learning groups of from 9 to 14 individuals. From the outset it was recognized that the make-up of the teams could affect the quality of the experience and hence the impact of the program. Therefore, teams were configured so as to have a mix in terms of gender, management levels, and home departments. As it turned out, because of schedule and logistical problems the actual mix in each team differed from what was planned. Therefore, each team's actual composition was inventoried after the program. This information is being used as a variable in a study designed to assess the impact of the program on attitudes and behaviors once back on the job.

The measurement of leadership in groups usually has relied on process approaches (see below). However, as it relates to its status as an input factor, it seems reasonable to characterize the existence and nature of formal leadership roles. Groups may or may not have a formal leader. This would be important to index. Moreover, if there is a formal leader, research has pointed out it is relevant to note and record how that person came to the role (assigned, elected, through personal effort, etc.). This is related to the characteristics that the formal leader will possess: experience, power, authority, even gender. All of these have been found to be relevant to group process and outcome (Shaw, 1981).

When it comes to both composition and leader input variables, the issue is usually not one of how to measure variables, but just what one is to measure. While basic research on groups can provide some guidance, appropriate choices will depend upon knowledge of such factors as the task and the social or organizational context in which the group will be functioning.

In thinking of group effectiveness, then, it seems very appropriate to consider (and even measure) these input factors. To put it another way, an effective group may be defined as one that is organized, staffed, and led appropriately to get the job done.

Defining Group Process Factors

Group process refers to the behaviors that take place in the group, the patterning of those behaviors (across individuals and across time), and the immediate consequences of these behaviors and patterns (Steiner, 1972). While a review of all of group process theory is not feasible, it does seem useful to highlight a few concepts as they help clarify potential process indicators of group effectiveness.

Three factors associated with or caused by levels of effectiveness in group process include: group member effort, skills utilization, and strategies. (see Figure 7-2) These are discussed as follows:

1.   *Group member effort.* For ultimate group effectiveness, group members need to demonstrate an appropriate level and pattern of effort directed toward the task. It is important to note here that this does not imply giving extraordinary effort all the time or the same levels of effort (beyond a minimum) for everyone. Moreover, effort levels will be affected by group norms, the perceived importance of the group task, and group leadership. Clearly, group members' behaviors toward one another also will have a significant impact (Hackman, 1976).

2.   *Group member skills utilization.* Even where the group is composed of individuals with the requisite skills and abilities, it is possible for the group to make ineffective use of them. Group process can determine if those people with the best knowledge are allowed to contribute to group functioning or, alternatively, to promote a waste of time by those who have little of substance to offer (Hoffman, 1965).

3.   *Work group strategies.* There seems to be ample evidence that how the group approaches the job to be done will have important consequences for ultimate group success (Vroom & Yetton, 1973). While work group strategies will be affected by the input variables of structure and composition, it is still something that gets superimposed on these. At a minimum, work group strategies, as the plan to be followed by group members, must be compatible with these variables.

A focus on group process recognizes that it is important to the prediction and to the understanding of ultimate group success. In our view it also provides the manager or researcher with an intermediate way of defining effectiveness. Thus, an effective work group is not only one that is appropriately composed (via input factors) but one that allows or encourages critical processes to unfold.

Measuring Group Process

In its essence, *group process* refers to the series of actions or operations that take place in a group as they relate some goal or end (Steiner, 1972). Thus, process is reflected in behaviors. In attempting to measure group processes it is important to realize that it is probably impossible to produce a complete or total description of all that occurs in a group. It would have to include an enormous number of variables, some of which may only be manifest in the behavior of the minds of the people involved (i.e., their thoughts). But we rarely even try to do this. Instead, we are interested in certain fragments of process as we seek to discover what Steiner calls the *collective tidiness* of group phenomona.

In general we seek to detect and record such things as who acts and how often, to whom the acts are directed, what the acts are made of, when the acts occur, and why the acts occur. Thus, while it is possible that an investigator would approach the study of group process without any preconceived notion with regard to what to look for (for an example of an ethnographer, see Chapter 4), most of us go into an examination of group process with some framework in mind.

Systems for the Measurement of Group Process

The heart of any framework is a set of variables of interest and a system for recording them. The preferred techinque for measuring group process is to observe groups (in real time or as recorded on film or video). The system of recording often includes rules for observation as well (i.e., what to look for).

Weick (1985) refers to the use of a system as *explicit observing*. More specifically, he explains that "explicit observing is self-conscious, public, contestable, fully and clearly expressed, and capable of reconstruction. Explicitness is both a means, in the sense that it facilitates evaluation and replication, and an end, in the sense that certain techniques of observation are designed to make tacit understandings of informants more evident (p. 587)." Thus explicitness not only guides our observations, it contributes to our ability to assess the validity of the resultant data.

Explicit records of our observations imply some attention to detail. As a rule, the value of process data stems from the richness of details that it provides. The challenge to investigators of group process is to settle on what level of detail to attend to and record.

In this regard, it is useful to distinguish between narrative systems and checklists. Narratives can take the form of anecdotes. These are descriptions of behavioral episodes written in some detail. A type of narrative that has been found useful in applied work is the critical incident (see Chapter 6). A specimen record is a second type of narrative that is more continuous in nature. As written, it is a sequential description of behavior along with some contextual material. It is the sort of thing that we generate when we are setting up a story in a conversation. When used in the measurement of group process, these materials would constitute the raw material for content or thematic analysis (see Chapter 4).

In contrast, checklists provide greater structure to the measurement of process. Checklists often provide for the characterization of the setting of interest. This might include the number of people involved, the physical context (e.g., office or conference room), and the task or problem at hand. Action checklists describe behaviors rather than settings. Activity logs focus on clusters of activities as they relate to some purpose or goal.

One of the most well-known checklist systems for describing and measuring group process derives from the work of Bales (1950). During interactions, the acts initiated and received by group members are recorded according to a format that is pictured in Figure 7-4. Once the frequencies of acts are recorded they are converted to percentages. Not only does this allow for a description of events but the scores then can be used according to a scheme for interaction process analysis to infer levels of individual and group phenomenon (leadership, conflict, conformity, cohesiveness).

As mentioned in Chapter 4, when it comes to the use of the observation method a critical choice relates to the frequency with which to observe and record. In this regard, the nature of the study (its goals and the resources available) will dictate whether or not to use a sampling strategy. However, in most cases the amount of process data accumulates so rapidly that continuous records are rare. It also should be recalled that the process of observation and recording can be obtrusive. Thus,an investigator should consider the likely consequences of passive, participative, or hidden observation plans.

Group process data can be obtained by using techniques other than direct observation. Usually this involves getting information from the group participants themselves. In this regard, most of the methods described in the chapter on qualitative methods in this text could be

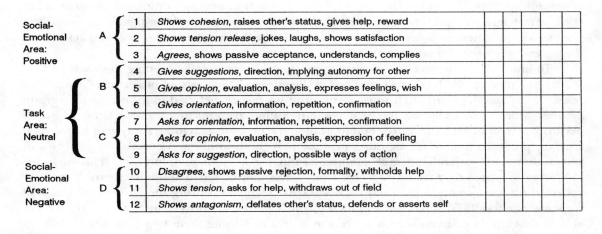

Social-Emotional Area: Positive	A	1	*Shows cohesion*, raises other's status, gives help, reward				
		2	*Shows tension release*, jokes, laughs, shows satisfaction				
		3	*Agrees*, shows passive acceptance, understands, complies				
Task Area: Neutral	B	4	*Gives suggestions*, direction, implying autonomy for other				
		5	*Gives opinion*, evaluation, analysis, expresses feelings, wish				
		6	*Gives orientation*, information, repetition, confirmation				
	C	7	*Asks for orientation*, information, repetition, confirmation				
		8	*Asks for opinion*, evaluation, analysis, expression of feeling				
		9	*Asks for suggestion*, direction, possible ways of action				
Social-Emotional Area: Negative	D	10	*Disagrees*, shows passive rejection, formality, withholds help				
		11	*Shows tension*, asks for help, withdraws out of field				
		12	*Shows antagonism*, deflates other's status, defends or asserts self				

a. problems of communication (6, 7)   A. Positive reactions
b. problems of evaluation (5, 8)   B. Attempted answers
c. problems of control (4, 9)   C. Questions
d. problems of decision (3, 10)   D. Negative reactions
e. problems of tension reduction (2, 11)
f. problems of reintegration (1, 12)

FIGURE 7-4 A System for Measuring Group Process
Source: Robert F. Bales, (1950). *Interaction process analysis.* Reading, MA: Addison-Wesley.

considered as potentially useful (e.g., individual and group interviews, diaries). Similarly, process information often can be accessed through the use of retrospective questionnaires. Thus, group members can be asked to respond to questions as to what happened in group sessions. Such questionnaires may be completed immediately after group sessions or after some time lapse. Further, group members can be forewarned that they will be filling out such an instrument before they meet as a group, or afterwards. Each of these options has advantages and disadvantages as they imply the potential for bias and memory lapses and, thus, relate to the quality of information you, the investigator, will receive (see Lord, Binning, Rush, & Thomas, 1978).

Field or Contrived Setting

The setting or context will clearly have an effect as to what kind of group process can be obtained and what methods are appropriate. A contrived setting is one created by the manager or investigator for specific purposes (in this case to get at group process). A contrived setting may be set up in a behavioral sciences labororatory. However, training and development contexts, assessment center contexts, or, specially called committee meetings all provide an opportunity to study group process. In general, contrived settings will present greater opportunities for direct and systematic observation. In field (organizational) contexts we are more likely to have to rely on alternative techniques (e.g., questionnaires).

In the assessment of the effectiveness of group process, the investigator would attempt to use any of the techniques reviewed in order to index the extent to which group member and leader actions and behaviors are, indeed, appropriate for the group, its members' attributes (knowledge, abilities, needs, etc.), the task at hand, and the resources available. Because there will be no single system for selecting the particular behaviors that are likely to promote or inhibit group member skills, effort levels or performance strategies, etc., the manager or investigator needs to use professional judgment in order to select or to develop the behavior recording system that will have the necessary content (or construct) validity.

To illustrate an approach to measuring group processes in a field setting the study by Katz (1982) might be recalled. He was interested in the effects of longevity on project performance of research and development (RD) work groups. But his theory included some attention to group process. More specifically, he felt that communication patterns would be related to group performance. In order to measure communication the professionals in his study kept a record on specially prepared lists, of all the other professionals (both within and outside the group) with whom they had work-related oral communication for a given sampling day. This included indicating to whom they talked and how many times they talked. These sociometric data were collected on a randomly chosen day each week for 15 weeks. During the 15 weeks the overall response rate was 93%, which was very high for such a labor intensive activity. Out of this he was able to develop six communication process measures and relate them to group productivity. In contrast, Gladstein (1984) used a combination of naturalistic observation, work flow analysis, and interviews to study group process in her study of 100 sales teams. In this way she was able to conclude not only what happened in each team but how they managed their relationships with other teams (boundary management). In her study she found that intra-group process rather than boundary management dynamics were significantly related to a subjectively rated team effectivess measure. Incidentally, team leadership (assessed by a questionnaire) also was found to be a strong predictor of effectiveness.

Group Outcome Factors

When defining group effectiveness, we usually are thinking in terms of how well the group has been able to accomplish certain group outcomes. This commonsense notion will be retained in this chapter. But we would like to expand the list of outcome factors to include some that are less obvious. The following have been culled from theoretical and empirical studies in the area.

1. *Objective group performance.* In some instances a case can be made that an appropriate measure of *group effectiveness* can be derived from counting what the group has produced or accomplished. In the United States, the effectiveness of most sports teams is defined in terms of the number of games won, points earned, etc. Similarly, in military settings, objective performance indicators may be available for use. For example, Tziner and Eden (1985) looked at the effects of crew composition on tank crew performance. In their study, tank crew performance was measured in terms of accuracy of gun fire, time lapse between target sighting and firing, and number of equipment failures attributed to poor maintenance. Finally, studying 100 different sales teams, Gladstein (1984) used actual sales revenue as an effectiveness measure.

   Objective performance data may be collected explicitly for the purpose of a study or may be taken from records already being kept by the group or the organization of which the group is a part. In the Tziner and Eden tank study, the latter strategy was used. Similarly, effectiveness indicators built on operational measures may make use of historical or archival records or contemporaneous observations. Gladstein made use of both current and archival data in her study.

   As in the case of individuals (Chapter 6), objective group performance may be couched in terms of absolute measures (e.g., "number of targets destroyed"), relative scores ("team performance is ranked third out of eight teams"), or with reference to standards.

In Gladstein's research, one effectiveness measure was the dollar amount of commissions that was earned by each sales team, where commissions were based on the revenue the team brought in above a specified objective (standard) determined at the start of each year (Gladstein, 1984).

2. *Subjective group performance.* In defining and measuring group performance it is not uncommon to obtain and use *subjective assessments.* That is to say, individuals with the opportunity to observe group outputs are asked to share or record their impressions. At times these individuals are managers or leaders. They may be the group members themselves. Or they may be experts or staff convened for the purpose of effectiveness measurement. In their tank crew study, Tziner and Eden (1985) asked military unit commanders to provide subjective performance rankings of crews. Gladstein (1984) asked sales team members to rate their own performance. She and her colleagues also made their own ratings based on interviews and extensive observations. Katz (1982), in his study of research and development project teams, interviewed each department manager and laboratory director to obtain their subjective assessment of the overall technical performance of all projects with which they were familar. Finally, Pritchard, Jones, Roth, Stuebing, and Ekeberg (1988) report a very elaborate group performance measurement system based upon the subjective assessment of the output of military maintenance and repair teams. In their system a score of zero would mean that personnel were just meeting expectations; their productivity was neither particularly good nor bad. The more positive the score, the more the teams were exceeding these expectations.

3. *Efficiency.* There are cases where group effectiveness has been conceptualized in terms of efficiency. While productivity is thought of as an index of what has been accomplished, *efficiency* refers to accomplishments relative to the resources utilized. Thus, efficiency is an output to input ratio (Pritchard et al., 1988). As in the case of productivity, efficiency indicators of effectiveness may be built around subjective or objective measurements. Thus, Katz (1982) used a seven-point rating scale to get at lab managers' impressions of a team's cost/performance ratios. In contrast, in a laboratory experiment examining the effects of task properties and interdependence, Shiflett (1972) was able to compute an efficiency score for each of the groups studied based on the number of units produced per unit of time.

4. *Quality.* Several authors (e.g., Maier & Solem, 1962; Vroom & Yetton, 1973) have argued that many group decisions and tasks require solutions that have a high quality component. Thus, it is not sufficient to produce something that is good enough to get the job done. The idea, product, or service must meet certain additional criteria—they must possess quality. While it is possible to index quality with reference to objective standards, on many occasions a quality determination must involve subjective assessments. These, in turn, may be obtained through ratings. Alternatively, inferences of quality can be made from the way group members behave relative to the group's decision or product. Thus, the speed and enthusiasm with which group decisions are implemented could serve to reflect the quality of group decisions (see White, Dittrich & Lang, 1980).

5. *Group emotional tone.* Most theories of group functioning imply that an effective group is one that meets or satisfies group member needs (Hackman, 1976, 1986; Shaw, 1981). That is to say, a reasonable indicator of an effective group can be found in the *emotional tone* of intragroup relations. More operationally, assessments of this tone can be made with reference to the group or to its members.

Indices of emotional tone focused at the group level can be obtained using any number of techniques. For example, Gersick (1988) observed and recorded meetings of groups over numerous sessions. She then had transcripts made that allowed her to create a group level indicator of energy spent on the task. Wicker, Kirmeyer, Hanson, and Alexander (1976) analyzed recordings of the interplay among members of their four-person laboratory groups in order to develop an index of comfort level. In a study of church groups, Wicker and Kauma (1974) recorded church service attendance levels over time to infer levels of satisfaction. As a final example, Blumberg (1980) measured satisfaction in work groups that had gone to a new style of worker development (job rotation) in a coal mining company. He created an index of job-switching behavior based on company records. He determined that this switching index did reflect anxiety and satisfaction levels in the work groups made up of people with particular job classifications.

Frequently, however, investigators attempt to get at estimates of emotional tone by interviewing or otherwise obtaining subjective assessments from individuals who belong to the groups under study. Group scores are thus created by aggregating or averaging individual scores. An illustration of this can be found in the field study reported by Wall, Kemp, Jackson, and Clegg (1986). They investigated the long-term effects of a new form of work group management in a candy manufacturing plant. Three waves of measurement were taken using questionnaires to get at worker self-reports of satisfaction and general mental health. In this study, the authors found that giving work groups greater autonomy with regard to job-related decisions had a positive impact on work-related satisfaction. However, there was no reliable effect on mental health. Work groups under all conditions reported similar and typical (for the working population) levels of stress and well being. Incidentally, there also was no real change in group productivity (e.g., indexed by hours worked per weight of output and deviation from targets). Similarly, in the Blumberg (1980) study, the answers to questionnaires completed by individuals provided the data for scales of satisfaction and job-related anxiety.

6. *Group member commitment.* In decision-making settings it is not only important to know that the quality of the solutions generated is good, it is also important to determine if the solutions will be adopted or implemented. To put it another way, an important outcome variable is group member committment. To illustrate, White, Dittrich, and Lang (1980) were very interested in the impact produced by three different types of group meeting procedures. In their study with a sample of nursing supervisors, they found that a structured method of conducting a meeting to deal with work-related problems produced a significantly greater rate of implementing group-derived solutions. This was true for both simple and complex problems. In contrast, unstructured discussions had a lot less impact in solution implementation back on the job. The authors speculate that the structured approach allowed for a more balanced participation on the part of group members. This involvement, in turn, was felt to increase commitment to seeing the solutions actually used on the job.

Context for Group Effectiveness Measurement

In the theory and practice of organizational sciences there are a wide variety of contexts wherein the manager or investigator would be interested in measuring effectiveness at the group level. At the outset of this chapter, we alluded to a few of these. At this point, however, it might be useful to identify a few situations where it would seem particularly appropriate to do so.

Incentive Plans. Lawler (1986) stresses how organizational reward programs can have a powerful impact on behavior in organizations. Under certain conditions of task interdependencies and management goals, he highlights the power of group bonus plans. Specifically, if cooperation in the workplace is felt to be very important, group bonus plans may be appropriate. In order to create such plans, defining and measuring effectiveness at the group level would be required.

As mentioned, Markham (1988) reports a study where the effects of a pay-for-performance plan could not be detected looking at the behavior of individual employees. However, because of his understanding of group norms and the way high levels of group cohesiveness can restrict the amount of variability in behavior, he looked at the same data, but aggregated at the level of groups. As predicted, he did find that the incentive plan had an impact but only as moderated by the attitudes and expectations of the first level supervisor. The supervisors' understanding and administration of the plan was crucial. Thus, the effect could only be detected at the group level.

Management Development. Every year, managerial training and development programs are implemented in most private and public organizations. A wide range of goals are held out for such efforts. For example, Burke and Day (1986) list self-awareness, problem solving, decision making, and general management as prevalent. However, it also is common to expect certain types of training and development to impact on leadership and the management of work groups. For example, Smith (1976) reports on a training program using behavioral modeling where the focus was on work group morale. Similarly, Woodman and Sherwood (1980) summarize several studies where training was aimed at producing managers who are effective in building teams. Hand and Slocum (1972) describe a human relations training program aimed at first-level supervisors where the improvement of group leadership was a goal. In many cases the manager or investigator not only is interested in the design, development, and delivery of a program, but in its impact as well. This immediately creates the need for group level measures of effectiveness.

Evaluating Changes in Policies and Practices. The management of organizations is regularly involved with developing and implementing new programs, policies, practices, or procedures. Many of these are aimed at improving work group functioning. When there is a need or desire to assess the impact of such programs, it is appropriate to use group level indicators of effectiveness. As mentioned earlier, Pritchard et al. (1988), assessed the impact of a new way of gathering and sharing information with work groups by using group performance criteria. Basadur, Graen, and Scandura (1986) evaluated a program designed to improve the creativity of teams of manufacturing engineers. Supervisors' ratings of group processes confirmed the success of the program under certain conditions (where the program involved intact work groups).

In general, whenever a model, a theory, or the assumptions underlying a change in organizational policies or practices imply an impact on group process or group outcomes, we would expect one or more approaches to determine and measure group effectiveness outlined above to be useful.

SPECIAL CONSIDERATIONS WHEN DEFINING AND MEASURING EFFECTIVENESS AT THE GROUP LEVEL

In doing research on groups or where group data are to be analyzed it is important to keep in mind that the unit of analysis is the group. Thus, the *sample size* is the number of groups involved in the investigation. This simple notion is sometimes forgotten, however, as the actual data often are generated by group members. A case in point is where satisfaction is a variable of interest. We usually obtain measures of satisfaction by asking individuals to complete a survey of some sort. If our study involves comparing the impact of two programs on satisfaction, it would be important first to compute team or group averages. To aggregate across all individuals exposed to one or the other program and use this as a basis for comparison would be inappropriate. This also becomes relevant when selecting the correct degrees of freedom for any statistical test of the differences between conditions. The use of the total numbers of individuals involved would be incorrect. In fact, this practice would lead to an error of inference (i.e., a Type I error).

It is not uncommon for the manager or researcher to think in terms of cause and effect. Thus, our study might examine the impact of group communication patterns (a cause) on group member satisfaction (the effect). However, the nature of group dynamics is such that feedback loops are quite numerous and tend to operate quickly (Hackman, 1976). Consequently, what is an effect might indeed become the cause. In the example offered here, this would mean that the levels of satisfaction felt by group members (initially the result of communication patterns) would, in turn, quickly influence the nature and amount of communication. Relationships in which variables may be both cause and effect are often referred to as instances of *reciprocal causation.*

These dynamics imply that it might be best to study group phenomona in contrived settings where we can take fine-grained measurements. That is to say, the investigator would be able to capture the sequences of the cause-and-effect forces involved. In any context, these reciprocal dynamics would seem to require some type of longitudinal research design (Gersick, 1988).

To this point in the chapter we have examined the nature of effectiveness at the group level of analysis. The brief introduction to the nature of groups, group dynamics, and group functioning has led to the conclusion that anyone interested in group effectiveness can attend to person, process, or product variables. It also may be clear by this point that many investigators find it beneficial to consider or take measures from all three perspectives in order to truly understand what is going on (e.g., Katz, 1982; Gladstein, 1984). If there is a message here it is that there is no one best approach in how to establish effectiveness at the group level.

DEFINING AND MEASURING ORGANIZATIONAL EFFECTIVENESS

As is the case in groups, organizations are complex by nature. Thus, it is not surprising that there exists a number of perspectives with which to approach the definition and measurement of effectiveness. After presenting a brief description regarding the nature of organizations, we will examine effectiveness using analogs to the person, process, and products framework. Once again you will discover that there is no single best way to think of effectiveness. Appropriate use of concepts and measures will depend upon informed judgment.

THE NATURE OF ORGANIZATIONS

Organizations can be thought of as "rational vehicles for accomplishing goals and objectives" (Scott, Mitchell, & Birnbaum, 1981, p. 25). By this, Scott et al. mean that they are created or designed by people in order to get something done— a product made or service delivered. Porter, Lawler, and Hackman (1975) elaborate by stating that organizations are entities made up of individuals and groups who are brought together in order to accomplish some goals and objectives by means of differentiated functions that are intended to be rationally coordinated and directed. They also point out that we also think of organizations as operating through time on a continuous basis.

Notice that we are talking about formal and complex organizations. While the concepts that will be emphasized could be used to characterize the corner drugstore or market, they would have to be adjusted considerably. In this regard, very small businesses (in terms of number of workers) might be better thought of in terms of the group concepts presented above.

The Structure of Organizations

Organizations often are characterized in terms of their structure. Traditionally this has meant that writers have focused on the formal configuration of roles, rules, and procedures that already exist. Practically, the emphasis has been on lines of authority regarding the integration of work tasks under a common manager (who reports to whom), and the amount of discretion individuals have as they go about doing their jobs (Dow, 1988). Thus, organizational structure is commonly equated to what is portrayed in a table of organization.

A little more operationally, structure is often described in terms of the following concepts (James & Jones, 1976):

1. *Interdependence.* The way the work flows from one department or unit to another.
2. *Centralization of decision making.* The locus or location of where important decisions are made.
3. *Specialization.* The division of labor that is employed as it relates to how unique or shared are the job duties.
4. *Standardization.* The extent to which the tasks to be done are specified in detail.
5. *Formalization.* How explicit or codified procedures are.
6. *Configuration.* The shape of the organization as it is determined by the nature of differentiation (specialization) that exists, the number of people working in the organization, the number of people typically reporting to a manager, and the number of levels of authority that are operative.

Thus, to characterize an organization in terms of its structure, an investigator would attempt to create, develop, or adopt measures of each of these factors.

Recently, however, the concept of structure has been augmented to refer to the particular patterns of activities and behavior that take place in the organization (Ranson, Hinings, & Greenwood, 1980). Writers have argued that the formal or prescribed frameworks described in any table of organization only are weakly related to what people actually do. In fact, most positions and job descriptions only are loosely defined. People are constantly interpreting and improvising as they fulfill their work roles. Individuals affect what other individuals do. And one group's functioning will have consequences for several others. It's not that the formal design of the organization isn't important; it's just that it should be viewed as merely setting the stage for what goes on there, perhaps even constraining actions somewhat. Thus, the operative structure is emergent and changing, rooted in the behaviors of individuals, and in the interpretations of events or the sense-making processes of the people involved (Dow, 1988; Ranson et al., 1980).

To get at this realized configuration (as contrasted to the prescribed configuration), writers with this view argue that an investigator cannot rely on formal organization charts or company documents. Instead, one would have to attend to and measure key behaviors and activities of individuals and groups involved.

Organizations as Open Systems

The characterization of organizations in terms of structure has a long tradition in the social sciences. However, several people have argued that it may not be the best way to understand the nature of organizations. In making their point, Porter et al. (1975) use the medical distinction between anatomy and physiology. In many respects, organizational structure can be thought of as anatomical in the sense that it provides the skeleton around which organizational life gets built. But a description of the human body would be incomplete and misleading by only referencing bone and muscle and organs. So, too, is a description of an organization. What is missing in both instances is some understanding of the physiology of the system.

An *open systems* view of organizations emphasizes the functioning (physiology) of organizations. It focuses on the patterns of activities of individuals and groups in an organization, not as an end in itself, but in order to uncover the extent to which (as in a healthy human body) these activities meet important needs or accomplish certain goals (Katz & Kahn, 1978).

In describing the open systems view, two other analogies to the human body can be made. First, much like a human, an organization must make sense of, interact with, and deal with its environment. Elements of the environment that must be considered include other organizations or entities with which there is some interdependence (suppliers of raw materials, customers, competitors), political and economic conditions, and emerging basic and applied technological developments (Katz & Kahn, 1978). The organization is an open system in that it must acquire things from the environment(raw materials, inventions, capital, etc.) and put things back into the environment (products, services).

This regular and necessary exchange with the environment is often overlooked by focusing on structure. In fact, the latter, with its emphasis on organizational features, often has been characterized as a closed system perspective. To put it another way, to understand why an organization functions the way it does and why it is more or less effective, open system theorists argue that you need to look beyond the organization's structure—to its environment—for explanations.

Finally, much like the human organism, a major goal for organizations is to grow, to remain healthy, and to live a long life. Thus, survival could be construed to be a very powerful goal or objective for most organizations. This observation will have greater significance when we examine what are considered to be the numerous hallmarks of organizational effectiveness. Clearly, an ultimate criterion of organizational effectiveness from the open systems view is longevity (Katz & Kahn, 1978).

What are key aspects of organizational functioning? While many have been identified, five seem to stand out. Katz and Kahn (1978) refer to these as subsystems of an organization. Five subsystems follow:

1. *Production subsystems monitor those activities most directly associated with producing the products, services, ideas, etc., that are bought or consumed by the public.* Organizations are often categorized by the nature of their production subsystems. Thus, terms like "hospitals," "schools," and "prisons" are used to describe particular types of organizations. All organizations have to attend to and develop ways to accomplish the production of objects or services. It's no coincidence, then, that the production subsystem gets so much attention and absorbs so much in the way of resources in most organizations.

2. *Boundary spanning subsystems monitor input to the organization and ensure that what is produced gets distributed, marketed, or sold.* Input can be thought of as the raw materials needed for producing products or services. But it goes beyond this. Boundary spanning activities

also are needed to obtain the necessary capital, energy, and people to make this happen. Sales, purchasing, and personnel departments are examples of units that might be especially involved in boundary spanning.

3. *Adaptive subsystems monitor or sense the nature of the environment in which the organization operates.* In general, organization decision makers need to be aware of what is going on and what changes are occurring. But the subsystem activities also imply a proactive function as well. Whenever possible, the organization (like any organism) seeks to influence what happens in its environment. Thus, while market research activities (reactive) are aimed at discovering what consumers need and want, marketing activities (proactive) focus on persuading consumers of the attractiveness of particular products or services.

4. *Maintenance subsystems monitor the internal functioning of the organization.* The goal here is to identify and smooth out problems as they occur. In general, maintenance subsystems deal with the people of the organization and ensure predictable and reliable behavior or performance. Thus, people in the human resources or education and training departments are most often involved.

5. *Managerial subsystems monitor activities associated with coordination, control, and leadership.* Some individuals in an organization must be concerned with general policy and strategy. Some members of the organization simultaneously need to have an internal and external perspective. Conflict among individuals and organizational units needs to be adjudicated in a timely and effective manner. Opportunities need to be recognized and seized upon. As implied, those with the title manager usually assume these coordination, control, and leadership responsibilities.

It is important to note that, in open systems theory, the subsystem functions described above need not be carried out by a single individual or unit. While this may sometimes be the case (e.g., the Personnel Department usually takes on maintenance subsystem goals), it is not at all unusual for many individuals or units to share a subsystem function. For example, in many organizations all employees are encouraged to look out for the best interests of the company as they interact with the public. That is to say, they are expected to perform (even in some modest way) adaptive subsystem functions.

On the other hand, systems theory is just as clear that if any of the subsystem functions are not attended to at some level, it is unlikely that the organization really will be effective, at least in the long run. This point will be developed further as we review alternative perspectives on organizational effectiveness.

Organizations as Social Systems

Our characterization of organizational structure as emergent and rooted in the interpretations of individuals reflects the fact that organizations are social systems. While behaviors and activities will be affected by the physical environment (buildings, offices, tools, and technologies), they are caused by attitudes, perceptions, beliefs, motivations, habits, and expectations of people as well. In a sense then, organizational realities are contrived in that they are made up by people as a result of, and in the furtherance of, relationships in the work setting (Katz & Kahn, 1978). This implies that organizations are dynamic entities, whose nature is subject to change with relatively short notice. It also suggests that the particular causes of organizational effectiveness, as flowing from structure and functioning, can change readily, as well.

What prevents organizations, as contrived social systems, from simply coming apart or disintegrating? We already have touched on some of the factors. Clearly, the product or service to be produced and the division of labor that gets established create forces fostering integration. These factors produce regularities in behavior and predictability. Similarly, the members of the managerial subsystem exist largely to develop and enforce rules for organizational behavior. Thus, information and control systems (Lawler & Rhode, 1976), coupled with the skillful application of incentives and rewards, constitute levers with which managers move diverse and balky groups of individuals in some desired direction. But it also turns out that the social forces themselves constitute the strongest "glue" in organizational life.

Katz and Kahn point out that roles, norms, and values reflect extremely important social dynamics in organizations and probably contribute greatly to system integration. *Roles* can be thought of as standardized patterns of behavior associated with a position, title, or office in an organization. They are expectations that we have for others with whom we interact and work with on a regular basis. While role definitions and expectations can be given to people, there is evidence that they really evolve out of personal interactions and exchanges over time. In most contexts they become established as a result of complex and often implicit negotiation processes between and among individuals (Graen, 1976). However, once they are established, roles constitute a basis for regularity and predictability in organizational life.

As discussed in this chapter in the section on the nature of groups, norms also are the basis for powerful social forces. While roles result in expectations for people in particular job positions, *norms* are more generalized expectations for all members in a social context (group or organization). Pivotal norms, especially, are communicated quickly to newcomers and are reinforced regularly by powerful individuals (Schein, 1968). Conformity to norms results in consistencies in not only what gets done but in the way work gets approached and carried out.

Systems values too add to these processes. As generalized, ideological, or justifications for goals, objectives, or behaviors, *values* promote a sense of community and purpose. Values also convey aspirations for outcomes and for goals. The latter can constitute a rallying point, a focus with which to align a heterogeneous work force (Ashforth, 1985; Katz & Kahn 1978).

The nature of organizational life and the possibility for effectiveness are strongly affected by the existence, nature and dynamic of roles, norms, and values. As you will see shortly, these constructs are closely tied to conceptual and operational definitions of effectiveness.

DEFINING ORGANIZATIONAL EFFECTIVENESS

"Effective organizations . . . are like elephants in the sense that they are identifiable when encountered, but very difficult to describe" (Spray, 1976, preface). By this we don't mean that we lack conceptual or theoretical views on the topic. In fact, as you will see, quite a variety of positions have been taken by writers in the field. At the current time, however, we do not have a consensus as to which model to adopt. This state of affairs is likely to continue for as new ideas have evolved, they have failed to displace older approaches (Spray, 1976). Even more problematic is that, while alternative positions can coexist in intellectual discourse, they frequently are incompatible in some very fundamental ways (Dubin, 1976). This means that, from a practical point of view, in doing research on organizational effectiveness, we often have to buy into and choose to use a framework that makes the most sense to the investigator (and the sponsor). The fact remains, however, people in our society (managers in particular) are not waiting around for theoretical clarification. They form and make use of assessments of organizational effectiveness all the time. They appear to make use of whatever indicators are at their disposal (Cameron, 1986).

A few years ago Steers (1975) reviewed 17 studies that had looked at or measured organizational effectiveness. He paid particular attention to the criteria used. What he discovered was that there was very little overlap among studies with regard to what the authors had chosen to measure. Figure 7-5 summarizes the frequency of use of the 14 different constructs that were used. He also points out that, without exception, the authors of the studies stated a priori what was good, desirable, or required for effectiveness. Thus, it is an area of research where the theoretical orientation or the personal values of the investigator play a key role.

More recently, Goodman, Atkin, and Schoorman (1983) highlighted several unfortunate trends in the area. Specifically, all too often researchers tend to rely on single indicators of effectiveness and ignore the relationships among multiple measures. When they do use appropriate measures they do not address the time frame implied by the criterion. The fact is, some manifestations of effectiveness (e.g., changes in market share) take longer to unfold than others (changes in worker attitudes). They also argue that there is an unfortunate tendency to apply particular criterion concepts or to use effectiveness indicators across dissimilar organizations without regard for their appropriateness.

In the section below, general approaches to the definition and measurement of organizational effectiveness are described. The clustering of alternatives reflects the way we see the development of current practices. There is no intent to imply that this is a typology or a taxonomy. Although there have been attempts to take a taxonomic approach, given the absence of a unified model of organizational functioning, this seems premature (for an example of such an attempt, see Cameron, 1978).

GOAL ATTAINMENT PERSPECTIVE

In light of the fact that, for many writers, organizations exist in order to accomplish some objective or achieve some goal, it seems reasonable that the definition and measurement of

Concept	Frequency of Use (Out of 17)
Adaptability/Flexibility	10
Productivity	6
Satisfaction of Employee	5
Profitability	3
Resource Acquisition	3
Absence of Strain	2
Control Over the Environment	2
Development of Employees	2
Efficiency	2
Employee retention	2
Growth	2
Integration	2
Open Communications	2
Survival	2
All Others	1

FIGURE 7-5 Alternatives in the Definition of Organizational Effectiveness
Source: Adapted with permission from Steers, R. M. (1975). Problems in the measurement of organizational effectiveness. *Administrative Science Quarterly, 20,* 546–558.

effectiveness should center on goal attainment (Georgiou, 1973; Thompson, 1967; Perrow, 1961). Most authors using this approach recognize that a goal perspective requires that attention needs to be given to resolving just what goals (e.g., publicly stated or operative goals) or whose goals (e.g., company owners or top management) are to be pursued before efforts at measurement can be undertaken.

The last point notwithstanding, many writers would grant that organizations need to produce a product or service and make a profit. The following are some specific indicators commonly used by managers and the general public that reflect this orientation.

Profit and Profit-Related Indices

Profit is the amount of revenue from sales left after all costs and obligations are met. Percent return on investment, percent return on assets, and measured operating income are *profit-related indices*. Price and Mueller (1986) refer to these indices as *financial viabilities* and argue that they are quite compatible with goal approaches to effectiveness. Figure 7-6 presents a variety of financial indicators that are commonly used to draw inferences regarding effectiveness by the financial community. As you can see, profit margin is one such indicator.

Productivity

Productivity usually is defined as the quantity or volume of the major product or service that the organization provides. We already have discussed this concept and its measurement at both the group and individual levels. Usually archival records are used to develop appropriate scores. Sometimes this is expressed as a rate (productivity per worker or per unit of time). Price and Mueller (1986) recommend an index of cost per unit of output. Figure 7-7 shows data on the productivity of an educational unit of a large organization.

Quality

Quality usually refers to the attributes of the primary product or service provided by the organization. It would have to be operationalized carefully in light of the specific product or service. In recent years it is not unusual in the restaurant and hospitality industries to rely on surveys of customers or clients to get data on perceptions of quality. In the specialty retail business and in banking trained observers may "shop" company and competitor stores and take notes to index quality of service delivery.

Growth

Growth refers to an index of such variables as plant capacity, assets, sales, profits, market share, or number of new products introduced. While it could be argued that growth is not always desirable, it is often viewed as a hallmark of effectiveness.

Efficiency

In most cases we think of *efficiency* in terms of a ratio that reflects a comparison of some aspect of performance relative to the costs incurred for that performance. Indices of efficiency can be derived from archival records. Damanpour and Evan (1984) created three efficiency measures in their study of libraries (e.g., circulation/size of holdings). Glisson and Martin (1980) calculated an efficiency measure for mental health professionals as "the number of clients served per week per $10,000 budget" (p.28). Hoy and Hellriegel (1982) distinguished between internal and external

Company/fiscal year end	Stock price 5-year high-low	32-month high-low	recent	Stock Perf. price change	relative to market	P/E 5-year high-low	P/E latest 12 months	P/E 1988 est	price/ sales	net profit margin	latest 12 months EPS	1987 EPS	1988 estimated EPS	% change '88 vs '87 EPS	indicated rate	yield	payout ratio	5-year growth rate
Abbott Laboratories/Dec	67- 18	67- 40	50 1/4	-21%	88%	28- 11	18.1	15.5	2.60	14.4%	$2.78	$2.78	$3.24	17%	$1.20	2.4%	36%	21%
Aetna Life & Cos/Dec	68- 27	68- 44	45 3/8	-32	76	37- 6	6.0	6.2	0.23	3.9	7.51	7.48	7.29	-3	2.76	6.1	37	0
Affiliated Pubs/Dec	84- 7	84- 41	64	35	152	20- 10	12.3	37.6	4.51	37.4	5.22	5.22	1.70	-67	0.40	0.6	8	20
HP Akmanson/Dec	29- 5	26- 13	15 1/2	-40	67	22- 4	7.6	7.2	0.58	7.6	2.03	2.03	2.15	6	0.88	5.7	43	27
Air Prods & Chems/Sep	54- 18	54- 29	47 3/4	2	114	20- 10	14.8	13.2	1.19	8.2	3.22	2.83	3.61	28	1.00	2.1	31	21
Alberson's/Jan	34- 11	34- 20	28 3/4	9	122	20- 10	15.3	13.8	0.33	2.1	1.88	1.88	2.08	11	0.56	1.9	30	12
Aice Health Services/Sep	26- 11*	21- 11*	18	-11	100	21- 7	12.1	11.8	0.12	1.0	1.49	1.39	1.53	10	0.12	0.7	8	0
Alce Standard/Sep	30- 14	30- 15	25 3/4	0	113	17- 8	13.3	12.3	0.32	2.4	1.94	1.81	2.10	16	0.68	2.6	35	4
Alexander & Alexander/Dec	42- 16	32- 16	21 7/8	-28	80	14- 9	14.3	12.8	0.82	5.8	1.53	1.53	1.71	12	1.00	4.6	65	0
Alexander & Baldwin/Dec	64- 11	64- 32	50 1/2	-3	115	15- 7	11.0	10.7	2.01	19.1	4.59	4.59	4.70	2	1.60	3.2	35	21
Allegheny Power/Dec	54- 22	45- 31	38 1/4	-12	99	13- 6	9.4	9.7	0.99	10.4	4.05	4.05	3.94	-3	3.00	7.8	74	4
Allegis/Dec	106- 28	106- 56	83 7/8	42	159	14- 4	13.9	30.7	0.57	4.0	6.02	6.02	2.73	-55	none	NA	NA	NA
Allied-Signal	49- 25	49- 26	32 1/2	-31	77	9- 6	9.2	10.9	0.44	5.4	3.55	3.55	2.89	-16	1.80	5.5	51	4
Allte/Dec	34- 13	34- 23	31	13	126	18- 7	10.1	10.8	1.39	14.2	3.07	3.07	2.88	-6	1.52	4.9	50	5
Altus Bank FSB/Dec	22- 5*	15- 5	6 1/2	-57	48	NM- 3	NM	NM	0.11	0.0	0.02	0.02	-0.14	NM	none	NA	NA	NA
Alcoa/Dec	65- 30	65- 34	46 3/4	5	118	19- 7	18.6	9.0	0.53	2.9	2.52	2.52	5.18	106	1.20	2.6	48	0
AMAX/Dec	33- 11	29- 13	18 7/8	4	117	22- 8	22.2	9.3	0.54	2.3	0.85	0.85	2.02	138	none	NA	NA	NA
Amdahl/Dec	50- 10	50- 19	34 3/4	-12	98	13- 7	12.7	10.3	1.21	9.4	2.74	2.74	3.36	23	0.20	0.6	7	7
Amerada Hess/Dec	42- 17	42- 22	30	-7	104	11- 6	11.0	9.4	0.52	4.9	2.73	2.73	3.19	17	0.60	2.0	22	0
American Breads/Dec	60- 23	60- 37	46 1/2	-8	103	17- 7	10.0	9.0	0.84	8.7	4.60	4.60	5.14	12	2.20	4.8	48	1
American Capital/Dec	10- 2*	6- 2	4 1/4	-11	100	NM- 5	NM	NM	0.14	0.0	-0.19	-0.19	NA	NA	none	NA	NA	NA
American Continental/Dec	13- 3	13- 5	6 3/8	-44	63	13- 3	7.3	NA	0.15	3.0	0.88	0.88	NA	NA	none	NA	NA	NA
American Cyanamid/Dec	57- 20	57- 29	51 3/8	5	118	26- 10	17.0	15.8	1.11	6.6	3.02	3.02	3.26	8	1.05	2.0	35	5
American Electric/Dec	32- 15	30- 23	28 3/4	-3	109	13- 5	11.1	9.8	1.16	10.5	2.60	2.60	2.93	13	2.26	7.9	87	0
American Express/Dec	41- 13	40- 21	26 1/2	-31	77	34- 10	22.1	9.6	0.63	3.0	1.20	1.20	2.76	130	0.76	2.9	63	6
American Family/Dec	19- 3	19- 10	15 3/4	14	127	21- 7	12.4	11.9	0.68	5.4	1.27	1.27	1.32	4	0.24	1.5	19	12
American General/Dec	47- 19	44- 27	36 1/4	-14	96	13- 7	9.3	9.5	0.66	7.9	3.86	3.88	4.25	10	1.40	3.9	36	12
American Health Prod/Dec	97- 43	97- 62	82	-10	101	19- 11	14.3	18.1	2.37	16.8	5.73	5.73	6.28	10	3.60	4.4	63	8
American Bell Group/Dec	94- 26	84- 54	59	-26	83	26- 9	9.3	9.0	0.86	9.4	6.34	6.34	6.53	3	0.30	0.5	5	9
American Medical/Aug	37- 11	21- 11	15	-21	89	13- 9	12.5	11.5	0.45	3.8	1.20	1.26	1.31	4	0.72	4.8	60	13

FIGURE 7-6 Profit Related Measures of Organizational Effectiveness
Source: Fortune Magazine (April 25, 1988).

Division Served	Number of "Student Training Days" Delivered					
	Jan	Feb	Mar	April	May	Year to Date
A	666	837	1189	641	712	4045
B	7626	7114	9612	6887	6532	37771
C	69	62	104	85	85	405
D	0	133	122	d102	63	420
E	0	912	1511	2503	1555	6481
F	0	196	846	1398	1567	4007
Total	8361	9254	13384	11616	10514;	53129

FIGURE 7-7   Effectiveness Defined as Output: The Case of the Education Department

efficiency in small business operations. However, most writers appear to feel that efficiency is an insufficient (deficient) indicator of effectiveness (Katz & Kahn, 1978).

Most goal-oriented approaches using one or more of the indicators include attempts to identify and operationalize the goals of particular individuals or groups of individuals. Typically, the needs, desires, and aspirations of the most powerful people, the *dominant coalition* (see Thompson, 1967; Georgiou, 1973; Pfeffer, 1973), would have to be determined. Campbell (1976) also points out that organizations using a management by objectives (MBO) program would be in a particularly good position to make use of the goal approach. Thus, organizational effectiveness would be indexed or defined as the extent to which managers at various levels and across departments have, in fact, reached their stated objectives for a particular time period. Of course, the construct validity of such an index would depend heavily on the quality of the MBO program and process (see Chapter 6).

OPEN SYSTEMS PERSPECTIVE

Our brief discussion of organizations as open systems implied a view of effectiveness that is somewhat different from the goal-attainment paradigm. In many ways investigators and managers taking an open systems view are as interested in effectiveness in organizational processes and functioning as in accomplishing organization outcomes.

The processes of interest are those involved in the various subsystem activities and functions described earlier. That is to say, to the extent that an organization is designed, structured, and managed to fulfill these functions, the open system proponent would argue that it is an effective organization.

Some open system effectiveness indicators that have been identified in the literature include survival, conflict, acquisition of resources, flexibility/adaptation, innovation, and distinctive competence.

Survival

Strictly speaking, *Survival* could be viewed as an outcome variable. It also is the ultimate criterion of an open system. Reimann (1982) studied 20 organizations over nine years using a survival criterion. Interestingly, he found that growth, decline, and disappearance could be predicted years before the fact from data obtained from key managers in interviews.

Conflict

Conflict over goals, values, and resources among organizational units is usually dysfunctional. High levels of conflict would, therefore, imply ineffectiveness. Cameron (1986) measured conflict with a questionnaire administered to school personnel, whereas Webb (1974) used structured interviews.

Acquisition of Resources

Acquisition of resources (e.g., capital, energy) follows directly from open systems theory. Yuchtman and Seashore (1967) and Cameron (1986) used this as a criterion variable. Opinions of senior staff were used to create an index of effectiveness in the acquisition of resources in the Cameron (1986) study.

Flexibility/Adaptation

Flexibility/adaptation refers to the organization's capacity to change its operating procedures in light of environmental demands. Georgopolous and Tannenbaum (1957) and Webb (1974) looked at this variable. While questionnaires have been used, it is possible to use interviews or observations to get at the speed and nature of response to threats or opportunities (Pettigrew, 1979).

Innovation

Innovation is the extent to which changes are intentionally introduced into the organization (Price & Mueller, 1986). While it is somewhat related to adaptation, innovation implies a certain proactivity that may allow an organization to preempt threats or take advantage of opportunities. Some authors distinguish between administrative and technological innovation (Damanpour & Evan, 1984). All agree, however, that the notion implies the successful implementation of new ideas. Blau and McKinley (1979) used a number of awards to index innovation in architectural firms; Damanpour and Evan (1984) created a relative measure (percentage) for both administrative and technical innovations in a library.

Distinctive Competence

Distinctive competence refers to those things that an organization does well relative to its competitors (Selznick, 1957). This is not just what an organization can do, but what it does particularly well (Andrews, 1971). As an aspect of systems effectiveness, it can be thought of as an analog to establishing an ecological niche. Snow and Hribiniak (1980) measured distinctive competencies in terms of the perceptions of top managers with regard to various organization functions (e.g., research and development, production, marketing) in four industries and found them to be related to the overall strategies that these managers were following.

MULTIPLE CONSTITUENCY VIEW OF EFFECTIVENESS

Some years ago, Friedlander and Pickle (1968) conducted a study of organizational effectiveness where specific measures taken from, or thought to reflect the view of, stockholders, workers, managers, suppliers, and customers were found to be related only to one another in modest ways. They pointed out that, like beauty, perceptions of effectiveness may, indeed, reflect ones vantage point. More recently, this observation has been developed into a fairly cogent framework for conceptualizing effectiveness (Connolly, Conlon, & Deutsch, 1980; Zammuto, 1984).

Zammuto (1984) argues that we should think of organizations as entities that come into existence and are maintained in order to satisfy the needs and views of diverse groups of people. What happens in organizational life then, is the result of the intersection of the decisions, actions, and behaviors of the various constituencies involved. Whether or not an organization is effective will depend on who wants what and how important it is that a demand be satisfied.

The measurement of effectiveness in a multiple constituency framework requires that the investigator establish the stakeholders in an organization. These are the individuals and groups whose viability is affected by organizational actions or decisions. Establishing the stakeholders might be done through analysis or field interviews. Some typical stakeholders include the following:

1. The owners of the business (private company),
2. The stockholders/shareholders (public company),
3. The workers,
4. The managers,
5. The customers/clients,
6. The suppliers,
7. The people and officials in the community (especially for small communities), and
8. The appropriate officials with the national government (in the case of large corporations)

The specific measures used to index the actual or likely satisfaction of these stakeholders will depend on the investigators' needs and the availability of relevant data. Either direct or indirect approaches might be used. For example, Friedlander and Pickle (1968) measured worker satisfaction using a questionnaire. They indexed supplier satisfaction in terms of volume of business generated by the company and the speed with which invoices were paid. On the other hand, shareholder satisfaction could be inferred from financial indicators, such as return on investment. Despite the likelihood that several and various operational indicators will be used in a study, it should be kept in mind that the central construct of interest is participant (stakeholder) satisfaction.

As complex as the measurement process might be, Zammuto (1984) points out that good data on various constituent needs satisfaction is not enough. It does not yet resolve the question of just whose needs and demands should be satisfied. In this regard, he identifies four alternatives.

1. *Relativism.* The investigator could identify and assess each constituency's preferences and satisfactions and merely make them available to the consumer of the research.
2. *Power.* It could be argued that claims to effectiveness should be related to the extent the needs and demands of the most powerful individuals and groups involved are being met.
3. *Social justice.* The position could be taken that the organization is effective to the degree that the needs and demands of the least advantaged constituents are being satisfied. This is sometimes called the *minimum regret principle* insofar as the organization minimizes those constituent's regrets over the consequences of participation with the organization.
4. *Evolution.* This implies that effectiveness is related to the extent to which diverse constituents are satisfied over the long run. Thus, the emphasis given to the various

stakeholders may shift depending on the organization's point in some evolutionary life cycle (birth, growth, maturity) or on the environmental pressures that it faces.

At the present time, there is no theoretical resolution as to which of these would be appropriate. However, Zammuto stresses that when it comes to this model of effectiveness, it is clear that the values of the investigator will have a strong impact as to which of the four approaches will be followed (see also Keeley, 1978 for a treatment of the moral and ethical considerations implied by participant satisfaction models). Another implication of the multiple constituency perspective is that it is a dynamic construct. Temporal (long- versus short-term) considerations exist.

ORGANIZATIONAL DEVELOPMENT (OD) PERSPECTIVE

This view of effectiveness can be found in the writings of a number of individuals who utilize a variety of behavioral science techniques (e.g., team building) to bring about planned organizational change (Campbell, 1976). In many ways, these authors consider and attempt to implement change where the goal is to bring about what might be considered a healthy organization. Figure 7-8 offers some of the end states that define an organization.

In many ways, the OD perspective is a process view. For practitioners in the area, profit or productivity outcomes are less interesting than appropriate processes. Moreover, appropriate or desirable processes are felt to be those that promote the physical, psychological, and social welfare of the individuals (both managers and workers) employed by the organization. Thus, in addition to the hallmarks listed in Figure 7-8, OD specialists look for and promote instrumental satisfaction, self-esteem, self-expression, and personal growth. There is a clear value orientation implied here.

Another generalization about this perspective is that investigators frequently use data gathered from individuals in order to index or infer effectiveness. While interview and observation techniques are not uncommon, paper-and-pencil surveys (questionnaires) have been the preferred method of many (Lindell & Drexler, 1979).

A prototype for measurement of organizational effectiveness as promoted by this perspective can be found in the work of Likert (1967) and his associates while he was at the University of Michigan. He created a framework for effectiveness that has been operationalized in a questionnaire called the Survey of Organizations. When completed by respondents in an organization, it allows the investigator to classify the organization as approximating a Type I,II, III, or IV. At the risk of over simplifying, Type IV organizations are considered to be more effective because they are characterized by people functioning well in areas of critical individual and interpersonal processes. Some of the dimensions of the survey, and hence of the organization's effectiveness, include the following:

1. Leadership processes used (e.g., autocratic or participative),
2. Motivational processes operating (e.g., intrinsic versus extrinsic),
3. Character of communication processes (e.g., downward, lateral, upward),
4. Character of interaction-influence processes (e.g., mutual influence and teamwork),
5. Decision-making processes (e.g., where decisions are made in the organization), and
6. Character of control processes (e.g., who gets what information).

Another well-developed approach to the measure of relevant processes has been offered by Tannenbaum (1968). In this case the emphasis is on the assessment and measurement of power

**SYNTHESIZED LIST OF END STATES SPECIFIED
BY OD THAT DEFINE A HEALTHY SYSTEM[1]**

1. "The total organization, the significant subparts, and individuals manage their work against *goals* and *plans* for achievement of these goals."
2. "Form follows function (the problem, or task, or project determines how the human resources are organized)."
3. "Decisions are made by and near the sources of information regardless of where these sources are located on the organizational chart."
4. "The reward system is such that managers and supervisors are rewarded (and punished) comparably for:
   —short-term profit or production performance.
   —growth and development of their subordinates.
   —creating a viable working group."
5. "Communication laterally and vertically is *relatively* undistorted. People are generally open and confronting. They share all the relevant facts including feelings."
6. "There is a minimum amount of inappropriate win/lose activities between individuals and groups. Constant effort exist at all levels to treat conflict and conflict situations as *problems* subject to problem solving methods."
7. "There is high 'conflict' (clash of ideas) about tasks and projects, and relatively little energy spent in clashing over interpersonal difficulties because they have been generally worked through."
8. "The organization and its parts see themselves as interacting with each other *and* with a *larger* environment. The organization is an 'open system.'"
9. "There is a shared value, and management strategy to support it, of trying to help each person (or unit) in the organization maintain his (or its) integrity and uniqueness in an interdependent environment."
10. "The organization and its members operate in an 'action-research' way. General practice is to build in *feedback mechanisms* so that individuals and groups can learn from their own experience."

FIGURE 7-8   OD Perspective of Organizational Effectiveness
Source: Reprinted with permission from Beckhard, R. (1969). *Organization development: Strategies and models.* Reading, MA: Addison-Wesley.

stratification and centralization (Price & Mueller, 1986). Specifically, survey data are gathered to allow for the creation of what are called Control Graphs.

Control graphs describe the amount and distribution of perceived influence in an organization. An example of a control graph is presented in Figure 7-9. In creating a control graph, individuals are asked to respond to the question, "In general, how much say or influence do you think each of the following persons has on what goes on in your office?" The number and nature of the "persons" would depend on the organization being studied. However, these "persons" normally correspond to major levels in the company's hierarchy. Scores from respondents are then averaged and graphed. Markham, Bonjean, and Corder (1984) studied the reliability of control graphs using a law enforcement agency sample. While it was found to be satisfactory, they did find that there was great variability in the perceptions of influence exerted by some groups of persons. Tannenbaum (1968) suggests a modification of the question posed to get at influence in key domains (e.g., policy decisions, budget, personnel actions) to enhance reliability and validity.

HUMAN RESOURCES ACCOUNTING PERSPECTIVE

In the United States in the 1970's there was discussion and debate regarding what came to be called the quality of work life (Lawler, 1982). The term *quality of work life* (QWL) was applied to

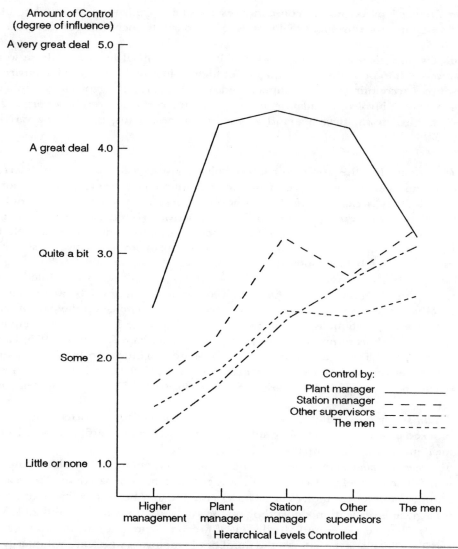

FIGURE 7-9   Describing Organizational Influence Using a Control Graph
Source: Tannenbaum, A. S. (1968). *Control in organizations*. New York: McGraw-Hill. Reprinted with permission.

working conditions and practices as they promoted (or frustrated) the creation of conditions in which democratic supervision is practiced, employees are involved in their work, and working conditions are safe (Lawler, 1982; Davis & Cherns, 1975). It also implied working conditions where individuals experience well being and personal satisfaction and growth. In many respects, the QWL approach is consistent with or similar to the OD model just described.

One distinguishing feature of the QWL approach, however, is that it did involve a concern for organizational effectiveness in terms of productivity and profitability. Thus, not only was the creation of a satisfied and committed work force a goal, but it was felt that such a state of affair also would have financial or economic consequences for the organization. A number of writers attempted to establish measurement techniques to demonstrate such linkages (Likert & Bowers, 1969).

Specifically, investigators attempted to establish the financial impact of those worker behaviors that were felt to occur as a consequence of high or low quality of work life environments. Human resources accounting then attempts to index and report an organization's human assets in economic terms. It involves calculating and indexing the costs incurred by an organization to recruit, select, hire, train, develop, and retain employees. Thus, several key variables are emphasized:

1. *Productivity.* For the workers or jobs involved, investigators attempt to determine the economic benefits to the company derived from poor, average, or superior performance. This is called *productivity.* The focus here is on estimating the dollar value associated with variability in worker productivity (Boudreau, 1983; Cascio, 1987; Schmidt, Hunter & Pearlman, 1982). In some cases, for some jobs this could be quite great. Macy and Mirvis (1976) indexed productivity levels relative to standards and estimated each below standard incident would cost the company $22,236.

2. *Absenteeism. Absenteeism* is nonattendance when an employee is scheduled to come to work (Price & Mueller, 1986). Often, it is common to distinguish between voluntary and involuntary absenteeism, where the former involves a choice on the part of an individual. More operationally, it usually is measured as time lost, and the frequency and number of short-term absences/calculated. (see Latham & Pursell, 1975; Hammer & Landau, 1981, for other alternatives). An absenteeism index created by Macy and Mirvis (1976) relating the number of absence days relative to the number of person-work days during one time period was costed out at $286,260 (at $55.36 per incident, at a 3.3% rate).

3. *Tardiness. Tardiness* reflects absenteeism for a period of time shorter than a day. When indexed as anything less than four hours, Macy and Mirvis (1976) computed a $4.86 per incident cost to the company.

4. *Turnover. Turnover* is the degree of individual movement into or outside of the organization (Price & Mueller, 1986). Most researchers examine separations. There are a large number of potential indices of turnover and one may be more suitable or appropriate for a given investigation, depending on the availability of data (Schmittlein & Morrison, 1983). However, Price and Mueller (1986) recommend quit rate and average length of service. *Quit rate* is the ratio of the number of employees who leave voluntarily during a given period to the average number of employees working for that same period. In contrast, the *average length of service* measure is reflected in the median length of service of all employees who leave voluntarily during a period. Estimating the economic consequences of turnover is quite complex. A large number of factors must be considered and many assumptions must be made. The following are some of these:

   a) Dollar value of the productivity of the individuals who leave,
   b) Salary costs of the people who leave,
   c) Cost of benefits of the people who leave,
   d) Recruiting costs,
   e) Salary costs of the replacements,
   f) Cost of benefits for replacements,

g) Costs associated with training replacements,

h) Dollar value of the lower levels of productivity of the replacements,

i) Speed with which replacements reach desired levels of productivity, and

j) Coordination costs associated with the need for experienced employees to adjust their work pace to that of replacements.

From this list it can be inferred that the economic costs of turnover will vary greatly depending on circumstances. Turnover of high performers who are hard to replace and train reflect a poor state of organizational effectiveness. Lawler and Rhode (1976) reported a situation in 1973 in which the costs associated with replacing a below-average performance sales associate was $31,600 while to replace an effective sales manager required $185,000. On the other hand, Dalton, Krackhardt, and Porter (1981) report that, under some circumstances, turnover of a certain rate (modest), and of the right sort (senior, low performing workers), is in the best economic interests of a company. In fact, they coined the term *functional turnover* to characterize this situation. As you can see, sophisticated human resource analyses are required in order to assess whether certain levels of turnover reflect high or low organizational effectiveness (see also Dalton, Todor, & Krackhardt, 1982).

5. *Accidents and work-related illnesses (both physical and emotional).* The quality of work life is thought to have an effect on the physical and mental well being of employees. The number, rate, and severity of accidents will have economic consequences for an organization in terms of insurance premiums, medical expenses, lost wages, temporary replacement costs, and even fines imposed by government agencies. At the time of this writing, a meat processing company had just received the largest fine ever levied ($4.6 million) by the Occupational Safety and Health Agency for repeated violations of safe working conditions.

6. *Grievances, strikes, and work stoppages.* These related events usually occur when individuals working under collective bargaining agreements feel that management practices or policies violate provisions of their agreement or that the workplace is unsafe. They can be variously indexed in terms of number, frequency, extensivity, severity, or duration. In any event, these manifestations of poor work life quality can be readily related to costs or expenses beyond what normally would be incurred in doing business. In their example, Macy and Mirvis (1976) calculated a per incident cost associated with grievances at $150.59. Factors that had to be considered included the time needed to resolve the grievance, the wages and salaries of those involved in processing the grievance (including human resource staff time or the hiring of a mediator), and the costs of settlement (e.g., past wages).

As noted, economic indices of those investigators emphasizing human resources accounting as described above often are considered in other approaches. For example, those concerned with organizational development usually will look at absenteeism, turnover, conflict (strikes and stoppages), etc., as evidence of poor or weak organizational processes and characteristic of an unhealthy organization. Similarly, the systems theorist could argue that these indicators are a symptom of the organization's ability to acquire and retain important (in this case human) resources. What distinguishes the human resources accounting perspective is its emphasis on translating things to what Nicholas (1982) refers to as hard criteria (i.e., dollars and cents).

CONTEXT FOR MEASURING ORGANIZATIONAL EFFECTIVENESS

There are a large number of situations where it would be desirable or necessary to define and measure effectiveness at the organizational level. While several already have been implied in this section, we will illustrate three additional applications: reward systems, planned organizational change, and theory building.

Reward Systems

Over the years, a norm has developed in the United States to compensate and reward top executives in a manner that bears some relationship to company performance (Lawler, 1981). The basic argument for this arrangement is that it offers incentive properties for chief executives; because they have something at stake, they work more diligently for company success (Ungson & Steers, 1984). For example, Pearce, Stevenson, and Perry (1985) measured the performance of executives of a public organization (the Social Security Administration) at the level of the district office with four indicators reflecting the speed and accuracy of providing money for claims to people making them. Using a sophisticated time series design they found no support for the impact of merit compensation on organizational performance.

More recently, however, a number of policymakers have recognized that the nature of organizational interdependencies makes it likely that organizational success requires the effort and cooperation of all employees, not just the top managers. Consequently, there is an interest in what have been called *gainsharing* plans (Bullock & Lawler, 1984). Under these arrangements (there are numerous types) organizational participants receive financial bonuses according to a formula that is driven by measures of organizational effectiveness. One of the oldest versions emphasized and rewarded employee efforts to make the company more efficient in the way business was done. The so-called Scanlon Plan involved a mechanism for indexing cost savings based on the adoption of suggestions generated by employees. The latter would get bonuses based on a percentage of such savings (White, 1979). Florkowski (1987) has reviewed a number of studies looking at the impact of profit-sharing plans and finds support for their use. However, in most instances, any program success is closely tied to the appropriateness of the specific effectiveness measures used. As White (1979) points out, measures that are contaminated and deficient (our terms) are quickly rejected by employees as the basis for incentives. They can reasonably ask, "Why put out effort where, because of the measures chosen, I can have little impact on the outcome?"

Planned Organizational Change

A second context in which it is common to use effectiveness indicators at the organizational level is where we are interested in assessing the impact of major planned organizational change. At times such measures are used by managers who have a genuine interest in learning about the consequences of their decisions so that they may be better prepared for the future. More often, the indicators are developed or selected by researchers who are motivated to learn more about change dynamics and perhaps develop a robust theory of the antecedents and mechanics of planned change (Beer, 1976; Katz & Kahn, 1978).

Lindell and Drexler (1979) highlight the fact that many investigators use the survey method to measure effectiveness and the impact of change because it fits into the OD model of effectiveness that underlies the change effort itself. And indeed, as pointed out above, many find the questionnaire a relatively direct way to get at levels of motivation and commitment. An example of this can be found in the work of Randolph (1982). In a study of planned change in a college student counseling center, he used a questionnaire to assess such indicators of effectiveness as levels of coordination, speed and accuracy of communications, and supervisory relations. He found reliable improvements in these areas as a result of a change program in an experimental center (when compared to a control center) using a time series design (see Chapter 11 for a description of time series designs).

Theory Building

To some extent, one could argue that any empirical study has the potential to contribute to the development or testing of a theory. However, in the present instance, we wish to emphasize the fact that a lot of interest in the measurement of effectiveness at the organizational level of analysis stems from the desire to explicitly contribute to theory building. Usually this means evaluating some aspect of a theory of organizations (see Scott et al., 1981). For example, Snow and Hribiniak (1980) used a measure of profitability, the ratio of total income to total assets, as a measure of organizational effectiveness in a study of corporate strategy. They found evidence that organizations whose top management adopted particular strategies (i.e., following a particular market-product orientation) outperformed the others, but only in highly competitive industries (e.g., semiconductors).

In all of these instances, the investigator will be interested in designing, adopting, or developing measures of effectiveness that are both valid and feasible. This chapter highlights several options.

SPECIAL CONSIDERATIONS IN DEFINING AND MEASURING ORGANIZATIONAL EFFECTIVENESS

As in the case of groups, using organization level measures requires sensitivity to special considerations.

Level of Analysis

Writers vary with regard to just what is the appropriate level of analysis when it comes to measuring organizational effectiveness (Cameron, 1978). Katz and Kahn (1978) argue that effectiveness must be viewed from the perspective of the supra system (larger society). Thus, agents or entities outside the organization should be the basis for effectiveness data. Others (e.g., Pennings & Goodman, 1977) prefer to look at the subunit (division or strategic business unit) as the appropriate level for analysis.

Problems of Aggregation

The above point notwithstanding, when studying organizational effectiveness, it is not unusual to obtain data from (or on) individuals, groups, departments, divisions, etc. How the data are combined can have an impact on the validity of the resulting index. The issues are sufficiently complex that the reader is encouraged to go to primary sources for guidance (e.g., Roberts, Hulin, & Rousseau, 1978; Dansereau & Markham, 1987).

Sample size

This is somewhat related to the issue of aggregation. The point here is that for theory building at the level of organizations, one needs to sample and study reasonable numbers of comparable entities. The difficulty associated with gaining access to reasonable numbers of organizations should not be underestimated.

Specific Versus Universal Criteria

We often characterize organizations in terms of their primary product or service (schools, hospitals, etc.). The fact is, these differing types of organizations will present differing challenges and opportunities for defining and measuring effectiveness. In some cases (e.g., manufacturing organizations), there is somewhat of a consensus regarding indicators of effectiveness. In other cases (e.g., schools), there is a greater need for the researcher to define and create measures of effectiveness (Cameron, 1978; Damanpour & Evan, 1984). In the latter case, this produces the unfortunate state of affairs wherein the results from different investigations may be hard to compare. It may be desirable, then, to attempt to use measures from prior investigations whenever possible.

Processes Versus Outcome Data

The various approaches to defining and measuring effectiveness differentially emphasize organizational processes or outcomes. The investigator must decide whether he or she is interested in the process of being effective or in the results of those processes.

Static Versus Change Data

As Cameron (1978) points out, most studies of organizational effectiveness involve static (one time) measurement efforts, although there are a few that examine effectiveness over time (Miles & Cameron, 1977 as cited in Cameron, 1978). One might form very different conclusions with one set of data versus another.

Subjective Versus Objective Measures

The various measurement options described above reflect a mixture of objective and subjective data. Each has strengths and weaknesses with regard to reliability and construct validity. An investigator has to determine the level of confidence to place in each. In particular, when both types of data are used, differing qualities may provide difficulties of inference (Cameron, 1978). Campbell (1977) takes the extreme position that, in the final analysis, effectiveness criteria always should reflect human judgments. But this still begs the question of who should provide such judgments (Cameron, 1978).

Global Versus Multiple or Composite Criteria

It is clearly recognized that organizational effectiveness is a complex and multifaceted construct. The investigator needs to resolve just what this implies for the project at hand. What seems likely, however, is that if multiple indicators are used, obtained scores are likely to covary in complex and often disconcerting ways. For example, Yuchtman and Seashore (1967) examined 76 organizational performance indicators for a sample of companies over an 11-year period. They found ten themes or dimensions embedded in the list. Seashore, Indik, and Georgopoulos (1960) report a correlation of -.56 between measured productivity and rated effectiveness for 32 departments.

Normative Versus Descriptive Criteria

Cameron (1978) points out that investigators differ in the extent to which they approach the definition and measurement of effectiveness with an a priori set of measures or develop or select measures based on what the people in the organization believe to be appropriate. The former can be thought to be normative in the sense that the researcher is imposing his or her values on the process. Clearly this issue relates to several of the others raised above.

Given the current state of affairs, it appears that there is no single conceptual model of organization effectiveness. But there is no shortage of possibilities as well. The investigator interested in measuring effectiveness at the level of the organization clearly needs to make choices. Some of the factors that should be considered in doing this include the following:

1. *Purpose of the investigation.* Theory building, theory testing, organization intervention, decision making, all imply differing measurement approaches.
2. *Beliefs and values of the investigator.*
3. *Multiple versus composite criteria.* There are times when there is a need or desire to have a global index of organizational effectiveness. The human resources accounting approach may be more appropriate here.
4. *Original data gathering.* There are cases when the investigator may wish to be able to use existent, operational indicators of effectiveness instead of gathering original data (for lack of time or resources).

ETHICAL ISSUES

Given the fact that almost any technique touched upon in this text can be used in the study and measurement of effectiveness at the group and organizational levels, it would be reasonable to refer you to the chapters covering specific techniques (e.g., hidden observation) for a discussion of ethical considerations. And, indeed, we recommend that you take the time to do this if you are working at these levels of analysis. However, beyond this advise we would like to highlight some concerns that derive from the fact that group and organizational effectiveness data usually are obtained in actual work settings.

Confidentiality

Because effectiveness data often are gathered in organizations, an important ethical consideration relates to just who will "own" or have access to effectiveness information. To be certain, if the investigator is a manager with proper authority, and/or if the data are from operational systems, this issue becomes moot. That is, the indicators are a matter of record and they will be shared as widely as policy or company norms allow. On the other hand, there are numerous instances where the investigator is an outsider, a consultant, or researcher based in a university and the effectiveness data are obtained especially for a project. Under these conditions, the question of data accessibility becomes more complex.

The most problematic case is where the measurement of effectiveness is built on individual opinions and perceptions. As noted above, this is a common strategy for those investigators adopting an organizational development model of effectiveness. Moreover, such data are obtained by using interviews or questionnaires administered just for that purpose. In most cases those conditions for producing high quality subjective data (confidentially) also are found to be unattractive to top managers. In our experience, there is a high probability that requests will be made that the information be released to such managers.

A special instance of these dynamics will occur when the data are being gathered as part of a time series designed for research that is aimed at rigorously assessing the impact of some intervention (see Chapter 11). Under these circumstances, not only does the researcher have to be concerned about the issue of confidentiality for its own sake, but also with what might occur to the integrity of the study if preliminary data were widely shared. To put it another way, the premature disclosure of the scores on effectiveness indicators might turn out to be a powerful intervention in and of itself.

There is no easy solution to these dilemmas. Perhaps the most forthright approach is to recognize the potential for disclosure under duress at the outset and to negotiate a clear understanding of the rights and obligations of all the parties involved (researcher, employees, top managers). Thus, the investigators' promise of confidentiality can be made with authority and can be kept.

Proprietary Nature of Measures

Another area where there is a potential ethical concern relates to the fact that some questionnaire measures of effectiveness and some systems for measuring process are proprietary. That is, they are based on the work of others who have chosen to obtain copyright protection. Thus, the Managerial Grid is a system for defining and measuring organizational effectiveness developed by Blake and Mouton (1964). To use it in practice or research would require permission (and, depending on the application, a fee) from the originators. On the other hand, the Survey of Organizations was developed by Likert (1967) to assess effectiveness while he was at the Institute for Social Research at the University of Michigan. While it is often treated as if the questionnaire is in the public domain, the institute (and his estate) still has a proprietary interest in it. Similar ambiguity is associated with the measure of effective group decision making (with its emphasis on quality and acceptance) developed by Vroom and Yetton (1973).

There are some clear benefits from using standardized and carefully developed measure of effectiveness. For example, it allows for the development of a normative data base and for the possibility of a cumulative science (see Chapter 12 on meta-analysis). Thus, whenever the opportunity presents itself, we encourage the adoption of standardized approaches. However, the investigator must be certain that he or she has the right to use a standard measure. It is not only desirable to contact the individual responsible for the instrument, but also to get permission in writing.

SUMMARY

This chapter has discussed issues of measurement at the group and organizational levels of analysis. In order to do this, however, we felt it necessary to review current theory on the nature of group and organizational functioning. In doing so we have tried to be very clear that the types of measures chosen by an investigator will be strongly influenced by the theoretical assumptions held or the type of model presumed to be valid. We also noted that in the area of assessing organizational effectiveness, personal values also will be relevant. In any event, as in the case of individual effectiveness measurement, the message that we want to leave you with is that, in an area filled with options, there is no substitute for informed choice. Appropriate measurement of the effectiveness of groups and organizations requires subject matter expertise, care, and skill.

ASSESSING THE POTENTIAL
FOR EFFECTIVE PERFORMANCE

In this chapter, we describe various methods whereby the human resource professional can assess the capability and motivation of members of their current work force or an applicant pool. In the case of each of the selection procedures discussed, we describe their advantages and disadvantages, including the cost and difficulty of their administration, their reliability and validity, and the degree to which these procedures are influenced by applicant subgroup status (i.e., minority or gender).

In Chapter 3, we described the criteria used to judge measurement instruments used in human resource management and research. In this chapter, we will discuss various measures of individual differences in human ability. In discussing their relative strengths and weaknesses, we will mention the validity and reliability of these instruments as well as the cost to develop and use them, and their potential for adverse impact. Formal legal definitions of adverse impact will be discussed in Chapter 9. In this chapter we will describe findings that indicate that the existence of sizable subgroup differences (male-female or minority-nonminority) are likely when a particular method is used to select employees.

THE LOGIC OF SELECTION DEVICES AND THEIR DEVELOPMENT

Selecting the right person for a job is a difficult and complex task. A fundamental problem is that we have so little on which to base a decision at the time of hire in the typical employment setting. If we had a great deal of time and were given ample opportunity to observe and to get to know each applicant, we might be in the best position to conclude something about his or her strengths and weaknesses and suitability for a particular job. Most of the time, however, this is not possible. Thus, human resource professionals have had to find ways to gather a great deal of job-relevant knowledge about the applicant in a timely and efficient manner. The several techniques to be reviewed in this chapter have been developed for this purpose.

Types of Information Desired

In general, the kind of information that is useful in selection contexts relates to the applicant's capacity to do the job and his or her tendency to approach and carry out the work in a motivated manner. Capacity is usually a function of the knowledge, skills, abilities, and other characteristics (KSAOs) a worker brings to a job. Motivation to work is strongly affected by the fit between the needs and values of the worker and the opportunities and rewards available on the job. Sometimes we think in terms of personality when we consider the likelihood that a person will be motivated in a given situation. Most often we are interested in uncovering what a person would typically do across situations. To put it into more colloquial terms, to predict successful job performance we must be convinced that the person both can and will do the job.

The various types of measures available to human resource professionals can be classified according to their usefulness in assessing maximum performance or ability and typical behavior. This has been done with regard to the devices covered in this chapter and the results are portrayed in Figure 8-1. However, it should be kept in mind that in most employment settings, it is not uncommon to use more than one approach, since each has its own strengths and weaknesses.

Determining What Information is Useful

One question you may have is how human resource professionals decide what KSAOs to measure, what procedures to use, and how to evaluate those procedures. In this area more than in any other human resource area, professionals have developed the most detailed and well-defined set of steps. The approach used in the development of selection procedures is outlined in Figure 8-2 and is sometimes referred to as the *criterion-related validation model* (recall the discussion of criterion-related validity in Chapter 3).

The first step in this process is to use a job analysis to define the tasks or responsibilities required of the job incumbent and the KSAOs necessary to adequately perform these tasks. Job analyses procedures were outlined in Chapter 4. These KSAOs and their relative importance as judged by job experts and the job analysts then become the blueprint for test construction. The researcher may choose from among existing selection procedures or tests those that index a particular KSAO or she or he may decide to construct a new measure. In either case, issues of content and construct validity as discussed in Chapters 1 and 3 must be considered.

Information on the required KSAOs will be important as the human resource practitioner makes decisions about who and where to recruit job applicants. The job analysis also will inform the researcher as to the types of job performance constructs that are relevant and how to measure those constructs. In this respect, the discussion of individual performance measures in Chapter 6 is relevant.

Type of Information Obtained	Type of Measure
Maximum Performance	Cognitive Tests
	Aptitude Tests
	Job Sample Tests
	Physical Ability Tests
	Assessment Centers
Typical Behavior	Biographical Data*
	Personality Measures
Both	Employment Interview
	Reference Checks

*Biographical data may be reflective of past maximum performance as well. Also, biographical data may be of a more demographic nature as contrasted with personality or attitudinal measures. For both these reasons, biographical data may fit elsewhere in this table as well.

FIGURE 8-1   Getting to Know You: The Types of Procedures Likely to Be of Use in Producing Maximum Performance or Typical Behavior Information

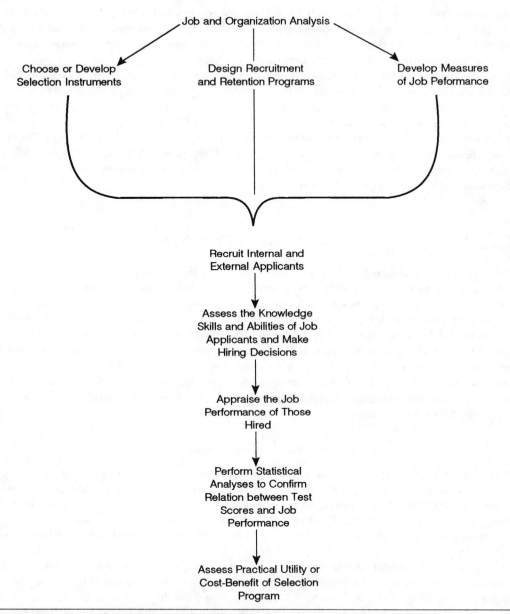

FIGURE 8-2 Diagram of the Steps in a Criterion-Related Validation Study

Job applicants are then recruited, their possession of relevant KSAOs is assessed, and individuals are selected (if a purely predictive research study is being conducted, recall that selection would be on a random basis). After some period of time, during which the newly hired persons learn their job and their performance stabilizes, job performance measures are collected. Statistical analyses are performed as outlined in Chapter 2 to ascertain the degree to which measures of KSAOs are related to subsequent job performance. Finally, using information on the cost of gathering information (KSAOs), the level of criterion-related validity, and the situation in which the procedures are being used, the researcher and practitioner draw conclusions about the practical utility of the selection procedures. Analyses of the practical utility of various human resource practices including selection are described in Chapter 9.

Occasionally, the full set of steps outlined in Figure 8-2 is not feasible or desirable. For example, see the discussion of the power of criterion-related validation and problems of low sample size, lack of reliability in the job performance measure, and predictor and criterion range restriction in the available study participants in Chapter 3. In these cases, the choice of selection procedures rests on the fact that they are measures of actual job behavior (repairing or rebuilding an automobile engine for an auto mechanic) or that the KSAO construct required by specific job tasks is the one measured by a test. In this context, the discussions of content and construct validity of the measures used (see Chapter 3) are relevant.

COGNITIVE ABILITY TESTS

The development of *cognitive ability tests* can be traced to the development of intelligence tests by Binet and Simon to diagnose children who were most likely to benefit from the typical school curriculum. The items for their tests were developed on the basis of observation (job analysis) and validated against teacher judgments of whether the students were fast or slow learners. The tests proved to be useful because Binet and Simon used the techniques discussed above and in Chapter 3 to construct and evaluate their measure. In particular, they were careful to construct content valid measures and to collect validity data on their items and to revise the testing instruments accordingly. Their tests were soon translated into various languages; the American version was called the Stanford-Binet. The Stanford-Binet and a similar set of tests, the Wechsler Adult Intelligence Scale, are individually administered tests.

General Ability Tests

As mentioned in Chapter 1, Yerkes and his colleagues developed a test called the Army Alpha which could be administered to groups of World War I Army recruits. Soon other group tests of general mental ability were developed, such as the Otis Quick-Scoring Mental Abilities Test, the Wonderlic Personnel Test, and the Purdue Adaptability Test. They became available to various organizations generating widespread use of tests by industry to select and promote individuals, especially supervisory personnel.

Tests of general mental ability have been shown to be valid in many industrial studies, particularly for the selection of sales personnel, managers, and supervisors (Hunter & Hunter, 1984; Schmitt, Gooding, Noe, & Kirsch, 1984). The mean validity of this type of test for the prediction of performance in various types of work is presented in the first column of Table 8-1. Columns 2 and 3 of Table 8-1 include validities for a wide variety of perceptual and motivational measures as summarized by Ghiselli (1973) and later reanalyzed by Hunter and Hunter (1984).

A couple of items, which are representative of the type of items found in these tests, are presented in Figure 8-3. The Wonderlic, which is fairly representative of these tests, is a 12-minute test that contains 50 items covering vocabulary, arithmetic reasoning, spatial visualization, number series, and other areas. While it may be appropriately argued that these general mental ability tests are valid measures of the potential to perform well at a large variety of jobs, and can be used effectively to make personnel decisions, these tests have been criticized heavily because members

TABLE 8-1
Validity of Different Test Types for Various Job Families

Job Families	Mean Validity*		
	Cog	Per	Mot
Manager	.53	.43	.26
Clerk	.54	.46	.29
Salesperson	.61	.40	.29
Protective Professions Worker	.42	.37	.26
Service Worker	.48	.20	.27
Trades and Crafts Worker	.46	.43	.34
Elementary Industrial Worker	.37	.37	.40
Vehicle Operator	.28	.31	.44
Sales Clerk	.27	.22	.17

*Cog refers to cognitive tests, Per indicates spatial or perceptual measures, and Mot refers to tests of motor skills. These data represent Hunter and Hunter's (1984) reanalysis of Ghiselli's (1973) work on mean validity of tests.
Source: Adapted with permission from Hunter, J. E., & Hunter, R. F. (1984). Validity and utility of alternative predictors of job performance. *Psychological Bulletin, 96,* 72–98.

of minority groups typically score much lower (the mean difference is often as large as one standard deviation) on these instruments than do Caucasians. Because of this difference, these tests result in significant *adverse impact*; that is, the proportion of minority applicants hired is much lower than the proportion of Caucasian applicants for any given score cutoff. The courts and the Equal Employment Opportunity Commission often react negatively to these tests even before the validity evidence is examined. The result may be that potentially useful and job-relevant information is ignored.

Although these intelligence tests or general mental ability tests originally were designed to measure an individual's general intellectual or cognitive level, it soon became apparent that these tests were quite limited in their coverage. In fact, most cognitive ability or intelligence tests primarily were measures of verbal ability and, to a lesser extent, of the ability to handle numerical and other abstract and symbolic relations. These tests actually became known in the 1920s as scholastic aptitude tests as American psychologists switched their attention to the development of special aptitude tests to supplement the general cognitive ability test.

Aptitude Tests

Beginning in the 1920s, as stated above, L. L. Thurstone and other American psychologists became disenchanted with general ability tests and began to develop *aptitude tests*—tests of specific abilities. Thurstone was interested in determining the number and type of factors needed to account for the intercorrelations among the various tests or items on ability tests. Using the factor analysis methods we described in Chapter 2, Thurstone (1922) identified seven primary abilities:

1. *Verbal comprehension.* Measured in tests of reading comprehension, verbal comprehension is tested through verbal analogies, disarranged sentences, verbal reasoning, and proverb matching.
2. *Word fluency.* Word fluency is tested through anagrams, rhymes, and tests requiring the generation of words in a given category.

1. The opposite of arrive is:
___ a. come
___ b. depart
___ c. friend
___ d. marry
___ e. resign

2. If a gallon of ice cream costs three dollars, three gallons would cost:
___ a. one dollar
___ b. thirty dollars
___ c. nine dollars
___ d. eighteen dollars
___ e. eight dollars

3. The next number in this series of numbers (1, 4, 16, 25) is:
___ a. 34
___ b. 50
___ c. 75
___ d. 36
___ e. 44

4. In what way do corn, asparagus, carrots, and beans go together?
___ a. they all are vegetables
___ b. they all are cloth
___ c. they all are stems
___ d. they all are roots
___ e. they all are yellow

5. The three figures on the left are similar in some way. Circle the letter of one figure on the right that goes with the first three.

FIGURE 8-3   Examples of Items in a General Mental Ability Test

3. *Number.* Speed and accuracy are assessed in simple arithmetic computation.
4. *Space.* Perception of space is tested through fixed spatial or geometric relationships and the visualization of changes in position.
5. *Associative memory.* Associative memory is tested through rote memory of paired associates.
6. *Perceptual speed.* Perceptual speed and accuracy are assessed in how well visual details, similarities, and differences are grasped.
7. *Reasoning.* Reasoning requires the subject to discover rules or principles underlying a set of facts or statements, and occasionally includes the use of syllogistic reasoning.

The development of specific aptitude tests for different occupations produced tests in the following areas: clerical, musical, sales, mechanical, etc. Items similar to those in the Minnesota Clerical Test are presented in Figure 8-4 and items similar to those in the Bennett Mechanical Comprehension Test are contained in Figure 8-5.

	Numbers/Letters		Same	
1.	3468251	3467251	YES	NO
2.	4681371	4681371	YES	NO
3.	7218510	7218520	YES	NO
4.	ZXYAZAB	ZXYAZAB	YES	NO
5.	ALZYXMN	ALZYXNM	YES	NO
6.	PRQZYMN	PRQZYMN	YES	NO

FIGURE 8-4   Items Similar to Those Appearing on the Minnesota Clerical Test Require the Test Taker to Indicate which Pairs of Numbers or Letters Are Exactly the Same

Multi-Aptitude Batteries

More recently, test developers have developed *multi-aptitude batteries*, which are sets of tests administered as a package and which yield aptitude scores on anywhere from eight to 14 or more potentially job-relevant dimensions. If a test user has job analysis information indicating the abilities essential for job performance, she or he may be able to use these multi-aptitude test

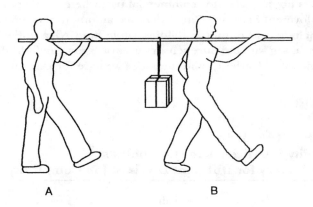

X

Which man carries more weight?
(If equal, mark C.)

A   B

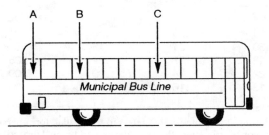

Y

Which letter shows the seat where the passenger will get the smoothest ride?

FIGURE 8-5   Mechanical Comprehension Test Items
Source: Adapted with permission from the Bennett Mechanical Comprehension Test

batteries to select personnel for a variety of jobs. Scores on tests requiring the specific subset of knowledge, skills, and ability required for job performance on a specific job would be used to make hiring decisions for that job only.

Perhaps because of the care taken in the development of the measures to ensure their reliability and their coverage of various aptitudes of relevance to a wide variety of occupations, studies relating scores on the tests to job measures indicate that they have substantial validity. Data on the validity of one such multi-aptitude battery (the General Aptitude Test Battery) are contained in Table 8-2 from Hunter and Hunter (1984).

Four of the better known multi-aptitude batteries include the following:

1. Differential Aptitude Tests (DAT),
2. Flanagan Aptitude Classification Tests (FACT),
3. General Aptitude Test Battery (GATB), and
4. Employee Aptitude Survey (EAS).

Table 8-3 presents the subtests offered in each. There is considerable overlap in content between the various multi-aptitude batteries. All four of those presented in Table 8-3 contain tests of more general intellectual factors, such as those described in the previous section on cognitive ability. The EAS is supported by excellent evidence of validity (Ruch & Ruch, 1980); in addition it takes only about one hour to complete. The DAT and FACT, on the other hand, require approximately four hours. The GATB is not available for commercial use; when used, applicants are generally tested only at State Employment Services. One difference among the four aptitude batteries is that the GATB and EAS include tests of motor abilities, while the DAT and FACT do not. These eye-hand coordination tests, along with the pure sensory tests of vision (including color blindness) and hearing, represent some of the earliest, valid measures we have for tasks involving a high sensorimotor component.

TABLE 8-2
Observed Validity Coefficients for the Subtests
of the General Aptitude Test Battery for Different Levels of Job Complexity

| | Validity* | | | |
Job Complexity	GVN	SPQ	KFM	Number of jobs
Set Up	.34	.35	.19	21
Synthesize/Coordinate	.30	.21	.13	60
Analyze/Compile	.28	.27	.24	205
Copy/Compare	.22	.24	.30	209
Feeding	.13	.16	.35	20

*GVN refers to the general intelligence, verbal, and numerical subtests: SPQ refers to the spatial, form perception, and clerical perception subtests; and KFM refers to the motor coordination, finger dexterity, and manual dexterity subtests of the General Aptitude Test Battery.
Source: Adapted with permission from Hunter, J. E., & Hunter, R. F. (1984). Validity and utility of alternative predictors of job performance. *Psychological Bulletin, 96,* 72–98.

TABLE 8-3
Some Multi-Aptitude Batteries and What They Test

DAT	FACT	GATB	EAS
1. Verbal reasoning	1. Inspection	1. General intelligence	1. Verbal Comprehension
2. Numerical ability	2. Coding	2. Verbal	2. Numerical ability
3. Abstract reasoning	3. Memory	3. Numerical	3. Visual pursuit
4. Space relations	4. Precision	4. Spatial	4. Visual speed and accuracy
5. Mechanical reasoning	5. Assembly	5. Form perception	5. Space visualization
6. Clerical speed and accuracy	6. Scales	6. Clerical perception	6. Numerical reasoning
7. Language usage (spelling)	7. Coordination	7. Motor coordination	7. Verbal reasoning
8. Language usage (sentences)	8. Judgment and comprehension	8. Finger dexterity	8. Word fluency
	9. Arithmetic	9. Manual dexterity	9. Manual speed and accuracy
	10. Patterns		10. Symbolic reasoning
	11. Components		
	12. Tables		
	13. Mechanics		
	14. Expression		

Locating Potentially Useful Aptitude Tests

Test publishers should produce a manual that describes the development of the test, how to administer it, and the data supporting its use. Most manuals for the tests discussed above report data on the validity of the tests in various situations for different groups of people. Additional information concerning many of these tests is available in the *Mental Measurements Yearbook* (Mitchell, 1986). This book publishes critical reviews of tests by one or more expert reviewers and is now undergoing its tenth revision; the first occurred in 1938. These yearbooks cover nearly all commercially available psychological, educational, and vocational tests published in English. A number of psychological and educational journals represent additional sources of current information about tests. New tests are regularly abstracted in *Psychological Abstracts* as are the articles published about tests.

Perhaps the most comprehensive reviews of the use of tests in personnel selection have been conducted by Ghiselli (1966; 1973). His reviews included summaries of studies done on the validity of tests for different occupations. His work provides a starting point for clues regarding the kinds of assessments most likely to be valid in particular occupational groups. Table 8-1 on page 257 presents a summary of some of these data by type of test for various occupations. While Ghiselli (1966) included the validity of each kind of test for both job performance measures and training success measures, Table 8-1 contains only the job performance data. The validities in this table are averages across concurrent and predictive criterion-related studies. Any one type of test (e.g., numerical ability) using Ghiselli's system of classification includes a large number of different tests, and a particular type of job performance measure may include several different measures. Further, within each broad occupational category (e.g., clerk, manager, etc.), there are a variety of jobs. The fact that the tests show validity at all after all of this averaging and collapsing of categories attests to their potential usefulness in a wide variety of situations.

As is the case with general cognitive ability tests, there typically will be large subgroup differences in the scores of verbal and numerical subtests of these multi-aptitude test batteries. Caucasians generally score higher than minority group members on these tests. Such subgroup differences are smaller or nonexistent for the psychomotor subtests and not nearly as large for spatial ability measures.

THE EMPLOYMENT INTERVIEW

In applying for most jobs in the U.S., job candidates likely will confront an employment interview. Estimates of the use of interviews by companies to select individuals range between 80% (ASPA, 1983) and 99% (Ulrich & Trumbo, 1965). Obviously, managers and personnel workers who use the interview have a great deal of faith in its usefulness and validity. Hundreds of "how to" books have been written on the interview telling the interviewer how to best conduct interviews. In addition, industrial psychologists have conducted extensive research on the interview designed to assess the reliability and validity of the interview, as well as the decision processes of the interviewer.

Research on the Employment Interview

During the last 30 years, six separate reviews of the interview research have been published, the most recent by Arvey and Campion (1982). These reviews have indicated that interview reliability (interrater reliability) and validity are low and variable. Hunter and Hunter (1984), using meta-analytic methods estimated the validity of the interview to be .14, although more recent meta-analyses (McDaniel et al., 1986; Wiersner & Cronshaw, 1988) are much more positive, especially about the validity of structured interviews. In the last 20 years, much of the literature on the interview has changed focus and researchers have tried to determine why, when, or how interview decisions are made (Webster, 1964; 1982). While some of this research has no direct implication for the validity of the selection interview, Schmitt's review (1976) did include the following suggestions for practicing personnel interviewers:

1. Use of a structured interview guide will improve interviewer reliability. In structured interviews, all interviewees are asked the same set of questions, which are designed to collect job-relevant information. Simply recording information and then returning to it later to make ratings or recommendations may serve to remove some of the effects of a good or bad interviewee's first or last answer (referred to as order effects in the research literature).

2. Knowing the requirements of the job for which an interview is conducted should help to focus on job-relevant information.

3. Interviewer training to avoid bias in ratings (Latham, Wexley, & Pursell, 1975; Wexley, Sanders, & Yukl, 1973) may be appropriate, although not much effort has been directed to this problem in the context of employment interviews. Vance, Kuhnert, and Farr (1978) found no training effects in reduction of error, and Heneman (1980) found training effects only for inter-interviewer reliability.

4. The interviewee is forming an impression of the interviewer (Schmitt & Coyle, 1976) and even when he or she is not an acceptable candidate, the interview may be employed effectively as a public relations vehicle.

5. Interpersonal skills and motivation of a job applicant are perhaps best evaluated in the interview (Ulrich & Trumbo, 1965); consequently, the interview likely will be employed most effectively when these elements are critical job performance requirements.

6. Allowing the applicant time to talk will provide a larger behavior sample. Studies by Webster and his colleagues (1964) indicate that interviewers talk far more than applicants in the typical employment interview.

7. Training of interviewers to relate effectively with members of other ethnic or sex subgroups may be appropriate, although no known effort to do this has been evaluated.

8. Attention should be directed to the purpose of the interview (i.e., whether it is intended as a final screen on several variables; an initial screening device, or whether its primary function is educational or of a public relations value).

Contemporary Approaches to the Employment Interview

More recently, validity data on the interview appear to be more encouraging. Arvey and Campion (1982) cite several instances in which researchers have reported encouraging results on the validity of the interview. Landy (1976) gathered data on 150 police officer candidates on three interview factors and correlated scores on these three factors with ratings on four job performance factors collected one year later. Four of the twelve validity coefficients were statistically significant and of modest magnitude (.26, .29, .33 and .34 with appropriate statistical correction). Anstey (1977) found civil service ranks correlated .35 with board interview ratings collected 30 years earlier. Arvey, Miller, Gould, and Burch (1987) reported the development of an interview for salesclerks that had a validity after one year of .34, and after two years of .51.

An innovative approach to employment interviewing is represented by the situational interview developed by Latham, Saari, Pursell, and Campion (1980). These authors began by using the critical incident approach to job analysis. Recall from Chapter 4 that critical incidents are reports by job experts of behaviors that they considered especially effective or ineffective. These critical incidents were translated into situational interview questions to which an applicant with no previous job experience was asked to indicate how he or she would respond. Each answer was rated independently by two or more interviewers on a five-point Likert-type scale with anchors describing good or bad responses (also provided by job experts). Interrater reliability was acceptable; concurrent validities for foremen and hourly workers were .30 and .46 respectively. Robertson (1987) has presented data on a managerial group that indicates observed validities of .28 and .31 against performance rating criteria collected 18 months after selection with a selection ratio of approximately .60 and corresponding range restriction. Likewise, Weekly and Gier (1987) reported a validity of .42 in selecting sales personnel.

One of your authors (Schmitt & Ostroff, 1986) developed a similar situational interview for the selection of emergency telephone operators. Examples of the interview questions and the critical incidents from which they were derived are given in Table 8-4. Interview rating scales also were developed using examples of good and bad answers to the interview questions as anchors. One important aspect of this approach is the careful link between interview questions and critical incidents job analysis data. The situational interview is consistent with Arvey and Campion's advice (1982) that interview use be preceded by thorough job analyses, development of a structured set of questions based on the job analysis, and the development of behaviorally specific rating instruments by which to rate applicants.

TABLE 8-4
Examples of Situational Interview Questions and Their Corresponding Critical Incidents Used for Selection of Emergency Telephone Operators

Critical Incident	Interview Question
1. Telephone operator tries to verify address information for an ambulance call. The caller yells at her for being stupid and slow. The operator quietly assures the caller an ambulance is on the way and that she is merely reaffirming the address.	1. Imagine that you tried to help a stranger, for example, with traffic directions or to get up after a fall, and that person blamed you for their misfortune or yelled at you. How would you respond?
2. A caller is hysterical because her infant is dead. She yells incoherently about the incident. The operator talks in a clear calm voice and manages to secure the woman's address, dispatches the call, and then tries to secure more information about the child's status.	2. Suppose a friend calls and is extremely upset? Apparently, her child has been injured. She begins to tell you, in a hysterical manner, all about her difficulty in getting babysitters, what the child is wearing, what words the child can speak, etc. What would you do?
3. A clearly angry caller calls for the third time in an hour complaining about the 911 service because no one has arrived to investigate a busted water pipe. The operator tells the caller to go to _____ and hangs up.	3. How would you react if you were a salesclerk, waitress, or gas station attendant and one of your customers talked back to you, indicated you should have known something you did not, or told you that you were not waiting on them fast enough?

Interview Dynamics

One feature that is obvious to most people who have gone through an employment interview is that it is what psychologists call a *mixed motive situation*. That is, both the applicant and the personnel interviewer usually have reasons to be both frank or honest *and* strategic or deceptive. Similarly, at times the candidate will be working with the interviewer and his or her needs to get an accurate fix on the former's strengths and weaknesses. But often this is not the case. Figure 8-6 highlights a common set of mixed motives that are operating in selection interviews.

To elaborate on Figure 8-6, one can imagine that an applicant's concerns with getting a job offer and maintaining self-esteem will cause him or her to be less than candid about weaknesses and to tend to encourage the exaggeration of accomplishments, perhaps even a distortion of interests or preferences ("Of course I have the knowledge, skills, and abilities to do the job!"). This, however, results in the dissemination of invalid information to the personnel specialist. A decision

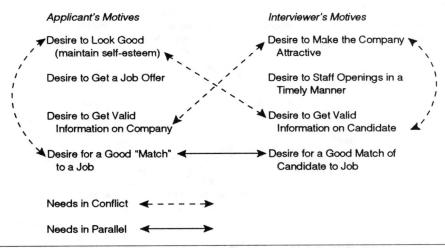

FIGURE 8-6   The Employment Interview as a Mixed Situation—Some Illustrations

or recommendation based on such information is likely to be wrong and to result in hiring someone who cannot or will not enjoy or be able to do the job. Similarly, a recruiter's desire to make the job seem attractive to entice a strong applicant will result in exaggerations or misleading comments that make it impossible for the candidate to formulate a valid decision regarding the suitability of a job opportunity. Also notice that both parties do agree with regard to the desirability of obtaining a good match between a new hire and the job in question. No applicant wants to take a job that is truly inappropriate or is likely to result in low satisfaction. Similarly, the recruiter does not want the company to hire someone who is likely to fail. Given this complexity, it's no wonder that it's difficult to account for the processes operating to affect the validity of the inferences and decisions made in the interview.

The mixed motive scenario just described makes it clear that it is difficult to get evidence of typical behavior in an employment interview. The candidate usually is on his or her "best" behavior. Rather than feeling that we have gained insight as to what he or she is really like, we might be safe to assume that what is portrayed is the result of maximum effort and attention. To put it another way, based on the interview, if a person appears to have the right answers to critical questions of appropriate on-the-job behaviors, we might be somewhat assured that he or she knows what to do. However, we should not infer that he or she would behave that way (make the same quality decisions or responses) on a day-to-day basis from information gathered only from the interview.

The Employment Interview as a Social-Psychological Phenomenon

One of the outcomes of research on the interview is an appreciation for the fact that the interview represents a complex social-psychological interaction. The complexity of the interview situation is represented by the various models researchers have drawn trying to depict the interview situation—one of which is produced as Figure 8-7. Dreher and Sackett (1983) argue convincingly that previous research supports the links in this model, but we believe that the model could serve as a valuable guide by which to direct future research as well. Further, we believe that much of the literature on information processing has never been evaluated in an actual interview. One recent study (Dougherty, Ebert, & Callender, 1986) serves as an example of how an information processing model might serve to illuminate actual interviewer decision making. They used regression

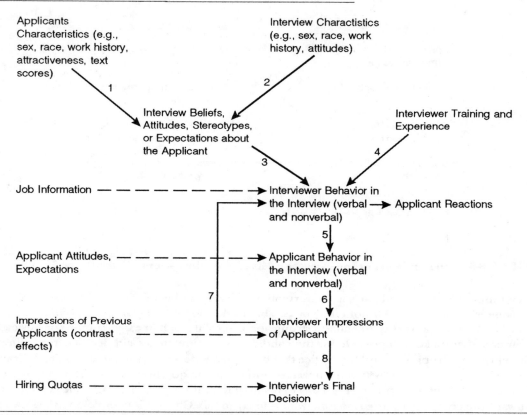

FIGURE 8-7   Hypothesized Model of Interviewer Information Seeking Receipt and Processing
Source: Reprinted with permission from Dreher, G. F., & Sackett, P. R. (1982). *Perspectives on employee staffing and selection: Readings and commentary.* Homewood, IL: Richard D. Irwin.

analysis to capture the way in which each interviewer used information in the interview and correlated the use of information with the validity of individual interviewer judgments. This approach could then be used to identify what is wrong with an interviewer's judgment process and to teach her or him to take corrective action. It should come as no surprise that in many respects, most of the recommendations for conducting a really good employment interview parallel those stressed in Chapter 4 for the research interview.

Developing a Potentially Valid Interview Program.

We have infrequently taken the information suggested in models like that in Figure 8-7 and the guidelines provided by Schmitt (1976) and others (Arvey and Campion, 1982) and constructed an interview and then reevaluated the validity of the interview. Given the interview appears to be most valid for interpersonal skills and motivation, it should provide information about job applicants that would not be as directly available in the cognitive paper-and-pencil measures discussed in the previous section of this chapter. Hence, it should, when properly developed and used, add significantly to the validity of employment decisions either when used in combination with paper-and-pencil ability tests or when used alone.

Campion, Pursell, and Brown (1988) report a very successful use of a structured interview in the selection of entry-level employees in a large pulp and paper mill. Their interview displayed interrater reliability of .88 and a validity of .34 (when corrected for range restriction and criterion unreliability r = .56). The steps they took in constructing and implementing their interview represent the best in current selection interviewing practice, hence we summarize them in the following paragraphs.

1. *Step 1: Develop questions based on a job analysis.* Any method of job analysis can be used, including the approach described in Chapter 5 as long as there is a determination of the KASOs required to perform important job tasks. These KASOs are used as the basis for the development of interview questions. Questions should not be based on the requirements of higher-level jobs nor on KASOs that are acquired after brief exposure to the job. Additionally, questions should be reviewed by minority job experts to avoid unintentional bias or misinterpretation.

2. *Step 2: Ask the same questions of every applicant.* If applicants' KSAOs are to be compared in a useful way, the interviewer must take steps to collect similar job relevant information from all candidates.

3. *Step 3: Anchor the rating scales used by the interviewers with examples of good and bad answers.* The critical incident approach developed by Latham et al. (1980) and illustrated by the Schmitt and Ostroff (1986) study of emergency telephone operators is one useful approach to the generation of these examples. Brainstorming with job experts, who have had experience interviewing candidates in the past, is another way to generate good or bad answers. Inability to generate such examples is often evidence that the question needs to be restructured or eliminated.

4. *Step 4: Have an interview panel record and rate answers.* Using more than one interviewer reduces the possibility or impact of idiosyncratic rater biases. If possible, the same interviewers should evaluate all applicants. They should meet in advance to review job duties and requirements, questions and answers, and ways to avoid various interview rating errors (Latham et al., 1975). Each panel member should independently record and rate candidate answers and the interview should be conducted before panel members review other information about the candidate.

5. *Step 5: Consistently administer the process to all candidates.* The same person should ask all questions and questions and answers should not be discussed between interviews to avoid changing standards or comparisons of candidates. After interviews are complete, large discrepancies are discussed and resolved if panel members feel that is appropriate. The final ratings of panel members are averaged.

6. *Step 6. Special attention throughout should be given to job relatedness, fairness, and documentation consistent with the Uniform Guidelines (1978) and SIOP's Principles* (Society for Industrial and Organizational Psychology, 1987).

Potential Bias in the Employment Interview and its Legal Status

One last issue concerning the employment interview is its legal status. Arvey (1979) provided an excellent summary of studies of bias in the interview. Evidence from research studies involving experimental participants, who were asked to evaluate resumes, indicates that women are evaluated more poorly than men, particularly when they are being considered for typically masculine jobs. However, when both the qualifications and sex of candidates are available to interviewer judges, it has been found that sex accounts for a small portion of the variability in interviewer judgments while qualifications are highly related to interviewer judgments. Attractiveness of candidates seems to be an important factor, but independent of gender. Interview ratings do not seem to be affected by applicant race, but applicant age exerts a strong effect on applicant ratings. Few studies of the effect of handicaps exist, but there is some indication that a handicapped person is judged to be more highly motivated than persons without handicaps.

Most of these studies of bias have been conducted with college students often using resumes or videotapes rather than "live" interviews, hence their generalizability may be severely limited. While relatively few lawsuits involving the employment interview have occurred, Arvey (1979) indicates that interviews are clearly vulnerable. Further, he predicts an increase in such suits and warns that organizations are likely to be ill-equipped to defend the interview because of the little attention given to quantifying and validating interviewer judgments. Arvey's view that the interview may be subjected to increased legal scrutiny is reinforced by a recent court case involving Fort Worth Bank & Trust in which a minority individual claimed she was discriminated against in the company's promotional process. The promotion decision in this case was based on a subjective performance appraisal not unlike the subjective appraisal frequently arrived at by an interviewer in the selection interview. While the implications of this case are still being debated (see Potter, 1989), one view is that the courts may now require that employers show that subjective evaluations (such as those arrived at in interviews and performance appraisals) are valid in the same way that they have been required to do in the case of more objective selection procedures (e.g., written tests). It should be noted that professional guidelines such as the *Principles for the Validation and Use of Selection Procedures* (1987) do indicate validation is necessary for all selection decisions.

PERSONALITY MEASURES AND INTEREST INVENTORIES

One alternative, or the source of complementary information, on job applicants' social and motivational dispositions is provided by *personality inventories*.

The Nature of Personality and Interest Measures

In responding to structured personality and interest inventories, an individual usually indicates how much they like or are interested in the stimuli referenced by a series of statements. An example of items taken from a measure of a personality variable called locus of control is presented as Table 8-5. Responses to items in inventories like this locus of control measure are neither right nor wrong but groups of items are written to measure persons' traits such as aggression, need achievement, sociability, or locus of control. The meaning of a person's score is derived by comparison to some reference group. For example, individual scores on interest inventories are usually compared to the scores of persons in similar or different occupations. For example, a high school student's score on a locus of control measure is "high" or "low" by comparison to the responses of large numbers of other high school students.

Structured personality inventories like aptitude batteries usually include several scales that purport to define and assess specific aspects of personality. Aside from the fact that these measures usually have not been developed for use in the work setting, another potential problem is that respondents may be able to figure out the responses needed to get the "right" scores on these tests. The ability to "outthink" the test may be particularly important in the work setting when employment or promotion is contingent on the test scores one receives.

TABLE 8-5
Locus of Control Measure

Indicate your response on the following scale:
 1 = Strongly Agree
 2 = Agree
 3 = Neither Agree nor Disagree
 4 = Disagree
 5 = Strongly Disagree
_____ Many of the unhappy things in people's lives are partly due to bad luck.
_____ Who gets to be boss often depends on who was lucky enough to be in the right place first.
_____ What happens to me is my own doing.
_____ The average citizen can have an influence in government decisions.

Source: Items reproduced with permission from Valecha, G. K. (1972). Construct validation of internal-external locus of control as measured by an abbreviated 11-item I-E scale. Unpublished doctoral dissertation. Columbus, OH: The Ohio State University.

Using Personality and Interest Measures

Mischel (1973) also argues that the use of personality tests is logically incorrect. He argues that behavior is a function of the situation with which an individual is presented. Since behavior is situationally unique or specific, personality trait measures cannot be predictive. A more moderate interactionist view is that a person's performance or behavior is a function of both the situation and her or his ability or personality. In any event, a significant additional problem for personality tests is their relatively low predictive validity in most work applications. Regardless of the research literature cited below and the view of many industrial/organizational psychologists that personality tests are not valid predictors of job performance, personality measures continue to be widely used.

The most recent example is the surge of interest in their use in screening potentially dishonest persons either prior to or after hiring (Sackett & Harris, 1984). This frequently involves the use of personality measures. For example, the Nuclear Regulatory Commission has proposed the use of the Minnesota Multiphasic Personality Inventory (traditionally used to assess and classify clinical patients) to screen job applicants for positions at nuclear plants where safety and security are important. Aside from the lack of demonstrated validity and the potential of faking answers on personality tests, your authors believe that serious invasion of privacy and ethical issues should be discussed and resolved prior to the use of personality tests for these purposes.

One successful use of personality tests for hiring has been reported recently by Bentz (1984). Bentz presented data collected for over 30 years at Sears Roebuck and Company. The conclusion Bentz drew from this research was that the pervasive academic bias against paper-and-pencil personality assessment is unjustified. Representative of the data he presented are the correlations in Table 8-6. These data were collected from a sample of 76 Sears store managers using the Guilford-Martin Personality Inventory. The average time between testing and gathering performance criteria was 17 years. Criteria included ratings of merchandising skills, operating ability, and people-related skills, as well as a general overall evaluation. Both merchandising and people-related skills are predicted at relatively high levels of validity. Prediction of overall effectiveness was not as good and operating ability was predicted significantly only by the dominance scale. In providing an interpretation of the prediction of the merchandising criterion, Bentz (p.11) offered the following comments:

TABLE 8-6
Relationship between Retail Store Manager, Sears Executive
Battery of Psychological Test Scores, and Job Performance Criteria

Performance Variables

Test Variables	Merchandising Ability	People-Related Ability	Operating Ability	General Overall Effectiveness
Sociability	-.331†	-.220	-.034	-.153
Reflectiveness	-.272‡	-.286‡	.044	-.157
Optimism	-.269‡	-.361†	-.024	-.148
Stability	-.099	-.215	-.141	-.097
Impulsive	.348†	.201	.084	.164
General Activity	.330†	.170	.173	.228*
Social Leadership	.269‡	.226	.110	.163
Dominance	.443	.391†	.213*	.301†
Self-Confidence	.318†	.324†	.077	.192
Composure	.134	.395†	.019	.082
Objectivity	.308†	.280‡	.107	.217
Agreeableness	.052	.170	-.002	.019
Tolerance	.169	.249	-.035	.093
N = Sample size	76	59	76	76

* A negative correlation is indicative of positive and more socially adaptive behavior.
‡ .05 Level of Significance
† .01 Level of Significance
Source: Adapted with permission from Bentz, V. J. (1984). Research findings from personality assessment of executives. Paper presented at meeting of Michigan Association of Industrial/Organizational Psychologists. Detroit, MI.

The store manager who effectively handles merchandising tasks is friendly, socially outgoing and at ease in most situations (Sociability = -.331). Naturally assertive, he readily takes over the leadership of any group of which he is a part (Social Leadership = .269) and functions with assured self-confidence (Self-Confidence = .318). He also has a kind of fast-moving, enthusiastic exuberance that allows him to express himself readily (General Activity = .330; Impulsive = .348) and carry others along with him. He likes excitement and change and may be somewhat impatient with those who do not function as quickly or as enthusiastically as does he. Sensitive to the subtleties and nuances of situations (Reflectiveness = -.272), his thinking is also closely tied to reality. His high objectivity is unlikely to let personal feelings or emotions color his evaluation of situations or ideas (Objective = .308). Cheerful and optimistic of mood (Optimism = -.269), he has the kind of emotionally robust outlook that allows him to encounter a wide range of situations without being personally bothered (Dominance = .443).

Projective Tests

Another type of personality instrument called a *projective test*, involves presenting examinees with one or more relatively ambiguous stimuli, usually pictures or the beginning words of a sentence. A respondent to these projective tests is asked to relate what he or she sees is happening in the picture or to complete the sentence provided. It is assumed that the examinee projects his or her own personality onto the ambiguous stimulus and by reporting what she or he experiences, reveals the kind of person she or he is. Two projective devices that have been used relatively frequently in industrial contexts are the Thematic Apperception Test (TAT) and the Miner Sentence Completion Scale (MSCS).

McClelland and his associates (McClelland & Boyatzis, 1982; McClelland, 1961) have used the TAT to assess the need for achievement (nAch), power, and affiliation. In measuring these constructs, the test administrator presents the examinee with a series of relatively ambiguous pictures and asks her or him to write a story about each picture, answering the following questions:

1. What is happening? Who is involved?
2. What has led up to this situation? That is, what has happened in the past?
3. What is being thought? What is wanted? By whom?
4. What will happen? What will be done?

The stories then are scored for achievement imagery; that is, for themes that suggest the person strives for accomplishment, ego enhancement, and recognition, or toward overcoming obstacles when confronted by possible failure. Numerous studies over several decades have indicated that achievement imagery is associated with performance on a variety of individual and societal criteria. Recently, McClelland and Boyatzis (1982) found low, positive correlations between the motivation patterns as identified using the TAT responses of senior managers at AT&T and the number of promotions they had received after eight and 16 years.

The Miner Sentence Completion Scale (MSCS) was developed specifically to assess motivation toward the performance of managerial work. Respondents to the MSCS (Miner, 1960) must complete sentences that begin as follows:

1. My family doctor. . . .
2. Police officers. . . .
3. Running for political office. . . .
4. Presenting a report at a staff meeting . . . .

To assess a candidate's motivation to manage, the MSCS provides scores for the candidate in the following six roles:

1. Successful interactions with superiors and the appropriate behaviors associated with such interactions;
2. Competitive situations;
3. Situations in which an active assertive role is demanded;
4. Situations in which the candidate must tell others what to do and enforce negative and positive sanctions;
5. Visible, attention-getting activities; and
6. Situations involving administrative tasks.

Miner (1978) reviewed 21 studies of the MSCS, all of which reported significant relationships between MSCS total score and a variety of managerial performance indices. Recently, Berman and Miner (1985) report similar results for a group of high-level executives. Cornelius (1983) reviewed the literature on the validity of the use of projective tests in industry. Of 14 studies (the 21 reviewed by Miner on the MSCS were not included), ten reported statistically significant validity coefficients.

However, most research on the use of personality and interest tests—both structured and projective—has been discouraging. The major tests of personality were not developed for use in the industrial setting; therefore, their typically unimpressive validity in distinguishing successful from unsuccessful employees is not surprising. Stogdill's early review (1948) of the predictability of leadership effectiveness using personality traits indicated little or no validity. Reviews by Guion and Gottier (1965) and by Ghiselli (1973) were equally negative regarding the use of personality tests in other work occupations. Attacks on the use of these tests are commonplace in the industrial psychology literature and in textbooks (Campbell, Dunnette, Lawler, & Weick, 1970; Korman, 1977; Landy & Trumbo, 1980; Muchinsky, 1987). More recent reviews of the validity of personality measures continue to yield evidence of low validity (Schmitt, Gooding, Noe, & Kirsch, 1984). The average of 62 validity coefficients for personality measures was only .15.

In summary, industrial/organizational psychologists and human resource personnel have not found personality tests particularly useful in the work setting. However, research such as that by McClelland and Boyatzis (1982), Miner (1978), and Bentz (1984) suggests that more thorough research be directed to the use of personality instruments. Schmitt and Schneider (1983) indicate several ways in which that research could be improved over earlier attempts. First, validation efforts should include larger samples and longitudinal data collection. Second, job analysis data should be used to develop more appropriate rationally derived hypotheses about what personality constructs are critical to job performance. Third, measures specifically constructed to measure these constructs in particular work settings should provide the largest possible validity coefficients and tests of hypothesized personality-performance relationships. One positive feature of personality inventories is that there is no evidence that scores on them are related to subgroup status.

REFERENCE CHECKS

A recent survey by ASPA (1983) indicated that the most frequently used selection procedure is a letter of recommendation or *reference check*.

The Nature of Reference Checks

Letters of reference usually are requested of former employees, but it is unusual to provide much guidance to the letter writer concerning the evaluations he or she should provide. McCormick and Ilgen (1980) have listed four conditions that they feel the letter writer must meet if letters of reference are to be valid predictors of job performance:

1. The letter writer must have an opportunity to observe the applicant on the job; to actually watch him or her perform.
2. The letter writer should have the technical competence to accurately judge the job applicant's performance.
3. The letter writer must be able to express clearly her or his evaluations; and
4. The letter writer must be willing to give a frank and open evaluation.

Problems with Reference Checks

The fact that any one of these conditions are not met may contribute to lowered validity for reference checks, but it is most likely that the last condition is the most significant. As a general rule, people are reluctant to write unflattering things about past employees. A further contribution to this problem is the fact that job applicants may retain their right to have access to letters of recommendation under freedom of information guidelines. A person writing a letter may be much more reluctant to write anything negative if he or she knows that the person who is the subject of the letter will have access to it. It also is becoming increasingly common for employers to record only job titles and dates of employment in letters of reference for fear of being sued for a bad letter of reference.

Attempts to overcome the reluctance to be frank and open in letters of recommendation have taken two forms. Employers have developed highly structured questionnaires in which they require the letter writer to answer specific questions about the applicant and to evaluate her or his past job behavior along specific dimensions. At least this type of recommendation provides standardized and comparable information across job applicants. A second approach is to simply call the letter writer and review the letter and applicant with the letter writer. Many individuals will provide a more open evaluation orally; in addition, statements in the letter can be pursued in more depth.

Muchinsky (1979) also reported the widespread use of the reference letter and reviewed studies of its validity. Validity tends to be greatest when the rater is well acquainted with the job applicant or the rater is the ratee's supervisor. The low average validity (.13) reported by Muchinsky (1979) may be partially attributable to low interrater reliability. Eighty percent of the reliabilities reported in an earlier study by Mosel and Goheen (1959) were less than .40. Muchinsky also makes the point that the reluctance of referees to say anything negative about job applicants is equivalent to a range restriction problem; that is, all but a few letters of reference are very good, thereby yielding very little variability in the scores derived from reference letters.

Another potential problem with the letter of reference is cited by Miner and Miner (1977) and was alluded to above. They point out that various laws and court decisions may be likely to constrain the use of references and background investigations in order to protect individual privacy rights. The possibility of legal problems exists, but a survey of major American employers indicated that few have encountered any problems as a result of reference checking practices (Levine & Randolph, 1977).

Schmidt, Caplan, Bemis, Decuir, Dunn, and Antone (1979) have developed a procedure to select employees that combines the usual application blank completed by job applicants and the reference check. The approach requires that job applicants cite instances of their own behavior that are particularly relevant to a given job requirement and that they indicate who might be able to evaluate their behavior in that instance. The basic assumption in this approach is that past behavior is the best predictor of future behavior; consequently, a great deal of emphasis is placed on the documentation and reliable rating of actual past achievements, rather than on education and credentials such as degrees, licenses or certifications. The development of the procedure begins with a job analysis designed to identify knowledges, skills, and abilities (KSAs) that differ-entiate between excellent employees and those who are minimally acceptable. This information is used to construct an application form and the applicant is asked to describe at least two achieve-ments that are relevant to each KSA dimension and to supply the following information:

1. The nature of the problem,
2. What the applicant actually did,
3. What the outcome was,
4. What percentage of the outcome he or she believes to be due to his or her efforts,
5. The names of persons who can verify these achievements.

In building rating scales by which to evaluate candidates' listed achievements, subject matter experts are used to judge achievements for use as anchors on the scales. In Figure 8-8 on pages 274 and 275, we present applicant instructions, responses, and a rating form for one dimension of a behavioral consistency form developed for the selection of attorneys by Hough (1984). The

---

USING KNOWLEDGE

Interpreting and synthesizing information to form legal strategies, approaches, lines of argument, etc.; developing new configurations of knowledge, innovative approaches, solutions, strategies, etc.; selecting the proper legal theory; using appropriate lines of argument, weighing alternatives and drawing sound conclusions.

Time Period: 1974–75
General statement of what you accomplished:
I was given the task of transferring our anti-trust investigation of   into a coherent set of pleadings presentable to   and the Commission for review and approval within the context of the Commission's involvement in shopping centers nationwide.

Description of exactly what you did:
I drafted the complaint and proposed order and wrote the underlying legal memo justifying all charges and proposed remedies. I wrote the memo to the Commission recommending approval of the consent agreement. For the first time, we applied anti-trust principles to this novel factual situation.
Awards or formal recognition:
none
The information verified by: *John   Compliance*

A. One Dimension of the Accomplishment Record Inventory and an Example of a Response

---

USING KNOWLEDGE

General Definition	Interpreting and synthesizing information to form legal strategies, approaches, lines of argument, etc.; developing new configurations of knowledge, innovative approaches, solutions, strategies, etc.; selecting the proper legal theory; using appropriate lines of argument, weighing alternatives and drawing sound conclusions.
Guidelines for Ratings	In USING KNOWLEDGE, accomplishments at the lower levels are characterized by the resolution of legal issues which lack impact and importance or issues easily resolved by existing case law or precedent. At progressively high levels, the complex legal strategies or the resolution of difficult legal issues which may be included in a case or procedures of substantial import. At the highest levels, accomplishments may refer to the assumption of significant personal responsibility in drafting major rules, regulations, proposed statutes, or like materials. Awards or commendations are likely.

B. Rating Principles for Dimension "Using Knowledge" of Accomplishment Record Inventory

---

FIGURE 8-8   Example of an Item from Hough's (1984) Accomplishment Record Inventory with a Response and Rating Guidelines and Form
Source: Reprinted with permission from Hough, L. (1984). Development and evaluation of the "accomplishment record" method of selecting and promoting professionals. *Journal of Applied Psychology, 6,* 135–146.

approach of Schmidt et al. (1979) was intended to make application blank data more job relevant, and their initial validation work, as well as that of Hough (1984), is encouraging. The approach also makes the reference checking process more systematic, more directly tied to job related issues, and, potentially, more valid.

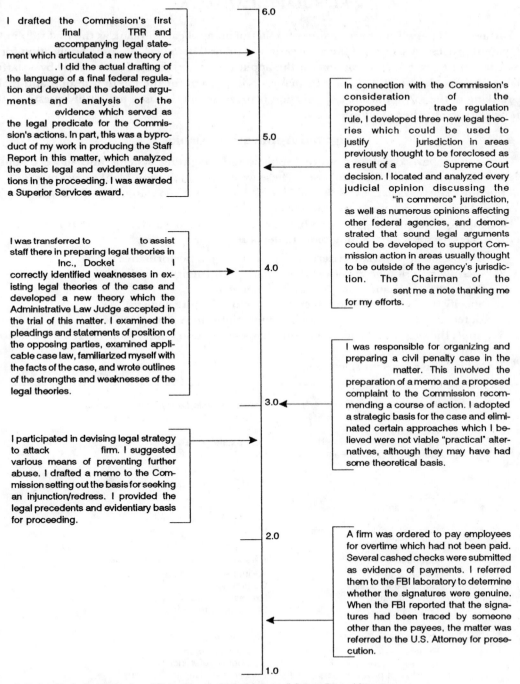

I drafted the Commission's first final   TRR and accompanying legal state-ment which articulated a new theory of   . I did the actual drafting of the language of a final federal regula-tion and developed the detailed argu-ments and analysis of the   evidence which served as the legal predicate for the Commis-sion's actions. In part, this was a bypro-duct of my work in producing the Staff Report in this matter, which analyzed the basic legal and evidentiary ques-tions in the proceeding. I was awarded a Superior Services award.

In connection with the Commission's consideration   of   the proposed   trade regulation rule, I developed three new legal theo-ries which could be used to justify   jurisdiction in areas previously thought to be foreclosed as a result of a   Supreme Court decision. I located and analyzed every judicial opinion discussing the   "in commerce" jurisdiction, as well as numerous opinions affecting other federal agencies, and demon-strated that sound legal arguments could be developed to support Com-mission action in areas usually thought to be outside of the agency's jurisdic-tion. The Chairman of the   sent me a note thanking me for my efforts.

I was transferred to   to assist staff there in preparing legal theories in   Inc., Docket   I correctly identified weaknesses in ex-isting legal theories of the case and developed a new theory which the Administrative Law Judge accepted in the trial of this matter. I examined the pleadings and statements of position of the opposing parties, examined appli-cable case law, familiarized myself with the facts of the case, and wrote outlines of the strengths and weaknesses of the legal theories.

I was responsible for organizing and preparing a civil penalty case in the   matter. This involved the preparation of a memo and a proposed complaint to the Commission recom-mending a course of action. I adopted a strategic basis for the case and elimi-nated certain approaches which I be-lieved were not viable "practical" alter-natives, although they may have had some theoretical basis.

I participated in devising legal strategy to attack   firm. I suggested various means of preventing further abuse. I drafted a memo to the Com-mission setting out the basis for seeking an injunction/redress. I provided the legal precedents and evidentiary basis for proceeding.

A firm was ordered to pay employees for overtime which had not been paid. Several cashed checks were submitted as evidence of payments. I referred them to the FBI laboratory to determine whether the signatures were genuine. When the FBI reported that the signa-tures had been traced by someone other than the payees, the matter was referred to the U.S. Attorney for prose-cution.

6.0

5.0

4.0

3.0

2.0

1.0

C. Rating Scale for Dimensions " Using Knowledge" of Accomplishment Record Inventory

FIGURE 8-8 (cont'd.)

BIOGRAPHICAL DATA

For most jobs, applicants are required to fill out an application blank as the first step in the employment process. A sample of the wide variety of items that appear on some application forms is presented in Figure 8-9. Information on the application blank is used subjectively by a staffing specialist who decides which type of information is important for the job in question and makes some ranking of the job applicants. Application blanks also may be used to identify questions that might be pursued further in an interview.

Weighted Application Blanks

Researchers have developed more sophisticated weighting systems and more extensive biographical forms for selection purposes. These weighted application blanks have proven to be one of the most valid alternatives (Reilly & Chao, 1982; Schmitt, Gooding, Noe, & Kirsch, 1984) to standardized tests, which have come under frequent legal attack.

Developing a weighted application blank is a complex process; Cascio (1987a), has summarized the necessary steps in choosing biodata items and their weights:

1. Choose an appropriate criterion (e.g., tenure, job performance).
2. Identify criterion groups (low versus high performing individuals).
3. Select the application blank items to be analyzed.
4. Specify the item response categories to be used in the analysis.
5. Determine item weights and/or scoring weights for each response option.
6. Apply the weights to a holdout group (cross-validation sample) and correlate total scores with criteria.
7. Set cutting scores for selection.

Personal
Age
Marital status
Number of years married
Number of dependents

General Backbround
Occupation
Occupation of relatives
Military service/rank
Parental family adjustment

Education
Level
Spouse's education
Subjects liked
Grades

Employment Experience
Previous occupations
Tenure on previous jobs
Number of previous jobs
Reason for quitting other jobs

Socioeconomic Level/Financial Status
Minimum current living expense
Debts
Real estate owned
Expected earnings

Interests
Hobbies
Sports activities
Prefer outside to inside work
Most important leisure activity

Personal Characteristics/Attitudes
Willingness to relocate
Confidence
Expressed personality needs
Stated job preferences

Miscellaneous
Source of references
Number of references
Relatives working in company
Availability

FIGURE 8-9 Examples of Biographical Items Used in Biodata Research

Reilly and Chao (1982) provide the most recent comprehensive review of the validity of biodata. They reviewed only studies that included a provision for cross-validation (Step 6 on page 276) of the scoring key. Their results indicate that biodata are a valid predictor for military occupations (mean $r = .30$), clerical workers (mean $r = .52$), management (mean $r = .38$), sales (mean $r = .50$), and scientific/engineering occupations (mean $r = .41$). Results were similarly encouraging across different types of criteria: tenure (mean $r = .32$), performance in training (mean $r = .39$), performance ratings (mean $r = .36$), productivity (mean $r = .46$), and salary progress (mean $r = .34$).

While the validation data generally have been encouraging, problems in the use of biodata do exist. Validity of biodata over a period of time seems to be less stable than for other selection instruments. Reilly and Chao (1982) did find evidence of lower proportions of minority groups and women being selected (adverse impact) when biodata were used. Dreher and Sackett (1983) also concluded that the use of biodata is relatively likely to produce adverse impact. There also are guidelines that restrict the types of questions one can ask in an application blank, biodata form, or interview. For example, the State of Michigan has an extensive list of questions that cannot be asked because of the potential to use the information from these questions in a discriminatory manner. In addition, Dreher and Sackett (1983) also noted a problem with the face validity of biodata items. They developed and validated a selection battery for a particular job, which had been commissioned by an industry consortium. When the validated battery was presented to the member organizations, a number of the participants refused to use the device because some of the items didn't make common sense (they lacked face validity).

Rational Approach to Biodata Content

Owens and his colleagues (Brush & Owens, 1979; Schoenfeldt, 1974; Owens & Schoenfeldt, 1979) have used scores on biodata factors to form life history subgroups that represent different life experience patterns. Membership in these life history subgroups is then related to performance and satisfaction with different kinds of work. For selection, one finds out which life history subgroups perform well and are satisfied with the work involved and selects members of those subgroups. This approach to the use of biodata is more rational than the usual empirical approach outlined above.

Pace and Schoenfeldt (1977) recommend that the most reasonable and justifiable approach is to base the choice of biodata items on a well-done job analysis, matching items to the knowledge, skill, and ability requirements of the job description. In other words, a move away from a strictly empirical approach toward a more rational approach may be necessary for legal defenses of the use of biodata information for personnel selection. This suggestion is certainly consistent with the approach to past achievements described in the section on reference letters on page 274 and if implemented may serve to correct the instability of validity coefficients derived from biodata. However, our discussion of this issue would not be balanced if we did not mention Mitchell and Klimoski (1982), who found that scoring keys developed with empirical keying as described by Cascio (1987a) were superior to those with the more rational approach described in this section.

JOB SAMPLE TESTS

A work or *job sample test* is one in which the applicant performs a selected set of actual tasks from the job. Job analyses serve to ensure that the tasks selected are representative of important tasks or problems actually encountered on the job. Procedures are standardized and scoring systems are worked out with the aid of experts in the occupation in question. Job sample testing has been used for years; some studies go back to the first quarter of this century (see Asher & Sciarrino, 1974, for a review). Early job sample tests in the clerical area include the Seashore-Bennett Stenographic Proficiency tests (Bennett & Seashore, 1946) and the Thurstone Examination in Typing (1922).

The Logic of Job Sample Tests

Increased interest in job sample tests is partly due to an article by Wernimont and Campbell (1968) in which they argued that samples of the kinds of behaviors or performances actually required on the job would be better predictors of future job performance than scores on aptitude or ability tests. They claimed that scores on aptitude and ability tests are merely "signs" that are statistically but very imperfectly related to future job performance. Their recommendation was to make the performance sampled by tests as similar as possible to the performance required by the job. This recommendation has received some support in a review of job sample research (Asher & Sciarrino, 1974) in which it was found that only biodata had a better record of validity than job samples. Work sample tests were found to be superior to both biodata and aptitude tests in a review by Schmitt, Gooding, Noe, and Kirsch (1984). Finally, Hunter and Hunter (1984) found that paper-and-pencil aptitude tests were about equally as valid as job samples.

Job samples also are popular because of the increasing level of criticism concerning the traditional ability and aptitude test. Much of this criticism is based on the fact that the content of aptitude and ability tests often appears to have little to do with the content of jobs. Job sample tests, if appropriately developed, are defensible on content valid bases and further, they look valid to the general public, to examinees, and to courts who frequently have little appreciation for statistical arguments related to validity.

Another potential advantage of a job sample test is that the difference between the scores of majority and minority group members is typically less for job sample tests than for written tests. A job sample test of apprentice skills in the machine trades was developed by Schmidt, Greenthal, Hunter, Berner, and Seaton (1977) and administered to a group of black and white apprentices. While minority apprentices took more time to complete the job sample test, their total score and two subscale scores were not significantly different from those of majority group members. Subgroup differences were observed, however, for a paper-and-pencil achievement test in the metal trades. When scores on a job sample test are based on the result of some effort on the part of a job applicant, there is little possibility of bias, but rater bias may exist when performance in the job sample is rated to produce scores (Guion, 1978). Brugnoli, Campion, and Basen (1979) examined the conditions under which race-linked bias in job sample ratings might occur. They found no evidence of racial bias when raters used a highly specific behavioral recording form or when making global evaluations. They concluded that careful development of job samples, and training and assistance for observers in focusing on and recording relevant behavior, eliminates the potential for bias in job samples.

Problems in the Development and Use of Job Sample Tests

There are some potential problems in using job samples, however. One is that they usually are expensive to develop and time consuming to administer, especially if raters are required. Second, job samples may not be practical because they are dangerous to the job applicant. This is especially likely in physically demanding jobs where job samples may be especially appropriate. An example of this type of practical problem is presented by Arnold, Rauschenberger, Soubel, and Guion (1982), who were interested in selecting workers in the steel industry. They solved the problem by using the job samples as performance criteria and developed simpler and safer physical tests on which performance was highly correlated with job sample performance.

Another very practical limitation occurs when the job applicants do not have the requisite KSAOs to complete the job sample. Siegel and his colleagues (Siegel, 1983; Siegel & Bergman, 1975) have dealt with this problem by constructing a miniaturized training test in which an applicant is trained to perform a sample of tests involved in the job for which he or she is an applicant, and following the training, is tested on her or his ability to perform these tasks. During training, applicants are allowed to proceed at different rates, they are given hands-on experience, and literacy requirements are minimized. A description of two miniaturized training tasks is presented as Figure 8-10. Schmitt and Ostroff (1986) have used this notion in developing a series of tests for emergency telephone operators. At early points in the examination procedure applicants are instructed to record critical information from telephone conversations onto forms similar to those which operators use to enter information into a computer. Later in the examination procedure, applicants are expected to use these forms in role-playing emergency calls.

Computation and Projection (CAP)

In the training aspect of the Computation and Projection (CAP) miniature training and evaluation situation, intercept course projection was taught. This included instruction about how to read a simplified plot diagram of the positions of two ships, their headings and speeds, and then how to extrapolate the new position of each ship after one hour and evaluate the danger of collision. Simple addition, subtraction, and ruler measurement were required to perform the work. After training and a practice session, problems were administered in a group session. Three subscores (projection, collision identification, and course change direction) were summed to derive a total subtest score.

Conceptual Integration and Application (CIA)

In the Conceptual Integration and Application (CIA) training session, the operation of an elementary, simulated electromechanical pumping system was explained and demonstrated. Potential malfunctions were diagnosed and the cause-effect relationships behind each diagnosis were explained. This ability to integrate facts and system relationships and to derive a conclusion about the cause of a malfunction is commonly termed "trouble-shooting." After the training session and a set of practice problems, 10 problems involving system malfunction symptoms were group administered. The task was to state the cause of each malfunction. Scoring on the subtest was determined by subtracting total wrong from total right.

Dual Task (DT)

The ability to share time between the performance of two or more different tasks is required for many Navy jobs. Watch keeping and equipment operation are examples. The simultaneous performance of two tasks was consolidated into the Dual Task (DT) exercise: simulated watch standing and fabricating a pipe assembly. In the watch standing aspect, the persons under evaluation attended to a series of "alarm" lights and recorded their time of occurrence. The pipe assembly task included assembly of a set of pipes in accordance with a schematic diagram.

During the training aspect of the exercises, schematic diagram interpretation and how to make the required measurements for completing the pipe assembly task were taught. In the evaluation aspect, the recruits were required to fabricate the pipe assembly while simultaneously monitoring the "alarm" lights and entering their time of activation on a simulated log form. The total score for the subtext was the sum of the pipe assembly and the alarm reaction scores.

FIGURE 8-10   Three Miniaturized Training Tests

Source: Reprinted with permission from Siegel, A. I. (1983). The miniature job training and evaluation approach: Additional findings. *Personnel Psychology, 36,* 41–56.

Clearly, job samples represent an attractive alternative to paper-and-pencil tests. However, a number of practical developmental and administrative problems need careful attention. Job samples also have been adapted to managerial positions in the form of assessment centers; in the next section of this chapter, we describe this technique and some of the research regarding its effectiveness.

ASSESSMENT CENTERS

Like other job samples, *assessment centers* are based on the behavior sampling assumption that the best predictor of future behavior or performance is present or past behavior or performance of the same type. Hence, efforts are made to construct assessment center exercises in a way that managerial job demands are replicated.

The Nature of Assessment Centers

A typical assessment center works something like the following. Based on nominations by their immediate supervisors, or, in some organizations, self-nominations, ten to 12 participants are chosen and sent to a central facility. For two or three days, they take part in exercises specially developed to reveal important manager behaviors. One popular assessment center exercise is the *leaderless group discussion* in which a group of candidates is presented with a problem (for example, a production scheduling problem) and told to solve it. The group's interactions are observed by specially trained raters who observe, record, and rate each participant's behavior. Another frequently used exercise is the *in-basket test* in which candidates are presented a set of memos, letters, telephone messages, etc. of the type that they likely would receive on the job and are asked to respond as they would in the event they had the job. Sometimes, candidates are required to play a particular role in an exercise; for example, a supervisor conducting a performance review with an employee. Traditional paper-and-pencil tests also are used, as are structured, in-depth interviews. Throughout all exercises, trained assessors, usually upper-level managers in the company, observe the candidates. These assessors spend two or more days after the center exercises are over preparing final evaluations of the participants, describing their strengths and weaknesses as future managers, and making recommendations concerning the candidates' promotability. In Figure 8-11, we present the schedule and a brief description of the exercises used in an assessment center to select school administrators. Two examples of the type of items appearing in the in-baskets used in this center are presented in Figure 8-12 on pages 282 and 283. The list of skills assessed in this center is listed in Table 8-7. This list is fairly typical of the skills assessed in many managerial centers.

Research on Assessment Centers

Perhaps the best research on the validity of the assessment center has been done at AT&T (Bray & Grant, 1966). In one study, 267 supervisory-level personnel were assessed, but the assessment center reports remained confidential, and were not used in any way. Eight years later, 82% of the college graduates and 75% of the noncollege graduate assessees who had been promoted to middle management were those identified by the assessment center as persons likely to be promoted to middle management. The ability of the assessment center to identify those who would not be promoted was even greater. Eighty-eight percent of the unsuccessful college graduates and 95% of the unsuccessful noncollege graduates were correctly identified. The critical feature of this study was that the results of the assessment center were not used in any way to make

Time	Activity	Description
Day 1: A.M.	In-Basket 1	Requires action on 24 in-basket items of a junior high principal.
Day 1: A.M.	In-Basket 2	Requires action on 30 in-basket items of a high school principal.
Day 1: P.M.	Assigned Role Exercise	Candidate is given a problem of decreasing student achievement scores and must prepare and present a report to the school board with the help of a resource person.
Day 1: P.M.	Role-Play	Candidate plays the role of a principal in a series of interactions with a dissatisfied parent, a poorly performing janitor, a student in trouble, etc.
Day 2: A.M.	Personal Interview	Interview covers educational and experience background as well as interests and hobbies and explores reasons for action taken on in-basket items.
Day 2: P.M.	Leaderless Group Exercise	Candidates discuss and come to consensus agreement about the strengths and weaknesses of the case study of a high school and its community.

FIGURE 8-11 Brief Description of a Two-Day Assessment Center Used to Select School Administrators

the promotion decision, so the results were truly predictive. Another important fact about the study, and subsequent followups of the same group of managers (Bray, Campbell, & Grant, 1974), is that sufficient time—eight years initially—was allowed for the managerial abilities of the assessees to display themselves in promotions. Especially when the number of promotions is the criterion, managerial ability may take time to display itself.

Assessment centers have been widely used and many other validity studies have been conducted. Meta-analyses of these studies (Schmitt, Gooding, Noe, & Kirsch, 1984) have indicated substantial validity—.41 across 21 studies. Gaugler, Rosenthal, Thornton, and Bentson (1987) also conducted a meta-analysis that included 107 validity coefficients from 50 studies. Average validity across all studies was .34. They also conducted a variety of analyses designed to assess the degree to which various factors might affect the level of validity. Validities were highest when ratings of

February 28

R.A. Howard, Principal
Avon High School

Dear Mr. Principal,

   I have observed a number of high school students smoking
dope on my property during and after school hours.

   Yesterday, I was startled to see a group of students
amusing themselves by breaking pop bottles in the empty lot
adjacent to my home. I went outside and yelled to them to get
off of my property.

   If you don't take any action I'm going to go to the police. I'm
fed up with this!!

                                                Jean Wagner

FIGURE 8-12 Type of Items Appearing in the In-Baskets Used in an Assessment Center

managerial potential served as a criterion, when the percentage of female assessees was high, when several evaluation devices were used, when assessors were psychologists rather than managers, when peer evaluation was used, and when the study was judged to be methodologically sound. A large number of other factors appeared to have no effect on the size of the validity coefficient. While Gaugler et al. (1987) concluded that the validity of assessment center ratings did generalize in the sense that validities were all well above zero, some unexplained variability in coefficients remained suggesting there are circumstances that may produce higher or lower validities.

Other Advantages of Assessment Centers

This selection technique has a number of other advantages in addition to the evidence supporting its validity. The "face validity" of the center is a major advantage; assessment center reports and the assessment process itself have been favorably accepted by large numbers of managers. Experience as assessors provides valuable training and experience of use to managers on their jobs. They learn how to systematically observe and evaluate management behavior, which may be frequently necessary in their work (Lorenzo, 1984). From the viewpoint of the assessee, the assessment center experience often stimulates self-development efforts by focusing the individual's attention on his or her training and development needs. An assessee also might learn much more about the job to which they seek promotion, allowing self-development efforts or even reevaluation of their career objectives. Finally, assessment centers usually have been favorably reviewed by courts

```
┌─────────────────────────────────────────────────────┐
│                 Mr. & Mrs. Bob Charles               │
│                 8420 Sleepy Hollow, NE               │
│                                                       │
│                                        March 8        │
│                                                       │
│                                                       │
│         R.A. Howard                                   │
│         Principal                                     │
│         Avon High School                              │
│         1022 Central Drive                            │
│                                                       │
│         Dear sir:                                     │
│                                                       │
│         I'm writing in regard to a book that has      │
│         been made required reading for 11th graders.  │
│         The book is Catcher in the Rye and it         │
│         contains several sexual scenes.               │
│                                                       │
│         As a parent, I feel I have the right to       │
│         decide if the content of what my child        │
│         reads is appropriate. I believe that the      │
│         content of this book is immoral. I demand     │
│         that my daughter, Janet, be given a           │
│         different assignment.                         │
│                                                       │
│         Sincerely,                                    │
│                                                       │
│         Jack London                                   │
│                                                       │
└─────────────────────────────────────────────────────┘
```

FIGURE 8-12 (cont'd)

concerned with violation of guidelines on equal employment opportunity (e.g., Uniform Guidelines on Employee Selection Procedures, 1978). In fact, in one case, a court required that assessment centers be used to eliminate bias against women and to increase their movement into managerial positions. A consent decree involving AT&T, the Equal Employment Opportunity Commission, and the Department of Labor resulted in the evaluation of 1634 women over a fifteen-month period and the judgment that 42% possessed the requisite managerial skills. Moses and Boehm (1975) reported virtually equal male and female performance in assessment centers involving over 13,000 candidates, one third of whom were women.

Criticisms of the Assessment Center and Center Research

There have been at least two major critical comments on the assessment center research. Klimoski and Strickland (1977) questioned the use of promotions as criteria, stating that these criteria have less to do with managerial effectiveness than they do with organizational survival and adaptation. Klimoski and Strickland contend that assessment center raters are rating highly those people who can maneuver their way upward in the organization rather than those who are the most effective. Few studies exist in which criteria other than the number of promotions or the rate of salary increases have been used, but in one study employing performance criteria, validities of .20 to .30 were found for prediction of success as secondary school administrators (Schmitt, Noe, Meritt, & Fitzgerald, 1984). Moreover, Jaffee, Bender, and Calvert (1978) report significant

TABLE 8-7
Assessment Center Dimensions and Descriptions

1. **Problem analysis.** Ability to seek out relevant data and analyze complex information to determine the important elements of a problem situation; searching for information with a purpose.
2. **Judgment.** Skill in identifying educational needs and setting priorities; ability to reach logical conclusions and make high-quality decisions based on available information; ability to critically evaluate written communications.
3. **Organizational ability.** Ability to plan, schedule, and control the work of others; skill in using resources in an optimal fashion; ability to deal with a volume of paper work and heavy demands on one's time.
4. **Decisiveness.** Ability to recognize when a decision is required and to act quickly (without an assessment of the *quality* of the decision.)
5. **Leadership.** Ability to recognize when a group requires direction, to get others involved in solving problems, to interact effectively with a group, to guide them to the accomplishment of a task.
6. **Sensitivity.** Ability to perceive the needs, concerns, and personal problems of others; tact in dealing with persons from different backgrounds; skill in resolving conflicts; ability to deal effectively with people concerning emotional issues; knowing what information to communicate and to whom.
7. **Range of interests.** Competence to discuss a variety of subjects (educational, political, economic, etc.); desire to actively participate in events.
8. **Personal motivation.** Showing that work is important to personal satisfaction; a need to achieve in all activities attempted; ability to be self-policing.
9. **Educational values.** Possession of well-reasoned education and philosophy; receptiveness to change and new ideas.
10. **Stress tolerance.** Ability to perform under pressure and opposition; ability to think on one's feet.
11. **Oral communication skill.** Ability to make a clear oral presentation of ideas and facts.
12. **Written communication skill.** Ability to express ideas clearly in writing; to write appropriately for different audiences—students, teachers, parents, other administrators.

---

validities between assessment center ratings and subordinates' absences, grievances, and visits to the infirmary. However, more recently, Turnage and Muchinsky (1984) reported a study in which assessment judgments were found to be predictive of promotability but were unrelated to job performance. Whatever the validity of the Klimoski-Strickland hypothesis, more studies of assessment center validity employing a variety of criteria of managerial effectiveness are needed. In a recent paper, Klimoski and Brickner (1987) explored the evidence for a variety of explanations of assessment center validity and concluded that while there is evidence that assessment centers yield valid predictions, we do not know why.

Another problem with assessment center research has been noted by Sackett and Dreher (1981). Earlier we noted that the center produces ratings on several skill dimensions as a result of performance in various exercises. Sackett and Dreher (1982) argued that if ratings on skill dimensions are meaningful, then ratings of the same skills obtained in different exercises ought to correlate highly with each other and ratings on different skills obtained from the same exercise should not correlate highly with each other. Sackett and Dreher (1982), Sackett and Harris (1983), and Turnage and Muchinsky (1982) all produce evidence contrary to this expectation; that is, correlations among different skills obtained in the same exercise were highly correlated and correlations between ratings of the same skill from different exercises were low. While this finding does not support the construct validity of the individual skill dimensions assessed in the center and calls into question the notion that the assessment center is defensible on content valid bases, it does not invalidate the criterion-related research on the validity of the technique.

PHYSICAL ABILITY TESTS

No discussion of employment testing would be complete without a section on physical ability testing.

Controversy over Physical Abilities Measurement

Physical tests usually have been the domain of medical personnel, whose primary concern was whether an applicant would experience any health risk on a job. Increased pressure to show the validity of all parts of the hiring process and the pressure to hire women in nontraditional jobs has stimulated a relatively large amount of work on physical abilities testing, particularly in the last decade. Fleishman's work on physical ability measurement began 25 years ago, but only recently has his work been used to develop selection procedures (Arnold, Rauschenberger, Soubel, & Guion, 1982; Cooper & Schemmer, 1983; Reilly, Zedeck, & Tenopyr, 1979). Campion (1983) has reviewed the literature on selection for physically demanding jobs.

In the past, organizations have used height and weight requirements as indicants of strength and ability to perform physically difficult tasks. However, these standards typically were set arbitrarily and their job relatedness was not demonstrated; hence, in many cases, they have been ruled illegal (e.g., see *Blake v. City of Los Angeles*, 1979). Given the likelihood of adverse impact against females and some ethnic groups, the need to validate physical abilities selection procedures against job performance is critical.

Research on Physical Abilities Measurement

In a series of experimental and correlational studies of the actual performance of participants on a wide range of physical tasks, Fleishman and his colleagues (Fleishman, 1979; Hogan & Fleishman, 1979; Hogan, Ogden, Gebhardt, & Fleishman, 1980) isolated 11 physical abilities that are listed and described in Table 8-8. The Fleishman abilities have been the basis for most selection research on physical abilities. He begins by measuring the physical requirements of jobs using a method called *physical abilities analysis* (Fleishman, 1978). Behaviorally anchored rating scales are constructed to assess the job requirements along each of the physical ability dimensions identified in his research as well as to measure upper and lower body strength.

One such behaviorally anchored rating scale used to assess flexibility requirements is presented as Figure 8-13. Each scale is defined and described with behavioral anchors with which raters should be familiar. In the Cooper and Schemmer (1983) study, physical abilities analysis was used by a group of knowledgeable, trained raters to rate the physical requirements of the tasks judged to be critical for job performance. Ratings over 4.00 were used to determine that five abilities—upper body static strength, upper body dynamic strength, trunk strength, equilibrium, and flexibility—were the most important.

Two simple tests to measure flexibility used by Cooper and Schemmer are pictured in Figure 8-14 on pages 288 and 289. All tests were relatively simple, required little in the way of equipment or administrator training, and little in the way of examinee time. Concurrent validation of these

TABLE 8-8
Definitions of Physical Ability Factors

Equilibrium. The ability to maintain or regain one's balance or stay up-right when in an unstable position. It is required to maintain balance while moving or standing still particularly when external forces act against stability.

Flexibility. The ability to bend, stretch, twist or reach out with the body or its appendages. It includes extending the limbs through a range of motion at the joints and making rapid, repeated flexing movements.

Upper Body Static Strength. The ability to use muscle force in the shoulder, upper back, arms, and hands to lift, push, pull, or carry objects for a brief period of time.

Lower Body Static Strength. The ability to use muscle force in the legs and feet to lift, push, pull, or carry objects for a brief period of time.

Upper Body Dynamic Strength. The ability of the muscles in the shoulder, upper back, arms, and hands to support, hold up, or move the body or external objects repeatedly for prolonged periods. It represents muscular endurance and emphasizes the resistance of the muscles to fatigue.

Lower Body Dynamic Strength. The ability of the muscles in the legs and feet to support, hold up, or move the body or external objects repeatedly for prolonged periods. It represents muscular endurance and emphasizes the resistance of the muscles to fatigue.

Upper Body Explosive Strength. The ability to use muscle force in the shoulder, upper back, arms, and hands to propel one's own body weight or external objects in one or a series of explosive acts or short bursts of effort.

Lower Body Explosive Strength. The ability to use muscle force in the legs and feet to propel one's own body weight or external objects in one or a series of explosive acts or short bursts of effort.

Trunk Strength. The ability to use the muscles in the trunk area (i.e., the abdominal and lower back muscles) to support part of the body repeatedly or continuously over time. It is characterized by resistance of the trunk muscles to fatigue.

Stamina. The ability of the cardiovascular and respiratory body systems to perform effectively over long periods of time.

Coordination. Frequently referenced as agility, this is the ability to coordinate the actions of different parts of the body simultaneously while the whole body is in movement.

Source: Cooper, M., and Schemmer, F. M. (1983). The development of physical ability tests for industry-wide use. Paper presented at the national convention of the American Psychological Association, Anaheim, CA. Reprinted with permission.

tests against supervisor ratings yielded a multiple correlation of .54. Careful analysis and examination of the physical ability requirements can result in practical and valid prediction instruments for selection in physically demanding jobs. There usually are large mean differences between men and women in most comparative studies. Use of these tests will, in all likelihood, result in adverse impact on women, thus evidence of their job relatedness/validity is critical.

INDIVIDUAL ASSESSMENT

One selection procedure (sometimes a combination of procedures) that is rarely discussed in textbooks is individual assessment. *Individual assessment* involves a psychological evaluation of an individual (usually to identify capability to perform managerial or high-level executive positions) by a single psychologist. While we see very little regarding such psychological assessments in the scientific literature, Miner (1970) indicated that such assessments actually may represent the single largest activity engaged in by industrial psychologists acting as consultants. Little evidence exists on the validity of these assessments, but recently Ryan and Sackett (1987) reported on a survey of

Flexibility
This is the ability to bend, stretch, twist, or reach out with the body, arms, or legs.

How Flexibility is Different from Other Abilities:
Involves the ability of the arms, legs, and back to move in all directions without feeling "tight" and includes being able to move to a desired position (e.g., toe touching, reaching high above one's head, crawling through a very small space). This is in contrast to stretch factors, the ability of the muscles to exert a force.

Flexiblilty

Requires a high degree of bending, stretching, twisting, or reaching out into unusual positions.	7	Do a split.
	6	
	5	Lean out a second story window to wash the outsides of the windows.
	4	Scrub a bathtub.
	3	
Requires a low degree of bending, stretching, twisting, or reaching out.	2	Reach for the salt and pepper shakers.
	1	

FIGURE 8-13 PAA Flexibility Scale
> Source: Reprinted with permission from Fleishman, E. A., & Hogan, J. C. (1978). A taxonomic method for assessing the physical requirements of jobs: The physical abilities analysis approach. Washington, D. C.: Advanced Research Resources Organization.

members of the Division of Industrial and Organizational Psychology of the American Psychological Association that described the type of assessments typically conducted, what methods are typically used and how they are chosen, how information is fed back to client organizations and assessees, and how these assessments are evaluated.

The 316 respondents reported that they used individual assessment most frequently for selection, promotion, development, and career counseling purposes with middle- and upper-level managers. About 70% of the respondents said these assessments took between two hours and a full day and over 75% indicated they used one or more of the following techniques: personal history form (83%), ability tests (78%), personality inventories (78%), and interviews (94%). Less frequently used were projective personality tests and simulations. Those ability tests most frequently mentioned as ones that these persons used included the Watson-Glaser Critical Thinking Appraisal, the Employee Aptitude Series, the Wesman Personnel Classification Test, and the Wechsler Adult Intelligence Scale. The most commonly used personality instruments were the 16PF, the Guilford Zimmerman Temperament Survey, the California Personality Inventory, the Minnesota Multiphasic Personality Inventory, the Myers-Briggs Type Indicator, and the Edwards Personal Preference Schedule.

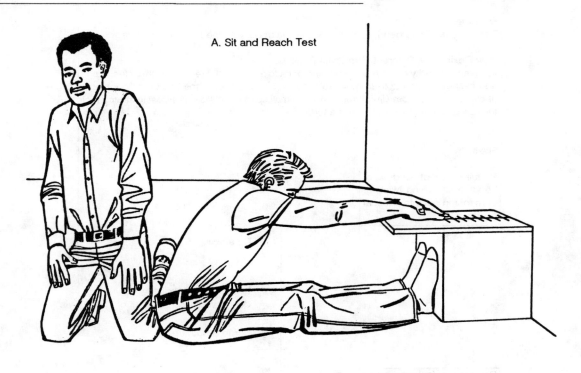

A. Sit and Reach Test

FIGURE 8-14 Physical Abilities Tests
Source: Reprinted with permission from Cooper, M., & Schemmer, F. M. (1983). The development of physical ability tests for industry-wide use. Paper presented at the national convention of the American Psychological Association, Anaheim, CA.

The various dimensions evaluated by persons conducting individual assessments are listed in Table 8-9. The basis for deciding that these dimensions were important was usually an informal conversation or interview with organizational members and rarely a standard or formal job analysis. Feedback to organizational clients most frequently consisted of follow-up phone calls or face-to-face discussions of reports with a list of the individual's strengths and weaknesses and developmental suggestions. About 60% of the Ryan and Sackett (1987) respondents also indicated that a narrative description of the individual with a specific recommendation was provided to client organizations. Self-reports of the evaluation of individual assessments by these respondents are presented in Table 8-10. A large portion (73%) of these respondents do indicate that they empirically validate their assessment process (though data as to how these validations are conducted is not presented) and virtually all (91%) report that they follow up with clients to monitor the performance of people they assessed. Moreover, a solid majority believe their procedures conform to the federal governments' *Uniform Guidelines* (1978) and the *Standards for Educational and Psychological Testing* published jointly by the American Educational Research Association, American Psychological Association, and the National Council on Measurement in Education (1985).

Because of the small sample sizes, the difficulty of collecting criterion data, the length of time it takes to collect meaningful criteria on middle- and upper-level managers, and perhaps because

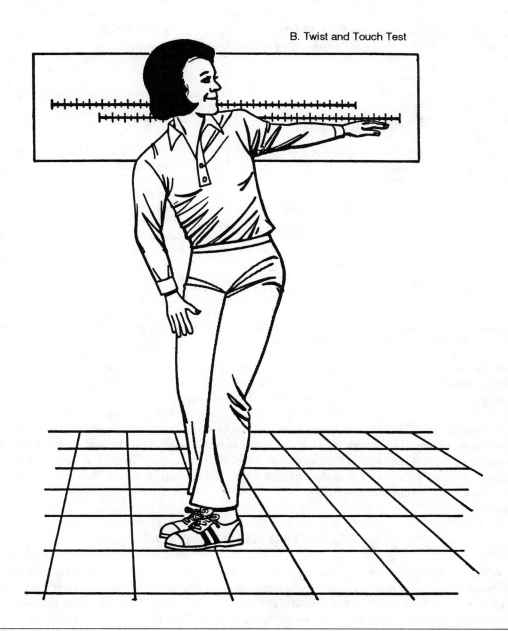

B. Twist and Touch Test

FIGURE 8-14 (cont'd)

of cost considerations there have been few attempts to empirically assess the relationship between data collected in an individual assessment and subsequent job performance. Of the few studies cited by Ryan and Sackett (1987), all but one were conducted over 25 years ago. Collection of additional data on the validity of these procedures would be useful. In the meantime, if we can take any lessons from research on other selection procedures, it seems that good job analysis informa-

TABLE 8-9
Dimensions Which Psychologists Attempt to Evaluate
When Conducting Individual Assessments

Work history	Flexibility
Verbal ability	Decision making
Motivation	Responsibility
Intelligence	Organization/planning
Judgment	Interest
Technical knowledge	Work orientation/habits
Leadership	Oral communications
Assertiveness	Sales ability
Goals/ambition	Stress tolerance
Communications (general)	Emotional maturity
Self-confidence	Self-insight
Energy/drive	Values/integrity
Interpersonal skills	Personality
Quantitative skill	Written communication
Supervisory skills	Creativity
Follow-through	

Source: Ryan, A. M., and Sackett, P. R. (1987). A survey of individual assessment practices by I/O psychologists. *Personnel Psychology, 40,* 455–488. Reprinted with permission.

tion ought to be gathered by the persons conducting the assessment and that that information ought to determine the nature of the information gathered and its weighting in any employment recommendation. Use of standardized, scorable data collection procedures and standardized ways of integrating information also seems necessary. While the clinical judgment of the assessor likely plays a role in many of these assessments, some attempt to recognize and document the importance of that judgment would be useful in any follow-up research and also may stimulate more systematic thinking about candidates' abilities and characteristics. As a very large number of high level positions are filled partly as a function of individual assessment, it seems that these procedures warrant much more research attention.

VALIDITY GENERALIZATION

While we have given the reader a general notion of the level of validity of various selection procedures across many studies, observed validity coefficients vary considerably from study to study even when jobs and tests appear to be similar or essentially identical. This variability has been taken as evidence that test validity is specific to a given situation. This means that to justify the use of a test, even a thoroughly researched test, a human resource specialist with adequate training must conduct a validation study whenever it is to be used in a different situation or company or with a different group of employees. This problem has been widely cited as the most serious shortcoming in the use of psychological tests to select employees (Guion, 1978) and has been labeled the *situational specificity hypothesis.*

Frank Schmidt, John Hunter, and their colleagues have reevaluated this situational specificity problem using meta-analysis (for a detailed description of meta-analysis, see Chapter 12) of

TABLE 8-10
Assessor Reports of the Evaluation of Individual assessment

1. Do you attempt to empirically validate the assessment process you utilize?
    Always   17.6 percent
    Often   28.8 percent
    Sometimes   29.6 percent
    Rarely   16.4 percent
    Never   10.7 percent
2. Do you attempt to follow up with clients to monitor the performance of individuals assessed?
    Always   26.9 percent
    Often   40.6 percent
    Sometimes   23.8 percent
    Rarely   5.0 percent
    Never   3.8 percent
3. For how long do you consider your assessment results valid (in months)?
                                              36.0 months
4. Do your assessment procedures conform to the Uniform Guidelines on Employee Selection
    Procedures?
    Yes   63.5 percent
    No   6.9 percent
    Uncertain   29.6 percent
5. Do your assessment procedures conform to the APA test standards?
    Yes   75.3 percent
    No   4.4 percent
    Uncertain   20.3 percent

Source: Ryan, A. M., and Sackett, P. R. (1987). A survey of individual assessment practices by I/O psychologists. *Personnel Psychology, 40,* 455–488. Reprinted with permission.

existing validation data (Hunter & Hunter, 1984; Schmidt & Hunter, 1977; 1978; 1980; 1981; Schmidt, Hunter, Pearlman, & Shane, 1979). Schmidt and Hunter held that true validity does generalize across situations and that observed differences among validity coefficients are statistical artifacts. The latter are due to various defects in the study, such as variability in the reliability of the job performance criterion and/or variability in the degree of range restriction that occurs when only a small portion of the job applicant population is available when data are collected to do a criterion-related validity study. The single largest source of variability among validity coefficients was attributed to small sample sizes used in most criterion-related work. In performing their meta-analytic work, Schmidt and Hunter pooled the results of validity studies for a given test type and a given job grouping and proceeded to determine how much of the variability in validity coefficients could be accounted for by these artifactual sources. If most of the variation in validities is accounted for by these "errors," then it is difficult to see how the situational specificity hypothesis holds, and the conclusion that validity is generalizable across situations is appropriate.

The meta-analytic procedure employed by Schmidt, Hunter, and their colleagues, as well as others (Callender & Osburn, 1980), is detailed in their various papers as well as in a book (Hunter, Schmidt, & Jackson, 1982). Their procedures also are summarized in Chapter 12 of this text.

Most of the validity generalization work has involved reviews of paper-and-pencil measures used in a wide variety of jobs, such as those described in this section. Hunter and Hunter (1984) and Schmitt, Gooding, Noe, and Kirsch (1984) have extended this work to other types of selection instruments as well. The major cognitive and perceptual tests always exhibit nonzero validities for virtually all jobs and most of the variability across situations in validity coefficients can be accounted for by statistical artifacts.

The data in Table 8-2 presented on page 260 represent the results of one such meta-analytic effort performed on 515 validation studies conducted on the General Aptitude Test Battery (GATB). While Hunter and Hunter clearly showed that the GATB subtests were valid across all job types, they did find variation in validities across jobs of differing complexity. Using the data and things categories from the Dictionary of Occupational Titles to derive a job complexity index, Hunter and Hunter found that the cognitive ability tests (GVN) were most predictive of job performance when job complexity was high, and that psychomotor tests (KFM) were most valid when job complexity was low. The pattern of validities for the perceptual ability subscales was similar to that of the cognitive ability subtests.

The primary conclusion that should be drawn from the validity generalization work is that paper-and-pencil cognitive ability tests are indeed valid and that there is no empirical basis for requiring separate validity studies for each job; tests can be validated at the level of general job families (Pearlman, 1980). Further, while tests can be used in many, if not all, contexts with confidence in their validity, the data in Table 8-2 indicate that there are substantial differences among validities for jobs which vary in complexity.

Validity generalization procedures continue to generate controversy (James, Demaree, Mulaik, & Mumford, 1988; Schmidt, Hunter, & Raju, 1988; Thomas, 1988) and the researcher needs to continue to update his or her knowledge of the literature on these procedures. We identify some of the controversial issues in Chapter 12. Another conclusion drawn by all who have attempted meta-analytic work is that research results should be described as fully as possible to produce maximally useful results for practitioners and scientists. Validation work should include information on (a) the type of firm or organization sponsoring the work; (b) the problem and setting about and in which the research is conducted; (c) the job title and code; (d) the job description; (e) sample size and sample characteristics; (f) the predictors—their reliability, intercorrelations and content; (g) the criteria and their psychometric characteristics; and (h) a full report of the data collected and analyzed to include any subgroup analyses.

After 85 years of aptitude testing and validation work, it seems we can derive some general principles of ability-performance relationships; appropriate reports of data collection efforts will contribute to the refinement and support of these principles.

ETHICAL ISSUES

Both in the administration of selection procedures and in the use of data generated from these procedures, the researcher and human resource personnel confront several ethical issues.

Professional Input

First, in selecting or developing instruments, someone must make the judgment that sufficient validation evidence as discussed in Chapter 3 exists to justify the use of the instrument to make selection decisions. This judgment should be made only after reading the evidence presented by way of validation and perhaps obtaining the advice of a professional. Such professionals usually will have at least a masters degree in industrial psychology or human resource management and most will possess a doctoral degree in one of these areas or a closely related field. They likely will be members of the Society for Industrial and Organizational Psychology (SIOP) (Division 14 of the American Psychological Association), the Human Resources Division of the Academy of Management, and/or a member of the International Personnel Management Association. Guidelines on the validation and use of tests have been published by the American Psychological Association and SIOP (American Educational Research Association, American Psychological Association, and National Council on Measurement in Education, 1985; Society for Industrial and Organizational Psychology, 1987). Particularly SIOP's *Principles for the Validation and Use of Selection Procedures* is a useful summary of the type of information that should be available about selection procedures and how these procedures should be used.

Appropriate Use

Information from a selection procedure should only be used for decisions for which it was intended and by persons qualified to make appropriate interpretations. The latter is particularly true when personality measures are used or when clinical information or interpretations are gathered as is done in the selection of security personnel. The need for confidentiality also is obvious in the case of letters of reference, but confidential safeguards are necessary for all test data. Organizations collecting such data on applicants or employees should have clearly defined procedures regarding who has access to the data and how it is to be used. These procedures also should include cautionary statements on the use of old information retained in files. Although selection test data may have some validity in predicting successful job performance or retention over a long period of time, it is likely that better measures, such as past and current job performance measures, may be available. Files should be retained for research purposes, but it would be unreasonable to use entry-level selection test scores to make personnel decisions ten years later. The span of time in which these data are appropriately used will vary with the organization, but the organization should take the responsibility of developing data regarding employee strengths and weaknesses that would be more appropriately and fairly used for subsequent decisions.

Privacy Issues

Use of some, perhaps all, selection procedures occasionally generate criticisms of an invasion of privacy. While this may be the case for personality tests and letters of reference, it also could occur for some interview questions and ability tests. Invasion of privacy criticisms can best be avoided by informing candidates fully (without compromising the test scoring or content) regarding the purpose of the selection procedure and how that purpose relates to the job for which the applicant is a candidate. In some instances, it may even be possible to allow the candidate alternative ways to document her or his skill when they find a particular technique or question objectionable. In all cases, access to information that might prove embarrassing to any of the parties involved should be protected carefully.

Reasonable Feedback

It also seems ethically appropriate that candidates be informed as to their relative level of performance in various selection procedures and the reasons why they were not selected in the event of rejection. We are not advocating release of test items or answers, but some explanation of how these scores relate to anticipated job performance might be helpful. In those cases in which large numbers of people are tested, it would be administratively or financially burdensome to routinely present this information to all applicants, but it still could be available to those who request that information. Reasonable feedback to applicants may satisfy an ethical requirement, but it also should contribute positively in the long run to the reputation of the organization among the individuals in the applicant pool.

Individuals who want additional information on ethical issues in selection and testing might consult the *Ethics Casebook* (Lowman, 1986), which includes various cases of appropriate and inappropriate test use and a discussion of the ethical considerations that apply to each case.

SUMMARY

In this chapter, we discussed various types of selection instruments beginning with paper-and-pencil measures of aptitude. The considerable evidence on the validity of those tests and the implications of recent validity generalization work was outlined. The validity and some potential limitations of various other selection devices to include personality measures, interviews, letters of reference, biodata, work samples, assessment centers, and physical abilities testing each were discussed in turn. In every case, we found evidence of useful validities when the use of a particular selection device was preceded by a careful job analysis delineating what workers did and what abilities were required, followed by subsequent development or selection of an instrument designed to measure those abilities in a job-related fashion. While many of these procedures and the methods used to validate their use (see Chapter 3) may seem beyond the reach of many small organizations or organizational units, they still may serve as a model of what should be done. Schneider and Schmitt (1986) provide suggestions as to how to meet this practical problem in the concluding chapter of their text. The literature also includes some good examples of relatively sophisticated procedures being implemented in small organizations (see Robinson, 1981; Schmitt & Ostroff, 1986). We concluded the chapter with a discussion of ethical issues involved in the development and use of tests.

DECISION MAKING ON HUMAN RESOURCE ISSUES IN ORGANIZATIONS

In this chapter, our focus is on procedures that are oriented to the use of human resource programs and their practical outcomes. While much of the literature in this area has dealt with the outcomes of selction programs, the practical utility of various human resource interventions, such as training and organizational development efforts, can be estimated using these procedures as well. In addition to the presentation of utility estimates, we also address communication of our results with other organizational personnel and human resource decision making in small organizations.

In the last chapter, we presented a model (see Figure 8-1, page 255) of the criterion-related validation model. Recall that the last step in this model was to assess the practical utility or cost benefit of the selection procedure introduced in the organization. Researchers and practitioners concerned with selection as well as other human resource issues, such as compensation strategy, training, and performance appraisal, are concerned with the practical outcomes of their efforts. Many of the procedures to assess utility described in this chapter were developed in the context of evaluating selection procedures. However, as we will see, the assessment of utility can be readily applied to other efforts to improve an organization's human resources.

In this chapter, we will describe how we use (a) the information we have collected about people and their performance, (b) the statistics we have regarding test-criterion relationships or the effectiveness of an intervention, *and* (c) information we have about the context in which work is to occur to make decisions about implementing a particular program or hiring and training people. As stated above, utility formulations were developed in the context of evaluating the practicality of selection procedures so our first examples relate to selection. However, we shall see that these discussions are equally applicable to other efforts to improve human resources.

PREDICTIONS OF JOB PERFORMANCE

Let's review the material on regression analysis presented in Chapter 2 using a hypothetical, but realistic, example in which we use the results of a criterion-related validity study of a test of simple arithmetic and an interview designed to measure interpersonal effectiveness to select sales clerks. The data from our validity study are summarized in Table 9-1. Since the validities reported in Table 9-1 are based on very large sample sizes (1200 persons) there will be very little shrinkage (Cattin, 1980) in the estimate of multiple correlation (see Chapter 2). In computing the regression equation (or prediction equation in this context), we applied formulas presented in Chapter 2. The formula for the regression weights was made simple because the correlation between the test

TABLE 9-1
Example of the Use of Results of a Criterion-Related
Validation Study to Predict Job Performance ($N = 1200$)

A. Means, Standard Deviations, Reliabilities, and Correlations between Test Scores, Interview Appraisal, and Job Performance Ratings

		$\bar{x}$	SD	Reliability	Intercorrelations (1)	(2)	(3)
Test score	(1)	15	5	.72	1.00		
Interview	(2)	8	4	.74	.00*	1.00	
Performance	(3)	22	10	.81	.35	.30	1.00

*As indicated in Chapter 2, computation of multiple R and regression weights when predictors are correlated is very complex. We present a simple case here.

B. Computation of Regression Equation †

Regression weight: Test = .35 (10/5) = .70
Regression weight: Interview = .30 (10/4) = .75
Regression constant = 22 - .70 (15) - .75 (8) = 5.5
Regression equation: y = .70 (Test) + .75 (Interview) + 5.5

† See Chapter 2 for formulas.

C. Predicted Performance for Persons with the Following Test Scores

	Test	Interview	Predicted Performance
A	15	8	22.0
B	10	4	15.5
C	20	12	28.5
D	20	6	24.0

D. $R^2 = .35^2 + .30^2 = .21$

E. $SE_{est} = 10 \sqrt{1 - .21} = 8.9$

score and interview appraisal was zero. Correlated predictors make these computations much more complex (see Ghiselli, Campbell, & Zedeck, 1981).

In part C of that table, we use the regression equation to compute predicted scores for three hypothetical applicants. The first, applicant A, has average scores on the interview and the test and, as we would expect, his or her predicted job performance equals the mean of the job performance ratings. The other two applicants have scores one standard deviation below and above the mean of the predictors; we find their predicted performance score equidistant from the mean, but in different directions. The squared multiple correlation (R^2) in the simple case of no predictor intercorrelation is the sum of the squared validity coefficients. Finally, recall that the standard error of estimate SE_{est} is the standard deviation of the errors we make using this prediction equation.

Compensatory and Noncompensatory Use of Test Data

The regression approach to the prediction of employee performance is said to be *compensatory*. This means that high scores on one selection instrument (i.e., a predictor variable) can compensate for low scores on another. For example, if we use the regression equation computed in Table 9-1 to predict the performance of an individual with a high test score (e.g., 25) and a low interview score (e.g., 2), we find that her or his predicted performance is 24.5, which is slightly above the average. If we have a person with a test score of 7 (quite low in this distribution) and an interview score of 18 (a high score), predicted performance would be 23.9. If we decide to hire individuals whose predicted performance levels are above 23, we would hire persons with quite different scores on the interview and test. In the first instance, the high test score compensated for a poor showing in the interview. The reverse was true for the second individual. In using multiple regression to make predictions about job performance, we are assuming that a person's relative lack of competence in one area can be made up for by her or his competence in another area.

For most human abilities, people can compensate for a low ability in one area with high abilities in other areas. For example, a relatively short basketball player may compensate for lack of height by quickness and superb ball-handling skills. Some abilities, such as eyesight, color vision, or physical strength, however, are likely to be critical in certain jobs. In these cases where a minimal level of an ability is critical, the compensatory regression model should be replaced by use of some noncompensatory or multiple cutoff approach to selection. In a *noncompensatory model*, minimal necessary levels of ability are determined and no one is selected who lacks these levels.

In Figure 9-1A, we indicate the outcomes associated with the use of two moderately correlated predictors (note that in Table 9-1 we had indicated a zero correlation between the test and interview measures so this figure represents a slightly different situation). This figure is a scatterplot of the relationship between a test and an interview with a line drawn across the scatterplot depicting the effect of a regression-based decision strategy. In this case, as above, we would select anyone whose predicted performance level was above 23. As is apparent in Table 9-1C and Figure 9-1A, there are a variety of combinations of test and interview scores that would produce a predicted performance level of 23 or above.

The multiple cutoff approach to the same situation is illustrated in Figure 9-1B. For our illustrative data, the interview cutoff might be set at 7 and the test cutoff at 14 (see our discussion later in this chapter regarding how cutoff decisions are made). Anyone scoring below one or both cutoff values would be rejected and those scoring above both cutoff scores would be accepted as indicated in Figure 9-1B.

A comparison between a regression approach to selection decisions and a multiple cutoff approach is depicted in Figure 9-1C. In this diagram the scatterplot between interview and test scores is represented by the oval in the diagram. A multiple cutoff approach would involve rejection of those below C_T and C_I represented by horizontal and vertical lines respectively. All those individuals whose combined scores lie above and to the left of the diagonal line in the diagram would be rejected using a regression strategy with a cutoff of $\hat{y} = 23$. The area labeled 7 in Figure 9-1C represents those test-interview score combinations that would be accepted using either decision strategy and areas 4, 5, and 6 represent score combinations that would result in rejections by both multiple regression and multiple cutoff strategies. Area 2, however, represents cases that would be rejected were the multiple regression strategy used and accepted if the multiple cutoff approach were applied. The reverse is true for cases in areas 1 and 3; that is, individuals with these

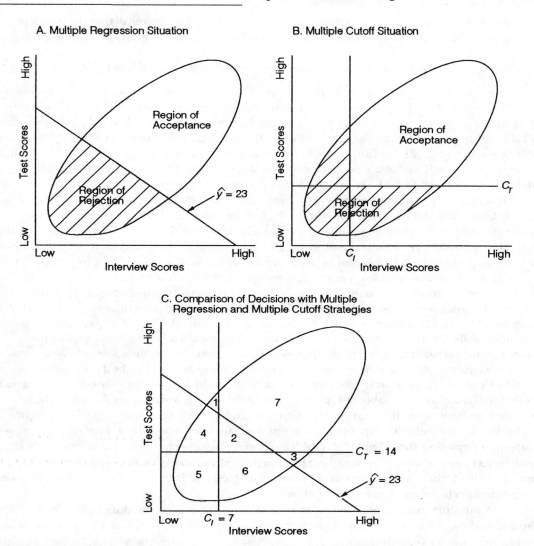

FIGURE 9-1   **Graphical Representation of the Effect of the Use of Multiple Regression and Multiple Cutoff Strategies of Selection with Two Moderately Correlated Predictors**

score combinations would be accepted if a multiple regression strategy was used but rejected if a multiple cutoff strategy was used. Person A in Table 9-1C would fall in area 2 while person D would fall in area 1.

As described above, a multiple cutoff approach is used when the abilities being measured are such that it seems appropriate. A *multiple hurdle* approach, which is similar to a multiple cutoff approach, also may be used for economic reasons. For example, the use of a simple paper-and-pencil screening test may be used to reject individuals who clearly do not possess the requisite skills and a more expensive assessment center technique can be used to evaluate the remaining candidates. The multiple hurdle approach differs from the multiple cutoff approach in that selection procedures are applied in sequential fashion making it unnecessary to evaluate persons eliminated by procedures used early in the evaluation sequence.

In using cutoffs, whether established on a composite score as in multiple regression or on individual tested abilities as in a multiple cutoff or multiple hurdle approaches, there are several things to keep in mind. First, what cutoff(s) are used should be based on the judgment of multiple job experts. Several techniques for establishing cutoffs are presented in the section below on decision making with content validation. Second, special attention should be given to reliability of measurement at the point in the scale at which the cutoff is set. Some type of banded scoring using the standard error of measurement (see page 100 in Chapter 3) may be advisable. Use of banded scoring involves treating all persons within a range or band of scores as identical in terms of the attribute being measured. We will discuss banded scoring in more detail later in this chapter in connection with cutoff scores. Third, if predictors are correlated and tests are used in a sequential multiple hurdle style, the range of tested ability on the latter tests in the sequence may be severely restricted. This restriction of range would diminish the validity and utility of the selection instruments used at the end of the sequential strategy.

This sequential strategy may be preferred because costs can be considerably reduced if, for example, an inexpensive general intelligence measure were used to screen out one-third of the candidates for managerial promotion prior to the administration of a much more expensive assessment center. If 600 candidates applied for promotion consideration and the assessment center cost $2000 per person (considering travel, accommodations, administrative costs, and off work salary time for candidates and assessors, this figure may be conservative), the savings would be $400,000 (1/3 X 600 X $2000) less the cost of administering the general intelligence measure. Using restriction of range formulas given in Chapter 3, we could estimate the effect on assessment center validity. For a full treatment of the implications of various strategies for establishing validity and utility, see Cronbach and Gleser (1965). Finally, if tests are used in a sequential, multiple hurdle fashion purely for economic as opposed to an administrator's well-reasoned judgment that a minimal level of competency on some dimension is essential, then special attention should be paid to the effects of these cutoffs on the employment of minority individuals and women.

Communication of Validity: Expectancy Charts

An especially useful way to communicate the results of a validity study is by means of expectancy tables. There are two types of expectancy charts; individual and institutional. The *individual* chart shows what percent of the employees fall into a priori categories usually given such labels as "above average" or "superior." The *institutional* chart shows the percent of superior or above average employees that will be obtained if only applicants above a certain cutoff are employed.

Four steps are involved in the construction of an individual expectancy chart:

1. Divide employees into high performing and low performing groups.
2. Divide the test score range into 5 to 8 categories in which there are approximately an equal number of scores.
3. Calculate the percentage of high performing people in each test score category.
4. Graph the results as shown in Figure 9-2.

This chart tells us that the 89% of the persons who scored in the 61 to 70 range were high performers; whereas only 23% of those scoring in the 10 to 14 range were so designated. Rarely do actual empirical expectancy charts provide as neat a progression of percentage successful candidates as in Figure 9-2 unless sample sizes are very large and the relationship between test and criterion is relatively linear (i.e., the test-criterion correlation is high). The empirical charts should

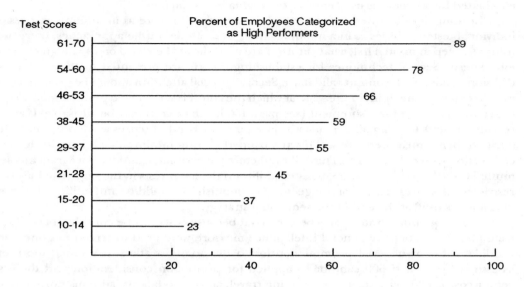

A. Individual Chart

Test Scores

Percent of Employees Categorized
as High Performers

61-70 ————————————————————————— 89
54-60 ——————————————————————— 78
46-53 ——————————————————— 66
38-45 ————————————————— 59
29-37 ——————————————— 55
21-28 ———————————— 45
15-20 —————————— 37
10-14 ———— 23

          20   40   60   80   100

B. Institutional Chart

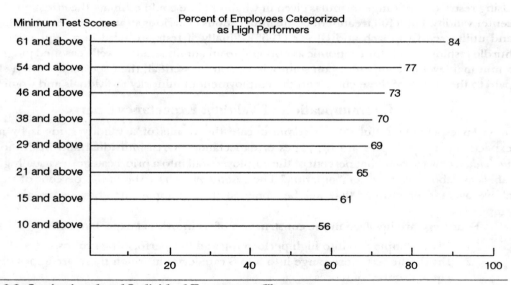

Minimum Test Scores

Percent of Employees Categorized
as High Performers

61 and above ———————————————————————————— 84
54 and above —————————————————————————— 77
46 and above ———————————————————————— 73
38 and above ——————————————————————— 70
29 and above —————————————————————— 69
21 and above ———————————————————— 65
15 and above —————————————————— 61
10 and above ————————————— 56

          20   40   60   80   100

FIGURE 9-2 Institutional and Individual Expectancy Charts

be converted to theoretical expectancy charts (Lawshe & Balma, 1966) in making predictions about a subsequent group of applicants.

The institutional chart is an illustration of what would happen if the labor market permitted selection of just individuals above certain test score points. If all the people in the group are considered, the percentage of people in the high performing group depends on how high and low performing individuals were identified. That is, the institutional chart in Figure 9-2 depicts a situation in which 56% of the people were considered high performers. If the company can afford to be very selective and hire only those persons whose test scores are above 61, 84% of the new employees would be classified as high performers. As such, the expectancy chart also can be used to specify the implications of a particular selection strategy for subsequent work force performance. With higher test score cutoffs, performance will improve more relative to the standard than if we are forced to use a low score cutoff because of labor market conditions or the inability to recruit highly qualified individuals. When this information is combined with information regarding the feasibility and expense of recruiting and/or training (if a lower cutoff than is desirable must be chosen), then a human resource manager can make much more informed decisions or recommendations.

Expectancy charts are simply a graphical illustration of validity. If there were no difference in percentage of high performers in the different test score intervals (in this case, 56% would be successful in all categories) or if the percentages scattered randomly above and below 56% then the validity would be zero. If the highest percentage of high performers occurred at low test scores and the percentage of high performers became progressively lower as the test scores went up, then we would have a negative validity.

Expectancy charts may be especially useful in detecting curvilinear relationships between test scores and performance measures. In the case of a curvilinear relationship, the highest percentage of high performers would occur at intermediate ranges of test scores while lower percentage of high performers would be observed at both high and low test score levels. Curvilinear relationships, however, are rare and when they do occur they often are due to statistical or sampling problems (see page 45–50 in Chapter 2). Consequently, human resource researchers should be especially wary of accepting an observed curvilinear relationship as a manifestation of the real relationship between variables unless these problems are first ruled out.

DECISION MAKING WITH CONTENT VALIDATION

As indicated at the beginning of this chapter, decisions about how to use test scores in selecting employees are made based on the empirical relationship between the test scores and a criterion. In a content validity study, we have no criterion on which to develop such strategies of selection. In this section, we consider in more detail two aspects of decision making that are part of content valid research—the weighting of components of a test battery and the establishment of test score cutoffs.

It should be noted that the issue of test cutoffs is also relevant for tests that have been validated in a criterion-related fashion. The fact that minimum test score cutoffs, as opposed to top-down selection of the best scoring individuals until all positions are filled, are used more frequently for tests for which use there exists only a content validation defense likely is due to a mistaken notion incorporated into the *Uniform Guidelines* (1978). The *Uniform Guidelines* state that selection in rank order from the best-scoring individual down until all available positions are filled is not appropriate for content valid tests and that such tests be used only with a minimum cutoff. However, the evidence for a linear relationship between ability and performance is overwhelming, and when this is true the expected job performance of a higher scoring person on a valid (by any strategy of evaluation) test is always greater than that of a lower scoring individual. Therefore, unless there is convincing evidence of a nonlinear test-criterion relationship selecting the best scoring persons is always the recommended approach.

The bases for weighting various components of a content valid battery are the ratings of various tasks or ability components from the job analyses discussed in Chapter 5. If, as should be the case, the content valid exams are built to represent major task dimensions, then their weighting in a test battery should be consistent with importance ratings as collected from job experts. These weights can be used to compile a weighted composite and applicants then can be ranked based on that composite. Selections then are made from the top down until all positions are filled. The test cutoff dividing selected persons and rejections is determined, in this case, by the number of job openings that exist. As stated on the last page, this approach to the use of tests in making selection decisions is likely the optimal one if our goal is to enhance organizational productivity.

Unfortunately, few problems are that simple. A very popular (although not scientifically based) notion of the human ability-performance relationship is that there is an identifiable level above which persons perform adequately, and below which their performance is substandard and unacceptable (recall our discussion of noncompensatory strategies of selection). Differences above this cutoff are typically ignored. This idea is most popular and most frequently used in civil service selection. Applicants take a selection battery and if they score above some point (usually 70% of the items), they are placed on a list of acceptable employees and then interviewed for positions or hired on the basis of some other criteria. Occasionally, the civil service will rank order people above the cutoff and then hire from the top down. This approach makes the cutoff relatively meaningless if the pool of acceptable individuals is large and the organization never hires the minimally acceptable employee. While our position is that for most human abilities there are unlikely to be easily defensible cutoffs, it is most likely that they will exist when physical abilities are considered. Eyesight is critical for many jobs; color vision is critical for reading color coded messages; some absolute level of strength may be necessary for police, fire, and heavy manufacturing work.

At any rate, test cutoffs are frequently required for administrative purposes in many organizations. If a human resource administrator is faced with the problem of hiring relatively small numbers of persons continually, it is hard to determine how many people should be tested so as to allow the use of a rank order strategy. Instead, the cutoff score allows the administrator to simply test people until enough individuals have passed at some score so as to fill the job vacancies. Job candidates, also, are much more familiar with pass-fail designations given similar usage in school; hence, it is easier to communicate the results of a selection procedure to applicants in this form. In this regard test score cutoffs can be established based on (a) judgments of the difficulty of test items or (b) based on the performance of persons whose ability to perform some task is known.

Several methods (Angoff, 1971; Ebel, 1972; Nedelsky, 1954) based on analysis of the difficulty of items have been proposed. Perhaps the most simple and applicable to employment situations is Ebel's method. Ebel proposed that expert judges make ratings of all test items on two criteria: difficulty (easy, medium, and hard) and relevance to job performance (essential, important, acceptable, and questionable). These two ratings produce 12 categories of items. For each of these categories of items, the judges are then asked to indicate what percent a borderline test taker would be able to answer correctly. The question posed to the judges is this: If a borderline test taker had to answer a large number of questions like these, what percentage would he or she answer correctly? In Table 9-2, we present a table that represents the type of judgments collected in this process. After these judgments have been collected from a group of experts, the percentages for each category are multiplied by the number of items in that category. The sum of these products for all 12 test item categories is the suggested passing score. An example of the calculations underlying Ebel's method is presented in Table 9-3.

An approach similar to the *Angoff procedure* (1971) was used by one of your authors to set a cutoff score for an in-basket examination used as part of a promotional procedure in a governmen-

TABLE 9-2
Example of Classification of Questions (Stage 1)
and Judgments (Stage 2) in Ebel's Method

Difficulty

Relevance:	Easy	Medium	Hard
Essential	Questions # 1, 4, 7, 8, 13	Questions # 11, 15, 22	Question # 21
	Judgment: 95% correct	Judgment: 85% correct	Judgment 80% correct
Important	Questions # 2, 6, 9	Questions # 10, 14, 20	Questions # 16, 25
	Judgment: 90% correct	Judgment: 75% correct	Judgment: 60% correct
Acceptable	Question # 5	Questions # 12, 18	Questions # 19, 23
	Judgment: 80% correct	Judgment: 55% correct	Judgment: 35% correct
Questionable	Question # 3	Questions: none	Questions # 17, 24
	Judgment: 50% correct	No judgment needed	Judgment: 20% correct

Source: Livingston, S. A., & Zieky, M. J. (1982). *Passing scores*. Princeton, NJ: Educational Testing Service. Reprinted with permission

tal organization. Each of 25 in-basket items was scored on a four-point scale with four being an indication of a superior answer and one being judged as a clearly inferior response to the in-basket item. A set of expert judges (supervisors of the position to which promotions were being made) were asked to review the in-basket items and to provide responses to the following question for each item:

> Consider a *minimally competent* applicant for a middle-level manager's position in state government. This is *not* an outstanding candidate, or even an average applicant but one that could perform tests at a *minimally* satisfactory level. Now look at each item and the scoring instructions for that item. What percent of these *minimally competent* applicants would receive a score of 4 on these items? What percent would receive a score of 3? Of 2? Of 1? The responses of one judge for one item might be as follows:
>
> | | |
> |---|---|
> | 4 = 0% | 2 = 70% |
> | 3 = 20% | 1 = 10% |

In this case the judge indicates that most (70%) of the *minimally competent* applicants can write a response to this in-basket item that would receive a score of 2. These results would be averaged over judges, and then totalled across all test items. This total would be the suggested cutoff. Obviously this procedure depends on the expert judges, but it does place appropriate emphasis on the merely acceptable performance level.

The contrasting groups method is another approach to setting a cutoff based on the idea that the test takers can be divided into a qualified and an unqualified group based on judgments of their knowledge and skills. Once the test takers (usually job incumbents in this method) have been divided into two groups, people with a particular test score can be considered and the percentage of qualified and unqualified test takers can be calculated. Assuming the test scores are related to their qualifications, then the highest proportion of qualified test takers should occur at high test score levels. As you go down the test score scale, the proportion of qualified test takers will become less than the unqualified proportion. One obvious choice for the selection of a cutoff is the point at which the proportions of qualified and unqualified candidates is equal. This choice of the cutoff,

TABLE 9-3
Example of Calculations from Ebel's Method Applied to a
Test Scored without Correction for Guessing

Category	Percentage Correct	Number of Questions	Expected score for category
Essential			
Easy	95	5	.95 x 5 = 4.75
Medium	85	3	.85 x 3 = 2.55
Hard	80	1	.80 x 1 = .80
Important			
Easy	90	3	.90 x 3 = 2.70
Medium	75	3	.75 x 3 = 2.25
Hard	60	2	.60 x 2 = 1.20
Acceptable			
Easy	80	1	.80 x 1 = .80
Medium	55	2	.55 x 2 = 1.10
Hard	35	2	.35 x 2 = .70
Questionable			
Easy	50	1	.50 x 1 = .50
Medium	*	0	.00
Hard	20	2	.20 x 2 = .40
			Sum = 17.75

Expected total score = 17.75

* Information not needed—no questions classified into this category.
Source: Livingston, S. A., & Zieky, M. J. (1982). *Passing scores.* Princeton, NJ: Educational Testing Service. Reprinted with permission.

however, assumes rejecting unqualified test takers is just as important as selecting qualified individuals which may not be the case. The cutoff may be adjusted up or down depending on the relative importance of rejecting unqualified persons versus accepting all qualified persons. The whole procedure is based on the assumption that appropriate judgments of the qualifications of some reference group of test takers can be made.

All three procedures to set cutoff scores involve the judgments of a set of experts. As noted above, use of a cutoff score also demands that the test used be highly reliable, especially at the cutoff point. These are particularly difficult problems for test constructors, but, in many practical instances, organizations or legal demands require that the cutoff points be established and that they be justified. Very little research on the use of cutoffs in the industrial context has been reported (see Cascio, Alexander, & Barrett, 1988).

ANALYSIS AND REPORTING OF AFFIRMATIVE ACTION AND EEO DATA

Any organization that directly or indirectly receives federal funding or remuneration for part or all of its work is required to report to the Office of Federal Contract Compliance regarding the effect of its hiring and promotion practices on women and minorities. The Equal Employment Opportunity Commission also requires an annual report of similar personnel data broken down by race and sex. An example of the type of data that need to be reported periodically are presented in Table 9-4. In this table, the number and percent passing in various sex and race subgroups are

TABLE 9-4
Impact of Hiring Practices on Minorities

Race	Test*	Cutoff	Male Pass	Male Fail	Female Pass	Female Fail
Hispanic	AR	70	33 (87%)	5 (13%)	85 (79%)	22 (21%)
	V	75	35 (92%)	3 (8%)	99 (93%)	8 (7%)
	N	65	35 (92%)	3 (8%)	98 (92%)	9 (8%)
	Al!		29 (76%)	9 (24%)	77 (72%)	30 (28%)
White	AR	70	343 (62%)	209 (38%)	1228 (74%)	440 (26%)
	V	75	508 (92%)	44 (8%)	1634 (98%)	34 (2%)
	N	65	459 (83%)	93 (17%)	1488 (89%)	180 (11%)
	All		305 (55%)	247 (45%)	1162 (70%)	506 (30%)
Black	AR	70	149 (60%)	100 (40%)	584 (68%)	276 (32%)
	V	75	232 (93%)	17 (7%)	833 (97%)	27 (3%)
	N	65	227 (91%)	22 (9%)	813 (95%)	47 (5%)
	All		143 (57%)	106 (43%)	567 (66%)	293 (34%)
Am. Indian	AR	70			3 (100%)	
	V	75			3 (100%)	
	N	65			3 (100%)	
	All				3 (100%)	
Asian	AR	70	21 (81%)	5 (19%)	26 (81%)	6 (19%)
	V	75	25 (96%)	1 (4%)	30 (94%)	2 (6%)
	N	65	24 (92%)	2 (8%)	31 (97%)	1 (3%)
	All		19 (73%)	7 (27%)	24 (75%)	8 (25%)

*Tests were Abstract Reasoning (AR), Verbal (V), Numerical (N). All refers to the employment of all three test score cutoffs in combination.

presented when three different tests, as well as all three in combination are used to make selections. These are numbers from a very large organization, but even in this organization, there were only three American Indian applicants and relatively few Asians (26) and Hispanics (38). These low numbers in a particular subgroup make tests of the impact of hiring procedures on any given group inconclusive.

In discussing various selection procedures, we expressed concern that on certain procedures large male-female or minority-majority differences were common and that use of these procedures would result in low hiring rates for the low-scoring subgroup. These low hiring rates produce what has become labeled as *adverse impact.* If there are no real subgroup differences in ability then hiring rates for different subgroups should be equal. The *Uniform Guidelines* have suggested that hiring rates for a minority group that are below four- fifths the hiring rate for the majority group should be used as evidence that an organization's hiring practices are potentially unfair (i.e., they are based on factors that have no bearing on the capacity to do a job). Failure to meet this four-fifths rule means an organization must then show that its procedures are valid and contribute in some major way to its continued economic viability.

A summary of the data for the groups in Table 9-4 and applications of the four-fifths rule are contained in Table 9-5. The numbers in Table 9-5 are for combined male and female subgroups for each racial group. As evidenced in the table, only the pass ratio for the black subgroup is below that of the white group, and, even in that case, the difference is small. The conclusion in this case

TABLE 9-5
Pass Rates and Application of the Four-Fifths Rule for Data Found in Table 9-4*

Race	N	% Pass	% Fail	Ratio of Pass Rates[†]
Am. Indian	3	100	0	—
Asian	58	74	26	74/66 > 1.00
Black	1109	64	36	64/66 = .97
Hispanic	145	73	27	73/66 > 1.00
White	2202	66	34	

* Ratios also could be computed for each sex-race subgroup against the white male group.
[†]A ratio of white passing rate to minority passing rate must not be lower than .80 to meet the four-fifths rule specified in the *Uniform Guidelines.*

is that these tests used in combination with the cutoffs designated in Table 9-4 are not producing hiring decisions that are unfair to either group of individuals. For a different outcome, see Table 9-6. Occasionally, human resource people have calculated tests of the significance of the difference in hiring rates, but the four-fifths rule seems to have been accepted by the courts and regulatory agencies. Clearly, with low numbers of people in a subgroup, computation of either a test of significance or a ratio of hiring rates should not be taken as conclusive evidence of anything. Further, calculations of the four-fifths rule and the test of significance for the difference in proportions (see Downie & Heath, 1970) lead to contradictions in various cases. In the top half of Table 9-6 we illustrate a case in which the four-fifths rule is clearly not met, but for low sample sizes (and low power, see Chapter 2), the test of significance of the difference between proportions yields a nonsignificant outcome. In the bottom half of Table 9-6, we illustrate an instance in which

TABLE 9-6
Illustration of the Difference between Application
of the Four-Fifths Rule and the Statistical Significance Test

No. of Candidates	No. of Minority Candidates	No. and Proportion of Minority Hired	No. of Majority Candidates	No. and Proportion of Majority Hired	Ratio of Pass Rates	Tests of Significance
20	4	1 (.25)	16	9 (.56)	.25/.56 = .45	Nonsignificant
60	12	3 (.25)	48	27 (.56)	.25/.56 = .45	$P < .05$
100	20	5 (.25)	80	45 (.56)	.25/.56 = .45	$P < .05$
200	40	10 (.25)	160	90 (.56)	.25/.56 = .45	$P < .05$
500	100	25 (.25)	400	225 (.56)	.25/.56 = .45	$P < .05$

No. of Candidates	No. of Minority Candidates	No. and Proportion of Minority Hired	No. of Majority Candidates	No. and Proportion of Majority Hired	Ratio of Pass Rates	Tests of Significance
20	5	2 (.40)	15	7 (.47)	.40/.47 = .85	Nonsignificant
60	15	6 (.40)	45	21 (.47)	.40/.47 = .85	Nonsignificant
100	25	10 (.40)	75	35 (.47)	.40/.47 = .85	$P < .05$
200	50	20 (.40)	150	70 (.47)	.40/.47 = .85	$P < .05$
500	125	50 (.40)	375	175 (.47)	.40/.47 = .85	$P < .05$

the four-fifths rule is met, but with larger sample sizes and greater statistical power, the test of significance yields the opposite conclusion; that is, a significantly smaller proportion of minority candidates are being hired. Various aspects of governmental regulation of personnel practices and their implications for decisions and practice are detailed in Ledvinka (1982).

One last issue regarding adverse impact relates to the earlier discussion in this chapter regarding the setting of cutoff points. If there are subgroup differences in scores, then the higher the cutoff on the test is set, the greater will be the adverse impact on the lower- scoring group. This effect is illustrated in Table 9-7 for a test developed by one of your authors as one criterion in making promotional decisions to mid-management positions in a state governmental department. A total of 177 were tested; 126 were white candidates, 51 were minority candidates. Scores ranged from 33 to 84. The result of setting cutoffs at various places in the test score range is depicted for both subgroups in Table 9-7. As can be seen, high cutoff scores result in very few individuals in the minority group passing relative to the majority group. As the cutoff score is lowered to 55 or lower, we see that the four-fifths criterion would be met. At higher cutoff scores, particularly 70 or above, it is clear that the proportion of minority applicants hired would be much lower than the proportion of white applicants hired.

There are various ways of adapting to the outcome. One approach is to establish a relatively low test score cutoff and randomly select above that point. This would have the effect of producing equal majority and minority hiring rates with relatively large numbers of people being selected. However, the disadvantage is that this approach ignores the often substantial individual differences in test scores and expected performance above the cutoff. A second approach is to rank order applicants in both groups and select from the top down. The number selected from both groups is equal to their proportional representation in the relevant labor pool. The latter approach maximizes predicted job performance while also satisfying the need to meet the social requirements related to equal opportunity. This approach, though, has been characterized as selection by ethnic status (and consequently is illegal) and was the object of study by a National Academy of Sciences panel. This panel (Hartigan & Wigdor, 1989) suggested consideration of a third approach: performance-based scoring. This approach adds a correction to minority scores equal to $(1-r^2)m$ where r

TABLE 9-7
Adverse Impact Analysis at Different Cutoff-Scores

Cutoff	Number Majority Passing	Number Minorities Passing	Percentage Majority Passing	Percentage Minorities Passing	Adverse Impact Ratio		
84	2	0	1.6	0.0	0.0 / 1.6	=	.00
79	6	1	4.8	2.0	2.0 / 4.8	=	.42
75	21	2	16.7	3.9	3.9 / 16.7	=	.23
70	42	4	33.3	7.8	7.8 / 33.3	=	.23
65	75	24	59.5	47.1	47.1 / 59.5	=	.79
60	94	29	74.6	56.9	56.9 / 74.6	=	.76
55	110	37	87.3	72.5	72.5 / 87.3	=	.83
50	120	43	95.2	84.3	84.3 / 95.2	=	.89
45	123	46	97.6	90.2	90.2 / 97.6	=	.92
40	124	49	98.4	96.1	96.1 / 98.4	=	.98
36	126	50	100.0	98.0	98.0 / 100.0	=	.98
33	126	51	100.0	100.0	100.0 / 100.0	=	1.00

is the test validity and m is the mean difference between majority and minority. This approach is little different than the within group scoring method with the usual level of test validity. As validity approaches 1.00, this approach yields results that are similar to top-down scoring.

ASSESSING THE PRACTICAL UTILITY OF SELECTION PROCEDURES

Researchers often have reported significant validity coefficients (relating scores on some selection procedure to some measure of job performance) as proof of the test's usefulness. The assumption was that managerial decision makers could see the great importance of human resource programs. Management is left the chore of comparing the assertions of human resources experts with those of organizational members who typically document their claims and requests in monetary terms. For example, a production manager comes with a request for new machinery and supports her or his request with projected increases in productivity and resultant decreases in unit production costs. The sales manager supports his or her request for a centralized computer system to process orders with figures concerning the amount of salesperson time saved and estimates of the increased amount of sales that could be generated during this time. Our point is that a personnel manager or human resource expert must compete for scarce organizational resources in the same language as her or his colleagues. A plea that human resource professionals learn and use the language of economists has been voiced repeatedly in recent years (Cascio, 1987b; Dunnette & Borman, 1979; Schmidt, Hunter, McKenzie, & Muldrow, 1979; Tenopyr, 1981; 1983). Their concern for *utility analysis* has resulted in the development of procedures by which validity coefficients can be translated into dollar and cent values.

These translations are important for three reasons. The importance of their use as a means of competing with other members of the organization we alluded to above. It also is important that we have better information concerning the relative cost/benefit of various human resource efforts such as training, selection, recruitment, career development, etc. Should we spend more money on training employees or selecting them when we open a fast food restaurant? How much money should we spend to select middle level managers who can manage people effectively or should we focus on career development plans? Finally, on a societal level, it is important that we be able to provide information concerning the relative costs and benefits of making different kinds of choices when confronted with conflicting goals regarding human resource allocation. A good example is the apparent conflict between productivity and affirmative action goals.

Some may object to utility estimation on the grounds that human resources should not be expressed in dollar terms. However, by failing to consider our actions in these terms, we are saying that the values that are the bases on which decisions are currently being made are fine; we assure maintenance of the status quo. All decisions, even a decision to leave things as they are, are based on a set of values. We believe it is best that all parties clearly articulate their values so that fully informed debate about which values are to be maximized can take place. Use of utility estimates promotes clear statements about values. We hope we have been convincing in our statement of the importance of utility estimation. In the remainder of this chapter, we will trace the development of ideas and methods in utility analyses and present techniques that have been found useful in various contexts.

Psychometric Definitions: Index of Forecasting Efficiency and Variance Accounted For

Most early attempts at describing the utility of a test focused on psychometric considerations rather than on dollars. The first proposal (Hull, 1928) compared the standard deviation of errors we make in predicting job performance levels using test information with the standard deviation of the errors that would result from the use of random selection or nonvalid information. This index was called the index of *forecasting efficiency* and is expressed as follows:

$$IFE = 1 - \sqrt{1 - r_{xy}^2} \tag{9.1}$$

where r_{xy}^2 is the validity squared. This formulation makes sense if we remember that the standard error of estimate (the standard deviation of prediction errors) is equal to the standard deviation of the criterion when validity is zero and zero when validity is one. IFE, then, is the percentage by which the standard error of estimate is reduced when we use a valid test. For example, if the validity of a test is .60, the IFE is .20; that is, the standard error of estimate is 20% lower than it would be if our test had no validity. In Table 9-1 on page 296, the standard error of estimate is equal to 8.9 while the standard deviation of the criterion is 10. The standard error of estimate is 11% lower than it would be if validity were .00.

A second measure of the utility of a test is the square of the validity coefficient, called the coefficient of determination. This coefficient is the amount of variance in the job performance measure that is accounted for by the selection procedure. A test with validity of .60 would be described as a measure that accounts for 36% of the criterion variance.

Neither of these measures provides a very positive interpretation of the usefulness of a test. More importantly, neither index bears any direct relationship to the actual economic value of a selection instrument. In addition, neither involves a recognition that the utility of a test varies as a result of several aspects of the situation in which the test is used. Both lead to the conclusion that test validities must be very high for the test to be useful. Their discussion is important for historical reasons and because some human resource professionals still incorrectly use them as indices of utility. We turn next to more complex, but more appropriate formulations of the utility of a selection procedure.

Taylor-Russell Tables

Taylor and Russell (1939) examined the impact of selection procedures on the percentage of successful persons in the work force. In addition to the validity of the selection procedure, the effect of the selection ratio (proportion of applicants hired) and the base rate (proportion of current employees considered successful) on the utility of the selection procedure were examined. Taylor and Russell developed tables to aid in the estimation of the value of a test. One such table is presented as Table 9-8. This table indicates the percentage of successful employees one can expect to select with varying levels of validity and various selection ratios given a situation in which half (base rate is .50) of the current work force is performing at acceptable levels. All other things being equal, the lower the selection ratio, the higher the proportion of successful candidates who will be chosen at any given level of test validity.

The base rate usually is determined subjectively and is used only as a standard against which to compare the performance of some other group of people (new hires) or previous performance. Occasionally, the base rate may be more objective as it might be if a company were interested in reducing the current level of accidents involving bodily injury. The base rate also can be changed by changing recruiting practices. If a company can recruit in a way that allows for more highly qualified applicants, then any selection procedure will produce better results. Alternatively, if there is increased pressure to recruit applicants from any source, then a given selection procedure may do less well than indicated by the Taylor-Russell tables.

TABLE 9-8
Proportion of Employees Considered Satisfactory = .50 Selection Ratio

r	.05	.10	.20	.30	.40	.50	.60	.70	.80	.90	.95
.00	.50	.50	.50	.50	.50	.50	.50	.50	.50	.50	.50
.05	.54	.54	.53	.52	.52	.52	.51	.51	.51	.50	.50
.10	.58	.57	.56	.55	.54	.53	.53	.52	.51	.51	.50
.15	.63	.61	.58	.57	.56	.55	.54	.53	.52	.51	.51
.20	.67	.64	.61	.59	.58	.56	.55	.54	.53	.52	.51
.25	.70	.67	.64	.62	.60	.58	.56	.55	.54	.52	.51
.30	.74	.71	.67	.64	.62	.60	.58	.56	.54	.52	.51
.35	.78	.74	.70	.66	.64	.61	.59	.57	.55	.53	.51
.40	.82	.78	.73	.69	.66	.63	.61	.58	.56	.53	.52
.45	.85	.81	.75	.71	.68	.65	.62	.59	.56	.53	.52
.50	.88	.84	.78	.74	.70	.67	.63	.60	.57	.54	.52
.55	.91	.87	.81	.76	.72	.69	.65	.61	.58	.54	.52
.60	.94	.90	.84	.79	.75	.70	.66	.62	.59	.54	.52
.65	.96	.92	.87	.82	.77	.73	.68	.64	.59	.55	.52
.70	.98	.95	.90	.85	.80	.75	.70	.65	.60	.55	.53
.75	.99	.97	.92	.87	.82	.77	.72	.66	.61	.55	.53
.80	1.00	.99	.95	.90	.85	.80	.73	.67	.61	.55	.53
.85	1.00	.99	.97	.94	.88	.82	.76	.69	.62	.55	.53
.90	1.00	1.00	.99	.97	.92	.86	.78	.70	.62	.56	.53
.95	1.00	1.00	1.00	.99	.96	.90	.81	.71	.63	.56	.53
1.00	1.00	1.00	1.00	1.00	1.00	1.00	.83	.71	.63	.56	.53

Source: McCormick, E. J., & Ilgen, D. R. (1985). *Industrial and organizational psychology* (8th ed.). Englewood Cliffs, NJ: Prentice Hall. Reprinted with permission.

Consider a case in which the validity of a test is .50 and the selection ratio is .30. The percent of successful employees in this situation would be .74. With a test of .00 validity, the percentage would be .50 (the base rate), so the test results in an increase of "successful" employees equal to 24%. Or, the same test used in a situation in which the selection ratio is .80 would yield a group of job incumbents, 57% of whom are considered successful. An examination of the rows of Table 9-8 indicates that the percent successful is always greatest when selection ratios are low and that tests of even quite low validity can be useful if the selection ratio is low. Alternately, use of a highly valid test when the selection ratio is high will result in little improvement in the work force.

Tables for other levels of base rates are available in McCormick and Ilgen (1985). Examination of these tables for various base rates indicates that we achieve maximal increases in absolute percent successful when the base rate is close to .50. At low base rates, there will be small changes in absolute percent successful but large relative changes. For example, when the base rate is .10, the selection ratio is .50, and the validity of the test is .40, the percent successful when employing the test is 16. This represents an absolute increase in successful employees of 6% but a relative increase of 60% [(16-10)/10]. Therefore, at low levels of base rate one expects relatively small absolute changes although the relative changes may be quite substantial.

While the Taylor-Russell tables represent a significant improvement in utility estimation by showing the benefits of using selection procedures under different circumstances, there are two distinct disadvantages associated with their use. First, the Taylor-Russell approach neglects any consideration of (a) the cost of gathering information concerning applicants (that is, testing, interviewing, checking references, etc.), and (b) the cost of recruiting an applicant pool that is of similar quality but is much larger. Recall that the utility of a test is greatly influenced by the selection ratio and that to maintain a low selection ratio one must recruit and test many applicants. Discussions of the Taylor-Russell tables often leave the impression that the selection ratio is stable and/or the organization has little control over the selection ratio. However, labor market conditions are almost always variable, which means that an organization may need to vary the proportion of applicants it hires. Or, if it wants to maintain a given selection ratio, it may need to expend more time and resources in recruiting applicants. With heavy emphasis on recruiting, the organization must concern itself with the level of ability of the applicant pool (or as indicated above, changes in the base rate). Clearly, determination of the selection ratio is a complex issue.

Second, using the Taylor-Russell tables necessitates the placement of workers into successful and unsuccessful categories. When we are forced to "dichotomize the criterion" in this fashion, we treat all the employees in the successful group as equally successful and all those in the unsuccessful group as equally unsuccessful. Obviously, this does not reflect reality because employees perform at more than two different levels of effectiveness and the contributions of those at different levels are lost when we dichotomize the criterion (Cronbach & Gleser, 1965, pp. 123–124). If a base rate is determined by an organization, it is perhaps best identified as an organizational goal. That is, the organization decides that it wants some percentage of its employees exceeding a given level of performance. People who do not exceed that level are not absolutely useless, but simply do not meet some arbitrary goal set by the organization. The base rate becomes a standard against which to judge the effect of selection strategies, or other human resource efforts for that matter.

Brogden's Formulation of Utility

Brogden's treatment of utility did not necessitate a splitting of the group into two performance categories. Further, Brogden (1946) showed that the validity coefficient is a direct index of utility. He assumed that both predictor and criterion are continuous (not discretely categorized), that predictor and criterion distributions are the same, and the relationship between predictor and criterion is linear. When these conditions are met, a test with a validity of .50 could be expected to produce 50% of the gain in utility that would result if we had a test of perfect validity, or a test of validity equal to .25 would have half the utility of a test with a validity of .50. So, if an organization had turnover costs of $500,000 yearly, a test with a correlation of .50 with turnover could be used to make turnover predictions that would save the company $250,000 annually, or half the amount saved if perfect prediction of turnover could be achieved.

Brogden also showed how the selection ratio and the standard deviation of job performance in dollars (SD_y) influence the utility of a selection procedure. The change in utility per person selected is equal to the product of (a) the validity of the test; (b) the standard deviation of job performance expressed in dollars; and (c) the mean standard score on the test of those persons selected. (Note that the lower the selection ratio, the higher will be the average test score of the persons selected.) Multiplying this number by the number of persons hired yields the total annual gain, which accrues from the use of the test.

The implications of Brogden's derivation were worked out for various levels of validity and selection ratios by Brown and Ghiselli (1953) and are reproduced as Table 9-9. (A similar approach has been presented as the Naylor-Shine tables in Blum & Naylor, 1968.) The values in this table are the mean standard score of those persons selected. Using the table for the situation in which test validity is .40 and selection ratio is .20 shows us that the average standard criterion score of those hired is .56. By comparison, the average standard criterion score of a randomly selected group or one selected with a nonvalid test would be .00. If the standard deviation of job performance in

TABLE 9-9
Mean Standard Criterion Score of Selected Cases in Relation to Test Validity and Selection Ratio

Selection Ratio	Validity Coefficient																				
	.00	.05	.10	.15	.20	.25	.30	.35	.40	.45	.50	.55	.60	.65	.70	.75	.80	.85	.90	.95	1.00
.05	.00	.10	.21	.31	.42	.52	.62	.73	.83	.94	1.04	1.14	1.25	1.35	1.46	1.56	1.66	1.77	1.87	1.98	2.08
.10	.00	.09	.18	.26	.35	.44	.53	.62	.70	.79	.88	.97	1.05	1.14	1.23	1.32	1.41	1.49	1.58	1.67	1.76
.15	.00	.08	.15	.23	.31	.39	.46	.54	.62	.70	.77	.85	.93	1.01	1.08	1.16	1.24	1.32	1.39	1.47	1.55
.20	.00	.07	.14	.21	.28	.35	.42	.49	.56	.63	.70	.77	.84	.91	.98	1.05	1.12	1.19	1.26	1.33	1.40
.25	.00	.06	.13	.19	.25	.32	.38	.44	.51	.57	.63	.70	.76	.82	.89	.95	1.01	1.08	1.14	1.20	1.27
.30	.00	.06	.12	.17	.23	.29	.35	.40	.46	.52	.58	.64	.69	.75	.81	.87	.92	.98	1.04	1.10	1.16
.35	.00	.05	.11	.16	.21	.26	.32	.37	.42	.48	.53	.58	.63	.69	.74	.79	.84	.90	.95	1.00	1.06
.40	.00	.05	.10	.15	.19	.24	.29	.34	.39	.44	.48	.53	.58	.63	.68	.73	.77	.82	.87	.92	.97
.45	.00	.04	.09	.13	.18	.22	.26	.31	.35	.40	.44	.48	.53	.57	.62	.66	.70	.75	.79	.84	.88
.50	.00	.04	.08	.12	.16	.20	.24	.28	.32	.36	.40	.44	.48	.52	.56	.60	.64	.68	.72	.76	.80
.55	.00	.04	.07	.11	.14	.18	.22	.25	.29	.32	.36	.40	.43	.47	.50	.54	.58	.61	.65	.68	.72
.60	.00	.03	.06	.10	.13	.16	.19	.23	.26	.29	.32	.35	.39	.42	.45	.48	.52	.55	.58	.61	.64
.65	.00	.03	.06	.09	.11	.14	.17	.20	.23	.26	.28	.31	.34	.37	.40	.43	.46	.48	.51	.54	.57
.70	.00	.02	.05	.07	.10	.12	.15	.17	.20	.22	.25	.27	.30	.32	.35	.37	.40	.42	.45	.47	.50
.75	.00	.02	.04	.06	.08	.11	.13	.15	.17	.19	.21	.23	.25	.27	.30	.32	.33	.36	.38	.40	.42
.80	.00	.02	.04	.05	.07	.09	.11	.12	.14	.16	.18	.19	.21	.22	.25	.26	.28	.30	.32	.33	.35
.85	.00	.01	.03	.04	.05	.07	.08	.10	.11	.12	.14	.15	.16	.18	.19	.20	.22	.23	.25	.26	.27
.90	.00	.01	.02	.03	.04	.05	.06	.07	.08	.09	.10	.11	.12	.13	.14	.15	.16	.17	.18	.19	.20
.95	.00	.01	.01	.02	.02	.03	.03	.04	.04	.05	.05	.06	.07	.07	.08	.08	.09	.09	.10	.10	.11

Source: Brown, C. W., & Ghiselli, E. E. (1953). Percent increase in proficiency resulting from the use of selective devices. *Journal of Applied Psychology, 37,* 341–345. Reprinted with permission.

dollars per year is $2000, then the average gain per person selected is $1120 ($2000 X .56). Further, if ten are selected, the total gained is equal to $11,200 in the first year these people are employed.

Obviously, a critical feature of this analysis is the standard deviation of job performance in dollar terms. For jobs in which the contribution of individual employees to the organization is widely different, valid testing will result in large dollar gains; in those situations in which individual contributions are relatively similar, even a valid testing procedure and a low-selection ratio will not result in large dollar gains. Validity is linearly related to increases in the standard score on the criterion. Recall that the standard score is expressed in terms of the number of standard deviations a given score is away from the mean. Hence, we must know the value of the standard deviation of performance differences in order to make estimates of utility.

Brogden (1949) also addressed the role of information gathering costs in the determination of utility. Tables 9-8 and 9-9 indicate that utility increases without limit as the selection ratio decreases. However, Brogden pointed out that, for very low selection ratios, an organization incurs tremendous testing costs since many applicants are tested to hire relatively few people. At high selection ratios, we are testing many applicants to reject a few. In both situations, the SD_y must be large or the net gain in utility becomes negative.

Contributions of Cronbach and Gleser

In, 1965, Cronbach and Gleser published a book titled *Psychological Tests and Personnel Decisions* that presented detailed and sophisticated formulations concerning utility that had been built on the work of Brogden. In particular, Cronbach and Gleser pointed out that much of the previous work considered the cost/benefit of only one of the outcomes of a selection decision; namely, the benefit that came from hiring a successful employee. In addition, three other outcomes may result from this decision: rejection of individuals who would have succeeded, rejection of those who would have failed, and the hiring of individuals who subsequently fail. These four outcomes are displayed in Figure 9-3. Cronbach and Gleser (1965) maintained that the utility of a selection procedure was a function of the combined utilities associated with each of these outcomes and the probability of the occurrence of each of these outcomes. The probability of the two outcomes representing a mistake, is low, of course, when the test is highly valid, whereas the probability of desirable outcomes is high with high test validity.

One outcome of selection procedures that has been largely neglected by human resource professionals has been the false negative, the rejected person who could do well. The current legal pressure to hire minorities and women is in part a recognition of the costs associated with this outcome. The societal costs associated with false negatives may be very high, but personal costs in lowered self-esteem and lower quality of life (if all higher level occupations are closed) also may be high. Even with the current emphasis on translating utility estimates into economic terms, the costs associated with this outcome are rarely discussed.

Cronbach and Gleser (1965) also pointed out that selection was frequently a matter of passing several hurdles; that is, the process may begin with a campus interview followed by a job interview followed by the administration of a battery of tests. In this situation, the utility of any given component is more problematic. They also detailed utility estimates in which employees are classified rather than selected or rejected. In a classification strategy, the organization has multiple jobs and the task involves the assignment of individuals to jobs in such a way as to maximize productivity while ensuring the required number of workers are assigned to each position. Classification usually involves multiple predictors and a separate prediction equation for each job. The job for which a person's predicted job performance is highest is the obvious assignment for that person unless vacancies in other job areas are more critical. The gain in utility that results from

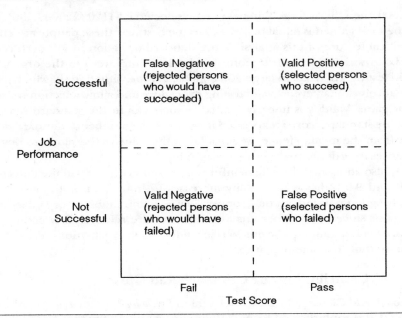

FIGURE 9-3   Four Possible Outcomes Resulting from Selection Decisions

a classification strategy comes from the fact that selection ratios for any given job are likely to be much smaller if there are many jobs with openings. Also of importance in considering the utility of classification systems is whether prediction equations for different jobs are sufficiently dissimilar and whether the SD_y for different jobs vary. Classification, of course, is possible only when an organization has many different jobs with large numbers of openings. The only application of classification strategies of which the authors are aware have occurred in a military context.

As we have detailed the various developments in utility analyses, one question likely has presented itself. How do you estimate the economic contribution of various employees, especially in more complex or people-oriented jobs? This question also has been difficult for researchers; in fact, little application of the notions of Brogden or Cronbach and Gleser occurred until recently. In the next section, we describe methods whereby researchers have obtained estimates of SD_y, the standard deviation of employees' dollar contribution to the organization.

Estimation of Employee Worth

In 1979, Schmidt, Hunter, McKenzie, and Muldrow reported a pilot study in which they derived estimates of SD_y for budget analysts. Supervisors were asked to judge the worth of their budget analysts because they were thought to have had the best opportunities to observe actual performance and output differences among employees. The *Schmidt et al.'s method for the estimation of employee worth* was based on the following reasoning: If job performance in dollar terms is normally distributed (see Chapter 2, for a description of the normal curve), then the difference between the value to the organization of the products and services produced by an average employee and the products and services produced by an employee at the 85th percentile (one whose performance is as good or better than 85% of the employees) is equal to SD_y. Similarly, the estimated difference between the average performer and the person who performs at the 15th percentile (as good as or better than only 15% of the employees) ought to be equal to SD_y. The 15th and 85th percentiles are approximately one standard deviation below and above the average or 50th percentile. The supervisors of budget analysts (Schmidt et al., 1979) were asked to estimate the contribution of employees at both the 50th (average) and 85th percentile and these values were averaged over 62 supervisors. The average SD_y was $11,327 for the budget analyst position.

Since the instructions to the judges who make the estimates are a critical element of the procedure, the instructions Schmidt et al. (1979) used are reproduced in Figure 9-4. Schmidt et al. claim that these instructions appeared to be meaningful to the supervisor-judges who asked very few questions about the procedure. Idiosyncratic tendencies, biases, and random errors of the judges can be minimized by averaging over a large number of judges.

Consider the following situation. A new selection procedure has been developed for the position of emergency telephone operator in an urban area. The telephone operator takes calls from citizens, secures the information needed to make an appropriate response, and enters the information into the computer. Another telephone operator assigns the call to an emergency unit and monitors the response to the emergency. Still a third component of this job is to secure information on cars or people that may be of importance in responding to police or fire requests. Eight supervisory personnel (all that were available) using the Schmidt et al. procedure provided a mean estimate of SD_y for this position equal to $10,000. The validity of the tests used to select these emergency telephone operators was .40. The cost of testing per applicant was $300. There were 75 applicants for the 15 position openings that occurred annually, so the selection ratio was .20 (15/75). Using Table 9-9 on page 312 to estimate the standard criterion score of those persons selected when the selection ratio is .20 and the validity of the test is .40 yields a value of .56. The average gain per person hired is .56 times $10,000, or $5,600. Since 15 are hired annually, the annual gain in utility is $84,000, assuming the previous selection procedure had no validity. The cost of testing is $22,500 (75 x $300). The net gain is $61,500. Similar analyses can be carried out for different selection ratios or different levels of test validity, or we can compare the utility of the new selection procedure with one that is less valid.

Since the introduction of the Schmidt et al. method for the estimation of employee worth, a great deal of work on utility estimation has been conducted. Cascio (1987b) wrote a book in which he described another method of utility analysis and detailed utility analyses for a wide variety of human resource development attempts. Boudreau (1983a; 1983b) has examined the impact of the introduction of a new selection procedure over a number of years incorporating the economic concepts of discounting, variable costs, and taxes. Other researchers have begun to compare the Schmidt et al. method with other judgmental methods of estimating SD_y and with cost accounting data such as sales commissions. While this research suggests some refinements to the initial approach to utility estimation, most researchers have concluded that the Schmidt et al. method provides a reasonable approximation of the variability in employees' organizational worth. In the next section, we describe the application of utility analyses to various human resource problems.

APPLICATION OF UTILITY ANALYSES TO HUMAN RESOURCE PROBLEMS

Most utility estimation work has been done in the context of personnel selection, but the concepts can be usefully applied to other human resource interventions as well. In this section, we give examples of the application of utility analyses to estimate the cost benefit outcomes of various programs.

The instructions to the supervisors were as follows:

The dollar utility estimates we are asking you to make are critical in estimating the relative dollar value to the government of different selection methods. In answering these questions, you will have to make some very *difficult judgments*. We realize they are difficult and that they are judgments or estimates. You will have to ponder for some time before giving each estimate, and there is probably no way you can be absolutely certain your estimate is accurate when you do reach a decision, But keep in mind three things:

1. The alternative to estimates of this kind is application of cost accounting procedures to the evaluation of job performance. Such applications are *usually* prohibitively expensive. And in the end, they produce only imperfect estimates, like this estimation procedure.

2. Your estimates will be averaged in with those of other supervisors of computer programmers. Thus error produced by too high and too low estimates will tend to be averaged out, providing more accurate final estimates.

3. The decisions that must be made about selection methods do not require that all estimates be accurate down to the last dollar. Substantially accurate estimates will lead to the same decisions as perfectly accurate estimates.

Based on your experience with agency programmers, we would like for you to estimate the yearly value to your agency of the products and services produced by the average GS 9-11 computer programmer. Consider the quality and quantity of output typical of the *average programmer* and the value of this output. In placing an overall dollar value on this output, it may help to consider what the cost would be of having an outside firm provide these products and services.

> Based on my experience, I estimate the value of my agency of the average GS 9-11 computer programmer at _____ per year.

We would now like for you to consider the "*superior*" *programmer*. Let us define a superior performer as a programmer who is at the 85th percentile. That is, his or her performance is better than that of 85% of his or her fellow GS 9-11 programmers, and only 15% turn in better performances. Consider the quality and quantity of the output typical of the superior programmer. Then estimate the value of these products and services. In placing an overall dollar value on this output, it may again help to consider what the cost would be of having an outside firm provide these products and services.

> Based on my experience, I estimate the value to my agency of a superior GS 9-11 computer programmer to be _____ dollars per year.

Finally, we would like you to consider the "*low performing*" *computer programmer*. Let us define a low performing programmer as one who is at the 15th percentile. That is, 85% of all GS 9-11 computer programmers turn in performances better than the low performing programmer, and only 15% turn in worse performances. Consider the quality and quantity of the output typical of the low-performing programmer. Then estimate the value of these products and services. In placing an overall dollar value on this output, it may again help to consider what the cost would be of having an outside firm provide these products and services.

> Based on my experience, I estimate the value to my agency of the low performing GS 9-11 computer programmer at _____ dollars per year.

FIGURE 9-4 Instructions for the Estimation of SD_y
  Source: Reproduced with permission from Schmidt, F. L., Hunter, J. E., McKenzie, R., & Muldrow, T. (1979). Impact of valid selection procedures on workforce productivity. *Journal of Applied Psychology, 64,* 609–626.

Selection

Schmidt, Mack, and Hunter (1984) present utility estimates for the selection of park rangers in the National Park Service using a test with an estimated validity of .51 as opposed to an unstructured interview for which validity was estimated as .14. They also estimated the utility that would result when different modes of test use were employed: (a) top-down selection, (b) random selection of those persons scoring above the mean, and (c) random selection of those persons who meet a minimum score equal to one standard deviation below the mean. Their estimate of the standard deviation of the dollar contribution of park rangers was $4450.74 based on the average of two estimates from the responses of 114 head rangers. Directions to these rangers required that they make dollar estimates of the contribution of an average ranger, of a ranger working at the 85th percentile, and of a ranger working at the 15th percentile. Two standard deviations were then computed as we described above and averaged to arrive at the $4450.74 estimate.

Utilities were estimated by the following equation:

$$\Delta U = [TN_s (r_1 - r_2) (\phi/p)] - [N_s (C_1 - C_2)/p] \tag{9.2}$$

where

ΔU = the gain in productivity in dollars from using the test for one year,

T = tenure in years of the average selectee,

N_s = number selected per year,

r_1 = the validity of the test (.51),

r_2 = the validity of the interview (.14),

C_1 = per applicant cost of the test,

C_2 = per applicant cost of the interview,

SD_y = the standard deviation of the dollar contribution ($4450.74),

p = proportion selected, and

ϕ/p = average standardized test score for those selected. For those in which only the top persons were selected (10% in this case) this value was 1.758. It was .7978 when random selection above the mean was employed and .2877 when the minimum test score of one SD below the mean was applied.

So, if 80 people are selected per year using the test and their average tenure is five years and we select the best 10% of the applicants, assuming that the expense of administering the test and the interview is approximately equal, then the expected change in utility would be as follows:

$$\Delta U = [(5 \times 80)(.51 - .14)(\$4450)(1.758)] - [80 (0)/.10]$$
$$= \$1,157,819.$$

The Schmidt et al. (1984) analysis and others like it show that the economic benefits of valid selection procedures can be very great. They also show that the way a test is used can affect the utility realized. For example, if a cutoff score is set at the mean of the test and we select randomly from those above the mean and we still are interested in hiring 10% of the applicants, the utility gained drops from the $1,157,819 computed above to just over $525,000. If a very low cutoff is used (e.g., one standard deviation below the mean), then utility drops to $190,000 over the average five-year tenure of the 80 selected candidates. Of course, if the selection procedure remains in use and the organization continues to employ 80 new applicants per year, then the utility associated with each of these new cohorts also would be realized. As we shall see below, additional complications arise in estimating the utility of human resource problems, but the Schmidt et al. (1979) procedure represented a significant breakthrough in this area and has stimulated a remarkable number of additional research studies.

Training

Our second example of the estimation of benefits accruing from human resource activities involves the estimation of the effects of training. In a typical evaluation study, the performance of a control group and an experimental group is compared using a t-test or analysis of variance which tells us whether group differences are statistically significant (see pages 45–50 in Chapter 2). The significance test, however, doesn't tell us what dollar value of the impact that the training program might have. Schmidt, Hunter, and Pearlman (1982a) provide a hypothetical example of the evaluation of a training program for computer programmers in which 100 serve as an experimental group and 100 serve as the control group. Cost of training was $500 per person. Supervisors were not told who had received training, but they were asked to rate the quality of the programs produced by each employee each month for a six-month period. The six-month composites were standardized against the control group performance so that mean performance equaled 50 and the standard deviation 10.

The following formula was used to estimate the utility of the training program:

$$\Delta U = TNd_t\, SD_y - NC \tag{9.3}$$

where

ΔU = the dollar value of the program

T = the number of years the training has a continued effect on performance,

N = the number trained,

d_t = the true difference in job performance between the average trained and untrained employee in standard deviation units,

SD_y = the standard deviation of job performance in dollars of the untrained group, and

C = the cost of training each programmer.

In the example, the mean of the trained group was 55 so d equaled .5 ((55-50)/10). Schmidt et al. (1982a) further corrected d for unreliability in the performance ratings used. Their estimate of reliability was .60, hence d_t = .65 (.50/$\sqrt{.60}$). Occasionally, d is estimated from a meta-analysis of previous studies in which the only data presented are significance tests or correlations. Schmidt et al. (1982a) provide formulas by which these statistics can be converted to d.

The SD_y can be estimated using procedures described above or by those presented by Cascio and Ramos (1986). The appropriate reference group in making those estimates would be untrained employees. Schmidt et al. (1982a) used a previously derived estimate of the SD_y of computer programmers equal to $10,413. The length of time an organizational intervention lasts must be estimated; in this example, the estimate was two years. So, use of the formula above to assess the economic benefit of the training program was as follows:

$$\Delta U = 2(100)(.65)(\$10,413) - 100(\$500)$$
$$\Delta U = \$1,303,690$$

The expected return on this training program for each 100 employees trained is over one million dollars. For those cases in which we can derive estimates of d for an organizational intervention, these procedures can be readily used to estimate the degree to which a particular program is worth pursuing. Kopelman (1986) and Guzzo, Jette, and Katzell (1985) provide comprehensive reviews of various types of organizational interventions from which d may be estimated.

Performance Evaluation

A third application of utility formulations is presented for performance evaluation and feedback by Landy, Farr, and Jacobs (1982). They modify the Schmidt et al. (1984) formula presented on the previous page to estimate the utility of a performance evaluation and feedback program as follows:

$$\Delta U = N \, d_f \, SD_y - NC_1 \tag{9.4}$$

where

ΔU = represents the benefit of the program,

N = number of persons receiving evaluation and feedback,

d_f = true difference in performance for the average person in the experimental group and the average person in the control group, and

C_1 = cost of the evaluation and feedback program.

Landy et al. (1982) present the following estimates of the parameters of this equation for a large manufacturing firm that employs 500 middle level managers. SD_y was estimated at \$20,000. They estimated the cost of delivering the performance evaluation system at \$700 per manager. Their cost estimate included development of the program, the time required to train supervisors to implement the program, and the actual time required of supervisors and subordinates in giving and receiving feedback. Finally, their review of the performance evaluation and feedback literature suggested a correlation of .30 to .50 between feedback and subsequent job performance. This value was transformed to d_f using a formula provided by Schmidt et al. (1982a).

Using these values and the formula presented above yields the following:

$$\Delta U = 500(.64)(\$20,000) - (500 \times 700)$$
$$= \$6,050,000$$

Clearly, given the estimates above are reasonable, and they certainly seem to be, the economic advantage of an effective performance evaluation and feedback program can be considerable.

Comparing Different Solutions to Human Resource Problems

Recently, legal factors also have influenced the way decision makers use selection procedures. We alluded to the problem of unequal hiring rates for minority and majority groups, or adverse impact, earlier in this chapter and also in Chapter 7 when we discussed various selection instruments. The Brogden and Cronbach-Gleser approaches to utility clearly show that, with linear ability-performance relationships, organizations will benefit the most if they pick those persons who score highest on valid selection instruments. This goal of maximizing organizational productivity frequently is inconsistent with the social and legal demand for equal representation of minorities and, in some cases, of women, in the organization's work force. Mathematical and empirical analyses of this problem (Cronbach, Yalow, & Schaeffer, 1980; Schmidt et al., 1984; Schmitt & Noe, 1986) indicate that the best solution is to set quotas (hire equal proportions of minority and majority applicants), but hire the best of both groups, rather than establish minimal competence levels and hire a fixed proportion of individuals randomly (or with some nonvalid procedure) who score above that point. However, as we stated above, this approach has been challenged on legal grounds as constituting selection on the basis of subgroup status unrelated to job performance.

The legal system also has been very involved in the setting of compensation rates. Both the Equal Pay Act (which applied to male-female comparisons) and Title VII of the Civil Rights Act require that performance of jobs that are equal in skill requirements, effort, responsibility, and working conditions must be paid equally. Not many would argue that two individuals working equally well in the same job in the same organization should be paid differently. However, to a considerable extent, women occupy different jobs than men and jobs held by women are, on average, paid less than are jobs held by men (Milkovich, 1980).

However, ambiguity arises when we try to determine the comparability of jobs occupied by one gender group as opposed to another (e.g., nurses versus engineers). Job evaluation as described briefly on pages 45–46 in Chapter 2 is the procedure that most directly addresses the question of job comparability for purposes of pay. Increasingly, however, there is a concern that job evaluation procedures themselves might be responsible for perpetuating sex discrimination in pay (see Heneman, Schwab, Fossum, & Dyer, 1983). Job evaluation procedures are inherently subjective as they are the outcome of some "experts" judgments about the requirements of a job and its worth. The claim is that these judges are influenced by the sexual composition of the job evaluated, its current market rate (which is often lower for female jobs), as well as various objective job requirements.

Frequently, moderated multiple regression is used to assess whether job evaluation procedures are biased for or against men or women. This approach was described on pages 64–69 in Chapter 2; in this application sex is a moderator, the assigned pay rate is the dependent variable, and the various factors (effort, training, responsibility, etc.) used to evaluate the job are independent variables. Significant effects due to sex or interactions with sex are taken as evidence of some sort of unfair discrimination in the way pay rates are set. Recently, Barrett, Alexander, Anesgart, and Doverspike (in press) have described the various regression models that have been used to address this problem. They identified several problems in using the regression approach to identify cases of pay discrimination. Instead, they recommend that the factors actually used by the company to determine salaries be identified and measured, that cases of overpayment or underpayment be identified, and that these cases be carefully examined to determine the possible causes of such discrepancies.

Finally, Rynes, Weber, and Milkovich (1989) report an exceptionally thorough study of the extent to which market survey rates of pay for job performance, job evaluation data, the proportion of men or women typically engaged in a job, and the sex of the compensation administrator judges influence the wage rates assigned to jobs by 406 compensation administrators. These compensation personnel assigned new pay rates to nine jobs in one of two matched job sets: either predominantly female or predominantly male. These two sets of jobs were matched on current pay, estimate of market rate for the same job in other local organizations, and the points a job received as a result of a job evaluation procedure like that described in Chapter 2. Recommended pay rates for these jobs were not related to "irrelevant" factors (job or judge gender) or the order in which the job was presented. Market rates and job evaluation data did affect pay recommendations with the size of the market rate effect being substantially larger than that of the job evaluation results. When both market rate and job evaluation were high, the recommended pay rates were highest, indicating an interaction between these two variables. While Rynes et al. (1989) felt that the results of their study regarding job gender and the gender of the compensation administrator were encouraging with respect to the assignment of fair compensation rates, they still point to the possibility of indirect discrimination through market rates or the results of job evaluations. Unfortunately, there is no ultimate criterion (see page 160 in Chapter 5) of job worth. Research on job evaluation (Arvey, 1986) and market surveys (Rynes & Milkovich, 1986) is especially difficult because of the absence of an objective standard of job worth or any societal consensus on the criteria by which the worth of jobs should be judged. As a result, there has been, and will probably continue to be, considerable legal (U.S. Supreme Court, *County of Washington, Oregon v. Gunther*, 1981) and sociopolitical (Treiman & Hartmann, 1981) controversy regarding the comparable worth of jobs.

We have presented examples of the application of utility concepts to three different concerns of human resource management: selection, training, and performance appraisal. Cascio (1982) presents other examples, such as anti-smoking and accident prevention efforts. Clearly, these are tools with wide applicability that human resource managers and researchers should have at their disposal. However, as you might have guessed, there are a variety of issues regarding these techniques that researchers have addressed. We present some of these issues in the next section.

RESEARCH ON UTILITY ESTIMATION

Boudreau (1983a) argued that the Schmidt et al. (1979) model ought to include economic considerations that are applied to other management decisions. Specifically, the concepts of variable costs, taxes, and discounting are introduced into the formulas presented earlier. *Variable costs* occur when the cost of producing a unit varies either positively or negatively with productivity. For example, a salesperson might receive a larger commission or bonus when he or she sells more. Or, the cost of equipment remains the same whether it is being operated by a high or low producing individual.

Taxes also increase with a firm's level of net profit, hence in order to compute a firm's tax liability, we must know their marginal tax rate. Boudreau (1983a) estimated this marginal tax rate varied from 0 to 55%—undoubtedly, too high given recent revisions in the U.S. tax code, but the principal that increased profits result in increased tax rates still applies.

Discounting refers to the fact that present monetary values can't be directly equated with future values. A benefit received two years from now must be decreased by the percent of interest one could earn with that money were he or she to receive it now. So, a promise of $1000 in two years is really worth only about $826 assuming 10% interest can be earned on the money $\{[1 / (1 + .10)^2]($1000)\}$. If one simply multiplies the utility expected in one year by the number of years a procedure is to be used, a relatively large overestimate of utility is made. Applying all three of the

Boudreau modifications to the utility of the training program example of Schmidt et al. (1982a) presented on page 318 reduced the utility estimate from $1,303,690 to $584,937. While Boudreau was making armchair estimates of each of these values, it is clear their impact on utility estimates can be substantial and they must be considered in utility calculations.

In another article, Boudreau (1983b) examined utility when a program is instituted, continued over a number of years, and applied to several sets of employees. His formulations show that even when discounting, taxes, and variable cost problems are included, the benefits of human resource programs are likely higher than earlier estimates by Schmidt et al. (1982a; 1984). These earlier estimates had extended utility estimates for one set of employees over some estimate of the number of years of their tenure, but they had ignored the estimate of the impact of the program being extended to new sets of employees every year. Boudreau and Berger (1985) also extended utility formulas to include issues of turnover or employee flow.

Another complication in applying utility analyses has been investigated by Murphy (1986). He pointed out that previous utility formulations assumed that, when a job offer was made to a group of applicants, they accepted the offer. Because some offers are declined offers must be extended to lower scoring individuals and the average ability of those selected will be correspondingly lower. Murphy (1986) developed formulas and considered three separate possibilities: (a) cases in which offers are declined at random, (b) cases in which the highest scoring applicants decline, and (c) cases in which test scores are related, but imperfectly so, to the probability of accepting an offer.

Murphy (1986) used an example previously presented by Hunter and Schmidt (1982) in which they had estimated the utility of a test to select 2000 budget analysts at $8,133,012 in a single year. If 10% of the original offers are declined, utility drops to $7,248,147 under case 1 conditions, to $5,973,859 under case 2 conditions, and to $6,881,152 when case 3 conditions apply. If half of the original offers are declined, corresponding figures are $2,416,049, $0.00, and $1,617,019 for cases 1, 2, and 3 respectively. Clearly, rejected offers have a huge impact on the utility of a selection procedure.

Murphy (1986) claims that under realistic circumstances utility formulas that do not take account of rejected offers overestimate utility gains by 30–80%. Rejected offers may be minimized if special efforts are made to recruit a more highly qualified labor pool or if special efforts are made to get those persons first offered a job to accept. These efforts, however, will cost money and those expenditures should be included in estimates of the recruiting and selection process. Boudreau and Rynes (1985) have developed utility formulas that explicitly include recruitment costs and the effects of different recruitment strategies.

While the previous studies have been primarily concerned with modifications to the basic utility formulas (i.e., taxes, recruitment, discounting, etc.), another set of studies has dealt with the issue of the appropriateness of estimates of SD_y. Recall that we mentioned that a lack of such estimates was the main reason utility formulas presented much earlier by Cronbach and Gleser (1965) never received much use. Schmidt and Hunter (1983) accumulated empirical data from 18 different sources that reported actual empirical figures for the mean and standard deviation of employee production and output. For piece-rate jobs, the standard deviation of output was about 15% of average performance; for nonpiece-rate jobs, the standard deviation was about 20% of the average output. Based on earlier estimates using the procedure for estimating SD_y developed by Schmidt et al. (1979), a lower bound estimate of SD_y was 40% of salary. Given the fact that in the United States economy, wages and salaries make up approximately 57% of the total value of goods and services, the estimate of 40% of mean salary as an estimate of the value of employee contribution is not greatly different from the actual output figures [i.e., .40 (.57) = 20%]. Or, taking

57% of the actual range of the estimates produced by the earlier work (Hunter and Schmidt, 1982), which were 42 to 60%, produces a range of estimated standard deviation of output between 24% (.42 x .57) and 34% (.60 x .57). These figures are slightly higher than the actual estimates based on the research reviewed by Schmidt and Hunter, but these estimates certainly lend credibility to the earlier estimates produced by judges using the Schmidt et al. (1979) directions.

Weekly, Frank, O'Connor, and Peters (1985) compared the Schmidt et al. (1979) procedure described above with an estimate of 40% of annual salary and a third estimate produced by a method described by Cascio (1982) and Cascio and Ramos (1986). In the Cascio method, average annual salary is partitioned among a job's principal activities so that each activity is assigned a portion of the salary equal to its weight in the job analysis results. Rated performance of each individual on these activities is multiplied by the proportion of annual salary associated with these activities and the products are summed across all job activities. This sum is taken as the employee's worth and the standard deviation of these employee worth values across employees is taken as the estimate of SD_y. These three estimates were developed for a group of convenience store supervisors. The Cascio method and the 40% estimate were similar, but the estimate based on the Schmidt et al. procedure (1979) produced an estimate considerably higher ($13,967 versus $8489 for the 40% rule and $7700 for the Cascio method).

Research by other authors (Burke & Frederick, 1984; 1986; Bobko, Karren, & Parkington, 1983) has produced similar results. There are differences among methods with the Schmidt et al. procedure (1979) producing somewhat higher estimates. Further, some judges have difficulty making the judgments at all and some judges make very high or very low estimates, perhaps indicating they do not understand what is being asked of them. However, the general conclusion should be that with a large group of judges (perhaps greater than 20), one can achieve a reasonably good estimate of the SD_y using any of the judgmental estimates and that these estimates are reasonable given actual empirical output. Given these procedures yield similar estimates, other considerations such as the ease and acceptability of the use of the procedures should be given consideration.

Some researchers have begun to attend to the variability in utility estimates and the degree of risk or uncertainty associated with the outcomes of human resource interventions in organizations. Rich and Boudreau (1987) presented a very sophisticated model of the factors influencing utility, but Cronshaw, Alexander, Wiesner, and Barrick (1987) showed that the variability in utility estimates was associated primarily with how many people were selected (and by implication exposed to other interventions as well).

Finally, and perhaps most importantly, Rauschenberger and Schmidt (1987) have begun to consider how best to communicate the results of these utility estimates on human resource programs to other members of the organization. This particular problem deserves much more attention if human resources personnel are to make maximum use of the procedures described in this chapter.

Where do all these modifications leave us with respect to the use of utility in personnel decision making? First, in estimating total utility, appropriate consideration should be made regarding variable cost, discounting, and tax issues when they apply. In the case of selection, the cost of recruiting and the ability to hire the desired applicants must be considered. In making estimates of SD_y, it is perhaps best to rely on more than one estimate and to be conservative. It seems best not to risk the credibility of estimates of human resource programs with an overestimate. Even conservative estimates of the utility of most human resource efforts have produced very handsome estimated returns. Finally, when a program is continued over a number of years or repeated, the benefit accruing from additional cohorts of employees should be estimated.

SELECTION AND DECISION MAKING IN SMALL ORGANIZATIONS

Most of the methods discussed in this chapter are applicable when we are dealing with organizations that employ large numbers of people. However, small organizations also need to make selection decisions. Can human resource specialists provide anything that is of use to these organizations? The answer is certainly positive and we provide an example of the use of some of the principles discussed in this and earlier chapters to the selection of a single person in a small business setting.

Robinson (1981) reported a case in which a construction superintendent was hired for a general contracting firm that had built about 60 single family homes and six multifamily projects in 1979. It had 10 employees and sales of about $10 million. Their work consisted of drawing plans for buildings, making cost estimates, inviting subcontractor bids for various aspects of the work, and then supervising the construction of the dwellings.

A job analysis panel consisting of the company president, production and financial vice presidents, and the construction superintendent identified 11 broad objectives and 71 tasks, of which 20 were judged critical. Job objectives were ranked independently from most to least important by the panel members and a composite ranking was computed.

Based upon consideration of the critical tasks, an assessment battery was constructed using work sampling procedures. The test battery consisted of the following tests:

1. *Blueprint Reading Test.* The applicants were asked to mark the location of common architectural drawing errors.
2. *Scrambled Subcontractor Test.* The examinees were given a list of subcontractors (e.g., electrical, plumbing, roofing, etc.) and were asked to rank order their appearance on the work site. Order of appearance was critical in avoiding unnecessary construction delays.
3. *Construction Error Recognition Test.* The candidates were required to examine a specially constructed shed noting common and expensive construction errors that had been deliberately built into the shed.
4. *Scheduling Test.* The applicants were required to change the job assignments of the people they supervised. They were rated by a team of company assessors on their ability to plan, organize, schedule, anticipate, and analyze problems.
5. *Structured Interview.* The president and production vice president covered aspects of the relationship between the superintendent and building inspectors, safety procedures, company philosophy, and business ethics.

A newspaper ad produced the resumes of 49 applicants of which 17 seemed to fit the job objectives. These 17 all agreed to go through the examination process. One eliminated himself after reviewing the set of job tasks. Eight more were eliminated by the Blueprint Reading Test, one by the Scrambled Subcontractor Test, and four by the Construction Error Recognition Test, leaving three for the Scheduling Test and the Structured Interview. After administration of these two procedures, one candidate seemed clearly superior and was hired. After more than a year on the job, the fit appeared satisfactory.

While we cannot rigorously evaluate the outcome and utility of these procedures in small businesses, they certainly apply in this context as well as larger organizational contexts. Also obvious is the fact that these procedures take time and effort to implement successfully. If we consider the implications of the four outcomes depicted in Figure 9-4 for this small construction company, we may realize some notion that this relatively complicated process was worthwhile even for the hiring of a single person. Perhaps the effects of a "false positive" would be most dramatic. Hiring a person who reads a blueprint incorrectly could produce the need for expensive modifications in building. A superintendent who cannot organize work teams effectively will produce delays in finishing building projects during which time the contractor is paying interest on large amounts of borrowed money. A person who can't deal effectively on an interpersonal level with inspectors, customers, and members of different work teams will almost certainly create work slowdown in the short term and fewer customers in the long term. So, hiring the right or wrong person in this small firm could mean the difference between success and failure of the business. False negatives also may be costly if those individuals go to competing construction firms. In addition, this investment in human resources may, itself, pay huge dividends and will likely have significant side benefits. Applicants will be more clearly informed regarding the job requirements, there may be clearer definition of company objectives, and there may be significant implications for training and compensation. Another similar example of selection in a small organization is provided in Schmitt and Ostroff (1986).

SUMMARY

In this chapter, we have provided an explanation of how the validity of the test and information about the test scores of individuals can be used to make predictions about their job performance. Multiple hurdle and multiple cutoff strategies of personnel selection were described. We outlined the use of expectancy charts to aid in the interpretation of test validity. Also described were methods to weight various elements of a selection test battery and procedures to select and justify cutoff points for a selection procedure. Analysis and reporting of data regarding personnel decisions involving women and minorities were presented.

In the last section of this chapter, we outlined methods whereby the practical implications of the introduction of some organizational intervention may be assessed. We began with purely psychometric methods of utility assessment, then discussed the theoretical contributions of Taylor and Russell, Brogden, Cronbach and Gleser. Finally, we described a method to assess employee worth, which made the earlier theoretical contributions applicable. We gave several examples of utility analyses of different human resource interventions and described research on the basic utility formulas and the estimates of SD_y. We concluded the chapter with an example of decision making, in this case the hiring of a supervisor in a small company.

ASSESSING EMPLOYEE
ATTITUDES AND OPINIONS

We begin this chapter with a description of the practical and scientific concerns addressed by survey research on human resource issues. We then discuss the planning of a survey and the writing of survey items. The consideration of who and how many should respond and how to solicit their cooperation receives a great deal of attention. Some guidelines on how to analyze survey data so as to ensure quality data that serve to answer important theoretical and practical questions are presented. Use of surveys as an organizational intervention and in training needs analysis are outlined. Finally, we include a section on special concerns (method bias, confidentiality, etc.) in the use of survey instruments. Throughout the chapter we emphasize the fact that the various practices we suggest contribute to the construct validity of the survey measures and to the internal validity of the survey research effort as a whole.

HOW ORGANIZATIONS AND ORGANIZATIONAL
RESEARCHERS USE SURVEY RESEARCH

A very popular method of gathering information regarding the perceptions people have of some object or phenomenon is to use a survey. Surveys also are used to measure people's attitudes, beliefs, and intentions, or to collect demographic and experience data. A survey usually is a series of questions requiring a written response in either a structured or open-ended format on some topic of concern. An example of some survey questions is presented in Figure 10-1.

Organizational researchers and practitioners in human resource management use the survey for several reasons. First, it might be the basis for an evaluation of some training program or organizational intervention. As noted in Chapter 11 on page 390, such reactions criteria are the most frequently employed dependent variable in training evaluation studies. Second, a survey itself may serve as the basis of an organizational intervention. For example, a survey might ask questions about worker concerns, such as supervision, work conditions and work procedures, pay and promotion policy, etc. These responses are then summarized for various work units, and discussed with members of those units, hopefully generating some action plan whereby any important problems or dissatisfactions are addressed. Third, surveys might be used by one organization to assess what is happening in other organizations in the human resource area, as is the case with a market rate survey in compensation. Fourth, the survey measures might be collected for research purposes or as a means of generating a longitudinal data base regarding employee opinions on various matters. Occasionally, the survey serves more than one purpose. In organizations such as IBM and Sears, data regarding employee opinions have been collected for many years. The data

A. Open-Ended Questions
   1. What are the most dissatisfying features of your job?
   2. What aspects of your job are most likely to make you happy?
   3. If you had a choice, how would you change your job?

B. Structured Questions
   Indicate in the space to the left of each item how happy you are with each of the following aspects of your job using the response scale below:

   > 5 = Very happy
   > 4 = Happy
   > 3 = Neutral, neither happy nor unhappy
   > 2 = Unhappy
   > 1 = Very unhappy

   _____ 1. The work you do
   _____ 2. Your supervisor
   _____ 3. Your coworkers
   _____ 4. The conditions in which you work
   _____ 5. The employee cafeteria
   _____ 6. Your work hours

C. Structured Questions with an Open Response Option
   Circle the number that best represents the reason you arrive at work late.
   1. I never come late
   2. Problems with car
   3. Problems with bus or train
   4. Family problems at home
   5. Illness
   6. Other (please specify) _____

FIGURE 10-1 Example of Structured and Open-Ended Survey Questions

are used for survey feedback purposes as well as a basis by which various research hypotheses can be evaluated. Longitudinal data collection of this type also allows the identification of trends in employee opinion.

Surveys can be either of an interview or questionnaire type. However, since most organizations use questionnaires in collecting survey data and because interview methods were discussed elsewhere in this text (see Chapters 3 and 8), we will discuss issues relevant primarily to written surveys.

Written surveys are popular because of the ease and low cost of their administration and reponse analysis. Recently, some organizations have computerized their surveys. Survey questions are presented and employee responses are obtained via the desktop computer or Touch-tone telephone. Computerization has significant advantages—it eliminates the need for paper and mailing costs and eliminates errors associated with the coding or reading of answer sheets. Perhaps of greatest advantage, however, is the fact that data collected by computer can be analyzed more quickly and made available as feedback to employees and/or organizational decision makers.

Because of the ease with which questionnaire data are collected from relatively large groups of people, survey data are probably used more frequently than they should be in organizational research. They may also be used in instances in which other methods of investigation (e.g., observation) might be more appropriate. In considering whether to conduct survey research some of the following points should be considered. Will survey data satisfy the *objectives* of the research?

Is the purpose of the research to generate hypotheses about some organizational problem? If so, then it might be more appropriate to use some combination of observations and informal unstructured interviews. Does the study call for the collection of data that might be available through other sources, such as company records? If so, then there would be few defensible reasons to collect these data by questionnaire unless company records were flawed in some way. Are we interested in testing causal hypotheses? If so, we might be better advised to consider an experimental design like those discussed in Chapter 11, although survey data, especially when collected at appropriate time intervals, can be used to test the plausibility of causal hypotheses.

Studies in which all variables are collected via survey are called *percept-percept studies*. That is to say, both presumed causal variables and dependent variables are gathered at the same time in the form of employee perceptions. These studies are especially susceptible to what researchers term *response bias*, that is, measures of all variables are influenced to some degree by the fact that they are collected via questionnaire. Consequently, inferences that correlations between these measures reflect a real relationship between underlying constructs are likely to be flawed. This weakness of self-report data is discussed further in Chapter 11.

Another question that is relevant to the decision to use survey research techniques is the degree of detail desired regarding ongoing social interactions in organizations. When a great deal of detail is desired about such process issues, it is usually better to consider participant observation or some form of the qualitative research techniques described in Chapter 3. For example, an in-depth probing interview might yield adequate information about such process issues.

Second, a researcher must consider the construct validity of data collected by surveys or questionnaires. Recall the discussion of construct validity on pages 107–112 in Chapter 3. In most scientific endeavors, researchers strive to secure measures that are representative of all possible measures of a particular construct. We might be confident that a rating of some person's work motivation has some objective basis if many different people give similar ratings of that person's motivation. Or, we'd be comfortable with questionnaire measures of the complexity of a job if they correlated highly with interview measures and ratings of complexity based on observations of individuals performing the jobs.

Validity is enhanced by several factors. The degree to which we can *quantify* our measures allows for objective comparisons across individuals and organizations. Construct validity is also enhanced when measures are *replicable*; that is, they produce similar results across time or in a different setting. The *qualitative depth* of the measure also contributes or detracts from validity. Questionnaires often are criticized for a lack of qualitative depth. For example, to know that a particular unit is not happy with supervision does not tell us why. To understand the nature of the supervision problems it may be necessary to interview both supervisors and employees, examine archival data, and observe the work situation. Qualitative depth concerns in a questionnaire also need to be balanced against concerns about the number of questions asked and the effect of a lengthy instrument on response rate and validity of responses.

Finally, validity of questionnaire responses may be affected by the simple fact that certain questions are asked. An organizational survey that contains items on employees' smoking behaviors may suggest to the employees that they ought to take smoking problems seriously because the organization is expending time and money on the problem. The mere fact that certain questions are asked, then, influences attitudes and responses. In these instances, the measure is said to be *reactive*. In deciding whether or not to use a survey, it is important to consider whether the validity of measurement of the attitudes or variables in which you are interested will be affected in any of these ways.

On the positive side, survey research is perhaps the easiest and least expensive way to collect information from large numbers of people. In comparison to other methods of data collection (e.g., interviews or participant observation), the researcher knows that the questions asked of all participants are precisely the same. Even well-trained interviewers may not treat all respondents in exactly the same way. In the next section, we review briefly the theoretical research that underlies some of the survey research conducted on human resource issues.

THEORETICAL BACKGROUND OF SURVEY RESEARCH

Surveys are used to investigate theoretical issues in leadership, motivation, and attitude formation, as well as other basic human resource issues. Because we believe that an appropriate understanding of the constructs one hopes to measure is fundamental to good survey research, we briefly review research in these areas. Obviously investigators interested in one of these areas or other aspects of human resource issues should consult these bodies of literature in more detail when they plan research. We briefly outline the basic issues addressed in those research areas in which surveys are frequently used.

Attitude Research

Theoretical literature on attitudes usually recognizes that attitudes have three components: a knowledge or cognitive component, an affective or feeling component, and a behavioral component. So, for example, we may know that yogurt is nutritious (cognitive), we may genuinely like yogurt (affective), and we frequently may eat yogurt (behavioral). In this instance, the three attitudinal components are consistent with each other, but this is not always true. In fact, attitude-behavior consistency and the lack thereof has been the subject of considerable research (Mischel, 1973) and controversy.

Various balance theories (Festinger, 1957; Heider, 1958; Osgood & Tannenbaum, 1955) predict that individuals who experience inconsistency between their feelings, beliefs, and behaviors are motivated to restore balance. A person who hates his or her job and knows that these feelings about the job also are affecting his or her behavior at home and that other jobs are available will be strongly motivated to leave.

This belief on the part of researchers that attitudes (as measured in surveys) have important implications for behavior in organizations is implicit in various areas of human resource research. Organizational commitment, climate, and culture are constructs that almost always have been operationalized in surveys and reflect the notion that the affective reactions to organizations and beliefs about organizations measured in surveys have significant behavioral correlates that impact on organizational efficiency. Job satisfaction research was originally initiated (Hoppock, 1935) partly because of the belief that a happy worker was more productive. While subsequent research has failed to produce evidence of a substantial relationship between job satisfaction and performance (Iaffaldano & Muchinsky, 1985), job satisfaction does seem to be related to attendance at work (Steers & Rhodes, 1978), to turnover (Mobley, Horner, & Hollingsworth, 1978), and to unionization activity (Friedson, 1985). In fact, the relationship between survey measures of job attitudes and pro-union voting behavior is so strong that surveys are used by some organizations and consultants in their efforts to keep organizations union-free. The ethicality and legality of this use of survey data has been questioned. The interested reader is referred to Friedson (1985) for a full discussion of the issues.

In any event, organizations and researchers usually collect survey data on the assumption that the expressions in these surveys do have behavioral implications. If all measures in a study are survey measures of attitude, perceptions or intentions, however, we have not provided any test of the attitude-behavior relationship. The scientific and practical contribution of these types of studies may be limited.

Motivation Research

In motivation research, surveys frequently are used to assess the strength of needs (Alderfer, 1972; Wahba & Bridwell, 1976), the various components of expectancy theory (Vroom, 1964), the perceptions of equity (Adams, 1965), and goal acceptance and commitment in tests of goal setting research (Locke, Shaw, Saari, & Latham, 1981). A brief introduction to these theories as background to our discussion of survey research methods follows.

Need Theory. Perhaps the first major discussion of *need theory* in the industrial/organizational context concerned the application of Maslow's theory (1954; 1970), although Maslow originally was not concerned with work motivation. Maslow maintained that needs were biological or instinctive, that people behaved in ways that satisfied these needs, and that when one need was satisfied, another took its place. He maintained that there were five major needs: physiological, safety, social, self-esteem, and self-actualization; and that these needs were arranged in hierarchical order. Maslow felt that once a person's physiological needs were met, safety needs would become most important, and that once safety needs were satisfied, social needs would dominate, and so on until one reached their full potential at the self-actualization stage. Maslow formulated his theory based on his observations of people; subsequent researchers have tried to test the existence of the needs postulated by Maslow and his notions of a need hierarchy.

Porter (1961) developed a need satisfaction questionnaire to assess the degree of fulfillment and importance of the five needs. Using a seven-point scale, Porter asked people to indicate (a) how much of a given need is present in their lives now; (b) how much of this need there should be; and (c) how important the need is. The difference between (a) and (b)—what people have and what they want—was used as a measure of relative deficiency. Wahba and Bridwell (1976) reviewed the results of two dozen studies of this type and found little clear or consistent support for the theory. There was support for the presence of some of the basic needs, but not for the full set of five; and, there was little support for the hierarchical proposition.

In response to the shortcomings of Maslow's theory, Alderfer (1972) proposed his *ERG theory*, so named because he suggested the presence of only existence, relatedness, and growth needs. Existence needs were defined as those associated with food, water, pay, fringe benefits, and decent working conditions; relatedness needs were defined as those associated with social interactions with coworkers, family, and friends; and growth needs were defined as those associated with a desire for unique personal development. In addition to his positing only three groups of needs, Alderfer also arranged those needs on a continuum ranging from the concrete (existence needs) to the abstract (self-actualization). While he agreed with Maslow that people moved up in the hierarchy as lower level needs became satisfied, he felt people also could move downward because of frustration in satisfying higher level needs.

While Alderfer's theory has received some support (Wanous & Zwany, 1977), it has the same problems as does Maslow's need approach. The psychological and physiological bases of needs are still unclear. If inherited, then little can be done to motivate workers other than to select and place them in the ideal motivating circumstances. Nothing is said about the relative strength of various needs; for example, should we expect employees to work harder if they are motivated by existence or growth needs. And, it has been very difficult to document the progressive changes in motivation up or down the hierarchy.

Equity Theory. Adams (1965) proposed what he called *equity theory*—that how hard a person worked was a function of the comparisons he or she made with the effort of others. Basic to equity theory are the perceptions a person has of himself or herself in relation to others. A person evaluates his or her inputs (such as their education, skill, seniority, effort) and outcomes (pay, benefits, working conditions, status, etc.). The ratio of inputs to outcomes is evaluated relative to perceptions of other workers' input-outcome ratio. If these ratios are equal, then the situation represents *equity*. If another person, however, is getting a greater share of outcomes for the same input level, the situation is unfair or inequitable.

According to Adams, people are motivated to reduce the tension that arises from inequity and can do this by varying the effort they invest in a job as well as by changing their interpretation of their own or others' inputs and outcomes. One of the interesting implications of equity theory occurs in conditions in which outcome exceeds input or overpayment occurs. Overpayment on an hourly basis should lead to greater effort and increased quantity and quality of production, while on a piece-rate basis fewer pieces of a higher quality would be made. Underpayment in hourly conditions would stimulate lessened effort and lowered quantity and quality production; in piece-rate pay conditions, workers should produce more pieces of lower quality.

Laboratory research has been supportive of equity theory, but the motivation resulting from overpayment does not tend to last long (Carrell & Dittrich, 1978) when the predicted effects occur at all. Further, deliberate manipulation of equity raises moral and ethical questions. Perhaps the greatest contribution of equity theory is to draw attention to its importance. People are especially sensitive to underpayment; perceptions of inequity lead to job dissatisfaction, which in turn leads to increased absenteeism and turnover. Notions of equity also are of great concern in compensation issues. Organizations strive to maintain both *external equity* (relative to salaries and wages of other employers in the area) and *internal equity* (salary and wages of people within the company).

Expectancy Theory. Vroom's book (1964), *Work and Motivation*, introduced expectancy theory to persons interested in work motivation. Expectancy theory assumes the worker rationally appraises her or his situation to determine how much effort to expend. In this rational appraisal, there are five major components, all of which are frequently measured in surveys in tests of the theory. These five major components are job outcomes, valence, instrumentality, expectancy, and force.

Job outcomes is what an organization provides in return for work. They include such things an individual derives from work as feelings of accomplishment, or things that one must sacrifice as a result of engaging in work, such as time with one's family. Attached to each of these outcomes is a *valence*, which is the employee's feelings (positive or negative) about the attractiveness of the outcome. A person is also influenced by their perception of *instrumentality*; that is, their belief that performance on the job is related to the attainment of outcomes. Instrumentality is typically measured as a probability; for example, a performance-pay instrumentality of .0 would mean that attainment of a given level of pay had no perceived connection to performance, while an instrumentality of 1.0 would indicate that pay is totally dependent on work performance. *Expectancy* is the perceived relationship between effort and performance. Also expressed as a probability, expectancy is high when a person believes that the harder she or he works, the better she or he will do. Finally, *force* is the effort one exerts at work. Force (F) is the summed (Σ) product over all outcomes (i) of valence (V), instrumentality (I) and expectancy (E) as follows:

$$F = E \left(\sum_{i=1}^{N} V_i\, I_i \right). \tag{10.1}$$

An example of the computation of force for four outcomes that might be associated with a nurse's job is contained in Figure 10-2A. In Figure 10-2B we present examples of items that might be used to operationalize expectancy, instrumentality, and valence for each outcome. Operationalizations of these components of the model are fully discussed by Mitchell (1974). Each instrumentality is multiplied by a corresponding valence, these products are summed, and then multiplied by expectancy to arrive at a prediction of a given nurse's effort.

In various research studies, this theory-predicted estimate of effort has been correlated with self-assessments of effort or time spent at some task or supervisor and peer assessments of effort. While the results of these studies generally have been positive, it is unlikely that people go through the calculations suggested by expectancy theory; certainly there are large differences in the rationality of subjects in their choice behavior (Muchinsky, 1977). However, each of the components of expectancy seems reasonable and the entire formulation represents a highly rational view of persons deciding how hard to work.

In doing studies on expectancy theory, researchers have come to recognize that this theory is a within-subjects approach to motivation; that is, the theory deals with how a single subject compares her or his options. Also, because of the multiplication of various components of the model in making predictions about effort, the theory demands measurement at the ratio level (Schmidt, 1973; Ilgen, Nebeker, & Pritchard, 1981). The latter two issues have been the source of considerable debate in motivation research and have been the source of criticism of many studies of expectancy theory hypotheses.

Goal-Setting Theory. *Goal-setting theory* (Locke, 1968) is based on the notion that people have goals that they consciously try to attain. These goals serve to motivate and direct behavior. These goals should influence performance if the individual is aware of the goal and what must be accomplished and accepts the goal. Goals may be rejected when they are seen as too easy or difficult or because the person doesn't know what to do to attain the goal. Knowledge about the goal and goal acceptance usually are measured by questionnaires in studies of goal setting while the experimenter sets the goals. Specific goals that are difficult are most effective in enhancing task performance.

Locke, Shaw, Saari, and Latham (1981) reviewed 12 years of goal-setting research and found goals improved task performance when (a) subjects have sufficient ability, (b) feedback is provided on progress toward meeting goals, (c) rewards are given for goal attainment, (d) management is supportive of workers' goals and goal-setting programs, and (e) individuals accept assigned goals. While this early research was done with relatively simple concrete tasks in which an identifiable product was produced (so progress toward meeting goals could be measured and was evident), more recent research has extended the concepts of goal setting to the investigation of much more complex behavior (Earley, Wojnarski, & Prest, 1987; Huber, 1985).

In assessing each of these theories of motivation, researchers frequently rely on questionnaire or survey measures of key constructs. It is necessary that these survey measures are valid measures of the construct as it is represented in theoretical statements. While we have given you the broad outlines of these theories, a researcher always should read the previous research and original statements of a theory when constructing survey instruments to ensure the construct validity of the measures (see the discussion of construct validity on pages 107–112 in Chapter 3) and that

A. Computation of Elements of Expectancy Theory

Job Outcome	Valence (-10 to 10)	Instrumentality (.0 to 1.0)	Expectancy (.0 to 1.0)	Effort
1. Need to work different shifts	-8	.0	.7	4.13
2. Interesting, important work	9	.5		
3. Pay	5	.6		
4. High work demands	-4	.4		

$$\sum_{i=1}^{N} V_i I_i = (-8 \times .0) + (9 \times .5) + (5 \times .6) + (-4 \times .4)$$

$$= 5.9$$

$$\text{Effort} = .7 (5.9)$$

$$= 4.13$$

B. Example of Items Operationalizing Expectancy Theory Constructs

Instrumentality
If you do your current job assignments well, how *likely* is it that you will receive more *interesting and important* tasks?
-3 = Much less likely
-2 = Less likely
-1 = Slightly less likely
 0 = Neither more nor less likely
 1 = Slightly more likely
 2 = More likely
 3 = Much more likely

Expectancy
How probable is it that if you work hard at your job that you will be able to perform job-related tasks well? Indicate the probability that this will happen using zero to indicate that there is no probability and 1.00 to indicate that you are certain that if you work hard, your job tasks will be accomplished. Your response may be any probability between .00 and 1.00 (e.g., .2, .4, .8, .9).

Valence
How desirable is it that you do interesting and important tasks at your job?
-3 = Very undesirable
-2 = Undesirable
-1 = Slightly undesirable
 0 = Neither desirable nor undesirable
 1 = Slightly desirable
 2 = Desirable
 3 = Very desirable

FIGURE 10-2 An Example of Expectancy Theory Computations of Effort with Four Job Outcomes for the Job of Nurse

important nuisance variables can be measured and/or controlled. In the next section, we turn to a brief overview of work and theory in leadership in organizations, which has depended on survey measures.

Leadership Research

Theory and research on leadership usually has been represented as involving one of three hypotheses: (a) effective leaders possess the requisite traits or abilities (trait theory), (b) effective leaders are those who engage in appropriate leader behavior (behavior theory), or (c) effective leaders are those who understand themselves and the leadership situation in which they find themselves and adapt their behavior accordingly (situational theory).

Trait theory is the oldest approach to the study of leadership. In studies of trait theory, some a priori determination of which leaders were effective and ineffective was made and then demographic and personality (authoritarianism, dominance, intelligence, etc.) differences between the two groups were described. While this approach is popular with laypersons who believe that some individuals are born with the "right stuff," this approach to leadership is not currently popular with most human resource researchers. First, there are no rational guidelines as to which traits to examine, hence most trait studies are of the shotgun type; that is, investigators compare ineffective and effective leaders on whatever data are available. Second, the approach presumes knowledge of an effective leader because it demands some means of identifying good and bad leaders. Third, the trait approach does not help explain why certain leadership traits operate as they do or how these traits develop.

Behavior theory began in the 1950s when researchers at Ohio State first examined those behaviors that seemed to be characteristic of good and bad leaders. Factor analyses of the evaluations of leader behavior yielded two major factors: consideration behaviors and initiating structure behaviors. *Consideration behaviors* reflected a concern for members' needs, mutual trust, and respect and included such behaviors as allowing subordinates more participation in decision making and encouraging two-way communication. *Initiating structure behaviors* included behaviors in which the supervisor organizes and defines activities, assigns tasks, plans ahead, and develops ways of getting things done. Two questionnaires were developed as a result of this research. One called the Leader Opinion Questionnaire is completed by a supervisor and asks her or him to describe her or his beliefs about good leader behavior. The second called the Leader Behavior Description Questionnaire is completed by a subordinate who describes how a supervisor behaves in certain situations.

A great deal of research has been conducted on the psychometric properties of these measures and on the relationship of consideration and initiating structure with other desired outcomes, such as subordinate job satisfaction, absenteeism, and turnover. While the two dimensions are clearly not independent (Kerr & Schriesheim, 1974), they do appear to be discriminable dimensions of leader behavior, and they are related to important organizational criteria (Fleishman & Harris, 1962; Korman, 1966; Kerr & Schriesheim, 1974). The behavioral approach represented an advance over trait approaches as it focused attention on what leaders do. Implications for training leaders were obvious and widely used interventions to develop better leaders grew out of the approach (Blake & Mouton, 1985).

Recently, Lord and his colleagues (Lord, DeVader, & Alliger, 1986; Lord, Foti, & DeVader, 1984; Lord, Foti, & Phillips, 1982) have criticized much of the leadership literature conducted from both the trait and behavior theory perspectives. As briefly noted in Chapter 6, their notion was that people have stereotypes of appropriate leader characteristics and behavior and that these stereotypes or categories of leader characteristics determine the responses of people who provide information on leaders. This implicit theory of leadership suggests, then, that the determinant of an observer's report about leader behavior and traits is the preconceived notion of a leader in the observer's head. Work on implicit theories of leadership has demonstrated widely shared beliefs about leader behaviors and traits that guide an observer's encoding of relevant information, their formation of leader perceptions, and their recall of leadership information (Lord, DeVader, & Alliger, 1986). This criticism of leadership research based on responses to questionnaires has implications for the validity of survey research in general.

Fiedler (1964) has developed *situational theory*—the view that there is no one best leader or set of leader behaviors but that the effectiveness of a leader also was the function of the situation in which a leader was placed. He identified three aspects of a situation as being of particular importance: (a) *leader group relations*—how well the leader and the group get along, (b) *task structure*—the clarity of the steps required to accomplish a task, and (c) *leader position power*—the amount of legitimate power and sanctions possessed by the leader. If all three aspects of the situation are favorable (i.e., good leader-member relations, high task structure and position power), then the leadership task is simple. Conversely, when leader-member relations are poor and task structure and position power is low, leadership is difficult. If situations are depicted quite simplistically as being high or low on each of these three aspects, then we have eight possible situations.

Fiedler maintains that the degree to which a leader does well in one or the other of these situations is a function of the degree to which the leader describes her or his least preferred coworker (LPC) in favorable or unfavorable terms. Fiedler has used a short survey instrument to measure leaders' descriptions of their LPC and hypothesizes that a person who describes an LPC in favorable terms should do best as a leader in situations that are of intermediate favorability, while those who describe their least preferred coworker in relatively unfavorable terms will do best either when the situation is very favorable or very unfavorable. These two hypotheses are based on the notion that those who give unfavorable ratings of their LPC will exercise more autocratic styles of leadership while those high in LPC will be more participative. Further, Fiedler posits that in very favorable situations, the autocratic leader is likely to be most effective because there is no need for participation while in the very unfavorable situation, the leader must quickly exercise control and direction to get things accomplished before the group disintegrates.

Of central importance to Fiedler's theory is the construct validity of his LPC measure. There have been numerous critical commentaries regarding the measure (Stinson & Tracy, 1974; Rice, 1978; Shiflett, 1981). Perhaps the most accepted interpretation of the LPC measure is that a person whose LPC is very low is task-oriented and derives satisfaction from the accomplishment of work tasks while the high LPC enjoys the relationship with other people demanded by a job. Also of importance to Fiedler's approach is an appropriate measure of situations, but the research on Fiedler's theory usually has involved manipulations of aspects of the situation. Fiedler also has developed leadership training, called Leader Match, which seeks to make leaders more cognizant of their own leadership style *and* the situation and to make efforts to modify the situation so as to make it more favorable to their particular LPC score (e.g., Fiedler & Mahar, 1979). Once again, survey data is used for this purpose. Support for the theory is debatable (Graen, Alvares, Orris, & Martella (1970); Fiedler, 1971; Vecchio, 1977) but Fiedler's approach to leadership did mark the beginning of a broader discussion of the importance of the situation in which leaders are placed (see House & Mitchell, 1974; Vroom & Yetton, 1973, for other examples of contingency approaches to leadership).

It should be clear that survey or questionnaire measures are central to the investigation of various theoretic issues of interest to human resource researchers. We certainly could give more examples of research in these and other human resource areas. Our point in this discussion is that very central to the use of surveys in all these areas is the issue of construct validity and that good measurement of variables cannot be separated from theoretical issues. Researchers must understand the constructs they wish to measure prior to the construction of their instruments.

Once a researcher has clearly identified the constructs of interest and has considered various data collection options and has decided to collect data via a written questionnaire or survey, he or she then must plan the survey. Planning the survey involves a consideration of the survey's goals, strategies to obtain valid measures of the constructs in which we are interested, and methods of data analysis. This is a critical phase since changes to questionnaires and sampling plans are impossible after the instruments are distributed. (This is less true for interview research or participant observation methods which frequently can be modified given the type of information uncovered during the research). In the next section, we outline some of the issues one should consider when planning a survey. The remainder of this chapter is devoted to many practical issues in survey construction, administration, data analysis, and interpretation. The guide to solving these problems lies in the theoretical or conceptual rationale for conducting the survey. Hence, survey research should always be preceded by consideration of the underlying theoretical issues involved as it is in this chapter.

PLANNING THE SURVEY

In planning a survey, it is most useful to consider the final needs for data and to work backwards to the beginning of the survey research process, as outlined in Figure 10-3. With a clear understanding of the need for data, one can consider the type of analyses and tables that would be useful in answering those needs. This will lead us to a consideration of the subgroups we will want to include in the survey, the items that will unambiguously identify those subgroups, and whether the potential available sample will allow separate analyses by all subgroups. Consideration of the type of respondents required will lead to issues involving sampling from various subgroups and how the reading level and perceptions of individuals in these subgroups will affect questionnaire items.

Many questionnaire projects in actual organizations are initiated with only a vague notion that something is wrong and that a survey might identify the nature of the problem (for example, turnover, absenteeism, or high accident rates). Frequently unstated at early stages of survey research projects is the desire that the survey will tell organizational decision makers what to do about the problems that are identified. In order to make informed policy recommendations based on survey results, appropriate questions must be included in the questionnaire. This demands that the authors of the survey understand the issues well enough through interviews, literature reviews, or participant observation that they can ask questions that will allow the evaluation of relevant hypotheses. In planning a survey, there are a number of questions that must be asked. In the remainder of this section, we will pose some of these questions using the example of a hypothetical company seeking to reduce turnover among its highly trained computer scientists.

What Are the Survey Objectives?

The first, and arguably, the most important questions that require detailed answers during the planning phase is what information the survey is supposed to supply, and what the organizational sponsors or researchers expect to get from the survey. A researcher typically will want to address theoretical questions while an organizational client usually will want to know why some problem has occurred and what can be done about the problem. For example, the organization manager concerned about the turnover of computer science personnel undoubtedly will want to know why people are leaving and what actions can be taken to decrease the turnover rate. In planning the survey it would be useful to find out what the current rate of turnover is, how that

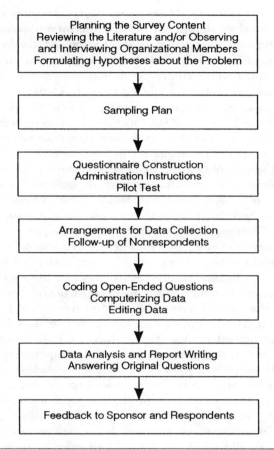

FIGURE 10-3 Steps in Survey Research

rate compares with other similar companies, and, if possible, to compile information about the performance and demographic characteristics of those who recently had left the organization. This information would tell us whether the organization's turnover is unusual, whether turnover is functional (that is, the least competent leave), and whether there are any subgroups that should be surveyed to clarify the problem.

Interviews with people who recently have left, might lead to hypotheses about the following: role of pay, department supervision, promotion opportunities, attractiveness of alternate job opportunities, opportunities to increase work-related skills and knowledge, and so on. Questioning those individuals about what might have made them stay may lead to the development of survey questions that have direct policy implications. Perhaps this initial gathering of information will lead to hypotheses that suggest that education, marital status, gender, or ethnic status play a role in turnover rates. These hypotheses will lead to questions which will allow the breakdown of data into the relevant subgroups and also will have implications for decisions regarding the nature of the respondent sample as well as information on the constructs relevant to the issue of turnover. The use of focus group interviews described on page 147 in Chapter 4 may be helpful in this stage of planning.

Once we have the answers to these questions we are ready to formulate some of the questions in the survey. Before we proceed we should ask whether the survey is necessary. Because of the widespread use of surveys, they have a significant nuisance value and should be used sparingly. Will the survey design provide the information needed? For example, if a survey that is designed to examine turnover includes only current employees, it may not generate information about the actual reasons for job changes. Alternatively, a literature review, a handful of exit interviews, and a consideration of the labor market and where people go when they leave may tell company administrators what they need to know about the turnover problem in order to initiate actions to change turnover rates. They then may decide to evaluate such actions using one of the experimental or quasi-experimental research designs suggested in Chapter 11.

Is the survey the best way to obtain the needed information? Frequently, much relevant information about a problem already is available in company archives. For example, the organization should have information on educational background, gender, absenteeism, tardiness, performance, and marital and family status that might suggest some potential explanations of the turnover problem. The use of surveys often is criticized as providing only a superficial understanding of a problem. If one is interested in the process whereby individuals finally come to a decision to leave an organization, it might be necessary to use a series of in-depth interviews with employees or retrospective interviews with former employees. We believe, however, that these interviews ought to be carried out in preparation for questionnaire construction. If the problem is so simple that the interviews provide the needed answers, fine. Most frequently, however, there will be a desire to gather information from a broader group of people in a less expensive and less time-consuming way than through interviews. Questionnaires, for which appropriate planning has taken place, include questions that should be responsive to the superficiality criticism.

Finally, there should be a consideration of all the likely stakeholders in a survey research project. In addition to policy makers or personnel who want specific information from the survey and may even want to use the survey results to promote a particular point of view or program, individual workers also may use the survey to "get even." The union almost always will have concerns about a survey and may want access to survey data. Questions about who has access to the data or who owns the data should be clearly spelled out prior to survey administration. The sequence of feedback to survey participants, degree of feedback, and who will give feedback should be considered so as to plan adequately for this critical aspect of survey research. Finally, the level of aggregation of the results (i.e., supervisory unit, work group level, department, etc.) must be determined prior to survey administration to ensure appropriate safeguards regarding confidentiality and to provide appropriate expectations regarding the level of feedback possible.

What Is to Be Measured?

After defining the goals of the research and deciding that a survey is an appropriate means of data collection, the researcher then must decide how to translate the general concepts or terms expressed in the research objectives into actual questionnaire items. Some variables such as sex, age, and level of education may be quite concrete and easily translated into a questionnaire item with discrete options as possible answers. Even variables such as these, however, are occasionally difficult to place in structured format (see the discussion on questionnaire design with regard to item formats that follows). Variables such as job satisfaction, social skills, and achievement motivation are abstract constructs that require careful conceptual consideration as they are translated into questionnaire items. Some variables, such as marital status or employment status, may appear fairly concrete but also require careful definition. For example, marital status defined as single, married, divorced, and widowed may appear fine but individuals who are divorced or widowed also are single and some of those who are married may have been divorced. Also neglected in this classification are individuals who live with each other but who never have been formally married. These persons likely would respond "single" to the marital status question but be more like married persons in various ways that are relevant to the research. In considering employment status, we must decide how many hours a person must work to be considered fully employed. Also, are members of a family business all considered employed? How are seasonal workers treated? In many areas, standard definitions (e.g., codes used by the U.S. government) are available. Unless there is good reason to do otherwise, the adoption of accepted (and presumably construct valid) items is to the investigators' advantage. In the case of all items, there is no substitute for clear conceptual definitions. We must consider the realm of behaviors represented by a particular concept; for example, job satisfaction, and then include items that sample the domain in which we are interested. This, of course, again represents an issue of construct validity that we discussed on pages 107–112 in Chapter 3.

In all survey research projects in which your authors have participated, the issue of the inclusion of *exploratory items* has been raised. Exploratory items are questions in which someone expresses some interest, but about which there are neither specific hypotheses nor plans for data analyses. To decide whether or not to include such items we must consider at least two conflicting objectives: (a) the desire to keep the survey as short as possible to maximize response rates and the level of seriousness with which all questions are answered, and (b) the desire to use the questionnaire as a means of testing new ideas. Since most questionnaires suffer because they are too long, our opinion is that the interest and rationale in such exploratory items must be extremely convincing. Exploratory items frequently are never analyzed because those who requested their inclusion are no clearer as to the rationale for their inclusion after data has been collected than they were before. Lacking any clear rationale for the items, they also fail to provide any clear plan for data analysis.

In deciding which questions to ask and how to ask them, it often is quite useful to seek the opinions and input of the individuals who will use the survey results. Oftentimes, people will try to explain away survey results which indicate the need for change or an unfavorable reaction to some policy on the grounds that the question was worded in a way that they think demands a negative response. If these individuals participate in advance in writing the questions, they feel more involved and are more likely to use the data once it comes back. Of course, a researcher who wants to use existing scales so as to be consistent in measuring a previously researched construct could not tolerate this kind of participation. For research purposes, most often it is advisable to use existing measures so as to allow comparisons across research studies. In this case, involvement in other aspects of the study may be feasible, however.

Who Will Answer the Survey?

Once we have clear conceptual definitions of the variables in which we are interested, it is time to consider the groups of people to whom the survey is appropriately directed. The findings of a survey are applicable only to the population from which we draw a sample. Human resource practitioners very often are interested in the results of a survey applied to a particular organization. Survey questions should be directed to some or all of the following groups:

1. persons working in different geographic locations;
2. persons working in different functional units (sales, marketing, finance, production, research and development, etc.);

3. persons working in different supervisory units; and

4. persons working at different hierarchical levels (hourly versus salary employees).

Consideration of the nature of the variables one is interested in measuring may dictate that the survey does not apply to one or more of these groups. For instance, questions regarding the availability of public transportation would be inappropriate in a rural community. Or, questions regarding the boring nature of work might not be relevant for a research and development section.

If one's interest is making more general statements about working people (i.e., statements with external validity), the question of who to survey is even more difficult. If we're interested in the degree to which people working at different occupational levels experience role ambiguity, we would want to make sure our sample included members of a range of occupational levels. If we want to investigate the degree to which physicians experience stress, we would be interested in sampling physicians who serve a variety of patients under different types of working situations (i.e., physicians working with other physicians, physicians working in a research institution, health maintenance organization employees, or physicians practicing alone). In the latter example, we are suggesting that stress might be affected by the degree to which responsibility and working hours are shared. Whether this hypothesis is correct or not the point is that the type of respondent we seek to include is dictated by the variables in which we are interested.

Once we have decided that a particular group of people is to be the target of our survey, it is very likely that this group will be too large to allow that each person be surveyed. In this case, we will want to select a sample from the population whose responses we would like to be able to represent. In the next section, we will discuss the development of sampling plans. We will find that we can achieve very accurate estimates of population statistics from samples containing a relatively small proportion of the population. While accuracy of estimates often can be achieved with a small sample of a total population, it may be desirable to include all potential respondents when the survey is to be used as an intervention (see the discussion of survey feedback research that follows). Telling a group of employees that survey results come from a sample may lead to attributions that the results do not represent their answers but those of someone else.

THE SAMPLING PLAN

For a sample to be a useful representation of some larger group, it must reflect the similarities or differences found in the larger group or population. Very frequently, human resource researchers use what is called a *convenience sample*. This means that we use a sample that is easy to obtain, a sample of people that we think will respond, or one for which we have been able to achieve organizational approval. Despite the prevalence of this practice, we recommend against it. Instead, the best way to achieve a representative sample is to select randomly the respondents from the population of interest. Without random sampling of respondents, the results may be biased in some unknown or unanticipated way. We will describe the basics of sampling and the confidence with which we can make inferences about a population from a sample. We also will indicate some ways in which one might be able to check on the representativeness of a sample when circumstances force the use of the nonrandom selection of respondents.

In discussing sampling, it is important to remember that the *population* is the total group about whom we are interested in gaining information. The *sample* is the set of respondents from this population from whom we actually collect information. From the measurements taken from this sample, we *estimate* the characteristics of the population.

Random Sampling and Population Estimates

To obtain a random sample of some group of people we first must have a complete list of all the people in the population. In most organizations, such a list would be relatively easy to compile. If one is interested in the members of a community or state or the unemployed in a particular region such lists are more difficult to come by. When this list is compiled, people are selected in such a way that each person has the same chance to be selected. Names of individuals can be drawn from an urn which included all individual names or one could use random number tables (Games & Klare, 1967; Winkler & Hays, 1975). Or, if the set of respondents is computerized, most software packages include a random sampling routine that would save a great deal of work.

Note that random sampling is not the same as taking anyone that is available on a street corner or who happens to leave a particular exit at a workplace. Random sampling means each and every specific person or element in the population has exactly the precise same probability of being included in the sample.

It also is true that we rarely get responses from the first randomly selected subjects. Some of them cannot be located or some refuse to participate. In some instances, researchers try to select replacement subjects who match the characteristics of the persons who cannot be located. This is apt to be undesirable, since there usually are many variables on which a match may be desired and the process of matching rapidly becomes unmanageable. It is best to randomly select additional persons until the desired sample size is achieved.

After collecting data from this sample, we will compute averages, standard deviations, correlations between items or variables, and other descriptive statistics. We then are interested in making statements about the degree to which these summary statistics apply to the population as a whole. For example, we may have sampled 200 people from the marketing division of a large organization and are now interested in saying that their responses represent the opinions of the marketing division. In Chapter 3, we introduced the notion of the standard error of measurement and said that with a less than perfectly reliable measuring instrument, we would expect some variability in actual measured values around a true value. If a person could be measured many times, the standard error would be the standard deviation of the observed values we would have expected to see. In this case, the standard error represents the standard deviation of the values we would expect to get if we took similar measures from an infinite number of samples of size 200. The standard error of the mean (the descriptive statistic we're most frequently interested in) is given as follows:

$$\overline{S}_x = \sqrt{(N - n/N)\,(s^2/n)} \qquad\qquad (10.2)$$

where S_x equals the estimated standard error,
N equals the population size,
n equals the sample size,
and s^2 equals the variance of the sample.

Let's say the average age of the 200 sample respondents was 32, the standard deviation of their ages was 6, and the total marketing division consisted of 2000 employees. In this case, the standard error would be computed as follows:

$$\overline{S}_x = \sqrt{(2000 - 200/2000)\,(36/200)} = .40.$$

The average age of the 200 respondents was 32, but it would be unlikely that the average age of all 2000 marketing employees was 32. However, we would know that the chances are 95 out of 100 that the average age of the population lies between $32 \pm (1.96(.4))$ or the average age is between 31.22 and 32.78. (Recall here the normal curve and the confidence interval introduced on page 41 in Chapter 2 and on pages 99–101 in Chapter 3).

Obviously, it is in our interest to get very accurate estimates of the population values or to decrease the width of the confidence interval. A relevant question in deciding on sample size is whether we ought to be concerned about absolute sample size (n) or the proportion of the sample size (n/N) from whom data are collected. In Table 10-1, we assume a sample standard deviation of 10, a population size of 10,000, and calculate the standard error of the mean.

An inspection of Table 10-1 and a calculation of the standard error for other examples yields three important conclusions. First, the standard error of the mean decreases more rapidly as a function of increases in absolute sample size than do similar increases in the proportion sampled. Practically, this means we should always be concerned most with the absolute number of survey respondents. Alternatively, increases in the sample size have a bigger payoff in decreased standard error than do similar increases in the proportion sampled. This influence of absolute sample size as opposed to proportion sampled explains why organizations that conduct polls regarding citizens' voting behavior can be very accurate when they are polling a very small proportion of the total voting population.

Second, Table 10-1 indicates that adding additional sample size yields diminishing returns as sample size gets large. So, for example, collecting data from 250 instead of 100 people results in a standard error .51 smaller in our example, while increasing sample size to 500 results in additional drop in standard error equal to .37 (.99 - .62).

Third, while we may have drawn a total sample of 2000, estimates of the means of some variable for members of different ethnic groups will be less accurate in terms of standard error of the mean than will estimates based on an N of 2000. Since the standard error of the mean depends on the absolute size of the subgroup sample, the more subgroups we analyze, the smaller are the subgroups and the larger the total sample size must be to keep the sampling error of the mean within tolerable limits.

Modifications of Random Sampling

Sometimes the requirements of random sampling cannot be met because some unit(s) will not cooperate with a research project or there is no complete or up-to-date listing of all the persons in a given community, occupation, or area. Occasionally, too, one may have information from previous work that indicates random sampling in a particular unit is not that important.

One modification to random sampling involves the use of stratification. *Stratification* involves dividing the population into subgroups and then selecting randomly from these groups. Use of stratification usually is undertaken to ensure the representativeness of the sample on some critical variable(s). For example, an organization might want to sample equal proportions of people from different supervisory or functional units. Or they might want representative proportions of different sex, ethnic, or tenure subgroups. Simple random sampling might not give exactly representative samples, particularly if the total sample size is relatively small and the number of different critical subgroups is large. Occasionally one subgroup of particular interest may be over sampled or different selection procedures will be applied because of data collection problems with a particular group.

A second modification of simple random sampling is *cluster sampling*, in which participants are chosen as members of a group rather than as individuals. Let's imagine we are interested in the adoption of safety procedures among workers who handle asbestos. If we randomly sampled all such workers, the project would be tremendously costly and might involve negotiating permis-

TABLE 10-1
An Illustration of the Effect of Sample Size and the
Proportion Sampled on the Standard Error of the Mean*

Proportion of Sample (n/N)	Sample Size (n)	Standard Error
.002	20	2.24
.005	50	1.40
.010	100	.99
.025	250	.62
.050	500	.44
.100	1000	.30
.250	2500	.17
.500	5000	.10

*Population size in this example was 10, 000 and the sample standard deviation was 10.
Source: Warwick, D. P., & Lininger, C. A. (1974). *The sample survey: Theory and practice.* New York: McGraw-Hill. Reprinted with permission.

sion to survey workers in a very large number of organizations. If we had a list of work sites or facilities at which asbestos poses a safety hazard, a possible solution would be to randomly select organizations as opposed to individuals. This approach to sampling may be a convenient, cost effective way to conduct research on human resource issues. Only these randomly selected organizations would be asked to cooperate and when one refused either another would be randomly selected or an organization similar (in type of product manufactured, demographics of the work force, size, etc.) could be selected.

The major disadvantage in using cluster sampling is the effect it has on the sampling error of the statistics computed. In the extreme case, if all the individuals in a particular cluster, or organization, were identical on a key variable and totally different from members of other organizations, then the sample size would be equal to the number of organizations, rather than to the number of people in those organizations. At the opposite extreme, all of the organizations would show the same variability on key variables as a simple random sample. In practice, Warwick and Lininger (1975) indicate sampling errors 1.5 times as large for cluster samples as for simple random samples and Kish (1965) provides computational formulas for standard errors for various clustering situations.

Another approach to selecting a sample is to order the people in the group to be sampled, to decide on the portion of the sample needed to achieve a desired sample size, then randomly to select a start point, and then to select every 5th, 10th or 20th person after that point. For example, in an organization of 2000 employees, we might decide to survey 200; hence every 10th person in an alphabetized listing would provide N equal to 200. If random selection of numbers between 1 and 10 produces 7, we would select the 7th, 17th, 27th, etc. This systematic selection is essentially equal to random selection if the potential respondents are *not* ordered on any characteristic that is related to the variables of interest. It is unlikely that an alphabetical list would be ordered in this fashion.

Occasionally, it might be desirable to sample unequally from certain subgroups. For example, if one's analysis objectives include the capability to describe a very small group then a large portion of that group will need to be included in the respondent sample in order to get reliable data on that subgroup. However, when the research objective is to describe the total population the responses of this one subgroup would be overweighted. In this latter instance, some type of compensating weights must be applied to the underrepresented individuals. For example, if an organization were particularly interested in the responses of a small minority group, it might sample from that group at three times the rate of the remaining members of the organization. In computing organizational level descriptive statistics, such as the mean, median, and percentages, the responses of the majority should be weighted three times the responses of the small minority. In computing the standard error of these weighted statistics, however, the actual population and sample sizes should be used.

Assuming we've developed a satisfactory sampling plan, one additional complication arises when not all of the sampled persons respond to the survey or we replace our original randomly selected respondents with others either themselves randomly selected or matched to the non-respondent in some way. The question of the representativeness of the final sample then arises. There is, perhaps, no way of ascertaining that the sample is completely representative, although in many cases we are likely to have data regarding the characteristics of the population as a whole. These data can be compared with similar data collected on the sample to check the possibility of nonrepresentativeness. An example of such a check on the results of a survey of business locations conducted by one of your authors (Schmitt, Gleason, Pigozzi, & Marcus, 1987) is presented in Table 10-2. In this case, the potential respondents included companies with 50–2000 employees who were members of the Michigan Chamber of Commerce. Four hundred thirty-eight organizations responded. Table 10-2 presents the respondent, their Chamber of Commerce membership, and the Department of Commerce statistics for Michigan regarding the type and size of business. As can be seen in the table, organizations working in fabricated metals are overrepresented while those in machinery were underrepresented in the respondent sample. Both the Chamber of Commerce and the respondent sample included larger organizations than the Department of Commerce figures indicate are available. This is not surprising since the Department of Commerce's statistics included many sole proprietor or family owned businesses that were usually smaller than the target companies (i.e., those with 50–2000 employees).

In comparing the respondent sample and the population sample, it is of interest to include comparison variables that might potentially influence the variables in which one has a substantive interest. For example, the survey from which the example statistics found in Table 10-2 were taken was conducted to assess the determinants of business relocations to states other than Michigan. It may have been useful to compare geographic location, location of other organizational facilities, and organizational profitability. As stated above, without random sampling and a high response rate (perhaps above 80%) we will never be sure of the representativeness of our sample, but with some obvious comparisons of sample and available population data, we can assess in some degree the relative representativeness of the sample. When these comparisons reveal a nonrepresentative sample on key variables then appropriate reservations should be made when data are interpreted. Finally, it is often a good idea to include in the survey itself questions that allow these comparisons with known population characteristics. When surveying individuals, these questions are often demographic in nature (e.g., gender or age of respondent).

There also are times when, because of the homogeneity of a sample, nonrandom sampling makes no difference. For example, unless one believes or has evidence that role ambiguity is experienced differently by men and women, it might not be disturbing that a sample contains more men than women. Such assumptions, however, should be made only with a thorough knowledge of the construct one is measuring and how it might be influenced by the other characteristics of the individuals in the population.

TABLE 10-2
Sample Characteristics (in Percentages)

Characteristic	Organization Population*	Chamber of Commerce Membership[†]	Respondent Sample
Standard Industrial Classification Category[‡]			
Food and kindred	5.4	8.0	7.9
Lumber, wood, furniture, paper (24, 25, 26)	11.9	12.0	12.3
Chemicals, rubber, plastics, etc. (28, 29, 30, 32, 33)	19.7	27.0	19.4
Fabricated metals (34)	20.2	20.0	42.9
Machinery (35, 36)	38.2	27.0	11.9
Transportation (37)	4.5	8.0	5.5
Firm Size (No. of Employees)			
0–100	91.0	40.4	37.2
100–500	7.4	49.4	48.4
500–1000	0.8	7.2	7.6
1000+	0.8	3.0	6.7
Sample Size	11,176	950	438

* U.S. Department of Commerce (1984) Table 1B.
† Michigan Chamber of Commerce (1984) membership list.
‡ Numbers in parentheses represent the Standard Industrial Classification code.

QUESTIONNAIRE DESIGN

Now that we've decided on the variables and sample to be measured we must begin to write questions and design the survey itself. Frequently, researchers and practitioners are interested in constructs that have been widely researched elsewhere and for which existing measures are available. Particularly when one of the objectives is to contribute to the scientific literature, existing measures should be used unless there is a compelling measurement (lack of reliability, too many items, etc.) or conceptual reason to develop a new measure. Use of previously existing measures, even when the primary objective is a local, practical, or policy one, will allow comparability of survey results across organizations and situations. The spectrum of previous literature is an aid to the interpretation of findings.

One group of large firms, called the Mayflower group, has organized their survey research efforts so as to take maximum advantage of survey results. The members of this group use a common core of questions across organizations and across time. This practice allows them to make interorganizational and longitudinal comparisons of survey results and to evaluate the possible impact of external or internal change on the survey results.

Structured Versus Open-Ended Items

If the choice is to develop one's own items, then one of the basic decisions is whether or not to use structured or open-ended questions. Examples of these two item types are contained in Figure 10-1 (see page 327). In making this decision, the primary considerations include the type of respondent, the purpose of the research, and the type of question. If the respondents are not likely to be very involved or if they are not likely to be accustomed to writing, open-ended questions will yield low response rates and incomplete surveys. In this instance it would be better to use structured questions. If the purpose of the research is primarily exploratory and you want the respondents to give their opinion on issues without a great deal of "prompting" or "leading" by the question itself, then it might be better to use open-ended questions.

Frequently the responses to open-ended questions are obtained from a small pilot sample whose responses are used as a basis for developing structured items. If the question is such that obvious options exist (sex, ethnic identity, state or country of residence), there is little reason for an open-ended format. Sometimes it is likely that not all options can be specified or anticipated. In these instances, it may be best to use an item similar to that in Figure 10-1C in which one of the options allows for an unanticipated response.

Finally, it is certainly true that a major consideration is the number of respondents one expects and the time and money available to code and analyze the open-ended responses. Our strong feeling is that, at least in mail surveys, all possible options be included and that the open-ended format be used sparingly. Experience with responses to open-ended formats indicates that the time expended in development of codes that somehow categorize the responses and the usual low interrater agreement in use of those codes usually means that the responses to these items are not even analyzed even when the respondents bother to answer them. Their primary advantage is the freedom allowed the respondent to express the depth of their feeling about an issue or some unconventional response.

In a study in which one of your authors used the survey method, respondents were given a space on the last page to write in comments that they wanted the sponsor to see. These pages were torn off and given to the sponsor unedited in order to provide qualitative insights to the issues involved (in this instance, salary and benefits). Interestingly, 22% of the sample of 800 chose to write comments.

Writing Items

The primary aim in item writing is to obtain complete and accurate information about the object of interest. At the same time, item writers must be sensitive to the need to maintain the potential respondents' cooperation and goodwill and to recognize their privacy and dignity. One of your authors once sent a questionnaire to a large group of women and asked a question regarding their ethnicity using the male term as the option for Mexican-Americans. Such mistakes only can be avoided by thorough pilot testing before distribution (see a more extensive discussion of pilot testing below).

While item writing is as much an art as a science, there are various guidelines against which it is useful to evaluate questionnaire items. The reader should be aware, however, that little research to evaluate these guidelines has been conducted. Remember that the primary objectives in writing items are to represent faithfully the constructs in which you are interested (recall again the discussion of construct validity on pages 107–112 in Chapter 3) and to rule out nuisance variables. Finally, note that many of the requirements for good survey items are similar to those for interview questions in general (see Chapter 4). The list of guidelines that follows is adapted from Warwick and Lininger (1975):

1. *Make sure all words are simple, direct, and familiar to potential respondents.* Sometimes researchers include technical jargon in items without recognizing that they do so. For example, instead of the word "feedback", it might be better to ask how often a supervisor or coworker tells you "how well you are doing your job." Or a question regarding the degree of "personal initiative" one can exercise in one's job might be rephrased to ascertain whether or how often the worker "can decide how to do a task" or "which task will get done."

2. *Make the question as clear and specific as possible.* In most instances, a lack of clarity results when the respondent is given an inadequate frame of reference for an answer. If we ask a worker how many people work with her or him, we may get answers that indicate how many workers are in the company, a supervisory work unit, a work group, etc. If we ask how many times someone comes in late for work, the item should specify whether we mean in a year, a month, a week, etc. "How long did you look for a job?" is a question that might generate respondent questions such as: "When? My first job? My current job?"

3. *Avoid double-barreled items.* Double-barreled items address two issues. They usually elicit an answer to only one of the two issues addressed, even when the question is open-ended. When structured response options are given, it is, of course, impossible to address both issues at once. Consider the following items:

   Do you plan to leave your job and look for another one during the coming year?
   Do you plan to retire and travel?
   Are you unemployed because of a lack of training?

4. *Avoid leading or loaded questions.* Questions can be leading when one or more option is listed with the question as in the following item:

   How often do you complain about some aspect of your work, such as the pay you receive? If all options are listed, as should be the case for an item with a structured format, then the item would not be subject to this bias.
   Another leading item might read like this one:
   How often do you drink to excess?

   This item makes the presumption that the respondent has indeed drunk too much on occasion. Again, a structured format with a "Never" response option would correct this item.

   Leading questions frequently are used by political candidates in surveys of constituents' opinions. Consider the following:

   Do you agree with my opponent's support of legislation, which would infringe on your rights, such as gun control legislation?
   Do you feel it is OK for a Congressman to own a townhouse in Washington and a condo in Florida and only rent an efficiency in the district he serves?
   Do you agree with my opponent's support of tax breaks for big business?

   These are questions actually addressed to one of your authors in an opinion poll. Not surprisingly, the results of the poll strongly supported the politician's preconceived positions, but developing campaign issues based on the results of questions formulated in this way is almost certainly misdirected. Each question is phrased so as to make it difficult for the respondent to disagree with the politician's position, whatever voters' real positions. For example, the tax breaks referred to may have positive implications for individuals as well as business and while no one likes to lose their rights, gun control legislation may not affect individual rights.

It also is possible and tempting to ask such questions on organizational attitude surveys. It is good to have top-level input into a survey, but frequently there is a strong temptation to frame questions in such a way that the survey indicates support for controversial organizational policies espoused by the organization leaders.

5. *Be sure the question is applicable to all respondents.* Questions to single respondents asking how long they have been married or to unemployed persons about how long they have worked on their current jobs are typical examples. Sometimes the question is applicable to all respondents, but the options in a structured item are not.

For example, consider the question in Figure 10-4. Persons working full-time in the home might well object to this question. Sometimes people will respond to one of the options simply to oblige the questioner or to avoid embarrassment. This often occurs when they are asked their opinion on some topic they have not previously considered and for which they really have no opinion.

The most convenient way to handle the problem of questions and their applicability to some subset of the potential respondents is to use a branching or skip format, such as that depicted in Figure 10-5. In the first question, individuals answering any of the first three options are directed to question 43A, which asks them additional detailed questions regarding which alternatives were eliminated and which criteria were used to make those eliminations. Individuals who did not decide on a business relocation in this manner would find those questions meaningless, hence, they are directed to question 44.

In question 46 in Figure 10-5, those answering "Yes" are asked for more specific information regarding the business relocation. Those who have not recently opened a facility are directed elsewhere. Note that in this case there even is an instance of further branching within the first branch (46e). Using instruments such as these can become quite complicated and requires extensive pretesting to ensure that all possible branches are included and that respondents are not confused by the rather complex directions.

The necessary pretesting and planning for surveys using branching is worthwhile, however, as it makes unnecessary the development of several sets of instruments for different types of respondents and the identification of the respondent subsamples which may be impossible prior to the administration or mailing of a survey.

It also should be noted that one of the strengths of computer-administered surveys is that such branching is done automatically as the respondent sees only those questions that are relevant to them based on their prior answers.

6. *The likelihood of response styles should be considered and appropriate steps taken to minimize their effects.* A response style is the tendency by a respondent to choose a certain response category regardless of the item's content. Your authors frequently have encountered

---

How would you describe your current employment status?

A. Unemployed
B. Part-time employment (less than 30 hours/week)
C. Full-time employment (30 or more hours/week)

FIGURE 10-4 A Question with an Incomplete Set of Options

42.   How many alternative sites did you consider?
      _____ alternative sites

      One way to select a site for a new business location is to establish a set of minimum
      criteria that the alternative must meet or exceed in order to be considered. (Examples
      might be the existence of adequate sewage-treatment facilities or a maximum cost per
      acre of land.) Did you do this when you were making your decision?

      _____ Yes, we did this to eliminate some alternatives and then looked at the remaining
               alternatives in more detail. (Go to question 43a)

      _____ Yes, we did this, and only one alternative that we looked at exceeded all the
               minimum criteria. (Go to question 43a)

      _____ Yes, we did this, but none of the alternatives that we looked at exceeded all the
               minimum criteria. (Go to question 43a)

      _____ No, we did not establish minimum criteria. (Go to question 44)

46.   In the past five years, has your company opened any new facilities?
      _____ Yes (Go to Question 46a)   _____ No (Go to Question 47)

46a. *If yes*, where is the newest facility located?
      City or County _____   State _____

46b. When was the *decision* concerning the location of this new facility actually made?
      Month _____   Year _____

46c. When was the new facility opened? Month _____   Year _____

46d. About how many full-time employees does this new facility employ?
      _____ full-time employees

46e. Was this new facility the relocation of an existing facility, that was then closed?
      Yes _____   No _____   (Go to question 47)

46f. If this was a relocation, where was the previous facility located?
      _____ City or County   _____ State

**FIGURE 10-5   Example of Items Directing Different Groups of Respondents to
Different Questions**

computerized answer sheets in which the responses form a series of straight lines
indicating the respondent likely read only one item (if any) from each set of items,
decided on a response, and then responded the same to all items.

Two response sets have been extensively studied by researchers using surveys to measure
attitudes. *Acquiescence response styles* are characterized by persons who indicate a positive
response to all statements in a scale. (Sometimes these yea sayers are distinguished from
nay sayers who indicate negative responses to all questions.) The most frequently
recommended way to minimize this response set is to word some items positively, and to
word others negatively. This supposedly forces the respondent to read all items to
discern their negative-positive nature and hopefully their content.

Recently, Schmitt and Stults (1985) drew attention to the fact that this practice may not work as intended but also may have produced frequent recognition of factors (recall the discussion of factor analysis on page 79–81 in Chapter 2) consisting of all negatively worded items. Perhaps a much more effective way of avoiding or minimizing these types of response bias is to maintain their motivation to respond carefully, for example, by keeping the survey short. People are more apt to read items rapidly and cursorily when an instrument is long and boring as a result of the repetitive nature of some response formats (i.e., strongly disagree to strongly agree).

A second major response style has been labeled *social desirability*. People who respond in a way that they think will present them in a favorable light are answering in a socially desirable way. For example, it is socially desirable for some people to say that they like challenging work, that they like opportunities to learn at work, or that they like to be able to exercise their own initiative at work. One way of dealing with the social desirability response style is to use a forced choice format, described in connection with performance evaluation instruments on pages 193–194 in Chapter 6. Unfortunately, this solution has not proven completely effective (for a full discussion of research on this topic see Zavala, 1965). Another attempt to minimize social desirability has been the development and use of *content specific anchors* as opposed to *agree-disagree* or *high-low continua*. An example of the difference between these formats is provided in Figure 10-6. Similar attempts have been used in performance ratings and are called *behaviorally anchored rating scales* (see pages 194–196 in Chapter 6). Another attempt to minimize both social desirability and acquiescence is to intermingle the items measuring a given construct throughout a survey. While this forces a person to read and think about each item independently, it may add to the confusion and frustration of respondents.

Anyone who has conducted survey research certainly could add to this list of six guides for writing items. A similar list of suggestions for writing attitude items has been compiled by Edwards (1957) and is presented in Figure 10-7A. A list of guides for multiple-choice knowledge items is contained in Figure 10-7B. However careful one is in following these or similar guidelines to produce what is felt to be a readable survey,

---

I would be willing to buy a foreign car.

General	*Content-Specific*
A. Certainly	A. I definitely prefer foreign cars and would never buy American autos.
B. Probably	B. I would be more likely to buy a foreign car but may look at American autos as well.
C. No Preference	C. I would shop for both American and foreign cars to compare their relative merits.
D. Probably not	D. I might look at some foreign cars but I prefer to buy an American model.
E. Never	E. I would never consider or look at a foreign car.

FIGURE 10-6 Example of Content-Specific Anchors in an Attitude Item

A. Attitude Items
   1. Avoid statements that refer to the past rather than to the present.
   2. Avoid statements that are factual or capable of being interpreted as factual.
   3. Avoid statements that may be interpreted in more than one way.
   4. Avoid statements that are irrelevant to the psychological object under consideration.
   5. Avoid statements that are likely to be endorsed by almost everyone or by almost no one.
   6. Select statements that are believed to cover the entire range of the affective scale of interest.
   7. Keep the language of the statements simple, clear, and direct.
   8. Statements should be short, rarely exceeding 20 words.
   9. Each statement should contain only one complete thought.
  10. Statements containing universals such as *all, always, some, none,* and *never* often introduce ambiguity and should be avoided.
  11. Words such as *only, just, merely,* and others of a similar nature should be used with care and moderation in writing statements.
  12. Whenever possible, statements should be in the form of simple sentences rather than in the form of compound or complex sentences.
  13. Avoid the use of words that may not be understood by those who are to be given the complete scale.
  14. Avoid the use of double negatives.

B. Multiple-Choice Knowledge Questions
   1. Use either a direct question or an incomplete statement as the item stem. A test's relationship to an external criterion is termed its:
     a. validity
     b. reliability
     c. utility
     d. reproducibility
   2. In general, include in the stem all words that otherwise would be repeated in each alternative.
   3. Avoid a negatively stated item stem if possible. This is especially bad when one of the distracters also contains a negative because it produces a double negative. If it is necessary to use a negative in the stem, underline or put the negative in capitals.
   4. Provide a response that competent critics agree is the best.
   5. Make all responses appropriate to the item stem. Verb and subject must be both singular or both plural. If question (stem) requires reasons, distracters should all be reasons.
   6. Make all distracters plausible and attractive to examinees who lack the information or ability tested by the item. Each distracter should attract examinees who make a specific kind of error as in the following. The ratio of 25 cents to $5 is:
     a. 5/1
     b. 1/20
     c. 1/5
     d. 20/1
     e. none of these
   7. Avoid highly technical distracters.
   8. Avoid responses that overlap or include each other.
     Average height of adult U.S. males is:
     a. less than 5'3"
     b. less than 5'5"

FIGURE 10-7 Guidelines for Item Writing

(continued on page 352)

    c. more than 5'7"
    d. less than 5'9"
9. Use none of these only when an absolutely correct answer can be given. Use as an obvious answer early in the test but sparingly thereafter. It is also inappropriate when student is looking for a best answer or a "completely correct answer."
10. Arrange responses in logical order, but don't use the same correct alternatives consistently. The average validity of personality tests is:
    a. near zero
    b. .2–.4
    c. .41–.60
    d. above .60
11. If an item is a definition, include the term in the stem and use alternate definitions as distracters.
12. Do not present a collection of True/False items as a multiple-choice question.
13. Avoid "all of the above" or b & c, c & d, a but not b & c alternatives.

FIGURE 10-7 (cont'd)

for a pilot test of the survey with a sample of the people to whom the survey will be directed.

Response Options in Likert-Type Scales

When structured response options are used, an important consideration is whether respondents use all of the options presented or only a portion of the total options presented, either all at one end of the scale, in the middle, or at both ends. This lack of variability, or *bimodal responding*, has important measurement consequences as we've already seen in Chapter 2. In human resources research, we make a great deal of use of judgments of amount and frequency. In some performance evaluation instruments, the rater judges amount—how much or how often the behavioral statements apply to an employee. The respondent to an attitude questionnaire judges frequency—how much or how frequently the statements reflect her or his opinion.

Bass, Cascio, and O'Connor (1974) have collected information about a large number of frequency and amount descriptors. Their objective was to provide descriptors that were equally spaced along a continuum. While their work was introduced in Chapter 6, it is presented in greater detail here. The results of their work are portrayed in Figure 10-8 for scales with four to nine anchors. If one is using scales of frequency and amount, these verbal descriptors would be optimal. Recently, Reagan, Mosteller, and Youtz (1989) have presented useful data on the comparability of meaning represented by various expressions of probability including quantitative expressions. It also may be advisable to objectify the anchors if it is reasonable to expect that respondents can reply accurately. For example, a frequency scale might include anchors, such as "once a week," "twice a week," "once a day," "twice a day," or "many times a day."

The data in Figure 10-8 also raise the issue of what would be an optimal number of scale points on structured survey questions of this type. Research on this issue (Lissitz & Green, 1975) indicates that reliability will increase up to five points, but that it levels off beyond that point, so that adding additional scale points gains little or nothing.

A final issue regarding questionnaire design has to do with its layout, instructions, and the ordering of items in the survey. If structured items are used and respondents are asked to indicate their answers on computerized answer sheets or directly into a computer terminal, detailed instructions with examples (see Figure 10-9) should be provided. These instructions should be

A. STATISTICALLY OPTIMAL SCALES OF FREQUENCY
(WITH PERCENTAGE OF OVERLAP BETWEEN SCALE POINTS)

No. points in scale					
9	8	7	6	5	4
8 Always 24%	7 Always 24%	6 Always 24%	5 Always 5%	4 Always 2%	3 Always <1%
7 Continually 21%	6 Continually 21%	5 Constantly 4%	4 Frequently, if not always 8%	3 Very often 12%	2 Often <1%
6 Very often 24%	5 Very often 13%	4 Often 25%	3 Quite often 1%	2 Fairly many times <1%	1 Sometimes <1%
5 Quite often 42%	4 Rather frequently 2.5%	3 Fairly many times 6%	2 Sometimes 10%	1 Occasionally <1%	0 Never
4 Fairly many times 6%	3 Sometimes 45%	2 Sometimes 10%	1 Once in a while 2%	0 Never	
3 Sometimes 45%	2 Now and then 16%	1 Once in a while 2%	0 Never		
2 Occasionally 16%	1 Not often 7%	0 Never			
1 Not very often 7%	0 Never				
0 Never					

B. STATISTICALLY OPTIMAL SCALES OF AMOUNT
(WITH PERCENTAGE OF OVERLAP BETWEEN SCALE POINTS)

No. points in scale					
9	8	7	6	5	4
8 All 44%	7 All 39%	6 All 18%	5 All 10%	4 All 2%	3 All <1%
7 An exhaustive amount of 18%	6 Almost entirely 31%	5 An extraordinary amount of 7%	4 Almost completely 16%	3 An extreme amount of 3%	2 A great amount of <1%
6 An extreme amount of 29%	5 An extreme amount of 8%	4 A great amount of 17%	3 Very much 2%	2 Quite a bit of <1%	1 A moderate amount of <1%
5 A great deal of 20%	4 A lot of 7%	3 Quite a bit of 5%	2 Fairly much <1%	1 Some <1%	0 None
4 Quite a bit of 5%	3 Fairly much 9%	2 A moderate amount of 12%	1 To some degree <1%	0 None	
3 An adequate amount of 32%	2 Some 9%	1 Somewhat 2%	0 None		
2 Some 5%	1 A limited amount of 4%	0 None			
1 A little 6%	0 None				
0 None					

Note. Each percentage shown represents the overlap in distribution between the accompanying entry's scale point and the scale point directly below that entry. For example, there is 44 % overlap in response distributions between response at Point 7 and response at Point 8 for the 9–point scale.

FIGURE 10-8 Numerical Equivalents for Expressions of Frequency and Amount
Source: Reprinted with permission from Bass, B. M., Cascio, W. F., & O'Connor, E. J. (1974). Magnitude estimations of frequency and amount. *Journal of Applied Psychology, 59,* 313–320.

This questionnaire contains 236 items in five parts dealing with your background, attitudes, and activities concerning education, employment, and life in general. Most of the questions are followed by several possible answers which are numbered below each question. Please pick the answer that best describes you and, using a number 2 pencil, fill in the space along the right side of the page which corresponds to your answer:

FOR EXAMPLE:

A.   Are you a high school graduate?

   1.   Yes

   2.   No

                                                  A.   ■ | |
                                                      1   2

Assuming you have graduated, darken the space above the number 1 as shown above.

In some cases a set of answers applies to a group of questions. In this case the instructions will indicate to which questions the answers apply.

If no possible answer is correct, you may write your own answer directly in the questionnaire booklet.

In some cases you are to *write your answer* in the blank space provided in the questionnaire. In all other cases enter your answer in the space in the right hand margin.

FIGURE 10-9 Instructions for Computerized Structural Survey Items

pilot tested as many older and less educated respondents may have had no previous exposure to computerized answer sheets and will almost always be wary or confused with the requirements of these forms.

The physical layout of the survey should be attractive, easy to use, *and* easy to code (if it is not read by computer) and otherwise process. There must also be some means to identify each survey and each page of the survey in the case of multiple pages and the possibility that the survey parts will become disconnected. To reduce paper and mailing costs, it is tempting to reduce the physical size of the survey by reducing print size or by cramming many items on a single page, but this should never be done at the expense of readability. Numbering of items should be consecutive throughout the questionnaire not restarted in different sections. Numbering sections separately increases the possibility for respondent confusion and errors in coding the data. Changing type faces, boxes, asterisks, and underlining can be very useful in alerting respondents to branches in the surveys, special instructions, negative wording, important exceptions, etc.

Pretesting the Survey

In the development of survey items, it certainly is useful to include members of the respondent population in discussions regarding readability and even item content when the survey is to address policy issues. In addition, the final version of the survey should be given to a small number (perhaps 20) of potential respondents. These people should be directed to answer the survey, but also to note any problems, confusions, and ambiguities. Pretests of components of the survey should be conducted face-to-face by someone who is working on the preparation of the survey. The pilot respondents who are answering the preliminary completed drafts of the survey should be encouraged to raise any issues that arise and need clarification as they proceed through the survey.

As a next best alternative to personal interviews, pilot respondents could be asked to tape-record their comments as they are responding. No matter how thoroughly the development phase is conducted, we can guarantee a pilot will reveal additional problems. It is an indispensable part of survey research.

Optimizing Return Rate

Gathering information by means of a survey is an extremely low cost method relative to individual or group interviews or telephone surveys, hence it is the most frequently used approach. The major disadvantage of a survey is that people can and do simply ignore it. The effects of a lack of perfect return rate on a carefully selected sample are difficult to assess, although as we indicated above, we often can compare the characteristics of the respondents with the population and the sample to which the survey was mailed if we have access to such information. In this section, we will discuss ways to maximize the return rate on surveys. The interested reader also may want to consult various issues of the *Public Opinion Quarterly* for research on various attempts to secure responses and a brief, early summary of this literature by Roeher (1963). A more recent summary of this research is contained in Heberlein and Baumgartner (1978).

In organizational research, surveys frequently are distributed at the workplace. In these instances, return rates can be enhanced by support from top-level executives and/or union officials. Such support can come in the form of an accompanying letter or previous announcements in newsletters or at worker meetings. Returns also can be increased if time is allocated at work for the completion of the survey, although this may result in feelings of coercion. The respondent should have the option to refuse without any real or perceived penalty. Certainly the most important determinant of return rates to surveys is the degree to which a work force believes in the value of the research. When it comes to problem-solving survey research, this feeling is enhanced when respondents believe that real and timely feedback regarding the results of this survey will be provided and that action on problems that the survey may identify will be taken. We will address these issues in more detail below.

Mailed surveys often are the only alternative, especially when the interest is in obtaining the responses of persons working in different organizations. In general, it seems the best returns come from surveys that look professional. Inclusion of a stamped, pre-addressed return envelope, personally-typed cover letter, use of first class mail, (Armstrong & Lusk, 1987 found that first class mail resulted in 9% higher return than business mail in a meta-analysis of experimental research on this issue), and a well-prepared and structured questionnaire all contribute to this professional appearance. Occasionally, we have used a postcard "warning" of the coming survey and asking for an indication of the respondent's willingness to respond. Postcard follow-ups, used as reminders to nonrespondents, have been used with mixed success. In one recent use of the postcard reminder sent specifically to nonrespondents, the return rate was increased from 48% to 66%. However, there are additional time and costs involved. It is likely that, by the time the post card arrives, the individual has lost or discarded the survey, and unless a new copy is provided, he or she cannot respond. In our experience most responses to survey research come within 2–4 weeks after the surveys are mailed. An additional important determinant of return rates is the length of the survey; we already alluded to the fact that long surveys also may detract from the quality of the information obtained as well.

If the respondents are personally involved or have an intrinsic interest in the subject matter addressed in a survey, return rate may be increased. One of your authors sent a mailed survey ten pages in length to business executives on their perceptions of business climate and business incentives. Perhaps reflecting their interest in this topic, nearly 50% returned completed surveys even though the survey was long and they likely were very busy. In the cover letter, there should be a convincing, but realistic, statement of how the survey is potentially relevant to the respondent and what purposes the survey is intended to serve.

Paying respondents can have an effect with some groups. In a survey research project with high school students, one of your authors increased response rates to a 400-item survey by 25% with an offer of $5.00 per completed and returned survey. This incentive certainly would not be expected to have a similar effect with business executives, although in one case we used a promise of sending $10.00 to a designated charity to enhance returns from a group of school principals. Recently, Berry and Kanouse (1987) reported higher response rates when a check was included with the mailed survey even with a relatively lengthy survey to a group of physicians.

Electronic Mail

With the increased availability of personal computers, the possibility of conducting survey research via electronic mail (Sproull, 1986) also exists. Electronic mail uses computer text-editing and communications tools to provide a high-speed message service. Anyone with a computer account can use a terminal to compose a message and send it to anyone who has a setup to receive messages on that computer or any other computer that communicates with the sending computer. According to Sproull (1986), organizations such as AT&T, Bank of America, Digital Equipment Corporation, Hewlett-Packard, IBM, 3-M, Westinghouse, and Manufacturer's-Hanover Trust have been using electronic mail for as many as ten years.

The primary advantage of electronic mail is, perhaps, its speed; in addition, as noted, an electronic survey can include branching and prompts that may be difficult or impossible to incorporate in a mailed survey. Further, there is no need to transcribe or score data, thereby eliminating the time and errors associated with these tasks in a typical written survey.

Sproull, (1986), however, identifies three issues relevant to the use of electronic mail as a research tool. Obviously, respondents must have access to a computer and large segments of the working population still do not. Respondents must be willing to use this mode of data collection and their responses should not be different than responses gathered via other more traditional methods of data collection.

In a study conducted with divisions of a large firm, Sproull (1986) found that electronic mail produced a 73% response rate, certainly higher than typical of mailed questionnaires (Heberlain & Baumgartner, 1978) but lower than participation rates among a similar group whose cooperation was requested by telephone and who were then interviewed. The time of response was less than a week (about half that of the conventional method); incomplete data occurred on about one percent of the items; subjects were fairly neutral toward this method of data collection but did indicate willingness to participate in a similar study in the future; and perhaps, most importantly, there were no substantive differences in mean responses to questions when compared to the interview-administered questionnaire method.

The questions in the Sproull (1986) study were relatively factual in content; in another study (Kiesler and Sproull, 1986) in which items were more subjective or attitudinal in nature, the authors reported that responses were more extreme and less socially desirable (Kiesler, Siegel, & McGuire, 1984). The potential for greatly facilitating the collection of survey data and perhaps enhancing the quality of the data is apparent, but data comparability as well as ethical issues discussed later in this chapter must be considered when developing the capacity to use electronic mail.

DATA ANALYSIS AND REPORT WRITING

Data analysis and report writing should have been planned prior to the conduct of the survey research. If such planning took place, then most of the work described in this section is a relatively mechanical execution of these plans. Prior to these planned analyses, there are a number of steps that should be taken to ensure the quality of the data being analyzed.

Preliminary Data Cleaning

The data analysis begins with a check of the forms for inconsistencies and obvious errors. If data are collected by computer-scored answer sheets, this checking should include a scan of answer sheets to make sure important identifying information (ID numbers, department, organization, city, etc.) has been included. At this stage, such information may be obtained from the envelope or from other sources from which the data has been sent. If physically damaged, answer sheets may be copied to another sheet, thereby making computer scoring possible and saving the respondent's answers. Also, answer sheets that were filled out in a careless manner should be discarded. These might include answer sheets in which the same response option always was used, the same pattern (1, 2, 3, 4, 3, 2, 1, 2, 3, 4 etc.) was used throughout, or even on which a picture or figure was drawn. A count of these discarded sheets should be kept and reported. Another common problem involves the respondents' use of pens as opposed to pencils, which makes the form unreadable. These answer sheets can be saved by copying responses to another sheet in pencil.

Answers that require an open-ended response entail much more work, assuming these answers will be translated into some quantifiable form. Coding categories must first be established and will most likely be developed by reading all or a large number of the responses and establishing a tentative list of mutually exclusive and exhaustive categories. These then must be described fully and rules for assigning a response to one category or another must be written. (See pages 130–135 Chapter 4.) The appropriateness of the categories is then tested by the degree to which independent coders can use the categories and can agree on the type of response given. When there is a low degree of intercoder agreement or the coders are unable to assign a large portion of the responses to any response category, the system of categorizing is inadequate.

As we stated above, the great deal of work involved in processing open-ended questions dictates that they be used sparingly. They can, however, be useful in explaining responses to structured responses (Dunham & Smith, 1979). For example, lowered scores on a job satisfaction scale may be explained by a large number of comments about a new work procedure. One of the reviewers of our text also suggested that he had used open-ended surveys in which the respondents helped code their own open-ended responses. If an employee wrote in a comment about his or her supervisor, the respondent entered the code for supervisor, then indicated whether the comment was positive or negative. People found it easy to code their own responses quickly and accurately and those responses were quickly tabulated by the codes that were used.

Once data are computerized, a listing of the file should be obtained and scanned. Data are usually input in a fixed format; that is, the answers to a particular item always are in the same place on a record and there always are the same number of responses on each record. This means that responses that are out of the input field can be readily recognized and often indicate a problem with the computerized scoring of the sheets, coder or keypuncher inaccuracy, or a respondent who failed to place answers in the correct position on the answer sheet. These problems occasionally indicate an entire record (or major portion thereof) has been incorrectly read or coded. A scan of the data listing also can reveal out-of-range responses; for example, 7s and 8s appearing in a field in which there should be only responses from 1–5 should be checked and corrected.

The next step is to compute basic descriptive data on all questionnaire items. Counts of the responses to all response options for all items should be checked for out-of-range responses (7, when the response options ranged from 1–5) or unreasonably large numbers in a given response category. Inspection of item means can direct one to a coding or formatting problem. For example, a mean of 6.6 to an item with response options of 1–5 is impossible and would alert one to some type of problem. Likewise, a standard deviation that is unreasonably large or small may represent some problem with data coding. If the range of possible responses is 6, then the standard deviation is likely to be about 1.5 (6 divided by 4, because two standard deviations on either side of the mean include most cases).

One also can detect potential problems by comparing the responses to items with one's knowledge of the respondent sample. If the survey indicates 80% of the respondents are male and you know the sample included an approximately equal proportion of males and females, some checking should take place. The problem could be a mistake in coding or scoring the data, differential male-female response rates, or inadequate sampling. When all of these potential problems or inconsistencies are checked, one is ready to begin the analyses related to the original objectives of the survey.

Analyzing and Interpreting Data

In analyzing and interpreting the results of surveys, comparisons of basic descriptive data are usually conducted and are necessary to make the results meaningful and to use them to initiate appropriate policy changes. At least four types of comparative data are possible: (a) comparisons of different departments, locations, occupational groups, etc., within an organization; (b) comparisons with similar groups in other organizations; (c) comparisons of the responses of similar groups across time; and (d) comparisons of the same group to different aspects of some content area, such as a training program or a work situation. Without such comparative data, the survey is of little or no use. Examples of all of these types of comparisons is presented in Figure 10-10.

In Figure 10-10A, the responses of people in different divisions in an organization are compared. One question that presents itself is whether the mean differences and percentile differences are meaningful. Statistical tests of significance can address the question of whether differences this large could be attributable to chance, but equally important (especially when N's are very large) is the practical significance of the difference. This is a more difficult determination to make and it probably always involves a value judgment. Here, it may be a judgment as to whether the relatively low job satisfaction in manufacturing and maintenance is a significant problem for the organization. Are these groups characterized by abnormally high rates of turnover, product sabotage, absenteeism, or grievances? If so, then the organization would want to further explore the reasons for low job satisfaction. Or perhaps there is no evidence that this low job satisfaction is being translated into unproductive behavior but the organization is interested in positive work reactions among its employees.

These questions of practicality can be better answered when other types of comparative data also are available. For example, Figure 10-10B contains comparative data for the research and development and manufacturing units in similar organizations (data from organization A is pictured in Figure 10-10A). As we can see, the figures from the research and development unit in organization A don't look very good in these comparisons and figures from the manufacturing area don't appear to be very negative. Both groups appear relatively average compared to similar groups in organizations B, C, and D.

A. Comparisons Across Departments within an Organization

Employee Job Satisfaction

Department	N	X	SD	Percentile (Corporate Wide)
				10 20 30 40 50 60 70 80 90
1. Sales	78	13.8	5.3	
2. Research & Development	22	21.7	6.1	
3. Manufacturing	238	10.2	4.8	
4. Maintenance	39	11.1	5.9	
5. Finance	18	18.9	6.1	

B. Comparisons of Similar Units Across Different Organizations

Research & Development

Organization A	22	21.7	6.1	
Organization B	13	23.2	7.1	
Organization C	48	18.6	5.9	
Organization D	38	19.8	6.3	

Manufacturing

Organization A	238	10.2	4.8	
Organization B	417	11.3	3.9	
Organization C	321	9.8	3.7	
Organization D	162	10.5	4.1	

C. Comparisons Across Time: Job Satisfaction

Research & Development (Percentiles Based on Responses of R & D Only in Various Organizations: 1980)

				10 20 30 40 50 60 70 80 90
1983	18	19.8	5.9	
1985	21	20.9	6.3	
1987	22	21.7	6.1	

Manufacturing (Percentiles Based on Manufacturing Personnel Only in Various Organizations: 1980)

1983	321	14.1	5.1	
1985	281	13.8	6.0	
1987	238	10.2	4.8	

D. Comparison of Responses of Manufacturing Group to Specific Job Satisfaction Dimensions

Satisfaction with	N	X	SD	Percentiles Based on Manufacturing Personnel in Various Organizations
Work	321	12.2	5.1	
Coworkers	328	11.3	5.3	
Pay	325	8.9	3.2	
Supervision	323	7.6	4.0	
Promotions	322	10.5	4.7	

FIGURE 10-10 Various Possible Comparisons of Survey Responses

Further comparisons of the research and development and manufacturing groups' responses indicate that the research and development group has remained relatively stable over the period during which surveys have been conducted while the manufacturing group has experienced a relatively sizable decline in job satisfaction. In this case, the job satisfaction instrument contained items related to various aspects of work as depicted in the Job Description Inventory (Smith,

Kendall, & Hulin, 1969). This allowed for the comparisons in Figure 10-10D which indicate that the manufacturing respondents' dissatisfaction relates primarily to supervision and pay. The survey, then, has identified a potential problem area and, as described below, the organization must proceed to develop more concrete notions of the nature of the problem and to develop interventions that provide solutions to these problems.

Several aspects of these hypothetical data analyses are important. First, data gain meaning only by virtue of relevant comparisons. To allow these comparisons to take place, one must plan for them by asking appropriate questions of the respondents (i.e., their department, work group, tenure, sex, ethnic status, job classification, etc.). Second, survey data can be much more useful if there is a large comparative data base collected over a period of time. Changes can be noted and in some instances related to specific events. For example, it appears as though the manufacturing work force in organization A is declining (see the sample sizes in Figure 10-10D). This decline in the workforce may be the reason (direct or indirect) for the lower levels of satisfaction with supervision and pay. Third, it should be obvious that survey research can serve as one means by which to identify and localize problems. Finally, Figure 10-10 should serve as an illustration that pictorial data can be very useful in communicating the results of surveys. A useful discussion of do's and don'ts of communicating results to various members of an organization is contained in Dunham and Smith (1979).

When we present survey data in cross tabulation form as in Figure 10-10 or in correlational form in research papers, one temptation is to infer that one of the variables is causing the other. For example, in Figure 10-10A, it looks like working in the manufacturing area might cause lower job satisfaction; we may draw the conclusion that this is because of something for which management in the manufacturing sector is responsible. This, of course, appears not to be the case as the comparisons in Figure 10-10B indicate a more plausible explanation is that these within-corporation differences are associated with the occupation or work group and that the satisfaction of the employees in the manufacturing unit is similar to that of manufacturing employees in other organizations. The important point is that any causal interpretations should be made with a great deal of caution. A more complete discussion of the appropriateness of causal attributions is contained in Chapter 2 (see pages 55–57).

Finally, as mentioned at the beginning of this chapter, survey data frequently are used to test theoretical or research issues as well. In these instances, concerns about internal consistency reliability or the appropriate operationalizations of some concepts (their construct validity) are of greater concern than they might be if results were to be used only within a single organization. Analyses might include the full range of techniques discussed in Chapter 2 (correlations, factor and cluster analyses, and regression analyses). Use of these techniques may be made in survey research at the organizational level, but the communication of the results of those analyses must minimize jargon, emphasize implications, and use simple tables, graphs, and terms.

SURVEY FEEDBACK AS AN ORGANIZATIONAL INTERVENTION

Employees in organizations, as well as respondents to surveys that do not have specific organizational concerns, usually want to know the results of a survey. If the survey includes questions regarding organizational policy or problems, employees will want to know what impact the survey results have on organization policy and programs. Successful reporting of results depends on how well the feedback process is designed and implemented, as well as on how well the organization can implement changes suggested by the results of the survey. Survey feedback research, then, may be a useful means to organizational change. Like all organizational change efforts, ineffective use of surveys can produce negative motivational outcomes for the organization and will certainly destroy the utility or feasibility of conducting survey research in the future.

In Table 10-3, French and Bell (1978) compare what they call a *traditional attitude survey* with a *survey feedback approach*. Most notably, approaches are different in the degree to which all employees are given detailed feedback on the survey and are asked to derive solutions to problems. It is our position that a survey researcher is ethically obligated to provide *at least* the information implied in the French and Bell traditional approach. If the only interest in conducting a survey is to examine research hypotheses, it might be expedient to provide only a short overall summary of the research findings to respondents. However, even in this instance, such a strategy would seem shortsighted. Surveys are widely used and, if we are to expect serious responses, we must be prepared to provide feedback at the level of detail desired by respondents. Sometimes an overall summary of the findings, their implications, and any planned action is sufficient if we also provide the option of obtaining additional data.

TABLE 10-3
Two Approaches to the Use of Attitude Surveys

Basis of Comparison	Traditional Approach	Survey Feedback or OD Approach
Data collected from	Rank and file, and perhaps supervisors	Everyone in the system or subsystem
Data reported to	Top management, department heads, and perhaps employees through company newsletter	Everyone who participated
Implications of data are worked on by	Top management (maybe)	Everyone in work teams, with workshops starting at the top (all superiors with their subordinates)
Third-party intervention strategy	Design and administration of questionnaire, development of a report	Obtaining concurrence on total strategy, design and administration of questionnaire, design of workshops, appropriate interventions in workshops
Action planning done by	Top management only	Teams at all levels
Probable extent of change and improvement	Low	High

Source: French, W. L., & Bell, C. H. (1978). *Organization development: behavioral science interventions for organization improvement.* Englewood Cliffs, NJ: Prentice-Hall.

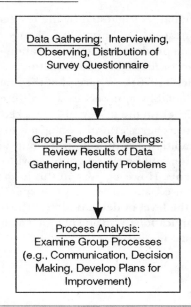

FIGURE 10-11 The Survey Feedback Process
  Source: Adapted with permission from Beer, M. (1980). *Organization change and development*. Santa
  Monica, CA: Goodyear.

When survey feedback is used as the basis of a change effort, there usually are three distinct phases to the process. These stages (Beer, 1980) or phases are presented in Figure 10-11. In this chapter and consistent with the book's objectives, we have described the data gathering stage of this organization development process. Thus, consistent with the techniques outlined in Chapter 2, data are analyzed and descriptive statistics for various groups are presented and the change agent (consultant) prepares a summary of the results for group feedback sessions. The various parts of a feedback report described in Figure 10-12 are taken from Dunham and Smith (1979).

The feedback meetings usually involve members of two or three organization levels. These groups are kept small to enable individual input and interaction. Meetings usually begin with top management and then progressively include employees at lower levels of the organization until all employees have participated in a feedback group. These sessions usually are led by the group manager rather than by a human resource department or an outside consultant to enable the transfer of data "ownership" from the consultant (who may actually have done the work) to the manager. The human resource professional may still help the manager to prepare for the meeting by reviewing the data and suggesting ways of stimulating discussion, identifying problems, and generating solutions. Feedback consists of average scores on attitude scales and profiles of the group's attitudes on various dimensions as well as comparisons with other groups in the organization as provided in Figure 10-10. Guidelines for managers leading these sessions are contained in Figure 10-13.

In the process analysis stage, action plans for improvement are developed. The group may examine its method of making decisions, communicating, and accomplishing its work. Usually, the consultant contributes to this discussion. Occasionally, several sessions are required before groups can come to concrete improvement plans. Usually, some member of the group is asked to monitor the degree to which these plans are implemented and to encourage that implementation.

1. *Brief Introduction.* This includes an expression of appreciation to respondents for their participation, a brief explanation of when and why the survey was carried out, and an endorsement
   of the program by the manager. If the report is to be read, it is helpful to comment on the reason
   for reading it rather than discussing it informally. A suggested approach might be, "I hope you
   will pardon me if I read this report to you. As you know, the survey dealt with a number of areas
   and I want to make sure I cover all of them."

2. *Statement of Favorable Areas.* It is usually best to begin with the areas that received favorable
   responses to let people know that the focus of the session is not on negative points only. In fact,
   a common misconception of employees and management is that surveys are only concerned
   with problem areas. The majority of surveys yield a balance of praise and criticism about the
   organization, and a responsible manager will want to present both sides. Organizational
   strengths are of equal or greater importance than weaknesses and should be emphasized in
   feedback sessions.

3. *Statement of Mixed Areas.* In most surveys, there are categories that receive a balanced
   reaction of positive and negative feelings and others that receive, on the average, responses
   of mild approval or disapproval. It is important to explain to respondents that there are
   differences of opinion on some issues and that others are not of major concern to most people
   in the organization.

4. *Statement of Negative Areas.* This is frequently the most difficult area for managers to handle,
   since they are likely to be sensitive to any criticism of their units or operations. It is important that
   all such areas are covered, however, because any attempt to avoid them may cause resentment
   among respondents. (Several suggestions on how to handle some of the most sensitive
   problems appear later in the chapter.)

5. *Statement of Planned Actions.* Respondents want to learn the results of a survey, but frequently
   they are more interested in knowing what actions will result. Therefore, managers should
   indicate which actions they can and will take, which actions they can but will not take, which
   actions will have to be taken by managers at a higher level, and which actions will require the
   cooperation of both managers and employees. Usually, the most immediate action that
   managers take in response to survey results involves a tangible aspect of the work situation or
   one that is most important to many respondents. Other actions may take more time and money,
   but it is very important to communicate any contemplated actions in the feedback session. In
   addition, actions desired by employees which cannot be initiated for economic or other reasons
   should be communicated along with the explanations of why such actions cannot be carried
   out. This will not please most respondents, but people generally accept a straight answer if it
   is explained reasonably.

6. *Call for Discussion.* The preceding steps involve one-way or downward communication. If this
   information is presented in an authoritarian manner, the survey feedback process can
   disintegrate into a passive reception of information by employees. This, of course, defeats the
   main purpose of survey feedback. By requesting questions and encouraging discussion of the
   points raised in the report, managers can prevent this problem.

FIGURE 10-12   Suggestions for Content and Organization of Survey Feedback Report
Source: Reprinted with permission from Dunham, R. B., & Smith, F. J. (1979). *Organizational surveys.*
Glenview, IL: Scott-Foresman.

USE OF SURVEYS IN TRAINING NEEDS ANALYSIS

Before initiating training programs in organizations, an analysis of the training needs of an
organization is recommended (see Chapter 11; Goldstein, 1986; Wexley & Latham, 1981). A *needs
analysis* is designed to identify where in the organization training is needed, what a trainee must
learn in order to perform the job effectively, and which employees need training. A thorough
analysis of training needs usually involves an analysis and survey of the organization, the employ-

1. *Avoid a Defensive Posture when Dealing with Criticism.* This will encourage discussion. Managers who can accept criticism or suggestions about their units usually generate a great deal of respect and are likely to open up important channels of communication with their subordinates. This is not to suggest that managers must agree with or act upon all critical comments, but they should treat them as a valid and valuable source of information. Trying to dismiss an observation reported in a survey is unwise and usually stifles the discussion. It should be remembered that human perceptions rather than objective facts are reported in a survey. These perceptions often determine behavior; they are valid in the minds of the individual respondents regardless of whether they are, in fact, accurate or inaccurate.

2. *The Use of Humor Can Contribute Greatly to the Ideal Climate in a Feedback Meeting.* It relieves tension and can be an effective means of dealing with difficult situations. If it is directed at individuals or used as a way of dismissing problems, however, it actually becomes dysfunctional. This point is often overlooked by managers who are uncomfortable discussing a given section of the survey report. In an effort to release their own tensions, they are likely to resort to some joking comment or sarcastic remark.

3. *Managers Should Avoid Treating any Subject Area as Frivolous.* The fact that it was highlighted in the survey report indicates that it represents the attitudes of a substantial group of people. If these results are dismissed or treated as a minor issue, employees may feel that managers are talking down to them or shutting them off.

4. *A Real Effort Should be Made to Treat Criticism of Management or the Management Staff as Constructive Information.* Managers should neither apologize for nor defend their leadership: they should attempt to face the issue directly. In doing so, it is not necessary to describe the details of the criticisms or the personalities of the supervisors involved. In fact, it would be as great a mistake to identify staff members who may have been criticized as it would be to ignore the subject altogether. However, the general subject can be discussed to show employees that their complaints have been heard and are being seriously considered.

FIGURE 10-13 Suggestions for Manager's Conduct of a Survey Meeting
Source: Reprinted with permission from Dunham, R. B., & Smith, F. J. (1979). *Organizational surveys.* Glenview, IL: Scott-Foresman.

ees, and the employees' tasks. Recall also the discussion of criterion development and measurement of individual and organizational effectiveness in Chapter 5, Chapter 6, and Chapter 7.

Organization analysis involves questions regarding how the organization interfaces with its external environment, whether it is accomplishing its stated objectives, and the attitudes and perceptions of its members. The primary purpose of organization analysis is to ascertain where in the organization training is needed. Information on the ages and skill levels of employees in various departments and jobs obviously is central in a determination of where training is needed. In addition, it often is useful to assess the organizational climate or environment to ascertain whether or not employees are satisfied with various aspects of organizational policy and what perceptions they have of the organization's efforts and policies. These perceptions almost always are measured via survey and can play an important role in determining whether employees will cooperate with or resist training efforts.

In task analysis, the focus is on a determination of which tasks an employee must perform and the knowledge, skill, and ability requirements associated with these tasks. Further, the task analysis should reveal what tasks an employee should be expected to perform when hired as opposed to those tasks he or she would learn to perform after having been hired. Finally, of the latter tasks, some determination must be made regarding which tasks (and the accompanying knowledge, skills, and abilities) can be best imparted through a formal training program and which will be acquired through on-the-job training and experience. We described some of the methods and rating scales used in task analysis in Chapter 5 (see page 163–167). Use of job descriptions and observation would be used to identify the tasks in a training needs analysis and these tasks might comprise the items that would be evaluated on various scales in a survey conducted with expert job incumbents. These judgments regarding tasks would then be translated into training objectives.

The person analysis is designed to catalog the human assets (knowledge, skills, abilities, and other characteristics) of the current work force. To do this adequately, one might use performance evaluations (see Chapter 6), performance or skill tests (see Chapter 8), and occasionally surveys of employee opinions or attitudes. Occasionally, also, the person analysis involves a self-assessment by survey of the type of training needed (see Ford & Noe, 1987, for an example). One such set of training need survey items is contained in Table 10-4.

Clearly, the use of surveys is an important aspect of training needs analysis and the application of the principles outlined in this chapter ought to contribute to the utility and accuracy of the information acquired in a training needs analysis.

SPECIAL CONCERNS FOR USE OF SURVEYS IN RESEARCH

Throughout this chapter, we have emphasized the usefulness of surveys in providing research that would provide answers to various practical and theoretical questions or as a guide to organizational policy decisions. In this section, we try to highlight issues that are particularly important in survey research. Some of these issues have been mentioned previously at various points in this chapter. Our intent in addressing them again here is to draw special attention to their importance.

Earlier in this chapter we indicated the need to keep questionnaire instruments short. This requirement often means that researchers are tempted to use only certain items from existing measures. So, an 11-item locus of control measure will be shortened to three items, or a 50-item climate scale will be reduced to ten items. While the measures from which these items are derived may have desirable psychometric characteristics and may have a degree of construct validity, subsets of items may or may not be appropriate representations of the same construct. It is not

TABLE 10-4
Examples of Training Need Survey Items

Basic Management Skills (Organizing and Planning, Delegation, Problem Solving)
    Setting goals and work objectives
    Developing realistic time schedules to meet work requirements
    Identifying and weighing alternative solutions
Interpersonal Skills (Developing Subordinates, Motivating Others, Building Teamwork
    Resolving interpersonal conflicts
    Creating a developmental plan for employees
    Identifying and understanding individual employee needs
Administrative Skills (Labor Relations, Safety, Equal Employment Opportunity)
    Ensuring maintenance on equipment, tools, and safety controls
    Understanding and interpreting national/local agreements and shop rules
Quality Control (Statistical Process Control)
    Analyzing and interpreting statistical data
    Constructing and analyzing charts, tables, and graphs
    Using statistical software on the computer

Source: Ford, J. K., & Noe, R. A. (1987). Self-assessed training needs: The effects of attitudes toward training, managerial level, and function, *Personnel Psychology, 40*, 39–53. Reprinted with permission.

correct to cite earlier studies on the full scale as support for the reliability and validity of shortened scales. If the survey instrument gets too long in these instances, it may be better to reduce the number of variables (or scales) included in the survey or find alternate methods of measuring some variables.

A second problem that occurs in survey research has been labeled the percept-percept problem (mentioned also in the evaluation of organizational interventions on pages 378–381 in Chapter 11). Researchers doing theoretical research usually are interested in determining the interrelationships between the variables they measure. For example, a researcher interested in organizational commitment might think job satisfaction, organizational climate, and job perceptions all contribute to people's commitment to an organization. However, if all these variables are measured in a single instrument, any mood or general response tendency possessed by the respondents will affect their responses to all measures and serve to inflate the observed correlations between variables. The fact that correlations between questionnaire measures tend to be positive and relatively high may be due at least in part to this percept-percept problem. This problem is, of course, important when the researcher hypothesizes a functional relationship between variables; that is, one or more of the variables measured is a dependent variable and the others are conceptualized as causes or independent variables. This problem will serve to destroy the construct validity of the measures used and the internal validity of the entire study.

Some measures can be taken to minimize or eliminate the percept-percept problem. The best solution, of course, is to consider whether all variables ought to be measured by questionnaire. The best guide here is to consider whether you are theoretically interested in the research participants' perceptions or some other "objective" reality. If the latter, then an alternate form of measurement ought to be considered. In task design research we might be interested in perceptions of job or task design, but at some point in a program of research one would almost certainly want to take some objective measurements of how the work is arranged.

If one does decide to measure all or part of the variables in a survey then it might be best to separate those items measuring independent variables from those measuring dependent variables. Or, it may be wise to collect the two sets of variables at different points in time. In this way, any temporary mood or reaction on the part of participants will not serve to inflate correlations between measures, although there still may be some inflation in observed relationships due to stable personal dispositions that are not relevant to the measured constructs.

Separation in time of measurement of the variables also may help the researcher establish some causal sequence in the observed relationships between variables. If job satisfaction at time 1 is correlated with turnover intentions at time 2, we are somewhat more comfortable with the assertion that job satisfaction causes subsequent turnover intentions than we would be if both measures were collected at the same point in time. Of course, the timing of these two data collection efforts also would affect the appropriateness of causal attributions. At the very least, it would not be likely that turnover intentions caused job satisfaction. Such issues of research will be the focus of Chapter 11.

If data are collected at two different times, then the researcher also must take care to identify the respondents to allow matching their answers in the two instruments. This, of course, raises issues regarding the confidentiality of answers. Occasionally, your authors have asked that each respondent use an identification number (such as his or her mother's birthdate) so as to allow matching across time and yet retain the anonymity of the respondents. If this type of solution is impossible or unsatisfactory, then respondents must be informed as to how their identity is being established and what confidentiality safeguards are being employed.

In survey research, as in other types of research, it is important to consider what other "nuisance" or contaminating variables might affect the measures and variables in which you are interested primarily. Age, sex, experience, education, socioeconomic status and/or organizational policies are examples of variables that may be related to various measures of interest to organizational researchers or these variables may affect the range of scores on other measures or interrelationships between variables of interest. Careful review of the literature, a clear conceptual understanding of the variables of interest, and knowledge of the respondent sample will suggest what these nuisance variables might be. Measures of these variables must then be included in the survey so as to enable an assessment of their effect; or, some alternate means must be taken to eliminate or minimize their effect.

Finally, theoretical research also necessitates a careful consideration of the scale anchors used with each item or set of items to ensure that respondents will exhibit some response variability. In applied research, it may be appropriate to have questionnaire respondents indicate "Yes" or "No" to items indicating whether they have experienced certain stress symptoms. A finding that none or all of the respondents have experienced a stress symptom would be useful knowledge. Theoretically, however, this variable would be of no use since it has no variability. Only prior knowledge of the variable being measured or a pilot effort will tell a researcher whether there is likely to be any response variability on items with a certain response scale.

ETHICAL CONCERNS IN SURVEY RESEARCH

The conduct of survey research usually involves at least three significant concerns. First, the participants must be informed adequately as to the objectives of the research and the intended use of the data generated by the survey. Second, adequate safeguards must be taken to preserve the anonymity of the respondents. If it is necessary to identify the respondents who gave certain answers (as it might be when data are gathered from other sources as well or data collection is part of a longitudinal effort), then precautions to safeguard the identity of particular individuals must be taken. Sometimes it is possible to let the respondents supply such an identification code (last four digits of a social security number, birth date, mother's birthdate, etc.) if your interest is only in tracking respondents across time. Third, as indicated above, the ethics of survey research demand some type of feedback be given or made accessible to the respondents.

Regarding the first issue above, there usually is no reason to hide the objectives of survey research or, if there is, it is quite likely that respondents will guess or form their own hypotheses regarding the purpose of the survey. If it is anticipated that results be broken down in various ways, it might be useful to indicate this information in a cover letter. By the same token, it probably is advisable to tell the respondents what concepts you are interested in measuring with a set of items. If the survey is concerned with organizational or product loyalty, job involvement, satisfaction with promotion opportunities, then tell the respondents that these are issues of concern. Aside from ethical concerns, it likely is true that a respondent who is informed about the purpose and nature of the questions asked will be better able and more motivated to provide accurate responses.

Many times respondents are concerned that management or the people responsible for conducting a survey have some method to identify them. Obviously, this becomes more likely under conditions of organizational stress and/or as we increase the number of demographics we ask of the respondents and the size of the group in which they are located is relatively small. In a group of 20, there probably are not many female workers, aged 35, with three children and a master's degree. Ultimately, trust that responses will indeed be treated confidentially is a function of many organizational-employee interactions and no assurance of confidentiality will suffice in an atmosphere of low trust. It is usually true that data become less valuable and interpretable as we aggregate over larger and larger groups. The need for confidentiality and the need for specificity are often in conflict. Again both because of ethical concerns and for reasons of collecting quality data on other occasions, it is mandatory that confidentiality of responses be scrupulously protected.

A special case of a threat to anonymity occurs when survey data results are to be broken down by work unit or department in such a way that the effectiveness of particular managers is implied. Because many survey items convey an evaluative tone (e.g., "How well does your group work together?"), this is very easy to do. Thus, average scores on items like this may be computed for each work group, published, and compared. The end result is that specific managers may appear to look better than others.

There is no easy resolution to this dilemma. However, the investigator should be certain that there indeed is some legitimate business or scientific need for such an analysis. If there is not, perhaps some other way of aggregating the same data should be tried. If there is such a need, participants/respondents all must be told at the outset that such clustering and reporting is intended. It also may be possible to code work groups so that while differences may be seen, only the members of a work team will know of their specific identity. As stated above, people have the right to know what will be done with the survey information that they provide.

Finally, we believe the researcher has an obligation to provide feedback to respondents or to provide access to such feedback. In those instances in which no feedback is possible or intended the respondent should be informed prior to answering the survey. The desired degree of specificity of the feedback will vary with the level of respondent interest in the survey and perhaps their ability to understand the research data. We usually have used three- to five-page feedback reports which provide very general findings and implications (if the survey is intended as an organizational intervention, we use the general outline pictured in Figure 10-12), and offer to send more detailed reports to individuals who request them.

SUMMARY

We began this chapter with a discussion of why organizational researchers do survey research. We then described some research areas in which surveys are commonly used. Our view is that a clear formulation of survey objectives and the theoretical constructs of interest dictate what questions will be asked of what group of people and how their responses will be analyzed. We then discussed in more detail how one samples from a population (so as to realize an adequate representation of the population without depleting the resources to conduct the study) and how to write questionnaire items and construct a readable instrument with clear directions. In this section, we also included a discussion of how to secure the responses of the targeted sample and the use of electronic mail.

In our section on data analysis and reporting, we described ways in which typical data processing errors might be detected and how to analyze and interpret survey data. We then briefly outlined methods in the use of survey feedback to initiate organizational change. The chapter was concluded with a recognition of ethical concerns in survey research.

EVALUATING ORGANIZATIONAL INTERVENTIONS

An important aspect of doing quality human resources research is the plan or design that is followed. This chapter reviews several common research designs with an emphasis on the capacity to make strong inferences (conclusions) from a study. In particular, concepts and strategies are introduced by showing how an investigator might use different designs in order to assess the impact of an organizational intervention involving training and development. Because there is no one best design, we stress the importance of a careful analysis of the goals of the research before selecting or adapting a particular approach. Finally, in the conduct of research, we argue that the principles of good design covered in the chapter will be as important as the use of any single design form.

This chapter examines several approaches to the systematic evaluation of ongoing or newly initiated human resources interventions, practices, or programs. The "need to know" may be driven by scientific curiosity or management's desire for accountability. Training program implementation is a common form of organizational intervention and thus will be used as a vehicle for illustrating key points. However, it is important to realize that the logic and strategies discussed generally will be relevant and useful for learning about the nature and impact of any intervention that has as its goal some change (usually improvement) in or some better understanding of the functioning of individuals, groups, or the organization as a whole.

The key to evaluating the importance or impact of organizationally relevant variables or programs is to have a plan. As stated earlier, in this book (see Chapter 1), a research design is a plan for conducting a study in such a way as to answer certain questions. In this chapter we assume the fact that, for many investigators and consultants, the question of primary interest has to do with assessing the degree of (causal) impact of some theoretically interesting variable, or some manipulation, intervention, or intentional change. Thus, the emphasis will be on designs (plans) that allow us to interpret the results of our study with a minimum amount of equivocality.

TRAINING AS AN INTERVENTION

An organization's interests in training program design and evaluation will be used to illustrate the concepts of research design in this chapter.

The Logic of Using Training

Training will be the focus of this chapter for several reasons. First, training represents a major recurring intervention in organizations, one that is largely under the control of management. Thus, many variations in design are feasible. Second, training can take place in extremely artificial settings (e.g., a laboratory) or it can occur *in vivo*. This implies needing to deal with issues associated with the four types of validity as described (see page 28 in Chapter 1). Third, research on training can be done for both applied and theoretical reasons. We may want to know not only if training had an impact, but why. This will promote different choices in design and will be a major theme in this chapter. Fourth, by highlighting training program evaluation in a chapter on design we might promote more frequent and systematic efforts in this direction. Despite the enormous amount of money spent by modern organizations on the training and development of employees (Lusterman, 1985), more than one writer has lamented the fact that if research on evaluation is done at all it is not carried out well (Goldstein, 1986). We hope that this text will help to change this situation by showing the many reasonable options open to any one charged with training program design and development activities.

Criteria Used for Training Effectiveness

Evaluating a training program as an intervention implies that we have some notion of training effectiveness. That is to say, when we ask the question, "Did the training work?", we may be thinking of any number of things. The fact is, there are a variety of potential criteria or dependent variables that we might use in an investigation in this area.

What standards or criteria should be used when evaluating a training program? The answer lies in the objectives that were defined for the program to begin with. The criteria used should correspond to these objectives. For example, if the objective is to change work-related attitudes, then we would look for shifts in measures of these attitudes as a result of training. Put another way, the criteria used to measure training program effectiveness are likely to differ from one instance to another, depending on training objectives.

This point notwithstanding, however, most evaluations tend to use one or more of the following classes of data in any evaluation effort (Kirkpatrick, 1967; Wexley & Latham, 1981):

1. *Reactions.* This refers to how well the trainees and others associated with the training program liked it. Reactions also include beliefs and opinions about program features and their potential value. As noted, reaction data can be obtained from the trainees, the training program staff, or from managers responsible for approving the use of the program. Usually this is done with surveys using paper-and-pencil questionnaires. Levels of satisfaction also can be determined through post-training discussions or even can be inferred from a program's popularity (i.e., how many people sign up for it) or by session attendance patterns (for multi-day programs).

2. *Learning.* Most training involves the acquisition of new knowledge or skills. A learning criterion would be one that allows for the assessment of the extent to which learning has occurred. Once again, the actual measures can take many forms. A common measure used for this purpose is the achievement test. Trainees might be examined for their new knowledge using a paper-and-pencil exam. Their scores on the exam become the index of learning.

   Alternatively, if new skills are the goal of training, the amount of learning could be determined by requiring trainees to exhibit or to demonstrate targeted skills under controlled conditions. For example, Latham and Saari (1979) and Hicks and Klimoski (1987) had trainees in management skills development programs demonstrate their new learning in role-play sessions after training. They were videotaped while doing this. The success of training was inferred from the levels of skill reflected in these sessions as judged by experts.

3. *Job behavior.* Training may be evaluated in terms of on-the- job behavior. Are the graduates of a program now behaving or performing differently as the consequence of the program? The trainees themselves might be asked about this through surveys or interviews of what their behavior is like in relevant areas. Or they may be asked to identify aspects of behavior change. The trainee's supervisor, peers, or subordinates (where appropriate) also can be used as sources of information. Finally, individuals might be recruited and sent to the trainee's work setting as observers in order to assess the effects of training on behavior.

   In organizations where performance appraisal systems are well developed and implemented, carefully monitored, and behaviorally based, we might look for the impact of training on the scores given to trainees on appraisal instruments. However, in most cases the training specialist interested in evaluations probably would be the one to design, implement and carry out an appraisal for that specific purpose (Wexley & Latham, 1981).

4. *Results.* One can presume that the ultimate objective of many training programs is increased trainee effectiveness on the job. Thus, we might look to typical operational indicators of effectiveness for any evidence of improvement. Measures of individual productivity, waste, lost time, unit performance in relation to budget (in the case of managers), might be reviewed for change in the expected direction. While training usually is aimed at individuals, there are times when it is part of a planned organizational change effort.

5. *Improved system functioning.* Usually we would not expect training efforts aimed at an individual or at a small group of individuals to result in increased organization-wide effectiveness. However, in instances where the entire work force is put through a training program, such effects could occur. Impact might then be reflected in measures of system performance (in contrast to individual job performance). For example, training given to all first-level managers might have an effect on employee grievance rates or turnover systemwide. Still, one has to be careful not to expect too much by way of system change from training interventions.

There exists a fair amount of disagreement as to which of these criteria to use when evaluating training programs (Campbell, Dunnette, Lawler, & Weick, 1970). In particular, there are those who see little value in relying on reactions data for assessing training success. Others maintain that only improvements in actual job performance should be considered. Another point of view is that these alternatives represent a form of hierarchy. Thus, you would need to produce some impact on attitudes (favorable) and on learning before you could hope to demonstrate a program's impact on job behavior or productivity.

This still begs the question of how effectiveness at one level relates to another. For example, Campion and Campion (1987) conducted a rigorous evaluation of an interviewee skills workshop designed and produced for workers of an electronics firm who were about to become unemployed as a result of the closing of a business unit. While they found that trainees improved in terms of attitudes and learning, no reliable impact on their behaviors in simulated interviews could be detected. Moreover, the trainees received no greater number of job offers from actual interviews than those who were not trained. Finally, from a practical point of view, it might be argued that one should start with the former criteria but try to achieve the most demanding standards of impact possible. Our position, however, is that the particular measures (or set of measures) to be used should be linked logically to the training objectives themselves. This would imply that all five types of measures may be appropriate and have their place under certain circumstances.

RESEARCH DESIGNS

For a research design to be a good one it needs to meet several criteria. In earlier chapters we emphasized three: it must help us to answer questions of program impact or to test hypotheses, extraneous factors need to be dealt with or otherwise controlled, and the results must be generalizable. We also would like to add that a design should be efficient. By this we mean that we can get the information that we need with the resources (time, number of participants, staff, etc.) that we have. It also has to be feasible within the context of the research site. That is to say, the investigator must recognize legitimate constraints and plan accordingly.

Key Design Choices

The conduct of research involves a large number of decisions or choices on the part of the investigator. This is a point that we have made early in this text and have stressed throughout most of the chapters. Generally, the combination of choices made by the investigator will determine the quality of the data obtained and the kinds of inferences that can be (should be) made from the data. The results of all these choices will, in effect, also determine the kind of design involved. Before going into the types of designs commonly found in the human resources literature some important or key choices will be highlighted. Several of these have been touched upon already. However, because these constitute themes that cut across various design types, they deserve additional attention.

The Context for the Research The investigator has to decide just how important it is for the purposes of the research to conduct it in operational settings. In the area of training and training program impact, there are any number of questions that can be studied in laboratory or contrived situations. This is because for many investigators the goal is to establish the existence of (or the nature of) certain dynamics or processes that are presumed to be operative in most contexts. To put it another way, the investigator's model or theory places little emphasis on the importance of the specific setting in which the phenomenon occurs. In contrast, the researcher's interest, his or her theory, or the purpose for the research may place a premium on specific features of a setting as they directly affect or modify events.

The area of behavioral modeling might be used to illustrate this point. Behavioral modeling training has become extremely popular since being introduced by Goldstein and Sorcher (1974) into the human resource management literature. Behavioral modeling incorporates concepts from social learning theory (Bandura, 1977) which emphasize the key role of observational learning. In such programs, trainees are exposed to and are expected to learn from individuals who are demonstrating the behaviors to be mastered.

Decker (1984) argued that although behavioral modeling has been shown to be an effective technique, there had been little research aimed at understanding its components. Thus, he conducted a study in a laboratory setting to examine the impact of instructions given to subjects regarding what they should do as they watched the model. Specifically, different groups were given different "rules" to follow. One group was given a list of learning points. A second group was given what were essentially rule-oriented instructions designed to enhance generalizations from the specific example being acted out by the model. A third group was given behaviorally oriented learning points. And a fourth, which served as a baseline, was given no instructions whatsoever. To be brief, Decker found that both the rule- and behavior-oriented learning points subjects outperformed those in the no learning points condition.

This study has been used to characterize a case where the setting or context was largely irrelevant to the research question. In contrast, Meyer and Raich (1983) were specifically interested in how behavior modeling training would impact in an organizational setting under operational conditions. Thus, they needed a field setting for their research. They introduced a behavioral modeling training program for sales representatives in a consumer electronics company. The fourteen stores of the company were divided into matched sets of seven. Sales people from one set of seven were given the training, those in the other set were not placed in the program. The criterion variable of greatest interest was the level of sales performance achieved. Meyer and Raich found that sales associates who received the behavioral modeling training increased their sales by an average of 7% over the ensuing six-month period. In contrast, their counterparts in the control stores showed a 3% decrease in average sales. What is interesting to note in this study was the discovery that, in addition to the increased performance, the stores whose employees received the modeling training also had lower rates of turnover. This had not been predicted.

When it comes to the importance of context, Wortman (1983) uses a distinction highlighted by the Office of Technology Assessment of the government of the United States. They use the term *efficacy* to describe the impact of a program under ideal conditions of use. On the other hand, *effectiveness* is reserved for the program's impact under average or typical conditions of use. Thus, in making this design decision, the investigator needs to be clear whether he or she is interested in determining that a program *can* have an impact or whether the interest is in showing that it *does* have an impact in actual organizations.

The Nature of the Sample There will be occasions where the investigator may wish to study all of the people in a particular organizational context (e.g., all the employees of a small company). However, in most cases, research is done with a sample of people. Two features of the sample that are particularly important are the sample characteristics and its size.

The phrase *sample characteristics* is used to convey the nature of the sample relative to the population of interest. As detailed in Chapter 10, (see page 339), the sample may be constructed to be representative of the population or to have some known relationship to the latter. Thus, we may use random or stratified sampling strategies, or our sample may be one of opportunity or convenience. More to the point, our actual sample plan will determine whether or not we can legitimately generalize to the population from the data we obtain from research participants. Moreover, there is some evidence that lack of representativeness also can affect the construct validity of the measures that might be taken. For example, Mitchell (1985) points out that, if respondents in a study do not represent the groups for which the measures were designed, the data obtained might be quite misleading. This would be the case if study participants had ability or education levels very different from those on which the measure was developed or normed.

Sample size also will affect representativeness. That is to say, it is harder for a small sample (relative to the population) to be representative. Thus, larger samples drawn with a known sample plan allow for the greatest confidence in generalizing results. But sample size also affects the statistical power of a study to detect the true effects of an intervention or a variable (if there are any). Recall the discussion of power in Chapter 2 (see page 58). Arvey and his colleagues (Arvey, Cole, Hazucha, & Hartamo, 1985) recently have shown that the statistical power of training impact studies not only will be related to sample size but also will be a function of the effect size, the correlation among sets of measures used to detect change or improvement, and the specific type of analysis to be used. In their reanalysis of Burke and Day's (1986) review of 71 studies of managerial training, they calculated an effect size (see Chapter 12) of .40. This, by the way, is higher than they originally felt would be the case and implies that managerial training programs do seem to have an impact. Assuming an effect size of this magnitude, Arvey et al. (1985) feel that for three analytic approaches (e.g., analysis of covariance), a study with a sample size greater than 40 would yield a power greater than .50. (Note power of .50 may not be considered adequate in many instances.) The authors do warn us that, in a different area of training (e.g., basic skills), a larger sample size might be warranted.

Measure or Manipulate?

A major theme in Chapter 1 had to do with the nature of variables in research and how they are defined. At the risk of over-simplifying, we described how an investigator could choose to measure a variable of interest or actually attempt to create a phenomenon in order to study it. The reader is encouraged to go back to the relevant sections of the text if a review of the issues involved is needed (see pages 19–22). In any event, because this represents a major design choice, it is being mentioned again here. In the area of evaluating training programs, the full range of options exists in as much as the variables of interest lend themselves to both measurement and/or manipulation.

Data Sources

A research design usually implies just who (or what) is going to be measured, assessed, tested, or monitored. As emphasized throughout this text, an investigator has any number of options at his or her disposal. However, in human resources research, it is quite common to make use of self-reports.

Podsakoff and Organ (1986) found "the self report to be well-nigh ubiquitous as a form of data collection" (p. 531) in the human resource research area. According to their analysis, the uses of self-reports could be described using the following categories (p.532):

1. Obtaining demographic or otherwise factual data (e.g., years of work);
2. Assessing the effectiveness of instructions or experimental manipulations;
3. Gathering personality data;
4. Obtaining descriptions of a respondent's past or characteristic behavior, or how they would behave under hypothetical conditions;
5. Measuring internal or psychological states of respondents (e.g., work attitudes);
6. Assessing respondent's perceptions of context or organizational variables.

Despite its popularity, Podsakoff and Organ argue that investigators often do not appreciate important weaknesses of self-reports. In particular, they point out potential problems when measures of two or more variables in numbers 3, 4, 5, and 6 are collected from the same respondents and attempts made to interpret any correlations among them. This relates to the potential problem of common method variance. Because both measures come from the same source (and usually at the same time), variables may be spuriously (highly) related. This could be due to the fact that the measures make use of the same response format, are not perfectly reliable, or induce a desire on the part of respondents to be consistent across sections of a questionnaire. To put it another way, these dynamics may produce a failure to exhibit the discriminant validity of the measures.

In addition to a possible monomethod or percept-percept bias, self-reports have the potential to induce socially desirable responses. This is the tendency of the measure to motivate responses that are intended to make the respondent look good in the eyes of the investigator or society at large. Thus, to ask a person on a questionnaire or an interview if he or she "learned anything" as a result of going to a training program or workshop is likely to produce an affirmative answer. Most people will reason that, irrespective of the truth of the matter, they would look foolish if they did not answer "Yes" to this question.

The investigator can check on the possibility of distortion in self-reports and otherwise try to deal with it. For example, Podsakoff and Organ (1986) suggest that all the scores from the various measures could be placed in a factor analysis to see if a single factor solution is obtained. This would imply that respondents are not discriminating among the various scales or measures. Alternatively, researchers may use partial correlation procedures to try to deal with any multicolinearity across scales. This would allow for the determination of the unique relationship among, for example, training program features and several outcome variables.

The best advice for dealing with some of the dynamics produced with self-reports, however, may be to use a research design that involves separation of measures. This might imply obtaining self-report data at slightly different times. It might involve using different modalities (e.g., questionnaire and face-to-face interview). Or, it might require that some variables or some data be obtained from more than one source (e.g., the employee and his or her peers). To illustrate, in assessing the impact of a training intervention on learning, the investigator could develop and use a paper-and-pencil achievement test, could ask for self-evaluations of amount learned, and get assessments of displays of new knowledge as perceived by coworkers. We might then have more confidence that the actual impact of the program had been estimated accurately.

The magnitude or extent of bias or distortion in self-reports cannot always be established beforehand. It may not be a problem under certain conditions. For example, Spector (1987) examined the issue of method variance (percept-percept bias) in published studies involving measures of job satisfaction and perceived job characteristics. The former is often treated as a criterion or dependent variable and the latter as an independent (causal) variable. That is to say, any number of investigators have been interested in the (causal) impact of job characteristics on job satisfaction. In fact many studies apparently have found a positive correlation between them. However, as Spector points out, data on both variables usually are obtained from self-reports on a single questionnaire. Thus, he reasoned, instead of a true relationship between the two, the results are due to method bias. Based on published research he was able to perform what was, in effect, a multitrait-multimethod analysis. In his research, he found six studies that had assessed social desirability along with these measures. His conclusions were somewhat reassuring. In very few instances did he find evidence of method bias at either the item or the scale level. Consequently, the positive relationship between key job characteristics and worker reported job satisfaction that has been found is likely to be a true one. He also points out that these results may have occurred because of the quality of the particular measures involved. Both the Job Descriptive Index (the preferred measure of job satisfaction) and the Job Characteristics Inventory (the common measure of job attributes) have been carefully developed. Thus, he warns that the results may not be similar where scales with less demonstrated construct validity are used. (See Williams, Cote, and Buckley, 1989, for an opposing view of the seriousness of the method bias problem.)

One other aspect of self-reports deserves to be highlighted because of its relevance to the assessment of the impact of training programs. As described in detail later, in the context of a training program evaluation it is not uncommon to obtain self-reports on more than one occasion. More specifically, measures may be taken before and after training. But Sprangers and Hoogstraten (1989) point out that any comparison of pre and post scores from self-report measures may be misleading because of what is termed a *response shift bias*. This refers to a change in the internal standards used by a respondent in making a judgment about his or her level of knowledge or functioning. Simply stated, after a person has gone through training, he or she is likely to reconsider any self-reports or self-assessments (as given on a premeasure) in light of what is taught. Thus, participants may feel that they have *less* skill than they originally thought given the competency of the instructor, the rigorous nature of the course content, or the behavior of their classmates. This shift in standards becomes a bias when, paradoxically, people come to feel and report less competency after training. This also would lead to the uncomfortable conclusion on the part of an investigator that the training might have actually hurt rather than helped participants.

In their research on the effects of communication skills training, Sprangers and Hoogstraten (1989) demonstrate the existence and nature of these pretesting effects and go on to show the potential usefulness of what they call a retrospective pretest. In this procedure, participants are not asked for a self assessment prior to training. Instead, after training, they are asked to make two judgments: a post assessment and a judgment of how well they were functioning before the training. The authors point out that this approach ensures that both judgments will be based on the same (posttraining) standards, and that a comparison of the two will be meaningful.

In summary, while self-reports are and will continue to be important in evaluating training interventions, they must be used with skill. Otherwise, both motivational forces and information processing dynamics can and will affect the quality of the data obtained.

The Importance of Time and Timing

In many chapters of this book we have described aspects of research and the research process, which have implied gathering data according to a plan involving the element of time. For example, in examining approaches to the validation of selection tests, both concurrent and predictive approaches were referenced. In general, the issue of time and timing of data gathering is an important aspect of research design.

Rosenthal and Rosnow (1984) distinguish between synchronic (cross-sectional) and diachronic (longitudinal) research designs. Quite often an investigator is concerned with examining a variable or set of variables at one point in time. This is referred to as *synchronic research*. Alternatively, when a phenomena or variable (set) is observed in a way so as to uncover changes that occur over time or in successive periods of time, it is characterized as *diachronic research*.

Obviously, if one is interested in change or impact, a diachronic research strategy would be useful. But given that a diachronic approach is warranted, as you will see shortly, there will be many variations in designs to choose from. For example, if more than one measurement period is preferred when should they occur? How long should the intervals between measurements be? How many "waves" of measurements should be taken? Usually these and related questions cannot be answered for the general case but must be resolved with guidance from the theories or models guiding the research, with reference to practicality and, not infrequently, with some amount of intuition on the part of the investigator.

One other issue that comes up in diachronic research is that of subject mortality. As described in Chapter 1 (see page 31), in taking repeated measurements over time, a percentage of research participants may drop out of a study or become otherwise unavailable for participation. This means that measures taken later in time will be based only on a subgroup of original respondents. This shrinking sample size implies lower statistical power. But more importantly, if those who cannot be reached or who no longer want to continue with the study represent a particular class of individuals (e.g., less educated), it also creates the possibility of an inadvertent bias in results. To review earlier terminology, such a bias would be a threat to the external validity of the study. Or, if the subject dropouts were concentrated within certain parts of the study or in certain treatment conditions (i.e., training conditions that demand a great deal of effort), we would worry about a treatment by mortality interaction and its threat to internal validity.

NON-EXPERIMENTAL RESEARCH DESIGNS

Nonexperimental designs are weak in terms of providing a basis for making a strong argument that an intervention (or variable) like training did any good. Because they often are perceived as easiest to conduct or less costly and disruptive (to the routine of the organization) they probably are the most prevalent kind of evaluation plan used. Key examples of nonexperimental research designs include the case study, relational research, and the pretest-posttest design.

Case Sudy

As described in Chapter 4 (see page 121), a case study involves a narrative description of the effects of (in this instance) a training program. Usually this is done by the trainer (hardly an unbiased person) for purpose of promoting or justifying a particular program (hardly a scientific orientation). Testimonials frequently are used to show that the training was indeed worthwhile. If there are any data gathered, it is taken only after training is completed. Schematically, this could be portrayed as follows:

Training ————> Post measures/description taken

Any conclusions based on the nature of the testimonials (or even on scores on the postmeasures) would have to be tentative at best. For example, with this design we don't really know what people were like before training so postmeasures may reflect levels of prior knowledge rather than program effectiveness. There would be many threats to internal validity.

In some instances an investigator uses a case approach because he or she is interested in descriptive information about the nature of training program activity and only incidentally about its impact. In this regard, measures might be taken and data reported for such things as the number of class hours taught, the number of students enrolled, etc. When such data are obtained for a variety of organizations or over different periods of time, the design being followed is referred to as an *enumerative survey* (Rosenthal & Rosnow, 1984). Thus, the goal of complete description is enhanced with trend information.

It should be noted that the way the investigator obtains information in the descriptive or case design can be as varied as the methods covered in this book. It need not rely on self-reports produced by questionnaire, but could use archival records, observations, etc.

The goal of a case study is usually one of complete description. But as outlined in Chapter 4, this, too, may be a means to an end. More specifically, when done well, a case analysis can provide the groundwork that we need to orient us to a new area of research or practice. Similarly, it can provide insight regarding the boundaries of a research domain. Finally, it can be the source of ideas that can be more systematically examined or tested later.

Relational Research

When data are gathered on more than one variable or on the same variable over time, it is possible to index the extent to which variables relate to one another. This can be done using any of the indices of covariation touched upon in this book: contingency tables, chi square analyses, correlation analysis, regression analysis, path analysis, and structural modeling.

The objective of relational research, at a minimum, is a description of whether and how events or variables relate to one another. In practice, however, most investigators also seek an explanation of why such patterns of data come about (Rosenthal & Rosnow, 1984). In fact, as highlighted earlier in Chapter 1 (see page 16), it is quite common to move all too easily from evidence of correlation to inferences of causation.

A common design in relational research is the *analytic survey* (Rosenthal & Rosnow, 1984). While the enumerative survey is aimed at uncovering facts, the analytic survey is used to explore or establish relationships among variables. Once again, the methodology of the analytic survey can be quite varied. Questionnaires, interviews, observations, etc., are commonly involved. But whatever the method, the key is to include measures of the relevant variables. This implies both those variables of primary interest (analogous to independent and dependent variables) and those that we have labeled in earlier chapters as control or nuisance variables. It is from the pattern of the correlations between these variables that the investigator makes inferences, tests hypotheses, and offers potential explanations.

As noted, the analytic strategy of a relational study can vary. The key point is that the investigator relies on data from measured variables. To illustrate, P. B. Smith (1976) was interested in the impact of a sensitivity training program. This program had been given to a sample of about 200 professional workers. It was administered to groups of 9–11 individuals over the course of a week where the total amount of time involved at least 20 hours.

Sensitivity training programs were designed originally to increase interpersonal skills thought to be important to individual and organizational effectiveness (Smith, 1975). This program followed the norm. The program stressed the impact of both spoken and nonverbal communications, behavioral style, and self-awareness.

Smith was interested in the effects of the program. He also had theoretical reasons to investigate the role of individual differences as moderators of program impact. Specifically, he gathered self-reports regarding individual perceptions and beliefs about the program. This was done on the last day of each completed seminar. From this information he created an index that allowed him to classify each participant as an externalizer or as an internalizer. More to the point, he had theoretical reasons for predicting that the latter would show greater long-term benefits from the program than the former.

To test his ideas he obtained criterion information on program impact. On the final day of the program, participants rated themselves and the others of their group on a global program benefit scale. The trainers also rated each trainee with regard to the perceived benefits each trainee had received. Five months later, participants were again contacted and asked to provide a rating of program benefits to them.

Smith found that, immediately after training, all participants, regardless of their classification, reported similar and high ratings of program benefits. But five months later, as predicted, the internalizers reported significantly higher ratings. Operationally, the mean ratings of the internalizers (mean = 5.3 on a seven-point scale) were compared to the externalizers (mean = 4.3) using a test of significance and found to be reliably higher. Interestingly, the trainers rated the internalizers as having benefited more immediately after training as well.

A simple relational study that used the organization as the unit of analysis was reported by Russell, Terborg, and Powers (1985). These authors were interested in the relationship between organizational level measures of training and performance. Archival data were obtained from 62 stores of a merchandising firm. Two measures of training effort and two measures of organizational support for training were used to predict two measures of store performance.

More specifically, Russell et al. (1985) obtained records from the company's most recent employee attitude survey. From this they were able to create several of their key variables: subjective estimates of how seriously each store seemed to treat training responsibilities (training emphasis), how much supervisor support was perceived (supervisor support), how much effort each store seemed to spend on merchandising (merchandising support) and an index of store image. The latter was felt to be an index of store performance. While the authors acknowledge that it would have been preferable to have had such data from actual customers, employees' perceptions of image were felt to have some validity as well.

The other variables in this study also came from company records. An index of efficiency was computed for each store (sales volume per employee), and another index of training effort was defined and measured as the percentage of sales personnel who actually received training in sales procedures and techniques.

The authors theorized that the levels of training emphasis and support provided by the various stores in this chain should be reflected in store performance. That is, greater effort and support should correlate with higher store performance. Table 11-1 shows the results of their analysis. Based on the pattern of significant correlations in Table 11-1 (and a regression analysis not described here), Russell et al. concluded that training can contribute to the bottom line (sales volume and store image) of a company.

One final relational study will be reviewed because it represents a very sophisticated approach to the study of training dynamics in an operational setting. Furthermore, while the study is fundamentally a relational one, its authors have carefully wedded this design to an elaborate data base in order to produce some plausible evidence of causal impact among the key variables of interest.

TABLE 11-1
Means, Standard Deviations, and Intercorrelations
for Performance, Training, and Support Variables [a]

Variables	Mean	SD	(1)	(2)	(3)	(4)	(5)	(6)
1. Percentage trained	31.54	32.94	—	.27*	.23	.37*	.46*	.39*
2. Training emphasis	11.46	1.00		.83	.51*	.53*	.47*	.08
3. Supervisory support	16.58	1.07			.85	.67	.42*	.07
4. Merchandising support	12.36	.99				.85	.51*	.05
5. Store image[b]	28.12	3.60					(2)	.26*
6. Volume per employee	35,476	6,991						—

[a] Cronbach's alpha for self-report measures in diagonal; N = 62 stores; r = .25, $p < .05$.
[b] Store image is a composite of management (alpha = .83) and staff (alpha = .87) perceptions.
Source: Russell, J. S., Terborg, J. R., & Powers, M. L. (1985). Organizational performance and organizational level training and support. *Personnel Psychology, 38,* 849–863. Adapted with permission.

Mumford, Weeks, Harding and Fleishman (1988) attempted to build a causal model describing the relationships among trainee attributes (e.g., aptitude, educational level, age), course variables (e.g., course length, student faculty ratio, amount of practice involved), and training performance. The latter included such things as the quality of student performance and attrition. Measures of these variables were obtained in 39 training courses in the U.S. Air Force containing over 5000 students. With this data base, relationships among the variables were examined using formal structural analysis (analogous to regression modeling when one has multiple indicators of each underlying variable or construct). The resulting model was cross-validated on a sample of nine additional courses containing 890 students. In cross validation, the resulting model did a good job of predicting training outcomes so it was felt to be a reasonable description of the technical training process.

Mumford et al. (1988) concluded that student characteristic variables played a very big role in training performance. For example, they were found consistently to have a greater impact on student achievement and motivational outcomes than course content variables. But it also was the case that when it came to certain negative outcomes, such as student attrition or "washouts," both student and course content factors interacted to produce effects. It should be pointed out that their model was based on the general trends across the many courses surveyed. It may be that in specific instances, course features will turn out to be extremely relevant to student success.

In summary, this last study is a good one in that it began with a conceptual framework, involved a large sample of respondents and courses, made use of multiple measures of the variables of interest, employed an analysis that allowed for the assessment of the plausibility of different explanatory relationships, cross-validated the resulting model, and was conducted in an operational setting.

Generally, then, relational research designs attempt to identify how variables are connected. Investigators search for patterns and systematic linkages as they might inform theory or guide practice. And, under the right conditions, they allow us to establish plausible arguments (but not really test) for causation. Rosenthal and Rosnow (1984) also argue that a distinct advantage of relational research is that it allows us to make comparisons where time is the independent variable. Thus, we can see trends or changes. Finally, as highlighted in earlier chapters, relational research often is used in validation work.

Our position is that when relational research is done well it represents an excellent design and useful knowledge can be acquired. Unfortunately, many investigators are not very rigorous in their approach. Recently, Mitchell (1985) provided an excellent analysis and critique of the usefulness of correlational research conducted in organizations. While his paper is not focused on training research, the points he makes are very relevant and deserve to be summarized.

Mitchell (1985) argues that the kind of analysis offered by Cook and Campbell (1976) with regard to threats to validity in research, and reviewed in some detail in Chapter 1 (see pages 29–32), should be applied regularly to relational studies. Specifically, in his essay, he points out how common practice in relational research may in fact compromise the integrity or validity of a study. To illustrate, when it comes to internal validity many investigators assert that a (perhaps causal) relationship exists between two variables without examining the possibility of the impact of a third (truly explanatory) variable. The issue of the construct validity of measures is often ignored as newly constructed and untested measures are used or, as noted in Chapter 10, established scales are shortened or modified without regard for what this might do to the quality of data obtained. Statistical conclusion validity may be questionable in light of unreliable measures, too small a sample, restriction in the range of values, or the conduct of all-too-numerous statistical tests on the same data set. The construct validity of the study itself might be weakened by method bias. Finally, threats to external validity in relational research might include the use of an inappropriate (i.e., nonrepresentative) sample.

More specifically, Mitchell (1985) suggests that relational research should be designed or critiqued with a key set of questions in mind. These are reproduced in Figure 11-1. To the extent that we can answer "Yes" or in a positive way to all the questions on the checklist, we should feel that a given piece of research is of high quality. However, in applying this list to 126 relational studies published over a four-year period in three well known journals, he states that he obtained a very bleak picture. For example, over 80% of the studies reviewed used a *convenience sample,* that is, one that had been nonscientifically drawn. Over half of the studies did not report a response rate. Only one study actually examined discriminant validity as a way of establishing construct validity. While Mitchell believes that relational research can be and is a powerful research tool, he feels that must be conducted better than it has been in the past to realize its potential. We would agree.

The Pretest-Posttest Design

The pretest-posttest design specifically deals with initial levels of trainee knowledge, skill, or behavior. It can be diagramed as follows:

$$\text{Measures before} \longrightarrow \text{Training} \longrightarrow \text{Measures after}$$
$$\text{training} \qquad\qquad\qquad \text{training}$$

The logic of this design is that the effectiveness of training may be inferred from any change in scores observed by contrasting premeasures and postmeasures. But despite this advantage, we only can have limited confidence in our ability to interpret the meaning of any differences found. One reason is that it is possible that something else occurred contemporaneously with training, and it, not the training program, was responsible for the change in scores. For example, the

---

1. What was the sample: random, cluster, stratified, convenience?
2. What was the response rate?
3. Were respondents compared to nonrespondents?
4. Type of method used to gather data: personally administered questionnaire, mailed questionnaire, delivered (but not administered) questionnaire, personal interviews.
5. Type of reliability reported: alpha, test/retest, split half, interrater, none.
6. Was previous literature on reliability and validity cited?
7. Were there any tests for convergent or discriminate validity?
8. If #7 was yes, what procedure was used: multiple measures, multimethod, multitrait, factor analyses, or discriminate validity?
9. Was the assessment of A and B on measures with a similar format?
10. Were intercorrelations of independent and dependent variables reported as evidence for a lack of method variance?
11. If #10 was yes, were the coefficients significant?
12. Did the authors address the issue of method variance statistically (e.g., partial correlations, stepwise regression) or conceptually?
13. Was a holdout sample or cross-validation present?

FIGURE 11-1 Critical Questions of Relational Research
Source: Adapted with permission from Mitchell, T. R. (1985). An evaluation of the validity of correlational research conducted in organizations. *Academy of Management Review, 10,* 192–205.

company might have coincidentally instituted a new incentive pay plan at the time of the program. The incentive plan, not the training, might be the true cause of performance improvements. This would be a case in which "history" is a threat to the validity of the study, but is analogous to the third variable threat mentioned in our discussion of relational research.

The above designs have only limited potential for concluding that a training intervention has (causes) certain intended effects. A preferred strategy is to use true experimental designs to establish this.

EXPERIMENTAL DESIGNS

There are numerous "true" experimental designs available. However, only a few will be highlighted here to show how they can reduce equivocality in our inferences about the effects of a training intervention. These include the pretest-posttest control group design, the pretest-posttest control group with multiple post-measures design, the after-only control group design, and the Solomon four-group design.

The Pretest-Posttest Control Group Design

This design attempts to deal with the potential effects of outside influences by having a separate group of employees, who are not in training, provide a parallel set of data within the time frame of the program. Using a diagram, this design would be represented as follows:

Group 1:   Premeasures ——> Training ——— >Postmeasures
                            taken   taken
Group 2 (Control):   Premeasures ——————————————— >Postmeasures
                            taken   taken

Group 2 is referred to as a control group in this instance because it wasn't exposed to any training; rather it supplied a set of measures. By comparing and contrasting the groups' scores on the measures, one is in a better position to conclude that outside (of training) factors were not responsible for pretest-posttest changes. In a sense we are "controlling" for this possibility. Thus, if we were a training specialist using this plan, we would hope to see an increase in scores (pretest to posttest) for those in training but no such change for the untrained group.

An important assumption for experimental designs is that the employees in the training group and in the control group are from the same population. That is, they don't differ from each other in some important way that might affect the outcome in an unintended fashion (e.g., the training group might have a higher aptitude as a whole). As a practical matter, the best way to ensure this is to follow the standard experimental design expedient of random assignment. Operationally, this means that we might take the pool of eligible employees and divide them into the two groups according to some unbiased procedure. Those assigned to the control group then would be presumed to be similar in most ways to those in the training group. (One also could use a matching strategy as was done in the Meyer and Raich (1983) study described earlier.)

This pretest-posttest design also allows us to check on the assumption of unbiased assignment. We can do this by comparing the two groups on the basis of premeasure scores alone. If assignments were done properly, they should be equivalent. To summarize, our training specialist would be satisfied to obtain the following pattern of data with this design:

1. Group 1 and 2 premeasure scores are equivalent,
2. Group 1 posttest scores are better than the pretest scores,
3. Group 2 pretest/posttest scores remain the same.

Given the above data, we would be able to conclude that the training program had a desired impact.

To illustrate, in a study by Venardos and Harris (1973), clients at a rehabilitation center were assigned randomly to one of three conditions, two of which were designed to improve job interview skills. The third constituted the control. All participants in the study were videotaped twice as they went through a simulated interview. The first time this was done prior to any one receiving training; performance measures were taken a second time after those in the two experimental groups had completed ten hours of training involving either videotape feedback or role playing. Independent, impartial judges' ratings of the pretraining videotapes revealed no differences among the three groups at the outset of training (in fact, they were all deficient in the skill area). Thus, the researchers felt that the random assignment of participants to conditions was successful. And, there were significant training effects. All those in training improved about the same amount, however, regardless of the type of program they were in. That is to say, either videotape feedback or role-play strategies were successful. It is interesting that no attempt was made to see what the combined effects of these two approaches would have been.

Another example of this type of design can be found in the study by Hand and Slocum (1972). Their goal was to evaluate whether a managerial human relations training program could change attitudes and whether these changed attitudes would be reflected in organizational effectiveness. A control and experimental group were established and criterion data on measures of self-awareness, sensitivity to the needs of others, and leadership style were obtained once before the experimental group was exposed to the program and again 18 months after the program was concluded. The program itself involved 90-minute training sessions given once a week for 28 weeks and covered such topics as managerial styles and worker motivation. The authors found that the randomly assigned group of 21 managers who were exposed to training did develop a more positive attitude toward the human relations aspect of their job and that this, in turn, was reflected in positive changes in job performance (as indexed by ratings of job performance provided by the superiors of all the participants in the study). It is interesting to note that, in this study, the control group scores were a mirror image of those of the trained group. As trainee scores went up, control group scores actually went down. Finally, the authors speculate (but do not evaluate the notion) that in programs like this one it takes some time before induced attitude changes will be reflected in the job behaviors and job performances of the participants.

The importance of having pre and post data from training and control groups cannot be overemphasized when it comes to making strong inferences about the impact of a program. Eden (1985, pg. 94) clearly makes this point in his discussion of the effects of a team development program in the Israeli armed forces: "Although subjective after-only reports [the kind one might obtain in a case study] of the command personnel who had participated in the workshops were very positive, more rigorous before-after comparisons among command personnel and subordinates demonstrated that TD (team development) failed to improve organizational functioning."

The Pretest-Posttest Control Group with Multiple Postmeasures Design

The issue of time and timing in relation to research designs already has been raised. In evaluating interventions like training, investigators (like Hand & Slocum, 1972) may feel that it takes time for a program to take effect. Alternatively, the manager or researcher may be most interested in just how long a program's impact will persist. For these and other reasons, then, we might seek to continue our post-training measures.

In a study of the impact of an innovative program of mental training in the Swedish armed forces, Larson (1987) used a pretest-posttest design with a control group. Participants were assigned randomly to experimental or control conditions. The program itself involved developing deep relaxation and imagery skills (techniques borrowed from sports psychology) among new recruits. His criterion measures were relaxation and meditation behaviors, examination scores, and on-the-job task performance. The salient feature of this study, however, is that the measures were obtained 5, 15 and 25 weeks after training. Larson found that the program worked so well and was so cost effective (e.g., recruit training time could be reduced 5% and, with relaxation training, acceptable levels of performance still could be achieved) that it is now being implemented systemwide in basic training.

Similarly, Latham and Frayne (1989) sought to determine the long-term effects of self-management training given to state government employees. The program was designed to enhance self-efficacy and the capacity to cope with factors that had been found to interfere with regular job attendance. Thus, the authors measured both training and learning for experimental and control groups prior to training and at 3, 6, 9, and 12 months after training had been completed. They, too, were able to report persistence of effects. In particular, trained employees had significantly better attendance records and reported having fewer family and transportation problems that interfered with their coming to work even months after the program.

One variation on this multiple postmeasurement design is worth describing because it has practical, as well as scientific, implications. In general, it usually is a challenge to get organizational decision makers to support the extra effort that a control group design implies. Specifically, they have to agree to withhold training from some people and yet authorize the time needed to obtain premeasures and postmeasures from this group. From the workers' perspective, as well, there is the imposition of the inconvenience of responding to or participating in the measurement process. They might rightly complain, "What's in it for me?"

An approach used by some investigators to deal with these problems is to design the intervention and the study in such a way that members of the control group ultimately will receive the same treatment (e.g., training) as the experimental group. In the ideal format, all potential participants would be identified and invited to the program with the understanding that, for some of them, the actual training will take place somewhat later. Then individuals would be assigned randomly to a program or control group, the program would be implemented, and the necessary premeasures and postmeasures taken. After this, however, the people in the control group would be exposed to the training with still another set of measures taken. Thus, all participants end up having the training experience. When diagramed, this design looks like this:

	Time 1	Time 2	Time 3	Time 4	Time 5
Group 1: (Initial Experimental Group)	Pre measure	——Training—	Post measure	——Control—	Second Post measure
Group 2: (Initial Control Group)	Pre measure	——Control—	Pre measure	——Training—	Post measure

This design was used by Basadur, Graen and Scandura (1986) in their field experiment to test the effects of training on the attitudes of a group of engineers toward divergent thinking in problem solving. A second group served as a control group in the first part of the experiment and vice versa for the second part. A positive effect for training was detected by comparing the scores of the two groups at Time 3 and again at Time 5. As predicted in their study, the members of group one showed better performance (e.g., higher supervisor ratings on their tendency to resist premature closure on problem solutions) at measurement period 3, while at Time 5 both groups were about the same. It also turned out that the training program worked best if it was done with intact work groups rather than ad hoc groups of engineers who don't usually work together. This is because members of the former could support one another in the practice and application of the divergent thinking principles to current engineering projects. A version of this design also was used by Latham and Frayne (1989) in the study described above. The control group in their project also received delayed training in self-management, but between the 9- and 12-month measurement periods.

The After-Only Control Group Design

This approach relies on an assumption that participants are, in fact, randomly assigned to training and control groups or that they have been carefully matched on relevant factors. It can be diagramed this way:

	Time 1	Time 2
Experimental Group	Training————	>Measures taken
Control Group	———————————	>Measures taken

This design might be followed if there is not enough time to obtain measures prior to training. Or it might be used if there is some strong reason to assume that the completion of premeasures would itself constitute a *treatment*, that is to say, it would have its own effects ("testing" effects). For instance, asking questions of the members of the control group regarding their management style might cause them to become sensitized to this aspect of their behavior and, inadvertently, cause them to change their style in some systematic way (e.g., to become more open or participative with their subordinates). This was discussed earlier in the section on self-reports (cf. Sprangers & Hoogstraten, 1989). Later comparisons with a group of trainees might yield surprising similarities because of this inadvertent inducement to change. The inference that the program did not have an effect would be incorrect.

The Solomon Four-Group Design

This represents a complex plan to reduce equivocality in evaluations as much as possible. In it several groups are created in order to measure or control for some of the threats to internal validity that have been identified. This design can be outlined as follows:

	Time 1	Time 2	Time 3
Group 1	Premeasures —— >taken	Training ——>	Postmeasures taken
Group 2	Premeasures ————————taken		>Postmeasures taken
Group 3	————>	Training ————	>Postmeasures taken
Group 4	———————————————		>Postmeasures taken

The logic of comparisons as developed earlier would then be followed to infer the degree to which the training program had an impact. This design also allows us to assess the extent to which pretesting has any real effects for both the trained and untrained employees.

The complexity of this design makes it difficult to implement, however. The degree of management support needed is quite great. Large numbers of employees must be available. The patience of those not involved in training (groups 2 and 4) must be great to tolerate all the measurements taken. The results, themselves, can be difficult to interpret if they don't turn out as expected. Such was the case with one of the few published examples of the use of the four-group design reported in the published training research literature.

Bunker and Cohen (1977) conducted an evaluation of a training program for telephone technicians using this design. The program itself involved a mixture of classroom and fieldwork on electronic and telephone systems. Employees were assigned randomly to training and measurement conditions as prescribed by the design. Bunker and Cohen (1977) found that pretesting did have an effect, but in complex ways. It actually lowered posttraining performance on an electronics achievement test of those in the training program, but only for certain subgroups (those with medium and low numerical aptitude). In contrast, it facilitated a postmeasure performance for a subset of those in the untrained, control group (this time those with medium levels of aptitude!). While these findings were unexpected, the authors felt that the more complex design was worth the extra effort because its rich data set prevented them from concluding wrongly that the program did not work, as they might have. Instead, it was found to be effective but for particular groups of trainees.

QUASI-EXPERIMENTAL DESIGNS

There are many times when the training specialist wishes to evaluate a program's effectiveness but does not have the requisite conditions to use one of the experimental designs just outlined (e.g., there may be too few trainees involved, the investigator may not be able to create or manipulate the treatment of interest, random assignment to experimental conditions may not be feasible). *Quasi-experimental designs*, also called Patch-up and time-series designs, may provide a reasonable alternative (Cook & Campbell, 1979). The logic of quasi-experimental designs is to use whatever opportunities available to rule out the most likely threats to internal validity in particular. Quasi-experimental designs include nonequivalent control group designs, simple time-series designs, and multiple time-series designs.

Nonequivalent Control Group Design

A hallmark of a true experimental design is the capacity to rule out plausible, rival hypotheses, especially with regard to the internal validity of the study. As we have seen, a practical approach to dealing with possible biases due to individual differences (e.g., in aptitude, experience, motivation), to group differences (norms, leadership), or to organizational differences (structure, resources) is to randomly assign participants to research conditions. However, there are many instances where this is not feasible. For instance, there may be only certain groups available at a point in time when the training is offered. Because of this, they will get the training while others will not. Thus, when data are gathered and analyzed the investigator must be cautious because the results may be an artifact of the particular (nonrandomly selected) groups involved.

From a design point of view, the nonequivalent control group case looks a lot like some of the experimental designs already discussed. However, the difference is in the special care that the investigator must exert to address possible biases stemming from the use of intact or ad hoc groups.

In the study of mental training in the Swedish military described earlier, Larson (1987) found that he could not break up military units for his research nor randomly assign recruits to control or treatment conditions. Similarly, he found that he had to wait to gather control group data from the next incoming class. However, beyond this he had essentially a pretest-posttest control group design.

To rule out possible biases due to sample characteristics, Larson did make use of archival data. For example, he looked for and found no significant differences between the participants in his experimental group versus the control groups on the standard enlistment exam regarding either physical or psychological variables, including mental ability. Similarly, both groups were assessed with regard to their previous experiences with mental training and were found to be comparable. About 30% had been exposed to mental training or had tried it at one point in their lives (e.g., in sports). With all of this evidence in hand, Larson felt that he could rule out sample differences as an explanation for his favorable results.

In a nonequivalent control group study of a program aimed at modifying the driving behavior of truck drivers, Siero, Boon, Kok, and Siero (1989), took similar cautious steps. In this effort, drivers from one district were exposed to a complex intervention, a part of which was training in energy-saving driving behavior. The drivers from another district served as a control. Data on actual fuel consumption obtained for weeks after the program was concluded seemed to show that it did have an impact. The authors were concerned that it could have been argued that the results were due to some special characteristics of the drivers in the experimental district. However, the authors were able to deal with this "threat" by showing that there were no differences between the districts and their drivers before the intervention. This ruled out such alternative explanations as selection bias, history, instrumentation effects, etc. Furthermore, they looked for the possibility of communication between drivers from the two districts. This could have produced unintentional diffusion or imitation of the treatment, or alternatively, compensatory rivalry or demoralization (Cook & Campbell, 1979). But they found none. Thus, while every alternative could not be dealt with, the most likely ones were addressed. Based on the pattern of performance data and on careful measures of attitudes and group norms, the authors concluded that it was the program that really had a positive impact.

A third example of a design that involves a nonequivalent control group can be found in the study by Marks, Mirvis, Hackett, and Grady (1986). It too dealt with the possibility of rival hypotheses brought about because the authors could not control the assignment of individuals to the treatment of interest. They also were not the initiators of the treatment itself since it was a company sponsored program.

More specifically, Marks et al. (1986) were interested in assessing the impact of participation in a quality circle program on quality of work life attitudes, productivity, and absenteeism among direct labor employees in a manufacturing firm. Quality circle programs originated in Japan and involve small groups of employees who perform similar work who meet regularly on a volunteer basis (but usually on company time) to discuss, analyze, and propose solutions to work-related (quality) problems.

Participants and nonparticipants (n = 46 in each group) were surveyed before and after the introduction of the quality circle program. Analyses revealed that participant's scores on scales directly linked to quality circle activities (e.g., involvement in decision making, organizational communication) increased, whereas no such changes were detected in general work life areas. In fact, the scores for nonparticipants actually tended to go down between the two measurement periods so that the program might have been able to buffer participants from organizational conditions. An analysis of organizational records for a period of six months before to 24 months after the program had been adopted showed that quality circle participation was related to improvements in employee productivity and attendance rates as well. For example, Figure 11-2 shows their data for the variables (a) hours spent on production, (b) efficiency, and, (c) productivity. T scores (a form of standard score) were computed between the average scores of the two groups for the six months preceeding the quality circle program and the time 5 results (19–24 months after the program). As pictured, there were significant positive changes for the participant group but not for the control group over this period for each of these variables. Weaker, and nonsignificant effects were found for the attendance measure.

There are several aspects of this study that make it a good example of a quasi-experimental design. To begin with, the investigators were not the ones who initiated the intervention. It was initiated by a consulting firm at the request of management. Similarly, the quality of work life data were obtained from company records of a regularly administered organizational attitude survey. As chance would have it, a survey had been conducted by the company's Personnel Department just before and again 20 months after the implementation of the program. Finally, the data on productivity and attendance were obtained from company records. Thus, in effect, the authors did not actually create or control the treatment in the study nor could they design the particular measurements involved. But existing data were used in a very clever way for a program evaluation attempt.

Another feature of this study is that the participants in the program were all volunteers; they were not randomly assigned to quality circle training and involvement. Data from 46 of 53 of these voluntary participants could be obtained. Information and self-reports from 46 of the 56 employees who were invited but who chose not to volunteer comprise the control data. Because the authors were concerned about a *volunteer bias*, these two groups were scrutinized carefully. The researchers found that they were comparable in most regards (age, gender, years of service).

One final feature of this study that bears mentioning relates to the kind of analyses that were performed. The principle tool used to evaluate the impact of participation on work attitudes was stepwise multiple regression. In this case, the quality of work life scale score obtained at time 2 was used as the criterion. The first independent variable entered into the regression equation was the score of the same variable as measured at time 1. Then, in stepwise fashion, the participation variable was added (coded 1 or 0). By entering the time 1 score of the dependent measure first, the influence of the respondent's pre-program score could be removed from the post-program score. In effect, by doing this we end up with a partial correlation reflecting the contribution of the participation variable to the prediction of time 2 scores. And, as noted, this contribution to the variance accounted for by the participation factor in the regression equation was significant for several key quality of work life dependent variables.

Careful analyses of the data generated from quasi-experimental designs are required to cope with what is essentially a lack of experimental (design) control. Measurement and statistical analysis becomes a very important way to deal with rival hypotheses and to ensure internal validity.

Simple Time-Series Design

This design involves taking repeated measurements on a criterion of interest from a group of trainees. These are obtained over a period of time that brackets their participation in a training program. The actual interval between measures can vary between daily, weekly, and monthly and is determined by whatever is deemed to be appropriate. The time-series design works best where measurement occurs naturally or as part of operational reporting requirements (e.g., sales performance data gathered weekly). Otherwise the measurement burden becomes oppressive and may produce testing effects. In diagram form it looks like this:

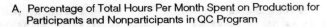

A. Percentage of Total Hours Per Month Spent on Production for
Participants and Nonparticipants in QC Program

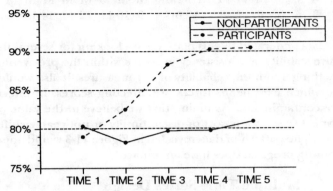

B. Efficiency Rates for Participants and Nonparticipants in
QC program (Number of Products Produced
Within Quality Specifications Divided by
Industrial Engineering Output Rate)

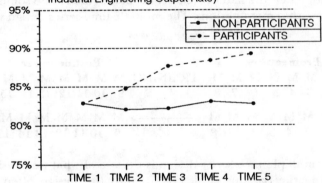

C. Productivity Rates for Participants and Nonparticipants in Quality
Circle Program (Total Hours Earned [Number of Actual Pieces of
Product Produced Divided by Number of Pieces of Product
Expected to be Produced] Divided by Total Hours Paid)

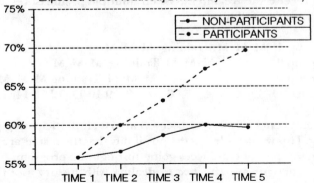

FIGURE 11-2 The Impact of a Quality Circle Program on the Measures of Performance
Source: Marks, M. L., Mirvis, P. H., Hackett, E. J., & Grady, J. F., Jr. (1986). Employee participation in a quality circle program: Impact on quality of work life, productivity and absenteeism. *Journal of Applied Psychology, 71,* 61–69. Reprinted with permission.

	Premeasures									**Postmeasures**								
Group 1:	M	M	M	M	M	M	M	M	Training	M	M	M	M	M	M	M	M	M
Time:	1	2	3	4	5	6	7	8	Occurs	9	10	11	12	13	14	15	16	17

In making use of the data generated by this plan, we are looking for several things. First, we are looking for some relative stability or consistency in scores within the pre-event measurement set. This would tell us something about the reliability of our measures. It also would give us some insight as to the extent to which extraneous forces are affecting scores. In effect, do we have criterion measures that are contaminated? Assuming that we believe in the value of the training program, we also would expect to see some sort of discontinuity or noticeable shift in scores just after the training experience. The pattern of data revealed in Figure 11-3 would appear to support the contention that the training program does have an impact.

Multiple Time-Series Design

This approach provides an extra margin of confidence by including data from individuals not involved in training. As illustrated in the Marks et al. (1986) study, these individuals serve as control subjects. Thus, we would hope that the latter reveal scores that demonstrate some consistency in premeasurement and postmeasurement periods. The multiple time-series design would look like the following:

	Premeasures									**Postmeasures**								
Group 1:	M	M	M	M	M	M	M	M	TRAINING	M	M	M	M	M	M	M	M	M
Time:	1	2	3	4	5	6	7	8		9	10	11	12	13	14	15	16	17
Group 2:	M	M	M	M	M	M	M	M	⟶	M	M	M	M	M	M	M	M	M
Time:	1	2	3	4	5	6	7	8		9	10	11	12	13	14	15	16	17

A special form of the multiple time-series design is the use of what we considered a *rolling control group*. As described in the Basadur et al. (1986) study this design often is used under circumstances where all organizational participants want or are ultimately to be scheduled to be exposed to an intervention (in this case, training), but whose involvement can be staged. Thus, a given group of participants can be construed to be in a control condition, but only for a period of time, after which they too receive the treatment. When multiple premeasures and postmeasures are taken, this can be diagrammed as follows:

Group 1:	M	M	M	Training	M	M	M								
Group 2:				M	M	M	Training	M	M	M					
Group 3:							M	M	M	Training	M	M	M		
Time:	1	2	3	4	5	6	7	8	9	10	11	12	13	14	15

The replication or consistency of effects observed across all participating groups in such a design would be reassuring. This would rule out the possibility that the results are due to particular features of the nonrandom samples of employees going through the program.

In general, time-series designs are effective in dealing with history as a threat to internal validity. Because of their temporal nature, they also help us get at the direction of the "causal arrow" as well. However, the emphasis on measurement also presents some liabilities. As mentioned, repeated measurements may create unintended testing effects. Similarly, if data are gathered

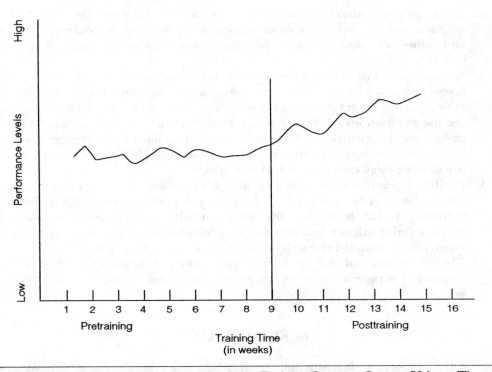

FIGURE 11-3 Idealized Pattern of Data Showing a Training Program Impact Using a Time-Series Design

through direct observations or self-reports, and are taken over long intervals, this increases the likelihood of instrumentation problems (Blackburn, 1987). Even archival measures may be affected when the period of time involved is long. Newer scales or methods for record keeping may come into being, calling into question the comparability of data sets.

CHOOSING A RESEARCH DESIGN

The previous section has illustrated the numerous options available to an investigator interested in assessing the impact of an organizational intervention such as training. Throughout, we have attempted to indicate both the advantages and the weaknesses of design alternatives and have used many illustrations. While we argue that certain designs have the potential for stronger causal inference, it is clear that there is no one best alternative. As pointed out by many writers (e.g., Dominowski, 1989), it is not only experimental manipulation that is the key to strong inference. The capacity to deal with alternative explanations is more important. Thus, there can be poor or weak "true" experiments and, conversely, very good or definitive relational studies in a particular topic area. The investigator always will have to make some choices as to which design(s) to use. The reader always will have to be alert to see if the study (irrespective of design) was done well.

In addition to the many potential factors influencing the choice of design that have been highlighted already, we wish to emphasize these additional considerations.

1. *Conceptual issues.* Above all else, a design should stem from the nature of the research question and the conceptual or theoretical issues involved. For example, the number and nature of control groups will be a function of the theorized relevant and nuisance variables.

2. *Costs associated with making a decision error.* As pointed out in Chapter 9 (see page 315), investigators, as a result of a study, may erroneously conclude that an intervention does (a false positive error) or does not (a false negative error) have a predicted impact. What are the implications of making either kind of error? To put it another way, certain designs may be adequate under circumstances of minimal consequences but would not be so where a lot is at stake. In particular, as Arvey et al. (1985) have stressed, the sample size must be large enough to detect true effects.

3. *Resources.* Resources include the time available for research, the number of participants (cases) that can be studied, and the money that exists for staff time, instruments, inducements, etc. More definitive designs usually consume more resources. As just noted, inferior or poor human resource decisions also can be very expensive. In any event, poorly designed research often can be as expensive as good research.

4. *The value system and skills of the investigator.* Some individuals are likely to be more committed to rigorous research designs and to possess the capability to execute them well.

SPECIAL ISSUES

In the next sections, we deal with philosophy/policy issues that can impact the type of design an investigator would use.

A Program Evaluation Perspective

Regardless of the type of design examined above, there is the potential that the question of the effectiveness or impact of an organizational intervention like training will be viewed rather narrowly. This limited view may be encouraged in our description of the types of measurements (reactions, learning, behavior, results) usually taken in research of this type. But this has been the traditional way of looking at training evaluation. More recently, however, there have been suggestions that we consider interventions like training in a larger perspective, one that acknowledges potentially diffuse and multiple consequences. In particular, several writers have advocated what has become known as a program evaluation research framework as an appropriate paradigm for assessing the impact of training (Goldstein, 1980; Wexley, 1984).

Program evaluation has been defined as "a set of procedures designed to systematically collect valid descriptive and judgmental information with regard to the ways in which a planned change effort has altered (or failed to alter) organizational processes. Thus, the result of program evaluation is a documentation of all relevant organizational behaviors that occur before, during, and after a planned organizational change" (Snyder, Raben, & Farr, 1980, p. 433). Important features of the program evaluation perspective include a systems-wide view, measurements throughout the process, and the acknowledged role of subjectivity.

A systems view implies that research on interventions should use multiple criteria or dependent variable sets, perhaps obtained from the various parties associated with the intervention. In the case of training, this would mean that we might assess a program's effects on trainees, on the training department, or on the whole company. The role of subjectivity is accepted as inherent in evaluations. The fact is most training programs are retained or scrapped based on judgments anchored in subjective feelings. Following the question: Does the training program work? We need to ask: From whose perspective? In doing so we should not be surprised to discover that assessed effectiveness is rarely an all-or-nothing prospect. In this approach values and value judgments will be explicitly acknowledged (Goldstein, 1980). Thus, different parties will expect and desire different things out of a research effort. This will be especially true in applied work (Boehm, 1980).

The assessment of organizational interventions from this perspective implies a continuing activity (Campbell et al., 1970; Snyder et al., 1980). You just don't carry out a pretest-posttest comparison of scores. The various steps associated with program design, development, implementation, and conclusion bring with them both subjective and objective assessments. Moreover, there is regular and systematic feedback after each stage to ensure that things are on track. For example, before we even try to carry out a training effort we need to know that the organization has the resources to support the proposed new skills and behaviors. Similarly, we should not attempt to evaluate a program prior to establishing that it is indeed being carried out as designed. Figure 11-4 diagrams the continuing cycles of evaluation favored by this approach. It should be noted that in this figure what Snyder et al. (1980) refer to as a summative evaluation comes closest to an evaluation as usually conceived by training specialists. Although the attention to training costs is relatively new, it too must be considered at the summative evaluation stage.

According to this view, the effectiveness of an intervention like a training program should be assessed relative to alternatives. For example, in attempting to establish a high quality workforce an organization could decide to emphasize more rigorous selection as an alternative to more or better training programs. If you hire people who already are capable of doing a job, training becomes less necessary. Similarly, the usefulness of a training program should be contrasted to other programs with the same objectives. As straightforward as this might seem, it still is not done very often (Campbell et al., 1970). Studies carried out comparing a particular type of training to a no training control group are all too common. It would be more appropriate to use a traditional or a less complex method of training as a control group condition. We do not need to rediscover that some type of training is better than none! Is a training program any good? Compared to what?

All this implies a consideration of training costs as well as the benefits associated with a program. When this kind of analysis is applied to the results of a training program we should be able to calculate its financial impact. Thus, we should consider improved performance due to training not only in terms of statistical significance, but also in light of its practical significance. A 10% gain in job performance might be statistically greater than alternatives. But is it enough to offset the costs associated with putting on the program? Figure 11-5 outlines the factors that might be considered in a cost effectiveness analysis (Cascio, 1982). Thus, as described in Chapter 9 (see page 315), economic analyses can appropriately be applied to training as well as other organizational interventions.

One final aspect of the program evaluation model that might be recognized is that it stresses the importance of a special orientation or attitude on the part of researchers and managers alike. That is to say, all parties must keep an inquiring mind regarding organizational interventions in general. There needs to be a genuine curiosity about effectiveness. This translates to cooperation and flexibility as the two groups go about designing an evaluation plan that balances rigor and pragmatism. Thus, while the program evaluation philosophy implies good program planning and good project management, it also stresses good research design. Whatever is agreed upon must be sufficiently rigorous to allow for some firm conclusions, yet not be so complex so as to be disruptive of the business enterprise. Evaluations should be a means to an end (improved individual or system functioning) and not become an end in itself (Snyder et al., 1980).

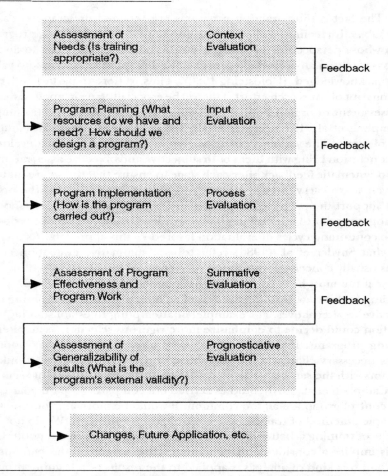

FIGURE 11-4 Program Evaluation Research Perspective on Training Impact Assessment
Source: Snyder, R. A., Raben, C. S., & Farr, J. L. (1980). A model for the systematic evaluation of human
resource development programs. *Academy of Management Review, 5,* 431–441. Reprinted with permission.

Idiographic Research

Much of the research in the social sciences has what might be considered a *nomothetic goal.*
That is to say, whether studying individuals, groups or organizations, the investigator seeks to
identify and refine a set of general rules or lawful relations that hold up over a wide variety of
circumstances. Thus, the implicit objective is to be able to predict, understand, and occasionally
control events in the typical or average case.

In contrast, there are theoretical, epistemological and practical reasons for focusing on the
specific instance (individual, group, or organization). Luthans and Davis (1982), for example,
argue for the intensive study of one or a few cases in order to build more complex and valid models
of human behavior that reflect more accurately the interaction between the person and his or her
environment. They also feel that it will allow us to build useful typologies of individuals. On a more

Training Costs:
1. Training development
   Needs analysis time ("people hours" used)
   Design time (people hours used)
   Material costs (includes supplies, staff preparation time)
2. Training materials (expendable costs of reproducing copies of developed program)
3. Training materials (unexpendable)
   Instructional hardware (e.g., projectors, cameras, etc.)
   Instructional software (manuals, videotapes)
4. Training time
   Trainee time (hours x salary) to reach competency
   Trainer time (hours x salary)
5. Production losses resulting from time in training by trainees
6. Training department overhead (pro-rata)

Training Returns:
1. Time to reach competency (time)
2. Job performance (rate, raw materials used, quality, down time)
3. Work attitudes (measured attitudes)

Evaluation: Returns – Costs = Cost Effectiveness

FIGURE 11-5 Costing Out Training Programs
Source: Cascia, W. F. (1982). *Costing human resources: The financial impact of behavior in organizations.*
Boston, MA: Kent

applied level, the intensive study of a single case would allow the investigator to predict with a high degree of accuracy what a specific individual (group, organization) will do under particular circumstances. These are the essential goals of idiographic (or so-called $n = 1$) research.

The approach described here goes beyond developing what are essentially the clinical insights of the qualitative researcher as described in Chapter 4 (see page 121). Instead, Luthans and Davis are advocating single case experimental designs that produce quantitative data upon which to build not merely hypotheses but actual causal models. Specifically, they emphasize the usefulness of reversal and of multiple baseline designs.

Reversal Designs. As implied by the phrase, *reversal designs* involve first the initiation of, and then the withholding of, some treatment or intervention. More specifically, as outlined by Luthans and Davis, the reversal design has these steps:

1. *Establish a baseline.* During this pre-intervention phase, the investigator takes measures (using observations, interviews or questionnaires) that permit establishing the normal or typical levels of the phenomenon of interest (e.g., individual performance).
2. *Establish the intervention.* The investigator then introduces and promotes the intervention (e.g., rewards) that he or she feels is likely to have the desired or predicted impact on the variable whose baseline was monitored. It is important that the phase is long enough for the intervention's effects to take hold and for them to be detected and stabilized as revealed in the measures taken.
3. *Withdraw the intervention.* At this point, the activities that make up the intervention are stopped but measurement of the relevant variables continues. The intervention is withheld for as long as it takes for the behavior or performance being monitored to stabilize at some (presumably lower) level.
4. *Reintroduce the intervention.* The consequence of doing this are then assessed.

The logic of the reversal design is that it allows the investigator to establish the extent to which a treatment or intervention produces a reliable impact. Ideally, the intervention should result in change in the measured variable to levels that are different (usually higher scores) than those seen at baseline conditions. A withdrawal should return performance or behavior to baseline, and so forth.

An example of the pattern of data predicted for a successful intervention can be found in Figure 11-6. In this study, Komaki and her associates were able to demonstrate that on-the-job working behaviors of an attendant in a game room were improved through the use of an intervention involving the application of valued consequences (e.g., time off with pay) that were made contingent on desired behaviors (Komaki et al., 1977).

Multiple Baseline Design. This approach also can be used with a single subject (individual, group, etc.). However, the emphasis in *multiple baseline design* is on the careful identification and measurement of two or more (dependent) variables that are felt to be differentially affected by one or more interventions (Luthans & Davis, 1982). The steps include the following:

1. *Baseline measurement.* Baseline data are obtained on two or more variables.

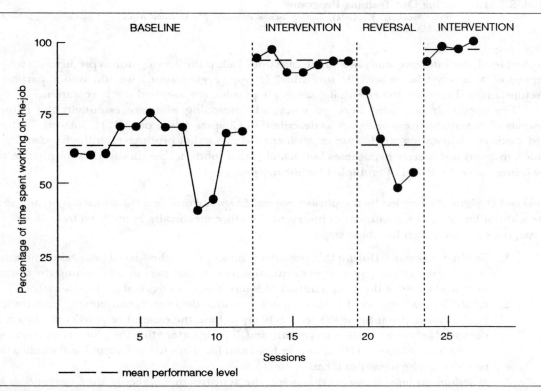

FIGURE 11-6 Illustrating Reversal Designs
Source: Komaki, J., Waddell, W. M., & Pearce, M. G. (1977). The applied behavior analysis approach and individual employees: Improving performance in two small businesses. *Organizational Behavior and Human Performance, 19,* 337–352. Reprinted with permission.

2. *Intervention "A"*. An intervention is made that is aimed at changing one of the dependent variables. Nothing is done to change intentionally the others being monitored. Ideally, they should remain at or near their baseline values.

3. *Intervention "B"*. Once the impact of the first intervention is stabilized, a second one is introduced. This one is aimed at a different dependent variable.

4. *Continued staggered interventions*. The investigator continues to introduce additional interventions until all variables of interest are targeted and assessed.

An example of this design (also from Komaki et al., 1977) is provided in Figure 11-7. In this case Komaki and her colleagues were able to demonstrate that particular interventions could be created to impact specifically on three different aspects of performance of grocery store workers. Notice, however, that fairly long periods were used to establish stable levels of baseline performance prior to an additional intervention.

Some Limitations. These two designs allow the investigator to study intensively a single individual, group, or organization. They produce data suitable for the application of traditional statistical treatments. However, they do have some limitations.

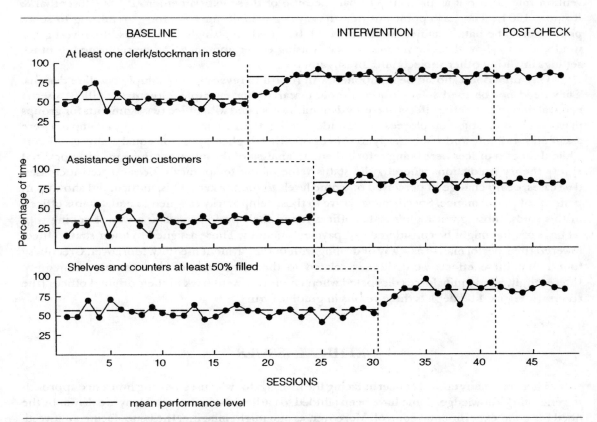

FIGURE 11-7 Illustrating Multiple Baseline Designs
Source: Komaki, J., Waddell, W. M., & Pearce, M. G. (1977). The applied behavior analysis approach and individual employees: Improving performance in two small businesses. *Organizational Behavior and Human Performance, 19,* 337–352.

Reversal designs, for example, assume no lingering consequences once the intervention has been withdrawn. This may be unrealistic for many types of organizational practices. For instance, once training is given, one cannot take away the knowledge accrued.

More to the point, the individual, once trained, is likely to continue to manifest the consequences in the measures taken. Thus, it is unlikely that we would see the person revert back to baseline levels of performance once the training intervention is stopped. Under these circumstances the investigator may conclude incorrectly that the intervention is not having the predicted impact.

Similarly, the multiple baseline design purports to eliminate the need for a reversal strategy by monitoring several dependent variables. However, it does depend on the independence of these variables. This, too, may be unwarranted. An intervention aimed at one variable may influence the others. This could lead to incorrect inferences regarding the effects of one or more interventions.

Luthans and Davis (1982) also highlight certain threats to the validity of these designs that would have to be dealt with in most applications. Most notably, the fact that they involve such intensive attention to the individual case may produce certain types of biases due to researcher expectancies and the demands that are (sometimes inadvertently) placed on subjects. The intervention may turn out as predicted in part because of these experimenter effects (Rosenthal & Rosnow, 1984). They also point out that these designs limit our basis for generalizing to some population. The data obtained would, after all, be based on a single case. Thus, the investigator would have to show that the results of a study using either approach can be replicated in other settings involving other subjects and investigators.

One final point should be mentioned with regard to reversal and multiple baseline designs. They need not be used solely in idiographic research. For example, Greenberg (1988) used a reversal design to test the effects of equity dynamics associated with office reassignments for groups of workers. In his study, employees in the underwriting department of an insurance company were assigned randomly and temporarily to offices of either higher, lower, or equal status coworkers while their own offices were being refurbished. An analysis of the impact of these moves supported equity theory predictions whereby the status value of the temporary offices created increases, decreases, or no change in perceived outcome levels to the workers. This, in turn, did show up in patterns of performance. Specifically relative to those temporarily assigned to equal status offices, in this study, those given higher status offices raised their performance as a way of coping with feelings of what might be considered overpayment inequity. Those assigned to lower status offices lowered their performance as a way of dealing with underpayment inequity. Moreover, Greenberg found that these effects were directly related to the magnitude of the amount of inequity. Interestingly, all inequity forces dissipated when employees went back to their original offices (the reversal). Figure 11-8 depicts these results in graphic form.

ETHICAL ISSUES

There are many ethical concerns facing the investigator who uses a strong inference approach to generating knowledge. Some have been alluded to earlier in this chapter. Many are driven by the need for good experimental control. Moreover, as one might imagine, the issues facing an investigator will vary depending on whether the research is to be carried out in a lab or a field setting. Good studies are much harder to conduct in organizational contexts, requiring at times extraordinary arrangements. Some of these imply difficult ethical choices (Cook & Campbell, 1976). Then

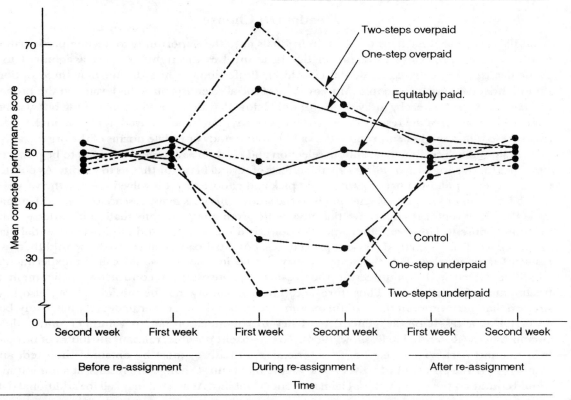

FIGURE 11-8 Mean Job Performance for Each Payment Group Over Time
Source: Greenberg, J. (1988). Equity and workplace status: A field experiment. *Journal of Applied Psychology, 73,* 606–613.

there is the notion of organizational norms. Investigators in university settings usually subscribe to professional norms regarding the treatment of participants in research. Moreover, they usually have institutional requirements for protecting the welfare of human subjects as well (Gardner, 1978). In fact, universities, as organizations receiving federal money, must set up elaborate mechanisms to review proposed research to assess in advance the extent to which participants are at risk and to mitigate such risk if the study were to be conducted (DHEW, 1975).

It is not that such review procedures are nonexistent in business organizations, but they are less inclusive and salient. Usually, company conducted research that clearly is likely to put subjects in physical danger will be the object of close scrutiny. But most often studies are not likely to be of this type. This places a greater burden on the investigator to attend to and to resolve any ethical dilemmas associated with experimentation involving organizational participants. Whether he or she is a manager, consultant, or staff researcher, personal or professional values must be invoked and brought to bear on choices among design and procedure options (some of which may imply tradeoffs regarding risk, costs, and the quality of the data that will be obtained). Many of these decisions will have to be made privately and without the benefit of external support.

These comments will serve as a backdrop for the set of issues selected for treatment in this section. The potential range of ethical concerns as they relate to experimental research that could be addressed is enormous. We only have space to highlight and illustrate a few.

Freedom to Choose

This refers to the extent to which individuals have the opportunity to decline participation in the research project. A variation on this issue involves the right to reject assignment to a particular treatment or experimental condition. Professional ethics dictate that these options should indeed be open to people. Moreover, most social scientists place high value in the process of *informed consent*, whereby individuals not only know that they are to be in a study but also are aware of the nature of the research and what risks (if any) might be involved. Yet for an investigator to do these things might compromise the validity of the study or violate norms of the organization.

It should be recalled that random selection and random assignment were felt to be powerful strategies for dealing with or mitigating the effects of several biases or threats to validity. As pointed out, however, if potential participants could pick and choose to get involved there is the very real possibility of an unknown bias entering into the study. This puts many researchers in a dilemma.

We argue that it is imperative that people be given adequate information in order to have informed consent. However, other things should be done to assess and minimize potential bias. First, as part of the informed consent procedures, potential participants should be told that, as a result of their involvement, they may or may not be in what we would call the experimental conditions. That is, by volunteering they realize that investigator control over assignment to treatments will be retained. Thus, threats to internal validity may be minimized. We also have stressed that it is important that careful measurements be taken in order to detect what, if any, bias occurred as a result of the general tendency to volunteer or not to volunteer under these circumstances (Rosenthal & Rosnow, 1984). To the extent possible, relevant attributes of nonparticipants and participants (e.g., age, experience, job tenure) must be obtained, indexed, and compared. While post study discovery of a sample bias cannot change the results, at a minimum it should condition the investigator's claims of generalizability. At most, it may call for additional data gathering.

In one field experiment, it actually was demonstrated that freedom to choose had additional effects on the impact of a training intervention itself. With the cooperation of top management, Hicks and Klimoski (1987) created two pools of "volunteers": those who actually volunteered and those who were "told" by their supervisors to attend a workshop designed to improve performance appraisal skills. Another experimental variable was the amount of information the managers had at the time that they were recruited for the workshop. Half of the managers were given a traditional pitch which, for this organization, was very brief and very positive about the benefits of attending. The other half were given a more complete and balanced description of what to expect. In this study it was found that those who had more choice regarding workshop attendance actually learned more (as reflected in test scores). This also was true of those who had more complete information about the program prior to entry.

Experimental research conducted in organizations brings with it a set of additional ethical concerns. Most organizations have norms that imply management control over many aspects of employee behavior. Here the professional's values may run up against management's need (and perhaps right) to know the consequences of an intervention. Indeed, some would argue that, because the latter (e.g., a change in work procedures) would be initiated or implemented regardless of whether or not it becomes part of a systematic investigation, no special consideration should be given to employees.

We feel that good management practices and ethical considerations are quite compatible. Managers should be educated with regard to the value of an empirical approach to decision making, one in which it makes sense for care to be given to employees as research participants. In the long run, the ethical values of social scientists, if adopted, are likely to create a climate conducive to organizational effectiveness. This implies that elements of informed consent and volunteerism should be part of assessing the impact of organizational interventions.

Interventions as Ameliorative Treatments

There are circumstances when the proposed research involves some intervention or treatment that is hypothesized to have beneficial effects for those who receive it. Moreover, this is widely believed by potential participants to be the case as well. Under these circumstances the investigator may be under tremendous pressure to allow all who wish to be involved the same treatment. And yet the researcher, in order to make strong inference, usually will require that some individuals be held out as a control group. Wortman, Hendricks, and Hillis (1976) point out how such pressures become exaggerated when both the beneficial nature of the intervention and the awareness of being in a control group are discovered by accident.

Cook and Campbell (1976) suggest that assignment to attractive treatments or interventions may be carried more easily out under certain circumstances:

1. When demand outstrips supply, there usually is a credible justification for some fair allocation mechanism (e.g., lottery).
2. When interventions cannot be delivered to all units at once, one might argue for a staged introduction.
3. When experimental units can be spatially and administratively separated, it may be feasible to justify withholding treatments.

While many of these alternatives may work, the investigator must still be sensitive to the possibility that delayed treatment may be one that is, in effect, denied. For example, an employee development intervention that takes some time to introduce and evaluate effectively forecloses on the opportunities of a whole group of cohort members who will not have the benefit of the experience at that particular (and possibly crucial) time in their careers.

Deception

It has been pointed out by Aronson, Brewer, and Carlsmith (1985) that it is an apparent paradox that experimental realism can be achieved through falsehood. In fact it is not uncommon to see deception used in research, especially on topics of a social psychological nature conducted in a laboratory. This has raised numerous ethical and methodological concerns (Kelman, 1967; Miller, 1972). For example, a researcher might wish to investigate the effects of failure on attitudes and behavior. Instead of creating conditions that will actually produce failure on a task, he or she uses a procedure that will lead the participant to *believe* that he or she failed (regardless of actual levels of performance). There are times when the investigator believes that deception is the most effective way to deal with the need for experimental control. It also may actually place the subject at risk to the smallest extent as well. But nonetheless, a deception has been carried out.

We would argue that deception (especially misleading or misinforming the subject, not just withholding information) should only be considered as a last resort. The investigator has an obligation to establish that alternatives (e.g., simulations, Klimoski, 1978; or role playing, Cooper, 1976; Miller, 1972) are not feasible or appropriate. If deception is used, it is imperative that, once the experimental session is over, the participants be carefully debriefed. This involves a description of what actually occurred in the study and why deception was involved. A number of writers have stressed how important this phase of experimental research is to both the participant and to the investigator (Holmes, 1976; Fromkin & Streufert, 1976; Tesch, 1977).

Pressure to Produce Findings

Although we would like to think otherwise, deliberate bias or fraud in scientific endeavors does occur. There are any number of personal and institutional pressures operating on researchers to produce results that support a particular point of view. While we find this unfortunate, we also would like to point out that the nature of research on organizational interventions has its own special pitfalls. In particular, the way that organizational interventions come about may set up additional pressures to report a preferred outcome of research.

Boehm (1980) implies that the investigator doing research in organizations often is the one responsible for developing, promoting, and implementing the intervention in question in the first place. In order to get top management to accept and underwrite the expenses of a program (e.g., a large-scale training effort), the organizational researcher often has to argue that the training will indeed have a desirable impact, even in the face of limited evidence. Moreover, when the research is done, the "real world" investigator then must be concerned with selling the results to decision makers. These realities hardly make for a disinterested position. As we have noted, it is no wonder that several writers can point out that the systematic evaluation of the most common form of intervention—training—is rarely carried out (e.g., Goldstein, 1986; Wexley, 1984). Our concern is that such forces also would create the potential for setting up weak or biased evaluation designs as well.

Quite clearly, it will take a strong sense of professional integrity, personal credibility, and skill to promote the notion of careful and systematic evaluation of interventions in organizational settings. This usually means working with top management to create an appreciation for differences in the quality of the data (and hence, of decisions) associated with weak versus strong designs. It also places an obligation on the organizational investigator to be flexible and resourceful in coming up with approaches to evaluation that will generate data of reasonable quality given very real constraints on resources or time. In particular, he or she should pay considerable attention to the potential of some of the quasi-experimental and $n = 1$ designs outlined in this chapter. They represent reasonable alternatives. Remember, there is no one best design. Each circumstance calls for informed judgment. The technology exists, but the investigator needs to be motivated to search for a workable solution.

SUMMARY

This chapter has reviewed the logic and many of the techniques associated with the rigorous evaluation of organizational interventions. Throughout, we have stressed the fact that there are any number of approaches that may be used, depending on the resources available and the level of certainty regarding causal inferences required. Thus, the investigator has many choices to make. It is hoped that the material in this chapter will allow the reader to make these choices in a more informed manner. Similarly, those who are responsible for supporting or evaluating research (or research claims) also should find this chapter helpful. The ideas presented can be used as checkpoints or benchmarks with which to critically review proposed or completed studies. In this sense it is hoped that, as a result of mastering the issues associated with design, the reader becomes a more informed consumer of human resources research.

SUMMARIZING AND INTERPRETING HUMAN RESOURCE RESEARCH USING META-ANALYSES

In this chapter, we emphasize the need to review and fully utilize the sizable research base available on various human resource issues. Specifically, we outline the methods used in meta-analytic reviews of research literature. These reviews serve as a basis to estimate the size of an effect one can expect when some human resource intervention is introduced in an organization. Further, these reviews can, in some instances, also indicate aspects of the situation that might magnify or minimize the expected intervention effect. Examples of previous meta-analyses, uses to which meta-analyses can be directed, cautions regarding its use, and guidelines for data reporting designed to facilitate future meta-analyses are described.

Given the large number of research studies that have been cited in this text and others that you have read, you are perhaps beginning to wonder why we need further research. Questions regarding the cumulative findings of research or what further questions can or should be addressed are the focus of literature reviews. Significant advances in the way literature reviews have been conducted and the way in which results are cumulated across studies have been made by several different research teams in the last decade (Glass, McGaw, & Smith, 1981; Hunter, Schmidt, & Jackson, 1982; and Rosenthal, 1978; 1984). In this chapter, we describe the need for these methods, present the basic methods of meta-analysis with some examples, and describe the current status of methods of meta-analysis. Throughout, we point to the ways in which the results of meta-analyses can be used in making decisions about the use of human resource interventions.

TRADITIONAL LITERATURE REVIEWS AND THE NEED FOR META-ANALYTIC METHODS

Many issues in social science research have been dealt with by dozens of researchers. These researchers frequently have slightly different purposes and methods of measuring key variables, and employ different procedures in data collection. Further, they often are faced with slightly different situational constraints (need for anonymity, sample size, sampling, etc.). As we shall see later in this chapter, sampling error alone can be expected to produce striking differences among the results of a set of studies that are similar in all other respects. Because of differences in the conduct of studies and the findings of those studies, researchers frequently have attempted to review and integrate studies on a topic so as to come to a general conclusion or in order to develop a theory that might explain inconsistencies in the results.

This task frequently can prove to be quite formidable. As early as 1949, Wagner (1949) reported 106 articles on the employment interview. Locke (1976) estimated that there had been between 2000 and 3000 papers on job satisfaction and Macoby and Jacklin (1974) reviewed 1600 published papers on the psychology of sex differences. Traditionally, these reviews involved a recording of the major variables investigated, the direction of the relationships, and the statistical significance (or lack thereof) of the relationships investigated. The reviewers also may have recorded particular features of the study, such as whether it was conducted in the field or the lab, how many subjects were involved, and their basic demographic statistics. They frequently counted the instances in which a significant relationship occurred under different research circumstances and drew their conclusions.

A good example of the way the results of a traditional literature review are presented is given by the excerpt from Schmitt (1976) contained in Table 12-1. Note that the study and major variable(s) investigated are listed, then some general notion of the number of studies reporting findings indicating the importance or irrelevance of this variable as a determinant of employment interview outcomes. Hunter, Schmidt, & Jackson, (1982) present a similar hypothetical example of a traditional narrative review to begin their text on meta-analysis. Their example involves a review in which there appear to be several factors that influence the degree of relationship between job satisfaction and organizational commitment when in reality the correlation in the data generated for the example was .33.

All variability in observed relationships, which seemed interpretable on the basis of study or sample characteristics, was due to sampling error. Recall from Chapter 2 (see page 57) that correlations computed in a sample will vary around a true or population value and that this variability is a function of sample size—the smaller the sample, the greater the expected variability. Later in this chapter, we will present a way to estimate the variability due to sampling error. The traditional review is, then, criticized primarily because it does not provide an index of the magnitude of observed relationships and, more importantly, the review actually may distort the findings of research because it does not take account of variability in study results due to sampling error and other artifacts.

Glass et al. (1981) cite a review of the practices and methods of research reviewers by Jackson (1978) that provides further criticisms of the traditional review. A listing of these criticisms follows:

1. *Reviewers frequently fail to examine critically the evidence, methods, and conclusions of previous reviews on the same topic.* They may cite those reviews, but they rarely take a second look at those reviews.

2. *Reviewers often focus their attention on a small subset of the articles they review.* It is not clear why their attention is focused in this way.

3. *Reviewers are very general or misleading in their descriptions of the findings of the studies they review.* For example, studies frequently are classified only as to whether or not their findings were statistically significant.

4. *Reviewers fail to recognize the role of sampling error in their findings.* Variability in results across studies is taken often mistakenly as conflicting evidence regarding some phenomenon.

5. *Reviewers frequently fail to assess the relationships between study findings and the characteristics of the study.* Failure to record these characteristics is important, because some reviewers simply eliminate some studies they consider flawed without considering the results of those studies in conjunction with the remaining papers.

6. *Reviewers often report very little about their methods of reviewing.* That is, they fail to report where they searched, what papers were included or excluded, etc.

TABLE 12-1
An Example of the Results of a Traditional Review on the Employment Interview

Variables	Studies	Conclusions
Attitudinal and racial similarity	Baskett (1973); Rand & Wexley (1975); Ledvinka (1971, 1972, 1973); Sattler (1970); Wexley & Nemeroff (1975); Peters & Terborg (1975); Frank & Hackman (1975)	Baskett (1973) reported that applicants' perceived similarity to the interviewer resulted in higher judgments concerning their competency and recommended salary, but no greater likelihood of recommended employment. Subsequent investigators have confirmed the effect of attitude similarity on interview ratings. Ledvinka (1972) reported that black interviewers were more likely to elicit responses of job rejection from black interviewees than were white interviewers in exit interviews.
Sex	Cohen & Bunker (1975); Dipboye, Fromkin, & Wiback (1975)	Similarity of sex appears to have some minimal effect on job resume ratings although Cohen and Bunker (1975) suggest sexual discrimination of a type that assigns individuals to sex role congruent jobs.
Contrast effects	Carolson (1968, 1970); Hakel, Ohnesorge & Dunnette (1970); Rowe (1967); Wexley, Yukl, Kovacs & Sanders (1972); Wexley, Sanders, & Yukl (1973); Landy & Bates (1973); Latham, Wexley, & Pursell (1975)	The majority of these studies found that an applicant's rating is at least partially dependent on the other individuals being rated at the same time. Landy & Bates (1973) and Hakel et al. (1970) have found the contrast effect to be minimal and Latham et al. (1975) found a workshop successful in the elimination of several ratings errors, including that of contrast effects.
Negative-positive nature of information	Springbett (1958); Bolster & Springbett (1961); Hollman (1972)	All three studies agree that negative and positive information are processed differently. Springbett and Bolster & Springbett (1961) maintain negative information is weighted too heavily; Hollmann (1972) concludes negative information is weighted appropriately, but positive information is not weighted heavily enough.
Temporal placement of information	Blakeney & MacNaughton (1971); Johns (1975); Peters & Terborg (1975); Farr (1973); Springbett (1958); Anderson (1960); Crowell (1961)	The early studies found primacy effects; Blakeney & MacNaughton reported negligible primacy effects and Farr (1973) reported recency effects. Peters & Terborg (1975) found favorable-unfavorable information sequence resulted in better applicant ratings than an unfavorable-favorable sequence. Solution may be an attention hypothesis that suggests interviewers use the information they are forced to attend to.
Interviewer stereotypes	Sydiaha (1959, 1961); Bolster & Springbett (1961); Rowe (1963); Mayfield & Carlson (1966); Hakel, Hollmann, & Dunnette (1970); London & Hakel (1974); Hakel (1971)	Interviewers seem to have a common "ideal" applicant against which interviewees are evaluated, although this generalized applicant may be the effect of halo (Hakel & Dunnette, 1970). Mayfield & Carlson (1966) also suggest that the ideal applicant may be at least partially specific or unique to the interviewer and Hakel, Hollman, & Dunnette (1970) found evidence for two clusters of stereotypes.

Source: Reprinted with permission from Schmitt, N. (1976). Social and situational determinants of interview decisions: Implications for the employment interview. *Personnel Psychology, 29,* 79–101.

In an experiment, which also illustrates the inadequacies of the typical narrative review, Cooper and Rosenthal (1980) divided 40 graduate students and faculty members into two groups and asked them to evaluate seven empirical studies on sex differences in persistence. The first group was told to read the studies and generate a single conclusion using whatever criteria they normally would in preparation of a review-type manuscript. The second group was given instructions as to how to quantitatively record the results of the seven studies and cumulate the results across studies. The reviewers in both groups were then asked to indicate their opinion of the likelihood that there was a relationship between sex and persistence. Nearly 75% of those relying on traditional review procedures concluded that sex and persistence were unrelated while only 31% of the group who had been given directions as to how to quantitatively cumulate the seven studies drew a similar conclusion.

Given that there are problems in a traditional review, you still might ask why or when a researcher in human resource management might be interested in meta-analytic methods. It is our position that, whenever a research base exists regarding the usefulness of a particular human resource intervention (selection, training, performance appraisal, changes in compensation practices, quality circles, survey feedback research), it would be advisable to first conduct a meta-analytic review. As we shall see later in this chapter, it may be that we no longer need another empirical study to make relatively accurate assessments of the impact of introducing some interventions (Kopelman, 1986; Schmidt & Hunter, 1980; Hunter & Schmidt, 1983).

In some instances an additional empirical study may be wasteful of valuable organizational resources (as a study of the validity of the General Aptitude Test Battery, for example) and, at the worst, one runs a highly probable risk that an incorrect conclusion about the value of a technique may be drawn when sample sizes of the planned empirical study are low. If one can conclude on the basis of a meta-analysis that a technique does have a high probability of having a positive effect on desired organizational outcomes, it would be better to use the effect size as estimated in the meta-analysis and make estimates of the utility of the procedure as outlined in Chapter 9. These utility estimates would then be used as a basis of deciding whether or not to introduce the intervention. Decisions regarding the use of a procedure could be analyzed in the same ways we outlined in Chapter 9 when it was assumed that the effect size estimate came from a single empirical study. When the data base is not very large and confidence in the precision of estimates of the effect size is not great, it may be best to proceed with the intervention but provide for an evaluation of its results using an appropriate research design and then report the results to allow for subsequent meta-analysis.

In the next section, we will briefly outline the techniques and quantitative formulas associated with meta-analysis.

META-ANALYTIC TECHNIQUES

The essential character of meta-analysis is that we attempt to statistically analyze the summary findings of many empirical studies. To this end a great deal of care should be taken to describe and code the empirical studies on relevant dimensions. Actually, the work of coding and analyzing the results of studies should be preceded by extensive preparation. Our view of the meta-analytic review process is outlined in Figure 12-1. The review process begins with a compilation of all the relevant empirical studies on the problem in which one is interested. The papers then should be read and the reviewer-researcher should formulate hypotheses about potential moderators or study characteristics that may affect the relationship between the variables being investigated.

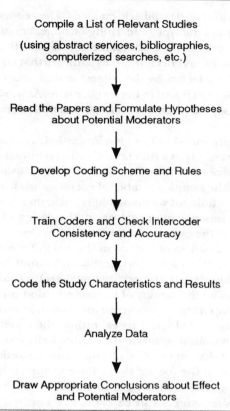

Compile a List of Relevant Studies

(using abstract services, bibliographies, computerized searches, etc.)

↓

Read the Papers and Formulate Hypotheses about Potential Moderators

↓

Develop Coding Scheme and Rules

↓

Train Coders and Check Intercoder Consistency and Accuracy

↓

Code the Study Characteristics and Results

↓

Analyze Data

↓

Draw Appropriate Conclusions about Effect and Potential Moderators

FIGURE 12-1 A Flow Chart of the Steps in a Meta-Analysis

One of the temptations of reviewers employing meta-analytic methods is to rush into the data coding part of the review without thoroughly reading the research or later simply scanning the relevant papers to find the numbers one needs to code data on the relevant variables. Very often, relevant aspects of the study and theoretical discussion can be missed if one proceeds in this fashion. The papers should be reviewed thoroughly to fully appreciate the sources of the data and the methods used to collect the data. From the hypotheses generated by this thorough reading of the relevant papers, a list of variables that need to be coded from each study is drawn up, along with coding rules to guide the coders. Coders are then trained, and their accuracy and consistency checked. Finally, these data are analyzed and summarized. In the next section, we use some examples to indicate what is important in describing and coding the studies in a meta-analytic review.

DESCRIPTION AND CODING OF STUDIES

What data are relevant certainly will vary with the substantive and methodological issues that are important to the reviewers and to the relationships being studied. Some examples may be useful here. Glass et al. (1981) provide data on 20 studies of the relationship between teacher style (discussion versus lecture orientation) and pupil achievement. They coded the number of teachers studied, the duration of the teaching, the type of learning or subject matter knowledge measured, the grade level of the students, and the type and value of the statistics reported. Clearly, their coding of these attributes of the studies reflected the hypotheses that the relative effectiveness of one style versus another might be affected by the subject matter taught, the grade level of the students, and how long students were exposed to the teacher style. As we shall see later, the number of subjects in the study (in this case, the teachers) is an important determinant of the variability in the observed effect size.

Another recent example is presented by Gaugler, Rosenthal, Thornton, and Bentson (1987) who examined assessment center validity as a function of various study characteristics. They coded the following characteristics: source of publication (journal, unpublished, convention presentation); percentage of minorities in the sample; number of exercises used; number of days of assessor operation; the type of assessor (psychologist versus manager); whether or not peer evaluations were collected; the purpose of the assessment center evaluation; the design of the validation study; and the type of criterion used, as well as the estimate of center validity. One or more authors previously had suggested that these variables had some effect on the magnitude of the validity coefficient and/or the quality of the center or validation effort. Similarly, Schmitt, Gooding, Noe, and Kirsch (1984) coded the type of validation design, the occupational group studied, the type of test, and the type of criterion used in assessing the validity of various selection procedures.

These studies indicate two important points about meta-analytic reviews. First, studies are not eliminated from the review on methodological bases; rather, their methodological features are coded and the influence of the variation in methods is empirically evaluated. Perhaps this is no more clearly evident or important than in the case of unpublished studies. Rather than automatically exclude such studies because of the feeling that failure to appear in the published research literature indicates a serious flaw, these studies are included so that the nature of differences between published and unpublished studies can be evaluated. Further, it requires that reviewers be especially thorough in locating the available empirical research. Various computerized search routines are now available to help locate existing research studies (see Table 7-1 of Hunter, Schmidt, & Jackson, 1982 and Chapter 3 of Glass et al., 1981), but additional efforts to locate unpublished studies may include letters and phone calls. Given the great deal of time and money expended in searching for relevant studies, it also is a good practice to record the sources of data with the review article. Second, all efforts should be taken in meta-analytic efforts to ensure accurate and reliable coding of study characteristics and results. Information such as the number and sex of the subjects and the effect size statistics are objective. There should be no disagreement, other than instances of recording errors, in this information. However, information such as the type of validation design in the Schmitt et al. (1984) study or the complexity of a job (Hunter & Hunter, 1984) may involve some subjective judgment on the part of the coder. In those cases, the rules for coding these variables, the extent of coder agreement, and the means by which coding inconsistencies are resolved should be stated clearly in the meta- analytic review.

Glass et al. (1981) provide a helpful discussion of issues regarding the reliability and validity of classifying and coding studies and examples from meta-analyses conducted in various substantive areas. Hunter and Hirsh (1987) provide a review of meta-analyses regarding human resource issues. We agree with Glass et al. (1981) that the validity and reliability of the coding of all but the simplest (most objective) features should be evaluated and reported. Coding reliability can be expressed as a correlation coefficient as it is in Chapter 3 (see page 93). If the data being coded are nominal (see page 53 in Chapter 2), a percent agreement or Kappa coefficient (Cohen, 1960; 1968) may be more appropriate indices of rater agreement.

Recently, Wanous, Sullivan, and Malinak (1989) have drawn attention to the various types of judgments meta-analytic researchers must make and how those judgments may affect the results and conclusions of a meta-analytic review. Wanous et al. (1989) summarize the critical points in meta-analyses in Table 12-2. Their paper showed how differences in judgments created differences in meta-analytic reviews of the job satisfaction-job performance relationship (Iaffaldano & Muchinsky, 1985; Petty, McGee, & Cavender, 1984), the relationship between realistic job previews and job survival (McEvoy & Cascio, 1985; Premack & Wanous, 1985), correlates of role ambiguity and role conflict (Fisher & Gitelson, 1983; Jackson & Schuler, 1985), and the job satisfaction and absenteeism relationship (Hackett & Guion, 1985; Scott & Taylor, 1985). Their conclusions in comparing these reviews were that judgment calls do affect the results of meta-analysis and that, by accounting for differences in the judgments made by meta-analysts, the results of the different reviews converged.

Their recommendations are consistent with our earlier remarks. Authors must consider their judgments at each of the steps outlined in Table 12-2; they must report the decisions they make with the greatest detail possible; and, whenever possible, they should test the effects of their decisions. Further, as mentioned above, two independent judges should make the judgments called for in Table 12-2 and the extent of their agreement (and how disagreements are resolved) should be reported. The practice of doing a good narrative review first, so as to be able to make intelligent decisions about what to code and what studies to include, should become standard practice. Finally, in some research areas, studies of a qualitative nature are common and it is difficult (and occasionally impossible) to quantify the study characteristics or findings. When this is true, it probably is good practice to include a narrative review of the qualitative studies along with the meta-analytic review.

In developing and testing theory, it often is important to read and to be knowledgeable of original research papers. In this regard, investigators perhaps can be too reliant on both narrative and meta-analytic reviews. While reviews, particularly meta-analytic reviews, often focus on simple bivariate relationships, we often find that rather complex, multivariate models are necessary to explain various phenomena (e.g., turnover, absenteeism, job satisfaction, job performance). An example of the use of meta-analytic results to test a multivariate model of job performance is provided by Schmidt, Hunter, and Outerbridge (1986). However, very few such evaluations of multivariate models are possible, because there are very few instances in which such multivariate models are evaluated in multiple studies. Consequently, the researcher interested in model or theory development must integrate the results of many studies and perhaps multiple meta-analytic reviews.

Estimating the Average and Variability of Effect Size

The actual estimates of effect size in meta-analytic reviews are easily obtained. The average correlation across studies is usually weighted by the sample size in the study that produced the correlation as follows:

$$\bar{r} = \Sigma[N_i \, r_i] / \Sigma N_i \tag{12.1}$$

where r_i is the correlation recorded from study i, Σ represents a summation over the total number of r_i, and N_i is the sample size in study i. The variance of the observed relationships across studies is given as follows:

$$\sigma_r^2 = \Sigma[N_i \, (r_i - \bar{r})^2] / \Sigma N_i \tag{12.2}$$

TABLE 12-2
Role of Judgment in Meta-Analysis

1. Define the domain of research (judgment call)
   a. By independent variable
   b. By commonly researched variable
   c. By causes and consequences of important variable
2. Establish criteria for including studies in the review (judgment call)
   a. Published versus unpublished study
   b. The time period covered in the review
   c. Operational definitions of variables
   d. The quality of a study
   e. And so forth
3. Search for relevant studies (judgment call)
   a. Computer search
   b. Manual search
4. Select the final set of studies (judgment call)
   a. Do individually
   b. Done by more than one person
5. Extract data on variables of interest, sample sizes, effect sizes, reliability of measurement, and other noteworthy characteristics of each study (judgment call)
   a. Use all the data when multiple measures are reported
   b. Use a subset of the data
6. Code each study for characteristics that might be related to the effect size reported in the study (judgment call)
   a. Research design factors
   b. Sample characteristcs
   c. Organizational differences
   d. And so forth
7. When there are multiple measures of independent and/or dependent variables, decide whether to group them a priori or not (judgment call)
   a. Theoretical diversity among variables
   b. Operational measurement diversity among variables
8. Determine the mean and variance of effect sizes across studies (calculations)
   a. Mean effect size weighted by sample size
   b. Between studies variance in effect sizes
   c. Estimate of artifactual sources of between-studies variance (sampling error, attenuation due to measurement error, and range restriction)
   d. Estimate of true between-studies variance
   e. Estimate of true mean effect size corrected for measurement error and range restriction
9. Decide whether to search for moderator variables (calculations)
   a. Significance test
   b. Amount of between-studies variance that is artifactual
10. Select potential moderators (judgment call)
    a. Theoretical considerations
    b. Operational measurement considerations
11. Determine the mean and variance of effect sizes within moderator subgroup (calculations): Procedure similar to Step 8.

Source: Wanous, J. P., Sullivan, S. E., & Malinak, J. (1989). The role of judgment calls in meta-analysis. *Journal of Applied Psychology, 74,* 259–264. Reprinted with permission.

Notice in the first formula, r_i is weighted by the sample size. This always will prove to be a better estimate of the population correlation except in those instances in which a single or small number of large sample size studies come from populations in which the effect size is different than in small sample size studies. We can check for this problem by doing separate analyses for the two sets of studies or by correlating sample size with effect size. In the event of differences or an effect size-sample size correlation, however, there are no guidelines as to what procedure to follow. Perhaps the best one can do is to report the problem so other researchers are aware that the results of studies differ in this way.

An example of a set of ten studies is presented in Table 12-3 with the calculations for $\overline{r}$ and σ_r^2. For these hypothetical data, half the studies were conducted when the weather was fair, the other half when it was stormy. In this case, the researcher had an a priori hypothesis about the effect of weather conditions on the size of the satisfaction-absenteeism relationship (see page 413). The weighted average correlation is .38 and its variance across studies is .0076. However, Hunter, Schmidt, & Jackson, (1982) point out that, in most cases, some of that variability is due to actual differences in population correlations and some is due to sampling error. To estimate the actual variance in population correlations, the value of σ_r^2 must be corrected for sampling error. The variance of the sampling error is given as follows:

$$\sigma_e^2 = [(1 - \overline{r}^2)^2 K] / \Sigma N_i \qquad (12.3)$$

where K is the number of studies. This formula uses $\overline{r}$ as an estimate of the population correlation. In the hypothetical data set, the estimate of the variance of sampling error is .0033, leaving .0043 as the estimate of actual variability in the satisfaction-absenteeism relationship. The value of .0043 is obtained by subtracting the variance of sampling error (.0033) from the total observed variance in the validity coefficient (.0076).

Schmidt, Hunter, and their colleagues list a variety of other artifacts that may produce variability in estimated coefficients, such as unreliability in the measured variables, differences in the variability of one or more measured variables across studies, differences in the factors measured across studies, and reporting errors. Schmidt, Hunter, and colleagues (Schmidt, Hunter, Pearlman, & Hirsh, 1985; Schmidt & Hunter, 1981) have argued that the largest portion of variability in effect sizes in personnel selection research is due to sampling error. However, the portion of variability due to sampling error also is clearly dependent on the sample size of the studies reviewed (McDaniel, Hirsh, Schmidt, Raju, & Hunter, 1986). With small sample sizes more of the variability will be accounted for by sampling error; as sample size increases a smaller proportion of the variability will be accounted for by sampling error. Given that actual data on these artifacts frequently is unavailable and its effect likely minimal for most of the sample sizes encountered, it may be best to settle for corrections due to sampling error only. However, correction formulas do exist (see Callender & Osburn, 1981, and Hunter, Schmidt, & Jackson, 1982) and for those research areas in which they are applicable and reasonable estimates exist, it would certainly be prudent to correct the σ_r^2 for these artifacts as well.

The remaining variance (.0043) in the estimates of the absenteeism-satisfaction relationship depicted in Table 12-3 can be used to compute a credibility interval regarding our expectation of absenteeism-satisfaction relationships in other situations. Taking the square root of the remaining variance leaves .066. The 95% credibility interval then would be .38 ± 1.96 (.066) or .25 to .51. This credibility interval means that we would expect to find a non-zero relationship between satisfaction and absenteeism when organizational conditions similar to those in the studies reviewed prevail.

TABLE 12-3
An Application of Meta-Analytic Formulas to the Satisfaction-Absenteeism* Relationship

Study	Year	Weather	N	r	Nr	$r_i - \bar{r}$	$N_i(r_i - \bar{r})^2$
1	1952	Stormy	57	.38	21.66	.00	.00
2	1971	Fair	72	.19	13.68	-.19	2.60
3	1968	Fair	98	.23	22.54	-.15	2.21
4	1973	Stormy	212	.41	86.92	.03	.19
5	1958	Fair	70	.23	16.10	-.15	1.58
6	1984	Stormy	580	.39	226.20	.01	.06
7	1979	Stormy	320	.50	160.00	.12	4.61
8	1956	Fair	79	.26	20.54	-.12	1.14
9	1981	Fair	412	.31	129.58	-.07	2.02
10	1983	Stormy	291	.47	136.77	.09	2.36
			2191		833.99		16.77

$$\bar{r} = (833.99)/2191 = .38$$
$$\sigma_r^2 = 16.77/2191 = .0076$$
$$\sigma_e^2 = 7.3/2191 = .0033$$

*Absenteeism is coded so that it really represents those who were at work. A positive correlation means that those who came to work tended to be more satisfied with the work situation.

Computation of credibility intervals is more complicated when corrections are made for other artifacts (e.g., lack of reliability and range restriction). Hunter, Schmidt, and Jackson (1982) supply these more complex formulations.

It also should be noted that, when corrections for range restriction and/or criterion un-reliability are made to the estimate of the population correlation, these corrections also must be made to the estimate of the standard deviation of this estimate (Schmidt, Gast-Rosenberg, & Hunter, 1980). In validity generalization work, one is normally interested in how consistently a test-job performance relationship would be observed across situations. To answer this question, we would compute the credibility interval.

Schmidt, Hunter, and colleagues usually report the lower bound of the 90% credibility value which, for our example, would be .30 (.38 - 1.28 (.066)). This credibility interval tells us whether moderators are likely to produce zero test-criterion relationships in some situations. Tests of the significance of an average observed correlation from a meta-analysis require the computation of a confidence interval (as distinguished from the credibility interval described above). Standard errors for the computation of confidence intervals in cases in which it is concluded that there are or are not moderators are provided in Schmidt, Hunter, and Raju (1988). Whitener (in press) has provided a detailed explanation of the difference between credibility and confidence intervals and to what questions each should be directed.

Examining Potential Moderator Effects

Computation of the total variance (.0076) in the validity coefficients and the variance attributable to sampling error (.0033) leaves a relatively large amount of remaining variability (.0043) and the resultant credibility interval (.25 to .51) is relatively large. The remaining variance may be due to other artifacts in the studies reviewed or it may be due to some moderator variable that causes differences in the correlations between two variables. If the remaining variance were close to .00, then any apparent moderator effects would be totally explained by sampling error.

In the hypothetical data presented in Table 12-3, the authors suspected that attendance at work and satisfaction were more highly correlated during stormy weather. Their rationale was that individuals who were unhappy with work would use the weather as an excuse to stay home, thereby increasing the absenteeism-satisfaction relationship. When the weather was fine, no excuse existed and absenteeism and satisfaction would be less highly correlated. To evaluate this moderator hypothesis, the researchers gathered archival data regarding weather conditions on the dates at which absenteeism data were collected and classified the weather as fair or stormy.

If weather is a real moderator we would expect that the average correlations for studies done in fair versus stormy conditions are different and that the corrected variance averages lower in the two subsets of data than in all ten studies. A summary of the data relevant to this question is contained in Table 12-4.

As we can see the average correlations of satisfaction and absenteeism in stormy weather (.43) is different from the same average correlation in fair weather. Further, within each subset of the data, sampling error accounts for more variance than is actually present in the observed correlations. This frequently occurs when the number of studies included in the review is small and is referred to as *second-order sampling error*. In any event, the data presented in Table 12-4 would be very consistent with the hypothesis that weather moderates the relationship between satisfaction and absenteeism.

Effect Sizes Expressed as a Function of Mean Differences

Frequently, evaluations of human resource programs produce results that are not reported in correlational form. For example, research such as that described in Chapter 11 usually would produce data regarding control and experimental group means and standard deviations and tests of the significance of the differences in group means (either t or F).

Glass et al. (1981) and Hunter, Schmidt, and Jackson (1982, Chapter 4) provide the formulas and a discussion of meta-analyses of program effects when the effect size is d. Glass et al. (1981) prefer to compute d as follows:

$$d = \frac{\overline{X}_e - \overline{X}_c}{SD_c} \tag{12.4}$$

TABLE 12-4
Summary of Moderator Analysis for the Absenteeism-Satisfaction Relationship

Fair Weather	Stormy Weather
$\overline{r}$ = .28	$\overline{r}$ = .43
σ_r^2 = .0019	σ_r^2 = .0022
σ_e^2 = .0063	σ_e^2 = .0028
σ_p^2 = -.0044	σ_p^2 = -.0008

*σ_p^2 indicates the population variability.

where $\overline{X}_e$ and $\overline{X}_e$ the experimental and control group means and SD_c is the standard deviation of the control group. The reason for using SD_c is that the experimental treatment may have affected the standard deviation as well as the mean. Hunter, Schmidt, and Jackson (1982) agree with this precaution but prefer, instead, to use the within-group standard deviation because it has the least sampling error. The within-group standard deviation (SD_w) is given by the following formula:

$$SD_w = [[\{[(N_e - 1)SD_e^2] + [(N_c - 1)SD_c^2]\}/(N_e + N_c - 2)]]^{1/2} \tag{12.5}$$

where N_e and N_c are the number of subjects in the experimental and control group respectively; and SD_e is the standard deviation in the experimental group. The equivalence (or lack thereof) of the two standard deviations $(SD_e$ and $SD_c)$ should be evaluated by meta-analyses carried out on the studies reviewed. If they are nonequivalent, then Hunter, Schmidt, and Jackson (1982) provide a formula to estimate d based on the control group standard deviation (see p. 100).

When t or F statistics are reported in the absence of group standard deviations, d can be calculated using two transformations. First, transform t to r as follows:

$$r = t/\sqrt{t^2 + (N_t - 2)} \tag{12.6}$$

where N_t is the total of the subjects in experimental and control groups. Then convert r to d as follows:

$$d = (1/\sqrt{pq}) [\sqrt{(N_t - 2)/N_t}] (r/\sqrt{1 - r^2}) \tag{12.7}$$

where p and q are the proportions of the total group in the trained and untrained groups respectively. Calculated in this fashion, d is based on the within-group standard deviation. When the outcome of studies is presented in statistics other than t, d, and r, the transformation formulas are more complex. Glass et al. (1981) provide transformations for some of these alternative statistics (see Chapter 5 of Glass et al (1981)).

Assume we have gathered the effect sizes from a group of experimental evaluations of an organizational intervention and made appropriate transformations. Then we would estimate $\overline{d}$ using the following formula:

$$\overline{d} = \Sigma[N_i d_i]/\Sigma N_i \tag{12.8}$$

where $\overline{d}$ is the average effect size,

N_i is the number of subjects in the study i, and

d_i is the effect size in study i.

The variance of the effect sizes across studies can be calculated as follows:

$$\sigma_d^2 = \Sigma[N_i(d_i - \overline{d})^2]/\Sigma N_i \tag{12.9}$$

Finally, the sampling error across studies is given by:

$$\sigma_e^2 = \{4[(1 + \overline{d}^2)/8]K\}/\Sigma N_i \tag{12.10}$$

where K is the number of studies, and ΣN_i is the number of subjects in all studies. The variance of effect size corrected for variability due to sampling error is the difference between σ_d^2 and σ_e^2. These formulas parallel those given previously for the cumulation of correlational data. When appropriate and when adequate estimates are available, d and variability in d can be corrected for other artifacts just as we can correct for correlational data. Hunter, Schmidt, and Jackson (1982, Chapter 4) provide these formulas.

An example of a meta-analysis conducted on a set of studies evaluating the number of cigarettes smoked per day by experimental and control groups after an anti-smoking campaign was conducted in the experimental group is presented in Table 12-5. In this case as in the example above in which we cumulated effect sizes expressed as correlations, we computed the average weighted effect size $(\bar{d})$, then the variance of this effect size (σ_d^2) and the variance attributable to sampling error (σ_e^2). In our example, there is substantial remaining variance; that is, $\sigma_d^2 - \sigma_e^2 = .0573$. If we take the standard deviation (.24) of this value and compute the 95% credibility interval we get -.12 to -1.06. The lower bound of the 90% credibility value would be -.28 [-.59 + 1.28 (.24)]. This value has been frequently used in meta-analytic research. It represents the value below which we can expect 10% of the validity coefficients. Our conclusion in this case is that the anti-smoking campaign does have an effect. However, less than 10% of the variance in effect sizes is explained by sampling error. The remaining variance could be due to variability in other artifacts or to some moderator of the effect of the anti-smoking campaign. Unfortunately, our example includes no other characteristics of the studies, the situations in which the studies were conducted, or the type of subjects studied, so moderator analyses cannot be carried out.

In the 1980s, a large number of meta-analytic studies were conducted on a wide range of human resource issues. In the next section, we summarize the results of these reviews and in so doing, we draw heavily on a similar recent review by Hunter and Hirsh (1987).

REVIEW OF META-ANALYTIC RESEARCH ON HUMAN RESOURCE ISSUES

Most of the meta-analyses that have been conducted explored various predictor-criterion relationships in personnel selection. This is not surprising since the use of meta-analyses of correlational data originated in the desire of Schmidt and Hunter (1977) to explore the degree to which results of many hundreds of criterion-related research studies could be generalized to other situations.

Both Hunter and Hunter (1984) and Schmitt et al. (1984) have produced comprehensive meta-analyses of selection research. Table 12-6 is taken from the Schmitt et al. (1984) paper and summarizes validity coefficients for various predictor-criterion combinations. The data in the table indicate that there are average positive correlations for all predictor-criterion combinations. The table does not include credibility values but their calculation did show that the 90% credibility value included .00 in only four relationships: personality-performance rating, general mental ability-turnover, biodata-achievement grades, and personality- status change. This means we can expect positive correlations in all other instances.

Percent variance left unexplained after correction for sampling error was substantial in some cases and larger than in previous reported meta-analyses although this can be accounted for by virtue of the fact that the Schmitt et al. studies had larger sample sizes than was true in previous meta-analyses. The number of times some predictor-criterion relationships have been studied is relatively small (< 10) and may prove to be a problem for meta-analyses which would be directed

TABLE 12-5
Example of a Meta-Analysis of Studies Evaluating Anti-Smoking Campaigns

Study	N_i^*	$\overline{X}_c$	SD_c	$\overline{X}_e$	SD_e	d_i[†]	$N_i d_i$	$d_i - \overline{d}$	$N_i(d_i - \overline{d})^2$
1	100	18	8	15	5	-.45	-45.0	.14	1.96
2	50	20	10	19	6	-.12	-6.0	.47	11.05
3	30	12	5	13	5	.20	6.0	.79	18.72
4	120	20	6	16	8	-.57	-68.4	.02	.05
5	240	18	8	12	8	-.80	-192.0	-.21	10.58
6	90	16	6	10	6	-1.00	-90.0	.41	15.13
7	150	14	5	12	6	-.36	-54.0	.23	7.94
8	180	17	6	13	7	-.61	-109.8	-.02	.07
9	60	22	10	16	8	-.44	-24.4	.15	1.35
10	80	12	4	8	6	-.78	-62.6	-.19	2.89
	1100						-646.0		69.74

$$\overline{d} = \quad -646/1100 = -.59$$
$$\sigma_d^2 = \quad 69.74/1100 = .0634$$
$$\sigma_e^2 = \{4[(1 + .59^2)/8]10\}/1100 = .0061$$

* N in the experimental and control group are assumed equal.
† In computing d, we used SD_w.

toward a study of moderator effects (see Sackett, Harris, & Orr, 1986 and the discussion of power on pages 421–423). The overwhelming conclusion of these studies, however, should be that various selection devices are related positively to a variety of criteria, that organizations can use these procedures with confidence, and that by doing so they will increase the effectiveness of their workforce.

Hunter and Hirsh (1987) present comparisons of the Hunter and Hunter (1984) and Schmitt et al. (1984) data. Direct comparisons are not appropriate, since Hunter and Hunter corrected estimates of the population validity for criterion unreliability and range restriction while Schmitt et al. did not. When the estimates from the Schmitt et al. paper were corrected using the same corrections Hunter and Hunter used, the average estimates were very similar and, of course, much larger.

While we believe these corrections are appropriate and endorse their use at other points in this text, we do not believe they are appropriate in the absence of data regarding the extent of range restriction and criterion unreliability in the studies reviewed. Hunter and Hirsh (1987) used a value of .67 for the ratio of the standard deviations of those who were selected to those who applied in correcting aptitude test validities. This ratio results in a correction that nearly doubles the estimate of population validity. As Schmitt et al. (1984) reported, almost none of the studies they reviewed reported the extent of range restriction. Over 40% (153) of the validity coefficients in the Schmitt et al. (1984) data base were concurrent criterion-related studies in which there would not have been direct restriction on the predictor. An additional 99 of these studies were purely predictive according to the authors, hence there should not have been any restriction. The remainder (114 validity coefficients) were from predictive studies in which there was some preselection of candidates, although the authors usually indicated this was minimal. Even the ratio of .67 used by Hunter and Hirsh (1987) does not apply to any one coefficient from the data base

TABLE 12-6
Results of Meta-Analyses of the Validities of Various Predictors for Different Criteria*

Predictor	Number of Validities	Total Sample	$\bar{r}$	σ^2_r	σ^2_e	σ^2_ρ	Percent Unexplained
Performance ratings							
Special aptitude	14	838	.162	.02841	.01584	.01257	44
Personality	32	4065	.206	.03531	.00722	.02809	80
Gen. mental ability	25	3597	.220	.01563	.00629	.00934	60
Biodata	29	3998	.317	.03566	.00587	.02979	84
Work sample	7	384	.319	.01081	.01471	—	0
Assessment center	6	394	.428	.00259	.01016	—	0
Supervisor/Peer evaluations	12	1389	.315	.03140	.00701	.02439	78
Turnover							
Personality	5	15927	.121	.00104	.00030	.00074	71
Gen. mental ability	8	12449	.141	.01877	.00062	.01815	97
Biodata	28	28862	.209	.01444	.00089	.01355	94
Physical ability	3	852	.154	.00762	.00336	.00426	56
Achievement/Grades							
Special aptitude	8	1093	.275	.03622	.00625	.02997	83
Personality	6	980	.152	.01406	.00584	.00822	58
Gen. mental ability	5	888	.437	.02209	.00369	.01840	83
Biodata	9	1744	.226	.07841	.00465	.07376	94
Work sample	3	95	.314	.01876	.02566	—	00
Assessment center	3	289	.312	.00692	.00846	—	00
Physical ability	4	976	.281	.00327	.00348	—	00
Productivity							
Biodata	19	13655	.203	.00362	.00128	.00234	65
Status change							
Personality	7	561	.126	.03139	.01208	.01931	61
Gen. mental ability	9	21190	.282	.00880	.00036	.00844	96
Biodata	6	8008	.332	.00144	.00059	.00085	59
Assessment center	8	14361	.412	.00151	.00038	.00113	75
Supervisor/Peer evaluations	9	4224	.512	.01537	.00116	.01421	92
Physical ability	3	245	.613	.00028	.00477	—	—
Wages							
Personality	10	1720	.268	.00903	.00501	.00402	45
Biodata	7	1544	.525	.01571	.00238	.01333	85
Work sample	4	1191	.438	.00547	.00219	.00328	60
Assessment center	4	301	.237	.00531	.00184	—	00
Supervisor/Peer evaluations	4	301	.206	.00737	.01219	—	00
Work sample							
Special aptitude	3	1793	.280	.00423	.00142	.00281	66
Gen. mental ability	3	1793	.426	.00660	.00112	.00548	83
Work sample	3	1793	.353	.01126	.00128	.00998	89
Physical ability	11	959	.419	.08924	.00784	.08140	91

*All predictor-criterion combinations for which less than three coefficients were available were ignored.
Source: Schmitt, N., Gooding, R. Z., Noe, R. A., & Kirsch, M. P. (1984). Meta-analyses of validity studies published between 1964 and 1982 and the investigation of study characteristics. *Personnel Psychology, 37*, 407–422. Reprinted with permission.

but rather to the average in studies of the General Aptitude Test Battery. These figures do not necessarily apply to all data. We believe corrections for range restriction should be made when data with which to make those corrections are available. In the absence of those data, we prefer the conservative observed validity. In either case (corrected or uncorrected coefficients), the contributions of selection procedures to important human resource outcomes is substantial.

The type of corrections discussed in the previous paragraph relate to corrections to the mean value of the validity coefficient. As we indicated above, corrections for variability in criterion unreliability and range restriction frequently also are made to the estimated variability of the validities. Recently, Raju, Pappas, and Williams (1989) have shown that the use of assumed distributions of these artifacts can seriously distort the estimate of the variability of validities and consequently our conclusions about validity generalization. The Raju et al. results, we believe, should indicate great caution in the use of hypothetical distributions in correcting the estimate of the variability of validity coefficients.

Table 12-7 summarizes the results of other meta-analyses directed to more specific questions in the personnel selection area. These studies indicate the variety of problems for which meta-analysis can provide reasonable answers, given the current data base. These studies, for example, indicate that (a) the training and experience inventory can be valid if it focuses on documentation of past behavior relevant to performance on the current job; (b) performance ratings may be biased when the raters and ratees are members of different racial/ethnic groups; (c) intelligence scores, as well as personality characteristics, are related to leadership ratings; and (d) age does not

TABLE 12-7
Results of Meta-Analyses on More Specialized Techniques and Questions

Study	Objective of Review	Result
McDaniel & Schmidt (1985)	Validity of training and experience inventories	Traditional inventory has $r_{xy} = .13$, behavioral consistency reviews have $r_{xy} = .49$.
McDaniel, Whetzel, Schmidt, Hunter, Maurer, & Russell (1986)	Validity of interview	r_{xy} for performance ratings = .29; r_{xy} for training success = .25.
Gaugler, Rosenthal, Thornton, & Bentson (1987)	Validity of assessment centers	Average $r_{xy} = .34$.
Lord, DeVader, & Alliger (1986)	Predictions of leader effectiveness	$r_{xy} = .52$ for intelligence; $r_{xy} = .15 - .34$ for various personality traits.
Ford, Kraiger, & Schechtman (1986); Kraiger & Ford (1985)	Racial bias in objective and subjective measures of performance	Performance of members of the same race is rated higher than members of different races; effect size is approximately .20.
Hunter & Hunter (1984); Waldman & Avolio (1986)	Age and performance ratings	$r = .01$ for USES studies $r = -.18$ for 13 nonprofessional jobs; $r = -.05$ for 5 professional jobs; r_{xy} was .26 and .27 for productivity and peer ratings.

appear to be related to job performance measures. All of these brief statements are perhaps oversimplifications of the authors' work, but they represent the type of general conclusions provided by a good meta-analytic review.

Guzzo, Jette, and Katzell (1985) and Kopelman (1986) provided reviews of different types of organizational interventions. Their results were presented in terms of *d* rather than as correlations. The primary results of the Guzzo et al. (1985) review are presented in Table 12-8. Effects of interventions were examined for each of three types of outcomes: (a) output, including quantity and quality of production; (b) withdrawal, including turnover and absenteeism; and (c) disruption, which included accidents, strikes, and other costly disturbances. Overall, workers who experienced the interventions listed in the top half of Table 12-8 improved their work performance by nearly one-half (.44) standard deviation, although there were large differences in effectiveness

TABLE 12-8
Effect Sizes and Intervention Programs

Type of Program	$\overline{X}$	N	95% Credibility Interval		Variance		
			Lower Bound	Upper Bound	Observed	Due to Sampling Error	Corrected
All programs combined	.44	330	.38	.50	.36	.04	.32
Selection/Placement	-.03	14	-.08	.02	.09	.05	.04
Training	.78	72	.56	1.00	.89	.06	.83
Appraisal and feedback	.35	26	.08	.62	.62	.12	.50
Management by objectives	.12	32	.10	.14	.24	.11	.13
Goal setting	.75	96	.57	.93	.91	.11	.80
Financial incentives	.57	13	-.10	1.24	1.65	.19	1.46
Work redesign	.42	18	.28	.56	.21	.13	.08
Decision-making strategies	.70	2	—	—	—	—	—
Supervisory methods	.13	18	.05	.21	.04	.01	.03
Work rescheduling	.21	27	.09	.33	.12	.02	.10
Socio-technical	.62	12	.54	.70	.03	.01	.02

Type of Criteria

Type of Outcome	$\overline{X}$	N	95% Credibility Interval		Variance		
			Lower Bound	Upper Bound	Observed	Due to Sampling Error	Corrected
Combined	.44	330	.38	.50	.36	.04	.32
Output	.63	218	.55	.71	.38	.04	.34
Withdrawal	.13	77	.07	.19	.07	.02	.05
Disruptions	.82	35	.45	1.19	1.34	.10	1.24

Source: Guzzo, R. A., Jette, R. D., & Katzell, R. A. (1985). The effects of psychologically based intervention programs on worker productivity: A meta-analysis. *Personnel Psychology. 38*, 274–291. Reprinted with permission.

across interventions. Selection/Placement which included mostly studies of realistic job previews had little or no effect, although subsequent meta-analyses of realistic job previews (McEvoy & Cascio, 1985; Premack & Wanous, 1985) report more positive outcomes. The effects of financial incentives were not as consistently positive either as the lower bound of the 95% credibility interval included zero. These results for financial incentives were much different when the studies were broken down by the type of criteria employed. For example, financial incentives had a major impact on output criteria ($d = 2.12$) and not as great an effect on other measures. Results for each of the three criteria, for organizations of different size and type (for-profit, nonprofit and government), and for different occupational groups are presented in Guzzo et al. (1985).

The effects of goal setting have been reviewed in meta-analytic form by four different reviewers (Chidester & Grigsby, 1984; Mento, Steele, & Karren, 1987; Latham & Lee, 1986; Tubbs, 1986). The primary area of agreement between three of these reviews (Latham and Lee did not estimate effect size) is that the effects of goal setting are much larger in laboratory than in field studies. They each also found sizable moderator effects. Future research should attempt to unravel the combination of moderator effects that seem to play a role in determining the outcomes of goal setting. Overall, however, goal setting does seem to have an effect (usually about .3 standard deviation) on organizationally relevant outcomes.

Some of the of literature on job satisfaction also has been reviewed using meta-analytic techniques. Petty, McGee, and Cavender (1984) and Iaffaldano and Muchinsky (1985) found average correlations between overall job satisfaction and performance ratings of .31 and .29, although Iaffaldano and Muchinsky (1985) found that correlations with components of satisfaction were lower ($r = .17$). Predictions of unionization activity from overall job satisfaction averaged .38 (Premack, 1984) and corrected correlations between role ambiguity and role conflict and job satisfaction averaged -.46 and - .48 respectively (Jackson & Schuler, 1985). Hackett and Guion (1985) found an average r of .14 between satisfaction and absenteeism.

Obviously, meta-analytic methods have made an important contribution to literature reviews and have added immensely to the utility of the current research base. However, as you might expect, a method that is as relatively new as is meta-analysis also has its critics. In our opinion, none of their criticisms are apt to change meta-analytic methods and the conclusions derived from the techniques to any significant degree, but they do represent issues of which the user should be aware. In some instances, our cautionary remarks refer to inadequacies in the current data base rather than in the meta-analytic formulations themselves.

CAUTIONS REGARDING THE USE OF META-ANALYSIS TECHNIQUES

In the following sections, we introduce the reader to some of the issues that are being debated actively in the research literature. In this area, in particular, it is important to read relevant current papers in the major journals. Most articles that consider meta-analytic precedures have appeared in the *Journal of Applied Psychology*.

Estimation of Variance

Perhaps the first methodological issue that surfaced was the discussion of the appropriateness of the equation used to estimate the variance of true validities (Callender & Osburn, 1980). While there has been a series of exchanges on this issue (Callender & Osburn, 1982; Schmidt, Hunter, & Pearlman, 1982b; Hunter, Schmidt, & Pearlman, 1982) and some modifications (Raju & Burke,

1983), the problem appears to be resolved and simulation studies indicate that the various formulations yield very small empirical differences. In fact, Schmidt et al. (1982b) hold that an equation that takes account of sampling error only (a *bare bones model*) is adequate to demonstrate validity generalization. However, they and others recommend the use of corrections for criterion unreliability, range restriction, and in some cases, predictor unreliability. Note that the equations we presented on pages 409–412 are their bare bones model. Equations that include corrections for these additional artifacts are available in Hunter, Schmidt, and Pearlman (1982) as are equations involving variations in assumptions about whether various artifacts are interactive (see Hunter, Schmidt, & Pearlman 1982, p. 92).

Power to Detect Moderators

A second question regarding meta-analysis techniques involves the power of these methods to recognize a moderator effect when in fact one exists. Recall from Chapter 2 (see page 58–59) that power is the probability of rejecting a null hypothesis when in fact it should be rejected. In this case, we are interested in rejecting the notion that there are no differences in effect size across groups of people or situations. This issue was first raised by Osburn, Callender, Greener, and Ashworth (1983) and has been addressed subsequently by Sackett et al. (1986) and Spector and Levine (1987). Osburn et al. (1983) examined the statistical power of meta-analysis as a function of number of subjects per study, number of studies in the meta-analysis, and true validity variance. They found low power to detect small to moderate true validity differences when the number of subjects per study was below 100.

Sackett et al. (1986) more thoroughly investigated power in a simulation study in which one dichotomous moderator existed such that half of the samples drawn were from a population with one effect size level and half from another effect size. The magnitude of the difference in true correlations between the two populations varied (.10, .20, .30) as did the number of studies included in the analysis (4, 8, 16, 32, 64, and 128), and the average sample size per study (50, 100, and 200). For each combination of these three variables (i.e., validity difference, number of studies, and sample size), 1000 samples were drawn and 1000 meta-analyses were conducted. Tests for moderator effects included (a) whether or not artifacts accounted for 90% or more of the variance in observed coefficients; (b) a χ^2 test for moderators presented by Hunter, Schmidt, and Jackson (1982); and (c) a simulation approach provided by Osburn et al. (1983).

The results of a portion of the Sackett et al. (1986) simulations are contained in Table 12-9. As can be seen in the table the power of the Schmidt-Hunter test is the best. None of the procedures have very high power (>.50) for most situations that are likely to apply; that is, power does not reach acceptable levels until we have 64 studies and average sample sizes of 200 when the true effect size difference is .1. Even at 128 studies, power is inadequate when sample sizes average 50. Lack of reliability in the variables being correlated further reduces power. This can be seen by comparing the top half of Table 12-9 in which reliability is assumed to be perfect and the bottom half of Table 12-9 in which reliability is less than perfect and variable. Other tables presented by Sackett et al. (1986) also show that this low power is not improved by corrections for attenuation due to unreliability. With larger differences in effect sizes, power is correspondingly greater, although even for differences of .20 we would require 16 studies with average sample sizes greater than 100 to achieve power greater than .80 across all three methods of testing for moderators.

The last three columns of Table 12-9 contain the probabilities of Type I error, which is the probability of falsely concluding that a moderator exists when all sample correlations came from the same population. While the Schmidt-Hunter procedure yields greater power, it does so at the expense of consistently high (most above .20) probability of Type I error. The other two methods

TABLE 12-9
Results of Sackett et al. Study of Power in Meta-Analysis

Power and Probability of Type I Error of the Schmidt-Hunter (S/H), Callender-Osburn (C/O), and Chi-Square (χ^2) Procedures for Testing the Hypothesis of No Difference with Perfectly Reliable Data

No. of Studies	Mean Sample Size Per Study	PD = .1			PD = .2			PD = .3			Probability of Type I error		
		S/H	C/O	χ^2	S/H	C/O	χ^2	S/H	C/O	χ^2	S/H	C/O	χ^2
	N = 50	.316	.105	.106	.501	.216	.204	.768	.469	.470	.266	.049	.053
4	N = 100	.380	.118	.122	.719	.386	.460	.945	.796	.805	.210	.048	.049
	N = 200	.501	.225	.224	.918	.718	.725	.999	.988	.990	.210	.051	.050
	N = 50	.412	.128	.113	.631	.302	.276	.905	.682	.655	.290	.069	.058
8	N = 100	.478	.159	.153	.873	.591	.600	.996	.948	.952	.269	.059	.056
	N = 200	.659	.289	.276	.994	.927	.929	1.000	1.000	1.000	.260	.050	.047
	N = 50	.428	.129	.111	.810	.476	.453	.978	.883	.881	.288	.059	.054
16	N = 100	.597	.188	.203	.969	.801	.812	.999	.997	.997	.276	.047	.049
	N = 200	.783	.448	.447	.999	.994	.995	1.000	1.000	1.000	.282	.058	.054
	N = 50	.492	.183	.188	.906	.669	.671	.999	.980	.984	.264	.046	.056
32	N = 100	.683	.315	.325	.999	.968	.974	1.000	1.000	1.000	.266	.054	.057
	N = 200	.906	.667	.680	1.000	1.000	1.000	1.000	1.000	1.000	.252	.048	.051
	N = 50	.492	.184	.189	.976	.860	.867	1.000	1.000	1.000	.211	.046	.047
64	N = 100	.789	.501	.506	1.000	.999	.999	1.000	1.000	1.000	.225	.055	.059
	N = 200	.979	.896	.872	1.000	1.000	1.000	1.000	1.000	1.000	.238	.071	.057
	N = 50	.600	.292	.332	.998	.983	.987	1.000	1.000	1.000	.178	.051	.059
128	N = 100	.869	.666	.688	1.000	1.000	1.000	1.000	1.000	1.000	.158	.045	.051
	N = 200	.998	.986	.987	1.000	1.000	1.000	1.000	1.000	1.000	.167	.043	.045

Note: Overall mean correlation = .3. PD = population difference.

Power and Probability of Type I Error of the Schmidt-Hunter (S/H), Callender-Osburn (C/O), and Chi-Square (χ^2) Procedures for Testing the Hypothesis of No Difference with Measurement Error Varying Across Studies

No. of Studies	Mean Sample Size Per Study	PD = .1			PD = .2			PD = .3			Probability of Type I error		
		S/H	C/O	χ^2	S/H	C/O	χ^2	S/H	C/O	χ^2	S/H	C/O	χ^2
	N = 50	.267	.067	.080	.416	.145	.162	.615	.283	.310	.222	.045	.054
4	N = 100	.313	.087	.099	.547	.244	.246	.831	.579	.583	.213	.047	.050
	N = 200	.428	.160	.168	.810	.507	.527	.975	.866	.872	.226	.054	.055
	N = 50	.319	.064	.073	.493	.166	.173	.741	.352	.380	.270	.043	.054
8	N = 100	.403	.107	.105	.728	.379	.376	.939	.745	.750	.276	.055	.054
	N = 200	.528	.200	.195	.913	.707	.695	.997	.979	.979	.278	.058	.052
	N = 50	.367	.111	.093	.616	.300	.269	.881	.598	.567	.292	.071	.061
16	N = 100	.474	.167	.147	.852	.592	.548	.989	.944	.937	.287	.067	.055
	N = 200	.671	.280	.285	.984	.889	.893	1.000	1.000	1.000	.299	.056	.061
	N = 50	.399	.091	.118	.741	.319	.368	.958	.788	.828	.256	.046	.058
32	N = 100	.536	.212	.198	.955	.785	.766	1.000	.996	.996	.282	.046	.058
	N = 200	.766	.399	.418	.998	.984	.989	1.000	1.000	1.000	.296	.053	.058
	N = 50	.422	.159	.164	.846	.555	.567	.995	.996	.973	.256	.062	.063
64	N = 100	.627	.286	.307	.992	.918	.925	1.000	1.000	1.000	.251	.052	.062
	N = 200	.877	.623	.620	1.000	1.000	1.000	1.000	1.000	1.000	.274	.071	.065
	N = 50	.391	.172	.169	.945	.817	.829	1.000	1.000	1.000	.183	.054	.054
128	N = 100	.688	.429	.465	1.000	.998	.998	1.000	1.000	1.000	.205	.053	.061
	N = 200	.952	.857	.859	1.000	1.000	1.000	1.000	1.000	1.000	.232	.078	.084

Note: r_{xx} = .80, r_{yy} = .80, standard deviation of reliabilities = .05, overall mean population correlation = .3. PD = population difference.

Source: Sackett, P. R., Harris, M. M., & Orr, J. M. (1986). On seeking moderator variables in the meta-analysis of correlational data: A Monte Carlo investigation of statistical power and resistance to Type I error. *Journal of Applied Psychology, 71*, 302–310. Reprinted with permission.

are designed to control Type I error at $p < .05$ and the simulation indicates figures very close to that value.

Table 12-9 and the other tables in Sackett et al. (1986) are not meant as a set of tables one consults to estimate power in a given situation. As Sackett et al. (1986) point out, various other factors also will impact on power, such as the possibility of multiple moderators, uneven proportion of studies in the populations sampled from, and lower reliabilities. However, they also caution that their paper does not represent a recommendation to do narrative reviews and single sample studies. Type I errors and power are not assessed easily for narrative reviews; the situation for narrative reviews is not likely to be better than in meta-analytic reviews and reliance on a single study as opposed to several past studies as an estimate of effect size clearly ignores the width of the confidence interval which is always larger for a single sample study given relatively equal sample sizes in all studies. The article does illustrate that meta-analysis can't consistently detect the presence of moderator variables given the current data base in many research areas.

Other Problems

Some other potential problems occur in meta-analyses when researchers conclude the residual variance in the estimate of the population effect size is large enough to suggest that meaningful moderators account for differences in effect sizes. If a great deal of data are coded from the individual studies, then the potential to study a large number of moderators exists and we have a new form of *brute empiricism*, that is, if we examine a large enough number of moderators, it is probable that one or more will be found to moderate effect sizes. Whether this is a real moderator of the relationship or a function of chance can't be determined without additional studies or provision for some form of cross validation. The best way to minimize this problem is to code and investigate only those moderators for which there is a sound practical, methodological, or theoretical basis.

A second problem that occurs in the search for moderators is that the moderators themselves are correlated. This would occur, for example, if one were investigating the moderator effects of gender and occupational group on performance-ability relationships and members of different gender groups were concentrated in particular occupations. In this event, gender and occupational group both might be independently identified as moderators when in fact only one may be the real moderator or there may be some interactive moderator effect. There is nothing one can do to remove the dependence or correlation between moderators, but its existence and implications should be recognized in the report of the meta-analytic results. Such a finding may actually suggest subsequent research which investigates the independent or joint effect of the moderator variables involved.

The quality of meta-analytic reviews obviously depends on the quality of the data-base that contributes to the review. If individual studies are inadequate, then the meta-analytic review may be inadequate. If the errors in individual studies are random and differ across studies, then the meta-analysis results are likely superior (but conservative) to any individual study, but if errors are systematic (that is, the same across a large number of the studies reviewed), then they will bias the results of a meta-analytic review in a given direction.

For example, Hunter and his colleagues have relied heavily on validation studies conducted by the U.S. Employment Service on the General Aptitude Test Battery (GATB). If these studies all were conducted by the same staff unit in a way that allowed for supervisors who provided performance ratings to have access to GATB scores, the possibility of criterion contamination that would raise all the sample coefficients exists. The average effect size from meta-analysis would then reflect this systematic inflation of the sample validity coefficients. Note there is no evidence that this actually occurred in the GATB validation studies or any others that have been the subject of meta-analytic review. However, it does mean that one cannot always accept an existing data base uncritically; maybe all studies are inadequate. Further, we believe a meta-analytic reviewer should be especially cautious when a large proportion of the studies on a particular relationship have been conducted by a single researcher or research group.

A series of articles (James, Demaree, & Mulaik, 1986; James, Demaree, Mulaik, & Mumford, 1988; Schmidt, Hunter, & Raju, 1988; Schmidt et al., 1985; Sackett, Schmitt, Tenopyr, Kehoe, & Zedeck, 1985) regarding other problems and procedures in meta-analysis have been debated. While the technical details of these debates and others (e.g., Kemery, Mossholder, & Dunlap, 1989; Rasmussen & Loher, 1988; Thomas, 1988) are beyond the scope of this textbook, it is important that the user of meta-analysis be aware of the developments in these techniques. Development of meta-analytic procedures is relatively recent and various adjustments are inevitable.

Finally, we would like to reiterate a note of caution regarding corrections to the average effect size for assumed (rather than directly estimated) levels of criterion unreliability and range restriction. Arguments pro and con on this issue have been presented elsewhere (Schmidt et al., 1985; Sackett et al., 1985; Q. & A. 26). Since we present equations for both corrections elsewhere in this text it is obvious that we feel they are appropriate when data exist regarding their actual levels. However, it is unreasonable to expect that a selection ratio of .60 or .67 applies in all occupational groups in all organizations, simply because it was found to be the average range restriction in a set of GATB validity studies. Moreover, this correction to the average effect size rather than correcting each validity coefficient with the appropriate estimate of range restriction or criterion reliability would be particularly troublesome if the sample size were related to the magnitude of these errors. Corrections for range restriction result in sizable upward estimates of effect size, hence it is very important that they be the best estimates available. As stated above, corrections to the variability in coefficients based on assumed or hypothetical distributions appear to be especially questionable (see Raju et al., 1989, for a full discussion). If such corrections are made, then we believe that both corrected and uncorrected coefficients should be presented, even though they may be redundant. Obviously these arguments about corrections would be unnecessary if adequate data regarding individual studies had been collected and/or reported. In the next section, we provide some guidelines regarding adequate reporting of individual studies.

GUIDELINES FOR REPORTING STUDIES TO FACILITATE META-ANALYSIS

Hunter, Schmidt, and Jackson (1982) provide a discussion of the data needed to conduct an appropriate meta-analytic review using a variety of data analysis techniques. Schneider and Schmitt (1986) provide a list of information for the case of validation studies that has been summarized in Table 12-10. Notice that this list includes basic descriptive data (means, standard deviations, intercorrelations, and reliabilities) but also a variety of data that may be of potential use in the event that some reviewer might want to assess moderator effects.

If one is reporting on a training evaluation study or on organizational intervention, it would be important to report sample sizes, means, standard deviations, and intercorrelations of variables and much of the information listed in Table 12-10. We also would want to know (a) how subjects were assigned to control and experimental groups, (b) when dependent variables were collected, (c) who did the training, and (d) how it was delivered, etc. Studies evaluating changes in pay systems ought to include, in addition to relevant data from Table 12-10, (a) what overall effect the

Table 12-10.
List of Information that Should be Reported in Validation Studies

1. **Firm.** The sponsor of the study and the organization or firm with which the study was done (or the type of firm when this information is proprietary).
2. **Problem and Setting.** The problem to which the study was addressed and the social, economic, organizational elements of the setting.
3. **Job Title and Code.** The title and code of the job performed as taken from the *Dictionary of Occupational Titles*.
4. **Job Description.** A description supplementing the *DOT* description when necessary.
5. **Sample.** The sample size and the characteristics of the people studied, i.e., their sex, age, education, ethnic status, job level, job experience, proportion of the total population represented in the sample and applicant versus study participant characteristics.
6. **Predictors.** The kinds of data being investigated for their usefulness in guiding personnel actions including appropriate reliability estimates and the intercorrelations among predictors.
7. **Criteria.** Detailed description of the criterion data collected (including their reliability) and a discussion of their relevance. If ratings were used, some estimate of the amount of contact the rater had with the employee should be reported; if production records were used, the duration of the data collection period should be reported.
8. **Data Reported.** The means, variances, and intercorrelations of variables for applicant and employee groups should be reported as fully as possible. The methods used to analyze the data, that is, regression, analysis of variance, contingency tables, etc., should be reported in detail.

Source: Schneider, B., & Schmitt, N. (1986). *Staffing organizations.* Glenview, IL: Scott-Foresman.

change had on pay levels, (b) how the decision to change was made, (c) what previous pay system the employees had been on, and (d) what the relative pay status of workers in the community and organization was, etc.

In short, the researcher should strive to describe the methods of research, the sample studied, and the organization in which the study was done along those dimensions that could conceivably influence the relationships observed. How much of this information is included is, of course, partly a function of the researchers' knowledge of the organizational intervention studied and her or his good judgment. Above all, the data should be reported as fully as possible including means, standard deviations, intercorrelations of all variables and their reliabilities or these data should be readily available to other researchers.

USE OF META-ANALYSIS

The results of meta-analyses are useful in a number of ways. The practitioner can consult meta-analytic reviews on various possible interventions to decide which of these interventions to use when trying to find a solution to a particular human resource problem. As stated earlier, effect size estimates can be used in utility analyses to decide what financial impact an intervention might have or if the expected financial gain will outweigh the expected costs. The practitioner also can consult meta-analytic reviews to determine whether enough data exist to support the use of an intervention without further empirical study. This usually would be the case, for example, when the credibililty interval around the mean effect size does not include zero.

Researchers also will benefit from meta-analytic reviews in several ways. First, they will be able to identify those relationships that are likely to be stable regardless of the situation or sample studied. Second, when the confidence interval around an effect size is large, they would expect to be able to find some moderator of the relationship even though all effect sizes may be relatively large and practically important. Third, when two variables which are correlated both moderate a relationship, as in the example of the sex and occupational group moderators presented earlier in this chapter, a researcher would realize that additional data would need to be collected to fully understand the relationships involved. In both of the latter two cases, the meta-analytic review would reveal deficiencies in the available data base. Research then should be directed to these issues rather than to more studies of relationships for which there is no indication of a possible moderator effect. Finally, of course, meta-analytic reviews allow researchers to make relatively more confident and specific theoretical statements about the variables they investigate.

SUMMARY

In this chapter we have described the deficiencies of the traditional narrative review and the basics of meta-analytic reviews. We also have indicated instances in which the researcher might want more complicated meta-analytic formulations (e.g., additional corrections for range restriction and reliability or transformations of test statistics to correlational or d measures of effect) and where those formulations can be found.

We provided examples of meta-analyses of hypothetical correlational and experimental data to include estimates of the population effect size and variability. Analyses designed to identify moderator effects also were presented.

A brief summary of meta-analytic research in the human resource area was provided and we discussed several different potential limitations or problems with meta-analysis. Finally, we provided some guidelines as to what should be reported in single sample research studies so as to facilitate subsequent meta-analytic review. A brief look at any research journal would indicate that the traditional narrative review has been replaced by the meta-analytic review. The content of this chapter is then crucial if one is to understand and perform integrative reviews in the future. The development and use of meta-analysis certainly is a positive development for social science in general and human resource research in particular.

EPILOGUE

This chapter concludes our presentation of the research methods we feel are important to the human resource practitioner or researcher. The need for expertise in using various research methods is absolutely essential for a researcher whose major goal is to contribute to the knowledge base regarding human behavior in organizations. As we stated at various points in the text we feel that even those who only intend to use the results of research to implement more effective human resource practices should be familiar with the techniques described in this book. Familiarity with research methods and data-analytic techniques allows the practitioner to make intelligent choices regarding the utility of possible interventions, to evaluate the outcomes of such interventions, and to appropriately assess the claims of consultants who are espousing a given intervention.

Another of our biases in writing this book was that people appreciate the importance of research methods best when those methods are used to answer questions of immediate relevance. Consequently, we have tried to use examples that would be of interest to human resource personnel. We have, in the process, addressed many of the content areas relevant to human resource personnel such as pay and compensation, training, attitude surveys, selection, performance appraisal, etc. Because of our own research and practice backgrounds, we probably have overemphasized certain areas while neglecting others. For those areas in which examples of the use of research are not as frequent, we hope the reader can see the potential application. We also would be interested in hearing from readers about any aspect of the book, but in particular we would like suggestions regarding ways in which we can more fully integrate discussions of human resource problem areas into our treatment of research methods.

There are a number of other relatively general comments about the research methods described in this book that we would like to make in closing. Many, if not all, of these comments have been made at various places in our text, but we believe they bear repetition at the conclusion of our text.

1. *Even without the capacity to do a completely controlled experimental field study, we believe it is always possible to collect data that will better inform decisions about people.* Sometimes we realize that the sample sizes we have do not justify generalizable conclusions. However, adequate documentation of the data we collect and use of measures that allow its future retrieval may allow some future study that can more adequately and definitively answer a question. In the short term, such data may alert us to consider options that had not presented themselves previously. In the meantime, such data should be used with a full realization of its limitations. In this context, bad research is worse than none at all. Many times, we are ready to be convinced by a single demonstration that a program is effective or ineffective forgetting in effect that we have a sample of one.

   At the beginning of this book, we stated a preference for an empirical, data-gathering approach to knowledge about human resource issues and organizational functioning. We hope that the book has reinforced this notion; in particular, we hope that the reader is now aware that there are many different ways to approximate elaborate, definitive research. These various methods provide valuable information and can be used given the competence and motivation to do so. In short, we do not want the reader to conclude that only expensive and elaborate field experiments that provide definitive conclusions regarding causality are worthwhile.

2. *In organizations, no single research method is likely to be adequate.* In defining problems, we will almost always make use of interviews, observations, surveys, and archival data. In more rigorous tests of theories about human resources, we almost always will want to resort to experimental or quasi-experimental approaches (see Chapter 11) to our questions. These various research methods should be used in a way that ensures that the information from each will more fully inform or complement the information obtained from other research approaches. In a completely developed program of research, most investigators use many of the methods described in this book.

3. *In considering research methods, it is important to distinguish between using a method badly which is never acceptable and recognizing the weaknesses that are inherent in the method used (McGrath, Martin, & Kulka, 1981).* Such weaknesses should be explicitly stated. All methods have flaws; different methods are flawed in different ways. This does not mean that a method should be abandoned because it can be used inappropriately. It does mean that multiple

methods should be employed perhaps by different researchers, each of whom is expert in the use of a given approach.

4. *The importance of theory and careful conceptualization can not be overemphasized in research efforts.* If we know what ought to be found in a research study so as to confirm or disconfirm a particular hypothesis, then we will know how to design our study, what variables on which to collect information, how to operationalize those variables, and which variables require statistical or experimental control. Most importantly, we are most likely to know how to interpret the results of our research, and what ought to be the next research effort given a less than definitive outcome. Time spent before conducting a research study on careful consideration of the theoretical base in the area in which the study is being conducted often can save considerable time and effort later or even make the difference between an effort that is really informative and one that is useless.

5. *Practical problems are symptoms that something needs to be done but frequently the symptoms present themselves in ways that are not indicative of the real underlying problem.* One of your authors was consulting with a law firm regarding the legality of one of their client organization's selection procedures. After some time, the law firm asked that a similar analysis of their selection of new law clerks be conducted. The law firm recruited a large number of law clerks every year to do library research and to write background papers on cases with which other members of the law firm were involved. After a year, it was expected that these persons would take on more significant roles in arguing cases and many failed. Because the consultant had convinced the law firm that selection procedures were very useful in enhancing the effectiveness of a work force, the lawyers perceived their problem with the young law clerks as one of selection. However, most young law clerks had not had much experience in the activities they were being asked to do after a year or more of library research. This experience was not provided the law school graduates. What the law firm needed to do was to provide training and development (or mentoring) for their young recruits. Selection would not solve the problem since none of the applicants had the experience the organization required.

    Human resource personnel must become good diagnosticians and they must appreciate the fact that interventions in one human resource area (i.e., pay incentives) may have implications for other areas of concern (i.e., performance appraisal). In the law firm example, additional training and mentoring may lead to expectations of earlier advancement in the law firm.

6. *A researcher must always be aware of previous research in an area.* Take time to review the literature. An informative review may lead to the conclusion that no additional research is required or the review may lead one to consider aspects of a problem that had not presented themselves previously. The effective researcher must be a competent consumer of research. One must be aware of the kind of choices an investigator makes when he or she operationalizes a construct, decides on a research design, or draws conclusions regarding the theoretical or practical significance of a research study. In this regard, it also is important to recognize that personal and professional values play a key role in research. An appreciation for the role of values and the implications for research is important. The researcher needs to understand both her or his values as well as those of others and, whenever appropriate, explicitly state those values in reporting research results.

7. *Research on research methods also is very important.* Some of the readers of our text may view the issues we raise, the shortcomings and weaknesses of various methods as the stimulus for their own research. Currently, a great deal of research is being conducted on methods of utility analysis, method bias, meta-analytic methods, and confirmatory factor analysis that should have significant impact on the way future researchers conduct their research and on the validity and usefulness of their conclusions.

Research efforts, particularly those in applied contexts, often are expensive and require huge commitments of time on the part of the researchers and research participants; this time and money should be spent in the best way possible. Research is cumulative and we hope that this text will in some small way facilitate a cumulation of knowledge on human resource issues and contribute to the effective functioning of individuals and organizations.

REFERENCES

Adams, J. S. (1965). Inequity in social exchange. In L. Berkowitz (Ed.), *Advances in experimental social psychology* (Vol. 2). New York: Academic Press.

Alderfer, C. P. (1972). *Existence, relatedness, and growth: Human needs in organizational settings.* New York: Free Press.

Alderfer, C. P., & Brown, D. L. (1972). Designing an empathic questionnaire for organizational research. *Journal of Applied Psychology, 56,* 456–460.

Altmann, J. (1973). Observational study of behavior: Sampling methods. *Behavior, 47,* 228–267.

American Educational Research Association, American Psychological Association, and the National Council on Measurement in Education. (1985). *Standards for educational and psychological testing.* Washington, DC: American Psychological Association.

Andrews, K. R. (1971). *The concept of corporate strategy.* Homewood, IL: Irwin.

Angoff, W. H. (1971). Scales, norms, and equivalent scores. In R. L. Thorndike (Ed.), *Educational measurement.* Washington, DC: American Council on Education.

Anstey, E. A. (1977). A 30 year follow-up of the CSSB procedure with lessons for the future. *Journal of Occupational Psychology, 50,* 149–159.

Aram, J. D., & Salipante, P. F., Jr. (1981). An evaluation of organizational due process in the resolution of employer/ employee conflict. *Academy of Management Review, 6,* 197–204.

Armstrong, J. S., & Lusk, E. J. (1987). Return postage in mail surveys. *Public Opinion Quarterly, 51,* 233–248.

Arnold, J. D., Rauschenberger, J. M., Soubel, W. G., & Guion, R. M. (1982). Validation and utility of a strength test for selecting steelworkers. *Journal of Applied Psychology, 67,* 588–604.

Aronson, E., Brewer, M., & Carlsmith, J. M. (1985). Experimentation in social psychology. In G. Lindsey & E. Aronson (Eds.), *The handbook of social psychology* (3rd ed.). New York: Random House.

Aronson, E., & Carlsmith, J. M. (1968). Experimentation in social psychology. In G. Lindsey & E. Aronson (Eds.), *The handbook of social psychology* (2nd ed., Vol. 2, pp. 1–79). Reading, MA: Addison-Wesley.

Arvey, R. D. (1979). Unfair discrimination in the employment interview: Legal and psychological aspects. *Psychological Bulletin, 86,* 736–765.

Arvey, R. D. (1986). Sex bias in job evaluation procedures. *Personnel Psychology*, *39*, 315–335.

Arvey, R. D., & Campion, J. E. (1982). The employment interview: A summary and review of recent research. *Personnel Psychology*, *35*, 281–322.

Arvey, R. D., Cole, D. A., Hazucha, J. F., & Hartamo, F. M. (1985). Statistical power of training evaluation designs. *Personnel Psychology*, *38*, 493–507.

Arvey, R. D., Miller, H. E., Gould, R., & Burch, P. (1987). Interview validity for selecting salesclerks. *Personnel Psychology*, *40*, 1–12.

Asher, J. A., & Sciarrino, J. A. (1974). Realistic work sample tests: A review. *Personnel Psychology*, *27*, 519–538.

Ashforth, B. (1985). Climate formation: Issues and extension. *Academy of Management Review*, *10*, 837–847.

ASPA. (1983). ASPA-BNA survey no. 45: Employee selection procedures. Washington, DC; Bureau of National Affairs.

Bales, R. F. (1950). *Interaction process analysis.* Reading, MA: Addison-Wesley.

Bandura, A. (1977). *Social learning theory.* Englewood Cliffs, NJ: Prentice-Hall.

Banks, C. O., & Roberson, L. (1985). Performance appraisers as test developers. *Academy of Management Review*, *10*, 128–142.

Baritz, L. (1960). *The servants of power.* Middleton, CT: Wesleyan University Press.

Barrett, G. V., Alexander, R. A., Anesgart, M. N., & Doverspike, D. (in press). Frequently encountered problems in the application of regression analysis to the investigation of sex discrimination in salaries. *Public Personnel Management.*

Barrett, G. V., Caldwell, M. S., & Alexander, R. A. (1985). The concept of dynamic criteria: A critical reanalysis. *Personnel Psychology*, *38*, 41–56.

Barrett, R. S. (1966). *Performance rating.* Chicago, IL: Science Research Associates.

Bartlett, C. J., Bobko, P., Mosier, S. B., & Hannon, R., Jr. (1978). Testing for fairness with a moderated multiple regression strategy: An alternative to differential analysis. *Personnel Psychology*, *31*, 233–242.

Basadur, M., Graen, G. B., & Scandura, T. A. (1986). Training effects on attitudes toward divergent thinking among manufacturing engineers. *Journal of Applied Psychology*, *71*, 612–617.

Bass, B. M., Cascio, W. F., & O'Connor, E. J. (1974). Magnitude estimations of expressions of frequency and amount. *Journal of Applied Psychology*, *59*, 313–320.

Becker, B., & Cardy, R. L. (1986). Influence of halo error on appraisal effectiveness: A conceptual and empirical reconsideration. *Journal of Applied Psychology, 71,* 662–671.

Beckhard, R. (1969). *Organization development: Strategies and models.* Reading, MA: Addison-Wesley.

Beer, M. (1976). The technology of organizational development. In M. D. Dunnette (Ed.), *Handbook of industrial and organizational psychology.* Chicago, IL: Rand McNally.

Beer, M. (1980). *Organization change and development.* Santa Monica, CA: Goodyear.

Beer, M., Ruh, R., Dawson, J. A., McCaa, B. B., & Kavanagh, M. J. (1978). A performance management system: Research, design, introduction and evaluation. *Personnel Psychology, 31,* 505–535.

Bennett, G. K., & Seashore, H. G. (1946). *The Seashore-Bennett stenographic proficiency test.* New York: Psychological Corporation.

Bentler, P. M., & Bonett, D. G. (1980). Significance tests and goodness of fit in the analysis of covariance structures. *Psychological Bulletin, 88,* 588–606.

Bentz, V. J. (1984). *Research findings from personality assessment of executives.* Paper presented at the meeting of the address to Michigan Association of Industrial and Organizational Psychologists, Detroit, Michigan.

Berkshire, J. R., & Highland, R. W. (1953). Forced-choice performance rating: A methodological study. *Personnel Psychology, 6,* 355–378.

Berman, F. E., & Miner, J. B. (1985). Motivation to manage at the top executive level: A test of the hierarchic role-motivation theory. *Personnel Psychology, 38,* 377–391.

Bernardin, H. J. (1977). Behavioral expectation scales versus summated scales: A fairer comparison. *Journal of Applied Psychology, 62,* 422–427.

Bernardin, H. J. (1978). Effects of rater training on leniency and halo errors in student ratings of instructors. *Journal of Applied Psychology, 63,* 301–308.

Bernardin, H. J., & Beatty, R. W. (1984). *Performance appraisal: Assessing human behavior at work.* Boston, MA: Kent.

Bernardin, H. J., Cardy, R. L., & Abbott, J. (1982). *The effects of individual performance schemata, familiarization with the rating scales and rater motivation on rating effectiveness.* Paper presented at the 42nd Annual Meeting of the Academy of Management, New York.

Bernardin, H. J., & Pence, E. C. (1980). Rater training: Creating new response sets and decreasing accuracy. *Journal of Applied Psychology, 65,* 60–66.

Bernardin, H. J., & Smith, P. C. (1981). A clarification of some issues regarding the development and use of behaviorally anchored rating scales. *Journal of Applied Psychology, 66,* 458–463.

Bernardin, H. J., & Walter, C. W. (1977). Effects of rater training and diary keeping on psychometric error in ratings. *Journal of Applied Psychology, 62,* 64–69.

Berry, S. H., & Kanouse, D. E. (1987). Physician response to a mailed survey. *Public Opinion Quarterly, 51,* 102–114.

Betz, N., & Weiss, D. J. (1987). Validity. In B. Bolton (Ed.), *Measurement and evaluation in rehabilitation.* Baltimore, MD: Paul Brookes Publishing.

Bickman, L. (1976). Observational methods. In C. Seltiz, L. S. Wrightsman, & S. Cook (Eds.), *Research methods in social relations* (3rd ed.). New York: Holt, Rinehart & Winston.

Blackburn, R. S. (1987). Experimental design in organizational settings. In J. W. Lorsch (Ed.), *Handbook of organizational behavior.* Englewood Cliffs, NJ: Prentice-Hall.

Blake v. City of Los Angeles. FEP 1441 (9th Cir.) (1979).

Blake, R. R., & Mouton, J. S. (1964). *The managerial grid.* Houston, TX: Gulf Publishing.

Blake, R. R., & Mouton, J. S. (1985). *The managerial grid III.* Houston, TX: Gulf.

Blau, J. R., & McKinley, W. (1979). Ideas, complexity, and innovation. *Administrative Science Quarterly, 24,* 200–219.

Blum, M. L., & Naylor, J. C. (1968). *Industrial psychology: Its theoretical and social foundations.* New York: Harper & Row.

Blumberg, H. H. (1972). Communication of interpersonal evaluations. *Journal of Personality and Social Psychology, 23,* 157–162.

Blumberg, M. (1980). Job switching in autonomous work groups: An exploratory study in a Pennsylvania coal mine. *Academy of Management Journal, 23,* 287–306.

Bobko, P., Karren, R., & Parkington, J. J. (1983). Estimation of standard deviations in utility analysis: An empirical test. *Journal of Applied Psychology, 68,* 170–176.

Bock, R. D. (1975). *Multivariate statistical methods in behavioral research.* New York: McGraw-Hill.

Boehm, V. R. (1980). Research in the "real-world"—a conceptual model. *Personnel Psychology, 33,* 495–504.

Bordens, K. S., & Abbott, B. B. (1988). *Research design and methods: A process approach.* Mountain View, CA: Mayfield.

Borman, W. C. (1974). The rating of individuals in organizations: An alternate approach. *Organizational Behavior and Human Performance, 12*, 105–124.

Borman, W. C. (1977). Consistency of rating accuracy and rating errors in the judgment of human performance. *Organizational Behavior and Human Performance, 20*, 238–252.

Borman, W. C. (1978). Exploring the upper limits of reliability and validity in job performance ratings. *Journal of Applied Psychology, 60*, 561–565.

Borman, W. C. (1979). Format and training effects on rating accuracy and rater errors. *Journal of Applied Psychology, 64,* 410–421.

Borman, W. C., Rosse, R. L., & Abrahams, N. M. (1980). An empirical construct validity approach to studying predictor-job performance links. *Journal of Applied Psychology, 65*, 662–671.

Bouchard, T. (1976). Field research methods: Interviewing questionnaires, participant observation, systematic observation, unobtrusive measures. In M. D. Dunnette (Ed.), *Handbook of industrial and organizational psychology.* Chicago, IL: Rand McNally.

Boudreau, J. W. (1983a). Economic considerations in estimating the utility of human resource productivity improvement programs. *Personnel Psychology, 36*, 551–576.

Boudreau, J. W. (1983b). Effects of employee flows on utility analysis of human resource productivity improvement programs. *Journal of Applied Psychology, 68*, 396–406.

Boudreau, J. W., & Berger, C. J. (1985). Decision-theoretic utility analysis applied to employee separations and acquisitions. *Journal of Applied Psychology, 70*, 581–612.

Boudreau, J. W., & Rynes, S. L. (1985). Recruitment effects on staffing utility analyses. *Journal of Applied Psychology, 70*, 354–366.

Brady, F. N. (1986). Aesthetic components of management ethics. *Academy of Management Review, 11*, 337–344.

Bramel, D., & Friend, R. (1981). Hawthorne, the myth of the docile worker and class bias in psychology. *American Psychologist, 36*, 867–878.

Brass, D. J. (1981). Structural relationships, job characteristics, and worker satisfaction and performance. *Administrative Science Quarterly, 26*, 331–348.

Bray, D. W., Campbell, R. J., & Grant, D. L. (1974). *Formative years in business.* New York: Wiley.

Bray, D. W., & Grant, D. L. (1966). The assessment center in the measurement of potential for business management. *Psychological Monographs, 80,* (Whole No. 625).

Brayfield, A. H., & Crockett, W. H. (1955). Employee attitudes and employee performance. *Psychological Bulletin, 52,* 396–424.

Brockner, J., & Guare, J. (1983). Improving the performance of low self-esteem individuals: An attributional approach. *Academy of Management Journal, 26,* 642–656.

Brogden, H. E. (1946). On the interpretation of the correlation coefficient as a measure of predictive efficiency. *Journal of Educational Psychology, 37,* 65–76.

Brogden, H. E. (1949). When testing pays off. *Personnel Psychology, 2,* 171–183.

Brogden, H. E., & Taylor, E. K. (1950). The dollar criterion: Applying the cost accounting concept to criterion construction. *Personnel Psychology, 3,* 135–154.

Brown, C. W., & Ghiselli, E. E. (1953). Percent increase in proficiency resulting from use of selective devices. *Journal of Applied Psychology, 37,* 341–345.

Brugnoli, G. A., Campion, J. E., & Basen, J. A. (1979). Racial bias in the use of work samples for personnel selection. *Journal of Applied Psychology, 64,* 119–123.

Brush, D. H., & Owens, W. A. (1979). Implementation and evaluation for an assessment classification model for manpower utilization. *Personnel Psychology, 32,* 369–383.

Buckley, M. R., & Bernardin, H. J. (1980). *An assessment of the components of an observer training program.* Paper presented at the annual meeting of the Southeastern Psychological Association, Atlanta, Georgia.

Bullock, R. J., & Lawler, E. E. III. (1984). Gainsharing: A few questions and fewer answers. *Human Resource Management, 23,* 23–40.

Bunker, K. A., & Cohen, S. L. (1977). The rigors of training evaluation: A discussion and field demonstration. *Personnel Psychology, 30,* 525–541.

Burke, M. J., & Day, R. R. (1986). A cumulative study of the effectiveness of managerial training. *Journal of Applied Psychology, 71,* 232–245.

Burke, M. J., & Frederick, J. T. (1984). Two modified procedures for estimating standard deviations in utility analysis. *Journal of Applied Psychology, 69,* 482–489.

Burke, M. J., & Frederick, J. T. (1986). A comparison of economic utility estimates for SD_y Estimation Procedures. *Journal of Applied Psychology, 71,* 334–339.

Calder, B. J. (1977). Focus groups and the nature of qualitative research. *Journal of Marketing Research, 14,* 353–364.

Callender, J. C., & Osburn, H. G. (1980). Development and test of a new model of validity generalization. *Journal of Applied Psychology, 65,* 543–558.

Callender, J. C., & Osburn, H. G. (1981). Testing the constancy of validity with computer-generated sampling distributions of the multiplicative model variance estimate: Results in petroleum industry validation research. *Journal of Applied Psychology, 66,* 274–281.

Callender, J. C., & Osburn, H. G. (1982). Another view of progress in validity generalization: Reply to Schmidt, Hunter, and Pearlman. *Journal of Applied Psychology, 67,* 846–852.

Cameron, K. (1978). Measuring organizational effectiveness in institutions of higher education. *Administrative Science Quarterly, 23,* 604–632.

Cameron, K. (1986). A study of organizational effectiveness and its predictors. *Management Science, 32,* 87–112.

Campbell, D. T., & Fiske, D. W. (1959). Convergent and discriminant validation by the multitrait-multimethod matrix. *Psychological Bulletin, 56,* 81–105.

Campbell, D. T., Kruskal, W. H., & Wallace, W. P. (1966). Seating aggregation as an index of attitude. *Sociometry, 29,* 1–15.

Campbell, J. P. (1976). Contributions research can make in understanding organizational effectiveness: Theory, research and application. In S. L. Spray (Ed.), *Organizational effectiveness.* Kent, OH: Kent State University Press.

Campbell, J. P. (1977). On the nature of organizational effectiveness. In P. S. Goodman, J. M. Penning, and associates (Eds.), *New perspectives on organizational effectiveness.* San Francisco: Jossey-Bass.

Campbell, J. P., Dunnette, M., Lawler, E. E. III, & Weick, K. E. (1970). *Managerial behavior, performance, and effectiveness.* New York: McGraw-Hill.

Campion, M. A. (1972). Work sampling for personnel selection. *Journal of Applied Psychology, 56(1),* 40–44.

Campion, M. A. (1983). Personnel selection for physically demanding jobs: Review and recommendations. *Personnel Psychology, 36,* 527–550.

Campion, M. A. (1988). Interdisciplinary approaches to job design: A constructive replication with extensions. *Journal of Applied Psychology, 73,* 467–481.

Campion, M. A., & Campion, J. E. (1987). Evaluation of an interviewee skills training program in a natural field experiment. *Personnel Psychology, 40,* 675–691.

Campion, M. A., Pursell, E. D., & Brown, B. K. (1988). Structured interviewing: Raising the psychometric properties of the employment interview. *Personnel Psychology, 41,* 25–42.

Campion, M. A., & Thayer, P. W. (1985). Development of an interdisciplinary measure of job design. *Journal of Applied Psychology, 70*, 29–43.

Carrell, M. R., & Dittrich, J. E. (1978). Equity theory: The recent literature, methodological considerations, and new directions. *Academy of Management Review, 3*, 202–210.

Carroll, S. J., & Schneier, C. E. (1982). *Performance appraisal and review systems.* Glenview, IL: Scott Foresman.

Carroll, S. J., Jr., & Tosi, H. L. (1973). *Management by objectives: Applications and research.* New York: Macmillan.

Cartwright, D., & Zander, A. (1968). *Group dynamics: Research and theory* (3rd. ed.). New York: Harper & Row.

Cascio, W. F. (1982). *Costing human resources: The financial impact of behavior in organizations.* Boston, MA: Kent.

Cascio, W. F. (1987a). *Applied psychology in personnel management* (3rd ed.). Englewood Cliffs, NJ: Prentice Hall.

Cascio, W. F. (1987b). *Costing human resources: The financial impact of behavior in organizations.* Boston, MA: Kent.

Cascio, W. F., Alexander, R. A., & Barrett, G. V. (1988). Setting cutoff scores: Legal, psychometric, and professional issues and guidelines. *Personnel Psychology, 41*, 1–24.

Cascio, W. F., & Ramos, R. A. (1986). Development and application of a new method for assessing job performance in behavioral/economic terms. *Journal of Applied Psychology, 71*, 20–28.

Cattin, P. (1980). Estimation of the predictive power of a regression model. *Journal of Applied Psychology, 65*, 407–414.

Champoux, J. E., & Peters, W. S. (1980). Applications of moderated regression in job design research. *Personnel Psychology, 33*, 759–784.

Chidester, T. R., & Grigsby, W. C. (1984). A meta-analysis of the goal-setting-performance literature. *Proceedings of the Academy of Management.* Academy of Management.

Clark, C. L., & Primoff, E. J. (1979). Job elements and performance appraisal. *Management: A magazine for government managers, 1*, 3–5.

Cohen, J. (1960). A coefficient of agreement for nominal scales. *Educational and Psychological Measurement, 20*, 37–46.

Cohen, J. (1968). Weighted kappa: Nominal scale agreement with provision for scaled disagreement or partial credit. *Psychological Bulletin, 70*, 213–220.

Cohen, J. (1978). Partialed products are interactions: Partialed powers are curved components. *Psychological Bulletin, 85*, 858–866.

Cohen, J. (1988). *Statistical power analysis for the behavioral sciences.* Hillsdale, NJ: Erlbaum.

Cohen, J., & Cohen, P. (1983). *Applied multiple regression/correlation analysis for the behavioral sciences.* Hillsdale, NJ: Erlbaum.

Connolly, T., Conlon, E. J., & Deutsch, S. J. (1980). Organizational effectiveness: A multiple-constituency approach. *Academy of Management Review, 5*, 211–217.

Cook, T. D., & Campbell, D. T. (1976). The design and conduct of quasi-experiments and true experiments in field settings. In M. D. Dunnette (Ed.), *Handbook of industrial and organizational psychology.* New York: Rand McNally.

Cook, T. D., & Campbell, D. T. (1979). *Quasi experimentations: Design and analysis for field settings.* Chicago, IL: Rand McNally.

Cooper, H. M., & Rosenthal, R. (1980). Statistical vs. traditional procedures for summarizing research findings. *Psychological Bulletin, 87*, 442–449.

Cooper, J. (1976). Deception and role playing: On telling the good guys from the bad guys. *American Psychology, 31*, 605–610.

Cooper, M., & Schemmer, F. M. (1983). *The development of physical ability tests for industry-wide use.* Paper presented at the national convention of the American Psychological Association, Anaheim, CA.

Cooper, W. H. (1981). Ubiquitous halo. *Psychological Bulletin, 90*, 218–244.

Cornelius, E. T., III. (1983). The use of projective techniques in personnel selection. In K. M. Rowland & G. R. Ferris (Eds.), *Research in personnel and human resources management.* Greenwich, CT: JAI Press.

Cornelius, E. T., Hakel, M.D., & Sackett, P. R. (1979). A methodological approach to job classification for performance appraisal purposes. *Personnel Psychology, 32*, 283–297.

Cotton, J. D., Vollrath, D. A., Froggatt, K. L., Longnich-Hall, M. L., & Jennings, K. R. (1988). Employee participation: Diverse forms and different outcomes. *Academy of Management Review, 13*, 8–22.

County of Washington, Oregon v. Gunther. 452 U.S. 161 (1981).

Cravens, D. W., & Woodruff, R. B. (1973). An approach for determining criteria of sales performance. *Journal of Applied Psychology, 57*, 442–447.

Cronbach, L. J. (1955). Processes affecting scores on understanding others and assumed similarity. *Psychological Bulletin, 52*, 177–183.

Cronbach, L. J., & Gleser, G. C. (1965). *Psychological tests and personnel decisions.* Urbana: University of Illinois Press.

Cronbach, L. J., Gleser, G. C., Nanda, H., & Rajaratnam, N. (1972). *The dependability of behavioral measurement.* New York: Wiley.

Cronbach, L. J., Yalow, E., & Schaeffer, G. A. (1980). A mathematical structure for analyzing fairness in selection. *Personnel Psychology, 33,* 693–704.

Cronshaw, S. F., Alexander, R. A., Wiesner, W. H., & Barrick, M. R. (1987). Incorporating risk into selection utility: Two models for sensitivity analysis and risk simulation. *Organizational Behavior and Human Decision Processes, 40,* 270–286.

Cudeck, R., & Browne, M. W. (1983). Cross-validation of covariance structures. *Multivariate Behavioral Research, 18,* 147–167.

Curtis, B., Smith, R. E., & Smok, F. L. (1979). Scrutinizing the skipper: A study of leadership behaviors in the dugout. *Journal of Applied Psychology, 64,* 391–400.

Dachler, H. P., & Wilpert, B. (1978). Conceptual dimensions and boundaries of participation in organizations: A critical evaluation. *Administrative Science Quarterly, 23,* 1–38.

Daft, R. L. (1983). Learning the craft of organizational research. *Academy of Management Review, 8*(4), 539–546.

Dalton, D. R., Krackhardt, D. M., & Porter, L. W. (1981). Functional turnover: An empirical assessment. *Journal of Applied Psychology, 66,* 716–721.

Dalton, D. R., & Todor, W. D. (1985). Composition of dyads as a factor in the outcomes of workplace justice: Field assessment. *Academy of Management Journal, 28,* 704–712.

Dalton, D. R., Todor, W. D., & Krackhardt, D. M. (1982). Turnover overstated: The functional taxonomy. *Academy of Management Review, 7,* 117–123.

Damanpour, F., & Evan, W. M. (1984). Organizational innovation and performance: The problem of organizational lag. *Administrative Science Quarterly, 29,* 392–409.

Dansereau, F., & Markham, S. E. (1987). Levels of analysis in personnel and human resources management. In K. M. Rowland & G. R. Ferris (Eds.), *Research in personnel and human resources management.* Greenwich, CT: JAI Press.

Davis, L. E., & Cherns, A. B. (1975). *The quality of working life* (Vols. 1 & 2). New York: The Free Press.

Dean, J. P. (1954). Participant observation and interviewing. In J. T. Doby (Ed.), *Introduction to social research.* Harrisburg, PA: The Stockpole Company.

Decker, P. (1984). Effects of different symbolic coding stimuli in behavior modeling training. *Personnel Psychology, 37,* 711–720.

DeCotiis, T., & Petit, A. (1978). The performance appraisal process: A model and some testable propositions. *Academy of Management Review, 3*, 635–646.

DeNisi, A. S., Cafferty, T. P., & Meglino, B. M. (1984). A cognitive view of the performance appraisal process: A model and research propositions. *Organizational Behavior and Human Performance, 33*, 360–396.

DeNisi, A. S., & Mitchell, J. L. (1978). An analysis of peer ratings as predictors and criterion measures and a proposed new application. *Academy of Management Review, 3*, 369–374.

Denzin, N. K. (1978). *The research act* (2nd ed.). New York: McGraw Hill.

Department of Health, Education, and Welfare (1975, March 13). Protection of human subjects. *Federal Register, 40*(50).

Dickinson, T. L. (1987). Designs for evaluating the validity and accuracy of performance ratings. *Organizational Behavior and Human Decision Processes, 40*, 1–21.

Dipboye, R. (1985). Some neglected variables in research on discrimination in appraisals. *Academy of Management Review, 10*, 116–127.

Dipboye, R. L., & Flanagan, M. F. (1979). Research settings in industrial and organizational psychology. *American Psychologist, 34*, 141–150.

Dominowski, R. L. (1989). Method, theory and drawing inferences. *American Psychologist, 44*, 10–78.

Dougherty, T. W., Ebert, R. J., & Callender, J. C. (1986). Policy capturing in the employment interview. *Journal of Applied Psychology, 71*, 9–15.

Dow, G. K. (1988). Configurational and coactivational views of organizational structure. *Academy of Management Review, 13*, 53–64.

Downey, H. K., & Ireland, R. D. (1979). Quantitative versus qualitative: The case of environmental assesment in organizational studies. *Administrative Science Quarterly, 24*, 630–637.

Downie, N. M., & Heath, R. W. (1970). *Basic Statistical Methods*, New York: Harper & Row.

Dreher, G. F., & Sackett, P. R. (1983). *Perspectives on employee staffing and selection: Readings and commentary.* Homewood, IL: Richard D. Irwin.

Dubin, R. (1976a). Theory building in applied areas. In M. D. Dunnette (Ed.), *Handbook of industrial and organizational psychology.* New York: Rand McNally.

Dubin, R. (1976b). Organizational effectiveness: Some dilemmas of perspective in organizational effectiveness. In S. L. Spray (Ed.), *Organizational effectiveness.* Kent, OH: Kent State University Press.

Dunham, R. B., & Smith, F. J. (1979). *Organizational surveys.* Glenview, IL: Scott-Foresman.

Dunnette, M. D. (1963). A note on the criterion. *Journal of Applied Psychology, 47,* 251–254.

Dunnette, M. D., & Borman, W. C. (1979). Personnel selection and classification systems. In M. R. Rosenzweig & L. W. Porter (Eds.), *Annual Review of Psychology, 30,* 477–525.

Earley, P. C., Wojnarski, P., & Prest, W. (1987). Task planning and energy expended: Exploration of how goals influence performance. *Journal of Applied Psychology, 72,* 107–114.

Eaton, N. K., Wing, H., & Mitchell, K. J. (1985). Alternate methods of estimating the dollar value of performance. *Personnel Psychology, 1,* 27–40.

Ebel, R. L. (1972). *Essentials of educational measurement.* Englewood Cliffs, NJ: Prentice-Hall.

Eden, D. (1985). Team development: A true field experiment at three levels of rigor. *Journal of Applied Psychology, 70,* 94–100.

Edwards, A. L. (1957). *Techniques of attitude scale construction.* New York: Appleton-Century-Crofts.

Ellsworth, P. (1977). From abstract ideas to concrete instances. *American Psychologist, 32,* 604–615.

Evered, R., & Louis, M. R. (1981). Alternative perspectives in the organizational sciences: "Inquiry from the inside" and "Inquiry from the outside." *Academy of Management Review, 6,* 385–395.

Feldman, D. C. (1984). The development and enforcement of group norms. *Academy of Management Review, 9,* 47–53.

Feldman, J. M. (1981). Beyond attribution theory: Cognitive processes in performance appraisal. *Journal of Applied Psychology, 6,* 127–148.

Ferguson, L. W. (1962). *The heritage of industrial psychology.* Hartford, CT: Findley Press.

Festinger, L. (1957). *A theory of cognitive dissonance.* Evanston, IL: Row, Peterson.

Fiedler, F. E. (1964). A contingency model of leadership effectiveness. In L. Berkowitz (Ed.), *Advances in experimental social psychology* (Vol. 1). New York: Academic Press.

Fiedler, F. E. (1971). Validation and extension of the contingency model of leadership effectiveness: A review of empirical findings. *Psychological Bulletin, 76,* 128–148.

Fiedler, F. E., & Mahar, L. A. (1979). A field experiment validating contingency model training. *Journal of Applied Psychology, 64,* 247–254.

Fisher, C. D. (1979). Transmission of positive and negative feedback to subordinates: A laboratory investigation. *Journal of Applied Psychology, 64,* 533–540.

Fisher, C. D., & Gitelson, R. (1983). A meta-analysis of the correlates of role conflict and ambiguity. *Journal of Applied Psychology, 68*, 320–333.

Fisicaro, S. (1988). A re-examination of the relation between halo error and accuracy. *Journal of Applied Psychology, 73*, 239–244.

Fleishman, E. A. (1978). *Physical abilities analysis manual.* Washington, DC: Advanced Resources Research Organization.

Fleishman, E. A. (1979). Evaluating physical abilities required by jobs. *Personnel Administrator, 24*, 82–91.

Fleishman, E. A. (1982). Systems for describing human tasks. *American Psychologist, 37*, 821–834.

Fleishman, E. A., & Fruchter, B. (1960). Factor structure and predictability of successive stages of learning Morse code. *Journal of Applied Psychology, 44*, 97–101.

Fleishman, E. A., & Harris, E. F. (1962). Patterns of leadership behavior related to employee grievances and turnover. *Personnel Psychology, 15*, 43–56.

Fleishman, E. A., & Hempel, W. E., Jr. (1954). Changes in factor structure of a complex psychomotor test as a function of practice. *Psychometrika, 19*, 239–252.

Fleishman, E. A., & Hogan, J. C. (1978). *A taxonomic method for assessing the physical requirements of jobs: The physical abilities analysis approach.* Washington, DC: Advanced Research Resources Organization.

Fleiss, J. L., Cohen, J., & Everitt, B. S. (1969). Large sample standard errors of kappa and weighted kappa. *Psychological Bulletin, 72*, 323–327.

Florkowski, G. W. (1987). The organizational impact of profit sharing. *Academy of Management Review, 12*, 622–636.

Ford, J. K., Kraiger, K., & Schechtman, S. L. (1986). A study of race effects in objective indices and subjective evaluations of performance: A meta-analysis of performance criteria. *Psychological Bulletin, 99*, 330–337.

Ford, J. K., MacCallum, R. C., & Tait, M. (1986). The application of exploratory factor analysis in applied psychology: A critical review and analysis. *Personnel Psychology, 39*, 291–314.

Ford, J. K., & Noe, R. A. (1987). Self-assessed training needs: The effects of attitudes toward training, managerial level, and function. *Personnel Psychology, 40*, 39–53.

Ford, J. K., Schmitt, N., Schechtman, S. L., Hults, B., & Doherty, M. L. (1989). Process tracing methods: Contributions, problems, and neglected research questions. *Organizational Behavior and Human Decision Processes, 43*, 75–117.

Fossum, J. A., & Fitch, M. K. (1985). The effects of individual and contextual attributes on the sizes of recommended salary increases. *Personnel Psychology, 38,* 587–602.

Frayne, C. A., & Latham, G. P. (1987). Application of social learning theory to employee self-management of attendance. *Journal of Applied Psychology, 72,* 387–392.

French, W. L. (1978). *The personnel management process.* Boston, MA: Houghton Mifflin.

French, W. L., & Bell, C. H. (1978). *Organization development: behavioral science interventions for organization improvement.* Englewood Cliffs, NJ: Prentice-Hall.

Friedlander, F., & Pickle, H. (1968). Components of effectiveness in small organizations. *Administrative Science Quarterly, 13,* 534–540.

Friedman, B. A., & Cornelius, E. T. (1976). Effect of rater participation in scale construction on the psychometric characteristics of two rating scale formats. *Journal of Applied Psychology, 61,* 21–216.

Friedson, A. S. (1985). The legality of employee attitude surveys in union environments. *Employee Relations Law Journal, 8,* 648–669.

Fromkin, H. L., & Streufert, S. (1976). Laboratory experimentation. In M. D. Dunnette (Ed.), *Handbook of industrial and organizational psychology.* Chicago, IL: Rand McNally.

Gael, S. (1988). *The job analysis handbook for business, industry, and government.* New York: Wiley.

Games, P. A., & Klare, G. R. (1967). *Elementary statistics: Data analysis for the behavioral sciences.* New York: McGraw-Hill.

Gardner, G. T. (1978). Effects of federal human subjects regulations on data obtained in environmental stress research. *Journal of Personality and Social Psychology, 36,* 628–634.

Gaugler, B. B., Rosenthal, D. B., Thornton, G. C., III, & Bentson, C. (1987). Meta-analysis of assessment center validity. *Journal of Applied Psychology, 72,* 493–511.

Geertz, C. (1973). *The interpretation of cultures.* New York: Basic Books.

Georgiou, P. (1973). The goal paradigm and notes towards a counter paradigm. *Administrative Science Quarterly, 18,* 291–310.

Georgopolous, B. S., & Tannenbaum, A. S. (1957). A study of organizational effectiveness. *American Sociological Review, 22,* 534–540.

Gersick, J. G. (1988). Time and transition in work teams: Toward a new model of group development. *Academy of Management Journal, 31,* 9–41.

Ghiselli, E. E. (1956a). Differentiation of individuals in terms of predictability. *Journal of Applied Psychology, 40,* 374–377.

Ghiselli, E. E. (1956b). Dimensional problems of criteria. *Journal of Applied Psychology, 40*, 1–4.

Ghiselli, E. E. (1966). *The validity of occupational aptitude tests.* New York: Wiley.

Ghiselli, E. E. (1973). The validity of aptitude tests in personnel selection. *Personnel Psychology, 26*, 461–477.

Ghiselli, E. E., Campbell, J. P., & Zedeck, S. (1981). *Measurement theory for the behavioral sciences.* San Francisco, CA: Freeman.

Gladstein, D. L. (1984). Groups in context: A model of task group effectiveness. *Administrative Science Quarterly, 29*, 499–517.

Glass, G. V., McGaw, B., & Smith, M. L. (1981). *Meta-analysis in social research.* Beverly Hills, CA: Sage.

Glisson, C. A., & Martin, P. Y. (1980). Productivity and efficiency in human service organizations as related to structure, size, and age. *Academy of Management Journal, 23*, 21–37.

Goldstein, A. P., & Sorcher, M. (1974). *Changing supervisor behavior.* New York: Penguin Press.

Goldstein, I. L. (1980). Training in work organizations. *Annual Review of Psychology, 31*, 229–272.

Goldstein, I. L. (1986). *Training in organizations: Needs assessment, development, and evaluation.* Pacific Grove, CA: Brooks/Cole.

Goodman, P. S., Atkin, R. S., & Schoorman, F. D. (1983). On the demise of organizational effectiveness studies. In K. S. Cameron & D. A. Whetten (Eds.), *Organizational effectiveness: A comparison of multiple models* (pp. 163–183). New York: Academic Press.

Gorsuch, R. L. (1974). *Factor analysis.* Philadelphia: Saunders.

Graen, G. B. (1976). Role making processes within complex organizations. In M.D. Dunnette (Ed.), *Handbook of industrial and organizational psychology.* Chicago, IL: Rand McNally.

Graen, G. B., Alvares, K., Orris, J. B., & Martella, J. A. (1970). Contingency model of leadership effectiveness: Antecedents and evidential results. *Psychological Bulletin, 74*, 285–296.

Greenberg, J. (1982). Approaching equity and avoiding inequity in groups and organizations. In J. Greenberg & R. L. Cohen (Eds.), *Equity and justice in social behavior* (pp. 389–435). New York: Academic Press.

Greenberg, J. (1988). Equity and workplace status: A field experiment. *Journal of Applied Psychology, 73*, 606–613.

Greenwood, R. G. (1981). Management by objectives: As developed by Peter Drucker, assisted by Harold Smiddy. *Academy of Management Review, 6*, 225–230.

Greller, M. M. (1980). The nature of subordinate participation in the appraisal interview. *Academy of Management Journal, 12*, 646–658.

Grey, R. J., & Kipnis, D. (1976). Untangling the performance appraisal dilemma: The influence of perceived organizational context on evaluative processes. *Journal of Applied Psychology, 61*, 329–335.

Guion, R. M. (1965). *Personnel testing.* New York: McGraw-Hill.

Guion, R. M. (1977). Content validity—the source of my discontent. *Applied Psychological Measurement, 1*, 1–10.

Guion, R. M. (1978). Scoring of content domain samples: The problem of fairness. *Journal of Applied Psychology, 63*, 499–506.

Guion, R. M. (1987). Changing views for personnel selection research. *Personnel Psychology, 40*, 199–214.

Guion, R. M., & Gottier, R. F. (1965). Validity of personality measures in personnel selection. *Personnel Psychology, 18*, 49–65.

Guzzo, R. A. (1986). Group decision making and group effectiveness in organizations. In P. Goodman (Ed.), *Designing effective work groups.* San Francisco: Jossey-Bass.

Guzzo, R. A., Jette, R. D., & Katzell, R. A. (1985). The effects of psychologically based intervention programs on worker productivity: A meta-analysis. *Personnel Psychology, 38*, 275–291.

Hackett, R. D., & Guion, R. M. (1985). A reevaluation of the absenteeism-job satisfaction relationship. *Organizational Behavior and Human Decision Processes, 25*, 340–381.

Hackman, J. R. (1976). Group influences on individuals in organizations. In M. D. Dunnette (Ed.), *Handbook of industrial and organizational psychology.* Chicago, IL: Rand-McNally.

Hackman, J. R. (1986). The design of work teams. In J. Lorsch (Ed.), *Handbook of organizational behavior.* Englewood Cliffs, NJ: Prentice Hall.

Hackman, J. R., & Morris, C. G. (1975). Group tasks, group interaction process, and group performance effectiveness: A review and proposed integration. In L. Berkowitz (Ed.), *Advances in experimental social psychology.* New York: Academic Press.

Hackman, J. R., & Oldham, G. (1976). Motivation through the design of work: Test of a theory. *Organizational Behavior and Human Performance, 16*, 250–279.

Hakel, M. D. (1971). Similarity of post-interview trait rating intercorrelations as a contributor to interrater agreement in a structured employment interview. *Journal of Applied Psychology, 55*, 443–448.

Hakel, M. D., Sorcher, M., Beer, M., & Moses, J. L. (1982). *Making it happen: Designing research with implementation in mind.* Beverly Hills, CA: Sage.

Hammer, T. H., & Landau, J. (1981). Methodological issues in the use of absence data. *Journal of Applied Psychology, 66*, 574–581.

Hand, H. H., & Slocum, J. W. (1972). A longitudinal study of the effects of a human relations training program on managerial effectiveness. *Journal of Applied Psychology, 56*, 412–417.

Hartigan, J.A., & Wigdor, A.K. (1989). *Fairness in employment testing.* Washington, DC.: National Academy Press.

Hayduk, L. A. (1987). *Structural equation modeling with LISREL.* Baltimore, MD: Johns Hopkins University Press.

Heberlein, T., & Baumgartner, R. (1978). Factors affecting response rates to mailed questionnaires. *American Sociological Review, 43*, 447–462.

Heider, F. (1958). *The psychology of interpersonal relations.* New York: Wiley.

Heilman, M. E., & Guzzo, R. (1978). The perceived cause of work success as a mediator of sex discrimination in organizations. *Organizational Behavior and Human Performance, 21*, 346–357.

Heneman, H. G., III. (1980). Self-assessment: A critical analysis. *Personnel Psychology, 33*, 297–300.

Heneman, H. G., III. (1985). Pay satisfaction. In K. M. Rowland & G. R. Ferris (Eds.), *Research in personnel and human resource management* (Vol. 3, pp. 115–139). Greenwich, CT: JAI Press.

Heneman, H. G., III, & Schwab, D. P. (1985). Pay satisfaction: Its multidimensional nature and measurement. *International Journal of Psychology, 20*, 129–141.

Heneman, H. G., III, Schwab, D. P., Fossum, J. A., & Dyer, L. D. (1983). *Personnel/human resource management.* Homewood, IL: Richard D. Irwin, Inc.

Heneman, R. L., & Wexley, K. N. (1983). The effects of time delay in rating and amount of information observed on performance rating accuracy. *Academy of Management Journal, 26*, 677–686.

Henry, R. A., & Hulin, C. L. (1987). Stability of skilled performance across time: Some generalizations and limitations on utilities. *Journal of Applied Psychology, 72*, 457–462.

Herriot, P. (1989). Selection as a social process. In P. B. Warr (Ed.), *Psychology at work*. Harmondsworth, England: Penguin.

Hicks, W. D., & Klimoski, R. J. (1987). Entry into training programs and its effects on training outcomes: A field experiment. *Academy of Management Journal, 30*, 542–552.

Hirsh, H. R., Schmidt, F. L., & Hunter, J. E. (1986). Estimation of employment validities by less experienced judges. *Personnel Psychology, 39*, 337–344.

Hoffman, L. R. (1965). Group problem solving. In L. Berkowitz (Ed.), *Advances in experimental social psychology* (Vol. 2). Orlando, FL: Academic Press.

Hogan, J. C., & Fleishman, E. A. (1979). An index of physical effort required in human task performance. *Journal of Applied Psychology, 64*, 197–204.

Hogan, J. C., Ogden, G. D., Gebhardt, D. L., & Fleishman, E. A. (1980). Reliability and validity of methods for evaluating perceived physical effort. *Journal of Applied Psychology, 65*, 672–679.

Holmes, D. S. (1976). Debriefing after psychological experiments: Effectiveness of post-deception dehoaxing. *American Psychologist, 31*, 858–867.

Holzbach, R. L. (1978). Rater bias in performance ratings: Superior, self, and peer ratings. *Journal of Applied Psychology, 63*, 579–588.

Hoppock, R. (1935). *Job satisfaction*. New York: Harper & Row.

Hough, L. (1984). Development and evaluation of the "accomplishment record" method of selecting and promoting professionals. *Journal of Applied Psychology, 6*, 135–146.

House, R. J., & Mitchell, T. (1974). Path-goal theory of leadership. *Journal of Contemporary Business, 3*, 81–98.

Hoy, F., & Hellriegel, D. (1982). The Kilmann and Herden model of organizational effectiveness: Criteria for small business managers. *Academy of Management Journal, 25*, 308–322.

Huber, V. L. (1985). Effects of task difficulty, goal setting, and strategy on performance of a heuristic task. *Journal of Applied Psychology, 70*, 492–504.

Huber, V., Neale, M., & Northcraft, G. B. (1987). Judgment by heuristics: Effects of ratee and rater characteristics and performance standards on performance-related judgments. *Organizational Behavior and Human Decision Processes, 40*, 149–169.

Hull, C. L. (1928). *Aptitude testing*. Yonkers, NY: World Book Co.

Humphreys, L. (1970). *Tearoom trade: Impersonal sex in public places*. Chicago, IL: Aldine-Atherton.

Hunter, J. E., & Hirsh, H. R. (1987). Applications of meta-analysis. In C. L. Cooper & I. T. Robertson (Eds.), *International review of industrial and organizational psychology*. New York: Wiley.

Hunter, J. E., & Hunter, R. F. (1984). Validity and utility of alternative predictors of job performance. *Psychological Bulletin, 96*, 72–98.

Hunter, J. E., & Schmidt, F. L. (1982). Fitting people to jobs: The impact of personnel selection on national productivity. In M. D. Dunnette & E. A. Fleishman (Eds.), *Human performance and productivity: Human capability assessment* (pp. 233–284). Hillsdale, NJ: Erlbaum.

Hunter, J. E., & Schmidt, F. L. (1983). Quantifying the effects of psychological interventions on employee job performance and work force productivity. *American Psychologist, 38*, 473–478.

Hunter, J. E., Schmidt, F. L., & Jackson, G. B. (1982). *Meta-analysis: Cumulating research findings across studies.* Beverly Hills, CA: Sage.

Hunter, J. E., Schmidt, F. L., & Pearlman, K. (1982). History and accuracy of validity generalization equations: A response to the Callender and Osburn reply. *Journal of Applied Psychology, 67*, 853–858.

Iaffaldano, M. T., & Muchinsky, P. M. (1985). Job satisfaction and job performance: A meta-analysis. *Psychological Bulletin, 97*, 251–273.

Ilgen, D. R., & Favero, J. L. (1985). Limits in generalization from psychological research to appraisal process. *Academy of Management Review, 10*, 311–322.

Ilgen, D. R., & Feldman, J. M. (1983). Performance appraisal: A process focus. In B. M. Staw & L. L. Cummings (Eds.), *Research in organizational behavior* (Vol. 5, pp. 141–197). Greenwich, CT: JAI Press.

Ilgen, D. R., & Knowlton, W. A. (1980). Performance attributional effects on feedback from superiors. *Organizational Behavior and Human Performance, 25*, 441–456.

Ilgen, D. R., Nebeker, D. M., & Pritchard, R. D. (1981). Expectancy theory measures: An empirical comparison in an experimental simulation. *Organizational Behavior and Human Performance, 3*, 157–189.

Ivancevich, J. M. (1979). Longitudinal study of the effects of rater training on psychometric error in ratings. *Journal of Applied Psychology, 64*, 502–508.

Jackson, G. B. (1978, April). *Methods for reviewing and integrating research in the social sciences.* Final report to the National Science Foundation for Grant No. DIS76-20309. Washington, DC: Social Research Group, George Washington University.

Jackson, J. (1965). A conceptual and measurement model for norms and roles. In I. D. Steiner & M. Fishbein (Eds.), *Current studies in social psychology*. New York: Holt.

Jackson, S. E., & Schuler, R. S. (1985). A meta-analysis and conceptual critique of research on role ambiguity and role conflict in work settings. *Organizational Behavior and Human Decision Processes, 36,* 16–78.

Jacobson, M. B., & Effertz, J. (1974). Sex roles and leadership perceptions of the leaders and the led. *Organizational Behavior and Human Performance, 12,* 383–396.

Jaffee, C. L., Bender, J., & Calvert, O. L. (1978). The assessment center technique: A validation study. *Management of Personnel Quarterly, 9,* 9–14.

James, L. R., & Brett, J. M. (1984). Mediators, moderators, and tests for mediation. *Journal of Applied Psychology, 69,* 307–321.

James, L. R., Demaree, R. G., & Mulaik, S. A. (1986). A note on validity generalization procedures. *Journal of Applied Psychology, 71,* 440–450.

James, L. R., Demaree, R. G., Mulaik, S. A., & Mumford, M. D. (1988). Validity generalization: Rejoinder to Schmidt, Hunter, and Raju (1988). *Journal of Applied Psychology, 73,* 673–678.

James, L. R., & Jones, A. P. (1976). Organizational structure: A review of structural dimensions and their conceptual relationships with individual attitudes and behavior. *Organizational Behavior and Human Performance, 16,* 74–113.

James, L. R., Mulaik, S. A., & Brett, J. M. (1982). *Causal analysis: Assumptions, models, and data.* Beverly Hills, CA: Sage.

Jenkins, G. D., Jr., Nadler, D. A., Lawler, E., & Cammann, C. (1975). Standardized observation: An approach to measuring the nature of jobs. *Journal of Applied Psychology, 60,* 171–181.

Jick, T. D. (1979). Mixing qualitative and quantitative methods: Triangulation in action. *Administrative Science Quarterly, 24,* 602–611.

Johnston, S. M., & Bolstad, Q. D. (1973). Methodological issues in naturalistic observation: Some problems and solutions for field research. In L. A. Hamerlynch, L. C. Handy, & E. J. Marsh (Eds.), *Behavioral change: Methodologies, concepts and practice.* Champaign, IL: Research Press.

Jones, A. P., Johnson, L. A., Butler, M. C., & Main, D. S. (1983). Apples and oranges: An empirical comparison of commonly used indices of interrater agreement. *Academy of Management Journal, 26,* 507–519.

Jones, E. E., & Davis, K. E. (1965). From acts to dispositions: The attribution process in person perception. In L. Berkowitz (Ed.), *Advances in experimental social psychology* (Vol. 2, pp. 219–266). New York: Academic Press.

Jöreskog, K. G., & Sorbom, D. (1984). *LISREL VI: Analysis of linear structural relationships by maximum likelihood, instrumental variables, and least squares methods.* Mooresville, IN: Scientific Software, Inc.

Kane, J. S., & Lawler, E. E. (1978). Methods of peer assessment. *Psychological Bulletin, 85,* 555–586.

Katz, D., & Kahn, R. L. (1978). *The social psychology of organizations.* New York: Wiley.

Katz, R. (1982). The effects of group longevity on project communication and performance. *Administrative Science Quarterly, 27,* 81–104.

Keeley, M. (1978). A social justice approach to organizational environment. *Administrative Science Quarterly, 23,* 272–292.

Kelley, H. (1973). The process of causal attributions. *American Psychologist, 28,* 107–128.

Kelman, H. C. (1967). Human use of human subjects: The problem of deception in social psychological experiments. *Psychological Bulletin, 22,* 1–11.

Kemery, E. R., Mossholder, K. W., & Dunlap, W. P. (1989). Meta-analyses and moderator variables: A cautionary note on transportability. *Journal of Applied Psychology, 74,* 168–170.

Keppel, G. (1982). *Design and analysis: A researcher's handbook.* Englewood Cliffs, NJ: Prentice Hall.

Kerlinger, F. (1973). *Foundations of behavioral research* (2nd ed., p. 129). New York: Holt, Rinehart & Winston.

Kerr, S., & Schriesheim, C. A. (1974). Consideration, initiating structure, and organizational criteria—an update of Korman's 1966 review. *Personnel Psychology, 27,* 555–568.

Kiesler, S., Siegel, J., & McGuire, T. (1984). Social psychological aspects of computer-mediated communications. *American Psychologist, 39,* 1123–1134.

Kiesler, S., & Sproull, S. E. (1986). Response effects in the electronic survey. *Public Opinion Quarterly, 50,* 402–413.

King, L. M., Hunter, J. E., & Schmidt, F. L. (1980). Halo in a multidimensional forced-choice performance appraisal scale. *Journal of Applied Psychology, 65,* 507–516.

Kirk, R. E. (1968). *Experimental design: Procedures for the behavioral sciences.* Belmont, CA: Brooks/Cole.

Kirkpatrick, D. L. (1967). Evaluation of training. In R. L. Craig & L. R. Bittel (Eds.), *Training and development handbook* (pp. 87–112). New York: McGraw-Hill.

Kish, L. (1965). *The survey sample.* New York: Wiley.

Klimoski, R. J. (1978). Simulation methodologies in experimental research on negotiation by representatives. *Journal of Conflict Resolution, 22,* 61–77.

Klimoski, R. J. (1983). Needs assessment for management development. *Personnel Selection and Training Bulletin, 4*(1), 7–17.

Klimoski, R. J., & Brickner, M. (1987). Why do assessment centers work? The puzzle of assessment center validity. *Personnel Psychology, 40,* 243–260.

Klimoski, R. J., & Inks, L. (1990). Accountability forces in performance appraisals. *Organizational Behavior and Human Decision Processes, 45,* 188–206.

Klimoski, R. J., & London, M. (1974). Role of the rater in performance appraisal. *Journal of Applied Psychology, 59,* 445–451.

Klimoski, R. J., & Strickland, W. J. (1977). Assessment centers— valid or merely prescient? *Personnel Psychology, 30,* 353–361.

Klimoski, R. J., & Strickland, W. J. (1978). *Comparative view of assessment centers.* Unpublished manuscript.

Knauft, E. B. (1948). Construction and use of weighted checklist rating scales for two industrial situations. *Journal of Applied Psychology, 32,* 63–70.

Komaki, J., Waddell, W. M., & Pearce, M. G. (1977). The applied behavior analysis approach and individual employees: Improving performance in two small businesses. *Organizational Behavior and Human Performance, 19,* 337–352.

Kondrasuk, J. N. (1981). Studies in MBO effectiveness. *Academy of Management Review, 6,* 419–430.

Kopelman, R. E. (1986). *Managing productivity in organizations.* New York: McGraw-Hill.

Korman, A. (1966). Consideration, initiating structure, and organizational criteria: A review. *Personnel Psychology, 19,* 349–361.

Korman, A. K. (1977). *Organizational behavior.* Englewood Cliffs, NJ: Prentice-Hall.

Kraiger, K., & Ford, J. K. (1985). A meta-analysis of rater race effects in performance ratings. *Journal of Applied Psychology, 7,* 56–65.

Krzystofiak, F., Cardy, R., & Newman, J. (1989). Implicit personality and performance appraisal: The influence of trait inferences on evaluations of behavior. *Journal of Applied Psychology, 73,* 515–521.

Kulik, C. T., Oldham, G. R., & Langner, P. H. (1988). Measurement of job characteristics: Comparison of the original and revised job diagnostic survey. *Journal of Applied Psychology, 73,* 462–465.

Landy, F. J. (1976). The validity of the interview in police officer selection. *Journal of Applied Psychology, 61,* 193–198.

Landy, F. J. (1978). An opponent process theory of job satisfaction. *Journal of Applied Psychology, 63*, 533–547.

Landy, F. J., & Farr, J. L. (1980). Performance rating. *Psychological Bulletin, 87*, 72–107.

Landy, F. J., Farr, J. L., & Jacobs, R. R. (1982). Utility concepts in performance measurement. *Organizational Behavior and Human Performance, 30*, 15–40.

Landy, F. J., & Trumbo, D. A. (1980). *Psychology of work behavior.* Homewood, IL: Dorsey Press.

Larson, G. (1987). Routinization of mental training in organizations: Effects on performance and well-being. *Journal of Applied Psychology, 72*, 88–96.

Larson, J. (1984). The performance feedback process: A preliminary model. *Organizational Behavior and Human Performance, 33*(1), 42–76.

Latham, G. P., Erez, M., & Locke, E. A. (1988). Resolving scientific disputes by the joint design of crucial experiments by the antagonists: An application of the Erez-Latham dispute regarding participation in goal setting. *Journal of Applied Psychology, 73*, 753–772.

Latham, G. P., Fay, C., & Saari, L. M. (1979). The development of behavioral observation scales for appraising the performance of foreman. *Personnel Psychology, 32*, 299–311.

Latham, G. P., & Frayne, C. A. (1989). Self-management training for increasing job attendance: A follow-up and replication. *Journal of Applied Psychology, 74*, 411–416.

Latham, G. P., & Lee, T. W. (1986). Goal setting. In E. A. Locke (Ed.), *Generalizing from laboratory to field settings.* Lexington, MA: D. C. Heath, pp. 101–118.

Latham, G. P., & Pursell, E. D. (1975). Measuring the absenteeism from the opposite side of the coin. *Journal of Applied Psychology, 60*, 369–371.

Latham, G. P., & Saari, L. (1979). The application of social learning theory to training supervisors through behavior modeling. *Journal of Applied Psychology, 64*, 237–246.

Latham, G. P., Saari, L. M., Purcell, E. D., & Campion, M. A. (1980). The situational interview. *Journal of Applied Psychology, 65*, 422–427.

Latham, G. P., & Wexley, K. N. (1981). *Increasing productivity through performance appraisal.* Reading, MS: Addison-Wesley.

Latham, G. P., Wexley, K. N., & Purcell, E. D. (1975). Training managers to minimize rating errors in the observation of behavior. *Journal of Applied Psychology, 60*, 550–555.

Lawler, E. E., III. (1971). *Pay and organizational effectiveness: A psychological view.* New York: McGraw-Hill.

Lawler, E. E., III. (1981). *Pay and organization development*. Reading, MA: Addison-Wesley.

Lawler, E. E., III. (1982). Strategies for improving the quality of work life. *American Psychologist, 37*, 486–493.

Lawler, E. E., III. (1986). The design of effective reward systems. In J. W. Lorsch (Ed.), *Handbook of organizational behavior*. Englewood Cliffs, NJ: Prentice Hall.

Lawler, E. E., & Rhode, J. G. (1976). *Information and control in organizations*. Santa Monica, CA: Goodyear.

Lawshe, C. H. (1975). A quantitative approach to content validity. *Personnel Psychology, 28*, 563–575.

Lawshe, C. H., & Balma, M. J. (1966). *Principles of personnel testing*. New York: McGraw-Hill.

Ledvinka, J. (1982). *Federal regulation of personnel and human resource management*. Boston, MA: Kent.

Levine, E. L. (1983). *Everything you always wanted to know about job analysis*. Tampa, FL: Mariner Publishing Co.

Levine, E. L., Ash, R. A., Hall, H., & Sistrunk, F. (1983). Evaluation of job analysis methods by experienced job analysts. *Academy of Management Journal, 26*, 339–348.

Levine, E. L., & Randolph, S. M. (1977). *Reference checking for personnel selection: The state of the art*. Berea, OH: American Society for Personnel Administration.

Levine, J., & Butler, J. (1952). Lecture vs. group decision in changing behavior. *Journal of Applied Psychology, 36*, 29–33.

Lewin, K. (1946). Action research and minority problems. *Journal of Social Issues, 2*, 34–46.

Light, D., Jr. (1979). Surface data and deep structure: Observing the organization of professional training. *Administrative Science Quarterly, 24*, 551–559.

Likert, R. (1967). *The human organization: Its management and value*. New York: McGraw-Hill.

Likert, R., & Bowers, D. G. (1969). Organization theory and human resource accounting. *American Psychologist, 24*, 585–592.

Lindell, M. K., & Drexler, J. A., Jr. (1979). Issues using survey methods for measuring organizational change. *Academy of Management Review, 4*, 13–19.

Lissitz, R. W., & Green, S. B. (1975). Effect of the number of scale points on reliability: A Monte Carlo approach. *Journal of Applied Psychology, 60*, 10–13.

Livingston, S. A., & Zieky, M. J. (1982). *Passing scores*. Princeton, NJ: Educational Testing Service.

Locke, E. A. (1968). Toward a theory of task motivation and incentives. *Organizational Behavior and Human Performance, 3,* 157– 189.

Locke, E. A. (1976). The nature and causes of job satisfaction. In M. D. Dunnette (Ed.), *Handbook of industrial and organizational psychology.* Chicago, IL: Rand McNally.

Locke, E. A., Mento, A. J., & Kutcher, B. L. (1978). The interaction of ability and motivation in performance: An exploration of the meaning of moderators. *Personnel Psychology, 31,* 269–280.

Locke, E. A., Shaw, K. N., Saari, L. M., & Latham, G. P. (1981). Goal setting and task performance: 1969–1980. *Psychological Bulletin, 90,* 125–152.

Loehlin, J. C. (1987). *Latent variable models: An introduction to factor, path and structural analysis.* Hillsdale, NJ: Erlbaum.

Long, J. S. (1983). *Confirmatory factor analysis.* Beverly Hills, CA: Sage.

Lord, F. M. (1984). Standard errors of measurement at different ability levels. *Journal of Educational Measurement, 21,* 239–244.

Lord, R. G. (1977). Functional leadership behavior: Measurement and relation to social power and leadership perceptions. *Administrative Science Quarterly, 22,* 114–133.

Lord, R. G., Binning, J. F., Rush, M. C., & Thomas, J. C. (1978). The effect of performance cues and leader behavior on questionnaire ratings of leadership behavior. *Organizational Behavior and Human Performance, 21,* 27–39.

Lord, R. G., DeVader, C. L., & Alliger, G. M. (1986). A meta-analysis of the relation between personality traits and leadership perceptions: An application of validity generalization procedures. *Journal of Applied Psychology, 71,* 402–410.

Lord, R. G., Foti, R. J., & DeVader, C. L. (1984). A test of leadership categorization theory: Internal structure, information processing, and leadership perceptions. *Organizational Behavior and Human Performance, 34,* 343–378.

Lord, R. G., Foti, R. J., & Phillips, J. S. (1982). A theory of leadership categorization. In J. G. Hunt, U. Sekaran, & C. A. Schriesheim (Eds.), *Leadership: Beyond establishment views* (pp. 104– 121). Carbondale, IL: Southern Illinois University Press.

Lorenzo, R. V. (1984). Effects of assessorship on manager's proficiency in acquiring, evaluating, and communicating. *Personnel Psychology, 37,* 617–634.

Lowin, A., & Craig, J. R. (1968). The influence of level of performance on managerial style: An experimental object lesson in the ambiguity of correlational data. *Organizational Behavior and Human Performance, 3,* 440–458.

Lowman, R. L. (Ed.). (1986). *Casebook on ethics and standards for the practice of psychology in organizations.* College Park, MD: Society for Industrial and Organizational Psychology, Inc.

Lundberg, C. C. (1976). Hypothesis creation in organizational behavior research. *Academy of Management Review, 1,* 35–42.

Lusterman, S. (1985). *Trends in corporate education and training.* New York: The Conference Board.

Luthans, F., & Davis, T. R. V. (1982). An idiographic approach to organizational behavior research: The use of single case experimental designs and direct measures. *Academy of Management Review, 7,* 380–391.

Mabe, P. A., III, & West, S. G. (1982). Validity of self-evaluation of ability: A review and meta-analysis. *Journal of Applied Psychology, 67,* 280–296.

MacCallum, R. (1986). Specification searches in covariance structure modeling. *Psychological Bulletin, 100,* 107–121.

MacKenzie, K., & House, R. (1978). Paradigm development in the social sciences: A proposed research strategy. *Academy of Management Review, 3,* 7–23.

Macoby, E. E., & Jacklin, C. N. (1974). *The psychology of sex differences.* Stanford, CA: Stanford University Press.

Macy, B. A., & Mirvis, P. H. (1976). A methodology for assessment of quality of work life and organizational effectiveness in behavioral-economic terms. *Administrative Science Quarterly, 21,* 212–226.

Madden, J. M. (1981). Using policy capturing to measure attitudes in organizational diagnosis. *Personnel Psychology, 34,* 341–350.

Magnusson, D. (1966). *Test theory.* Reading, MA: Addison-Wesley.

Maier, N. R. F. (1950). The quality of group decision as influenced by the discussion leaders. *Human Relations, 3,* 155–179.

Maier, N. R. F., & Solem, A. R. (1962). Improving solution by turning choice situations into problems. *Personnel Psychology, 15,* 151–157.

Markham, S. E. (1988). Pay-for-performance dilemma revisited: Empirical example of the importance of group effects. *Journal of Applied Psychology, 73,* 172–180.

Markham, W. T., Bonjean, C. M., & Corder, J. (1984). Measuring organizational control: The reliability and validity of the control graph approach. *Human Relations, 37,* 263–294.

Marks, M. L., Mirvis, P. H., Hackett, E. J., & Grady, J. F., Jr. (1986). Employee participation in a quality circle program: Impact on quality of work life, productivity and absenteeism. *Journal of Applied Psychology, 71*, 61–69.

Marsh, H. W., Balla, J. R., & MacDonald, R. P. (1988). Goodness-of-fit indexes in confirmatory factor analysis: The effect of sample size. *Psychological Bulletin, 103*, 391–410.

Marsh, H. W., & Hocevar, D. (1988). A new, more powerful approach to multitrait-multimethod analyses: Application of second-order confirmatory factor analysis. *Journal of Applied Psychology, 73*, 107–117.

Martin, S., & Klimoski, R. J. (1990). Use of verbal protocols to trace cognitions associated with self and supervisor evaluations of performance. *Organizational behavior and human decision processes, 46*, 17–25.

Martinko, M. J., & Gardner, W. (1985). Beyond structured observation: Methodological issues and new directions. *Academy of Management Review, 10*, 676–695.

Maslow, A. H. (1954). *Motivation and personality.* New York: Harper & Row.

Maslow, A. H. (1970). *Motivation and personality* (2nd ed.). New York: Harper & Row.

McAllister, D. W., Mitchell, T. R., & Beach, L. R. (1979). The contingency model for the selection of decision strategies: An empirical test of the effects of significance, accountability and reversibility. *Organizational Behavior and Human Performance, 24*, 288–344.

McCauley, C., Stilt, C. L., & Segal, M. (1980). Stereotyping: From prejudice to prediction. *Psychology Bulletin, 87*, 195–208.

McClelland, D. C. (1961). *The achieving society.* Princeton, NJ: Van Nostrand.

McClelland, D. C., & Boyatzis, R. E. (1982). Leadership motive pattern and long-term success in management. *Journal of Applied Psychology, 67*, 737–743.

McConkie, M. L. (1979). A clarification of the goal setting and appraisal processes in MBO. *Academy of Management Review, 4*, 29–40.

McCormick, E. J. (1976). Job and task analysis. In M. D. Dunnette (Ed.), *Handbook of industrial and organizational psychology.* Chicago, IL: Rand McNally.

McCormick, E. J. (1979). *Job analysis: Methods and applications.* New York: AMACOM.

McCormick, E. J., & Bachus, J. (1952). Paired comparison ratings: 1. The effect on ratings of reductions in the number of pairs. *Journal of Applied Psychology, 36*, 123–127.

McCormick, E. J., & Ilgen, D. R. (1980). *Industrial psychology,* Englewood Cliffs, NJ: Prentice-Hall.

McCormick, E. J., & Ilgen, D. R. (1985). *Industrial and organizational psychology* (8th ed.). Englewood Cliffs, NJ: Prentice-Hall.

McDaniel, M. A., Hirsh, H. R., Schmidt, F. L., Raju, N. S., & Hunter, J. E. (1986). Interpreting the results of meta-analytic research: A comment on Schmitt, Gooding, Noe, and Kirsch (1984). *Personnel Psychology, 39,* 141–148.

McDaniel, M. A., & Schmidt, F. L. (1985). *A meta-analysis of the validity of training and experience ratings in personnel selection.* Paper presented at the 93rd Annual Convention of the American Psychological Association, Los Angeles, CA.

McDaniel, M. A., Whetzel, D. L., Schmidt, F. L., Hunter, J. E., Maurer, S., & Russell, J. (1986). *The validity of employment interviews: A review and meta-analysis.* Unpublished manuscript. Washington, DC: U.S. Department of Personnel Management.

McDougall, W. (1908). *An introduction to social psychology.* London: Methaen.

McEvoy, G. M., & Cascio, W. F. (1985). Strategies for reducing employee turnover: A meta-analysis. *Journal of Applied Psychology, 70,* 342–353.

McGrath, J. E. (1984). *Groups: Interaction and performance.* Englewood Cliffs, NJ: Prentice Hall.

McGrath, J., Martin, J., & Kulka, R. (1981). *Better ways of making judgment calls in methodological decision making.* Workshop presented in APA Innovations in Methodology Conference. Greensboro, NC: Center for Creative Leadership.

McGregor, D. (1957). An uneasy look at performance appraisal. *Harvard Business Review, 35,* 89–94.

Mento, A. J., Steele, R. P., & Karren, R. J. (1987). A meta-analytic study of the effects of goal setting on task performance: 1966–1984. *Organizational Behavior and Human Decision Processes, 39,* 52–83.

Meyer, H. H., & Raich, M. S. (1983). An objective evaluation of a behavior modeling training program. *Personnel Psychology, 36,* 755–761.

Miles, M. B. (1979). Qualitative data as an attractive nuisance: The problem of analysis. *Administrative Science Quarterly, 24,* 590–601.

Miles, R. H., & Cameron, K. (1977). *Coffin nails and corporate strategies: A quarter century view of organizational adaptation to environment in the U.S. Tobacco Industry.* Working Paper No. 3, Business–Government Relations Series. New Haven, CT: Yale University.

Milkovich, G. T. (1980). The emerging debate. In E. R. Levernash (Ed.), *Comparable worth: Issues and alternatives.* Washington, DC: Equal Employment Advisory Council.

Miller, A. G. (1972). Role playing: An alternative to deception? *American Psychologist, 27,* 623–636.

Miner, J. B. (1960). The effect of a course in psychology on the attitudes of research and development supervisors. *Journal of Applied Psychology, 44,* 224–232.

Miner, J. B. (1970). Psychological evaluations as predictors of consulting success. *Personnel Psychology, 23,* 393–405.

Miner, J. B. (1978). Twenty years of research on role motivation theory of managerial effectiveness. *Personnel Psychology, 31,* 739–760.

Miner, J. B., & Miner, M. G. (1977). *Personnel and industrial relations.* New York: Macmillan.

Mintzberg, H. (1973). *The nature of managerial work.* New York: Harper & Row.

Mintzberg, H. (1979). An emerging strategy of "direct" research. *Administrative Science Quarterly, 24,* 582–589.

Mintzberg, H., Raisinghani, D., & Theuret, A. (1976). The structure of unstructured decision processes. *Administrative Science Quarterly, 21,* 246–275.

Mischel, W. (1973). Toward a cognitive social learning reconceptualization of personality. *Psychological Review, 80,* 252–283.

Mitchell, J. V., Jr. (1986). *The ninth mental measurements yearbook.* Lincoln: University of Nebraska Press.

Mitchell, T. R. (1974). Expectancy models of job satisfaction, occupational preference and effort: A theoretical, methodological, and empirical appraisal. *Psychological Bulletin, 81,* 1053–1077.

Mitchell, T. R. (1985). An evaluation of the validity of correlational research conducted in organizations. *Academy of Management Review, 10,* 192–205.

Mitchell, T.R., & James, L.R. (1989). Theory development forum. *Academy of Management Review, 14,* 330–407.

Mitchell, T. R., & Kalb, C. S. (1981). The effects of outcome knowledge and outcome valence on supervisor's evaluations. *Journal of Applied Psychology, 66,* 604–612.

Mitchell, T. W., & Klimoski, R. J. (1982). Is it rational to be empirical? A test of methods for scoring biographical data. *Journal of Applied Psychology, 67,* 411–418.

Mitchell, T. W., & Klimoski, R. J. (1985). *Accountability bias in performance appraisal.* Unpublished manuscript. Columbus: Ohio State University, Department of Psychology.

Mobley, W. H. (1982). Supervisor and employee race and sex effects on performance appraisals: A field study of adverse impact and generalizability. *Academy of Management Journal, 25,* 598–606.

Mobley, W. H., Horner, S. O., & Hollingsworth, A. T. (1978). An evaluation of precursors of hospital employee turnover. *Journal of Applied Psychology, 63,* 408–414.

Morgan, G., & Smircich, L. (1980). The case for qualitative research. *Academy of Management Review, 5,* 491–500.

Mosel, J. N., & Goheen, H. W. (1959). The employment recommendation questionnaire: III. Validity of different types of reference. *Personnel Psychology, 12,* 469–477.

Moses, J. L., & Boehm, V. R. (1975). Relationship of assessment center performance to management progress of women. *Journal of Applied Psychology, 60,* 527–529.

Moskowitz, M.J. (1977) Hugo Munsterberg: A study in the history of applied psychology. *American Psychologist, 10,* 824–842.

Muchinsky, P. M. (1977). A comparison of within- and across- subjects analyses of the expectancy-valence model for predicting effort. *Academy of Management Journal, 20,* 154–158.

Muchinsky, P. M. (1979). The use of reference reports in personnel selection: A review and evaluation. *Journal of Occupational Psychology, 52,* 287–297.

Muchinsky, P. M. (1987). *Psychology applied to work.* Homewood, IL: Dorsey Press.

Mulaik, S. A. (1972). *The foundations of factor analysis.* New York: McGraw-Hill.

Mumford, M. D., Weeks, J. L., Harding, F. D., & Fleishman, E. A. (1988). Relations between student characteristics, course content and training outcomes: An integrative modeling effort. *Journal of Applied Psychology, 73,* 443–456.

Munsterberg, H. (1913). *Psychology and industrial efficiency.* Boston: Houghton-Mifflin.

Murphy, G., & Likert, R. (1938). *Public opinion and the individual.* New York: Harper.

Murphy, K. R. (1986). When your top choice turns you down: Effect of rejected offers on the utility of selection tests. *Psychological Bulletin, 99,* 133–138.

Murphy, K. R., & Balzer, W. (1981). *Rater errors and rating accuracy.* Paper presented at the annual meeting of the American Psychological Association, Los Angeles, CA.

Mussio, S. J., & Smith, M. K. (1972). *Content validity: A procedural manual.* Minneapolis, MN: Civil Service Commission.

Nahavandi, A., & Malekzadeh, A. R. (1988). Acculturation in mergers and acquisitions. *Academy of Management Review, 13,* 79–90.

Nedelsky, L. (1954). Absolute grading standards for objective tests. *Educational and Psychological Measurement, 14,* 3–19.

Nemeroff, W. F., & Cosentino, J. (1979). Utilizing feedback and goal setting to increase performance appraisal skills of managers. *Academy of Management Journal, 22,* 566–576.

Nicholas, J. M. (1982). The comparative impact of organizational development interventions on hard criteria measures. *Academy of Management Review, 3,* 531–542.

Nunnally, J. C. (1978). *Psychometric theory.* New York: McGraw-Hill.

Olson, H. C., Fine, S. A., Myers, D. C., & Jennings, M. C. (1981). The Use of functional job analysis in establishing performance standards for heavy equipment operators. *Personnel Psychology, 34,* 351–364.

Organ, D. W., & Konovsky, M. (1989). Cognitive versus affective determinants of organizational citizenship behavior. *Journal of Applied Psychology, 74,* 157–164.

Osburn, H. G., Callender, J. C., Greener, J. M., & Ashworth, S. (1983). Statistical power of tests of the situational specificity hypothesis in validity generalization studies: A cautionary note. *Journal of Applied Psychology, 68,* 115–122.

Osgood, C. E., & Tannenbaum, P. H. (1955). The principle of congruity in the prediction of attitude change. *Psychological Review, 62,* 42–55.

Owens, W. A. (1976). Background data. In M. D. Dunnette (Ed.), *Handbook of industrial and organizational psychology.* Chicago, IL: Rand McNally.

Owens, W. A., & Schoenfeldt, L. F. (1979). Toward a classification of persons. *Journal of Applied Psychology, 46,* 329–332.

Pace, L. A., & Schoenfeldt, L. F. (1977). Legal concerns in the use of weighted applications. *Personnel Psychology, 30,* 159–166.

Parsons, H. M. (1974). What happened at Hawthorne? *Science, 183,* 922–932.

Pearce, J. L., Stevenson, W. B., & Perry, J. L. (1985). Managerial compensation based on organizational performance: A time series analysis of the effects of merit pay. *Academy of Management Journal, 28,* 261–278.

Pearlman, K. (1980). Job families: A review and discussion of their implications for personnel selection. *Psychological Bulletin, 87,* 1–28.

Pennings, J. M., & Goodman, P. S. (1977). Toward a workable framework. In P. S. Goodman & J. M. Pennings (Eds.), *New perspectives on organizational effectiveness.* San Francisco: Jossey-Bass.

Perrow, C. (1961). The analysis of goals in complex organizations. *American Sociological Review, 26,* 854–866.

Pettigrew, A. M. (1979). On studying organizational cultures. *Administrative Science Quarterly, 24,* 570–581.

Petty, M. M., McGee, G. W., & Cavender, J. W. (1984). A meta-analysis of the relationship between individual job satisfaction and individual performance. *Academy of Management Review, 9,* 712–721.

Pfeffer, J. (1973). Size, composition and function of hospital boards of directors: A study of organization-environment linkage. *Administrative Science Quarterly, 18,* 349–364.

Pfeffer, J., & Salancik, G. R. (1974). Organizational decision making as a political process: The case of a university budget. *Administrative Science Quarterly, 19,* 135–150.

Phillips, A. P., & Dipboye, R. L. (1989). Correlational tests of predictions from a process model of the interview. *Journal of Applied Psychology, 74,* 41–52.

Phillips, J. S. (1984). The accuracy of leadership ratings: A cognitive categorization perspective. *Organizational Behavior and Human Performance, 23,* 125–138.

Platt, J. R. (1964). Strong inference. *Science, 146,* 347–353.

Podsakoff, P. M., & Organ, D. W. (1986). Self-reports in organization research: Problems and prospects. *Journal of Management, 12,* 531–544.

Popper, K. R. (1959). *The logic of scientific discovery.* New York: Basic Books.

Popper, K. R. (1968). *The logic of scientific discovery.* New York: Harper & Row.

Porter, L. W. (1961). A study of perceived need satisfaction in bottom and middle management jobs. *Journal of Applied Psychology, 45,* 1–10.

Porter, L. W., Lawler, E. E., III, & Hackman, J. R. (1975). *Behavior in organizations.* New York: McGraw-Hill.

Potter, E. E. (1989). Employer's burden of proof may be reduced in testing cases. *The Industrial-Organizational Psychologist, 26,* 43–47.

Premack, S. L. (1984). Prediction of employee unionization from knowledge of job satisfaction. In J.A. Pearce and R.B. Robinson, Jr. (Eds.) *Academy of Management Proceedings.* Boston, MA.

Premack, S. L., & Wanous, J. L. (1985). A meta-analysis of realistic job preview experiments. *Journal of Applied Psychology, 70,* 706–720.

Price, J. L., & Mueller, C. W. (1986). *The handbook of organizational measurement.* Marshfield, MA: Pitman Publishing.

Pritchard, R. D., Jones, S. D., Roth, P. L., Stuebing, K. K., & Ekeberg, S. E. (1988). Effects of group feedback, goal setting and incentives on organizational productivity. *Journal of Applied Psychology, 73,* 337–358.

Pulakos, E. D., Schmitt, N., & Ostroff, C. (1986). A warning about the use of a standard deviation across dimensions within ratees to measure halo. *Journal of Applied Psychology, 71,* 29–32.

Raju, N. S., & Burke, M. J. (1983). Two new procedures for studying validity generalization. *Journal of Applied Psychology, 68,* 382–395.

Raju, N. S., Pappas, S., & Williams, C. P. (1989). An empirical Monte Carlo test of the accuracy of the correlation, covariance, and regression slope models for assessing validity generalization. *Journal of Applied Psychology, 74,* 901–911.

Randolph, W. A. (1982). Planned organizational change and its measurement. *Personnel Psychology, 35,* 117–139.

Ranson, S., Hinings, R., & Greenwood, R. (1980). The structuring of organizational structures. *Administrative Science Quarterly, 25,* 1–17.

Rapoport, R. N. (1970). Three dilemmas of action research. *Human Relations, 23,* 499–513.

Rasmussen, J. L., & Loher, B. T. (1988). Appropriate critical percentages for the Schmidt and Hunter meta-analysis procedure: Comparative evaluation of type I error rate and power. *Journal of Applied Psychology, 73,* 683–687.

Rassenfoss, S., & Klimoski, R. J. (1985). *Role of implicit personality theories in individual assessments.* Unpublished manuscript. Columbus: Ohio State University, Department of Psychology.

Rauschenberger, J. M., & Schmidt, F. L. (1987). Measuring the economic impact of human resource programs. *Journal of Business Psychology, 2,* 50–59.

Reagan, R. T., Mosteller, F., & Youtz, C. (1989). Quantitative meanings of verbal probability expressions. *Journal of Applied Psychology, 74,* 433–442.

Reilly, R. R., & Chao, G. T. (1982). Validity and fairness of some alternative employee selection procedures. *Personnel Psychology, 35,* 1–62.

Reilly, R. R., Zedeck, S., & Tenopyr, M. L. (1979). Validity and fairness of physical ability tests for predicting performance in craft jobs. *Journal of Applied Psychology, 64,* 262–274.

Reimann, B. C. (1982). Organizational competence as a predictor of long run survival and growth. *Academy of Management Journal, 25,* 323–334.

Rice, R. W. (1978). Construct validity of the least preferred coworker (LPC) score. *Psychological Bulletin, 85,* 1199–1237.

Rich, J. R., & Boudreau, J. (1987). The effects of variability and risk in selection utility analysis: An empirical comparison. *Personnel Psychology, 40,* 55–84.

Rizzo, J. R., House, R. J., & Lirtzman, S. I. (1970). Role conflict and ambiguity in complex organizations. *Administrative Science Quarterly, 15,* 150–163.

Roberts, K. H., Hulin, C. L., & Rousseau, D. M. (1978). *Developing an interdisciplinary science of organizations.* San Francisco: Jossey-Bass.

Robertson, I. (1987). *Validity of situational interviews for the selection of managerial personnel.* Unpublished manuscript. Manchester, UK: UMIST.

Robinson, D. B. (1981). Content-oriented personnel selection in a small business setting. *Personnel Psychology, 34,* 77–87.

Roeher, G. A. (1963). Effective techniques in increasing response to mailed questionnaires. *Public Opinion Quarterly, 27,* 299–302.

Roethlisberger, F. J., & Dickson, W. J. (1939). *Management and the worker.* New York: Wiley.

Rosenthal, R. (1967). *Experimenter effects in behavioral research.* New York: Appleton-Century-Crofts.

Rosenthal, R. (1978). Combining results of independent studies. *Psychological Bulletin, 85,* 185–193.

Rosenthal, R. (1984). *Meta-analysis procedures for social research.* Beverly Hills, CA: Sage.

Rosenthal, R., & Rosnow, R. (1984). *Essentials of behavioral research.* New York: McGraw-Hill.

Ruch, F. L., & Ruch, W. L. (1980). *Employee aptitude survey technical report.* Los Angeles, CA: Psychological Services, Inc.

Runkel, P. J., & McGrath, J. E. (1972). *Research on human behavior: A systematic guide to method.* New York: Holt, Rinehart and Winston.

Rush, M. C., Thomas, J. C., & Lord, R. G. (1977). Implicit leadership theory: A potential threat to the internal validity of leader behavior questionnaires. *Organizational Behavior and Human Performance, 20,* 93–110.

Russell, J. S., Terborg, J. R., & Powers, M. L. (1985). Organizational performance and organizational level training and support. *Personnel Psychology, 38,* 849–863.

Ryan, A. M., & Sackett, P. R. (1987). A survey of individual assessment practices by I/O psychologists. *Personnel Psychology, 40,* 455–488.

Ryan, R. T., Mosteller, F., & Youtz, C. (1989). Quantitative meanings of verbal probability expressions. *Journal of Applied Psychology, 74,* 433–442.

Rynes, S. L., & Milkovich, G. T. (1986). Wage rates: Dispelling some myths about the market wage. *Personnel Psychology, 39,* 71–90.

Rynes, S. L., & Miller, H. E. (1983). Recruiter and job influences on candidates for employment. *Journal of Applied Psychology, 68*, 620–631.

Rynes, S. L., Weber, C. L., & Milkovich, G. T. (1989). Effects of market survey rates, job evaluation, and job gender on job pay. *Journal of Applied Psychology, 74*, 114–123.

Sackett, P. R., & Dreher, G. F. (1981). Some misconceptions about content-oriented validation: A rejoiner to Norton. *Academy of Management Review, 6*, 567–568.

Sackett, P. R., & Dreher, G. F. (1982). Constructs and assessment center dimensions: Some troubling empirical findings. *Journal of Applied Psychology, 67*, 401–410.

Sackett, P. R., & Harris, M. M. (1983). *A further examination of the constructs underlying assessment center ratings.* Paper presented at the American Psychological Association convention, Anaheim, CA.

Sackett, P. R., & Harris, M. M. (1984). Honesty testing for personnel selection: A review and critique. *Personnel Psychology, 37*, 221–245.

Sackett, P. R., Harris, M. M., & Orr, J. M. (1986). On seeking moderator variables in the meta-analysis of correlational data: A Monte Carlo investigation of statistical power and resistance to type I error. *Journal of Applied Psychology, 71*, 302–310.

Sackett, P. R., Schmitt, N., Tenopyr, M. L., Kehoe, J., & Zedeck, S. (1985). Comment on forty questions about validity generalization and meta-analysis. *Personnel Psychology, 38*, 697–798.

Sackett, P. R., Zedeck, S., Fogli, L. (1988). Relations between measures of typical and maximum job performance. *Journal of Applied Psychology, 73*, 482–486.

Salancik, G. R. (1979). Field stimulation for organizational behavior research. *Administrative Science Quarterly, 24*, 638–649.

Salancik, G. R., & Meindl, J. R. (1984). Corporate attributions as strategic illusions of management control. *Administrative Science Quarterly, 29*, 238–254.

Sanday, P. R. (1979). The ethnographic paradigms. *Administrative Science Quarterly, 24*, 527–538.

Saunders, D. R. (1956). Moderator variables in prediction. *Educational and Psychological Measurement, 16*, 209–222.

Scarpello, V., Huber, V., & Vandenberg, R. J. (1988). Compensation satisfaction: Its measurement and dimensionality. *Journal of Applied Psychology, 73*, 163–171.

Schall, M. S. (1983). A communication-rules approach to organizational culture. *Administrative Science Quarterly, 28*, 557–581.

Schein, E. H. (1968). Organizational socialization and the profession of management. *Industrial Management Review, 9,* 1–16.

Schmidt, F. L. (1973). Implications of a measurement problem for expectancy theory research. *Organizational Behavior and Human Performance, 10,* 243–251.

Schmidt, F. L. (1977). *The measurement of job performance.* Unpublished manuscript. Washington DC: U.S. Office of Personnel Management.

Schmidt, F. L., Caplin, J. R., Bemis, S. E., Decuir, R., Dunn, L., & Antone, L. (1979). *The behavioral consistency method of unassembled examining.* Washington, DC: U.S. Office of Personnel Management.

Schmidt, F. L., Gast-Rosenberg, I., & Hunter, J. E. (1980). Validity generalization results for computer programmers. *Journal of Applied Psychology, 65,* 643–661.

Schmidt, F. L., Greenthal, A. L., Hunter, J. E., Berner, J. G., & Seaton, F. W. (1977). Job samples vs. paper-and-pencil trade and technical tests: Adverse impact and examinee attitudes. *Personnel Psychology, 30,* 187–197.

Schmidt, F. L., & Hunter, J. E. (1977). Development of a general solution to the problem of validity generalization. *Journal of Applied Psychology, 62,* 529–540.

Schmidt, F. L., & Hunter, J. E. (1978). Moderator research and the law of small members. *Personnel Psychology, 31,* 215–231.

Schmidt, F. L., & Hunter, J. E. (1980). The future of criterion- related validity. *Personnel Psychology, 33,* 41–60.

Schmidt, F. L., & Hunter, J. E. (1981). Employment testing: Old theories and new research findings. *American Psychologist, 36,* 1128–1137.

Schmidt, F. L., & Hunter, J. E. (1983). Individual differences in productivity: An empirical test of estimates derived from studies of selection procedure utility. *Journal of Applied Psychology, 68,* 407– 414.

Schmidt, F. L., Hunter, J. E., Croll, P. R., & McKenzie, R. C. (1983). Estimation of employment test validities by expert judgment. *Journal of Applied Psychology, 68,* 590–601.

Schmidt, F. L., Hunter, J. E., McKenzie, R., & Muldrow, T. (1979). Impact of valid selection procedures on work-force productivity. *Journal of Applied Psychology, 64,* 609–626.

Schmidt, F. L., Hunter, J. E., & Outerbridge, A. N. (1986). Impact of job experience and ability on job knowledge, work sample performance, and supervisory ratings of job performance. *Journal of Applied Psychology, 71,* 432–439.

Schmidt, F. L., Hunter, J. E., & Pearlman, K. (1982a). Assessing the economic impact of personnel programs on workforce productivity. *Personnel Psychology, 35,* 333–347.

Schmidt, F. L., Hunter, J. E., & Pearlman, K. (1982b). Progress in validity generalization: Comments on Callender and Osburn and further developments. *Journal of Applied Psychology, 67,* 835–845.

Schmidt, F. L., Hunter, J. E., Pearlman, K., & Hirsh, H. R. (1985). Forty questions about validity generalization and meta-analysis. *Personnel Psychology, 38,* 697–798.

Schmidt, F. L., Hunter, J. E., Pearlman, K., & Shane, G. S. (1979). Further tests of the Schmidt-Hunter validity generalization procedure. *Personnel Psychology, 32,* 257–281.

Schmidt, F. L., Hunter, J. E., & Raju, N. S. (1988). Validity generalization and situational specificity: A second look at the 75% rule and Fisher's z transformation. *Journal of Applied Psychology, 73,* 665–672.

Schmidt, F. L., Hunter, J. E., & Urry, V. W. (1976). Statistical power in criterion-related validation studies. *Journal of Applied Psychology, 61,* 473–485.

Schmidt, F. L., & Kaplan, L. B. (1971). Composite vs. multiple criteria: A review and resolution of the controversy. *Personnel Psychology, 24,* 419–434.

Schmidt, F. L., Mack, M. J., & Hunter, J. E. (1984). Selection utility in the occupation of U.S. park ranger for three modes of test use. *Journal of Applied Psychology, 69,* 490–497.

Schmitt, N. (1976). Social and situation determinants of interview decisions: Implications for the employment interview. *Personnel Psychology, 29,* 79–101.

Schmitt, N., & Bedeian, A. G. (1982). A comparison of LISREL and two-stage least squares analysis of a hypothesized life-job satisfaction reciprocal relationship. *Journal of Applied Psychology, 67,* 806–817.

Schmitt, N., & Coyle, B. W. (1976). Applicant decisions in the employment interview. *Journal of Applied Psychology, 61,* 184–192.

Schmitt, N., Gleason, S. E., Pigozzi, B., & Marcus, P. M. (1987). Business climate attitudes and company relocation decisions. *Journal of Applied Psychology, 72,* 622–628.

Schmitt, N., Gooding, R. Z., Noe, R. A., & Kirsch, M. P. (1984). Meta-analyses of validity studies published between 1964 and 1982 and the investigation of study characteristics. *Personnel Psychology, 37,* 407–422.

Schmitt, N., & Noe, R. A. (1986). Personnel selection and equal employment opportunity. In C. L. Cooper & I. Robertson (Eds.), *Review of industrial and organizational psychology.* New York: Wiley.

Schmitt, N., Noe, R. A., Meritt, R., & Fitzgerald, M. P. (1984). Validity of assessment center ratings for the prediction of performance ratings and school climate of school administrators. *Journal of Applied Psychology, 69,* 207–213.

Schmitt, N., & Ostroff, C. (1986). Operationalizing the "behavioral consistency" approach: Selection test development based on a content-oriented approach. *Personnel Psychology, 39*, 91–108.

Schmitt, N., & Schneider, B. (1983). Current issues in personnel selection. In K. M. Rowland & G. R. Ferris (Eds.), *Research in personnel and human resources management*. Greenwich, CT: JAI Press.

Schmitt, N., & Stults, D. M. (1985). Factors defined by negatively keyed items: The result of careless respondents? *Applied Psychological Measurement, 9*, 367–373.

Schmitt, N., & Stults, D. M. (1986). Methodology review: Analysis of multitrait-multimethod matrices. *Applied Psychological Measurement, 10*, 1–22.

Schmittlein, D. C., & Morrison, D. G. (1983). Modeling and estimation using job duration data. *Organizational Behavior and Human Performance, 32*, 1–22.

Schneider, D., Hastorf, A. H., & Ellsworth, P. C. (1979). *Person perception* (2nd ed.). Reading, MA: Addison Wesley.

Schneider, B., & Schmitt, N. (1986). *Staffing organizations*. Glenview, IL: Scott-Foresman.

Schoenfeldt, L. F. (1974). Utilization of manpower: Development and evaluation of an assessment-classification model for matching individuals with jobs. *Journal of Applied Psychology, 59*, 583–594.

Schoenfeldt, L. F., & Brush, D. (1980, August). *A content-oriented approach to the validation of a performance appraisal system*. Paper presented at the 40th annual meeting of the Academy of Management, Detroit, MI.

Schriber, J. B., & Gutek, B. A. (1987). Some time dimensions of work: Measurement of an underlying aspect of organizational culture. *Journal of Applied Psychology, 72*, 642–650.

Schuler, H., & Stehle, W. (1982). *The social validity of aptitude testing procedures: Recent developments in the assessment center approach*. Paper presented at the 31st International Congress of Applied Psychology, Edinburgh, Scotland.

Schuler, R. S. (1988). Human resource management choices and organizational strategy. In R. S. Schuler, S. Youngblood, & V. Huber (Eds.), *Readings in personnel and human resource management* (3rd ed.). St. Paul, MN: West Publishing Co.

Scott, K. D., & Taylor, D. S. (1985). An examination of conflicting findings on the relationship between job satisfaction and absenteeism: A meta-analysis. *Academy of Management Journal, 28*, 599–612.

Scott, W. A. (1960). Measures of test homogeneity. *Educational and Psychological Measurement, 20,* 751–757.

Scott, W. D. (1911). *Increasing human efficiency in business.* New York: Macmillan.

Scott, W. G., Mitchell, T. R., & Birnbaum, P. H. (1981). *Organizational theory* (4th ed.). Homewood, IL: R. D. Irwin, Inc.

Seashore, H. G. (1962). Women are more predictable than men. *Journal of Counseling Psychology, 9,* 261–270.

Seashore, S. E., Indik, B. P., & Georgopoulos, B. S. (1960). Relationships among criteria of job performance. *Journal of Applied Psychology, 44,* 195–202.

Seashore, S. E., & Katz, D. (1982). Rensis Likert (1903–1981). *American Psychologist, 37,* 851–853.

Selznick, P. (1957). *Leadership in administration.* New York: Harper & Row.

Shaw, M. E. (1981). *Group dynamics: The psychology of small group behavior* (3rd ed.). New York: McGraw-Hill.

Shen, E. (1925). The reliability coefficient of personal ratings. *Journal of Educational Psychology, 16,* 232–236.

Shiflett, S. C. (1972). Group performance as a function of task difficulty and organizational interdependence. *Organizational Behavior and Human Performance, 7,* 442–456.

Shiflett, S. C. (1981). Is there a problem with the LPC score in leader match? *Personnel Psychology, 34,* 765–769.

Shore, L. M., & Thornton, G. C., III. (1986). Effects of gender on self and supervisory ratings. *Academy of Management Journal, 29,* 115–129.

Sieber, S. D. (1973). Integration of fieldwork and survey methods. *American Journal of Sociology, 78,* 1335–1359.

Siegel, A. I. (1983). The miniature job training and evaluation approach: Additional findings. *Personnel Psychology, 36,* 41–56.

Siegel, A. I., & Bergman, B. A. (1975). A job learning approach to performance prediction. *Personnel Psychology, 28,* 325–339.

Siero, S., Boon, M., Kok, G., & Siero, F. (1989). Modification of driving behavior in a large transport organization: A field experiment. *Journal of Applied Psychology, 74,* 417–423.

Sisson, E. D. (1948). Forced choice: The new army rating. *Personnel Psychology, 1,* 365–381.

Smith, G. L., Jr. (1978). *Work measurement: A systems approach.* Columbus, OH: Grid Publishing, Inc.

Smith, H. W. (1981). *Strategies of social research.* Englewood Cliffs, NJ: Prentice-Hall.

Smith, P. B. (1975). Controlled studies of the outcome of sensitivity training. *Psychological Bulletin, 82,* 597–622.

Smith, P. B. (1976). Social influence and the outcome of sensitivity training. *Journal of Personality and Social Psychology, 34,* 1087–1094.

Smith, P. C. (1976). Behaviors, results, and organizational effectiveness: The problems of criteria. In M. D. Dunnette (Ed.), *Handbook of industrial and organizational psychology.* Chicago, IL: Rand McNally.

Smith, P. C., Budzeika, K. A., Edwards, N. A., Johnson, S. M., & Bearse, L. N. (1986). Guidelines for clean data: Detection of common mistakes. *Journal of Applied Psychology, 71,* 457–460.

Smith, P. C., & Kendall, L. M. (1963). Retranslation of expectations: An approach to the construction of unambiguous anchors for rating scales. *Journal of Applied Psychology, 47,* 149–155.

Smith, P. C., Kendall, L. M., & Hulin, C. L. (1969). *The measurement of satisfaction in work and retirement: A strategy for the study of attitudes.* Chicago, IL: Rand McNally.

Smith, P. E. (1976). Management modeling training to improve morale and customer satisfaction. *Personnel Psychology, 29,* 351–359.

Smither, J. W., Reilly, R. R., & Buda, R. (1988). Effects on prior performance information on ratings of present performance: Contrast vs. assimilation revisited. *Journal of Applied Psychology, 73,* 487–496.

Snow, C. C., & Hribiniak, L. G. (1980). Strategy, distinctive competence and organizational performance. *Administrative Science Quarterly, 25,* 317–336.

Snyder, R. A., Raben, C. S., & Farr, J. L. (1980). A model for the systematic evaluation of human resource development programs. *Academy of Management Review, 5*(3), 431–444.

Society for Industrial and Organizational Psychology, Inc. (1987). *Principles for the validation and use of selection procedures.* College Park, MD: Author.

Spector, P. E. (1987). Method variance as an artifact in self-reported affect and perceptions at work: Myth or significant problem? *Journal of Applied Psychology, 92,* 438–443.

Spector, P. E., & Levine, E. L. (1987). Meta-analysis for integrating study outcomes: A Monte Carlo study of its susceptibility to type I and type II errors. *Journal of Applied Psychology, 72*, 3–9.

Spool, M. D. (1978). Training programs for observers of behavior: A review. *Personnel Psychology, 31*, 853–888.

Sprangers, M., & Hoogstraten, J. (1989). Pretesting effects in retrospective pretest-posttest designs. *Journal of Applied Psychology, 74*, 265–272.

Spray, S. L. (1976). *Organizational effectiveness.* Kent, OH: Kent State University Press.

Sproull, L. S. (1986). Using electronic mail for data collection in organizational research. *Academy of Management Journal, 29*, 159–169.

Stagner, R. (1981). Training and experiences of some distinguished industrial psychologists. *American Psychologist, 36*, 497–505.

Steers, R. M. (1975). Problems in the measurement of organizational effectiveness. *Administrative Science Quarterly, 20*, 546–558.

Steers, R. M., & Rhodes, S. R. (1978). Major influences on employee attendance: A process model. *Journal of Applied Psychology, 63*, 391–407.

Steiner, I. D. (1972). *Group process and productivity.* New York: Academic Press.

Stevens, S. S. (1946). On the theory of scales of measurement. *Science, 103*, 677–680.

Stinson, J. E., & Tracy, L. (1974). Some disturbing characteristics of the LPC score. *Personnel Psychology, 27*, 477–485.

Stogdill, R. M. (1948). Personal factors associated with leadership: A survey of the literature. *Journal of Psychology, 25*, 35–71.

Stogdill, R.M. (1969). Validity of leader behavior descriptions. *Personnel Psychology, 22*, 153–158.

Stone, E. F. (1978). *Research methods in organizational behavior.* Santa Monica, CA: Goodyear.

Stone, E. F. (1988). Moderator variables in research: A review and analysis of conceptual and methodological issues. In K. R. Rowland & G. R. Ferris (Eds.), *Research in personnel and human resources management.* Greenwich, CT: JAI Press.

Stone, J. H. (1973). An examination of six prevalent assumptions concerning performance appraisal. *Public Personnel Management, 5*, 408–414.

Sulsky, L., & Balzer, W. K. (1988). Meaning and measurement of performance rating accuracy: Some methodological and theoretical concerns. *Journal of Applied Psychology, 73,* 497–506.

Sussman, G. I., & Evered, R. D. (1978). An assessment of the scientific merits of action research. *Administrative Science Quarterly, 23,* 582–603.

Sussman, M., & Robertson, D. U. (1986). The validity of validity: An analysis of validation study designs. *Journal of Applied Psychology, 71,* 461–468.

Taft, R. (1955). The ability to judge people. *Psychology Bulletin, 52,* 1–23.

Tannenbaum, A. S. (1968). *Control in organizations.* New York: McGraw-Hill.

Tatsuoka, M. M., & Lohnes, P. R. (1988). *Multivariate analysis: Techniques for educational and psychological research.* New York: Macmillan.

Taylor, H. C., & Russell, J. T. (1939). The relationship of validity coefficients to the practical effectiveness of tests in selection. *Journal of Applied Psychology, 23,* 565–578.

Tenopyr, M. L. (1977). Content-construct confusion. *Personnel Psychology, 30,* 47–54.

Tenopyr, M. L. (1981). Trifling he stands. *Personnel Psychology, 34,* 1–18.

Tenopyr, M. L. (1983). *Comments on symposium: Cost analyses of human resource interventions. Are they worth it?* American Psychological Association Convention, Anaheim, CA.

Tesch, F. E. (1977). Debriefing research participants: Though this be method there is madness to it. *Journal of Personality and Social Psychology, 35,* 217–224.

Tesser, A., & Rosen, S. (1975). The reluctance to transmit bad news. In L. Berkowitz (Ed.), *Advances in experimental social psychology* (Vol. 8). New York: Academic Press.

Tharenow, P., & Harker, P. (1982). Organizational correlates of employee self-esteem. *Journal of Applied Psychology, 67,* 797–805.

Thomas, H. (1988). What is the interpretation of the validity generalization estimate $Sp^2 = S_r^2 - S_e^2$? *Journal of Applied Psychology, 73,* 679–682.

Thompson, J. D. (1967). *Organizations in action.* New York: McGraw-Hill.

Thorndike, E. L. (1920). A constant error in psychological ratings. *Journal of Applied Psychology, 4,* 25–29.

Thorndike, R. L. (1949). *Personnel selection.* New York: Wiley.

Thorndike, R. L. (1971). *Educational measurement* (2nd ed.). Washington, DC: American Council on Education.

Thornton, G. C. (1980). Psychometric properties of self-appraisals of job performance. *Personnel Psychology, 33*, 263–271.

Thornton, G. C., & Zorich, S. (1980). Training to improve observer accuracy. *Journal of Applied Psychology, 65*, 351–354.

Thurstone, L. L. (1922). *Thurstone employment tests: Examination in typing.* New York: Harcourt, Brace, & World.

Tiffin, J., & McCormick, E. J. (1965). *Industrial psychology.* Englewood Cliffs, NJ: Prentice-Hall.

Tinsley, H. A., & Weiss, D. J. (1975). Interrater reliability and agreement of subjective judgments. *Journal of Counseling Psychology, 22*, 358–376.

Treiman, D. J., & Hartman, H. I. (Eds.). (1981). *Women, work and wages: Equal pay for jobs of equal value.* Washington, DC: National Academy Press.

Tubbs, M. E. (1986). Goal setting: A meta-analytic examination of the empirical evidence. *Journal of Applied Psychology, 71*, 474–483.

Tucker, L. R., & Lewis, C. (1973). The reliability coefficient for maximum likelihood factor analysis. *Psychometrika, 38*, 1–10.

Tunnell, G. B. (1977). Three dimensions of naturalness: An expanded definition of field research. *Psychological Bulletin, 84*, 426–437.

Turnage, J. J., & Muchinsky, P. M. (1982). Transituational variability in human performance within an assessment center. *Organizational Behavior and Human Performance, 30*, 174–200.

Turnage, J. J., & Muchinsky, P. M. (1984). A comparison of the predictive validity of assessment center evaluations versus traditional measures in forecasting supervisory job performance: Interpretative implications of criterion distortion for the assessment paradigm. *Journal of Applied Psychology, 69*, 595–602.

Tziner, A., & Eden, D. (1985). Effects of crew composition on crew performance: Does the whole equal the sum of its parts? *Journal of Applied Psychology, 70*, 85–93.

Ulrich, L., & Trumbo, D. (1965). The selection interview since 1949. *Psychological Bulletin, 63*, 100–116.

Ungson, G. R., & Steers, R. M. (1984). Motivation and politics in executive compensation. *Academy of Management Review, 9*, 313–323.

Uniform Guidelines on Employee Selection Procedures. (1978). *Federal Register, 43*, 38290–38315.

Valecha, G. K. (1972). *Construct validation of internal-external locus of control as measured by an abbreviated 11-item IE scale.* Unpublished doctoral dissertation. Columbus, OH: The Ohio State University.

Van Maanen, J. (1975). Police socialization: A longitudinal examination of job attitudes in an urban police department. *Administrative Science Quarterly, 20*, 207–228.

Van Maanen, J. (1979). Reclaiming qualitative methods for organizational research: A preface. *Administrative Science Quarterly, 24*, 520–526.

Vance, R. J., Kuhnert, K. W., & Farr, J. L. (1978). Interview judgments: Using external criteria to compare behavioral and graphic scale ratings. *Organizational Behavior and Human Performance, 22*, 279–294.

Vance, R. J., MacCallum, R. C., Coovert, M. D., & Hedge, J. W. (1988). Construct validity of multiple job performance measures using confirmatory factor analysis. *Journal of Applied Psychology, 73*, 74–80.

Vecchio, R. P. (1977). An empirical examination of the validity of Fiedler's model of leadership effectiveness. *Organizational Behavior and Human Performance, 19*, 180–206.

Venardos, M. G., & Harris, M. B. (1973). Job interview training with rehabilitation clients: A comparison of videotape and role playing procedures. *Journal of Applied Psychology, 38*, 365–367.

Vroom, V. H. (1964). *Work and motivation.* New York: Wiley.

Vroom, V. H., & Yetton, P. W. (1973). *Leadership and decision making.* Pittsburgh, PA: University of Pittsburgh Press.

Wagner, R. (1949). The employment interview: A critical summary. *Personnel Psychology, 2*, 17–46.

Wahba, M. A., & Bridwell, L. T. (1976). Maslow reconsidered: A review of research on the need hierarchy theory. *Organizational Behavior and Human Performance, 15*, 212–240.

Waldman, D. A., & Avolio, B. J. (1986). A meta-analysis of age differences in job performance. *Journal of Applied Psychology, 71*, 33–38.

Wall, T. D., Kemp, N. J., Jackson, P. R., & Clegg, C. W. (1986). Outcomes of autonomous workgroups: A long-term field experiment. *Academy of Management Journal, 29*, 280–304.

Walsh, W. B., & Betz, N. E. (1985). *Tests and assessment.* Englewood Cliffs, NJ: Prentice Hall.

Wanous, J. P., Sullivan, S. E., & Malinak, J. (1989). The role of judgment calls in meta-analysis. *Journal of Applied Psychology, 74,* 259–264.

Wanous, J. P., & Zwany, A. (1977). A cross-sectional test of need hierarchy theory. *Organizational Behavior and Human Performance, 18,* 78–97.

Warmke, D. L., & Billings, R. S. (1979). Comparison of training methods for improving the psychometric quality of experimental and administrative performance ratings. *Journal of Applied Psychology, 64,* 124–131.

Warwick, D. P., & Lininger, C. A. (1975). *The sample survey: Theory and practice.* New York: McGraw-Hill.

Weary, G. (1979). Self-serving attributional biases: Perceptual or response distortions? *Journal of Personality and Social Psychology, 37*(8), 1418–1420.

Webb, E. J., Campbell, D. T., Schwartz, R. F., & Sechrest, L. (1966). *Unobtrusive measures: Non-reactive research in the social sciences.* Chicago, IL: Rand McNally.

Webb, E. J., & Weick, K. E. (1979). Unobtrusive measures in organizational theory: A reminder. *Administrative Science Quarterly, 24,* 650–659.

Webb, R. J. (1974). Organizational effectiveness and the voluntary organization. *Academy of Management Journal, 17,* 663–677.

Webster, E. C. (1964). *Decision making in the employment interview.* Montreal, ONT: Eagle.

Webster, E. C. (1982). *The employment interview: A social judgment process.* Schomberg, ONT: S.I.P. Publications.

Weekly, J. A., Frank, B., O'Connor, E. J., & Peters, L. H. (1985). A comparison of three methods of estimating the standard deviation of performance in dollars. *Journal of Applied Psychology, 70,* 122–126.

Weekly, J. A., & Gier, J. A. (1987). Reliability and validity of the situational interview for a sales position. *Journal of Applied Psychology, 72,* 484–487.

Weick, K. E. (1968). Systematic observational methods. In G. Lindzey & E. Aronson (Eds.), *The handbook of social psychology* (Vol. 2, pp. 357–451). Reading, MA: Addison-Wesley.

Weick, K. E. (1985). Systematic observational methods. In G. Lindzey & E. Aronson (Eds.), *Handbook of social psychology* (3rd ed.). New York: Random House.

Wernimont, P. R., & Campbell, J. P. (1968). Signs, samples, and criteria. *Journal of Applied Psychology, 52,* 372–376.

Wexley, K. N. (1984). Personnel training. *Annual Review of Psychology, 35,* 519–551.

Wexley, K. N., & Klimoski, R. J. (1984). Performance appraisal: An update. In K. Rowland and G. R. Ferris (Eds.), *Research in personnel and human resources management* (Vol. 2). Greenwich, CT: JAI Press.

Wexley, K. N., & Latham, G. P. (1981). *Developing and training human resources in organizations.* Glenview, IL: Scott Foresman.

Wexley, K. N., Sanders, R. E., & Yukl, G. A. (1973). Training interviewers to eliminate contrast effects in employment interviews. *Journal of Applied Psychology, 57,* 233–236.

Wherry, R. J. (1952). *The control of bias in rating: A theory of rating.* Washington, DC: Department of the Army, Personnel Research Section.

White, J. K. (1979). The Scanlon plan: Causes and correlates of success. *Academy of Management Journal, 22,* 292–312.

White, S. E., Dittrich, J. E., & Lang, J. R. (1980). The effects of group decision-making process and problem-situation complexity on implementation attempts. *Administrative Science Quarterly, 25,* 428– 440.

Whitehead, T. N. (1938). *The industrial worker.* Cambridge, MA: Harvard University Press.

Whitener, E.M. (in press). A note on confidence intervals and credibility intervals in meta-analysis. *Journal of Applied Psychology, 75.*

Wicker, A. W., & Kauma, C. E. (1974). Effects of a merger of a small and a large organization on members' behaviors and experiences. *Journal of Applied Psychology, 59,* 24–30.

Wicker, A. W., Kirmeyer, S., Hanson, L., & Alexander, D. (1976). Effects of manning levels on subjective experiences, performance and verbal interaction in groups. *Organizational Behavior and Human Performance, 17,* 251–274.

Widaman, K. F. (1985). Hierarchically nested covariance structure models for multitrait-multi-method data. *Applied Psychological Measurement, 9,* 1–26.

Wiersner, W. H., & Cronshaw, S. F. (1988). A meta-analytic investigation of the impact of interview format and degree of structure on the validity of the employment interview. *Journal of Occupational Psychology, 61,* 275–290.

Williams, L. J., Cote, J. A., & Buckley, M. R. (1989). Lack of method variance in self-reported affect and perceptions at work: Reality or artifact? *Journal of Applied Psychology, 74,* 462–468.

Winer, B. J. (1971). *Statistical principles in experimental design.* New York: McGraw-Hill.

Winkler, R. L., & Hays, W. L. (1975). *Statistics: Probability, inference and decision.* New York: Holt, Rinehart & Winston.

Woodman, R. W., & Sherwood, J. J. (1980). The role of team development in organizational effectiveness: A critical review. *Psychological Bulletin, 88,* 166–186.

Wortman, C. B., Hendricks, M., & Hillis, J. W. (1976). Factors affecting participant reactions to random assignment in ameliorative social programs. *Journal of Personality and Social Psychology, 33,* 256–266.

Wortman, P.M (1983). Evaluation research: A methodological perspective. *Annual Review of Psychology, 34,* 223–260.

Yuchtman, E., & Seashore, S. E. (1967). A system resource approach to organizational effectiveness. *American Sociological Review, 32,* 891–903.

Yukl, G. A. (1981). *Leadership in organizations.* Englewood Cliffs, NJ: Prentice Hall.

Yukl, G. A. (1989). *Leadership in organizations* (2nd ed.). Englewood Cliffs, NJ: Prentice Hall.

Yukl, G.A., & Kanuk, L. (1979). Leadership behaviors and effectiveness of beauty salon managers. *Personnel Psychology, 32,* 663–675.

Zammuto, R. F. (1984). A comparison of multiple consistency models of organizational effectiveness. *Academy of Management Review, 9,* 606–616.

Zavala, A. (1965). Development of the forced-choice rating scale technique. *Psychological Bulletin, 63,* 117–124.

AUTHOR INDEX

INDEX